THE OXFORD ENGLISH
LITERARY HISTORY

Volume 10. 1910–1940

THE OXFORD ENGLISH LITERARY HISTORY

General Editor: Jonathan Bate

* already published

This series was conceived and commissioned by Kim Walwyn (1956–2002), to whose memory it is dedicated.

THE OXFORD ENGLISH
LITERARY HISTORY

Volume 10. 1910–1940

The Modern Movement

CHRIS BALDICK

OXFORD

UNIVERSITY PRESS

OXFORD

UNIVERSITY PRESS

Great Clarendon Street, Oxford OX2 6DP

Oxford University Press is a department of the University of Oxford.
It furthers the University's objective of excellence in research, scholarship,
and education by publishing worldwide in

Oxford New York

Auckland Bangkok Buenos Aires Cape Town Chennai
Dar es Salaam Delhi Hong Kong Istanbul Karachi Kolkata
Kuala Lumpur Madrid Melbourne Mexico City Mumbai Nairobi
São Paulo Shanghai Taipei Tokyo Toronto

Oxford is a registered trade mark of Oxford University Press
in the UK and in certain other countries

Published in the United States
by Oxford University Press Inc., New York

© Chris Baldick 2004

British Library Cataloguing in Publication Data
Data available

Library of Congress Cataloging in Publication Data
Data available

ISBN 0-19-818310-0

10 9 8 7 6 5 4 3 2 1

Typeset by Regent Typesetting, London
Printed in Great Britain
on acid-free paper by
Biddles Ltd,
King's Lynn, Norfolk

For Hayley

Acknowledgements

This book has been nearly eight years in the making, and it would have been longer still without institutional support in the form of sabbatical leave. I am grateful, then, to the Research Committee of Goldsmiths' College for granting me three periods of research leave, and to the Arts and Humanities Research Board for supporting a further term's leave in which to complete the work. I am fortunate too in having been sustained by the patience of Sophie Goldsworthy at the Oxford University Press, by the guidance and enthusiastic encouragement of Jonathan Bate as OELH series editor, and by the team spirit of the OELH authors, among whom Randall Stevenson has been especially generous with his advice. Rowena Anketell has contributed clarifications of my text as copy-editor. Several of my colleagues past and present at Goldsmiths' College have offered, or inadvertently let slip, valuable tips and leads: Lucia Boldrini, Helen Carr, Bill McCormack, Bart Moore-Gilbert, Len Platt, Jean Radford, and Derval Tubridy. Jane Desmarais and Conor Carville contributed precious assistance with the bibliographies, and Lindsay Martin divulged the arcana of Bloomsbury. Joshua, Zoë, Ella, and Bethany recycled reams of early drafts with creative zest. It has been a long journey, but in such company a fully rewarding one.

C. B.

Goldsmiths' College, London
April 2004

General Editor's Preface

The Oxford English Literary History is the twenty-first-century successor to the Oxford History of English Literature, which appeared in fifteen volumes between 1945 and 1997. As in the previous series, each volume offers an individual scholar's vision of a discrete period of literary history.[1] Each has a distinctive emphasis and structure, determined by its author's considered view of the principal contours of the period. But all the volumes are written in the belief that literary history is a discipline necessary for the revelation of the power of imaginative writing to serve as a means of human understanding, past, present, and future.

Our primary aim is to explore the diverse purposes of literary activity and the varied mental worlds of writers and readers in the past. Particular attention is given to the institutions in which literary acts take place (educated communities, publishing networks, and so forth), the forms in which literary works are presented (traditions, genres, structural conventions), and the relationship between literature and broader historical continuities and transformations. Literary history is distinct from political history, but a historical understanding of literature cannot be divorced from cultural and intellectual revolutions or the effects of social change and the upheaval of war.

We do not seek to offer a comprehensive survey of the works of all 'major', let alone 'minor', writers of the last thousand years. All literary histories are inevitably incomplete—as was seen from the rediscovery in the late twentieth century of many long-forgotten women writers of earlier eras. Every literary history has to select; in so doing, it reconfigures the 'canon'. We cast our nets very widely and make claims for many works not previously regarded as canonical, but we are fully conscious of our partiality. Detailed case studies are preferred to summary listings.

A further aim is to undertake a critical investigation of the very

---

[1] Since Volume 1, *to 1350*, covers many centuries, it is co-written by two scholars.

notion of a national literary heritage. The word 'literature' is often taken to refer to poems, plays, and novels, but historically a much wider range of writing may properly be considered as 'literary' or as belonging within the realm of what used to be called 'letters'. The boundaries of the literary in general and of *English* literary history in particular have changed through the centuries. Each volume maps those boundaries in the terms of its own period.

For the sake of consistency and feasibility, however, two broad definitions of 'English Literary History' have been applied. First, save in the polyglot culture of the earliest era, we have confined ourselves to the English language—a body of important work written in Latin between the fourteenth and the seventeenth centuries has been excluded. And secondly, we have concentrated on works that come from, or bear upon, England. Most of the writing of other English-speaking countries, notably the United States of America, is excluded. We are not offering a world history of writing in the English language. Those Americans who lived and worked in England are, however, included.

So too with Scottish, Irish, Welsh writers, and those from countries that were once part of the British Empire: where their work was produced or significantly disseminated in England, they are included. Indeed, such figures are of special importance in many volumes, exactly because their non-English origins often placed them in an ambivalent relationship with England. Throughout the series, particular attention is paid to encounters between English and other traditions. But we have also recognized that Scottish, Welsh, Irish, African, Asian, Australasian, Canadian, and Caribbean literatures all have their own histories, which we have not sought to colonize.

It would be possible to argue endlessly about periodization. The arrangement of the Oxford English Literary History is both traditional and innovative. For instance, the period around the beginning of the nineteenth century has long been thought of as the 'Romantic' one; however we may wish to modify the nomenclature, people will go on reading and studying the Lake Poets and the 'Shelley circle' in relation to each other, so it would have been factitious to introduce a volume division at, say, 1810. On the other hand, it is still too soon for there to be broad agreement on the literary-historical shape of the twentieth century: to propose a single break at, say, 1945 would be to fall in with the false assumption that literature moves strictly in tandem with events. Each volume argues the case for its own period as a period, but at the same time beginning and ending dates are treated flexibly, and in many cases—especially with respect to the twentieth century—there is deliberate and considerable overlap between the temporal boundaries of adjacent volumes.

The voices of the last millennium are so various and vital that English literary history is always in the process of being rewritten. We seek both to chart and to contribute to that rewriting, for the benefit not just of students and scholars but of all serious readers.

Jonathan Bate

Contents

List of Figures and Tables

Figures

Tables

A Note on References

Brief biographical information on selected authors will be found at the end of the volume, together with bibliographies covering their major works and some of the most notable modern scholarship concerning them. In addition, there are suggestions for more general reading relevant to the literary history of the period. The bibliographies are intended as starting points for further study, not comprehensive listings of the kind found in the *Cambridge Bibliography of English Literature* and other sources (the majority of which are now published in electronic form). Whenever possible, the Author Bibliographies include recommended modern editions. An asterisk indicates the edition that has been used in the main body of the book.

Quotations in the texts from works written in the period are usually followed by a reference in parentheses. Where possible, these are given in a form that does not depend on access to a particular edition (e.g. chapter, or book and line number), but for works without convenient subdivision, the citation is of the page number of the edition asterisked in the relevant Author Bibliography. Where there is no modern edition, references are to the first edition, unless otherwise stated. Longer references, e.g. to secondary sources, are given in footnotes, but if a source is referred to more than once in a chapter, subsequent references appear in the text in parentheses.

Since the ellipsis (. . .) is a significant feature of prose style in this period, I have adoped the now common practice of indicating my own omission of any portion of a quotation by placing my ellipses in square brackets. Where an ellipsis appears without square brackets, it is to be found in the original passage quoted.

Different forms of surname will be found for two authors who are discussed in this book. Cecil Day-Lewis used the unhyphenated name 'C. Day Lewis' for his published work as a poet, translator, and critic; and the pen-name 'Nicholas Blake' for his detective novels. I refer to him by these names in the contexts of these works, but as Day-Lewis otherwise, and I list him in the Author Bibliographies under Day-Lewis. Ford Madox Ford, as we now usually know him, was known as Ford Madox Hueffer before he changed his name in 1919, so he is referred to as Hueffer in pre–1919 contexts, but otherwise as Ford, under which name he is listed in the Author Bibliographies.

The dates given in this book for stage plays indicate the year in which they were first performed in Britain. In some cases this will differ from the date of the world premiere; in others it will differ from the date at which the script was published.

Introduction: Modern Beginnings

New Words, 1910–1940

contextualize   coverage   Edwardianism   intro
mappable   old hat   out-of-dateness   periodization
post-Victorian   reappraisal   update

We may begin with Ursula Brangwen, the restless heroine of D. H. Lawrence's *Women in Love* (1920). She has thrown up her job as a schoolteacher and, without her parents' blessing, hurriedly married Rupert Birkin, with whom she has begun a new life of uncharted wandering on an Alpine holiday at a hotel near Innsbruck. Passing a cowshed among the mountains, she is reminded uncomfortably of the farm on which she grew up in the English Midlands.

She wished it could be gone for ever, like a lantern-slide which was broken. She wanted to have no past. She wanted to have come down from the slopes of heaven to this place, with Birkin, not to have toiled out of the murk of her childhood and her upbringing, slowly, all soiled. She felt that memory was a dirty trick played upon her. What was this decree, that she should 'remember'! Why not a bath of pure oblivion, a new birth, without any recollections or blemish of a past life. She was with Birkin, she had just come into life, here in the high snow, against the stars. What had she to do with parents and antecedents? She knew herself new and unbegotten, she had no father, no mother, no anterior connections, she was herself, pure and silvery (ch. 29)

In this baptismal invocation of a new self bathed clean of all murky histories, we hear the distinctively modern voice declaring itself self-begotten from willed obliviousness to its origins, uncompromisingly severed from any allegiance to the past. Such a passage could not have been written before the early twentieth century, which is not to say that it is typical of its time. It is an extreme case, as almost any paragraph of Lawrence's writings is an extreme case, this one taken from a narrative full of fierce denials and repudiations. Yet it presents in especially pure form an indication of the new volatile energies at work in modern literature.

That a strange new sense of disconnection from the past was now a general condition of modern literary awareness, we may confirm from the calmer testimony of Virginia Woolf's collection of critical articles, *The Common Reader* (1925), in which the concluding essay, entitled 'How It Strikes a Contemporary', deliberates upon what it meant for her generation to be 'modern' in literature:

There is something about the present which we would not exchange, though we were offered a choice of all past ages to live in. And modern literature, with all its imperfections, has the same hold on us and the same fascination. It is like a relation whom we snub and scarify daily, but, after, all, cannot do without. It has the same endearing quality of being that which we are, that which we have made, that in which we live, instead of being something, however august, alien to ourselves and beheld from the outside. Nor has any generation more need than ours to cherish its contemporaries. We are sharply cut off from our predecessors. A shift in the scale—the war, the sudden slip of masses held in position for ages—has shaken the fabric from top to bottom, alienated us from the past and made us perhaps too vividly conscious of the present. Every day we find ourselves doing, saying, or thinking things that would have been impossible to our fathers. [. . .] No age can have been more rich than ours in writers determined to give expression to the differences which separate them from the past and not to the resemblances which connect them with it. It would be invidious to mention names, but the most casual reader dipping into poetry, into fiction, into biography can hardly fail to be impressed by the courage, the sincerity, in a word, by the widespread originality of our time. (*The Essays*, vol. 4, p. 238)

Woolf captures here a fact of central importance for her literary contemporaries, especially after the Great War of 1914–18: their sense of living and writing in a drastically changed world, a modern world which they regarded as radically different from the Victorian cultural order to which their parents had belonged. She is careful, however, to hint that the modern writers' emphasis on their separation or alienation from the past involves a certain partiality, a distortion of perspective in which real continuities are overlooked amid the celebration of novelty and originality.

The hint is worth taking, because our inherited conceptions about the shape and direction of literary history between 1910 and 1940 are still strongly marked by just such emphases on radical breaks and unprecedented innovations. In academic literary studies especially, the major development in literature during these three decades is presented—commonly to the exclusion of all else—as the triumph of the revolution that we call modernism. There are perfectly sound reasons for dwelling in this way upon the achievements of the modernist innovators: much of their work is, as Woolf indicates, courageously original, and much of it also deserves the attention which critics have in its defence lavished upon it. Even so, if we allow our view of literature in this period to be engrossed by the heroism of a small band of modernist pioneers—James Joyce, T. S. Eliot, Ezra Pound, Virginia Woolf—then we lose sight not only of a wealth of creative work by their contemporaries but also, self-defeatingly, of the very distinctiveness of the leading 'modernists' themselves, to appreciate which requires some awareness of the mainstream from which they diverged.

Although it now dominates our map of the literary scene in these decades, modernism was in its own time a minority current. What may now seem to us the most important publications of the age— the more experimental fictions of Joyce and Woolf, Eliot's poems, avant-garde periodicals like *The Egoist* and *The Criterion*—reached at first an audience of only a few hundred people, while the novels of H. G. Wells and Arnold Bennett and the poems of John Masefield sold in their tens of thousands. That this discrepancy now applies entirely in the opposite direction is the result of a vigorous and pro- longed campaign of critical reconstruction, starting with the essays and manifestos of Pound, Eliot, and Woolf themselves, which are passed down to us as defining statements of modern literature's onward movement. As this campaign on behalf of the experimental minority was taken up by academic commentators in later years, the label 'modernist' was applied retrospectively to its works, giving the impression that the writers so designated had shared a common revolutionary purpose and programme not just with one another but with French painters, Russian film-makers and choreographers, Italian sculptors, and Austrian composers. Presenting the cultural history of the early twentieth century in this way usually has the effect of separating a few favoured literary innovators sharply from other authors who were using the same medium and the same language in more traditional forms. If, however, we were to set such distinctions aside for a moment, we might recognize that a 'modernist' novelist such as Dorothy Richardson or D. H. Lawrence has more in common with a 'traditionalist' practitioner of the same art, such as E. M. Forster or Arnold Bennett, than with a Stravinsky, a Picasso, or a Dalí.

The appearance of the terms 'modernist' and 'modernism' in literary discussion before 1940 is something of a rarity. Only one significant critical work of this period, *A Survey of Modernist Poetry* (1927) by Robert Graves and Laura Riding, makes prominent use of them, and the few writers who consequently picked up the terminology kept these words within the sceptical quarantine of inverted commas. In their own time, the writers we call the modernists, along with many others from whom we withhold the honour, regarded themselves as participants in a rather larger and looser enterprise which was then more commonly known as 'the modern movement'. Some idea of this movement's accepted breadth may be gleaned from Cyril Connolly's nearly contemporaneous account in his *Enemies of Promise* (1938), which is partly a memoir and partly a survey of trends in modern writing; it includes lists of 'Some Books in the Modern Movement' from 1900 to 1932. What is now very striking about these lists is that they include works not just by writers now regarded as the eminent modernists (and by some modernists now forgotten, such as Edith Sitwell) but also by 'realist' novelists such as Arnold Bennett, H. G. Wells, W. Somerset Maugham, John Galsworthy, Hugh Walpole, and E. M. Forster; by the Ibsenist playwright Bernard Shaw; by 'Georgian' poets like Rupert Brooke and other 'traditionalists' in verse such as Robert Bridges and A. E. Housman; and by an assortment of authors—Hilaire Belloc, Robert Graves, Aldous Huxley, Noël Coward, Evelyn Waugh—who cannot sit comfortably within our definitions of modernism.[1] The modern

---

[1] Cyril Connolly, *Enemies of Promise* (Penguin, 1961), 39–41, 73–5.

movement, then, as understood by writers who had grown up with it, was a broad church that embraced a variety of forms, techniques, styles, and attitudes, all of which were in some way innovative and in some way representative of new twentieth-century modes of awareness. 'Within literary studies', Alison Light has pointed out, 'we have perhaps suffered from a surfeit of "modernism" and a dearth of studies of modernity.'[2] This does not mean that the contrasts often highlighted between the more experimental modernist works and the more traditional realist novels or Georgian poems are in themselves irrelevant or misleading; only that they can be given a false significance if they tempt us to forget that there are many ways of being modern, or to believe that the experimental and the traditional can be segregated cleanly. As the modernist writers themselves understood very well, every literary experiment is necessarily traditional in some sense, just as every 'traditionalist' work of any value is also a new experiment.

In this book I shall be offering a fresh survey of a thirty-year phase of this broader modern movement. Without, I hope, indulging in any ostentatious revisionism that would devalue the achievements of the leading modernist writers, the following chapters will reinstate Woolf, Eliot, Joyce, and the others within the contexts not only of minor modernist work but also of those literary currents that were modern in less obvious ways; and so they will discuss 'highbrow' writing alongside 'middlebrow' writing, symbolist poems and stream-of-consciousness novels alongside rural elegies and family sagas. They will offer also some impression of the range of innovative work that was produced in non-fictional genres, and notice at least some of the more important developments in the realm of light reading, including children's books and crime thrillers. One of my purposes here, apart from that of encompassing such a wider sample of modern writing, is to get back behind our more recent preoccupation with the small modernist vanguard and to recover at least some impression of, in Woolf's phrase, how it struck a contemporary. (Woolf in fact took her title from that of a poem by Robert Browning, as if to acknowledge the debt that all modern authors inevitably owed

---

[2] Alison Light, *Forever England: Femininity, Literature and Conservatism between the Wars* (Routledge, 1991), 216.

to the Victorian past.) This will involve somewhat less reference than is usual to the manifestos and other self-justificatory writings of the eminent modernists, and in its place the calling of other witnesses from within the period: writers such as Cyril Connolly, Arnold Bennett, Elizabeth Bowen, Winifred Holtby, Robert Graves, W. Somerset Maugham, George Orwell, and Frank Swinnerton, all of whom, as well as being practising novelists, had a shrewd and considered grasp of contemporary literary trends and problems, but whose valuable testimony is now too seldom heard.

This account begins somewhat abruptly from the year 1910, which, like all beginnings, is arbitrary, although it has more to recommend it than, say, 1908 or 1912. If this were a full survey of modernism or of the larger modern movement, it would certainly need to start somewhere in the second half of the nineteenth century. As it claims only to review a relatively distinct phase of the movement, though, it may begin with a date that seemed to some modern writers to mark the opening of such a new phase. Virginia Woolf was not the only author to nominate 1910 as the appropriate dawn, but her essay 'Character in Fiction' (1924; separately reprinted as *Mr Bennett and Mrs Brown*) has become the most famous statement of the case. In that essay, she justifies the experiments of her own generation of novelists by claiming that the methods of the previous generation for presenting human character, in the novels of Arnold Bennett and others, have become obsolete because 'in or about December 1910 human character changed'. Expanding upon, but partly retreating from this startlingly precise chronology, she asserts further that

All human relations have shifted—those between masters and servants, husbands and wives, parents and children. And when human relations change there is at the same time a change in religion, conduct, politics and literature. Let us agree to place one of these changes about the year 1910. (*The Essays*, vol. 4, pp. 421–2)

One of the important events of 1910, at least for British subjects, was the death of King Edward VII and the accession of George V in May of that year, which thus drew a line between the Edwardian period and the new Georgian era; and Woolf uses these terms to distinguish 'Edwardian' novelists from her own 'Georgian' generation of writers. Her reference to December rather than to May, however, has seemed to most commentators to indicate that Woolf had in mind the Post-Impressionist Exhibition of works by Gauguin, Van Gogh, Cezanne, Matisse and Picasso, held in London from November until the January of 1911. As this exhibition was organized by her friend Roger Fry and other Bloomsbury associates, it is likely to have been as significant for her as it was momentous for British perceptions of modern painting. But because Woolf invokes a wholesale shift in human relations, it is worth looking briefly at the ways in which 1910 also marks a turning point in the larger social and political spheres.

On the broadest scale, relations 'between masters and servants' were reshaped by the political crisis of 1910. There was a wave of unofficial strikes that year in the coal and rail industries, which announced the new strength of organized labour; and in November the police staged their first violent clash with Suffragette demonstrators outside the Houses of Parliament, provoking an escalation of arson attacks by campaigners for women's suffrage. Inside Parliament, Lloyd George's 'People's Budget' of 1909 had proposed a series of increased taxes upon the incomes of large landowners in order to pay for old-age pensions for the poor, and in response the House of Lords had broken with constitutional convention by voting down the Budget in a flagrantly self-interested attempt to preserve its own members' wealth. This forced the governing Liberal Party of H. H. Asquith (with which most literary intellectuals were aligned) to call two general elections in 1910, both of which gave the balance of power to Irish nationalists and representatives of Labour. The second of these elections, in December, was fought on the question of 'the peers against the people': the proposed Parliament Bill was to abolish the Lords' power to veto the elected House of Commons' legislation, reducing this to a delaying power only. The Lords gave way in 1911, conceding with bitter reluctance their obsolescence in the face of a democratic mandate. The classic account of this crisis, George Dangerfield's *The Strange Death of Liberal England* (1935), suggests that Britain narrowly escaped revolution in the 1910–14 period. In any case, the showdown between Lords and Commons in 1910 opened up a new political landscape for the next thirty years, which included the enfranchisement of women (1918, 1928), the partition of Ireland (1921), and the first Labour governments (1924,

1929). Literature in this period is coloured in various ways by the recognition that, on the one side, 'mass' democracy, with all its cultural consequences, had established itself, and on the other, the aristocracy's traditional roles, including patronage of the arts, were now doomed. W. B. Yeats's famous poem 'The Second Coming' (1920) employs an image drawn from the aristocratic sport of falconry:

> The falcon cannot hear the falconer;
> Things fall apart; the centre cannot hold;
> Mere anarchy is loosed upon the world

This poem is, with good reason, usually understood as a response to the Great War, but it is also, like 'Upon a House shaken by the Land Agitation' (1910) and many of Yeats's other poems in this period, a lament for the passing of the aristocracy's cultural authority, in which the 'best' landed families provided the central standard of manners and 'breeding', before the clamour of modern democracy broke their spell.

While modern authors were sharply aware of themselves as participants in a new cultural order that was in many ways radically disconnected from that of the past, most were unwilling to endorse the cult of the new. There were a few poets, including those of the Auden group, who were prepared to celebrate some of the forms of technological and scientific progress, and Arnold Bennett enthused about the benefits of modern domestic plumbing, but the more usual literary responses to the world of mass newspapers, advertising, the cinema, tinned foods, and industrial mass-production were either elegiac withdrawal or satiric revulsion. The Shakespearian title of Aldous Huxley's *Brave New World* (1932) is heavily ironic, and the book extrapolates from contemporary ideals of industrial efficiency and consumer satisfaction a vision of a future false utopia in which everybody is cheerful but in which the nobility of human suffering and of high art has been eliminated. The modernity of the modern writer, then, was established less often by the embracing of the new world than by a disavowal of the old.

Literature in the years after 1910 defined its own modernity most obviously by its stance of anti-Victorianism. Most modern authors had grown up in the late Victorian period and were now eager to repudiate its pieties, its moralism, its cult of dutiful self-renunciation, its imperialism, and above all its patriarchal forms of family life. Anti-Victorianism was of course not invented in 1910: the major writers of that age, from Dickens to Wilde, whom we loosely call 'the Victorians', were themselves anti-Victorian in their dissent from their contemporaries' orthodoxies. For later generations, though, 'Victorianism' could more easily be imagined as a single monstrous entity. Following the Edwardian examples of Samuel Butler's novel *The Way of All Flesh* (1903) and Edmund Gosse's memoir *Father and Son* (1907), the modern writers embodied their view of the Victorian age in the figure of the tyrannical paterfamilias, who becomes a recurrent character-type, and sometimes a stock figure, in the novels and plays of this period, as he attempts to stifle the emotional and spiritual growth of his children: Edwin Clayhanger in Arnold Bennett's *Clayhanger* (1910), or Mr Ramsay in Virginia Woolf's *To the Lighthouse* (1927), for example. The miseries of a late Victorian upbringing were a favoured subject for semi-autobiographical fiction including W. Somerset Maugham's *Of Human Bondage* (1915) and most of the novels of Ivy Compton-Burnett. Indeed the dominant theme of this period's fiction is the painful birth of modern consciousness from the shell of Victorian conventions. This is most visible in such family sagas as D. H. Lawrence's *The Rainbow* (1915), John Galsworthy's *The Forsyte Saga* (1922), and Virginia Woolf's *The Years* (1938); but it asserts itself too in novels of emergent individuality (*Bildungsromane*) like Dorothy Richardson's *Pilgrimage* sequence (1915–38) and May Sinclair's *Mary Olivier* (1919).

The indiscriminate smashing of Victorian icons could be heard most loudly in the telegrammatic imprecations of Wyndham Lewis's magazine *Blast*:

BLAST / years 1837 to 1900 / Curse abysmal inexcusable middle-class / (also Aristocracy and Proletariat). / BLAST / pasty shadow cast by gigantic Boehm / (imagined at introduction of BOURGEOIS VICTORIAN VISTAS). / WRING THE NECK OF all sick inventions born in that progressive white wake. / BLAST their weeping whiskers—hirsute / RHETORIC of EUNUCH and STYLIST—/ SENTIMENTAL HYGIENICS / ROUSSEAUISMS (wild Nature cranks) / FRATERNIZING WITH MONKEYS[3]

---

[3] *Blast*, 1 (June 1914), 18.

Less violently but just as decisively, the literary critic F. R. Leavis wrote off Tennyson and most other Victorian poets as insipid day-dreamers in his *New Bearings in English Poetry* (1932). The most influential work of post-War anti-Victorianism, though, was Lytton Strachey's *Eminent Victorians* (1918), a sequence of linked bio-graphical essays on four of the idols of the Victorian age—Cardinal Manning, Florence Nightingale, Dr Thomas Arnold of Rugby, and General Gordon of Khartoum. Strachey makes no overt anti-Victorian declarations in these essays, but inflicts more damage by the corrosive irony in his treatment both of individuals and of institutions. The four heroes' shared sense of providential purpose is regarded as a symptom of manipulative monomania, while the received idea of the Victorian period as a great age of Reform is over-turned in repeated accounts of official incompetence and bureaucratic obstruction. From the theological confusions of the Church and the stultifying conformities of the public schools to the administrative shambles of the Army and the diplomatic service, the structures of the British Empire emerge from this book as little more than pitiful impostures. Cyril Connolly was a schoolboy at Eton when *Eminent Victorians* was published, and he later recalled that it caused a sensation there, undermining as it did the patriotic values which the school had tried to instil in its pupils during the Great War.

The War itself provided a second, more catastrophic 'shift' in human relations. Younger writers such as Siegfried Sassoon and Robert Graves returned from the trenches with a hardened contempt for the bankrupt ideals of their elders, helping to establish Strachey's anti-heroic scepticism as the dominant mood of inter-war litera-ture. Even among those who had not experienced combat, there was a general conviction that the old world lay in ruins. Katherine Mansfield, for example, wrote in 1919 of the significance of the War for writers that 'I feel in the *profoundest* sense that nothing can ever be the same—that, as artists, we are traitors if we feel otherwise: we have to take it into account and find new expressions, new moulds for our new thoughts and feelings' (*Letters and Journals*, p. 147). In this kind of post-War mood, Stracheyan anti-Victorianism often modulated into anti-Edwardianism of two kinds. The first involved an imaginative diagnosis of the ills of pre-War England, which implies that it fully deserved to be bombed out of its complacencies.

Bernard Shaw's play *Heartbreak House* (1921) presents a group of idle aristocrats, millionaires, and socialites who, in the last act, welcome the arrival of airborne bombs to put an end to their frivolity. Osbert Sitwell's satirical novel *Before the Bombardment* (1926), based upon a real incident in which the German navy in 1915 had somewhat ludicrously shelled the seafront hotels of Scarborough, offers a view of Edwardian life as a phase of senile dementia in which the worst Victorian prejudices enjoy a ghastly afterlife among a cast of pettily scheming septuagenarians.

A second form of anti-Edwardianism took the form of a split within the broad modern movement of literature, in which some of the younger writers rounded upon their elder colleagues and accused them of not being modern enough for these drastically changed times. There are signs of such impatience already in Edwin Muir's first collection of essays, significantly titled *We Moderns* (1918), which complains that Arnold Bennett and other senior writers have failed to break out of Victorian conventions and values. Six or seven years later, the grumbling about Bennett and his generation had become something of a campaign. Virginia Woolf's *Mr Bennett and Mrs Brown* begins by grouping modern writers into two 'camps', the Edwardians (Bennett, Wells, Galsworthy) and the Georgians (Forster, Lawrence, Strachey, Joyce, Eliot, and Woolf herself), and goes on to claim that the so-called Edwardians are not really interested in human beings but only in their incomes, their costumes, or their houses. This is demonstrably slanderous, but it has been repeatedly cited with respect, as if it were a seriously defensible critical judgement. Woolf's labelling of the senior novelists as 'Edwardians' in fact condemns them in advance: it has no real meaning in literary-historical terms (Edward's reign lasted less than ten years, and it is hard to find any significant author whose work is confined within it), but is a way of saying that they have no place in the post–1910 world and no capacity for new creative work—against all the evidence of their recent triumphs in *The Forsyte Saga* (1922) and Bennett's *Riceyman Steps* (1923). In the next year, 1925, Edwin Muir returned to the assault upon Bennett as an outdated purveyor of Victorian ideology: 'He is the representative', Muir wrote in the *Calendar of Modern Letters*, 'of an era of almost universal and absolutely naïve optimism, which is now past.'[4] Muir's essay was part of a series of critical 'Scrutinies' of established reputations by the young iconoclasts of the *Calendar*, which continued after the magazine's demise in a collaborative volume, *Scrutinies by Various Writers* (ed. E. Rickword, 1928). Here most of the respected 'Edwardian' writers are lined up and shot down: J. M. Barrie, G. K. Chesterton, H. G. Wells, John Masefield, and Walter de la Mare are all condemned for childish evasions of reality; Bernard Shaw for his anaemic rationalism; Galsworthy (in an essay by D. H. Lawrence) for vulgar cynicism; and Rudyard Kipling (by Robert Graves) for hysterical imperialism. This was a kind of show trial in which the young zealots arraigned their elders for the 'Victorian' sins of being materialistic, sentimental, naïvely optimistic, and gallingly popular. It was also a way of defining by negation the truly modern stance of fastidious disillusionment. As in the fictional case of Ursula Brangwen's fantasized obliteration of her parents in the self-fashioning 'bath of pure oblivion', to be ultra-modern meant adopting the symbolic stance of the parricide.

Ursula reinvents herself as a modern spirit not just by renouncing her past but by leaving England, as her creator, D. H. Lawrence, himself had done. Lawrence's later life of uprooted exile in such different places as Australia, Ceylon, and Mexico is again an extreme case, but all the same a representative one, of a general literary condition of his times. As we shall see in more detail in Chapter 3, migration, resettlement, cosmopolitanism, and cultural hybridity are major facts of literary life in this period on a scale never seen before in what we please to call English Literature. In the previous generation, immigrants from the United States or Poland (Henry James, Joseph Conrad), and writers who had come from the outposts of the Empire (Rudyard Kipling, Olive Schreiner), had assumed important places in the English literary scene; but after about 1910 we have a far more extensive pattern of authorial displacement, with American and Scottish writers working in London, Irish writers in Paris, and English writers scattered around the Mediterranean sea. The secure link between writers' locations and their *œuvres* which had been such a prominent feature of nineteenth-century English Literature

---

[4] Edwin Muir, 'Scrutinies (4): Arnold Bennett', *Calendar of Modern Letters*, 1 (1925), 296.

from William Wordsworth and Jane Austen to George Eliot and Thomas Hardy has by now been broken so often that the author 'rooted' in the same place about which she or he writes is the exception and not the rule. If the typical modern writer has a nineteenth-century precursor in this respect it is the roving exile Lord Byron. Arnold Bennett's best Staffordshire novels and stories were written in France; and the greatest novel of Dublin life was written in Trieste, Zurich, and Paris, and named after the archetypal exile Ulysses.

Under these conditions of dislocation, English Literature is no longer a 'national' literature harvested from its shires and supplemented by the tributary offerings of Edinburgh and Dublin, but an Imperial literature, which means that it is at once more dispersed and more centralized. Major works of poetry were no longer published from Bristol, as *Lyrical Ballads* had been in 1798, and the Edinburgh periodicals which had been so powerful in the early nineteenth century had ceded their influence to the all-consuming vortex of London. There was still a Scottish publishing trade, but its leading houses, such as Nelson & Sons or Collins, conducted most of their literary operations from those small streets in the English metropolis where the reading matter of the world's largest empire was determined. The scope of my account of English literary history in these three decades is defined by this complicated modern configuration, in which authors belong to the same Republic of Letters less by virtue of birthplace or residence than by incorporation within a system of publishing, reviewing, and dramatic performance that was heavily concentrated in the centre of London. This survey will cover the work of English writers wherever they lived, of non-English writers who operated in the English literary sphere, and even of some writers who hardly spent any time in England, provided that they used London as a principal centre of publication: James Joyce, for instance, most of whose major works apart from *Ulysses* first appeared there. On the other hand, literary works in English that were written and produced as contributions to secessionist projects are left out of my account. As the literature of the United States, the first major secession from London's literary empire, lies outside the scope of this series, so the work of Sean O'Casey and others at Dublin's Abbey Theatre, the Anglo-Welsh revival led by Caradoc Evans, and the Scottish Renaissance led by Hugh MacDiarmid and

Neil M. Gunn will not be treated in this volume, as it would insult the nationalist motives of these bodies of writing to corral them into a realm from which they were determined to escape. Much else, of course, will have to be passed over for lack of space, or glimpsed only fleetingly, but I hope to have charted at least the salient lines of literary development and offered a starting point for further explorations.

The chapters that follow are organized in three parts. In the first, the infrastructural components of the literary world are reviewed, starting with readers and publishers, then moving on to authors and the language they used. Part II surveys modern developments in the various literary genres and forms, proceeding from poetry and drama to various kinds of prose fiction and then to the non-fictional genres. In Part III, a number of important topics that attracted significant literary treatment in this period are considered; the approach here is thematic, ranging across different genres to explore representations of childhood, of sexuality, of Englishness, and of the Great War. This organization of material is designed to provide a broad view of this period's literature, not a series of intensive critical analyses of individual authors and works. By contrast with J. I. M. Stewart's *Eight Modern Writers* (1963) in the old Oxford History of English Literature series, this book takes into account the work of about two hundred modern authors, but cannot dwell upon any of them at length. Guides to further reading on one hundred of them, though, are provided in the Author Bibliographies.

Part I

Elements

1

The Modern Literary Market

New Words, 1910–1940

blurb   break-even   contractually   mark-up
mass medium   newspaperland   obtainability
percentage-wise   prepublication   pricey
promotional   publicize   stockist

With levels of literacy in this period reaching about 80 per cent, England boasted a potential 'reading public' of about twenty million adults. What these millions read, for the most part, were newspapers and magazines. Mass-circulation daily papers like the *Daily Mail*, *Daily Express*, *Daily Mirror*, and *Daily Herald*; Sunday papers such as the *News of the World*; and influential local papers such as the London *Evening Standard* provided the most regular and most formative relationship between the majority of the population and the written word. Almost everything else that was written, and most of what was read in this period, was in some way shaped by the overwhelming commercial and cultural dominance of these publications. Few novelists or poets could make a living without engaging in some form of journalism, and fewer still could reach a significant readership unless their works were commended by the reviewers, at least in the more respectable papers. In the late Twenties, booksellers would wait to see which books had been recommended by Arnold Bennett—the country's highest-paid book reviewer—in his regular Thursday literary column in the *Evening Standard* before placing their orders. Newspapers could pluck obscure writers from the review shelves and turn them into widely discussed authors in a few days, then transform them into 'celebrities'. As the dailies strove to reach the coveted two-million circulation figure, attained by both the *Express* and the *Herald* in 1933, they offered their readers more enticements, including those of a literary kind. They published poems and stories, and serialized whole novels, plays, and biographies. The *Daily Telegraph*, for example, serialized T. E. Lawrence's *Revolt in the Desert* over the Christmas holiday of 1926–7, Noël Coward's patriotic play *Cavalcade* appeared in the *Daily Mail* in December 1931, and the *Daily Express* ran Agatha Christie's *The ABC Murders* in 1935, inviting readers to send in their solutions to the mystery before the final chapter appeared. These papers could also afford to send talented young writers like Evelyn Waugh to remote parts of the world to satisfy the growing demand for travel-writing. Outbidding the weekly magazines, whose sales declined accordingly, they offered substantial payments to essayists and short-story writers.

Most people would now read at least one newspaper or magazine a week, and a book from time to time, but very few—perhaps about two percent of the adult population—would buy newly published books from a bookseller. Most books were borrowed, usually from a variety of commercial libraries catering to different levels of the market. The public library service, although expanding significantly, was poorly stocked outside the major cities, conservative rural taxpayers being unwilling to subsidize the novel-reading habits of their servants. The reason for the predominance of borrowing was that book prices were fairly high, compared with those in Europe and North America, and relative to average incomes. The most helpful figure to keep in mind for these comparisons is the average male manual worker's weekly wage in the Twenties, which was about 60s. (sixty shillings; that is, £3). Women workers usually earned about half this amount, or still less if they were lowly domestic servants or shop assistants; and the maximum old-age pension was 10s. a week.

A new novel would usually cost you 7s. 6d., while a substantial work of history or biography would commonly be sold at twice or even four times this price. Books of verse ranged in price from 2s. 6d. for a slim volume to 7s. 6d. for a more substantial collection or anthology. On the other hand, you could borrow *Tarzan of the Apes* or an Edgar Wallace thriller from a local shop for twopence or three-pence. And reprints, either of the classics or of relatively recent best-sellers, were reasonably priced: you could have an Austen novel or an edition of Milton in hard covers for 2s. in the Everyman's Library series, or a modern popular novel at the same price from Hodder & Stoughton or Nelson & Son; and there were cheaply produced romances and westerns on sale in Woolworth's for sixpence. New novels were not, as they had been until the 1890s, entirely beyond the pocket of the working population, although it still made more sense to borrow them rather than to purchase outright. Arnold Bennett, as a shrewd observer of the book trade, put the matter a little differ-ently:

Tell me not that average persons can't, in practice, read. They can. They read with earnestness and understanding, at certain hours of the day, the prophecies of gifted men about the relative speeds of horses at certain later hours of the day. Nor tell me that they can't afford to buy books. The aver-age adolescent and adult person spends on alcohol at least £15 per annum, a sum which would enable him to buy forty new novels, or ten volumes of history or biography or philosophy. (*Evening Standard Years*, p. 320)

Bennett was by no means a censorious puritan, and he tended to place the blame for the small size of the book-buying public less on the bad habits of the undeserving poor than on the sloth of publishers and booksellers—in particular their failure to reduce the price of books or to advertise them more attractively.

Like many other sectors of British trade and industry in the early twentieth century, the book trade had forsaken the risks of open competition for the security of a controlled market. The business of publishing and selling books was regulated by price-fixing arrange-ments between the Associated Booksellers (founded in 1895) and the Publishers Association (founded 1896), embodied in the Net Book Agreement (NBA) of 1899. The point of the NBA was to protect established businesses on both sides against the arrival of newcomers who might undersell them, so its signatories agreed not to trade with rogue price-cutters outside the system. At first, the NBA had applied only to non-fictional books, but novels—by far the largest category of newly published books, amounting to more than 1,000 titles a year—were brought into the system from 1914. This meant that if, at the end of the year 1910, you had seen an advertisement for *Howards End* published at 6s., you could still have expected to buy a copy from a bookseller, under the old discounting scheme, for 4s. 6d., of which the bookseller would have kept sixpence, leaving the publisher with 4s. But after the War, you would pay for a newly published novel the full advertised price of 7s. 6d., of which the retailer would keep between a quarter and a third, leaving the publisher with something over 5s. These bare figures might suggest a lucrative racket, but if we adjust them for inflation, book prices actually fell in the years following the War, and they remained stable until the end of the Thirties. Booksellers certainly enjoyed higher margins, but the overriding problem for publishers was that they now had to sell perhaps twice as many copies—for a novel, 1,000 rather than 500—of a given book in order to recover its production costs and author's royalties, which were usually 10 to 15 per cent, but in some cases as high as 25 per cent. The degree to which such increased sales could be achieved through the established booksellers was limited. As writers and publishers complained, there were many large towns in England which had not a single shop devoted exclusively to the sale of books. Publishers therefore relied heavily both upon reprints rather than on the riskier trade in new titles, and upon their ability to sell large numbers of copies, at least of their more popular new titles, to the public and commercial libraries, and in the 1930s to the book clubs. In the eyes of the artistic minority, the result seemed to be a dangerous dependence upon a 'commercialized' public taste, as publishers neglected higher literary standards in their search for the best-sellers that could keep them afloat.

Along with the NBA, the second pillar of the modern book trade was the Copyright Act of 1911, which for the first time secured for authors effective control over the rights to reprint or perform their works during their lifetimes and for fifty years after their deaths—a substantial extension to the old seven-year term. The new Act, and its application throughout most of the British Empire, was a victory for the authors' pressure group, the Society of Authors, and of obvious benefit to writers and their dependants, especially in the realm of performance and adaptation rights, the potential of which increased upon the arrival of radio broadcasting (1922) and of the talking pictures (1928). Just as important for many writers were the easier arrangements for British authors to secure copyright in the USA, achieved by American legislation in 1909: novelists such as D. H. Lawrence and Virginia Woolf relied heavily upon American sales of their work, the home and Imperial markets being too small and conservative to sustain their radical experiments. The extension and entrenchment of copyright had important, if less obvious, consequences for publishers as well. Reprints of classic works such as the plays of Shakespeare allowed publishers a fairly safe income, but no individual publishing firm could expect to gain any significant advantage over its competitors in this market. If, on the other hand, one had sealed a contract with an Agatha Christie or a P. G. Wodehouse for the sole rights to publish and sell their popular books, one had a small-scale but real monopolistic advantage, upon which the firm might survive for the next few decades, retaining or selling off these rights as its fortunes required. The 1911 Copyright Act underlined the importance for publishers of discovering and retaining a 'stable' of popular living authors, the profits from whose books would allow them to take risks with new writers and to continue publishing prestigious but loss-making works by poets and philosophers.

The market in books was, then, stabilized and regulated by deals between the Society of Authors and the Publishers Association on copyright and royalty terms, and between the Publishers Association and the Associated Booksellers or the libraries on sales and discounts. It was also, as never before, a stratified market, that could even be described as a hierarchy of relatively distinct reading publics broadly parallel with the different readerships of the mass-circulation newspapers and of the 'quality' press. This becomes evident if we examine the variety of the commercial libraries, or 'circulating libraries' and 'subscription libraries', as they were called. The powerful duopoly of Mudie's Library and W. H. Smith & Sons, which had shaped the reading habits of the Victorians, had by now given way to a variegated field of small and large operations serving different levels of the rental market. In the late Twenties, the Cambridge scholar Q. D. Leavis conducted her doctoral research into the history and current state of novel-reading in England, later publishing this as *Fiction and the Reading Public* (1932). Her conclusions, prophesying the impending extinction of true literature by a flood of cheap trash, were hastily alarmist, and her research methods were unsystematic; but her investigations nonetheless provide a useful impression of the various levels of the book-buying and book-borrowing markets. She found that working-class readers were relying less on the public library service than on local book-hire shops known as Twopenny Libraries. George Orwell worked in one of these shops in the early Thirties, and describes one in his novel *Keep the Aspidistra Flying* (1936). Owners of these little backstreet businesses told Leavis that many of their customers, mostly women, came back every day to exchange their books, which were almost all cheap romances and thrillers. For the lower middle class, there was the Boots' Booklovers' Library, set up by the chain of retail chemists and boasting a quarter of a million members paying an annual subscription of half a guinea (10s. 6d.) for a more varied diet of light reading available in its 340 local branches; and there was a similar service provided by W. H. Smith & Sons at more than 600 shops and railway station stalls. Elizabeth Bowen has one of her fictional characters in *The Death of the Heart* (1938) work as a librarian in Smoot's—a composite of these two big chains. The upper middle classes were served by such organizations as Mudie's and Day's in London (both used by Virginia Woolf) or Harrod's department store and the Times Book Club, which both sent out packages of books to their provincial subscribers and allowed them a wider choice of titles. The head of Boots' Booklovers' Library attested that his organization bought more than a million books a year, most of them novels. Subscribers would read two books a week on average; a new novel would be in strong demand for the first fortnight, and then hardly ever ordered after three months. After novels, the books most often requested were biographies and travelogues, while political works and plays were reasonably popular.[1] The retail sales of books showed a similar division between working-class readers who bought sixpenny reprints at newsagents or in Woolworth's, and lower middle-class readers who found novels for 2s. or more in the better class of newsagent.

There had come about, then, a noticeable stratification of the market into three levels, which Leavis and other commentators,

---

[1] F. R. Richardson, 'The Circulating Library', in John Hampden (ed.), *The Book World: A New Survey* (Nelson, 1935), 195–202.

borrowing the American usage, designated the 'highbrow', 'middle-brow', and 'lowbrow' reading publics. On the basis of circulation figures for magazines addressed to these different readerships, and of some informed guesswork about sales figures for recent novels pitched at distinct levels, Leavis estimated the sizes of the three reading publics at about four thousand, ten thousand, and two hundred thousand respectively. There is little doubt that her figures are gravely underestimated, derived as they are from sales of individual novels and of specific periodicals, rather than from aggregated sales and from library membership figures. On a different interpretation of the available evidence, one could easily arrive at figures of sixty thousand 'highbrows', two million 'middlebrows', and at least ten million 'lowbrow' readers of fiction. And it should not be forgotten that, beyond the regular book-borrowers, almost every person came into some sort of contact with literature, through their schooling, by reading poems and stories in newspapers and magazines, by listening to the 'wireless' (radio), or by seeing adaptations in the cinema.

Leavis and others, employing rather selective comparisons, contrasted the divisions among readerships with the homogeneity of the reading public of the mid-Victorian period, in which Dickens and Tennyson had appealed to all levels of the literate population at once, or of the later Victorian decades, in which Hardy and Kipling had achieved something similar. Leavis blamed this cultural disaster on the mass-circulation newspapers, and on 'middlebrow' journalistic authors such as Arnold Bennett, who had promoted second-rate pseudo-literature at the expense of the more challenging works of the very best writers. Bennett himself, who died before Leavis's book appeared, shared a similar general view of the stratification of reading publics, but he refused to treat middlebrow reading, or even the violent lowbrow thrillers of Edgar Wallace, as an evil, and, despite his disappointments about the slow rate of increase in book-buying, he eschewed the pessimism of the highbrows: 'This is no more a decadent age, in literary terms, than any other age', he wrote in 1929. 'On the contrary, in no previous age have so large a proportion of the populace shown such discrimination among books, such intelligent interest in good books, as obtains to-day' (*Evening Standard Years*, p. 333). While the avant-garde literary minority was convinced that the influence of the newspapers had brought about a debasement or 'levelling-down' of culture, publishers and librarians generally agreed with Bennett's more cheerful view. They could point to the weekly *Times Literary Supplement*, which, as an independent publication from 1914, reached more than thirty thousand sales and probably twice as many actual readers; or to the ten thousand readers of such literary monthlies as the *London Mercury* and the *Bookman*. The latter magazine, which merged with the *Mercury* in 1934, provided plentiful reviews of recent novels and non-fictional works, profiles of 'celebrity' authors with photographs of their houses and families, and advertisements for fountain pens, desks, and other bookish paraphernalia. It was 'middlebrow' indeed, but provided more evidence for the growth of bibliomania than for any predicted death of literature.

For publishers, however, the market in the finer kinds of literary work, especially poetry, was precarious enough to require some insurance, in the form of popular best-sellers or school textbooks. The firm of Edward Arnold, which published E. M. Forster's novels and paid him generous royalties for them, could do so because it also traded well in school books and published the standard textbooks on gynaecology and obstetrics. One of the most forward-looking London publishers in this period was Gerald Duckworth, Virginia Woolf's half-brother. His company published Woolf's first two novels, D. H. Lawrence's *Sons and Lovers* (1913), and the novels of Dorothy Richardson and Ronald Firbank; but it also had the good sense to publish the scandalous sex-novels of Elinor Glyn and the early romances of Barbara Cartland. Likewise the firm of Methuen took the risk of publishing T. S. Eliot's volume of critical essays, *The Sacred Wood* (1920), a landmark in literary criticism, but of interest only to a small minority, and the more disastrous gamble of Lawrence's *The Rainbow* (1915), most copies of which were confiscated and destroyed by the police. They did so, though, on the basis of the safety provided by the solid sales of Kipling's poems, Bennett's *Clayhanger* trilogy (1910–16), and a strong list of children's books which later included *Winnie-the-Pooh* (1926) and the Tarzan series.

The risks of operating without such safety nets can be seen in the fates of two other imaginative publishers. The house of Martin Secker was founded in 1910, starting off with a strong fiction list that eventually included most of D. H. Lawrence's works after 1920. It issued some good poetry anthologies, and won a favourable reputation for its translations of modern European writers including Kafka and Thomas Mann. These books made a loss, however, and because Secker had only one really popular author on his list—Rafael Sabatini, writer of swashbuckling pirate romances—he could keep afloat only by selling off his D. H. Lawrence titles, to Heinemann for £7,000, before eventually sliding into insolvency in 1935. A year later, the Bodley Head, noted for its literary exploits in the 1890s, also went into receivership, publishing the first British edition of James Joyce's *Ulysses* in a final defiant fling before it was bought out by a consortium of rivals. This publishing house had taken its bold risks in the recent past, publishing the modernist manifesto-cum-journal *Blast* in 1914, and John Cowper Powys's *A Glastonbury Romance* (1932), but in the early Twenties had prudently signed up a new detective writer called Agatha Christie. Fatally, though, it lost her in 1926, when she became convinced that the Bodley Head owed her more in royalties than its official accounts showed; she decamped to Collins and made them a fortune. Holding on to your most valuable authors once you had found them was a problem for several other publishers, especially with celebrities who knew how to play the system. H. G. Wells was notorious for squeezing the best terms from publishers by hopping among several rivals for his famous name, and he ended his career having used no fewer than thirty different firms. An unusual but effective method of retaining a valued author was to offer the comparative security of a long-term contract. Chatto & Windus struck such a deal with Aldous Huxley, under which he agreed to write a given number of books for them over a period of three years in return for estimated royalties paid in advance in the form of an annual 'salary'; the agreement satisfied both sides, and was renewed every three years.

The Publishers Association had a membership of nearly a hundred firms, of which about twenty-five had significant literary interests in this period. These can be divided into firms specializing in light entertainment of a middlebrow-to-lowbrow kind, and firms catering to the higher literary tastes. At the lower level, the most power-ful purveyor of light fiction to the commercial libraries was Hodder & Stoughton, which had an unrivalled team of prolific entertainers including Edgar Wallace, 'Sapper', John Buchan, and the queen of romancers, Berta Ruck. The firm of Ward Lock published little of note apart from the comical tales of Dornford Yates, while Herbert Jenkins had the invaluable property of P. G. Wodehouse, and John Murray acquired in 1917 the works of Arthur Conan Doyle. Hutchinson & Co boasted a large team of best-selling authors including Barbara Cartland and Ethel M. Dell. At a slightly higher middlebrow level were found the house of Benn, which published the early detective novels of Dorothy L. Sayers and some of Noël Coward's plays; Cassell, which combined popular best-sellers by Ernest Raymond and Warwick Deeping with more advanced material such as Bennett's later novels and works by Wyndham Lewis, Robert Graves, and Radclyffe Hall; and Heinemann, who likewise balanced the historical romances of Georgette Heyer against more serious works by such authors as John Masefield, John Galsworthy, and W. Somerset Maugham. The new publishing firm of Victor Gollancz, founded in 1928, traded well in detective fiction by Sayers and others, and in middlebrow novels by A. J. Cronin and Daphne du Maurier, which allowed it to publish also the more prestigious authors Elizabeth Bowen and George Orwell.

Of publishing houses willing to invest in the more challenging kinds of literary work, there was a healthy array. Some of these were well-established firms which tended to rely on older authors: Macmillan had the invaluable rights to Thomas Hardy and Henry James, and acquired those to W. B. Yeats and Sean O'Casey; Methuen had the poems of Kipling and the essays of G. K. Chesterton; Constable acted as distributors of the works of Bernard Shaw (who insisted on dealing directly with the printers as a self-publishing author), while adding Walter de la Mare and Katherine Mansfield to their list; and Sidgwick & Jackson published the poems of Rupert Brooke and John Drinkwater. The more adventurously 'modern' publishers, though, were, with one exception, those newly launched in this period or relatively recently: Gerald Duckworth (1898), Martin Secker (1910), the Hogarth Press (1917), Jonathan Cape (1921), and Faber & Faber (1925, as Faber & Gwyer). The exception was the older house of Chatto & Windus, which in the post-War years had the strongest array of new talent: they published Wilfred Owen, Aldous Huxley, Rosamond Lehmann, Richard Aldington, T. F.

Powys, David Garnett, Lytton Strachey, Sylvia Townsend Warner, R. H. Mottram, F. R. Leavis, and the Scott Moncrieff translation of Proust, and reprinted many of these in attractive pocket editions at 3*s.* 6*d.* in their 'Phoenix Library' series. Jonathan Cape's distinguished list included Robert Graves's *Good-bye to All That* (1929), T. E. Lawrence's *Seven Pillars of Wisdom* (1935), the children's books of Arthur Ransome, and eventually the principal works of James Joyce. Like Chatto & Windus, Cape had, from 1926, an extensive series of 3*s.* 6*d.* pocket editions called the Travellers' Library. While Chatto and Cape were noted for their fiction lists, the newer house of Faber, with T. S. Eliot as an active editorial director, rapidly cornered much of the market in modernist poetry with a list headed by Eliot himself and including Ezra Pound, W. H. Auden, Stephen Spender, and Louis MacNeice; it also published Joyce's *Finnegans Wake* and the prose works of Siegfried Sassoon.

The unwillingness of most of the major publishers to hazard the publication of poetry or certain kinds of experimental fiction left a vacuum which was filled by smaller publishing operations based in bookshops or even private homes. The *Georgian Poetry* anthologies (1912–22) were published by Harold Monro's Poetry Bookshop in Bloomsbury, and Joyce's *Ulysses* (1922) was published by Sylvia Beach from her bookshop, Shakespeare & Co., in Paris. The most successful and lastingly valuable of these small concerns was the Hogarth Press, founded in 1917 by Leonard and Virginia Woolf in their house at Richmond as a therapeutic hobby. Using a hand press, they set up and printed short works like Katherine Mansfield's *Prelude* (1918), T. S. Eliot's *Poems* (1919), and a limited edition of his *The Waste Land* (1923), selling these to friends or private subscribers. For longer works, including Virginia Woolf's own novels and essays, they began to hire outside printers, and then established themselves with proper business premises in Bloomsbury, taking on a paid assistant in 1924, when they started publishing the English versions of Sigmund Freud's works. By 1940, when their offices were destroyed by bombing, they had also published the important poetry anthology *New Signatures* (1932) and some interesting new novelists including Christopher Isherwood and Henry Green.

The Hogarth Press, however, was unusual in becoming a relatively successful small business. The more typical publishing enterprise of the advanced literary minority was the aesthetically vibrant but financially hopeless 'little magazine' which struggled to stay alive for long on a circulation of less than four thousand, even when propped up by subsidies from rich patrons. The vitality and audacity of these little magazines, and their importance in providing openings to new and experimental writers, are striking features of this period. A succession of imaginative editors packed into their pages some of the best in contemporary poetry, short fiction, and criticism: A. R. Orage as editor from 1907 to 1922 of *The New Age*, John Middleton Murry during his editorships of *The Athenaeum* and *The Adelphi* in the Twenties, T. S. Eliot at *The Criterion* (1922–39), Edgell Rickword at the *Calendar of Modern Letters* (1925–7), and Desmond MacCarthy as editor (1928–34) of *Life and Letters*. There were little magazines of a predominantly literary-critical nature, such as *Scrutiny* (1932–53), edited by F. R. Leavis and others from a private house in Cambridge; and others devoted to aggressive avant-garde self-advertisement, such as Wyndham Lewis's *Blast*, of which there were only two issues (1914–15) announcing the positions of 'Vorticism'. Little noticed at the time, one of the most distinguished vehicles for literary modernism in London during the Great War was *The Egoist* (1914–19), which had formerly been a feminist review entitled *The New Freewoman*, edited by Dora Marsden, but was converted, under Ezra Pound's influence, into a literary showcase for 'Imagist' poetry, the critical essays of T. S. Eliot, and the fiction of James Joyce. Under the editorship of Harriet Shaw Weaver, the magazine serialized the latter's *A Portrait of the Artist as a Young Man*, and portions of *Ulysses*. It then collapsed under its debts, having failed to attain a circulation of more than four hundred. The little magazines that lasted longer tended to be those enjoying covert patronage from wealthy sponsors: *The New Age* was sustained by anonymous benefactors, and Eliot's *Criterion* could not have come into existence without the funds provided by Lady Rothermere, wife of the *Daily Mail*'s proprietor—another sign of the literary power exerted by the riches of Fleet Street.

Despite such unacknowledged links between the big newspapers and the little magazines, the more visible contrast between the popularity and power of the former and the obscurity and fragility of the latter tended to entrench the open hostilities between the two camps.

From Fleet Street and from such conservative literary monthlies as J. C. Squire's *London Mercury*, it appeared that the avant-garde of the little magazines was a self-regarding and self-appointed elite which had arrogantly uprooted itself from the healthier culture of the majority. From the other side, the younger modernist vanguard regarded itself as the embattled defender of artistic integrity against the commercialism of 'mass' culture and its herd mentality. It seemed that to be truly artistic was to be unpopular, and so to be popular was almost certainly to be guilty of selling out to the commercial interests of journalism, advertising, and shallow mass-entertainment. Writers who had acquired some celebrity and wealth—Wells, Shaw, Bennett, Galsworthy, Maugham, Buchan, Wodehouse, Wallace—were thus to be regarded not as artists but as journalists or lesser entertainers; and almost any publication with a circulation of more than five thousand could safely be assumed to be indifferent or hostile to artistic integrity.

The modernist minority nursed a kind of appalled fascination with the brazen commercialism and cheapened language of the public press. Of all the major modernist works, Joyce's *Ulysses* is the most thoroughly obsessed with this world. Its hero, Leopold Bloom, is an Everyman figure, but one with a particular job, soliciting advertisements for a Dublin newspaper whose offices are presented, in the 'Aeolus' chapter, as an enormous windbag of stale rhetoric. One of Bloom's first actions in the book is to ease his bowels in the exterior water closet of his house, while reading a prizewinning short story in the popular magazine *Tit-Bits*:

Asquat on the cuckstool he folded out his paper turning its pages over on his bared knees. Something new and easy. No great hurry. Keep it a bit. Our prize titbit. *Matcham's Masterstroke*. Written by Mr Philip Beaufoy, Playgoers' club, London. Payment at the rate of one guinea a column has been made to the writer. Three and a half. Three pounds three. Three pounds thirteen and six.

Quietly he read, restraining himself, the first column and, yielding but resisting, began the second. [. . .] It did not move or touch him but it was something quick and neat. Print anything now. Silly season. He read on, seated calm above his own rising smell. Neat certainly. *Matcham often thinks of the masterstroke by which he won the laughing Witch Who now.* Begins and ends morally. *Hand in hand.* Smart. He glanced back through what he had read and, while feeling his water flow quietly, he envied kindly Mr Beaufoy who had written it and received payment of three pounds thirteen and six. (pp. 66–7)

Having finished *Matcham's Masterstroke*, Bloom then wipes himself with it, thereby clinching the slyly equivocal identification of the magazine column with the turd. This little episode exacts a kind of revenge, on behalf of the original but unremunerated artist, against the commercial culture in which each predictable word has an equally predictable cash value. When Joyce had eventually found a publisher for his short-story collection *Dubliners* (1914) after years of frustrated effort, the book had sold fewer than 400 copies, and he had made no money from it.

The growing commercial spirit in the world of letters was nonetheless unstoppable, as the novelist and critic Frank Swinnerton mockingly observed: 'Even poets and aesthetes complain of their small returns in royalties, as if they had one eye on these, instead of having both eyes upon the stars.'[2] Many writers were now indeed prepared to repudiate the unworldliness expected of them, and to speak plainly of the financial necessities of their craft. Virginia Woolf estimated in *A Room of One's Own* (1929) that a writer of fiction or poetry needed a private room to work in and an income of £500 a year, this sum being about ten times the annual wage of most domestic servants. A lower figure was suggested by the Anglo-Irish critic Cyril Connolly in his book *Enemies of Promise* (1938), which declares that nobody should embark upon a literary career without first having found 'some way however dishonest of procuring with the minimum of effort, about four hundred a year.'[3] Arnold Bennett, whose first literary earnings had come from winning a short-story prize in *Tit-Bits* magazine, railed in his *Evening Standard* column against the 'revolting artistic snobbishness' of the dilettanti who held that artists should not concern themselves with money:

These parasites on society cannot, or apparently will not, understand that the first duty of, for instance, a poet is not to write poetry but to keep himself in decency, and his wife and children if he has them, to discharge his current obligations, and to provide for old age. [. . .] Artists yearn to

[2] Frank Swinnerton, 'Authorship', in Hampden (ed.), *The Book World*, 23.
[3] Connolly, *Enemies of Promise*, 148–9.

be appreciated. The best proof of appreciation is the receipt of cheques, notes, or coin. If people genuinely appreciate a thing they will pay money for it to the extent of their means. If not, not. A comfortable earned income should be a matter of pride to an artist. (It is.) Artists who affect to contemn a comfortable income, when they can't make it, are nincompoops in addition to being liars. (*Evening Standard Years*, p. 56)

In a similar spirit, Bernard Shaw encouraged his fellow writers to fight for every penny they could extract from theatres and publishers, and himself acted as a tough negotiator on behalf of the Society of Authors. The Society had more than two thousand fee-paying members who were entitled to use its royalty collection service or its legal advice on contractual matters. Specialist offshoots of the Society such as the League of Dramatists (1931) and the Screenwriters' Association (1937) were established to protect minimum royalty terms in these areas.

Most established writers were now additionally employing the services of a professional literary agent—a recent arrival on the publishing scene, but increasingly indispensable in the modern world of film rights, broadcasting rights, serial rights, and complex foreign copyright stipulations. Authors who lived abroad, like D. H. Lawrence and Somerset Maugham, could not have negotiated simultaneously with publishers, magazine editors, and theatrical producers without hiring the expertise of a powerful agency such as Curtis Brown or J. B. Pinker. The four volumes of Arnold Bennett's *Letters* include one whole volume of nearly 400 pages made up of his letters to the Pinker agency. Books of advice to aspiring authors, such as *The Commercial Side of Literature* (1925) by Michael Joseph, who worked for Curtis Brown before becoming a publisher, stressed the importance of using a good agent. One serious suspicion about the intervention of the literary agent, sometimes voiced by the Society of Authors, was that it was in the agent's interest to concentrate on the most lucrative deals, especially in film rights, at the expense of such trivial business as placing poems in magazines. But the same could be said of authors themselves, who might just decide to set aside work on the great novel or the slim volume of verse when offered a Hollywood contract. Maugham made more than $35,000 on the film rights of his short story 'Rain' in 1923, and in the later period of the talkies the opportunities were of course all the greater: Aldous

Huxley and Christopher Isherwood both settled in Hollywood as highly paid screenwriters, and P. G. Wodehouse spent a year there, earning huge sums for little but sitting by a swimming pool. There was money to be made too, on a smaller scale, from the expansion of radio broadcasting in the Thirties, either from talks and perform-ance fees or from articles in the successful BBC literary magazine *The Listener*.

The commercialization of literature was widely discussed and lamented in this period, often in terms either of writers selling their souls to Hollywood or Fleet Street, or of the best-selling novelist pan-dering to the lowest tastes of the multitude—the xenophobic brutal-ity of the Bulldog Drummond thrillers by 'Sapper', or the masochistic titillations of E. M. Hull's *The Sheik* (1919), which was the basis of Rudolph Valentino's most famous starring role in Hollywood. Less often remarked, although it was an important publishing trend, was the exploitation of sequels, usually on the basis of the popularity of a well-recognized fictional character. This in turn was a symptom of a general hardening of generic categories (historical romance, detec-tive fiction, schoolgirl stories) in the popular market, in response to patterns of demand recorded by the commercial libraries. The most celebrated earlier victim of this process was Arthur Conan Doyle, who had attempted to finish off Sherlock Holmes once and for all by having him plunge down the Reichenbach Falls in 'The Final Problem' (1893), but had been urged to resurrect him ten years later. Despite the title of *His Last Bow: Some Reminiscences of Sherlock Holmes* (1917), Doyle, feeling himself increasingly enslaved to his own creation, was still grinding out Holmes stories as late as 1927 with *The Casebook of Sherlock Holmes*. Formulaic repetition was most obvious in the crime genre, in which a successful practitioner would invent a distinctive detective figure and then stick to it, as Agatha Christie did with Hercule Poirot. But the same pattern is highly visible in children's fiction, in such long-running series as Elinor Brent-Dyer's Chalet School stories (from 1925), Richmal Crompton's William books (from 1922), and W. E. Johns's Biggles cycle (from 1931). Writers of comical tales for adults, notably P. G. Wodehouse and Dornford Yates, established a loyal following for the same sets of characters in countless reappearances, becoming vic-tims of what Wodehouse called 'the Saga habit' (*Blandings Castle*,

p. 7); and the thriller writer John Buchan put his hero Richard Hannay through a further four exhausting adventures after *The Thirty-Nine Steps* (1915). At the higher levels of serious fiction, the obvious value to publishers of the multi-volume family saga was borne out by the success of Hugh Walpole's *Herries Chronicle* (1930–3) and by that of John Galsworthy's long sequence of novels and tales about the linked Forsyte and Charwell families. Arnold Bennett published three profitable sequels to his *Clayhanger* (1910), and the War novelist R. H. Mottram followed up *The Spanish Farm* (1924) with two further works to form a trilogy, selling the film rights to Hollywood and retiring from his job in a bank to become a full-time writer.

Even though newspapers, literary agents, and an increasing number of reputable authors acknowledged that literature was, among other things, necessarily a trade, the book trade itself was unwilling to adopt modern marketing methods. The older booksellers conducted their business with a modest amateurism that placed it above the ranks of groceries and pharmacies, while publishing was a profession for gentlemen who could not stoop below the more discreet kinds of advertising. This started to change with the Wall Street Crash of 1929, which seems to have concentrated minds on the need to stay in business, even if it meant adopting new American techniques of promotion. In the United States, the Book of the Month Club had been launched successfully in 1926, its first selection being *Lolly Willowes*, by the British writer Sylvia Townsend Warner. Three years later, the first of several book clubs in Britain, the Book Society, was inaugurated with a selection committee including Hugh Walpole and J. B. Priestley; one of its earlier selections was Richard Hughes's *A High Wind in Jamaica* (1929). Publishers, having secured an agreement that these clubs would not undercut NBA prices for newly published works, were attracted by the prospect of bulk sales through this new outlet, although booksellers were at first hostile. In the event, it seems that the book clubs did no damage to the retailers, and merely expanded the book-buying habit by mail to readers who had no local bookshop. A further innovation of direct benefit to the retailers was the invention of the Book Token, devised by Chatto & Windus and launched by the Associated Booksellers in 1932.

Two of the more imaginative publishers in the Thirties brought about a modernization of the design and marketing of books. Victor Gollancz left the house of Benn in 1928 to set up his own firm, and persuaded the detective writer Dorothy L. Sayers, an advertising copywriter by profession, to follow him. He promoted her books aggressively with a series of tantalizing and boastful advertisements in the newspapers, in a style considered vulgar by the more genteel publishers. Gollancz's books made a strong visual impact in their standard canary-yellow jackets; the colour was disturbingly similar to that of Hodder & Stoughton's cheap thrillers, although the designs were more chastely 'modern'. At the Bodley Head, Allen Lane, nephew of the firm's founder, decided in 1935 to launch a reprint series of books in paper covers at the perilously low price of sixpence, which meant that each title would have to sell 20,000 copies if it were to recover its costs. In the circumstances of the Bodley Head's own impending bankruptcy, this was a daring gamble, but, with the decisive help of Woolworth's, who were accustomed to trading in sixpenny books of an inferior sort, Lane's new company, Penguin Books, had sold a million books by the end of the following year, both creating and cornering the market in good-quality paperbacks—which soon meant the end of the 3s. 6d. clothbound reprint series. Most of the first Penguins were reprints of books published a few years earlier by Jonathan Cape, and several of them, including crime novels by Sayers, Christie, and Dashiel Hammett, were of a 'middlebrow' flavour. At this stage, Penguin Books represented neither literary innovation nor the highest literary quality but the democratic promise of an expanded reading public which could at last afford to buy fairly reputable novels, biographies, plays, and travel books.

Paperbacks, and the enormous new demand for reading matter during the Second World War, helped to create that new reading public in later years. In the short term, the new war brought unforeseen setbacks. From April 1940, the book trade had to cope with the official rationing of paper supplies, more severe than the limited controls enforced in 1916–19. The heart of the London book trade was located in Paternoster Row and Ave Maria Lane, on the north side of St Paul's Cathedral, where twenty publishers had their premises, along with the offices of the Associated Booksellers and the warehouse of the country's largest book wholesaler, Simpkin Marshall.

On the night of 29 December 1940, the Luftwaffe devastated these streets with incendiary bombs, destroying millions of books and bringing this phase of British publishing history to a spectacular conclusion.

2

Modern Authorship

New Words, 1910–1940

*Bloomsburyite   cattiness   cultish   exclusivity
fan-mail   high-ranking   marginality   socialite
uprootedness   white-collar*

In a magazine article in 1911, H. G. Wells, the son of humble shop-keepers but now a successful journalist and novelist, declared that

The literary life is one of the modern forms of adventure. Success with a book, even such a commercially modest success as mine has been, means in the English-speaking world not merely a moderate financial independence, but the utmost freedom of movement and intercourse. One is lifted out of one's narrow circumstances into familiar and unrestrained intercourse with a great variety of people. One sees the world.[1]

More authors than ever before were indeed seeing the world, in the sense of travelling to other lands, either professionally as screen-writers and travel writers, or because they had earned enough to travel for pleasure. Others gained access to 'the world' of high society and political power in ways that their parents could never have imagined. Arnold Bennett, raised in a lower middle-class provincial family, dined regularly with cabinet ministers. Michael Arlen, the son of Armenian immigrants, could be seen, after the huge success of his novel *The Green Hat* (1924), gliding around Mayfair in his yellow Rolls Royce. Aristocratic hostesses made a point of inviting

---

[1] 'Mr Wells Explains Himself', *T. P.'s Magazine* (December 1911), 3.

young poets to mingle with politicians and plutocrats at weekend parties. Noël Coward, the son of a suburban piano-salesman, was rumoured to have become one of the many lovers of Prince George, later the Duke of Kent, at a particularly wild party in New York in 1924. Even a writer of working-class origin like D. H. Lawrence, who did his best to become a social outcast, could call upon friends in high places. When *The Rainbow* was suppressed by a police raid on his publishers in 1915, he was driven by the Prime Minister's daughter-in-law Lady Cynthia Asquith to the House of Commons to meet the Liberal MP Philip Morrell, who then confronted the Home Secretary with a question in the House challenging the legal basis of the police action. Lawrence was later able to approach Winston Churchill's private secretary Edward Marsh—an admirer of his verse, which he had included in his *Georgian Poetry* anthologies— for help in obtaining a passport. In some ways, literary talent was itself a passport.

While literary authors, even those from modest backgrounds, were seeing more of the world, the world was also seeing more of them, at least in the newspapers. Bennett, who was accustomed to being pestered by autograph hunters, commented in 1928 upon the oddities of modern literary celebrity:

If a prominent author enters a restaurant or a theatre people are sure to put their heads together and murmur: 'Look! There's so and so.' They will even point fingers at the fellow defenceless against their impolite curiosity. Whereas the Governor of the Bank of England, or the head of a great trust or mercantile concern, or an illustrious barrister would pass unnoticed anywhere.

People want to know even what authors eat and drink and how they dress. If a prominent author uses a handkerchief in a public place he will read of the event next day in the press. Such items are 'news,' and para-graphists earn their living and keep wife and children in comfort by sup-plying them. (*Evening Standard Years*, p. 213)

It is hard to imagine now, but celebrity authors were held in higher esteem, and usually earned more, than footballers or singers. They became accustomed to receiving fan mail and begging letters from anonymous cranks. Rosamond Lehmann claimed to have received 'literally hundreds of letters' in response to her first novel, several of them containing sexual propositions (*Swan in the Evening*, pp. 66–7). An extreme case of such intrusion was the frantic news-paper coverage of Agatha Christie's mysterious eleven-day dis-appearance in December 1926: when she was found at a hotel in Harrogate, the *Daily Mail* went to the length of chartering a special train in the hope that she could be rushed to London for an exclusive interview; she refused, although the episode did no harm to her public career. Perhaps in the hope of avoiding such attentions, an unusual number of authors, especially those with respectable bourgeois par-ents, concealed themselves behind pseudonyms: Cissie Fairfield took the name of the Ibsen heroine 'Rebecca West', Kathleen Beauchamp became 'Katherine Mansfield', Gwen Williams remade herself as 'Jean Rhys', Henry Yorke as 'Henry Green', Eric Blair as 'George Orwell'. The poet C. Day Lewis disguised himself as 'Nicholas Blake' when writing middlebrow detective novels.

Although a few writers made fortunes and several more enjoyed the mixed blessings of fame, literary authorship was by no means typically a 'rags-to-riches' story. The social origins of authors in this period lie overwhelmingly among the middle classes. There is no exact science in such things, but a trawl through the biographies of about two hundred of the foremost figures shows that between 85 and 90 per cent of them can be described as middle class in origin. Most were sons and daughters of lawyers, doctors, schoolmasters, politicians, clergymen, stockbrokers, industrialists, architects, pro-fessors, bankers, diplomats, and Imperial administrators; a few were born among the inferior ranks of artists, estate agents, journalists, and shopkeepers. This preponderance of middle-class authors is neither a new nor a surprising feature of this period, as it matches fairly closely the sociological patterns of Victorian and Edwardian authorship. The remaining 10 or 15 per cent comprised on the one side the children of the aristocracy, like Vita Sackville-West, and the landed gentry (Edith Sitwell and her literary brothers, for instance), and on the other the sons—not, in this category, the daughters—of smallholders, artisans, and labourers. Until the 1930s, hardly any writers emerged from the industrial working class in the strict sense, apart from D. H. Lawrence, the son of a coal miner, and Edgar Wallace, the adopted son of a Billingsgate fish porter. A few other authors had endured real destitution: before becoming a 'Georgian' poet, W. H. Davies had one leg amputated and lived as a tramp; and

WOMAN WINS OUR £400 PICTURE PUZZLE PRIZE

DAILY SKETCH

INCORPORATING THE DAILY GRAPHIC

No. 5,518. Telephones { London—Museum 8141. Manchester—City 6561. LONDON, WEDNESDAY, DECEMBER 15, 1926. [Registered as a Newspaper] ONE PENNY.

20 Pages
DARK
BLUES
AGAIN
ROUTED
AT
TWICKENHAM

MRS. AGATHA CHRISTIE FOUND ALIVE

Colonel Archibald Christie, who throughout the long suspense resolutely declined to believe that his wife was dead. " I want to believe she is alive," he said.

A diver making ready for the renewed search which was to have been made to-day for the novelist in pools on the Surrey Downs—plans which are, of course, now cancelled.

Missing for eleven days, Mrs. Agatha Christie, the novelist, of whom this is one of the latest photographs, was found yesterday at Harrogate. Following on police information her husband, Colonel Christie, travelled earlier in the day to the Yorkshire resort from Sunningdale, from which Mrs. Christie disappeared on the evening of Friday, December 3. To-day a search of the Surrey Downs over an area of 40 square miles was to have been made, and divers were to have descended pools and wells near Newlands Corner, where the novelist's car was found abandoned the day after she left home. Inset : Mrs. Christie with her little daughter Rosalind.

The lonely hut, near Newlands Corner, in which police, searching for Mrs. Christie, discovered a torn-up postcard and a fur coat. The hut was subsequently placed under police guard.

Fig. 1. The front page of the *Daily Sketch* for 15 December 1926 announces the safe discovery of Agatha Christie at a hotel in Harrogate, following an eleven-day disappearance during which she had been feared dead.
(British Library, Newspaper Library LD19)

the war poet Isaac Rosenberg grew up in a family of seven living in one room in Stepney while his mother took in washing and his father scraped a living as a pedlar.

One should not assume, from the bare fact that most writers' fathers were in the more prosperous professions, that these authors were all nurtured in conventional middle-class stability and comfort. Some indeed were blessed with financial security, familial support, and stimulating education; but a common pattern in these writers' lives is that of a childhood disrupted by the death, desertion, or financial ruin of the father. W. Somerset Maugham, for example, was orphaned at the age of 10, suffering thereafter from a lifelong stammer. The list of writers bereaved in childhood is extensive: Hilaire Belloc, Agatha Christie, C. Day-Lewis, Norman Douglas, E. M. Forster, and Christopher Isherwood lost their fathers; and Elizabeth Bowen, John Masefield, Louis MacNeice, J. B. Priestley, and Virginia Woolf mourned the early deaths of their mothers. Wyndham Lewis, Siegfried Sassoon, Radclyffe Hall, and Rebecca West were brought up by their mothers, their fathers having absconded. Dorothy Richardson grew up amid the opulence of the idle rich, but her father was bankrupted and her mother slit her own throat with a kitchen knife, leaving her to fend for herself by working as a dental receptionist. Sudden financial ruin also afflicted the families of Bernard Shaw and May Sinclair, whose fathers were both alcoholics. John Masefield's father, a solicitor, suffered financial losses that led to his insanity; the future Poet Laureate joined the merchant navy at the age of 13 and subsequently lived for a while as a vagrant in America. There were other private griefs and disasters to endure: Virginia Woolf was sexually molested by her half-brothers, Aldous Huxley was nearly blinded by an eye infection in boyhood, and Graham Greene attempted suicide as a schoolboy. In various ways, the apparently comfortable backgrounds of middle-class writers were often in fact marked by profound disturbances and, as we shall see, dislocations.

Despite its domination by children of middle-class professionals, literary authorship was of course not itself a secure profession requiring regular educational qualifications, like medicine or the law. This indeed was a major part of its attraction for the nonconformists and misfits who were drawn to it, and for those who had not been through higher education—especially women and lower middle-class men. Journalism still provided the usual route into authorship, although novel-writing and travel-writing were increasingly becoming graduate careers, this being a significant shift from the nineteenth-century pattern in which leading poets came out of the universities while leading novelists did not. The growing participation of women in higher education speeded this new trend, especially at Somerville College, Oxford, where Vera Brittain, Winifred Holtby, Rose Macaulay, and Dorothy L. Sayers all studied. In all, roughly half of the prominent authors of this period had had some experience of university or college, although few of these had studied literary subjects. Most were qualified in history, law, philosophy, mathematics, or medicine. There were a few who had studied modern languages (James Joyce, Dorothy L. Sayers) or classics (Ivy Compton-Burnett, Louis MacNeice), but even though English Literature had been available at Oxford since 1893 and at Cambridge from 1917, only a tiny minority of writers had taken degree courses in this subject: these included Edmund Blunden, Robert Graves, Rosamond Lehmann, Aldous Huxley, Henry Green, and W. H. Auden, whose first year at Oxford was spent as a student of biology. A leading author at this time was more likely to have a training in the sciences, like H. G. Wells, W. Somerset Maugham, Naomi Mitchison, Arthur Ransome, and David Garnett, or in music or fine art (Katherine Mansfield, Agatha Christie, Wyndham Lewis, W. B. Yeats) than in English Literature.

The most striking new feature of authorship in this period is to be found in the patterns of migration and geographical dispersal which shaped the lives and public careers of many writers, setting them at a remove from English culture. The novelist and critic Frank Swinnerton, surveying the contemporary literary scene in 1934, observed that 'an extraordinary number of English writers are Americans, Frenchmen, Scotsmen, Irishmen, Welshmen, Jews, South Africans, Australasians, and Poles'.[2] Recent interest in the 'postcolonial' dimensions of works by writers born at the outposts of the British Empire has highlighted the cases of the New Zealander Katherine Mansfield and of Jean Rhys, born and raised in the

---

[2] Frank Swinnerton, *The Georgian Literary Scene* (Dent, 1938), 79.

Caribbean island of Dominica. To be reminded of the origins of such figures is helpful, but it hardly begins to indicate the momentous extent of deracination, expatriation, and cultural hybridity among authors of this period. A traditional form of internal migration, in which the ambitious Scottish, Welsh, or Irish writer gravitates towards London as a literary and publishing centre, continues in this period: the Dubliners Bernard Shaw and W. B. Yeats had already broken into the London literary scene, along with the Scots Arthur Conan Doyle and J. M. Barrie; and the newer Celtic arrivals included John Buchan, Edwin Muir, Louis MacNeice, and Dylan Thomas. Following the example of Henry James, a few American writers settled in the old country either permanently (T. S. Eliot, from 1914) or temporarily (Ezra Pound, from 1908 to 1920). Some writers had migrated from the colonies in late adolescence (Rhys, Mansfield, Roy Campbell, P. L. Travers), while many more had been sent or brought to England as children. George Orwell had been born in Bengal, Harold Nicolson in Tehran, Hugh Walpole in New Zealand, and the poet Harold Monro in Belgium; but all had been sent 'home' to endure an English public-school education. Maugham had grown up in Paris until the age of 10, and his first language was French; similarly, William Gerhardi had passed his boyhood in St Petersburg speaking Russian and French. Rose Macaulay had spent most of her childhood in Italy, while Enid Bagnold's early years were spent variously in Jamaica, Switzerland, France, and Germany. Apart from such children of British expatriates, there were several writers of mixed or entirely foreign parentage: Max Beerbohm, Ford Madox Ford, and Robert Graves all came from half-German families; Hilaire Belloc, born near Paris, was Anglo-French; Norman Douglas was born in Austria of Scottish-German parentage, and German had been his first language; Michael Arlen had been born as Dikran Kouyoumdjian in Bulgaria, to Armenian parents who brought him to England as a child.

As outsiders came in, insiders departed. The Irishman James Joyce regarded exile as an artistic virtue, and passed nearly all his adult life in Trieste, Zurich, and Paris. The best-known of the English literary emigrants was D. H. Lawrence, who turned his back on England after the Great War and lived with his German wife in Italy, Australia, Mexico, the United States, and Ceylon before dying in

France. Although rooted, like Lawrence, in the English Midlands, Arnold Bennett married a Frenchwoman and lived for many years in her country, and Francis Brett Young wrote his Midlands novels in his home in Italy. Aldous Huxley married a Belgian refugee, and they spent most of the years between the wars in France and Italy before settling in California. Edmund Blunden had an academic post in Japan, William Empson was a professor at the University of Peking, and Robert Graves, briefly professor of English at Cairo, spent most of his adult life in Majorca. By the end of the Thirties, W. H. Auden, Christopher Isherwood, the playwrights Dodie Smith and R. C. Sherriff, and the novelist James Hilton had all, like Huxley, emigrated to the United States. Ford Madox Ford settled in Paris in 1922, and Edith Sitwell made the same move two years later. Richard Aldington went into European exile in 1928, and in the same year Somerset Maugham bought a villa near Monte Carlo as his permanent residence. Michael Arlen settled in the south of France shortly afterwards, as did P. G. Wodehouse in 1934. Some of the writers who had arrived in England from overseas moved abroad again: Rhys to Paris, Pound to Paris and then Italy, Mansfield to Italy and France, Roy Campbell to Spain. Although there were a few notable writers who stayed in one place for most of their lives—F. R. Leavis in Cambridge, T. F. Powys in Dorset—British authors were usually well travelled. Even Rupert Brooke, who gave us the phrase 'for ever England' and the playfully nostalgic image of teatime in Grantchester, actually wrote most of his poems on his travels in Germany, the United States, and Tahiti.

Migration and international travel had their obvious cultural value for imaginative writers. Besides, as the Romantic poets before them had known, it was cheaper to live in Italy than in England, and the food, wine, and weather were better. Continental Europe was also, as it had been for Byron and Shelley, the obvious refuge for sexual outlaws. Katherine Mansfield abandoned her husband within a few hours of marrying him and, pregnant by another man, disappeared to an obscure Bavarian spa. Bavaria was also the destination of D. H. Lawrence when he eloped in 1912 with Frieda Weekley, the wife of his former tutor. Robert Graves left his wife and four children to set up a home with the American poet Laura Riding in Majorca. Norman Douglas was able to tour southern Italy in 1911 accompanied by a 12-year-old catamite, but he could not get away with seducing a teenage boy in London five years later: charged with gross indecency, he jumped bail and fled back to the Mediterranean. For homosexual men in particular, exile was both safer (the trials of Oscar Wilde were still within living memory) and more exciting: the nightclubs of Berlin were a home from home for Christopher Isherwood, while Noël Coward enjoyed the company of sailors at the various ports of call on his international tours, and E. M. Forster was provided by his Indian employer in 1921 with his own 'barber' for sexual purposes.

In cases such as these, the strikingly migratory condition of authors in this period converges with a second prominent feature of their way of life, which is the prevalence among them of unorthodox sexualities and irregular ménages. At least a quarter of the prominent writers of the time may be categorized as homosexual or bisexual, and among the heterosexuals there were several parents of illegitimate children (Rebecca West and H. G. Wells in concert; James Joyce, Wyndham Lewis, Ezra Pound, and Dorothy L. Sayers severally), adulterers of various kinds (Edmund Blunden, Jean Rhys, Rose Macaulay, John Galsworthy), and notorious womanizers including H. G. Wells, who—to twist his words quoted above—indeed had familiar and unrestrained intercourse with a great variety of people. Male homosexuality or homoerotic feeling is notable among the war poets (Owen, Sassoon), among the Bloomsbury Group (Strachey, Forster), among successful playwrights (Maugham, Coward), and among the younger writers of the Thirties (Auden, Spender, Isherwood). Some of the prominent women writers of the time were evidently confirmed lesbians (Radclyffe Hall, Sheila Kaye-Smith, Charlotte Mew, Vita Sackville-West, Sylvia Townsend Warner) or had significant lesbian affairs (Virginia Woolf, Katherine Mansfield, Mary Butts). Recent lesbian scholarship has extended this list to include other women writers who were given to intense female friendships, Ivy Compton-Burnett, Ruth Pitter, Angela Brazil, and Elizabeth Bowen among them.

The sexual dimension of modern authorship has an importance beyond that of historical gossip, not as a mere aggregation of individual 'orientations' but as a genuine subculture of emancipation in which erotic and artistic exploration often went hand in hand. The playfulness of Virginia Woolf's *Orlando* (1928), for instance, arises directly from her affair with Vita Sackville-West. Such continuities between personal and literary forms of rebellion against censorious 'Victorianism' were by no means confined to the networks of homo-sexuals and 'bohemian' modernists. Among the so-called Edwardian writers, John Galsworthy drew upon his ten-year affair with his cousin's wife, whom he eventually married, for the main plot and for the humane moral intention of his *Forsyte Saga*, which is essentially a liberal-feminist novel about the conflict between sexual and aes-thetic liberty on the one side and bourgeois forms of property on the other.

The dynamics of literary culture in this period were shaped by a remarkable sharpening of generational differences and conflicts. Antagonism between old and young may be a perennial problem of human life and a commonplace theme of fiction and drama, but it quite suddenly assumes a central importance in literature at the time of the Great War. At the age of 25, Wilfred Owen wrote a shocking verse travesty of the Biblical story of Abraham and his son Isaac, entitled 'The Parable of the Old Man and the Young'. As in the Biblical account, Abraham passes God's test of loyalty by preparing, as commanded, to sacrifice his son, and is then told at the last minute by an angel to kill a ram instead. Owen's topical version ends:

> But the old man would not do so, but slew his son,
> And half the seed of Europe, one by one.
>
> (*The Poems*, p. 151)

In the view of Owen and of much of his generation, the War was an unforgiveable act of ritual filicide for which the Old Men as a whole stood condemned. This accusation recurs in such poems as Richard Aldington's 'The Blood of the Young Men' and Osbert Sitwell's 'Hymn to Moloch' (both 1919). As Robert Graves recalled, he and Siegfried Sasson had agreed in 1917 that the continuation of the War 'seemed merely a sacrifice of the idealistic younger generation to the stupidity and self-protective alarm of the elder' (*Good-bye to All That*, p. 202). George Orwell too recollected of the revolu-tionary mood of 1918 that among the young a 'dominance of "old men" was held to be responsible for every evil known to humanity'

(*Road to Wigan Pier*, ch. 9). Even some of the old men agreed: at the age of 63, Bernard Shaw wrote in his Preface (1919) to *Heartbreak House* that in the War 'the young, the innocent, the hopeful expiated the folly and worthlessness of their elders' (p. 16). Through the post-War decades, the younger writers' gerontophobic resentment simmered on.

The official mechanisms of the War itself, under the Military Service Act of 1916, divided the male population of Great Britain neatly into three categories: those who had been born before 1875 and who were too old to be conscripted; those who had been born in the last quarter of the previous century, who were, by the time of the November 1918 Armistice, liable to conscription (unless exempted under various provisions including those for 'conscientious objectors'); and those born in or after 1900, who were too young to serve. Most of the authors active in the 1910–40 period belonged to the generation that was liable to military service, having been born between 1875 and 1899. As a convenient date from which to chart the relevant ages, we may take Sunday, 15 August 1915, when the government conducted a census, or 'National Registration' of all men and women aged between 15 and 65, ostensibly for the purpose of assessing and rationalizing its industrial requirements. On that date, all but three of the writers whose works are considered in this book were alive.[3] Some, however, were more alive than others: Thomas Hardy, revered as the Grand Old Man of English letters, was 75 years old, while Dylan Thomas was still a babe in arms. Apart from Hardy, the other Grand Old Men were Henry James (aged 72) and the serving Poet Laureate Robert Bridges (70). Senior figures on the literary scene included Edmund Gosse (65), Bernard Shaw (59), Joseph Conrad (57), Arthur Conan Doyle (56), A. E. Housman (56), and the patriotic poet Henry Newbolt (53). W. B. Yeats had recently celebrated his fiftieth birthday, and there was a clutch of established writers who were in their late forties: Arnold Bennett, John Galsworthy, Rudyard Kipling, and H. G. Wells. Also above the maximum conscriptable age of 40 were G. K. Chesterton, W. H. Davies, Walter de la Mare, Ford Madox Hueffer, W. Somerset Maugham, John Cowper Powys, Dorothy Richardson, and May

[3] The exceptions were the poets James Elroy Flecker and Rupert Brooke, who had both died earlier in the same year, and the playwright Stanley Houghton (d. 1913).

Sinclair. Hueffer, later surnamed Ford, did in fact serve in the War, having concealed his true age when he volunteered.

At the other end of the scale lie the younger writers who emerged in the late 1920s, like Rosamond Lehmann and Evelyn Waugh, or in the 1930s, like W. H. Auden and Daphne du Maurier. These authors had still been children during the War, and had grown up as fully 'modern' spirits, born in the new century itself. Between these extremes of age and youth we find the great majority of this period's authors, including the leading modernists, who were in their early thirties (Joyce, Lewis, Woolf) or late twenties (Eliot, Mansfield, Pound) on National Registration day; the Bloomsbury Group writers E. M. Forster (36) and Lytton Strachey (35); and most of the women writers who emerged in the 1920s, Elizabeth Bowen (16), Agatha Christie (24), Radclyffe Hall (35), Jean Rhys (24), Vita Sackville-West (23), and Mary Webb (34) among them. Everybody, old or young, was affected by the War; but it was this middle generation that bore the brunt, experiencing combat itself, or witnessing the resulting injuries and derangements, as did the many women writers who served as volunteer nurses, or mourning the deaths of brothers, lovers, and close friends.

Quite apart from the divisions exposed by the War, the resentments of younger writers were inflamed by the visible prosperity of some of the senior authors. Shaw, Wells, Galsworthy, Maugham, Bennett, Buchan, and Wodehouse were all known to have earned fortunes from their writings, while Pound, Joyce, Eliot, and a host of junior literati lived either on handouts from patrons or by whatever job they could find in teaching, journalism, advertising, or banking. A simple reason for the disparity was that it usually took many years to establish oneself as a financially self-supporting author. Joseph Conrad, for example, had written all his major novels and reached the age of 56 before he benefited from his first commercial success with his novel *Chance* in 1913. Virginia Woolf did not start to earn significant sums from her novels until *Orlando* did well in America, by which time she was 47 years old. Arnold Bennett made his breakthrough in 1912, and recorded it in his journal for that year, at the age of 45:

All my five later plays have been performed this year. About 1,155 p[erforman]ces altogether. I received (less agents' commissions) about £16,000 during the year, which may be called success by any worldly-minded author. It is apparently about as much as I had earned during all the previous part of my life. And I bought a car and a yacht, and arranged to buy a house. (*Journals*, p. 358)

Bennett had become indeed one of the country's highest earners in any profession. He was never forgiven by younger writers for that yacht; but he had been writing novels and plays for fourteen years to earn it. It is worth noting here that although Bennett is now remembered as a novelist, he earned more in some years from his plays than from his books. His case is one of several that tend to show that the most prosperous literary careers, such as those of Galsworthy, Maugham, Wodehouse, and Wallace, were those that combined stage plays with novels. As any competent literary agent knew, the best way to follow up the success of one's novel was to take advantage of the performance rights enshrined in the 1911 Copyright Act by adapting the book speedily for the stage, in collaboration with an experienced playwright. Margaret Kennedy, for instance, did this successfully with her *The Constant Nymph* (1924, dramatized 1926), and Walter Greenwood did the same with his *Love on the Dole* (1933, dramatized 1934); both went on to earn yet more from the film rights.

To become a really successful author, it was best to be prolific. Bennett usually wrote between one and two thousand words a day, and all before breakfast. Edgar Wallace could turn out one of his thrillers in a matter of days, and he managed sixteen of them in the year 1926 alone. But even if one were merely to make a modest living as an author, one would usually have to write in a number of different forms addressed to different readerships. Just as publishers needed to compensate for their losses on highbrow material by producing larger runs of middlebrow books, so authors had to support their more experimental work by writing in safely remunerative forms as well. The case of D. H. Lawrence illustrates this particularly well. The disastrous suppression of his novel *The Rainbow* in 1915 threatened to cut short a promising career, which he salvaged by writing essays, reviews, short stories, travel books, and even a school history book, all pitched at a more popular level than the poems and novels which these works allowed him to continue writing. Virginia Woolf meanwhile relied upon regular book-reviewing for the *Times Literary Supplement* and upon the modest profits of the Hogarth Press. Robert Graves and C. Day-Lewis sustained their careers as poets in the Thirties by writing popular historical and detective novels, Edith Sitwell by writing newspaper articles and popular biographies.

Most novelists and virtually all poets failed to become self-supporting authors. They were part-time writers only, living on their salaries from other employments. Although there were a few books of verse that achieved best-seller status, such as John Masefield's *Collected Poems* of 1923 and Robert Bridges's *The Testament of Beauty* (1929), most of the poets had to support themselves by other means. T. S. Eliot worked for Lloyd's Bank before joining a firm of publishers, Auden and Day-Lewis worked as schoolteachers, Blunden and MacNeice as university lecturers. One of the fictional characters in Aldous Huxley's *Those Barren Leaves* (1925) is a poet who earns his living as editor of the *Rabbit Fanciers' Gazette*, an irony derived from Huxley's own former employment by the firm of Condé Nast on *House & Garden* magazine, and from the more general reliance of poets upon income from journalistic hack-work. Novelists too usually needed a second career to support them, and often enough this was journalism, either of a literary kind, as with Ford Madox Ford, Rebecca West, and J. B. Priestley, or on the regular staff of newspapers, like Graham Greene, who was a sub-editor on *The Times*. John Buchan combined journalism with publishing, David Garnett was a bookseller and publisher, Henry Green worked on the shop floor of his father's factory, and R. H. Mottram worked in a bank, while Dorothy L. Sayers and Eric Ambler were both copywriters in advertising agencies. George Orwell moved from schoolteaching to bookselling and then to market gardening.

Without such a second income, the financial security required in order to write came from inherited family wealth (as with Radclyffe Hall), or from marriage, or from patrons. Ben Travers became the most successful writer of farces in the West End because his marriage to a wealthy woman allowed him to engage in full-time authorship. Daphne du Maurier married a Guards officer who later became a member of the Royal Household, and Enid Bagnold became Lady Jones by marrying Sir Roderick, chairman of Reuters News Agency. Harriet Weaver, the business manager of *The Egoist*, was the munificent patron of James Joyce, to whom she paid more than £20,000 over a period of nine years from 1914, receiving in return a few thank-you letters and the manuscript of *A Portrait of the Artist as a Young Man*. Another important 'angel' of London modernism was John Quinn, a New York lawyer and collector of literary rarities, who subsidized Yeats, Conrad, Eliot, Pound, and Joyce, often by purchasing their manuscripts; by 1924 he had amassed a collection that included the manuscripts of *The Waste Land* and *Ulysses*, which he then sold, their value having been enhanced by the critical endorsement of the little magazines which he also patronized.

Literary prizes were not of direct benefit to the indigent author, as the only one with significant cash value, the Nobel, was awarded to writers of long-established reputations: Yeats in 1923, Shaw in 1925, Galsworthy in 1932. The award of a prominent literary prize could, however, launch a young writer's career. The Hawthornden Prize, established in 1919, was reserved for authors under 41 years of age. David Garnett, for example, won it in 1923 for his romance *Lady into Fox*, which also took the James Tait Black Memorial Prize for the best novel of the previous year. The Shropshire novelist Mary Webb won the Femina Vie Heureuse Prize in 1925 for *Precious Bane*, but this did little for its sales. Only after the Prime Minister, Stanley Baldwin, praised the book in a speech at a literary event three years later were her novels widely noticed and reprinted, by which time Webb herself had died.

Behind the public world of literary honours there lay a private realm in which Mr Eliot was 'Tom', Mr Forster was 'Morgan', Mr Maugham was 'Willie', Mr Wodehouse was 'Plum', Mr Garnett was 'Bunny', and Miss Radclyffe Hall was 'John'. This was a remarkably small world, in which most authors would already know some others through connections of family or school, or would come to know fellow writers through shared publishers, agents, hostesses, or regular social and professional gatherings. An entry in Arnold Bennett's journal for 1919 indicates something of the diversity of such social networks: 'Dined at Osbert Sitwell's. Good Dinner. Fish before soup. Present, W. H. Davies, Lytton Strachey, [Leonard]

Woolf, [Robert] Nichols, S. Sassoon, Aldous Huxley, Atkin (a very young caricaturist), W. J. Turner, and Herbert Read (a very young poet)' (*Journals*, p. 437). Here, writers whom we might think of as belonging in separate compartments marked 'realist', 'modernist', 'Bloomsburyite', 'Georgian', or 'war poet' were in fact mixing freely. The small size of the literary-artistic community in London, and the numerous interconnections between its three principal centres— Bloomsbury for intellectuals, Mayfair for fashionable socialites, Chelsea for artists and lesbians—made this kind of encounter between young authors and old authors, experimental authors and traditionalist authors almost inevitable. At the same time, authors did form themselves into groupings and coteries of the like-minded, often through little magazines or anthologies with distinctive positions, and through the literary salons or looser social networks that sustained these projects.

Much of the story of London modernism, for instance, can be told as a succession of busy efforts by Ezra Pound to make friends and influence people. He had started by joining Yeats's Monday salon, moved on to T. E. Hulme's Thursday salon, made contact both with Ford Madox Hueffer's *English Review* and with A. R. Orage's *New Age*, gathered his own Tuesday salon of 'Imagists' including his former inamorata Hilda Doolittle and Richard Aldington, become Yeats's secretary, and through this connection been put in touch with James Joyce. By 1914, he had unofficially taken effective control of *The New Freewoman*, converted it into *The Egoist*, and installed Aldington as deputy editor, meanwhile joining in Wyndham Lewis's magazine *Blast*, to whose position he gave the name 'Vorticist', and 'discovering' T. S. Eliot, to whom he later gave Aldington's job on *The Egoist*. He spent the next years vigorously promoting the work of Joyce, Eliot, Yeats, and Lewis to publishers, patrons, and magazine editors, and publicizing the work of his sculptor friend Henri Gaudier-Brzeska. Richard Aldington later remarked that 'Whenever Ezra has launched a new movement, he has never had any difficulty about finding members. He just calls on his friends.'[4]

The most important of the social groupings of writers and artists was the Bloomsbury Group, which comprised both an inner sanctum

---

[4] Richard Aldington, *Life for Life's Sake* (Viking, 1941), 135.

of close friends and an extensive periphery of sympathizers, guests, and hangers-on, including the literary-artistic salon of Lady Ottoline Morrell at Garsington Manor near Oxford. At the centre of this group, which had begun to coalesce as a Thursday-evening discussion circle in 1905, were the artist Vanessa Bell and her husband Clive Bell, along with Vanessa's sister Virginia Stephen, and Clive's Cambridge friends Lytton Strachey, Maynard Keynes, Leonard Woolf, and Desmond MacCarthy. The internal dynamics of this group assumed a new complexity in 1909, when Virginia's and Vanessa's brother Adrian Stephen brought in his homosexual lover, the artist Duncan Grant, who had previously had affairs with Strachey and Keynes. The voracious Grant later had a long affair with Vanessa, who had a daughter by him in 1918, but not before she herself had fallen in love with the art critic Roger Fry, who was drawn into the group in 1910, shortly before E. M. Forster, another Cambridge-educated homosexual, became a new member of the expanded circle. Before taking up with Vanessa in 1911, Fry had had a brief affair with Ottoline Morrell, who then took as her lover the Cambridge philosopher Bertrand Russell. By the time Leonard Woolf, having returned from a posting in Ceylon, married Virginia Stephen in 1912, the group had accommodated both a bewildering complexity of sexual entanglements and a formidable range of intellectual talent, some of it yet to be established on the public stage: Fry had made his name as an art critic, partly through his Post-Impressionist Exhibitions of 1910–11 and 1912, and Forster had won a reputation for his novels, but it was some time before Strachey became famous as a biographer, Clive Bell as an art critic, Keynes as an economist, and Virginia Woolf as a novelist, critic, and publisher.

The Bloomsbury Group had no formal creed, doctrine, or manifesto, but it cultivated a recognizably coherent set of values: liberal pacifism, feminism, and anti-imperialism in politics, agnosticism in religion, abstract form rather than moralizing content in art and literature, and the primacy of personal friendships over public obligations. It constituted a centre of 'civilized' rebellion against the moral code of Victorianism, especially in its toleration of unorthodox sexual arrangements and in its endorsement of the unpopular pacifist position in the Great War. During the War, Bloomsburyites aided conscientious objectors by getting them employment as land workers. Thus the young David Garnett was taken on as a labourer by Vanessa Bell and Duncan Grant at their country house in Sussex; he too was added to Grant's list of lovers. Meanwhile Ottoline Morrell and her husband, the pacifist MP Philip Morrell, had moved to Garsington Manor, where they employed Clive Bell and Aldous Huxley on the farm. Here, Huxley was introduced to Ottoline's other protégés, including D. H. Lawrence, T. S. Eliot, John Middleton Murry, Katherine Mansfield, and the artist Mark Gertler, as well as the Bloomsbury set itself. It was through Lady Ottoline that Eliot was first introduced into English literary society, and that Huxley was introduced both to his wife Maria Nys and to his future employer Murry. Her assistance to Lawrence, Huxley, and others, though, did not spare her from later satiric assaults on her eccentricities: she almost sued for libel upon learning that the character of Hermione Roddice in Lawrence's *Women in Love* (1920) was based on her, and she later appeared as the gushingly 'soulful' hostess Priscilla Wimbush in Huxley's novel *Crome Yellow* (1921), and as the pretentious Mrs Aldwinkle in *Those Barren Leaves* (1925). As we shall see in Chapter 12, the world of such literary coteries and salons, with their compounded elements of sexual intrigue and artistic pretension, provided rich materials to the satirists of the age.

Few major writers of the Twenties escaped the orbit of Bloomsbury. Bernard Shaw, for instance, met the Woolfs in 1916 while he was writing *Heartbreak House*, and in the same year Siegfried Sassoon and Robert Graves visited the Morrells; T. E. Lawrence became friends with Forster, Noël Coward was invited for tea and mutual admiration by Virginia Woolf in 1928, and Rosamond Lehmann's brother John was employed by the Woolfs at the Hogarth Press, having befriended their nephew Julian Bell at Cambridge. Personal relations constituted the highest value for the Bloomsburyites, and they were the principal mode by which their tentacular influence was felt. Having no doctrine to proclaim, they had no need for sectarian anthologies or little magazines, especially since they had in the Hogarth Press their own publishing house, and had ready access to the pages of the weekly *New Statesman*, of which Desmond MacCarthy was literary editor. It has been claimed that the

Bloomsbury influence on educated opinion in England lies behind the revolution of sexual and cultural attitudes in the 1960s. With more certainty it can be shown that it sponsored some of the leading writers of the next generation in the Thirties. The Hogarth Press published C. Day Lewis's first volumes of verse, and then the anthology *New Signatures* (1932), which brought the poetry of Auden, Spender, and Day Lewis to wider notice. The Woolfs' protégé John Lehmann, who had commissioned this anthology, went on to promote the verse of the Auden group in his periodical *New Writing* from 1936. Meanwhile Christopher Isherwood's novels were being published under the Hogarth imprint, and Forster was becoming a close friend and mentor to the younger novelist. The Auden-Spender-Isherwood-MacNeice circle was itself, like the Bloomsbury group, a sort of conspiracy of friends: not only did they often collaborate (Auden and Isherwood on plays, Auden and MacNeice on *Letters from Iceland*, 1937), they repeatedly dedicated their books to one another, incorporated private references and pet names into their writings, adopting the manner of a schoolboy gang. As they began to dominate the literary scene in the Thirties, they came to be seen as an Old Boys' network, favoured, for instance, by Forster's homosexual friend Joe Ackerley, literary editor of *The Listener*. From the inside, the Bloomsbury Group and the Auden group were centres of modern enlightenment, but to indignant observers on the outside, such as the Leavises in Cambridge, both groups appeared to be cliques of effete poseurs dedicated chiefly to self-promotion.

The literary world was so small, so narrow in its social base, and so taken up with its own company, that it should not surprise us to find it marked also by vicious snobbery and backbiting. If one reads through the letters and diaries, and even the published writings, of some of this period's leading authors—not just those who sympathized with Fascism, like Yeats, Lawrence, Eliot, Lewis, Pound, and Radclyffe Hall, but 'civilized' liberals like Aldous Huxley and Virginia Woolf—one is disconcerted to come across frequent complaints about the stupidity of servants, the smelliness of the lower orders, the vulgarity of Jews and lower middle-class types, and the 'commonness' of just about anybody outside the writer's own caste. These are symptoms of a larger cultural problem, which is the strong conviction among most literary intellectuals that they constituted an elite of sensitive and discriminating souls who scarcely belonged to the same species as the automatized 'herd' of semi-educated clerks and gullible cinema-goers who thronged the expanding suburbs—the likes of Leonard Bast in *Howards End* or the typist and her spotty boyfriend in 'The Waste Land'. John Carey's book *The Intellectuals and the Masses* (1992), despite the injustice in its use of Adolf Hitler as a point of comparison, has demonstrated the prevalence among this period's authors not just of petty snobberies but of violent fantasies of extermination or selective breeding directed at the swarming multitudes of modern democracy. Many authors, although certainly not all, regarded themselves as members of a sort of spiritual aristocracy which—like the real landed aristocracy after the 'People's Budget' of 1909—was threatened with extinction by the commercialized culture of the suburban hordes. Such views were shared by Bloomsburyites like Clive Bell in his book *Civilization* (1928) and by sworn enemies of Bloomsbury condescension like F. R. Leavis in his *Mass Civilization and Minority Culture* (1933): both maintained that the preservation of culture depended upon the vigilance of that small cultivated minority which was capable, as the 'masses' were plainly not, of discriminating true art from mere entertainment or journalism.

The vigilance maintained by this aristocracy of taste in reinforcing the line between true art and pseudo-art could easily turn into an orgy of critical recrimination in which no literary reputation was safe from accusations of fraudulence. The writings of Wyndham Lewis are animated by a compulsion to expose virtually all other writers and artists as charlatans, while the critical essays of Ezra Pound and F. R. Leavis display a fanatic exclusiveness in reducing the number of living writers who were worthy of being described as 'serious' artists to a tiny handful. Among the younger modernists, only a few modern masters—Henry James, T. S. Eliot, Ezra Pound, D. H. Lawrence, James Joyce—were above suspicion of compromise with 'mass' culture, but in some quarters even Lawrence and Joyce were held to be blemished by vulgarity. Unseemly feuds broke out between rival authors: Edith Sitwell never forgave Noël Coward for writing a revue sketch in which she was sent up as 'Hernia Whittlebot', and Somerset Maugham offended Hugh Walpole by portraying him as a self-promoting mediocrity in his novel *Cakes and Ale* (1930), a satire on the vanities of novelists. Authorship remained a great adventure, but there was a price to be paid for it in the form of envy and malice. As George Orwell concluded, 'it is not easy to crash your way into the literary intelligentsia if you happen to be a decent human being' (*Road to Wigan Pier*, ch. 10).

3

Modern English Usage

New Words, 1910–1940

*articulacy   commercialese   headlinese   legalese
lexicalize   metalanguage   non-standard   officese
sloganize   standardizable   translatorese   trilingualism*

The processes of change in early twentieth-century life are most commonly presented in terms of technological inventions such as those in motorized transport, aviation, and radio, or sometimes by reference to new theoretical models such as Relativity and Psychoanalysis. But there were innovations in the sphere of language as well. Although now scarcely remembered as an event of any cultural significance, the arrival of the crossword puzzle in 1924 may be seen as marking a new kind of relationship between the literate public and the vocabulary, orthography, and morphology of the English language. It started as a newspaper craze, fomented by the offer of cash prizes, but it soon established itself as a national institution, confirmed by the inauguration in 1930 of *The Times* crossword. By this time, crossword fiends were beginning to appear in fiction, too: Sidney Quarles in Aldous Huxley's *Point Counter Point* (1928), and two nameless mariners in the opening chapter of Evelyn Waugh's *Vile Bodies* (1930), for example. Whether there is a connection between the crossword craze and the simultaneous boom in detective fiction, with its prominent puzzle-solving appeal, is a matter of conjecture; more certainly the crossword encouraged a widespread fascination with words for their own sakes. From their newspapers, readers were thus sent hurrying to their lexicons, and librarians complained that they had repeatedly to replace dictionaries, which were being mauled or even stolen by crossword addicts. For the crossword relies strongly upon prior linguistic regulation, including standardized spellings and the availability of 'authoritative' dictionaries such as the *Concise Oxford Dictionary* (1911) or the handier *Pocket Oxford Dictionary* (1924), both of them derived in part from the gigantic *New English Dictionary on Historical Principles* (1928), better known from 1933 as the *Oxford English Dictionary* or *OED*.

The completion—if it can really be called that—of the *OED* in 1928 after seventy years of toil by professional lexicographers and amateur word-hunters was an event of national significance: the first copy was presented to King George, and the Prime Minister of the day toasted the editors at a celebratory banquet. Arnold Bennett jokingly commended the dictionary as the longest sensational serial ever published—a reference to the fact that it had been appearing in paperbound instalments since 1884. It was already lagging well behind its original schedule even at that stage, and by 1910 the *OED* team had still only reached the letter *R*. The final stages of this great Victorian project bear some comparison with the contemporaneous British expeditions to the Antarctic, as the dictionary's heroic chief editor, Sir James Murray, died in 1915, having completed *T*, and his followers staggered on through the inhospitable wastes of *S*. C. T. Onions wrote the final entry, 'zyxt', in 1921, but *U* and most of *W* had yet to be conquered after the death of Murray's successor Henry Bradley in 1923. Even when 'completed' in twelve huge bound volumes in 1928, the dictionary required a thirteenth volume (1933) to accommodate more words that had been overlooked or had recently arrived in the language. Apart from new importations and coinages, with which it could never keep pace, the *OED* also deliberately excluded two notorious 'four-letter' words. By a happy coincidence, these two words were exhibited prominently in another book published (but not legally available in Britain) in 1928, *Lady Chatterley's Lover*. In this respect, Lawrence's novel constitutes an unauthorized supplement to the *OED*, complete with word definitions: in the twelfth chapter the gamekeeper Mellors offers his explanations of the two words to Lady Chatterley as she struggles to learn his dialect.

This unusual division of labour between Onions the lexicographer and Mellors the gamekeeper illustrates an important tension in this period between propriety and impropriety in language. On the one side was a quest for some authoritative standard of 'proper' English which was sought in such reference books as Daniel Jones's *English Pronouncing Dictionary* (1917), H. W. Fowler's *Modern English Usage* (1926), and the *OED* itself. On the other side, a number of writers tested the artificial boundary between what people really said and what could appear in print or on the stage. One form of this problem is presented in an innocuously comical fashion by Bernard Shaw's play *Pygmalion* (1914), in which the phonetician Professor Higgins accepts the challenge of passing off a Cockney flower seller, Eliza Doolittle, as a duchess by training her pronunciation. His first attempt to bring her into polite society, in his mother's drawing room in the third act, comes to grief because although Eliza's elocution is polished her idiom and the substance of her conversation—about her father's violent drinking bouts—are out of place. Unaware of the discrepancy, Eliza makes her famous exit:

LIZA [*perfectly elegant diction*] Walk! Not bloody likely. [*Sensation*].
  I am going in a taxi.   [*She goes out*].
  Pickering gasps and sits down.

The most interesting consequence of Eliza's little 'sensation' is that one of the young middle-class witnesses to it, Clara Eynsford Hill, immediately adopts the expletive as a refreshingly modern form of rebellion against Victorian linguistic prudery, which she condemns as 'bloody nonsense'. In this, Clara represents fairly accurately the 'advanced' view of the younger generation of women on their conversational liberties. By the Twenties, it had become a mark of 'the modern girl' that she swore freely. The opening dialogue of Agatha Christie's *The Murder on the Links* (1923) begins with a teenage girl shouting 'Hell!' in front of a stranger on a train; the stranger is Captain Hastings, who eventually marries her. Similarly Jennifer Baird in Rosamond Lehmann's *Dusty Answer* (1927) punctuates her speech with 'Christ!' and 'bloody', to the discomfort of the more prudent heroine. Reticence in speech had been more generally disrupted by the return of servicemen from the Great War, where some had come into contact with the lively invective employed by their

Australian comrades (they gave us *poofter*, for instance), and nearly all had learned to enliven their speech with words inadmissible to the dictionaries.

The gap between real usage and the official lexicon was to be bridged by an ex-soldier, the New Zealander Eric Partridge. Some years after serving with Australian forces at Gallipoli, he set out both to explore the riches of colloquialism and to shame the prudes of the *OED*, first with his *Songs and Slang of the British Soldier* (1930) and later with his pioneering *Dictionary of Slang and Unconventional English* (1937). On a much smaller scale, George Orwell too became a collector of slang terms: the thirty-second chapter of *Down and Out in Paris and London* (1933) comprises his observations on London slang, criminal patois, and swear words used by tramps with whom he had lived. The section on swearing, though, was rendered unintelligible in parts by his publishers' insistence on replacing the crucial words with dashes.[1]

Given the problems of official censorship by the police, the libraries, and the Lord Chamberlain (who still vetted theatrical productions), and the resulting timidity of publishers, little of the vernacular pungency relished by modern writers could find its way into literature, or into public print of any kind. Frederic Manning, an Australian who had served with a British regiment in the Great War, produced in 1929 a war novel, *The Middle Parts of Fortune*, the realism of which includes extensive use of all the strongest swear words by soldiers, and some of the newest playful forms, such as *abso-bloody-lutely*. But this was for private circulation only; the published version, entitled *Her Privates We* (1930), was expurgated. Richard Aldington tried at the same time to record the real speech-habits of the infantry in *Death of a Hero* (1929), but his publishers substituted asterisks for several expletives, and systematically misspelt one of them, with the result that soldiers in this novel tell one another to *muck off*. Laxity of speech, though, could be exploited in literary form if it avoided the obscene. Certain kinds of best-selling middlebrow fiction, like the Jeeves and Wooster stories of P. G. Wodehouse, and the schoolgirl adventures of Angela Brazil, depended for their special appeal upon the cultivation of slang, usu-

---

[1] Orwell's original words have been restored by Peter Davison in the *Collected Works* and in the subsequent Penguin edn.

ally of an old-fashioned kind, and the hero of H. G. Wells's *History of Mr Polly* (1910) endeared himself to readers by mispronouncing long words and employing 'Right O' as his habitual affirmation. The popularity of Waugh's *Vile Bodies*, like that of Noël Coward's early plays, had much to do with its capturing of the catchphrases ('darling, how too, too divine!' and the like) of the fashionable young.

Self-appointed defenders of 'pure' English meanwhile worried themselves less about schoolgirls saying *ripping* than about the debasement of public discourse, especially in journalism, advertising, and political rhetoric. For most of them, to say *bloody* was good earthy English, but to say *eventuate*, *finalize*, *intensive*, or *mentality*, or to use *contact* or *feature* as verbs was a capitulation to the empty verbiage of bureacrats—although one shouldn't say *bureaucrat* either, this being a mongrel coinage from two different languages. The fact that the principal campaigns for linguistic purity were directed not against blasphemers or people who dropped their aitches but against the euphemistic pomposities of the commercial and journalistic worlds helps to explain why so many imaginative writers signed up to join the Society for Pure English (SPE), which was founded in 1913 by the newly appointed Poet Laureate, Robert Bridges. The Society's membership list for 1925 included several other poets (Hardy, de la Mare, Sassoon), dramatists (Shaw), novelists (Wells), literary critics (A. C. Bradley, F. R. Leavis), lexicographers (Henry Bradley, H. W. Fowler), and other notables (the former Prime Minister Lord Balfour, the leading British psychoanalyst Ernest Jones), alongside various schools, colleges, and publishers. Acting independently, the novelist A. P. Herbert wrote for the jocular magazine *Punch* a series of lamentations about dreadful modern coinages, collecting these in his book *What a Word!* (1935). Herbert openly regrets the faint-hearted neutrality of the *OED*, and hopes 'that some virile new lexicographer will arise and make a *Good English Dictionary* showing us not only what is said but what is sound'.[2] His chamber of lexical horrors is occupied mainly by bureaucratic euphemisms such as *eventuate*, *maximize*, and *transpire*, but he also revolts against the coining of new verbs from nouns, as in *to service*, *to position*, or *to audition*.

[2] A. P. Herbert, *What a Word!* (Methuen, 1935), 49.

As for Bridges's Society for Pure English, its aims were modest and realistic enough: not to impose the purist whims of 'experts' upon the living language, but to provide advice upon problems of English usage based on sound linguistic knowledge, and to encourage clarity of communication by resisting confusing 'corruptions' of the language. The clearest statement of the SPE position is Bridges's pamphlet *The Society's Work* (1925), in which he argues that, given the centralization of the publishing world (newspapers and publishing houses now all had their manuals of 'house style'), the language could be made consistent in the light of the philological knowledge embodied in the *OED*. Bridges predicted that the SPE's most important influence would be upon newspaper editors. In fact only one major newspaper, the liberal *Manchester Guardian*, had subscribed to the SPE's publications, and it was the BBC that turned to the Society for assistance in compiling its handbook of pronunciation, through an advisory committee chaired by Bridges and then by Bernard Shaw.

The SPE itself published only a series of short tracts, but its purposes were embodied most fully in H. W. Fowler's substantial reference book *Modern English Usage*. This is in parts an eccentric work, some of whose longer entries have titles like 'Battered Ornaments' and 'Out of the Frying Pan', illustrated with countless solecisms perpetrated by the newspapers. Fowler certainly laments, in his entry on 'Presumptuous Word-Formation', the arrival of many malformed coinages: *pacifist*, for instance, should have been *pacificist*. But he is not a diehard purist, as he dismisses several of the shibboleths of 'correct' usage as ignorant superstitions: sentences can begin with *But*, it is better to straightforwardly split an infinitive than to artificially contort your syntax, and a preposition is as good a word as any other to end a sentence with. Fowler has some lively opinions on general matters of style, and a typically modern horror of cliché—of which he lists literary examples under 'Novelese'—but the bulk of his entries are short recommendations on the preferred spellings, pronunciations, and plural forms of individual words, especially foreign words. *Modern English Usage* was quickly adopted by journalists and other writers as the arbiter in these doubtful cases, supplementing the publisher's or newspaper's rules of house style.

The lengths to which the quest for linguistic uniformity and consistency was taken can be illustrated from the case of T. E. Lawrence's *Revolt in the Desert* (1927), the popular abridgement of his *Seven Pillars of Wisdom* published by Jonathan Cape. Cape's proof reader noticed that Lawrence had spelt several Arabic proper names in different ways, and wrote to him to ask which variant should be adopted consistently throughout the corrected text. Lawrence would have none of this, insisting that there was no basis for preferring one transliteration to another. Eventually Cape decided to publish a prefatory disclaimer in which Lawrence's responses to the proof reader were tabulated:

Q.	A.
Slip 20. Nuri, Emir of the Ruwalla, belongs to the 'chief family of the Rualla'. On Slip 23 'Rualla horse', and Slip 38, 'killed one Rueili'. In all later slips 'Rualla'.	Should have also used Ruwala and Ruala.
Slip 28. The Bisaita is also spelt Biseita.	Good.
Slip 47. Jedha, the she-camel, was Jedhah on Slip 40.	She was a splendid beast.
Slip 53. 'Meleager, the immoral poet'. I have put 'immortal' poet, but the author may mean immoral after all.	Immorality I know. Immortality I cannot judge. As you please: Meleager will not sue us for libel.

(*Seven Pillars*, Preface)

This was a heroic last stand against the rule-book, a kind of continuation of the Arab Revolt against alien codes of conformity. Most other writers found their peculiarities ironed out by the proof reader, which at least saved the blushes of Radclyffe Hall and W. B. Yeats, whose spelling was always chaotic. Only a few authors could evade such standardization: Bernard Shaw dealt directly with his printers, and so he could exhibit his own system of reformed spelling, in which *cigarette* became *cigaret*, and *can't*, confusingly, became *cant*. Robert Bridges as Poet Laureate was allowed to exhibit his own rationalized spellings in *The Testament of Beauty* (1929).[3] Another special licence was granted to the juvenile. One of the best

[3] For a sample, see p. 77 below.

selling novels of 1919, *The Young Visiters*, had been written by Daisy Ashford at the age of 9, and was thus as delightfully innocent of conventional spelling as it was of biology. Its happy ending sees a newly wed couple return from their six-week honeymoon 'with a son and hair', while the bride's jilted suitor vents his frustration in 'bad languige'.[4]

While the conventions of spelling were too firmly entrenched to permit much inventive latitude, there remained to the imaginative writer the traditional privilege of word formation. Even here, however, the poets had ceded much of the initiative to scientists and advertising copywriters. Most of the new words coming into the language were born in the realms of technology and commerce, although a significant new body of psychological terms also emerged in this period, both from clinical jargon (*empathize*, *extrovert*, *narcissistic*, *obsessive*, *schizophrenia*, *voyeurism*) and from lay sources (*fantasize*, *uptight*), and was more rapidly adopted into modern diction, including literary language. The novelist Hugh Walpole, for instance, seems to have been the first author to employ *sadist* as an adjective, Bernard Shaw being the first to use the adverb *sadistically*. In general, though, the poets and novelists played only a minor role in the creation of new words for general circulation. Virginia Woolf in her essay 'American Fiction' (1925) pointed out that lexical productivity in English was now strongest in American slang, whereas in England, 'save for the impetus given by the war, the word coining power has lapsed; our writers vary the metres of their poetry, remodel the rhythms of prose, but one may search English fiction in vain for a single new word' (*The Essays*, vol. 4, p. 278). How mistaken Woolf was about this the second (1989) edition of the *OED* now reveals abundantly. English journalists and scientists were indeed still coining new words, and there were neologisms to be found even in novels, plays, and poems: James Joyce is credited with the first printed use of *poxy*, Ford Madox Ford with *scatological*, Winifred Holtby with *self-deprecation*, Aldous Huxley with *sex-starved*, H. G. Wells with *careerist*, P. G. Wodehouse with *unscramble*, and Evelyn Waugh with *sick-making*. Among the poets

---

[4] Daisy Ashford, *The Young Visiters; or, Mr Salteenas Plan* (Chatto & Windus, 1919), 84–5.

W. B. Yeats takes the credit for *life-span*, Louis MacNeice gave us *unzip*, W. H. Auden introduced the written use of *shagged* to mean 'exhausted', and Robert Graves minted as many as six new compound adjectives in a single short poem ('The Bards', 1933). Given the inevitable incompleteness of *OED2*'s data, and its persistent literary bias, some of its attributions to notable authors need to be distinguished from original coinages: while it is almost certain that Yeats alone dreamed up the nonce-adjective *gong-tormented* (who else would need it?), it is most unlikely that Shaw really coined *headscarf*, or that Coward was the first to write down *salami sandwich*. And Auden was plainly not the originator of *ticket barrier* in 1939, as *OED2* records: Coward had used the term eight years before in a stage direction for *Cavalcade*, but even he must have picked it up from some anonymous railway official.

Literature may have contributed few coinages to common parlance, but one novelist in particular was so bold as to forge a literary diction all of his own. There are various ways of accounting for the pre-eminence of James Joyce among the prose writers of his time, but the more convincing of them start from his prodigious appropriation of the English language as an instrument upon which he could perfect a full repertoire of styles, registers, rhetorical acrobatics, and word games. Each of his longer works is designed to parade the range of his linguistic virtuosity: as *A Portrait of the Artist as a Young Man* (1916) begins with babytalk and ends with the diary of a philosophical aesthete, so in *Ulysses* (1922) we find one chapter that includes examples of every known device of rhetoric, and another that illustrates the development of English prose from its beginnings to the present time. His even more ambitious *Finnegans Wake* (1939) stretches the language beyond recognition in a display of multilingual puns and deliberate Freudian slips, in which words blend and interbreed promiscuously on the dizzying brink of nonsense. Joyce's favoured mode of word formation in *Ulysses* is agglutinative, as we see on the novel's third page, where the mock-Homeric epithets *snotgreen* and *scrotumtightening* are applied to the sea. But this delight in verbal compounds is taken a step further by the coining of 'portmanteau' words, in which two known words are fused to form a punning third, as in this sentence in the penultimate chapter: 'He kissed the plump mellow yellow smellow melons of her rump, on each plump melonous hemisphere, in their mellow yellow furrow, with obscure prolonged provocative melonsmellonous osculation' (p. 686). In among the various tricks of rhyme, alliteration, and metaphor here, the portmanteau word *smellow* (meaning smelly/yellow/mellow) is further entangled with the nonce-word *melonous* to form the more complex compound *melonsmellonous*. It is this kind of lexical alchemy that dominates the protean vocabulary of *Finnegans Wake*, in which logical distinctions collapse and opposites are merged. Whereas in *Ulysses* the double identity and dual cultural inheritance of Leopold Bloom is evoked in the compound 'greekjew' (p. 474), in *Finnegans Wake* Joyce outdoes himself by applying to Shem the Penman the multi-continental epithet 'Europasianised Afferyank!' (p. 191). To describe the language and style of this book there are no terms quite adequate, save for those offered by the *Wake* itself: 'abcedminded', 'rhubarbarous', 'alphabettyformed verbage', or 'once current puns, quashed quotatoes, messes of mottage' (pp. 18, 171, 183).

It should be noted in passing that wordplay is not entirely the monopoly of modernist experimenters such as Joyce. In H. G. Wells's romance *The History of Mr Polly*, for instance, a hurried wedding ceremony is recorded in this garbled notation: 'D'bloved we gath'd gether sighto' Gard'n face this con'gation join gather Man Whom Ho Mat'mony whichis on'bl state stooted by Gard in times mans in'cency. . . .' (ch. 6, pt. 4). In this kind of mimickry, Wells was following the example of Charles Dickens, of whom he was the principal modern imitator. Wells was also noted for his unorthodox punctuation, in which a sentence would be strung together with dashes and would trail off with an ellipsis (. . . .), as in the example above. He may indeed have given the cue to several younger modernists to adopt the ellipsis as a favoured device of their prose. Dorothy Richardson, who acknowledged Wells as a pioneer in her 1924 article 'About Punctuation',[5] employed ellipses in her *Pilgrimage* sequence, at first to indicate hesitancy or digressive transitions of her heroine's thoughts, especially when in states of reverie or semi-wakefulness; but then more freely as her so-called 'stream-of-consciousness' style evolved—as here in the sixth chapter of *Honeycomb* (1917):

---

[5] Dorothy Richardson, 'About Punctuation', *Adelphi*, 1/11 (Apr. 1924), 990–6.

Flags of pavement flowing—smooth clean grey squares and oblongs, faintly polished, shaping and drawing away—sliding into each other. . . . I am part of the dense smooth clean paving stone . . . sunlit; gleaming under dark winter rain; shining under warm sunlit rain, sending up a fresh stony smell . . . always there . . . dark and light . . . dawn, stealing . . . (*Pilgrimage*, vol. 1, p. 416)

A number of other novelists—May Sinclair, Ford Madox Ford, Osbert Sitwell, and Rosamond Lehmann among them—adopted the device, in search of a more fluid style that would no longer represent the world as a matter of certainties and fixed categories; while Virginia Woolf used the ellipsis in this way even in her non-fictional writings, as Rupert Brooke had done in several of his poems. The ellipsis is by no means a signature of modernist innovation, though: several non-modernist writers apart from Wells use it too, including E. M. Forster, the adventure-story author P. C. Wren, and the comic novelist Dornford Yates. Again, such modern techniques have their nineteenth-century precedents: few modern texts are quite so riddled with ellipses as Walt Whitman's 1855 Preface to *Leaves of Grass*.

If we set aside Joyce's experiments in word formation as a special case, it is in this realm of punctuation that the modern literary relaxation of linguistic conventions is most generally felt. In this too, Joyce was, alongside Richardson, a leading example. He regarded quotation marks as an intrusive eyesore in passages of dialogue, and preferred to use the French system by which direct speech is indicated by an initial dash. More important, though, was the greatly admired feat of *Ulysses*'s final chapter, which gives us Molly Bloom's interior monologue in a continuously unpunctuated 'stream' flowing for forty pages until we reach the only full stop. One of the purposes of this spectacular exercise was to provide a distinctively 'feminine' form of language in answer to the predominantly masculine voices of the earlier chapters. Joyce's particular conception and impersonation of the 'feminine' here may be open to question, but Dorothy Richardson, for one, applauded the principle in her Foreword to the 1938 collected edition of *Pilgrimage*, declaring that 'Feminine prose, as Charles Dickens and James Joyce have delightfully shown themselves to be aware, should properly be unpunctuated, moving from point to point without formal obstructions' (vol. 1, p. 12). Virginia Woolf had already commended Richardson herself for her achievements in this feminizing of prose, remarking in 1923 that the author of *Pilgrimage* had invented, or at least consciously developed 'a sentence which we might call the psychological sentence of the feminine gender' (*The Essays*, vol. 3, p. 367).

Some writers, at least, were now casting their punctuation and syntax in self-consciously 'masculine' and 'feminine' forms. Of the 'masculine' style and its forced clarity of staccato assertion, Wyndham Lewis was the most deliberate exponent. The second chapter of part 5 in *Tarr* (1918; rev. 1928) begins thus:

The following is the manner in which Tarr had become acquainted with Kreisler. Upon his first return from his exile in Montmartre he had arrived at Bertha's place about seven in the evening. He hung about for a little: in ten minutes' time he had his reward. She came out, followed by Herr Kreisler.

These are decisive statements, typically separated into compartments by colons, and lacking in adjectival colour. As the 'feminine' opposite to such a style, one might nominate Richardson's 'stream-of-consciousness' passage quoted above, or, in more orthodox form, this long sentence from her *Backwater* (1916):

They would go their favourite midday walk, down the long avenue in the park through the little windings of the shrubbery and into the chrysanthemum show, strolling about in the large greenhouse, all the girls glad of the escape from a set walk, reading over every day the strange names on the little wooden stakes, jokes and gigglings and tiresomenesses all kept within bounds by the happiness that there was, inside the great quiet steamy glass-house, in the strange raw bitter scent of the great flowers, in the strange huge way they stood, with all their differences of shape and colour staring quietly at you, all in the same way with one expression. (*Pilgrimage*, vol. 1, pp. 339–40)

The sentence itself is punctuated, although its adjectival phrases are not. It hangs clause upon clause, and adjective upon adjective, according to no 'set' structure of subordination but in sympathy with the relaxed 'strolling' exploration that it describes.

Language is of course always a primary concern of professional writers, but it does not always pose such ominous questions as it seemed to do in the wake of the Great War. To many writers and intellectuals at that time, the whole relation of language to thought and action had become an urgent problem. The War appeared to have demonstrated that careless talk costs lives, in the sense that the public rhetoric of King and Country, Heroism, Sacrifice, Loyalty, Valour, Gallantry, Honour, and Glory had swept the country into irrational endorsement of mass slaughter, while draping the results in chivalric euphemism (the corpses decomposing on the barbed wire of the Western Front were 'the fallen'). Language in its most powerful public forms of slogan and shibboleth, as wielded by politician and journalist, had shown itself to be a deadlier weapon than poison gas. The consequences among the younger generation in particular were a horror of 'Victorian' public cant and euphemism, and a distrust of such emotionally charged abstractions as Home, Love, or Duty. D. H. Lawrence's Connie Chatterley feels the effects of this deflation: 'All the great words, it seemed to Connie, were cancelled for her generation: love, joy, happiness, home, mother, father, husband, all these great, dynamic words were half dead now, and dying from day to day' (*Lady Chatterley's Lover*, ch. 6). To Anthony Beavis in Aldous Huxley's *Eyeless in Gaza* (1936), such words appear to be a filthy burden waiting to be cleansed: 'There ought to be some way of dry-cleaning and disinfecting words. Love, purity, goodness, spirit—a pile of dirty linen waiting for the laundress' (ch. 2). Language needed somehow to be purified or decontaminated to rid it, not of solecism or obscenity, but of the far more dangerous vocabularies of idealism, as philosophers and critics at Cambridge also thought.

On Armistice Day, 1918, a Cambridge bookshop owned by C. K. Ogden, editor of the semi-pacifist *Cambridge Magazine*, was smashed up by a crowd of patriotic rioters. That same night, Ogden sat down with his friend I. A. Richards and decided to sort out the problems of language and meaning that he believed had contributed to the ideological madness of the previous four years. The result was their collaborative book *The Meaning of Meaning* (1923), which assaulted the superstition that words have essential or inherent meanings by virtue of some magical bond with things. As Ogden and Richards argue in this founding work of British semiotics, words 'mean' nothing in themselves but are given meanings by their various contexts and uses; and a careful discrimination among such contexts and uses might lead to clearer communication and to our liberation from bondage to irrational propaganda. Their central distinction here was between the 'referential' function of language, which made true or false statements about the world, and the 'emotive' function, which produced what Richards later called 'pseudo-statements' expressing moods or attitudes that can be neither true nor false; confusion between these radically different functions was especially dangerous. Ogden furthered his campaign for more efficiently decontaminated communication by promoting as a world language and elementary teaching aid a skeletal form of English called Basic English, which had a vocabulary of only 850 words, a mere eighteen of these being verbs. If Ludwig Wittgenstein's *Tractatus Logico-Philosophicus* (1921) was right to declare (in an English translation commissioned by Ogden) that 'The limits of my language mean the limits of my world',[6] then the world of Basic was as limited as one could get, although of course it was never intended to replace the full range of English except in the special contexts of the beginners' class or the business conference. In the Thirties, Basic English, endorsed by Bernard Shaw, Ezra Pound, and some other literary figures, became an international business, its teaching system officially adopted in Chinese schools.

Richards helped in the promotion and refinement of Basic English, but his more important work as a lecturer in the newly established school of English at Cambridge was the development of a 'scientific' modern theory of poetry in *Principles of Literary Criticism* (1924) and its application in *Practical Criticism* (1929). In these works, which laid the foundations of the influential 'Cambridge School' of modern critical analysis, he called for and demonstrated a new kind of detailed attention in the reading of poetry to the 'words on the page' rather than to a poem's paraphrasable doctrine. As the Cambridge emphasis upon 'close reading' of poems evolved in the Thirties, in the work of Richards's student William Empson and of other contributors to F. R. Leavis's journal *Scrutiny*, an inherited 'Victorian' conception of poetry as the melodizing of noble sentiments was discarded as a typically moralistic fallacy. The key to poetry was no longer its moral message but its linguistic medium, poetry being the

---

[6] Ludwig Wittgenstein, *Tractatus Logico-Philosophicus* [trans. F. P. Ramsey] (Routledge & Kegan Paul, 1922), proposition 5.6.

most powerful and the subtlest way of combining the resources of the language. Leavis's iconoclastic book *New Bearings in English Poetry* (1932) revalues the English poets not according to their philosophies but according to the verbal texture of their verse: Milton, Shelley, and Tennyson are condemned for using an artificial and anaemic poetical language detached from the living rhythms of common speech, while the better poets—Donne, Keats, T. S. Eliot, and the recently discovered Gerard Manley Hopkins—make us feel their words as if they were physically palpable and alive. After commenting upon Hopkins's poem 'Spelt From Sybil's Leaves', Leavis remarks that, by comparison with this, 'any other poetry of the nineteenth century is seen to be using only a very small part of the resources of the English language' (ch. 5). Such new critical approaches implied that the central value of literature in the modern world was as a reaffirmation of linguistic range and energy, not just against the exhausted traditions of the past but against the cheap clichés of advertisers and journalists in the present day. Literature had a new post-War mission, which was to reinvigorate the English language, to reconnect it both with its former richness and with contemporary actuality.

Part II

Forms

4

Modern Poetry

New Words, 1910–1940

Audenesque   counter-rhythm   emote
hypersensitivity   Imagism   off-rhyme   pararhyme
pasticheur   plangently   Yeatsian

The critical priorities of 'modernism' in some accounts of this period's literature have encouraged a general assumption that English poetry underwent a profound revolution between about 1910 and the mid-Twenties. Such assumptions, though, mistake revolutionary intentions for revolutionary results, confusing innovation and icono-clasm, for which there is patchy evidence, with an actual overturning of centuries-old traditions in verse, for which there is none. They also tend to rely upon a further conflation of the interconnected but still distinct tradition of American verse, which had indeed been more radically experimental, with that of verse in Britain and Ireland, which more readily obeyed the gravitational pull of tradition. One of the aims of this chapter in its brief survey of leading figures and trends in the period's poetry is to qualify the legend of heroic modern-ist insurrection by placing its novelties within a larger context of continuities. Another is to propose that the salient tendency of poetic practice in England between 1910 and 1940 is not adequately to be described in terms of 'modernism' at all.

Verse Technique

Formal and technical liberties were indeed declared in principle and taken in practice by a significant minority of poets, but there was no wholesale or widespread abandonment of inherited poetic forms. The flexibility of *vers libre* ('free verse') was proclaimed in manifestos by Ezra Pound, D. H. Lawrence, and others, but even these radicals wrote many of their poems in conventional metres, sometimes also in conventional rhyme schemes. Free verse appears more often in this period than before, but as a supplementary resource of the modern poet, an extension of possibilities in English verse rather than a displacement of its traditional forms. Even Michael Roberts's *Faber Book of Modern Verse* (1936), of all the period's major anthologies the most avant-gardist to the point of sectarianism in its exclusion of Hardy, Housman, and most of the 'Georgian' poets, exhibits free verse in only a quarter of its chosen poems; and if one subtracts the many American poets represented there, the proportion diminishes to less than one-fifth. In non-modernist anthologies, the visibility of free verse shrinks markedly: Edward Marsh's *Georgian Poetry 1920–1922* (1922) includes only two poems in free verse, against ninety-six in standard metres. Even as late as the mid-Thirties, the averagely well-read poetry lover might have encountered contemporary free verse only in a few anthologized selections from T. S. Eliot and D. H. Lawrence; or in critical dismissals of it such as G. K. Chesterton's essay 'The Romance of Rhyme' (1923), in which he quips that *vers libre* 'is no more a revolution in literary form than eating meat raw is an innovation in cookery' (*Selected Essays*, p. 209).

It would also be a mistake to identify 'experiment' in this period's verse too closely with a particular generation of poets, or with free verse alone. The Victorian age in poetry had itself been a great period of experiment, providing new metrical patterns in the work of Tennyson, Swinburne, and Hopkins; and that tradition of experimenting within the realms both of metrical regularity and of stanzaic form prolongs itself into our period through the efforts of the older poets—Robert Bridges and Thomas Hardy—who had learned their craft while Tennyson was still alive. As Dennis Taylor has demonstrated in his book *Hardy's Metres and Victorian Prosody* (1988), the Dorset poet was a prolific inventor of new verse forms and stanzaic patterns, right up to his last collection, *Winter Words* (1928). Bridges meanwhile began in 1913 to break away from the inherited accentual principle of English metres, in which the stresses are counted, and towards the purely syllabic principle used in French, which counts only the number of syllables to the line. His remarkably popular long poem *The Testament of Beauty* (1929) illustrated both Bridges's system of reformed spelling and, as he felt, the flexibility of an English twelve-syllable line:

> Thus hath man's Reason dealt since he took spade in hand,
> either by wit of the insect or of the engineer:
> and they who hav come to think that in remotest times
> Eve delved and Adam span, can show matriarchy of sorts
> had precedent in natur, ostensibly among birds,
> whose males more gaudily feather'd wil disport their charms
> and dance in coquetry to win the admiring hens:
> Verily it well may be that sense of beauty came
> to those primitiv bipeds earlier than to man.

(3. 385–93)

In his old age Bridges here launched the modern tradition of English syllabic metre, continued in the 1930s by his daughter Elizabeth Daryush, and later taken up by Dylan Thomas, W. H. Auden, Thom Gunn and others.

If we detect a general tendency for poetic experiment in this period to take the form of extensions and variations upon traditional regularity, not of 'rejections' or 'abandonments' of it, we will find the principle amply confirmed within the realm of rhyme. Most poets worked, most of the time, with rhymed line-endings, although a few of them redefined what rhyme could involve. There is a good case for claiming that the more important emancipation of modern verse technique from earlier constraints lies not in free verse but in the adoption by several leading poets of half-rhyme (terminal consonance without assonance: *love/have*) and pararhyme ('rich' consonance without assonance: *love/leave*) as possible substitutes for full rhyme (terminal consonance with assonance: *love/dove*). Like free verse, half-rhyme and pararhyme have their precedents in some nineteenth-century poets, in earlier traditions such as Old

Welsh verse, and in the accepted licence of eye-rhyme (*love/prove*). In this period their revival represents a significant compromise between recognized sound patterns and the impulse to reach beyond exhausted pairings so familiar from the traditions of full rhyme (*eyes/ sighs*, *world/hurled*, and the rest).

The rediscovery of half-rhyme coincides with the beginning of our period, at least in the highly influential work of W. B. Yeats. Before 1910, the incidence of half-rhymes in his verse is negligible, but *The Green Helmet and Other Poems* (1910) exhibits a markedly more frequent appearance of such rhymes as *mouth/truth*, *blood/ proud*, and *charm/form*. With each successive collection, the resort to half-rhyme becomes more noticeable, until we reach the celebrated 'Easter, 1916' (1917) with its reliance upon pairs like *death/faith* and *come/name*. Here and in later poems employing the same device— 'Among School Children' (1927), 'Coole Park, 1929' (1931), or 'Parnell's Funeral' (1934)—full rhymes still predominate over half-rhymes, which are used opportunistically as the occasion demands. In this sense, Yeats's half-rhyming is a half-measure, compared with the full-blooded pararhyming of the younger poets Wilfred Owen, W. H. Auden, and Dylan Thomas. Owen's distinction was to have made the recurrence of pararhymes, sometimes interspersed with half-rhymes, the principal pattern of some of his wartime poems (published posthumously as *Poems*, 1920). Thus 'Strange Meeting' gives us a sequence of pararhymed couplets (*hall/Hell*, *grained/ ground*, etc.) to the exclusion of any full rhyme, while the 12-line poem 'Arms and the Boy' exhibits pararhymes in its first six lines (*blade/blood*, *flash/flesh*, *leads/lads*) and half-rhymes in its last six (*teeth/death*, *apple/supple*, *heels/curls*). Owen also employed a new form of half-rhyme in which final unstressed syllables are matched while the preceding stressed syllables are not (*brothers/withers*, *progress/tigress*), and this further stretching of the basis of rhyme was developed inventively by Auden, by Thomas, and by Auden's associates Stephen Spender, Louis MacNeice, and C. Day Lewis.

Many of Auden's early poems exploit half-rhyme, usually more persistently than in Yeats. Auden even gives himself licence to rhyme solely on 'open' unstressed final syllables, as in the pairs *beauty/early* and *quinsy/virginity*. The most dedicated practitioner both of half-rhyme and of pararhyme, however, was Dylan Thomas, all but one of whose fifty-nine poems in his first three collections use these devices. Like Auden, Thomas stretches rhyme to accommodate pairings of unstressed syllables, as in 'My hero bares his nerves' (1934), which half-rhymes *shoulder* with *ruler*, *paper* with *hunger*, and *Venus* with *promise*. In other poems, open stressed syllables may half-rhyme, as *sea* with *sky*; in others, such as 'I dreamed my genesis' (1934), final unstressed syllables are discounted so that disyllabic words may rhyme with monosyllables: *driving* with *nerve*, *metal* with *night*, *journey* with *man*. Taken as a whole, the revival of half-rhyme shows an impressive record of creative innovation in this period, having given us such memorable works as Yeats's 'Easter, 1916', Owen's 'Strange Meeting', Thomas's 'And death shall have no dominion' (1936), MacNeice's 'Bagpipe Music' (1937), and Auden's 'Lay your sleeping head, my love' (1937; later entitled 'Lullaby').

The modernity of modern English verse, then, is not a matter of any revolution in techniques and forms, although certain modest technical innovations did play their part in breaking old habits. The modern element resides rather in an extended range of diction and of 'unpoetical' subject matter, in a deliberate avoidance of 'Victorian' moralizing and ornate poeticism, and in less tangible qualities such as tone, attitude, mood, and authorial 'voice'. The rest of this chapter will aim to highlight these features and their evolution in a few major representatives of four generations of modern poets. Before reviewing this parade of poetic modernity, though, it is worth issuing further cautions against regarding it as some sort of triumphal procession. Modern poetry did not sweep away the nineteenth-century inheritance, in part because a certain inevitable inertia prevailed in the poetry-reading public, for most of whom Tennyson was still the defining example of poetic greatness, Palgrave's *Golden Treasury* (1861) and Quiller-Couch's *Oxford Book of English Verse* (1900) still the formative anthologies. However much the modern poets repudiated the moralizing, rhetorical, and didactic strains in Victorian verse, the public seemed to crave more of the same: the single most popular English poem of this period, and of the century, according to surveys conducted in the 1990s, was Rudyard Kipling's 'If—' (1910), one of a series of his unashamedly didactic poems that includes 'The Gods of the Copybook Headings' (1919) and 'The Female of the Species' (1911). Another factor is a backward-looking tendency among several of the more talented poets themselves. Even such an aggressively modernist periodical as the *Calendar of Modern Letters* could be found publishing as late as 1925 a sonnet by Edmund Blunden which includes the lines

> And many a girl by tinkling pastures stood
> With primrose brow toward eve's single gem[1]

Like much of Blunden's work, this echoes elegantly the 'poetical' conventions of late eighteenth- and early nineteenth-century pastoral verse. Finally, as we shall see more clearly below, the modernizing trend itself was in many respects a continuation of the programme for poetic realism announced by Wordsworth in 1800, especially in its pursuit of a more chastely colloquial language shorn of florid ornaments.

Hardy and Yeats

Thomas Hardy and W. B. Yeats cannot be yoked together as members of any poetical school or generation. While Yeats's work derives from the high prophetic strain of English Romanticism in Blake and Shelley, filtered through Pre-Raphaelitism and French symbolism, Hardy's comes out of the plainer rural tradition of Wordsworth and the Dorset dialect poet William Barnes. Hardy's world-view was formed by scientific naturalism, Yeats's, on the other hand, by occult forms of mysticism. Hardy had started writing poetry before Yeats was born, and had passed his seventy-fourth birthday by the time Yeats's landmark collection *Responsibilities* (1914) appeared shortly before Yeats's forty-ninth. Despite these and other striking differences between the two, they may still be linked as Victorians who made themselves post-Victorian, as powerful influences on younger poets such as Auden, as twin examples of modern poetic integrity. Both succeeded in renouncing the melodious sententiousness of

---

[1] Edmund Blunden, 'Shepherd's Calendar', *Calendar of Modern Letters*, 1 (1925), 345; later retitled 'Another Spring', in Blunden's *Poems* (Cobden-Sanderson, 1930), 108–9.

much Victorian verse in favour of a more colloquial, even awkward style of impassioned deliberation or self-questioning. Each was able to subdue his private griefs and obsessions to the discipline of poetic craft, then to turn towards public themes in a modestly meditative fashion devoid of Kiplingesque hectoring or opinion-mongering—in Yeats's 'Easter, 1916', for instance, or in Hardy's poem on the sinking of the *Titanic*, 'The Convergence of the Twain' (1912).

Hardy's poetry is at first unlikely to strike the reader as especially modern: written in stanzaic forms, its diction is studded with archaic words and conventional poeticisms ('Yonder a maid and her wight', for example, in a poem of 1913); and it rarely ventures into a specifically twentieth-century world, preferring to treat familiar themes of love, death, grief, and the vanity of human wishes within rustic settings. Apart from its sardonic distance from the consolations of Christian belief—which alone made it too distressingly modern for some readers—its modernity is an unobtrusive quality of restraint and reticence. Hardy eschews lavish emotional gestures in favour of an intensity wrung from plainness both of language and of situation, notably in the 'Poems of 1912–13 ' written after the death of his first wife ('The Voice', 'After a Journey', 'At Castle Boterel', and others). He likewise abandons the smooth-running line of Tennyson or of Swinburne for the sake of a cunningly irregular rhythm that suggests the halting, tentative movement of confessional self-communion. And although several poems suggest or allude to a philosophical stance, as in 'The Convergence of the Twain', they carefully refrain from moralizing.

At their best, Hardy's poems of this period vindicate the tested virtues of stanzaic patterning through artfully modulated repetition. 'During Wind and Rain' (1917), the most-often admired of these, deserves quotation in full on this account.

> They sing their dearest songs—
> He, she, all of them—yea,
> Tenor and treble and bass,
>   And one to play;
> With the candles mooning each face. . . .
>   Ah, no; the years, O!
> How the sick leaves reel down in throngs!

> They clear the creeping moss—
> Elders and juniors—aye,
> Making the pathways neat
>   And the garden gay;
> And they build a shady seat. . . .
>   Ah, no; the years, the years;
> See, the white storm-birds wing across.
>
> They are blithely breakfasting all—
> Men and maidens—yea,
> Under the summer tree,
>   With a glimpse of the bay,
> While pet fowl come to the knee. . . .
>   Ah, no; the years O!
> And the rotten rose is ript from the wall.
>
> They change to a high new house,
> He, she, all of them—aye,
> Clocks and carpets and chairs
>   On the lawn all day,
> And brightest things that are theirs. . . .
>   Ah, no; the years, the years;
> Down their carved names the rain-drop ploughs.

There is no declared 'message' here, and certainly no moralizing: everything is given to us in perceptible 'images' (perhaps literally, in that the poem may be inspired, like other Hardy lyrics of this period, by a family photograph album) culminating in the eroded gravestone; and despite the conventional poetic symbolism of the 'rotten rose', we have no sentimental elaboration. Instead, the emotional force of the anguish in each penultimate line is held fast and thus amplified by the strictly patterned and blankly descriptive context. In these respects, 'During Wind and Rain' conforms inadvertently but almost perfectly to the canons of post-Victorian poetic taste, as a 'modern' poem in spite of itself.

While Hardy's poetry from the 1860s to the 1920s shows almost no change in style, tone, or subject matter, the career of Yeats is altogether different. The author of 'He Wishes for the Cloths of Heaven' and other much-anthologized love lyrics of the 1890s had seen his adored muse Maud Gonne married to a rival in 1903 and then issued his *Collected Works* in 1908, as if to concede that he was

Fig. 2. William Butler Yeats photographed in July 1911
by G. C. Beresford.

a spent force in the new century. However, his astonishing capacity for self-reinvention carried him through a difficult period of transition (roughly, 1903–17) into a new phase of mature work that reaches its peak in *The Tower* (1928), *The Winding Stair* (1933), and some of the *New Poems* (1938). Against the odds, Yeats remade himself not just into a twentieth-century poet but into the major English-speaking lyric poet of the age, as his contemporaries soon acknowledged (see Table 1 below). Yeats's work is too various and too ambiguous to be dragooned under any critical label, especially 'symbolism' or 'modernism', without severe distortion. All that we can attempt here is the sketching of a few general features of this paradoxical, shape-shifting writer, under the constant warning that of almost anything one says about Yeats the opposite will also be true.

To summarize the general themes and preoccupations of Yeats's poetry as those of permanence and impermanence ('Sailing to Byzantium', 'Among School Children', 'Byzantium'), of the cyclical patterns of world history ('The Second Coming', 'Leda and the Swan', 'Two Songs from a Play'), of contemplation and action ('An Irish Airman Foresees His Death', 'A Dialogue of Self and Soul', 'Long-Legged Fly'), of body and soul ('Michael Robartes and the Dancer', 'Crazy Jane Talks with the Bishop'), of art and the artist ('Ego Dominus Tuus', 'The Circus Animals' Desertion') would be incomplete but still sufficient to indicate the degree to which he adopts the mantle of the great Romantics, confidently assuming the power of poetry to illuminate weighty principles in tones of high prophetic seriousness. As Yeats indeed wrote of himself and his poetic generation,

> We were the last romantics—chose for theme
> Traditional sanctity and loveliness
>
> ('Coole and Ballylee, 1931')

and one of his notable contributions to modern verse technique was the revival of the *ottava rima* stanza favoured by Byron, Keats, and Shelley. It will not do, though, to cast Yeats as an Irish Shelley stranded in the wrong century. Among the important Yeatsian themes left out of the list just offered are some that betray particular cultural and political pressures of his own lifetime and that make him a different kind of poet, concerned with the opposites of traditional sanctity and loveliness. These are the hostility of the philistine modern world to the Artist ('September 1913', 'The Fisherman', 'Under Ben Bulben') compared with the gracious patronage bestowed by the landed gentry and aristocracy ('At Galway Races', 'Coole Park, 1929', 'The Municipal Gallery Revisited'); and the violence, betrayals, and guilt of living Irish history ('Easter, 1916', 'Meditations in Time of Civil War', 'Nineteen Hundred and Nineteen', 'Parnell's Funeral'). Yeats may have dreamed of being a late Romantic or a Pre-Raphaelite, but what brought the best out of his art was that he was, in his words, 'thrown upon this filthy modern tide' ('The Statues').

The significance of the *Responsibilities* collection as a turning point in Yeats's work is that it shows a conscious breaking out from the limits of his earlier poems of love and folklore, and a willingness to immerse himself in that filthy modern tide. As if to strip himself for the effort, Yeats also carries out a denuding of his poetic language. The short poem 'A Coat' (1914) discards the embroidered garment of his earlier manner in favour of 'walking naked', and thereby announces Yeats's new, barer style, unencumbered by romantic colouring, half-colloquial in diction, and even apparently casual in tone. This new note can be heard throughout Yeats's later verse, and it was picked up by his readers as an audibly 'modern' quality. Yeats's own aim in adopting this style, partly influenced by his experience in the theatre, was to stay closer to common speech and to the integrity of the spoken voice, shunning the ornate confections of rhetoric. This second, anti-rhetorical strand of Yeats's self-modernizing programme is announced in a fascinating dialogue poem, 'Ego Dominus Tuus' (1917), amid his unfolding of the doctrine of Self and Anti-Self:

> The rhetorician would deceive his neighbours,
> The sentimentalist himself; while art
> Is but a vision of reality.

Yeats here identifies the twin hazards of the late Victorian poetic culture in which he had shaped his early work, resolving now to evade them both in forging a poetry that is at once realistic and visionary. This repudiation of rhetoric, though, is itself a rhetorical gesture, a fact that may help us discriminate between what Yeats was renouncing (the Tennysonian role of poet as mouthpiece of public opinion) and what he was all the more jealously retaining (the semi-magical power of figurative language).

Like any position adopted by Yeats, the apparent rejection of rhetoric is part of a moving masquerade in which temporary costumes and masks are donned and discarded in turn. For after the self-imposed leanness of this middle period, and after the reawakening prompted by Yeats's marriage to the young Englishwoman Georgie Hyde-Lees in 1917, there follows a sumptuous feast of rhetorical effects in the Twenties and Thirties, when the ageing poet employs the full range of his masks and voices, from facetious drinking song to visionary incantation. The celebrated final stanza of 'Among School Children' may illustrate the spellbinding quality of his high rhetorical manner:

> Labour is blossoming or dancing where
> The body is not bruised to pleasure soul,
> Nor beauty born out of its own despair,
> Nor blear-eyed wisdom out of midnight oil.
> O chestnut tree, great-rooted blossomer,
> Are you the leaf, the blossom or the bole?
> O body swayed to music, O brightening glance,
> How can we know the dancer from the dance?

Summoned in dizzying succession here are trope upon trope (personification, metaphor, synecdoche) and figure upon figure (parallelism, alliteration), culminating in Yeats's favoured coda, the rhetorical question—which may or may not here also be *aporia*, the figure of indecision. The frequency with which Yeats rounds off his more challenging poems with questions is striking: 'No Second Troy' (1910), 'Demon and Beast' (1920), 'The Second Coming' (1920), 'Leda and the Swan' (1924), and 'A Nativity' (1938), among several others. The device provides some clue to a central paradox of Yeats's poetic tone, because it is one that allows him to be assertive and tentative, brazen and modest at the same moment, thus reconciling the diffidence of his private Self with the bold confidence of his artistic Anti-Self. There are a number of false moves we can make in approaching Yeats's poetry: one is to take fright at the allusions to his personal circle, to Irish politics, or to occult lore; another is to assume that the poems are expressions of Yeats's personality or his system of beliefs. We come better prepared if we take the poems as dramatic impersonations, and as phases in a process of self-questioning that can shrug beliefs and systems away at whim, subordinate as they are to the conjuring of new selves.

Masefield, Brooke, Thomas, and 'Georgian' Poetry

Stirrings of impatience with the insipid legacy of late Victorian verse made themselves felt in the years 1910–14, almost in parallel with the social and political restlessness of the times. The earliest signs that the poetry of George V's reign would distance itself from Victorian decorum came in an outbreak of poetic realism in 1911. When the *English Review* published a lengthy narrative poem, *The Everlasting Mercy* by John Masefield, a minor sensation broke out in response to its rough colloquial energies: the recurrence of the word 'bloody' (replaced by blanks in the magazine but restored in the book version of the same year) seemed at the time to be a bold rejection of Victorian inhibition, and a promising reconnection of poetry with the vitality of popular speech. A celebrated passage at the start of the poem captures the idiom of the narrator, a hard-drinking poacher named Saul Kane, here quarrelling with a rival:

> Now when he saw me set my snare,
> He tells me 'Get to hell from there.
> This field is mine,' he says, 'by right;
> If you poach here, there'll be a fight.
> Out now,' he says, 'and leave your wire;
> It's mine.'
>   'It ain't.'
>   'You put.'
>   'You liar.'
> 'You closhy put.'
>   'You bloody liar.'
> 'This is my field.'
>   'This is my wire.'
> 'I'm ruler here.'
>   'You ain't.'
>   'I am.'

'I'll fight you for it.'

'Right, by damn. [. . .]'

(*Collected Poems*, pp. 89–90)

Admirers of the poem, some of whom chanted it aloud in pubs, tended to overlook its glaringly 'Victorian' tale of moral redemption—in which Kane's sinfulness is overcome both by his conscience and by a female Quaker missionary, so that he embraces religion and accepts the social order—and the fact that the profanity of the working man had already been versified more convincingly by Rudyard Kipling. Nevertheless, Masefield became identified as the leading exponent of modern poetic realism. The success of *Dauber* (1913) and *Reynard the Fox* (1919), established his reputation as a popular narrative poet, consolidated by the best-selling *Collected Poems* (1923) and by his accession to the Laureateship upon the death in 1930 of Robert Bridges.

Less noticed at the time as a portent was the appearance of the first collection by the younger poet Rupert Brooke, simply entitled *Poems* (1911). This volume included a number of pieces offensive to the delicate sensibilities of older poetry-loving generations, showing a deliberate exploitation of realistic 'unpleasantness'. The first part of his double sonnet 'Menelaus and Helen', for example, presents in a lofty heroic manner the rediscovery of Helen by her husband at the end of the Trojan war, closing with a Pre-Raphaelite tableau of the hero kneeling in adoration, 'The Perfect Knight before the perfect Queen'. The second part, though, offers a cruelly deflatory sequel:

> So far the poet. How should he behold
>   That journey home, the long connubial years?
>   He does not tell you how white Helen bears
> Child on legitimate child, becomes a scold,
> Haggard with virtue. Menelaus bold
>   Waxed garrulous, and sacked a hundred Troys
>   'Twixt noon and supper. And her golden voice
> Got shrill as he grew deafer. And both were old.
>
> Often he wonders why on earth he went
>   Troyward, or why poor Paris ever came.
> Oft she weeps, gummy-eyed and impotent;
>   Her dry shanks twitch at Paris' mumbled name.

So Menelaus nagged; and Helen cried;
And Paris slept on by Scamander side.

(Poetical Works, pp. 125–6)

The anti-heroic debunking of legend here includes an explicit rebuke
to the idealism of the poetic tradition: the poet, restricted by codes
of honour and virtue, can venture only 'so far' towards representing
the whole truth, whereas Brooke leads us all the way into the territory of the modern novelist, stressing the disillusionment and de-
crepitude that lie beyond the happy endings of epic or romance. In a
further outrage against poetical decorum, Brooke's *Poems* included
a sonnet called 'A Channel Passage' that plays upon the parallels
between lovesickness and seasickness, as the speaker recalls his lost
love while struggling with physical nausea aboard ship: 'Retchings
twist and tie me, | Old meats, good meals, brown gobbets, up I throw'
(*Poetical Works*, p. 113). The reviewers were all the more disgusted
in that Brooke had chosen the form of the sonnet, associated as it
was with the purest flights of spiritual transcendence, as the basis
for his display of physical grossness. Those who accused Brooke
of immature bravado had a point. These exercises in realism rely
heavily upon their shock effect, yielding much less on a second reading; they tend merely to turn idealistic conventions on their heads
rather than transform them—most obviously in 'Sonnet Reversed',
which begins with a climactic couplet expressing erotic bliss, then
trails off into an octave on suburban domesticity.

Such are the ironies of literary legend that Rupert Brooke the
crudely upsetting realist of 1911 has subsequently been transformed
into an exemplar of naïve idealism, largely on the strength of his un-
characteristic wartime sonnets, and of a phrase about teatime from a
poem ('The Old Vicarage, Grantchester') that is in fact more satirical
and self-mocking than quotation out of context suggests. Comparison of Brooke's 'The Soldier' (1915) with a poem by Wilfred Owen
or Siegfried Sassoon on the horrors of trench warfare has become a
standard classroom exercise, designed to illustrate the gulf between
the poetry of abstract cliché and the poetry of felt experience. The
injustice of this lies in the fact that the realism which we appreciate in
Owen's or Sassoon's war poems was made possible and acceptable
chiefly by Brooke's prior example: both Owen and Sassoon started

off as feeble late Romantic poetasters before they adopted Brooke's realistic idiom.

Brooke himself died of blood poisoning while on military service in the Aegean in April 1915, and was instantly elevated to the status of national hero. His posthumous *1914 and Other Poems* (1915) and *Collected Poems* (1918) were widely sold and read, contributing to the larger boom in sales of contemporary poetry reported by publishers between 1915 and 1919. During the last years of his short life, though, Brooke had made his own deliberate efforts to boost public awareness of the post-Edwardian poetic revival. His vehicle for this campaign was a series of anthologies entitled *Georgian Poetry*, edited by his friend the well-connected civil servant Edward Marsh, and published by the poet Harold Monro. This series, inaugurated in December 1912, eventually ran to five volumes (1912, 1915, 1917, 1919, 1922), each including recent work by English and Welsh poets of the kind regarded as promisingly modern by Marsh and his advisers. These 'Georgian' poets did not form a coherent school but rather a mutual promotion society in which each anthology included lists of their recent publications and was set up to be reviewed by friends—often by contributors themselves—in the more influential papers and literary journals. The results were more than satisfactory in terms of sales, although eventually this success attracted resentful assault from rival coteries. Nevertheless, there are some common characteristics to be found among the central group of early contributors to Marsh's anthologies.

The original Georgian team comprised Lascelles Abercrombie, Gordon Bottomley, Rupert Brooke, W. H. Davies, Walter de la Mare, John Drinkwater, Wilfrid W. Gibson, John Masefield, Harold Monro, and James Stephens. (James Elroy Flecker and D. H. Lawrence, both of them rather marginal to the main current, were also represented in the first two volumes.) Several of these authors had become associated with poetical realism: not only Masefield and Brooke, but also Davies and Gibson, both of whom had lived in poverty and written some studies of 'low life', as in Gibson's collection *Daily Bread* (1910). Abercrombie and Bottomley wrote verse dramas incorporating 'brutal' passages that offended many readers: Abercrombie's 'The End of the World', for example, which appeared in the second (1915) Georgian anthology, carried a description of boys crushing frogs under cartwheels. The remaining poets, along with some latecomers, may be characterized broadly as realists in the Wordsworthian sense, content to observe and celebrate the humbler aspects of rural and domestic life in plain language and unassuming tones. Eschewing the grand romantic gesture, the Georgians settled for quiet meditation upon treasured places or unglamorous animals and plants.

While the prevailing spirit of the first two Georgian anthologies, prepared under Brooke's influence, was one of realism and a certain buoyant vitality, the initial sense of purpose seemed increasingly to be lost in the final three volumes. The third anthology (1917) was notable for the arrival of some promising young soldier-poets (Sassoon, Robert Graves, and Isaac Rosenberg; followed in 1922 by Edmund Blunden); but with these Marsh also brought in some inferior talents such as J. C. Squire, who increasingly set the tone for the two post-War collections—in which Masefield refused to participate. The principal historian of the Georgian group, Robert H. Ross in his book *The Georgian Revolt* (1967), makes a useful distinction between the original Georgians and these 'neo-Georgian' latecomers, or the 'Squirearchy' as they were named by their modernist adversaries. The change of personnel was significant, especially in that the vehemently anti-modernist and anti-realist Squire acted as a red rag to the modernist school, attracting severe critical censure from John Middleton Murry, Edith Sitwell, and others. More important, though, were the escalating slaughter of the War and the devastated condition of the post-War world, in which context the moonlit meditations and comfortable rustic tranquillity, not just of the Squirearchy but of several founding Georgians, began to look irresponsibly trivial. By the late Twenties, Georgianism was repeatedly being pronounced dead, by lapsed Georgians like Robert Graves among others, and dismissed wholesale as an episode of facile, harmless escapism in English verse. This standard retrospective verdict, reinforced by Squire's later verses about dog-walking, cosy country inns, and rugby matches, is, as we have seen, drastically incomplete, and requires some further qualification.

Georgianism forfeited its implied claim upon the future, but it did not slink away and die. It retained its popular following, for example in the reception of Vita Sackville-West's long poem *The*

Land (1926), a deeply old-fashioned work hymning the cycle of the agricultural year in the style of eighteenth-century georgics. And although the critical standing of Abercrombie, Bottomley, Davies, Drinkwater, Gibson, Monro, and others was eventually to lapse irrecoverably, the reputations of most Georgian poets survived through this period; in particular, the more distinctive voices of de la Mare and Blunden. De la Mare had turned out many a trifling nature study of the kind that gave Georgianism a bad name—'The Linnet' (1918) or 'Titmouse' (1921)—but at his best he could also provoke eerie foreboding and nightmarish disturbance, as in the title poem of *The Listeners* (1912), or in 'The Marionettes' (1918), 'Drugged' (1921), and the macabre 'Dry August Burned' (1938). Blunden's antiquated diction (*oft*, *fain*, *wingèd*, and the like) set him well apart from the avant-garde, but he has commanded respect for his war poems and for the more sinister of his rural pieces, notably 'Winter: East Anglia' (1920) and 'The Midnight Skaters' (1925).

Even more highly respected now than those Georgian survivors is the poetry of Edward Thomas, who wrote verse for only three years before he was killed by a shell blast at Passchendaele in April 1917. Thomas was not a war poet in the accepted sense, but a practitioner of rural contemplation in the tradition of Wordsworth, of Hardy, and of his immediate mentor, the American poet Robert Frost. Edward Marsh's refusal to include samples of Thomas's work in the *Georgian Poetry* series was one of his gravest mistakes, because the body of verse collected posthumously in *Poems* (1917) and *Last Poems* (1918) is in the best sense more Georgian than the Georgians themselves: strictly plain in diction, modestly local in focus, quietly unrhetorical, and inconclusive in tone. His commitment to the unsung and commonly unregarded secrets of rural life is seen in such poems as 'Swedes' and 'Sedge-Warblers', and declared openly in 'Tall Nettles': 'As well as any bloom upon a flower | I like the dust on the nettles'. This is a characteristic preference of Georgian realism, but it is pursued with more honest diligence and discipline than it is among the Marsh–Monro circle. A more distinctive virtue of Thomas's poetry is that it is able to expand from such homely materials into shadowy realms of wonder and brooding perplexity, as in 'Old Man', which takes us from the smell of a common shrub into puzzled deliberations on memory. 'Adlestrop', a poem deservedly favoured by anthologists, illustrates this unemphatic germination of mood:

> Yes, I remember Adlestrop—
> The name, because one afternoon
> Of heat the express-train drew up there
> Unwontedly. It was late June.
>
> The steam hissed. Someone cleared his throat.
> No one left and no one came
> On the bare platform. What I saw
> Was Adlestrop—only the name
>
> And willows, willow-herb, and grass,
> And meadowsweet, and haycocks dry,
> No whit less still and lonely fair
> Than the high cloudlets in the sky.
>
> And for that minute a blackbird sang
> Close by, and round him, mistier,
> Farther and farther, all the birds
> Of Oxfordshire and Gloucestershire.
>
> (Collected Poems, pp. 71–3)

After a cursory glance through this poem, one might write it off as a facile celebration of rural 'Englishness' evoked through an idealized Cotswold village, though pretty enough in its way. Further attention to its craft reveals more: artful sleights of enjambment that produce a naturally 'spoken' account, syntactical parsimony that makes us wait and listen as the train passenger has done, and crucially a withholding of incident that throws the reader's attention back upon itself. No quaint village scene is offered for celebration; only a sign and a platform whose blankness surprises the mind into an exposure of its own forms of awareness. Thomas's exploitation here of 'unwonted' silence and the extended vigilance it affords is Wordsworthian in inspiration, and the same may be said of de la Mare's frequent uses of a similar 'listening' motif. In a larger perspective, the understated plainness both of Thomas's work and of the Georgians' points us forward to the anticlimactic tones of Auden's verse and eventually to those of Philip Larkin, whose poem 'The Whitsun Weddings' (1964) echoes some of the effects of 'Adlestrop'.

Imagism and After: Pound, Eliot, Sitwell, and Lawrence

The death of Algernon Swinburne in 1909 was taken by some younger poets as an occasion for at last burying the worn-out poetical inheritance of Pre-Raphaelitism and of the late Victorian 'decadence', and for moving on. Attempts to venture beyond that tradition, however, took various forms: as we have seen, Yeats fashioned for himself a leaner, more colloquial voice, while the Georgians abandoned the wilting orchids of the late Victorian poetical hothouse in search of wild flowers and a bracing, sometimes Wordsworthian realism. A more aggressive campaign of radical demolition began to take shape among a few writers in London associated with the *English Review* and *The New Age*, especially Ford Madox Hueffer (later surnamed Ford) and T. E. Hulme. In these reviews, and in lively debates among poets in Soho restaurants, these two men argued that most verse in the Romantic nineteenth-century tradition up to the present was hopelessly wordy, vague, sentimental, and disconnected from contemporary reality. Hueffer insisted that poetry should become less 'poetical' in the accepted sense and emulate the clarity of good prose; Hulme longed for an end to gushing emotionalism and for a new poetry of clear, 'hard' classical precision. Neither of them produced poetry of any significance in fulfilment of these hopes, but their provocations pointed towards a possible renewal, if only some bolder spirit could develop them.

The American poet Ezra Pound had arrived in London in 1908, and before long had established contact with Yeats, Hulme, and Hueffer. He would not have seemed a promising iconoclast at this time, steeped as he was in the Victorian exoticisms of Robert Browning, D. G. Rossetti, Swinburne, Symons, Dowson, and the early Yeats. Readers of his early work, in which *thee*s and *hath*s abound, up to and including the *Canzoni* (1911) and the *Ripostes* (1912), could have been forgiven for classifying him as a belated Pre-Raphaelite with a charming antiquarian devotion to the medieval troubadours. Edward Marsh even approached him in 1912 to ask whether the first *Georgian Poetry* anthology could reprint Pound's 'Ballad of the Goodly Fere' (1909), a poem that casts Jesus of Nazareth as a hearty drinking companion. In some respects Pound remained a Pre-

Raphaelite at heart—especially in his politics, with disastrous later results; in others he managed after years of self-discipline to renounce Swinburne, remaking himself simultaneously into a creator, arbiter, catalyst, and salesman of the modern element in poetry. During much of his transitional London period (1908–20), though, Pound seems less to be developing his own poetic identity than dissolving it in translation, dramatic impersonation, and exotic pastiche of other writers, as he scours the Western and Eastern poetic traditions for models: translating from Old English and Old French poets in *Ripostes*, then adapting verses from eighth-century Chinese authors in *Cathay* (1915), imitating Greek epigrams in *Lustra* (1916), and Englishing a Roman poet in *Homage to Sextus Propertius* (1919). By the time of *Lustra*, though, and even more clearly in *Hugh Selwyn Mauberley* (1920), this self-imposed course of multilingual training has indeed forged a distinctive Poundian voice, mischievously ironic and at last capable of addressing the contemporary scene.

Modernizing his own style by apparently paradoxical immersion in the ancients was not enough for Pound, whose revolutionary ambitions required the recruitment and mobilization of other writers around him. His first and most memorable exercise of this kind was the invention in 1912 of *Imagisme* or Imagism. Pound began in April 1912 by announcing to his friends Hilda Doolittle and Richard Aldington in a Kensington tea shop that they were, unwittingly, *Imagistes*, which meant that their poems met his new standard of modern taste, derived from the anti-Romantic opinions of Hueffer and Hulme. In the winter of 1912–13 Pound started spreading the news to American readers through Harriet Monroe's Chicago-based magazine *Poetry* that the very latest thing in London was a 'school' of *Imagistes* who insisted upon precision in verse. This baseless rumour was followed up in the March 1913 issue of *Poetry* with a sort of manifesto in the name of the English poet F. S. Flint but actually written by Pound, which called for directness of treatment, the avoidance of unnecessary words, and the use of musical rather than metronomically measured rhythms; an appended list of 'A Few Don'ts By an Imagist' in Pound's own name offered practical instruction in how to avoid the worst vices of contemporary poetry: 'Use no superfluous word, no adjective, which does not reveal something. [. . .] Go in fear of abstractions. [. . .] Use either no ornament or good ornament' (Pound, *Literary Essays*, pp. 4–5). At this stage, Imagism was merely a set of negative injunctions, an imprecise demand for precision coupled with an implicit defence of free verse. Pound had to back this up with some positive exemplification, and so put together an anthology of short poems by himself, Doolittle ('H.D.'), Aldington, Flint, and a few others including Hueffer, James Joyce, William Carlos Williams, and Amy Lowell, which eventually appeared in 1914 in New York and then in London (published by Harold Monro) as *Des Imagistes*, a would-be rival to the success of *Georgian Poetry*. By the summer of 1914, though, Pound had defected to a more noisily rebellious group around Wyndham Lewis's *Blast* journal and cast ridicule on the 'Amygisme' of Amy Lowell, who took over the direction of the Imagist circle in three further anthologies, all entitled *Some Imagist Poets* (1915, 1916, 1917).

The Imagist poem as represented in these four anthologies is a miniature, rather delicate performance that often echoes the fragile poignancy of a Japanese haiku, a Greek epigram, or the slighter kind of late symbolist lyric written in the 1890s. Presenting as concisely as it can a single visually clear metaphorical suggestion, it offers no discursive or rhetorical expansion or supplementary emotional effusion. Here, for instance, is 'Nocturne, V' by the otherwise unknown Skipwith Cannell, which Pound included in the 1914 anthology:

> I am weary with love, and thy lips
> Are night-born poppies.
> Give me therefore thy lips
> That I may know sleep.[2]

Although more redolent of Nineties languor than some other Imagist poems, this one is characteristic in its reliance upon a slight enigmatic tremor. By 1917, the flower, the leaf, the petal, the rippling pond, and the goldfish had become clichés of Imagist miniaturism, and easy prey for parodists or lazy imitators. Although it had a considerable impact upon the development of modern American free verse, Imagism was a temporary episode, an approach whose self-imposed restrictions limited its poetic scope and its further potential. It enjoyed some success as a publicity stunt—no more disreputably in this respect than the *Georgian Poetry* venture—and helped through

---

[2] Peter Jones (ed.), *Imagist Poetry* (Penguin, 1972), 59.

its manifestos to define for later poets what was unacceptable to modern taste in the bad habits of the late Romantic verse tradition.

Pound never abandoned his injunctions against 'sloppiness'; but he came to see the Imagist style of free verse in the 1912–17 phase as an inadequate solution that brought its own risks of sloppiness with it. A new revelation of the possibilities of modern poetry appeared to him in September 1914 when he met the American poet T. S. Eliot, who had recently arrived in England. Reading the manuscript of Eliot's 'The Love Song of J. Alfred Prufrock' (1915), he was delighted to find a poet who had both mastered his technique and fully modernized his style. Pound had long admired the dramatic monologues of Robert Browning, and had written numerous dramatic lyrics himself, using a variety of 'personae' (masks); but here in Eliot's 'Prufrock' he encountered a new kind of monologue, one that disintegrates character into mood. The speaker is a painfully hesitant young man, emotionally paralysed by self-consciousness, his sense of self crumbling into disconnected and overpowering images. The combined comedy and pathos of this figure is rendered through an assured command of variable rhythm, vivid but mysterious imagery, and curious disjunctions between formal and conversational, melancholic and blasé tones. The unique verbal music of 'Prufrock' establishes it as the first masterpiece of English-language modernism, almost matched among Eliot's early poems by the evocations of urban tedium in 'Preludes' and the enigmatic lyricism of 'La Figlia Che Piange'. These poems, collected in *Prufrock and Other Observations* (1917), were more convincingly modern than anything so far produced by Pound or the Imagist group. In part this arises simply from Eliot's study of more recent models—notably the French symbolist poet Jules Laforgue—than those imitated by the Imagists. The derivation, though, cannot fully account for his uncanny ability to transmute the unpoetical materials of modern urban life into genuinely poetical effects, in the street scenes of 'Prufrock' and 'Rhapsody on a Windy Night', and most strikingly in the evocation of grime and squalor in 'Preludes'. It is significant that Pound's review of *Prufrock and Other Observations* in *Poetry* particularly praised the book for 'its fine tone, its humanity, and its realism; for all good art is realism of one sort or another' (*Literary Essays*, p. 420).

Most of the poems in Eliot's first collection are regarded as exercises in 'free verse', for lack of any more careful distinction; but Eliot was suspicious of the term, partly because his verse was in fact 'unfree', closely bound both to recognized metrical patterns and to rhyme, while enjoying a certain licence in the variation of line lengths. In their continuing discussions of the new direction to be taken in modern verse, it seems that Eliot and Pound agreed that some reversion to more craftsmanlike metrical and stanzaic forms was needed. The result was a sequence of lighter sardonic poems in quatrain form published in Eliot's second and third volumes, *Poems* (1919) and *Ara Vos Prec* (1920). These display Eliot's gift for improbable polysyllabic rhyming, along with a sophisticated kind of 'wit' that in some of its features (anti-Semitic assumptions, a squeamish revulsion from the human body and from common humanity) now inspires more unease than amusement. This is coterie verse designed to raise a knowing chuckle among a highly educated circle for its allusively ironic treatment of gulfs between body and spirit, high culture and low commerce. The same may be said of Pound's *Hugh Selwyn Mauberley* (1920), in which a partial return to quatrain form goes along with a disdainful tone of superiority to modern cheapness. This short sequence of poems embodies Pound's ironic review of his early career, his farewell to London, and his lament for the self-destruction of Europe in the 1914–18 war.

The sense of a whole culture in ruins that is evoked in *Hugh Selwyn Mauberley* in turn helped to inspire Eliot's most ambitious and intriguing work, 'The Waste Land' (1922). This poem of 434 lines was at one stage of composition more than twice as long, but was whittled down by Pound's astutely judged excisions. The strong elements of pastiche and multilingual mimicry in this poem also echo Pound's earlier example; but the command of varied rhythmic effects, and the orchestration of fragmentary images and contrasting voices, are all Eliot's own. The immediate and highly unusual origins of 'The Waste Land' lie in the nervous breakdown with which Eliot was afflicted in 1921, and in periods of attempted recuperation at Margate, during a prolonged drought, and at Lausanne. From the opening lines, in which spring is encountered not joyously but with trepidation as a disturbing catalyst of memory and desire, the emotional substance of the poem is an agitated compound of exhaustion, despair, disgust, and dread, its modes of speech dominated alternately by lamentation and prophecy. Something which might be a terrifying resurrection, or might equally be a merciful obliteration, is constantly awaited, but the voices of the poem cannot or dare not identify it, beyond hinting at its association with the element of water: a baptism, or a drowning?

Whatever the nature of Eliot's psychological crisis in 1921, 'The Waste Land' is composed of elements that pre-date that disturbance: within it appears to be concentrated his awareness both of comparative mythology and of literary traditions stretching back to the Bible and Sophocles. The waste land of the title is not, as many hastily assume, a patch of disused ground but a country devastated by some curse; its identity, though, is multiple—the Thebes of Oedipus as well as the oft-destroyed city of Carthage and the now disintegrating empires of Austria-Hungary and Britain. As in nightmare, distinctions of time and place have dissolved so that we are simultaneously in post-War London and in Dante's Limbo, listening now to Tiresias, the blind prophet of ancient Thebes, and now to his cheap modern counterpart, the fortune teller Madame Sosostris, while fragmentary quotations from Spenser, Kyd, Shakespeare, Marvell, Baudelaire, and Verlaine drift to the ear as ghostly interruptions and sinister echoes. Poetic styles of different periods are also, to use a cinematic term, intercut: those of medieval epitaph, Shakespearian eulogy, eighteenth-century satire, and contemporary jazz song. The most daring, and for most readers the most bewildering, feature of the poem is its rapid succession and juxtaposition of different 'voices', some of them self-identifying (Marie the German aristocrat, the 'hyacinth girl', Tiresias, the working-class woman in a pub), some that can be guessed at (a war veteran, the Fisher King, the mock-Wagnerian Thames-daughters), others that remain unplaced. The coherent single voice that we expect to hear in most kinds of poetry has abdicated, and we are left to find new ways of attending to a kind of operatic seance.

'The Waste Land' appeared in two periodicals in the autumn of 1922: the American *Dial*, and Eliot's own newly founded journal *The Criterion*. Preparing the poem for book publication in America (1922) and Britain (1923—hand-set by Leonard and Virginia Woolf for their Hogarth Press), Eliot added a series of explanatory notes, both to fill out the number of pages and to guard against accusations of plagiarism. This mock-pedantic supplement only confirmed the poem's reputation for formidable obscurity, and encouraged attempts to unravel its coded 'meaning', usually in terms of the Grail legend, fertility cults, sexual sterility, and the quest for spiritual salvation. Less concerned with meaning than with tone and mood, younger writers and enthusiastic students greeted 'The Waste Land' as the definitive statement of the post-War generation's 'disillusionment' or of the spiritual 'malaise' of the times, and quoted its more memorable phrases as badges of youthful despair: 'a handful of dust', for instance, ended up as the title of an Evelyn Waugh novel. Older writers including J. C. Squire at the *London Mercury*, on the other hand, dismissed it as simply incomprehensible, and thereby marked out a line of battle between 'Georgian' conservatism and the modernism of the Twenties.

With Pound having moved on to France and then to Mussolini's Italy, Eliot had now clearly assumed the leadership of literary modernism in London, backing up his authority with the important critical essays collected as *The Sacred Wood* (1920) and *Homage to John Dryden* (1924).[3] He was not the only experimental alternative to Georgianism, though. Even more boldly 'incomprehensible' than Eliot's work was that of Edith Sitwell, who had, with her brother Osbert and her friend Nancy Cunard, founded in 1916 the periodical *Wheels*, which functioned as an annual anthology of verse. Before it collapsed in 1921, *Wheels* served as a showcase for the Sitwells' verse and as a platform for their critical assaults upon the Georgian 'establishment'. The Sitwells were devoted to noisy rebellion against the Victorian aristocratic culture in which they had been brought up. Osbert wrote some rather shapeless verse satires on militarism and fox-hunting, while Edith attempted a more original kind of experiment in poetry. Like Eliot and Pound, she rejected the nineteenth-century Romantic tradition, especially its Wordsworthian ruralism, and claimed she was returning to the imaginative strengths of the Elizabethan age. Her early verse is colourfully crowded with mandolins, parrot-feathers, unicorns, exotic spices and fruits, peopled by clowns, dwarfs, and princesses, its rhythms seeking the impression of frenetic dance. It comes close to nonsense verse in its free associa-

---

[3] See Ch. 12, below.

tion of images through simile or mere sound, as here at the start of one of the *Façade* poems of 1923:

> SOMETHING lies beyond the scene, the encre de chine marine obscene
> Horizon
>   In
>   Hell
> Black as a bison
> See the tall black Aga on the sofa in the alga mope, his
> Bell-rope
> Moustache (clear as a great bell!)
> Waves in eighteen-eighty
> Bustles
> Come
> Late with tambourines of
> Rustling
> Foam.
>
> (*Collected Poems*, p. 157)

Despite her public hostility to the Georgians, there is a significant debt in many of Edith Sitwell's poems, as her biographer Victoria Glendinning has noticed, to the children's rhymes of Walter de la Mare published in his *Peacock Pie* (1913).[4] The public event that was meant to confirm the superiority of Sitwell's kind of modernism to the defunct Georgians, however, turned into a fiasco: a performance in 1923 of her *Façade* sequence, set to music by the young composer William Walton, and in which Sitwell chanted her verse through a megaphone, attracted widespread critical derision; and her subsequent reputation has never fully recovered from suspicions of self-promoting charlatanism. Echoes of her early boisterous wordplay could still be heard in the Thirties in the poems of her younger Welsh friend Dylan Thomas, but already Sitwell's own verse had mellowed into a quieter, more romantic and nostalgic mood in *The Sleeping Beauty* (1924) and *Rustic Elegies* (1927). At the same time, Eliot's voice was subsiding into the penitential monotone of 'The Hollow Men' (1925) and *Ash-Wednesday* (1930). The rebellious energy and even the strangeness of modernism were on the wane by the late Twenties.

---

[4] Victoria Glendinning, *Edith Sitwell: A Unicorn among Lions* (Weidenfeld and Nicolson, 1981), 88.

There remained for a while one lonely rebel, who had in any case been fighting a rather different battle. While Eliot and Pound had been attempting to overthrow nineteenth-century Romanticism in the name of some new 'classical' precision, D. H. Lawrence was renewing what they regarded as its worst individualist features of spontaneous fluidity, displaying in his free-verse poems the clear influence—again, the worst possible, on the Pound–Eliot view—of Walt Whitman. To Lawrence had fallen the unusual distinction of being included in both the Georgian and the Imagist anthologies, an honour that indicates on either side a premature misreading of his true poetic inclination. Even in the early collections *Love Poems and Others* (1913) and *Amores* (1916), where rhyme prevails and the influence of Hardy predominates, Lawrence's poems are already more intense than those of the Georgians, and more confessionally expansive than those of the Imagists. A new surge of emotional and creative self-confidence brought about by his marriage then launched him still further from those schools, into the unfettered free-verse style of *Look! We Have Come Through!* (1917) and the later books. Lawrence here reinvented his poetic identity as Yeats, Pound, and Eliot had, but in the opposite direction: away from their impersonal dramatic masks and their allusive obliqueness, and towards the unguarded, instinctive revelation of the self in its momentary raptures or rages. Lawrence attempted to justify the new manner in his essay 'Poetry of the Present' (1919), which renounces the 'static perfection' of metrical patterns and rhyme schemes:

Finished beauty and measured symmetry belong to the stable, unchanging eternities.

But in free verse we look for the insurgent naked throb of the instant moment. To break the lovely form of metrical verse, and to dish up the fragments as a new substance, called *vers libre*, this is what most of the free-versifiers accomplish. They do not know that free verse has its own *nature*, that it is neither star nor pearl, but instantaneous like plasm. It has no goal in either eternity. It has no finish. It has no satisfying stability, satisfying to those who like the immutable. None of this. It is the instant; the quick; the very jetting source of all will-be and has-been. The utterance is like a spasm, naked contact with all influences at once. (*Selected Critical Writings*, pp. 78–9)

Lawrence's delirious Whitmanesque phallicism here demands

nothing less than that the true free-verse poem be an orgasm. The risks of failure by such a standard are high indeed; and in most of Lawrence's later poems, especially in the *Pansies* (1929), the 'jetting source', unrestrained by traditional rhythms, either wilts into a detumescent prosiness or rushes to a premature ejaculation of mere opinion. There is often a liberating vitality to them, at least for the reader who feels able to trust to the impulsive urgency of Lawrence's rhetoric and does not mind being preached at. The more successful poems are those in which the usually insistent 'I' is reverently humbled before the otherness either of non-human life, as in the *Birds, Beasts and Flowers* collection (1923), or of death itself, in the posthumously published *Last Poems* (1932).

W. H. Auden and the Poetry of the Thirties

Lawrence was mistaken about the future of poetry, at least in England, where, after his death in 1930, free verse became less important, not more. It was not just the ex-Georgians—Graves, Sassoon, Blunden, de la Mare—who persisted in the use of traditional metres, rhymes, and verse forms, but the emerging generation too. The new poets who came to prominence in the early Thirties, in particular Auden, Day Lewis, Spender, and MacNeice, combined a modernity of subject matter, tone, and diction with an obvious respect for established verse forms both popular (ballad and song) and literary (sonnet, sestina, and villanelle). In this they display a determination to move beyond the esoteric remoteness of Yeats, Eliot, and Pound, and to leave behind the literary agenda of the 1890s which colours the work of those three poets. They cultivated instead a vernacular plainness of technique and diction that in some ways aligns them with Hardy and the Georgian poets, although their range of reference is more modernistic both in embracing the sights and sounds of contemporary urban and industrial life and in maintaining an intellectual detachment that owes something to Eliot.

These features of the Auden group may be accounted for both in terms of generational shift and by reference to changing political circumstances. Unlike the Georgians or the Imagists, this group of poets, who came to public attention in the anthologies *New*

Signatures (1932) and *New Country* (1933) and then published their work in the journal *New Verse* (1933–9), was 'new' in that its members had been born in the twentieth century itself and were clearly more at ease within a post-Victorian culture of motorized transport, aviation, and mass entertainment than any of their predecessors—which is not to say that they were satisfied with it. By contrast with Yeats, Eliot, and Pound, they were not inclined to bemoan the arrival of their century as a catastrophic Fall from the aristocratic glories of old into vulgar suburbanism. Suspicious of that kind of cultural nostalgia, they were more consistently modern in identifying their adversary as a moribund social order sliding into the atavistic politics of Fascism. They celebrated the modern technological power and beauty of the aeroplane, as in Spender's 'The Landscape Near an Aerodrome' (1933), and of the railways, as in Auden's 'Night Mail' (1938) and Spender's 'The Express' (1932), and they earned some notoriety for writing about gasworks and electricity pylons. Many of their poems are marked by colloquial levity and up-to-the-minute slang, notably in MacNeice's 'Bagpipe Music' (1937). At the same time they were happy to adapt verse techniques of considerable antiquity: alliterative patterns derived from Anglo-Saxon poetry in parts of Day Lewis's 'The Magnetic Mountain' (1933) and in Auden's Epilogue to *The Orators* (1932), or Chaucer's favoured rhyme-royal stanza in Auden's 'Letter to Lord Byron' (1937).

The *New Signatures* poets, then, and some others like MacNeice who arrived a little later, were modern in ways that set them apart from the high modernist poets of 1912–22. Their language was more democratically legible to readers of such large-circulation magazines as the BBC weekly *The Listener*, their imagery was more confidently contemporary, and their anti-romantic stance was, like Hardy's, friendlier to liberal conceptions of progress: they could write, for example, about the urban poor with sympathy rather than with disdainful alarm, as in Spender's 'An Elementary Class Room in a Slum' (1939) or MacNeice's 'Birmingham' (1934). In one respect at least, though, they learned from and developed the significance of such works as 'The Waste Land' and 'The Second Coming': they were prepared to assume the 'prophetic' function of the modern poet as Yeats and Eliot had done so powerfully, but at the same time they steered its emphasis away from lamentation and towards diagnosis.

Some of these poets had brought with them from their schooldays a private mythology of conflict between 'us' and 'them', a fantasy of clandestine resistance derived from spy thrillers in which young heroes would slip over frontiers to adventures behind enemy lines. In the new political context of the Thirties, marked by economic depression, ascendant Fascism in Europe, and the alignment of young intellectuals with Communist and Popular Front movements, these adolescent dreams could readily—and often naïvely—be projected onto the map of current affairs. The times lent poetry a new urgency and a new antagonistic spirit, in which the younger writers hurried to prophesy the impending doom of their corrupt and terminally sick civilization, as Day Lewis did in *The Magnetic Mountain*, concluding that

> It is now or never, the hour of the knife,
> The break with the past, the major operation.
>
> (*Complete Poems*, p. 162)

The surgical metaphor and idea that the time is up for the old order here echo, as so often in Day Lewis, the more original exploitation of these tropes in such early poems of Auden as 'Consider this and in our time' and 'Get there if you can . . .' (both 1930). Auden's early verse, collected in *Poems* (1930), is a poetry of enigmatic menace in which it is always too late for the complacent bourgeois to flee the imminent violence of invasion or revolt. The same kind of implied threat appears in 'O what is that sound' (1934), 'It's farewell to the drawing-room's civilised cry' (1937; later entitled 'Danse Macabre'), and many other poems of that decade. Auden did not only capture earlier than other poets the contemporary sense of looming catastrophe; he gave it a special imaginative force through his repeated use of medical imagery and a clinical tone. The personal background to this lies in his early scientific interests, from his childhood as a physician's son through his period as a student of biology to his readings in psychoanalysis, while the historical reference point often seems to be the great influenza pandemic of 1918–19. Throughout the decade, from the mock prayer of 'Sir, no man's enemy, forgiving all' (1930) to the gloomy meditations of 'September 1, 1939' (1939), Auden presented the crisis of contemporary civilization in terms of illness, infection, or neurosis, and especially in terms of 'psychosomatic' illness, a concept he had borrowed from the psychologists Homer Lane and Georg Groddeck. Like many writers of his generation, he wrote under the dual intellectual influences of Marx and of Freud. Unlike most of them, he forged poetically vivid connections between the personal and the political, between love and democracy, inhibition and authority-worship, whether in lyrics of private reflection such as 'Out on the lawn I lie in bed' (1934; later entitled 'A Summer Night') or in poems of public exhortation such as 'Spain' (1937).

Auden the prophet-clinician was to the fore in the early phase of his career, from 1928 to about 1935, but the remarkable years 1936–9 in which his work matured most impressively display a rich and varied development of his verse well beyond the perceived categories of 'public', 'political', or 'Leftist' poet. His poems of this phase include biographical and allegorical sonnets, philosophical love lyrics on natural perfection and human imperfection, macabre ballads, formal elegies—notably those on Yeats (1939) and Freud (1940)—and an extended comical verse epistle, the 'Letter to Lord Byron'. Amid this fertile variety one common feature asserts itself as distinctively 'Audenesque': a deliberately deflated tone of prosaic anticlimax, indicative both of anti-romanticism and of positive poetic realism. So, even in 'Spain', when Auden appears to rally his readers to a decisive encounter with History, the reality of anti-Fascist struggle is presented unheroically as 'the expending of powers | On the flat ephemeral pamphlet and the boring meeting' (*English Auden*, p. 212). The refusal to exaggerate or idealize extends to Auden's love poetry, in which the imperfection of the beloved is treasured, and to his elegies, in which the passing away of a great man does not shake the world but provokes only a pause for thought among a minority.

'The real world lies before us', Auden reminds himself in his poem 'May with its light behaving' (1935; *English Auden*, p. 152); and that recognition entails a responsibility for the modern poet to attend to the ordinary and the habitual as well as to the miraculous and the mythic, as he suggests in 'Musée des Beaux Arts' (1939). He wanted poetry to show more interest in plain facts, to become more prosaic, novelistic, or even journalistic. He had in 'Letter to Lord Byron' accused the poets in general of being lazily unobservant by comparison with the novelists, and he takes up the same unflattering contrast in his sonnet 'The Novelist' (1939). This poem likens the talent of the poets to the dazzling uniform of nineteenth-century cavalry officers, in contrast with the novelist, who 'Must struggle out of his boyish gift and learn | How to be plain and awkward' (*English Auden*, p. 238). The dominant metaphor of this sonnet is the historical gulf between old-fashioned military glory and a new epoch of war and revolution characterized by clandestine infiltration and anonymous intelligence work. The conspicuous, self-destructive romantic poet is defunct, Auden suggests, and needs to be replaced by self-effacing literary spies willing to immerse themselves like the novelists and the documentary film-makers in the destructive elements of boredom, dullness, and vulgarity. As Louis MacNeice had observed in his poem 'Hidden Ice' (1936),

> There are few songs for domesticity
> For routine work, money-making or scholarship
> Though these are apt for eulogy or for tragedy.
>
> (*Collected Poems*, p. 76)

It was MacNeice more than any of Auden's other associates who carried through this new programme for a poetry attentive to the mundane and the habitual in their connections to larger psychological and political problems, in his collection *The Earth Compels* (1938) and more impressively in the colloquial tones of his *Autumn Journal* (1939). A major implication of Auden's and MacNeice's work in the late Thirties is that poetry must humbly acknowledge its own diminished importance and learn from the now dominant prose arts.

Trends, Anthologies, and Reputations

The significance of Auden and MacNeice is not only a matter of individual talent. It involves also their absorption and creative development of the dominant tendency in this period's verse, which, as this chapter has repeatedly suggested, is not that of 'modernism' but of realism. The realistic trend in modern verse, as we have seen, is broad enough to accommodate a variety of individual tones ranging from the different kinds of irony found in the poems of Hardy, Eliot, and Sassoon; through the colloquialisms of Masefield, MacNeice, and even, at times, Yeats; to the quiet understatements of Edward Thomas and the anti-idealistic deflations of Brooke, Owen, and Auden.

To identify a mainstream, however, is to fulfil only half of the task of literary history in this sphere. Almost as important are the exceptions and counter-tendencies that complicate the full picture, many of these being neither minor nor eccentric. A strong 'romantic' tradition of verse persists in this period, with the major poet of the age, W. B. Yeats, at its head; D. H. Lawrence and Dylan Thomas clearly also fall under this description, while the playful free-associating style of Edith Sitwell places her beyond the pale of verse realism. The preoccupation of some poets, notably Walter de la Mare and Robert Graves, with the irrational realms of nightmare places them partly within this romantic camp too, despite their 'Georgian' avoidance of high rhapsody. Much of Pound's work displays more nostalgic Pre-Raphaelitism than modern realism, while two of the poets often mentioned in the same breath as Auden—C. Day Lewis and Stephen Spender—are distinctly more 'romantic' in tendency.

Most of the poetry of the Thirties, indeed, was not what we now commonly understand to be 'Thirties Poetry' at all: Yeats, Eliot, Blunden, de la Mare, and many other poets were publishing significant verse in that decade, and yet they do not feature in most anthologies and critical accounts of its literary scene. What we usually mean by 'Thirties Poetry' is in fact the work of a particular group of poets who emerged as a new wave in about 1930. The continuing work of older poets then tends to be eclipsed, and so does newer verse that fails to echo the Audenesque stance. In contrast to Auden's cool intellectual tone, there arose in the Thirties an opposing current of flamboyant irrationalism among the younger poets, most striking in the work of Dylan Thomas, but evident too in that of the surrealists David Gascoyne and Charles Madge. Nor was the poetry of that decade uniformly leftist in political inclination: apart from the conservatism of Eliot and Yeats, there was among the younger cohort Roy Campbell, the South African poet who expressed open support for the Fascist side in the Spanish Civil War, hymning the dictator Franco in his *Flowering Rifle* (1939).

Distortions of perspective in the history of modern poetry are produced by the understandable pressure, in academic courses and in surveys like this one, to concentrate on the major achievements and thus on a small band of major figures. The misleading impression may then be given that the poets passed over as 'minor' are in some way inferior versions of the eminent few. The true variety of the occluded or half-forgotten poetic voices in these decades is such that it cannot here be exhibited, but only obliquely indicated by reference to anthologies. Within this period itself, the 'common reader' of poetry would have been acquainted with works by many more living poets than we now recall or reprint; perhaps sixty or more names would have been recognized by such a reader as figures in the contemporary poetic scene, all readily sampled in the numerous anthologies of modern verse. This was a great age of anthologies, in which no publisher of literary distinction could afford to do without some selection of contemporary poetry on its list. As we have seen, certain anthologies, most importantly the *Georgian Poetry* series and the later *New Signatures* volume, fulfilled the vital function of bringing new generations of poets to public attention; others, like the Imagist series, declared the existence of controversial new schools of poetry. But beyond these there were general anthologies aiming at least to provide introductory selections of modern verse and its varieties. The English Association, founded to encourage the study of literature in schools, offered *Poems of To-Day* (1915; 2nd vol., 1922). The firm of Secker responded with *Selections from Modern Poets* (1921; 2nd vol., 1924), and Chatto & Windus with Harold Monro's *Twentieth Century Poetry* (1929). The Oxford University Press invited W. B. Yeats to edit an *Oxford Book of Modern Verse* (1936), which appeared in the same year as Michael Roberts's more exclusively modernist competitor, the *Faber Book of Modern Verse*. By the late Thirties, there could be little excuse for remaining in ignorance of a good range of modern verse, the work of the anthologists having consolidated a recognizable tradition of twentieth-century poetry that embraced both the older styles of Hardy, Yeats, and de la Mare and the newer experiments of Eliot, Lawrence, and Sitwell.

If we look more closely at the common ground of critical valuation embodied in these anthologists' selections, we will encounter some surprises. In academic contexts as elsewhere, our map of the poetic landscape in this period has long been shaped by the modernistic, anti-Georgian selections of Roberts's *Faber Book*, a work that, unlike its contemporary rivals, remained in print for decades, with some revisionary supplementation. Shown in Table 1 here is a list of the thirty-five modern British and Irish poets most often represented in six of those other general anthologies in the period 1933–41. Provided that they appear in at least five of these books, they are ranked here by the total number of poems or extracts appearing under their names.

Table 1. *Anthologized Poets, 1933–1941*

Author	No. of appearances in an anthology	Author	No. of appearances in an anthology
Yeats	44	Campbell	15
de la Mare	35	MacNeice	15
Bridges	29	Binyon	14
Eliot	29	Gibson	13
Davies	26	Flecker	13
Housman	26	Kipling	13
Hardy	25	Meynell	13
Turner	25	'AE' (Russell)	13
Day Lewis	24	Thomas, Edward	13
Sassoon	23	Chesterton	12
Lawrence	21	Joyce	12
Masefield	20	Abercrombie	11
Sitwell	19	Brooke	11
Auden	18	Church	11
Blunden	17	Read	11
Spender	17	Drinkwater	10
Moore	16	Mew	10
Monro	16		

Sources: Phyllis M. Jones (ed.), *Modern Verse, 1900–1940* (Oxford University Press, 1940); C. Day Lewis and L. A. G. Strong (eds.), *A New Anthology of Modern Verse, 1920–1940* (Methuen, 1941); Robert Lynd (ed.), *Modern Poetry* (Nelson, 1939); Harold Monro (ed.), *Twentieth Century Poetry* (Chatto & Windus, 1929; rev.1933); Denys Kilham Roberts (ed.), *The Century's Poetry, 1837–1937*, vol. 2. *Bridges to the Present Day* (Penguin, 1938); W. B. Yeats (ed.), *The Oxford Book of Modern Verse, 1892–1935* (1936).

What is likely to strike us first about this table is how few of these poets are now read or even recollected. They still have entries in the better reference works, and their books are familiar to second-hand book dealers, but our cultural memory has otherwise jettisoned the minor 'Georgian' poets Lascelles Abercrombie, James Elroy Flecker, Wilfrid Gibson, Harold Monro, and W. J. Turner, along with such traditionalist poets as Laurence Binyon, Robert Bridges, Thomas Sturge Moore, Richard Church, and the Irish poet 'AE' (George Russell), although Binyon's 'For the Fallen' (1915) still appears in anthologies of war poetry. Little attention is now paid even to the lesser modernists Edith Sitwell and Herbert Read, or to the poems— far more traditional than his prose works—of James Joyce. On the other hand, we might be puzzled too by the absence of some names more familiar to us, like those of Dylan Thomas (who emerged too late for two of the anthologies, but does have eight poems in the others), Wilfred Owen (who is represented by nine poems, but was excluded by Yeats and more reasonably on grounds of date by Day Lewis and Strong), Isaac Rosenberg, William Empson, and Robert Graves (who had not helped his cause by denouncing anthologies on principle). Odd as it may look to twenty-first-century eyes, Table 1 may be taken nonetheless as a fair reconstruction of a Thirties consensus about the leading practitioners of modern verse. These thirty or so poets, we may reasonably assume, were at the time the most often read, the most widely studied, recited, and admired.

The most significant feature of Table 1 is the overwhelming predominance of non-modernist poets who were continuing or quietly modifying late Victorian verse styles. Bridges, Hardy, Housman, and Moore, along with the Georgians de la Mare, Davies, Turner, Sassoon, Masefield, and Blunden, all rank high in the list, and are followed by such late Victorian and Edwardian traditionalists as Kipling, Meynell, 'AE', Flecker, and the light balladeer Chesterton. Even among the newer poets emerging in the war years, notably Edward Thomas and Richard Church, the Wordsworthian inheritance remains strong. As many as fifteen of these thirty-five poets had had poems published in the *Georgian Poetry* collections of 1912–22. It was not that the anthologists were overlooking the younger generations: C. Day Lewis, W. H. Auden, Stephen Spender, and Roy Campbell are all there, while Dylan Thomas (b. 1914) and George Barker (b. 1913) appear in four of the collections. It was more that they felt no obligation to debar such writers as Bridges, Kipling, Hardy, Housman, Meynell, and the throng of Georgians from the pantheon of modern poets, and no embarrassment at presenting the twentieth-century verse tradition inclusively as a continuation, in most respects, of the nineteenth-century legacy. By contrast, Roberts's *Faber Book of Modern Verse*, partly because of its policy of exhibiting American poets alongside the Irish and British, is provocatively eccentric. It includes only ten of the thirty-five poets listed in Table 1, and of these only two (Lawrence and Monro) had appeared in the *Georgian Poetry* series. A ruthless winnowing was under way, of a kind that is echoed in some influential, harshly anti-Georgian critical works of the period, notably F. R. Leavis's *New Bearings in English Poetry* (1932).

Triply occluded by the exclusiveness of the modernist canon, by the clubbishness of Edward Marsh's Georgian circle, and even by the more catholic anthologists of the Thirties are the English women poets. Only three of them, Edith Sitwell, Alice Meynell, and Charlotte Mew, appear in Table 1, and only one (Sitwell again) appears in the *Faber Book*, albeit alongside three American women. The first three *Georgian Poetry* anthologies had included no women poets at all, although the now forgotten Fredegond Shove appeared in the fourth, and Vita Sackville-West in the final volume. The more powerfully original poet Charlotte Mew would have been brought in, had Marsh accepted Harold Monro's advice; she was still, after Sitwell and Meynell, the most visible of modern women poets at the time, and her reputation has more recently benefited from new editions and from revived critical attention. Dorothy Wellesley, Duchess of Wellington, has not survived so well, although her work was anthologized and commended with enthusiasm by Yeats, who was for a while her lover. Lilian Bowes Lyon had some of her nature poems adopted by anthologists in the Thirties, and a few have re-appeared in later collections. Also represented rather sparsely by the Thirties anthologists were Frances Cornford, Stella Gibbons, Ruth Pitter, Anne Ridler, Sylvia Townsend Warner, and Anna Wickham. Gibbons and Townsend Warner, like Rose Macaulay, Winifred Holtby, and Naomi Mitchison, are all still honoured as prose writers, but the fact that they were also poets of some reputation in their day has been forgotten, although the same may now also be said of James Joyce, Aldous Huxley, and Ford Madox Ford. Later anthologies, including such otherwise valuable books as Robin

Skelton's *Poetry of the Thirties* (1964), in which Anne Ridler alone of the women appears, have pushed these poets further into an oblivion from which Jane Dowson's anthology *Women's Poetry of the 1930s* (1996) has done well to rescue them. Further labours of rediscovery and critical revaluation are needed in this area: the poems of Ruth Pitter and Elizabeth Daryush in particular merit serious attention. There is a precedent for the recovery of lost reputations from this period, in the case of Ivor Gurney, the war poet who was all but forgotten after his incarceration in a psychiatric hospital in 1922, but whose *Collected Poems*, edited by P. J. Kavanagh in 1982, dramatically enhanced his standing. Auden in his sonnet 'The Novelist' may have claimed that 'The rank of every poet is well known' (*English Auden*, p. 238), but he was only joking. The pantheon of this period's poets is almost certain to be disturbed and reordered afresh.

5

Modern Drama

New Words, 1910–1940
*black-out expressionistic forestage
improvisational off-stage on-stage post-Ibsenist
pratfall producership puppeteer
scenarist Thespianism*

The widening division evident in this period between minority art and majority entertainment was most visibly entrenched in the theatre. As in the late Victorian and Edwardian periods, so in these decades the English theatre was a large and generally prosperous business offering a harmless evening's diversion to urban middle-class audiences, principally in the forms of light comedy and melo-drama. Until the advent of radio drama (1924) and of the talking pictures (1928), it still enjoyed with the music hall a comfortable duopoly of dramatic entertainment; and in London at least, it man-aged to withstand the competition of these new rivals through the 1930s while the music hall succumbed to it. The theatre was com-mercially strong enough to make fortunes for astute producers, and sometimes even for playwrights, but this very prosperity and institutional solidity weighed heavily against the kinds of creative risks that poets or novelists could take. Playwrights were hemmed in both by the commercial caution of theatre managers and by an official censorship that restricted the treatment of sensitive religious, political, and sexual subjects. So the tried-and-tested formulas of light entertainment dominated both the West End of London and the provincial theatre, while the more adventurous or controversial kinds of new literary drama were confined to the margins, in private theatre clubs operating in small, out-of-the-way suburban theatres hired for one afternoon or evening. Devotees of 'serious' drama in London had commonly to forsake the bright lights of Shaftesbury Avenue and make their way out to the Court Theatre in Chelsea, the Everyman Theatre in Hampstead, the Lyric in Hammersmith, the tiny Mercury in Notting Hill, or across the Thames to the Old Vic, a converted temperance hall in Lambeth.

This division between the mainstream and the fringe dated back to the Independent Theatre Company's efforts (from 1891) to bring the works of Henrik Ibsen to English audiences, and of the Stage Society (from 1899) to promote the work of Bernard Shaw, Harley Granville-Barker, and other new dramatists. The 'New Drama' of the Edwardian period had offered impressive challenges to the timidity and triviality of the commercial stage, and breathed new imaginative life into the theatre outside London, notably in the adventurous repertory companies of Birmingham and Manchester. Its influence outlasted 1910, but the pioneering energies of its leaders were waning: Granville-Barker, for example, a pillar of the Stage Society as actor, playwright, and director, withdrew from the stage in 1914 to write a series of books on Shakespearian production; by which time another leading Stage Society playwright, St John Hankin, had drowned himself (1909) and the younger Lancashire dramatist Stanley Houghton had died from natural causes (1913). The heroic phase of Edwardian 'independent' drama, with its emphasis on controversial social problems, gave way after the Great War to a kind of truce in which the dominance of lightweight commercial theatre was unshaken but became permeable by the influence of the uncommercial fringe: experimental literary dramatists who had long been encamped on the margins could be welcomed in the West End to the extent that they employed the medium of comedy—as with the success of Shaw's *Pygmalion* (1914)[1]—while some other playwrights, notably W. Somerset Maugham and Noël Coward, abandoned the

---

[1] Dates given in this chapter and throughout the book for dramatic works are those of the first public performance in Britain. These often differ from the dates of a play's world premiere and of its publication.

unrewarding purity of the Stage Society milieu to enrich themselves in the West End while raising its accepted kinds of entertainment to those of literary art. Far from freezing out the literati, the managers of London's commercial theatres learned to co-opt their vitality, allowing the smaller fringe theatres to take the risks with unorthodox new plays and then reaping the profits from the best of them. Thus Noël Coward's early play *The Vortex* (1924), having narrowly escaped censorship by the Lord Chamberlain for its treatment of serial adultery and drug addiction, opened at the Everyman Theatre, Hampstead, where it garnered enough public notoriety and critical acclaim for it to transfer three weeks later to the Royalty Theatre in the West End, and later to two other West End theatres for two hundred performances before being taken over to New York.

In speaking of the gulf between minority and majority drama, it is important to be clear that this division is not between 'modernist' and 'traditional' forms, as it is in the poetry and prose fiction of this period. True to Somerset Maugham's dictum that 'intellectually, the theatre is thirty years behind the times' (*Summing Up*, ch. 37), modernism did not arrive upon the English stage until the 1950s, although there were some marginal experiments by W. H. Auden and Christopher Isherwood in the 1930s that deserve the name— and numerous non-naturalistic plays by Shaw, J. B. Priestley, T. S. Eliot, and others that do not. The truly pertinent line of division in this period is between an uncommercial 'literary' drama of ideas and social controversy, and a commercial drama of spectacle, sensation, and amusement. The minority tradition that survived from the ferment of the 1890s was for the most part inspired by the example of Ibsen's realistic stage representations of serious familial and social conflicts. Rejecting the frivolity of intricately plotted romantic intrigues in the nineteenth-century French tradition of the 'well-made play', it favoured instead the form of the 'problem play', which would bring to life some contemporary controversy of public importance—women's rights, unemployment, penal reform, class privilege—in a vivid but responsibly accurate presentation.

Problem plays of a fairly pure kind survive in the period 1910–40, from John Galsworthy's *Justice* (1910) to St John Ervine's play about a birth-control campaigner, *Robert's Wife* (1937). In between may be found 'problem' dramas treating in realistic or semi-melodramatic fashion a range of topical controversies such as industrial conflict (Ernest Hutchinson's *The Right to Strike*, 1920), divorce (Clemence Dane's *A Bill of Divorcement*, 1921), journalistic ethics (Galsworthy's *The Show*, 1925), euthanasia (Maugham's *The Sacred Flame*, 1929), the plight of war veterans (Maugham's *For Services Rendered*, 1932), and the impact of the depression upon business (Dodie Smith's department-store drama *Service*, 1932) and upon the unemployed (Lawrence Gow and Walter Greenwood's *Love on the Dole*, 1934). The problem play, though, occupies a minor place in the drama of these decades, which is dominated by various forms of comedy. The direct treatment of topical social questions in the problem play risked preaching to the converted, also suffering from obsolescence as public debate evolved and from audiences' desire to be entertained rather than appalled. Bernard Shaw vaulted beyond the limits of the problem play into a unique kind of intellectual comedy in which serious ideas could be brought before an audience in the diverting guise of what he called 'tomfoolery'. Meanwhile the comedy of manners as developed by Somerset Maugham and Noël Coward, although often berated for shallow cynicism, demonstrated that modern playwrights could still lure their audiences through laughter into significant engagement with the moral confusions of their time.

From Problem Play to Discussion Play

The last of the Edwardian problem plays, Galsworthy's *Justice* (February 1910, directed by Granville-Barker), illustrates well the typical virtues of Ibsenist realism as developed by its English exponents; and it reveals some of the restrictions that had prompted Shaw and others to venture beyond it. As a play with a specific purpose—to halt the routine use of solitary confinement in British prisons—it is unusual in that it actually helped to achieve its goal within a few months, in the shape of penal reforms introduced by the newly appointed Liberal Home Secretary, Winston Churchill, who attended the play and consulted Galsworthy about the details of revised prison regulations. *Justice*, then, rendered itself in the best sense redundant by the very success of its reformist mission; but Galsworthy maintained that his play had an importance surpassing the specific issue of solitary confinement, as a tragic demonstration of the judicial system's blindly destructive inhumanity. He subtitled his play 'A Tragedy in Four Acts', and although the traditional elements of tragic heroism and waste are lacking here (the protagonist, a junior legal clerk named Falder, is deliberately presented as a nervous weakling), the iron logic of events appropriate to tragic action is clearly marked out. This relentless chain of cause and effect begins with the decision of a solicitor, James How, to turn Falder over to the police upon discovery that he has forged a cheque, in a hasty attempt to elope with a married woman. Mr How is confronted here with a kind of moral dilemma that would not be beyond the experience of a middle-class theatre audience. Against the advice of his son, who pleads for clemency, this being the first offence of an overwrought young man, he invokes both the respectability of his legal practice and his responsibility to protect Society against embezzlers, thus propelling Falder irreversibly into the crushing machinery of the Law. The final act, also set in the offices of James & Walter How, sees the consequences of Mr How's decision returning upon him in horror, as the now virtually unemployable ex-convict Falder is rearrested for a minor infringement of his parole and jumps to his death. In the intervening acts, Galsworthy resists any easy melodramatic tipping of the scales: there are no heroes here (Falder is clearly guilty of the crime, and is personally unimpressive), and no villains either, the police, the judiciary, and the prison officials all being shown to be reasonable and even well-meaning men fairly observing the legal process. This important restraint, which is a mark of Galsworthy's realism, forces us to recognize the inherent insensitivity of the Law itself in the face of average human frailty, rather than to assign reassuring blame to cruel individuals. What the blindness of Justice cannot acknowledge, the clarity of realistic drama can expose to us: not just the inhumanity of the solitary confinement cell, brought before us here in a celebrated scene of painful mime, but the particular position of a harmless if erring human being in a moment of desperation, to which the Law's destructive response is appallingly disproportionate.

What dates this well-crafted and honourable play is not the fact that the worst excesses of solitary confinement were soon outlawed, so much as the contamination of the central issue of blind justice by moral categories of sexual purity and respectability. Falder's motive for the forgery is to get his beloved friend Ruth (with whom he has not, we are clearly informed, had sexual relations) and her two children beyond the clutches of her drunken, violent husband. This pitiful situation enlists our sympathies on Falder's side, but in the eyes of the judge at his trial, the same 'immoral' relationship counts against him, as it does when he applies to have his old job back; and the final straw that drives him to self-destruction is the discovery that during his term in prison Ruth has become the kept mistress of her employer. Falder dies in a state of sexual purity, and the play's final line declares 'He's safe with gentle Jesus!' (*Five Plays*, p. 169). Galsworthy intended those last words to be an ironic suggestion that modern society had followed the example of Pilate rather than of Christ, but it is scarcely possible to render them as anything but feeble consolation. Galsworthy worked diligently to expel Victorian melodramatic clichés from the legal drama of *Justice*, but they creep back in nonetheless through the sentimental sub-plot. The more resolutely anti-conventional dramatists of the time, led by Bernard Shaw, saw it as their task to challenge directly those moral notions of purity and respectability that Galsworthy had tended to leave undisturbed.

The more modern kind of problem play, such as Stanley Houghton's Lancashire drama *Hindle Wakes* (1912),[2] presents women characters more rebellious than Galsworthy's passively suffering Ruth. Houghton's colleague at the *Manchester Guardian*, Harold Brighouse, for example, showed in his comedy *Hobson's Choice* (1916) a strong daughter rebelling against her father, a self-important bootmaker, by marrying 'beneath' her and eventually buying out the family business. This post-Ibsenist figure of the strong woman in revolt against patriarchal constraints stands at the centre of this period's drama, from *Hindle Wakes* and *Hobson's Choice* to Rudolph Besier's *The Barretts of Wimpole Street* (1930) and Coward's *Design for Living* (1939), and especially in the plays of Bernard Shaw: *Misalliance* (1910), *Fanny's First Play* (1911), *Pygmalion* (1914), *Heartbreak House* (1921), and most emphatically *Saint Joan* (1924)

---

[2] See Ch. 17, below.

all exhibit the type in various forms, as several of his earlier works had done. Shaw's repeated use of the rebel-daughter figure reflects in part his personal philosophy of 'Creative Evolution', according to which Woman is the bearer of the Life Force, and Youth its advance guard; but it also echoes the activist feminism of the Suffrage campaigns, most obviously when the eponymous Fanny of *Fanny's First Play*, a student member of the Fabian Society at Cambridge, reveals herself to be a clandestine Suffragist who is writing to further the cause. Similarly, Shaw's Joan of Arc defends her adoption of masculine clothing much as a modern feminist dress-reformer would do, and she is openly compared with the socialist-Suffragist leader Sylvia Pankhurst in Shaw's preface to *Saint Joan*.

While Shaw was in sympathy with the emancipatory social agenda of the Edwardian problem-play tradition, he had long outgrown its dramatic limitations and its sometimes sentimental earnestness. The performance-within-a-performance of *Fanny's First Play* recapitulates the familiar Ibsenist revolt of the younger generation against the elders, but this time as farcical travesty: the young middle-class protagonists Bobby and Margaret are engaged to be married, but each has a minor brush with the police and is briefly imprisoned, so bringing shame upon both respectable families; as the parents come round to conceding that such minor blemishes on their respectability are not the end of the world, the youngsters cause further disgrace by bringing home their new-found admirers, a prostitute and a married French lieutenant. Once Margaret has broken off the betrothal as a result of her new self-awareness, fresh engagements are formed between Bobby and the cheerful streetwalker Dora, and between Margaret and the family butler Juggins, who reveals that he is the brother of a duke. The realistic sobriety of the orthodox problem play is thrown to the winds here as Shaw represents emancipation from bourgeois respectability in the forms of comic surprise, excess, and release.

Shaw's preference was not for realistic representation of social problems but for the provocative and paradoxical discussion of ideas, interspersed with implausible comic interruptions and unmaskings. His special innovation was the 'discussion play', in which a negligible plot serves as an excuse for a medley of extravagant debates, quarrels, and confessions that turn received opinions on their heads. Shaw's *Misalliance*, for example, which opened in February 1910 in the same theatre and as part of the same repertory season as Galsworthy's *Justice*, illustrates the gulf between the disciplined seriousness of the problem play and the free-ranging levity of the Shavian discussion drama. Subtitled 'A Debate in One Sitting', *Misalliance* scarcely achieves the coherence even of a debate, but sustains itself as a loose sequence of dialogues on the mutual incomprehension of parents and children, occasionally enlivened by some farcical and theatrically daring interruptions, including the arrival ex machina of a female Polish acrobat in an aeroplane that crashes just offstage. 'Lets argue about something intellectual,' one of the characters suggests almost as soon as the curtain rises, thus setting the tone (*Misalliance*, p. 114). The action takes place in the conservatory of a country house belonging to John Tarleton, a wealthy underwear magnate famed as a practical businessman but actually so devoted to ideas that he supplements his speeches with recommendations for further reading, referring his guests and relatives to the works of Ibsen, Browning, Whitman, Darwin, and other leaders of modern thought. The rebellious young heroine, Tarleton's daughter Hypatia, is impatient with the unending talk in her home, longing to become 'an active verb' (p. 145). She is engaged to be married to the obviously unsuitable weakling Bentley Summerhays, but a more promising catch is presented by the arrival of the aviator Joseph Percival with his Polish passenger Lina Szczepanowska. Displaying the customary boldness of the Shavian heroine, Hypatia takes Percival by the hand and invites him to chase her through the heather, if only to give her family something new to talk about. Further farcical complications ensue as Tarleton propositions Lina the acrobat and is amiably rebuffed, while a young socialist clerk who has arrived to assassinate Tarleton in revenge for the seduction of his mother attempts to blackmail Percival and Hypatia, having witnessed their outdoor frolics. Hypatia's fiancé Bentley is eventually hauled off by Lina, who has decided to make a man of him. There is a comic plot of sorts here, but it serves as little more than a peg on which to hang conversations about youth, age, marriage, democracy, and any other subject that may come up. Lina is a skilled juggler, but she is not permitted to practise her art on stage, where it is strictly ideas that are thrown in the air.

Misalliance was a failure at the box office and provoked bewilderment among the critics. Max Beerbohm complained in the *Saturday Review* that the play 'is about anything and everything that has chanced to come into Mr Shaw's head. It never progresses, it doesn't even revolve, it merely sprawls.'[3] Shaw had, not for the first or last time, gone too far in indulging his preference for discussion over the more reliable bases of dramatic interest. A similar disregard for the ordinary demands of an audience gave rise to his philosophically speculative five-part sequence *Back to Methuselah* (1923), which takes over eight hours to perform, spread over four nights and a matinée in its first production. Fortunately, Shaw sometimes stepped back from these excesses and constructed plays upon firmer foundations of comic appeal. One of these is his most commercially successful play, *Pygmalion* (1914), in which he revises the Cinderella myth so as to mock the English class system while replacing Prince Charming with an entirely unromantic professor of phonetics, and still more perversely renounces the expected dramatic climax of the ballroom triumph in favour of further discussion. *Androcles and the Lion* (1913) is another: an exuberantly disrespectful treatment of early Christian martyrdom that takes a mixed group of eager converts to the brink of violent death in the games of the Roman Colosseum, thus putting their faith to the supreme test. Serious matters are touched upon here, including the nature of religious faith and of its objects, but Shaw's handling of them is the reverse of solemn. The Christians' zeal for martyrdom offers a feast of gallows humour, while an unmistakable element of pantomime appears in the shape of a dancing lion. Intellectual discussion is still to be heard in the debates between the Christian beauty Lavinia and her godless admirer, the Captain; but it rarely impedes the dramatic momentum of the action. The dominant figure, indeed, is not a debater but a warrior, the strong man Ferrovius, who is torn between his innate fighting spirit and his new faith's injunction to turn the other cheek, eventually 'lapsing' so spectacularly into his truly combative self that he slaughters a whole team of gladiators and thereby converts Caesar himself to Christianity, although for disturbingly unchristian reasons.

---

[3] T. F. Evans (ed.), *George Bernard Shaw: The Critical Heritage* (Routledge, 1976), 202 (from *Saturday Review*, 26 February 1910).

Shaw's first major post-War play, *Heartbreak House* (1921) shows a partial return to the 'discussion' form, being a variation upon *Misalliance*: the setting is a country house again, although this one allegorically resembles a ship; there is a lower-class intruder, this time a burglar who deliberately gets caught in order to exploit his hosts' guilty consciences; and there is an aerial surprise, a Zeppelin raid replacing the crashed aeroplane of the earlier play. *Heartbreak House*, though, has more symbolic substance than *Misalliance*, and a more legible dramatic structure of successive disenchantments as the heroine, Ellie Dunn, unmasks each of her suitors as a sham before moving on to the next. Discussion is unleashed, on some of Shaw's favoured topics—marriage, money, the soul, age and youth, work and idleness—but its digressions and non sequiturs fail to divert the play's essential momentum as it reaches its ominous climax, in which the assembled house-guests greet the arrival of war as a release from their limbo of futile leisure.

Shaw was not the only dramatist to attempt the introduction of ideas onto the stage. The Yorkshire playwright J. B. Priestley wrote a series of plays in the Thirties that experimented with concepts of time proposed by the mathematician J. W. Dunne and the occultist P. D. Ouspensky. These 'time plays' present a comfortably naturalistic surface, but then introduce us to unsettling notions of recurrence or of the intrusion of the future into the present. His first play, *Dangerous Corner* (1932), a kind of informal inquest into a mysterious death, proposes alternative outcomes for the same series of events in the past. *Time and the Conways* (1937) concerns the hopes of a family looking forward to a new age of social reform and progress in 1919, but then finding its dreams dashed in 1937. The relation of these two times of action, though, is unusual in that the second act is offered as a kind of dream in which one of the characters who falls asleep in 1919 is privileged to occupy her future life in 1937, within which another character expounds an explicit time-philosophy according to which the passing of time is dismissed as an illusion:

ALAN: No . . . it's hard to explain . . . suddenly like this . . . there's a book I'll lend you—read it on the train. But the point is, now, at this moment, or any moment, we're only a cross-section of our real selves. What we *really* are is the whole stretch of ourselves, all our time, and when we come to the end of this life, all those selves, all our time, will be *us*, the real you, the real me. And then perhaps we'll find ourselves in another time, which is only another kind of dream. (*Time and the Conways*, p.153)

This sort of exposition may be clumsy, here and in the more overtly Ouspenskian play *I Have Been Here Before* (1937), but the time-shifting devices have a curious power, as in the traditional dramatic ironies of the final act of *Time and the Conways*; and they help to sustain Priestley's more substantial moral themes of choice and responsibility.

Like the problem play, the discussion play or play of ideas encountered scepticism among critics, theatre managers, audiences, and even playwrights about its legitimacy and longevity as genuine theatrical entertainment. It had a principled enemy in W. Somerset Maugham, who argued in the prefaces to his *Plays* (1931–4) and again in *The Summing Up* (1938) that an audience could be held by appealing to its perennial emotions, but not by invoking the latest versions of reason:

The disadvantage of ideas in the theatre is that if they are acceptable, they are accepted and so kill the play that helped to diffuse them. For nothing is so tiresome in the theatre as to be forced to listen to the exposition of ideas that you are willing to take for granted. [. . .] The dramatist of ideas loads the dice against himself. Plays are ephemeral enough in any case, because they must be dressed in the fashion of the moment [. . .] it seems a pity to make them more ephemeral still by founding them on ideas that will be stale the day after tomorrow. (*Summing Up*, ch. 37)

For these reasons, Maugham regarded Shaw's influence upon the modern English stage as 'devastating', and the play of ideas as 'responsible for the lamentable decadence of our theatre' (ch. 38). Championing the proven virtues of the 'commercial' theatre against what he regarded as the intellectual snobbery of the Shavian school, Maugham maintained that the uncommercial drama of the Stage Society tradition had failed, not because of philistine theatre managers or audiences, as Shaw had alleged in his Preface (1919) to *Heartbreak House*, but because it had arrogantly disregarded the essential basis of dramatic art—the audience's craving for emotionally satisfying entertainment. Subsequent critical accounts of modern drama, most of them 'modernist' in their favouring of formal innovation, minority experiment, and anti-Victorian rebellion, have almost unanimously taken Shaw's side in this debate, if they have bothered to notice Maugham's objections at all; and most have also dismissed Maugham as a fabricator of shallow 'conventional' plays. At the time, though, it looked rather different: the young Harold Hobson, who later became a prominent theatre critic, belonged in the mid-Twenties to a circle of stage-struck Oxford students who took it as read that the foremost dramatists of the day were Shaw and Maugham.[4]

Comedy of Manners: Maugham and Coward

Maugham had conquered the West End in the 1907 and 1908 seasons with a string of witty comedies, and after a wartime intermission had returned with *Home and Beauty* (1919), *The Circle* (1921), and further successes to resume his position as London's most acclaimed and best-rewarded playwright, until his retirement from the stage in 1933. Some of his works may be classed as melodramas (*The Letter*, 1927; *The Sacred Flame*, 1929), others as exotic spectacles or morality plays (*East of Suez*, 1922; *Sheppey*, 1933), and one of them, *The Unknown* (1920), is a play of ideas about religious belief and war; but Maugham's success rested chiefly upon his sardonic comedies, some of which invited comparisons with those of Oscar Wilde. Whether in the shape of farce, as in *Home and Beauty*, or in the more sophisticated form of the comedy of manners, as in *The Circle* or *Our Betters* (1923), these are finely crafted, consciously artificial works noteworthy for their satirical incisiveness. *Home and Beauty*, for example, treats farcically the situation of a fashionable young woman of extraordinary selfishness who has inadvertently acquired two husbands (the first, having been mistakenly reported dead in the Great War, returns to find his best friend occupying his place), and now proposes to divorce both of them in order to acquire a wealthier third. The fun here is laced with pointed satires on war profiteers and the bogus 'sacrifices' of other civilians in wartime, and on the absurdities of the English divorce laws as they then stood.

---

[4] Harold Hobson, *Theatre in Britain: A Personal View* (Oxford University Press, 1984), 38.

The strengths of Maugham's dramatic art are best illustrated by *The Circle*, whose structure, as the title suggests, is built upon a clear pattern of repetition. The play is old-fashioned in several ways, being a country-house 'society' drama set within the landowning political elite, and involving that stock stage figure of the 1890s, the Woman with a Past. It is plainly what Shaw was accustomed to call disparagingly a 'well-made play' in that it keeps the audience in suspense about the outcome of its intrigues, and concludes each act with a satisfyingly dramatic crisis. At the centre of the action is the unappealing figure of Arnold Champion-Cheney, a Member of Parliament who seems more interested in his hobby of collecting antique furniture than he is in his lively young wife Elizabeth. Arnold has refused to meet or even write to his scandalous mother, Lady Kitty, since she abandoned him in his infancy, deserting his father (also a politician) and eloping with Lord Porteous to Florence. Elizabeth, though, regards her mysterious mother-in-law in a much more romantic light as one who sacrificed everything for love, and has seized the opportunity of Lady Kitty's long-delayed return to England with Porteous to insist that she meet the exiled couple at the ancestral home while Arnold's father, Clive, is away. Clive, however, changes his plans and reappears unexpectedly as soon as his estranged wife and her consort have arrived, thus bringing Arnold's parents together for the first time in thirty years, and drawing the first act to an impressive close. The complications of the second act are subtly equivocal: on the one hand, Elizabeth's romantic image of Lady Kitty and Porteous is deflated by their irritable bickering and pettiness, much to the delight of the cynical Clive, while on the other hand her own romantic susceptibility is exposed as we see her falling in love with another house-guest, the energetic and sincere Teddie Luton, a young entrepreneur from Malaya. The question before us now is whether Elizabeth will repeat family history by 'bolting' with Teddie as Lady Kitty had done with Porteous, or whether she will learn from her mother-in-law's exhibition of vanity and ill temper that irregular passion ends in middle-aged humiliation. Clive, in an attempt to save his son from such a repetition of the family scandal, persuades Arnold to adopt a 'nobly' forgiving response to Elizabeth's love for Teddie, while also getting Lady Kitty to spell out to her the true consequences of exile and social ostracism inflicted upon runaway wives. Elizabeth falters for a while under this onslaught, but is won back to Teddie when he explains that he is offering her not a life of comfortable happiness, but a future of love and turmoil. Porteous and Lady Kitty, now touchingly reconciled as ageing lovers, look on in admiration as the young couple drive off into the night. History has repeated itself because the young cannot—and, it is implied, should not—learn from the mistakes of the old.

The denouement of *The Circle* balances carefully the claims of romantic escapism and realistic worldliness, sending the audience home with a happy, if unsettlingly 'immoral', ending while overshadowing this with the prospect of disenchantment embodied in the elder couple. The ending also involves an unusual surprise in that the cynical father, who has appeared all along to be the *raisonneur*—that is, the mouthpiece of the author's own wisdom—is shown finally to be blinded by his conceit of worldy wisdom, boasting of the inevitable success of his scheme when we have already seen it backfire. As in most of Maugham's plays, English high society, here embodied in the Champion-Cheney family, is shown up mercilessly as a stifling prison of insincerity and emotional repression, from which the most promising escape is to the open skies of the colonies.

Maugham had several lesser rivals in the realm of comedy, ranging from the whimsically sentimental A. A. Milne, now remembered only as a children's author, to the wittily accomplished Frederick Lonsdale, now remembered hardly at all, even for his big success, *The Last of Mrs Cheyney* (1925). Other comic dramatists carved out special niches of success, Eden Phillpotts in the production of West Country comedies such as *The Farmer's Wife* (1924) and *Devonshire Cream* (1930), and Ben Travers in laying the foundations of modern English bedroom farce at the Aldwych theatre with *A Cuckoo in the Nest* (1925) and *Rookery Nook* (1926). There was only one of Maugham's competitors, however, who was original enough to displace him: Noël Coward. A professional actor since the age of 12, this prodigy had placed himself at the head of the new generation of the 1920s in a succession of plays and musical revues, and had by 1928 begun to dominate the West End as Maugham had done twenty years earlier. Maugham saw what was coming, and before long quit the stage.

Coward's growing success in the Twenties, and its consolidation in the Thirties, mark the arrival at last of a distinctively modern form of drama, one that owes less to the traditions of the 1890s than Shaw, Galsworthy, or Maugham plainly do. It may even be taken as spelling the end of 'literary' drama as such, as Coward's work abandons the machinery of the playwright—plot, rhetoric, epigrammatic repartee—all the better to highlight the skills of the star performer, who was often enough himself. On the page, his plays may have a lightweight appearance of casual construction and of inconsequential dialogue, but they should be read as prompt books offering the actors scope to unfold their talents of gesture and timing. They are, in short, essentially theatrical in conception, whereas Shaw's plays in their published form, decked out with elaborate descriptions of character and setting and with lengthy prefaces (*Androcles and the Lion*, for instance, has a preface more than twice as long as the play itself), may be read almost as novels or tracts. Coward's modernity should not be overstated. His early works in particular display multiple debts to the dramatic tradition: *The Young Idea* (1923), despite its title, lifts its plot from Maugham's *The Circle* and its characters from Shaw's *You Never Can Tell* (1899), and *Easy Virtue* (1926) deliberately imitates A. W. Pinero's plays of the 1890s, while *The Vortex* offers clear echoes of Shakespeare's *Hamlet* and *Much Ado*, of Ibsen's *Ghosts*, and of the late Victorian 'well-made' melodrama. His most distinctive comedies of this period, though—*Hay Fever* (1925), *Private Lives* (1930), and *Design for Living* (1939)—show him shedding both the dramatic conventions and the associated moral assumptions of Maugham's generation, and refashioning in fully modern terms the interrelations of plot, situation, and dialogue.

Like Shaw, Coward came to reject the intricate plotting of the 'well-made' play; but unlike Shaw, who discarded it for the shapeless liberties of staged 'discussion', he distilled plot to an essential symmetry of action resembling either a dance or a game in its self-enclosed formal perfection. There are no intrigues, sub-plots, lost heirs, or intercepted love letters in these comedies, nor even a chain of cause and effect, but simply an elegantly artificial pattern of rearranged erotic pairings. In *Hay Fever*, each of the four members of the Bliss family invites a potential lover home for the weekend, but each guest then turns out to be temporarily adopted by the 'wrong' host before quitting the house paired with another guest. In *Private Lives*, the central characters, Elyot and Amanda, have divorced but now re-encounter one another while honeymooning with their new spouses at the same hotel; in parallel scenes, they each flee from the uninspiring prospect of the second marriage to renew their old relationship, culminating in a violent brawl of just the kind that had led to their divorce in the first place. *Design for Living* follows the permutations of a love triangle in which the absence of each member of an intimate trio in turn brings about the pairing of the other two, so that in parallel scenes one man unexpectedly emerges from the heroine's bedroom wearing the other man's pyjamas.

Such dance-like exchanges of partner are not merely random. They are governed in each of these plays by a fundamental division of the characters into contrasted groups of insiders and outsiders, a division that in turn provides the terms of Cowardian comedy's double-edged moral implications. The insiders typically belong to the small and self-regarding world of artistic bohemianism: Judith Bliss in *Hay Fever* is a retired actress, her husband a novelist, and her son an artist; the love triangle in *Design for Living* brings together Otto, a painter, Gilda, an interior designer, and Leo, a playwright; Amanda and Elyot in *Private Lives* appear to have no artistic vocation but nonetheless proclaim a bohemian hedonism. Ranged against them are the dully wholesome specimens of bourgeois decency, who intrude warily upon the private histrionics of the insiders but are finally ejected: the house-guests in *Hay Fever*, the new spouses of *Private Lives*, the significantly named art-dealer Ernest and his philistine customers in *Design for Living*. Viewed from one angle, the plays seem to expose the artistic types as monsters of narcissistic self-indulgence, especially in *Hay Fever*; but they may equally suggest that these insiders deserve, by virtue of their wit and vivacity, a special exemption from the moral obligations observed by others. For it is the flamboyant insiders, denounced as they may be by the outsiders as egotists and degenerates, who always dominate Coward's stage as performers, tempting the audience to suspend its everyday moral distinctions in favour of purely theatrical values.

An important feature of Coward's dramatic style that stood out more in his own time than it can in ours is its proximity to ordinary conversation. Older observers such as Maugham regarded his dialogues with dismay as naturalistic speech taken to its extreme; and by comparison with the operatic orotundity of Shaw's characters or the syntactically perfect paragraphs uttered by Maugham's own, the kind of conversation we find in Coward's plays is notably casual, nonchalantly unfinished, and rarely marked by rhetorical inflation. As illustration, here is the first encounter between Professor Higgins, identified at first as 'the Note Taker', and Colonel Pickering, in the first act of Shaw's *Pygmalion*:

THE NOTE TAKER. You see this creature with her kerb-stone English: the English that will keep her in the gutter to the end of her days. Well, sir, in three months I could pass that girl off as a duchess at an ambassador's garden party. I could even get her a place as lady's maid or shop assistant, which requires better English.

THE FLOWER GIRL. What's that you say?

THE NOTE TAKER. Yes, you squashed cabbage leaf, you disgrace to the noble architecture of these columns, you incarnate insult to the English language: I could pass you off as the Queen of Sheba. [*To the Gentleman*] Can you believe that?

THE GENTLEMAN. Of course I can. I am myself a student of Indian dialects; and—

THE NOTE TAKER [*eagerly*] Are you? Do you know Colonel Pickering, the author of Spoken Sanscrit?

THE GENTLEMAN. I am Colonel Pickering. Who are you?

By contrast, here is the kind of verbal informality with which Elyot and Amanda quarrel in Coward's *Private Lives*:

ELYOT: That sort of remark shows a rather common sort of mind I'm afraid.

AMANDA: Oh it does, does it?

ELYOT: Very unpleasant, makes me shudder.

AMANDA: Making all this fuss just because your silly vanity is a little upset.

ELYOT: Vanity: What do you mean, vanity?

AMANDA: You can't bear the thought that there are certain moments when our chemical, what d'you call 'ems, don't fuse properly.

ELYOT (*derisively*): Chemical what d'you call 'ems: Please try to be more explicit.

AMANDA: You know perfectly well what I mean, and don't you try to patronise me.

(Collected Plays: Two, p. 53)

Fig. 3. Noël Coward as Elyot Chase, with Gertrude Lawrence as
Amanda Prynne, in the first London production of *Private Lives*
at the Phoenix Theatre, September 1930.

Amanda's conversational imprecision here is a mark of the private informal codes and word games with which Coward's insider characters usually confirm their solidarity. These people know perfectly well what their friends and lovers mean without having to hear it enunciated to Professor Higgins's preferred degree of clarity.

Inexplicitness carries an important value in *Private Lives*, especially in the celebrated dialogue between Elyot and Amanda towards the end of Act One. Here they agree not to speak of their feelings for one another, Amanda instead asking Elyot trivial questions about his travels, until he interrupts her with a declaration of his love for her. The initial veto against reference to their real emotional situation here creates a curious ironic gulf between the audible superficiality of what they say without meaning and the 'subtext' of what they mean without saying. In varying contexts, Coward's comedies repeatedly play upon this discrepancy between small-talk and the unacknowledged tensions of the situation that it fails to mask. The house-guests in *Hay Fever* attempt in this way to cover their discomfort with flagging conversations about their travels; Elyot and Amanda in the last act of *Private Lives* conspire to repel their respective spouses with parodies of small-talk; and, more aggressively, Otto and Leo in the last act of *Design for Living* seek to drive away Gilda's guests by pushing a seemingly polite conversation into the realms of absurdity. Unlikely as the connection may seem at first sight, there is a thread running forward here to the menacing use of conversational gambits in the plays of Harold Pinter, another modern playwright who began as a professional actor.

Historical and Verse Drama

Meanwhile, those many dramatists who wished to maintain the rhetorical level of drama above that of Coward's realistic contemporary conversations found that the most convincing basis of such heightened speech lay in the historical or chronicle play, either in prose or in verse. John Drinkwater enjoyed some success at the Birmingham Repertory with a series of such prose plays on historical figures: *Abraham Lincoln* (1918), *Mary Stuart* (1922), *Oliver Cromwell* (1923), and *Robert E. Lee* (1923). Later, *Richard of*

Bordeaux by 'Gordon Daviot' (Elizabeth Mackintosh) became one of the big hits of 1933, with John Gielgud in the title role; and Laurence Housman's *Victoria Regina* (1937) won similar acclaim. The actress and writer 'Clemence Dane' (Winifred Ashton) came up with an ambitious play, *Will Shakespeare—An Invention* (1921), written partly in Shakespearian blank verse, which continues to attract critical respect. Noël Coward's most popular and most spectacular play, *Cavalcade* (1931), was a historical pageant of Britain in modern times, more reliant upon mime and song than upon rhetoric. The two historical plays that have survived the period most resiliently, however, have been studies of religious martyrdom: T. S. Eliot's verse drama *Murder in the Cathedral* (1935) and Bernard Shaw's prose chronicle *Saint Joan* (1924). The former play, written for the Canterbury Festival and performed in the Chapter House to commemorate the martyrdom of Thomas Becket, owes much of its longevity to its approval by the Church of England for production by schoolboys; in itself it is an interesting failure, ritualistically stiff and lacking in dramatic momentum or even, except in some of the choruses, in poetic vitality. By contrast, Shaw's dramatization of the story of Joan of Arc still resounds with heretical energy.

Although *Saint Joan* was not Shaw's final play—another ten lesser pieces would follow—it was his last major international success, and indeed the occasion for the award of his Nobel Prize. It stands as a concluding summation of his stage career and its preoccupations, bringing to a climax his earlier fascination with religious inspiration and militancy (in *Androcles and the Lion* and the earlier *Major Barbara* (1905)), casting the heroic embodiment of historical evolution yet again in the image of the rebellious virgin-daughter, and again mocking British imperialism, here represented by the myopic patriotism of the English chaplain de Stogumber. Ostensibly concerned with military and political conflicts of the fifteenth century, the play reverberates with the insurgencies of Shaw's own time: women's rights, Irish nationalism, and the exploits of T. E. Lawrence 'of Arabia', on whom Shaw's Joan was partly modelled. Brazenly anachronistic in its reinterpretation of Joan's divine voices and her miracles, it presents the Maid of Orleans as the unwitting herald of modern historical movements, Nationalism and Protestantism, obliging its characters to debate these as yet inconceivable developments. The play offers a colourful medley of comedy, in its first three scenes; of tragedy mixed with 'discussion' in its fourth, fifth, and sixth scenes; and of pure discussion in its Epilogue, where Joan reappears after her death to debate the significance of her rehabilitation and recent (1920) canonization. The tragic element is unusual for Shaw, and achieved here by his refusal to melodramatize Joan as a victim of wicked persecutors: her inquisitors are presented as genuinely pious in their efforts to save the heretic's soul. This underlines the implication that Joan and her like will be betrayed and sacrificed in every age, by normal well-intentioned people. *Saint Joan* thus requires its audiences to acknowledge both the historical ('evolutionary') necessity of heresy as the essence of what later becomes approved as sanctity, and the political inevitability of its suppression. As the Bishop of Beauvais concludes in the Epilogue, 'The heretic is always better dead. And mortal eyes cannot distinguish the saint from the heretic.'

The historical play was one obvious means of raising the drama from the prosaic levels of merely functional dialogue, of the drawing-room set, and of the uniformities of contemporary costume, into something reminiscent of its former glories. A more determined, and in a sense a more desperate, measure was to abandon the constraints of modern realistic prose drama altogether and to return to the ancient potencies of verse, music, and dance as the basis of a new 'poetic' theatre. In the Thirties, as it became clear that the moving picture was easily surpassing the stage in its capacity both for realistic representation and for sumptuous spectacle, even those playwrights who had clung successfully to realistic conventions began to fear that the game was up: Maugham, for example, concluded that the reign of realism was exhausted, and that if the stage play were to survive, 'the dramatist would be wise now to go back to the origins of modern drama and call to his aid verse, dancing, music, and pageantry so that he might appeal to all possible sources of entertainment' (*Summing Up*, ch. 39). He may well have been thinking of Coward's *Cavalcade*, which had been welcomed as a victory of the stage against the screen. Poets of the Left and the Right, equally convinced that the bourgeois civilization underpinning mainstream drama was doomed, dreamed of bypassing the middle-class audiences of the West End theatres and of constructing a new popular audience more responsive to incantation and gesture than to country-house repartee. From these ambitions grew a new experimental fringe, entirely antithetical to the Ibsenism of the earlier Stage Society movement, but markedly less successful or tenacious. It was embodied for seven years in the Group Theatre, founded in 1932 by the dancer Robert Doone, and joined by a number of artists, academics, composers, and poets, notably T. S. Eliot, W. H. Auden, Louis MacNeice, and Stephen Spender.

The omens for a revival of poetic drama were not at all favourable. Quite apart from the now overwhelming power of the cinema, the radio, and the theatrical establishment, the record of earlier verse plays in this period was a discouraging one. Several of the 'Georgian' poets—Gordon Bottomley, John Masefield, John Drinkwater, Lascelles Abercrombie, and W. W. Gibson—had written verse plays during the War and in the Twenties without significant success, most of these works being destined for production by students or other amateurs, although Laurence Binyon's *Arthur* (1923) had been put on at the Old Vic with music by Elgar. Apart from Clemence Dane's *Will Shakespeare*, the only new poetic drama to have made any impact in the West End had been *Hassan* (1923), an exotic melodrama produced eight years after the death of its author, James Elroy Flecker; and even this had relied less upon formal verse than upon lavish costumes and sets and upon a bombastic pseudo-levantine prose ('Alas, Master of the World, my eyes are dim from long confinement in a jewelled cage, and the wings of my soul are numb'[5]). The Group Theatre playwrights did distinguish themselves from their 'Georgian' predecessors with a more urgent contemporaneity and with more adventurous stage techniques, but they too were doomed to address only a restricted audience of fellow intellectuals for short runs either at the Arts Theatre, Cambridge, or at the small Mercury and Westminster theatres in London.

The most impressive aspect of this body of work is its readiness to absorb and mix styles derived so variously from contemporary French dance-drama, Russian ballet, agitation-propaganda ('agit-prop') performance, music-hall turns, German Expressionist drama, symbolist dream-play, and late medieval mystery plays and moral

[5] James Elroy Flecker, *Hassan* (Penguin, 1948), 89.

interludes, although the price of this eclecticism is often incoherence, undramatic abstraction, or propagandist woodenness. The most innovative of these works is Auden's *The Dance of Death* (1934), which combines allegorical ballet with agit-prop devices, representing the death wish of the middle class in the form of the Dancer, who transmutes variously into sun-god, demagogue, and heroic aviator before collapsing and being declared dead by Karl Marx. The dances and choric responses are framed by commentary from an Announcer, and interrupted by jocular heckling and slogans from actors placed among the audience itself. Auden's subsequent collaborations with Christopher Isherwood—*The Dog Beneath the Skin* (1935), *The Ascent of F6* (1936), and *On the Frontier* (1938)— are psychological morality plays of a surrealistic tendency, gesturing fitfully towards the irrationalities of Fascism in Europe. Along with Eliot's early verse works for the theatre, the fragmentary *Sweeney Agonistes* (1934) and the religious pageant *The Rock* (1934), these works retain some value as literary curiosities, but they did not turn out to be, as their authors had hoped, portents of a revolutionized drama.

Within an international perspective, the dramatic literature of this period in England does not stand up well to comparison with the best contemporary work of O'Casey in Ireland, of O'Neill in the USA, of Lorca in Spain, of Čapek in Czechoslovakia, of Pirandello in Italy, or of the young Brecht in Germany. In such company it looks, with few exceptions, anaemic or even trivial. It fails to exhibit, in particular, a single work of commanding tragic stature. If, though, we adopt a different comparison, say with the state of English drama in the early Victorian age, then the achievements of Shaw, Maugham, Coward, and a few others stand out more than creditably. This was clearly no Golden Age of drama, but its principal works do not deserve to be overshadowed quite as much as they have been by the celebrated poems and novels of the day.

6

Modern Short Stories

New Words, 1910–1940

*Chekhovian   durationless   gimmick   itsy-bitsy
punch-line   quickie   short-storyist*

The youngest of the recognized literary forms, and in other ways the most 'modern' in tendency, was the short story. Introducing her anthology, *The Faber Book of Modern Stories* (1937), Elizabeth Bowen highlighted this youthfulness, likening it to that of the cinema:

The short story is a young art: as we now know it, it is the child of this century. Poetic tautness and clarity are so essential to it that it may be said to stand at the edge of prose; in its use of action it is nearer to drama than to the novel. The cinema, itself busy with a technique, is of the same generation: in the last thirty years the two arts have been accelerating together. They have affinities—neither is sponsored by a tradition; both are, accordingly, free; both, still, are self-conscious, show a self-imposed discipline and regard for form[1]

Other commentators looked back on the growth of the modern short story as a kind of 'poetic' renaissance, admiring its emancipation from older traditions, in particular from the burdens of novelistic description and plotting. In his introduction to a rival anthology, *Modern Short Stories* (1939), John Hadfield declared that there was 'no other form of imaginative writing in which the twentieth century

---

[1] Elizabeth Bowen, 'The Short Story', *The Faber Book of Modern Stories* (Faber, 1937), 7.

has discovered so many new possibilities of art, interpretation of life, and entertainment'.[2] Arnold Bennett had claimed ten years earlier that 'though Britain took late to the short story, she has in thirty years borne a whole brilliant galaxy, school, and flying flock of short-story writers' (*Evening Standard Years*, p. 313). This kind of enthusiasm about modern achievement is not generally found in contemporary reflections on the state of the drama, of poetry, or even of the novel. The short story at this time enjoyed the status of a favourite child, embodying the promise of all that was new, hopeful, and 'free'. In addition to its youth, it accorded well with the new rhythms of modernity in being rapid, fleeting, weightless, ephemeral (most stories appeared first in magazines and newspapers), and imaginatively agile; in all these respects it was more novel than the novel.

The liberatory buoyancy with which the short story had become associated was defined most convincingly by another practitioner of the art, H. E. Bates, in his book *The Modern Short Story: A Critical Survey* (1941). For Bates, there has been a double emancipation, first from the Victorian distaste for sexual or otherwise 'improper' subject matter, secondly—and more specific to short fiction itself—from the clumsy narrative conventions of the nineteenth-century tale. These cast-off encumbrances he presents parodically:

Inessential paraphernalia has dropped away, the casual explanatory lead-up of the club arm-chair has gone ('Four of us were having a sundowner when Carruthers, apropos of nothing, remarked,' etc.), the moral-issue opening and the pompous philosophical statement have also gone ('We are all creatures of perverse circumstance, tossed willy-nilly by fate, ever cruel, but if ever there was a person who less deserved the arrows of outrageous fortune it was Edith Carstairs') and with them the sermon ending ('It is not for us to judge. But I believe if ever there was a good man it was Roger Carmichael,' etc.).[3]

The newly discovered flexibility of the modern short story, as Bates presents it, is one that dispenses with the scene-setting and 'framing' preliminaries of the traditional fireside yarn or moralizing tale. The

[2] John Hadfield (ed.), *Modern Short Stories* (Dent, 1939), p. vii.
[3] H. E. Bates, *The Modern Short Story: A Critical Survey* (Nelson, 1941), 217.

modern short narrative wastes less time in interpreting its events, instead placing more trust in the reader's ability to provide and complete their significance, as Bates contends, picking up Bowen's earlier comparison with cinematic art:

The story now described less, but implied and suggested more; it stopped short, it rendered life obliquely, or it was merely episodic; so that the reader, if the value of the story was to be fully realized at all, had to supply the confirmation of his own experience, the fuller substance of the lightly defined emotion, and even the action between and after the episodes. The short story, in fact, moved nearer the film, and the two arts, rendering life largely by suggestion, brief episodes, picture-sequences, indirect narration, and the use of symbolism, developed together. (*Modern Short Story*, pp. 206–7)

Youthful as these twin arts may have been, their appeal in this sense is of an adult kind, granting to the reader or viewer a developed skill in drawing rapid connections, a mature autonomy of imaginative synthesis, a readiness to take the indirect hint.

The artistic possibilities of the short form appealed to many of the period's writers, as did the speedy financial returns. It is one measure of vitality in this junior branch of fiction that so many authors better known as novelists, poets, or playwrights also turned their hands to the short story: the more popular novelists Michael Arlen, Arnold Bennett, John Galsworthy, Stella Gibbons, W. Somerset Maugham, and Hugh Walpole extended their reputations in this way, and so did a few of the poets, including Walter de la Mare and Dylan Thomas, who had before them the prominent example of Rudyard Kipling's dual career in verse and short prose fiction. Among the modernist or otherwise 'highbrow' minority there is an even stronger commitment to the short form in the contributions of Richard Aldington, Elizabeth Bowen, Mary Butts, E. M. Forster, Aldous Huxley, James Joyce, D. H. Lawrence, Wyndham Lewis, May Sinclair, Sylvia Townsend Warner, and Virginia Woolf. The readership of short stories was large enough even to sustain specialist writers who devoted themselves chiefly or exclusively to this genre: H. E. Bates, A. E. Coppard, and Katherine Mansfield, along with the humourists 'Saki' and Dornford Yates, and a few practitioners of the supernatural tale such as Algernon Blackwood, M. R. James, and

Arthur Machen. Several of the period's most rewarding works are short-story collections: Saki's *Chronicles of Clovis* (1911), Joyce's *Dubliners* (1914), Lawrence's *The Prussian Officer* (1914), Mansfield's *Bliss* (1920) and *The Garden Party* (1922), Maugham's *The Casuarina Tree* (1926), Bowen's *The Cat Jumps* (1934), and P. G. Wodehouse's *Blandings Castle* (1935) among them. Far from being a minor sidetrack of modern literature, the short story can claim to occupy a main road, both busy and varied.

Most observers of the short story in this period were agreed that there were, broadly speaking, two kinds of modern story, each derived from a model provided by European writers at the close of the nineteenth century. The first, indebted to the stories published in the 1880s by the Frenchman Guy de Maupassant, tended to rely upon the plotting of dramatic events; the second, inspired by the Russian author Anton Chekhov's stories of the 1890s, leaned towards the evocation of character and mood without emphasis on plot or dramatic climax. Reduced crudely to extreme positions equally unjust to the real merits of these pioneers, the Maupassantian narrative was understood to be a strongly plotted anecdote, at its worst a crude manipulation of suspense, the Chekhovian to be a 'plotless' character sketch, at its worst a flimsy brooding over non-events. Each of these foreign masters had, by the 1920s, found his disciples in England, the tradition of Maupassant being carried on by Maugham, from *The Trembling of a Leaf* (1921) to *The Mixture as Before* (1940), the Chekhovian influence showing through in Katherine Mansfield's strongest collections, *Bliss* and *The Garden Party*. Maugham was a firm believer in the 'French' virtues of dramatic unity and coherence exemplified in Maupassant's tales, and found little to admire in 'Russian' hypersensitivity. His kind of story was to have a beginning, a middle, and a conclusive ending. 'In short,' he recalled in 1938, 'I preferred to end my short stories with a full stop rather than with a straggle of dots' (*Summing Up*, ch. 56). Maugham seems to be taking a swipe here either at Joyce, two of whose stories in *Dubliners* end with ellipses, or at Mansfield, whose longest fiction, 'Prelude' (1918), like the final story in *The Garden Party*, 'The Lady's Maid', similarly closes with a row of dots. In the latter collection can be found 'Bank Holiday', a prose sketch composed in the present tense and without any of the recognized properties of a story; lacking not only plot but even characters, it describes a festive group of people in bustling movement. Its last sentence reads: 'Up, up, they thrust into the light and heat, shouting, laughing, squealing, as though they were being pushed by something, far below, and by the sun, far ahead of them—drawn up into the full, bright, dazzling radiance to . . . what?' Mansfield was evidently, here and in many other stories, more comfortable than Maugham could ever be with an inconclusive ending, and with a fragmentary, rather than a dramatically complete construction. In this she and Joyce answer, as they help to create, a 'modern' taste, whereas Maugham adheres to late Victorian narrative expectations.

Although such differences of approach were observable, we should not imagine that short-storyists, as Elizabeth Bowen called them, occupied starkly opposed camps. It is harder, indeed, to draw clear boundaries between traditional and experimental writers in the realm of this period's short fiction than it is in poetry or the full-length novel. Joyce was more radically experimental in *Ulysses* and *Finnegans Wake* than in the stories of *Dubliners*. D. H. Lawrence likewise stayed closer to inherited conventions in his tales than in his poems and novels, with the result that many critics preferred the restrained formal control of such stories as 'Odour of Chrysanthemums' (1911) to the looser construction of his verse and longer fictions. Certain forms of radical literary experiment need room to develop, which the short-story form tends to forbid; and this may be why both Joyce's *Ulysses* and Woolf's *Mrs Dalloway*, each of which was at first conceived as a short story, unfolded into much longer works. As Dominic Head rightly insists in his book *The Modernist Short Story* (1992), the modernist practitioners of the short story attempted not a revolutionary rejection of older methods but a subtler shift of emphasis in which 'plotted' action was not discarded but merely muted. Setting aside extreme cases such as 'Bank Holiday', most short fiction written by the modernist school does tell a sequential story, just as most of the tales written by non-modernist authors—apart from comical yarns—do explore the enigmas of human psychology.

Joyce's story 'Eveline', for instance, exploits traditional kinds of narrative expectation and suspense in telling of a shop girl who has agreed to elope overseas with her boyfriend but who finds herself unable to board the ship at the last moment. It also employs a technique often associated with modernist prose fiction, that of 'free indirect style', in which the narrative voice, while remaining in the third person, borrows the idiom and temporal references of the central character's own perspective on events, thus allowing both an immediacy of identification with that character's predicaments and a certain ironic distance from them. The carefully judged modulations of voice and viewpoint involved in the use of free indirect style are a central feature of the artistry shown in Joyce's *Dubliners* collection and in many of Katherine Mansfield's most successful stories; but they do not constitute a distinctively modernist method. The free indirect style may be found too in the novels of Jane Austen; and the more old-fashioned of the storytellers in our period can be found using it, as Maugham does in 'The Yellow Streak' (1925) or as Coppard does in 'The Man from the Caravan' (1926). Such writers would be more likely to close a story with a dramatic 'twist', as in Maugham's celebrated 'Rain' (1921), but then the modernist vanguard was not always above using such devices: several of Mansfield's stories rely upon delayed revelations and surprises, including 'The Child-Who-Was-Tired' (1910), 'The Sister of the Baroness' (1910), 'The Little Governess' (1915), and 'Bliss' (1918); and one of them, 'Feuille d'Album' (1917), even comes with a comic punchline.

Bearing in mind, then, that 'traditional' and 'experimental' approaches are not, in this genre, clearly ranged against each other, we may review first some of the features of the surviving older styles of storytelling, before moving on to look at more modern effects, and then briefly at a special sub-genre of short fiction.

Four writers who could be grouped at the 'traditional' end of the spectrum would be 'Saki', Kipling, Maugham, and Coppard. 'Saki' (H. H. Munro) was killed in the Great War, his best stories having been collected in the period 1910–14. Kipling had been a popular and influential storyteller since the 1890s, but his last three collections—*A Diversity of Creatures* (1917), *Debits and Credits* (1926), and *Limits and Renewals* (1932)—fall within our period. Maugham had established himself as a novelist and playwright before striking out successfully into short fiction in the 1920s. Coppard, an author highly regarded in his time but now undeservedly forgotten, devoted himself almost exclusively to the writing of short stories, following his first collection, *Adam and Eve and Pinch Me* (1921), with another eighteen volumes of tales before 1940.

Saki concentrated his talents within a particular sphere of comic cruelty, while Kipling's range is much broader, but these two short-storyists may be likened in one important respect: the frequent reliance of their tales upon patterns of revenge and retaliation. To this degree, plot, in the strong sense of 'intrigue', becomes central to their work. Kipling's tale 'The Village that Voted the Earth was Flat' (1913), for example, concerns a group of journalists and politicians caught in a motoring speed trap and fined by a rural magistrate; they then devise a campaign of hoaxes and rumours in order to make the magistrate's village the laughing stock of the world. His later story 'Dayspring Mishandled' (1928) likewise recounts an elaborate plan of revenge, in which an embittered literary man tries to destroy the reputation of his rival by forging a 'lost' Chaucerian poem. The wartime story 'Mary Postgate' (1915) earned Kipling some notoriety for its shockingly vindictive revenge-plot. Here a harmless English spinster employed as a lady's companion witnesses the effects of a stray German bomb dropped from an aeroplane, which kills a young girl. She then discovers in her garden the German airman, mortally wounded in baling out. Calmly ignoring his cries for help, she relishes his death agonies to the end, then treats herself to a satisfying hot bath.

Saki's elegantly witty stories often display a streak of vengeful malice, of which the usual victim is the respectable aunt who has encroached upon the sacred liberties of boys and animals. In 'The Music on the Hill' (1911) for example, a woman who has nagged her husband into moving to the country removes a bunch of grapes from a statue of the youthful god Pan, sees a mysterious boy watching her, and is gored to death by a stag. The more obvious revenge-drama of 'Sredni Vashtar' (1911) has a 10-year-old boy worshipping a polecat-ferret kept in a concealed hutch; when his female guardian, an honorary 'aunt', discovers his pet and goes out to remove it, the animal miraculously kills her, whereupon the boy celebrates by devouring extra portions of buttered toast. As with Mary Postgate's bath, this final bodily indulgence echoes the narrative satisfaction of a fitly concluded retribution, while obliquely acknowledging its primitive basis. The pleasure to be had from Saki's stories is usually of a punitive or arbitrarily destructive kind, the plot consisting in a practical joke or improbable outrage: his resourceful hero Clovis frightens a respectable old lady out of her home in 'The Stampeding of Lady Bastable' (1911) by pretending that a revolution has broken out, while in 'The Unrest-Cure' (1911) he livens up a dull household by posing as a bishop's emissary on a secret mission to massacre the local Jews. Saki's fictional world is insulated from normal sensitivities, and cheerfully permits the blowing-up of children by bombs (in 'The Easter Egg'), the murder of a musician by immersion in a vat of soup ('The Chaplet'), or the throwing of a naked boy into a nettle-bed ('The Remoulding of Groby Lington'). The act of storytelling itself is significantly driven by impulses of retaliation or competitive advantage. Thus the tale 'Esmé' (1911) is launched by Clovis's claim that all hunting stories are the same, to which his interlocutor, a baroness, responds by producing a hunting story quite unlike all others in its absurd violations of taste and of sporting codes: the hounds pick up the trail not of a fox but of an escaped hyena, which proceeds to eat a gipsy child before being run over by a car, thereby earning handsome financial compensation for the baroness. In 'The Story-Teller' (1914), a bachelor is visibly disgusted to overhear a group of children being told morally improving tales of infant virtue rewarded. The teller of these fables is, naturally, the children's aunt, who challenges the man to do better, which he manages by telling a story of a girl so 'horribly good' that a lion is attracted by her good-conduct medals and devours her. The children are delighted by the tale, while the now deflated aunt is aghast at its 'improper' tendency (*Complete Saki*, pp. 351–4). All of Saki's stories are in this sense gestures of retaliatory defiance against the Victorian aunts among whom he had grown up.

Another characteristic shared by Saki and Kipling is their willingness to use trick endings. Kipling's 'The Gardener' (1926) fools the reader into crediting the account given by the unmarried Helen Turrell of her 'nephew' whom she has brought up from infancy following his father's death in India. Reaching military age, the boy serves in the Great War, and is killed in action. Helen later travels to the cemeteries of Flanders in search of his grave, gets lost, and meets a mysterious Christlike gardener, who kindly says 'I will show you where your son lies' (*War Stories and Poems*, p. 320). There is a double revelation here: first, that Helen has concealed her child's illegitimacy from the world and from himself, and, second, that the presumed omniscience in which we have partaken as readers has been equally deceptive, trumped now by a higher knowledge. Saki likewise catches the reader out in his tale 'The Open Window' (1914), in which a nervous young man arriving for the first time at a country house hears from a teenage girl the tragic history of her aunt's bereavement: her husband and brothers set off hunting three years before, but were all drowned in a bog, since which time the aunt has kept a French window open for their return. A few minutes later, the husband and brothers do indeed arrive through the French window, prompting the young man to flee in terror, the victim not of ghosts but of a narrative prank by the quick-witted girl, who happens to enjoy making up grotesque tall stories on the spur of the moment. As in other tales by Saki, storytelling itself has the power to spread confusion and alarm like an anarchist's bomb.

Maugham's stories avoid the artificialities of the revenge-plot and the trick ending. They are more straightforwardly realistic studies of character and environment in which people are placed under intense pressures that show up their psychological flaws and hidden agonies. They tend, though, to be old-fashioned in other ways. Maugham's insistence that a story have a beginning, a middle, and an end gives rise to familiar features of construction: a beginning in which a first-person narrator explains how he came across an unusual acquaintance with a fascinating story to tell; a middle in which the yarn is spun or summarized; a coda in which some ironic reflection is provided upon the characters involved. Many of his stories, then, are 'framed' by preliminaries and by concluding flourishes. 'The Facts of Life' (1940), one of Maugham's most admired tales, begins with the arrival of a middle-aged man at his gentleman's club in an irritable mood; his cronies ask what is wrong, and he tells them the story of his son going to the fleshpots of Monte Carlo, ignoring all paternal warnings against gambling and loose women, and coming back not only unscathed but wealthier—a run of luck that has discredited the father's authority; we close with the friends laughing over this trick of fate.

The kind of story that could be told over a post-prandial glass of brandy or among intimates in a club is close to Maugham's ideal, which is why many of his short fictions are cast in the first person as confidential anecdotes. Many of his best tales, though, are unframed and told in the third person. They tend to include, however, a dispassionate observer who witnesses the violent turmoil of the central action while standing partly aloof from it. This is the position of the Singapore lawyer Mr Joyce in 'The Letter' (1924), who defends the poised and genteel English wife of a rubber-planter against a charge of murder as evidence piles up of her true guilt and of the adulterous passions behind it. In 'Rain', the observer is a sceptical doctor who witnesses the persecution of an American prostitute on a South Sea island by a fanatical missionary. In 'Lord Mountdrago' (1939) we have a psychoanalyst at work upon the disturbing case of a politician at the end of his tether. It becomes the painful privilege of these men to peer into the dark places of the soul and to confront the barbarities, terrors, and perversities hidden behind the masks of ostensibly civilized people. Maugham was sometimes criticized for his coldly clinical dissection of his characters' hypocrisies and egotisms, but a saving tolerance usually comes with the aloofness of his narrators and observers; they are almost always 'men of the world' who have seen too much of human self-deception to be shocked by it or to cast the first stone.

The storytelling of A. E. Coppard is so flagrantly old-fashioned as to signal a deliberate reversion to archaic forms of fable and folk tale. In his first collection we find one story that begins 'Long ago a princess ruled over a very tiny kingdom', and another that even opens with the phrase 'Once upon a time' (*Adam and Eve and Pinch Me*, pp. 95, 63); the later collection *The Field of Mustard* (1926) includes another that has the formulaic beginning 'Long, long ago there lived with her godmother a fair and pleasant girl named Sheila' (*Dusky Ruth*, p. 145). All three are marvellous fables, as is 'Piffingcap', a tale about a magically accursed shaving-cup; while the opening story of *Adam and Eve and Pinch Me*, 'Marching to Zion', is a kind of dream-vision narrated by a travelling minstrel. Although he wrote some stories of urban poverty, Coppard's fictional world is predominantly rural and pre-industrial, peopled by blacksmiths, vagrants, poultry-farmers, ragged urchins, circus performers, cobblers, pedlars, chimney sweeps, and, most frequently, by enigmatically silent virgins—as in three of his most admired tales, 'Dusky Ruth' (1921),

'The Black Dog' (1923), and 'The Higgler' (1925). All this may suggest a rather childish sort of romantic whimsy, but Coppard's handling of these materials is in fact far richer and more adult in its darker themes of loss, bewilderment, violence, grief, and waste. His narrative styles are colourfully and quirkily 'poetic', and his endings often surprise us with enigma rather than with any neat closure: even the marvellous fables refrain from pointing any obvious moral. He is even capable of writing a 'plotless' tale in which nothing happens except the revelation of a mood, as in 'The Field of Mustard'. His is a paradoxical case of a writer who achieves a kind of modern vitality by immersion in antique forms and devices. H. E. Bates in his *The Modern Short Story* treats Coppard and Mansfield as the two leading exponents of short fiction in the 1920s, but Coppard's name has tended to vanish from later surveys.

Turning now to the more self-consciously modern short-storyists, we may briefly identify elements in the work of Joyce, Mansfield, and Bowen, not so much of 'experimentation' or startling technical innovation, but of a certain sophistication and artful reticence.

Joyce's *Dubliners* collection has the distinction of raising the materials of nineteenth-century naturalist fiction—the stagnant lives and spiritual poverty of lower middle-class city-dwellers—to higher degrees of artistic treatment that are felt in its subtle word-music, its unobtrusive symbolism, and its precisely judged handling of narrative voice and perspective. It is also rounded off with the story upon which more critical acclamation has been lavished than upon any other short English-language narrative of its time, 'The Dead'. Joyce's aim in composing these stories was to build up through a sequence of intensely realized episodes a collective portrait of the native city he had repudiated, and of what he believed to be its atmosphere of moral paralysis. The book opens with the paralysis and death of a priest, and closes with the living and the dead of Ireland jointly blanketed in snow. In between we find recurrent representations of living deaths and deadly lives, beginning with a series of bleak first-person recollections of childhood and adolescence, then moving on to episodes of adult life in the uniformly dispiriting spheres of sexuality ('Two Gallants', 'The Boarding House'), domesticity ('Eveline', 'A Little Cloud'), culture ('A Mother'), politics ('Ivy Day in the Committee Room'), and religion ('Grace'). In these sketches occupying the middle of the collection, the deceptive artistry of Joyce's storytelling lies in its withholding of authorial interpretation, his ability to show the reader, through free indirect narration, the events of the tale through the eyes of the characters themselves, often in their own depleted and clichéd linguistic idiom, as in these sentences about Maria, the central character of 'Clay':

She used to have such a bad opinion of Protestants but now she thought they were very nice people, a little quiet and serious, but still very nice people to live with. Then she had her plants in the conservatory and she liked looking after them. She had lovely ferns and wax-plants and, whenever anyone came to visit her, she always gave the visitor one or two slips from her conservatory. There was one thing she didn't like and that was the tracts on the walls; but the matron was such a nice person to deal with, so genteel.

In this typical exploitation of narrative viewpoint, the controlling voice of the narrator appears to recede into neutrality, delegating the terms of valuation to Maria herself, who in turn draws them from a tamely limited vocabulary. An ironic discrepancy then opens up between the character's evidently restricted awareness and the reader's intuition of something beyond it. Joyce is careful both to respect the reader's autonomy of judgement by avoiding any overt narrative intrusion, and to deflect the irony away from any merely scornful mimicry of an unfortunate and well-meaning woman.

The impressive achievement of *Dubliners* as a whole lies less in its generation of ironic insights flattering to the intelligence of the reader than in persuading us to temper them with a humane indulgence, or with what is referred to at the end of the book as 'a strange friendly pity' (p. 175). The sharp edge of irony is unsheathed in the anticlerical satire of 'Grace', but in the finale of the collection a more compassionate mood envelops 'The Dead'. Here we begin the story with a cliché ('Lily, the caretaker's daughter, was literally run off her feet'), one that reflects the mentality of Lily and of her employers, the Misses Markan, who are hosting a Christmas party. But with the arrival of their nephew, Gabriel Conroy, an intellectual who has some resemblances to Joyce, we move into a realm of complex self-consciousness and eventually of painful self-awareness that has not been available in the earlier stories. 'The Dead' is enriched by an assortment of minor characters and by varied description of festive dance, song, oratory, and cuisine, but at the centre of this bustle is Gabriel's uncomfortable sense of his own failings, with which we are left alone after the party as his wife sleeps. The story's reflective coda is an exhibition of musical English prose unsurpassed even in Joyce's later writings.

Katherine Mansfield shares with Joyce a careful avoidance of narratorial interpretation or moral commentary and a preference for the immediacy and the ironic perspective afforded by free indirect narration, an approach whose benefits show especially well when she adopts the limited viewpoints of children, as in 'Sun and Moon' (1920), 'The Voyage' (1921), and in parts of 'Prelude' (1918); or of adolescents, in 'Her First Ball' (1921) and 'The Garden Party' (1922). Early reviewers of her work commended the freshness and psychological inwardness achieved by these means. Her larger and more varied body of stories shows a technical adventurousness fuller in range than that of Joyce's single collection. She can, for instance, successfully manage the difficult art of multiple viewpoint, alternating the narrative perspective between a husband and wife in 'The Man without a Temperament' (1920) and 'Marriage à la Mode' (1921), or distributing it among several characters in 'Prelude' and 'At the Bay' (1922). Some of her stories are even less tied to a sequence of plotted events than Joyce's are, being devoted rather to the evocation of place, character, and mood. Mansfield is often bolder, too, in the abandonment of preliminary scene-setting, as in the abrupt opening of 'A Dill Pickle' (1917): 'And then, after six years, she saw him again.'

Mansfield's stories come in different kinds, varying according to their settings and in response to evolving technical challenges. Her first collection, *In a German Pension* (1911), is dominated by a sequence of stories set in a Bavarian spa town, in which a first-person narrator barely distinguishable from the author satirizes the various guests who are taking 'the cure' with her. The book also contains, though, a few third-person narratives that foreshadow the special preoccupations of her later works—with the psychology of male vanity in 'A Birthday', and with the burdens borne by female servants in 'The Child-Who-Was-Tired'. The more often admired collections *Bliss and Other Stories* and *The Garden Party and Other Stories*

Fig. 4. Katherine Mansfield photographed in 1913.

combine fictions based upon Mansfield's upbringing and family life in New Zealand—notably 'The Garden Party' and the two extended stories 'Prelude' and 'At the Bay'—with shorter studies of contemporary life in London, Paris, or the French Riviera, some comical and satirical in tone, others more sombre. In these volumes, most of the stories are told in the third person, but observed through the eyes of an 'internal' character rather than from an externally omniscient standpoint; their effects are vivid, and are sometimes described as 'impressionistic'. Two posthumous collections overseen by her husband John Middleton Murry, *The Dove's Nest* (1923) and *Something Childish* (1924), gather previously uncollected pieces, most of them early sketches. Mansfield's work still feels much less dated than that of most of her contemporaries, in part because the fleeting, enigmatic impressions raised by her narration are usually not tidied up into a conclusive denouement, but still hang in the air after the story's end.

An aesthetic principle of narrative is at work in these more modern kinds of story, which calls to mind Oscar Wilde's bon mot about the pleasure of smoking a cigarette: it is exquisite, and it leaves one unsatisfied. This idea that a good story must somehow linger after the last sentence has been stubbed out was one maintained by Elizabeth Bowen, whose best short fictions of the Twenties and Thirties fully exemplify it. These stories lure us rapidly into fraught relationships of densely 'novelistic' complexity—often involving clashes between children and adults, between guests and hosts, or among members of disintegrating families in large houses—conjure from them darkly anxious forms of expectation, and then leave us floundering after an illumination that never arrives. This is approximately the predicament of the house-guest Alban in one of Bowen's finest stories, 'Her Table Spread' (1930), who suspects that he has been invited to a remote Irish mansion in order to be married off to the family's mad heiress. Some earlier stories show a similar teasing pattern of disorientation: 'Ann Lee's' (1924) has two women visit an exclusive London hat shop whose owner exerts the mysterious authority of a priestess; a man arrives on unspecified business, insisting that he has an appointment with Ann Lee; later, the women see him rush past in the street looking terrified, but they will never know quite why. In 'Human Habitation' (1926), two male students get lost in the dark on a walking trip, and seek refuge in a remote house where a young woman is anxiously awaiting the return of her unaccountably delayed husband; they resume their benighted journey before the mystery of the husband's lateness is resolved:

> 'She said the track was not long. We outstayed our time—think we'll get the bus, old fellow?'
> 'Don't know. Jameson, shan't we ever know if he came back?'
> There was no answer.
> They stumbled forward in the dark with tingling minds. (*Collected Stories*, p. 159)

There is in these concluding lines a kind of allegory of the effect that Bowen seeks by means of unanswered questions and unrelaxed apprehensions, the 'tingling' corresponding to the story's afterlife in the reader's thoughts.

The finely crafted exploitation of nameless unease in Bowen's stories gives evidence of her immersion in the late Victorian and Edwardian ghost-story tradition of J. Sheridan LeFanu, Henry James (*The Turn of the Screw* lies behind her often disturbing sketches of child psychology), and M. R. James. Some of her short fictions, like 'Foothold' (1929) and 'The Cat Jumps' (1934), are indeed ghost stories within that central tradition; most, however, involve less recognizable extensions and adaptations of its devices into entirely new kinds of trepidation and 'haunting' atmosphere. It is worth noting here that the nineteenth-century tradition of ghostly narratives and supernatural tales persists with some vigour in this period, sustained in part by the continuing Dickensian custom by which magazine editors expected to fill their Christmas issues with uncanny fiction. This kind of story was produced not just by genre specialists like M. R. James himself (in *A Warning to the Curious* 1925, and other collections), Oliver Onions (*Widdershins*, 1911), or Algernon Blackwood (*Strange Stories*, 1929, among many more volumes), but by writers associated with higher literary aspiration such as Maugham ('P. & O.', 1923), Coppard ('Polly Morgan', 1928), May Sinclair (*Uncanny Stories*, 1923), Violet Hunt (*Tales of the Uneasy*, 1911), Walter de la Mare (*The Riddle*, 1923), Mary Butts ('With and Without Buttons', 1938), and D. H. Lawrence ('The Border Line', 1924; 'The Rocking Horse Winner', 1926). One significant feature of the modern short story's development is the efforts of several writers to develop uncanny narratives that break out of the Victorian conventions into new realms of horror that would have been too strong to put before a pre–1914 readership. Robert Graves's story 'The Shout' (1929), set in the cricket ground of a lunatic asylum, is one such terrifying tale; Coppard's 'Arabesque: The Mouse' (1921), which weaves sinister thematic patterns around the motif of amputation, is another. Dylan Thomas's short stories of the mid-Thirties, composed in poetically heightened prose, whip up a powerful brew of violence, sexual obsession, and religious delirium in such unsettling narratives as 'The Burning Baby' (1936), in which a hellfire preacher incinerates the baby he has fathered upon his own daughter while his son cackles over a dead rabbit. The horror story was certainly crossing new frontiers here.

The brief survey of modern stories attempted here may point us to the conclusion that distinctions commonly made between 'traditionalist' and 'experimentalist' writing in this period do have a certain value if carefully applied, but that the short story is a something of a special case in which traditions are less fixed and experiments less disruptive. These distinctions might more pertinently be recast, then, in terms of a spectrum of narrative satisfaction and frustration. At one end we would place stories which are formally framed and morally interpreted, their events completed in a satisfyingly rounded pattern of which revenge-plots and retaliatory schemes, highlighted above, are strong cases. I have not found space to review the short stories of D. H. Lawrence here, but it can be observed in passing that many of them incline to this end of the scale in that they betray a vindictive impulse to punish or humiliate the central character: 'The Prussian Officer' (1914), 'Tickets, Please' (1919), 'England, My England' (1922), 'The Fox' (1923), and 'The Border Line' would all respond to such an analysis, as would the extraordinary story of ritual human sacrifice and symbolic race-suicide, 'The Woman Who Rode Away' (1925). Towards the other end of the spectrum we would then place stories that decline to complete their actions or to explain themselves, that leave us stumbling in the dark but tingling. Here we find a certain affinity, most obvious in Bowen's work, between the enigmatic inconclusiveness of the 'modernist' short narrative and the teasings of the ghostly or uncanny tale, in that both kinds of story exploit the advantage of 'the unexplained', leaving us in one sense (as with Wilde's cigarette) unsatisfied but all the more 'haunted' and thus securing for themselves an afterlife. The eminence of Joyce's 'The Dead', for example, might be accounted for in such terms: although, like many uncanny tales, it is set at Christmastime, there is nothing supernatural to it, but as the title implies, it concerns a kind of harrowing of the living by a dead man. It may indicate a more general, if unsensational, shift in modern taste, away from stories that give us 'satisfaction' (a term once used by duellists to mean vengeance) and towards stories that can be commended as 'haunting'.

7

The Modern Novel:
Principles and Methods

New Words, 1910–1940

*Conradian   Galsworthian   Joycean   Lawrentian
perspectivism   Proustian   relativize
sprawlingly   Wellsian   Woolfian*

The next three chapters, and parts of Chapters 11 and 13, will be devoted to various species of extended prose fiction. The purpose of the present chapter is to provide a preliminary sketch of this large field, partly in order to account for the ways in which I have distributed different kinds of novels and prose romances among later chapters. Our main objects of investigation here are the idea of 'the novel' as understood in this period; its relation to nineteenth-century traditions; its formal principles of composition and narrative perspective as debated in novelistic theory of the 1920s; and its competing responsibilities to art and to 'life'. I will look first at theories of the novel, and then review some modern fictions that press in various directions against the limits of novelistic construction.

In the nineteenth century, there had been novels, novelists, and novel-readers in abundance, but in the early twentieth century their shared innocence was disturbed by the encroachment of something known as 'the novel', a critical concept that brought with it the pains of self-consciousness, doubt, and dissension. A ferment of debate continued from the War years to the late 1920s, in essays, lectures, and books including H. G. Wells's 'The Contemporary Novel' (1914), D. H. Lawrence's 'The Novel' and 'Morality and the Novel' (both 1925), Elizabeth Drew's *The Modern Novel* (1926), E. M. Forster's *Aspects of the Novel* (1927), Edwin Muir's *The Structure of the Novel* (1928), John Carruthers's *Scheherazade; or the Future of the English Novel* (1928), and Ford Madox Ford's *The English Novel* (1930). In these and in other works by Percy Lubbock and Virginia Woolf, the questions at issue were not so much the merits and deficiencies of particular novels and novelists, but the nature, methods, and larger destinies of the genre. The world of the novel had become volubly self-analytical as never before.

Novelists fell out with one another over the purpose and direction of their craft. Henry James's article 'The Younger Generation' (1914) surveyed a number of living novelists and complained of H. G. Wells and Arnold Bennett in particular that they presented their readers with shapeless matter unformed by any artistic method. Wells fired back in his book *Boon* (1915) with a wickedly parodic assault on James's limitations both as a novelist and as a theorist of fiction, accusing the elder writer of sacrificing the real complexity of life to a fetish of artistic perfection, and of confusing the necessary heterogeneity of a novel with the formal unity of a painting. The exchange brought their previously cordial friendship to a sudden frosty end. Within a few months, James had died, but the campaign he had been conducting for decades against the inartistic clumsiness of the English novelists survived him, and the battle-lines established between him and Wells remained in place, with the champions of novelistic 'art' ranged against partisans of messy 'life'. Later skirmishes between Arnold Bennett and Virginia Woolf, between E. M. Forster and Percy Lubbock, and between Forster and Woolf tended to be fought over the same ground: could the novel be raised to the level of an art like sculpture by the conscious perfection of its techniques, or did its true vitality lie in its undisciplined fluidities and hybridities, its omnivorous capacity to chew and digest all manner of ideas and materials? Should it aspire to the condition of painting, or instead claim kinship with the prosaic arts of essay-writing, biography, and social history? Should English novelists learn the 'method' of the French master Gustave Flaubert, or could they trust to the unmethodical English examples of Austen and Dickens?

Henry James was revered as 'the Master' by a circle of devoted disciples including Ford Madox Hueffer (later Ford) and Percy Lubbock. Hueffer had written an effusive tribute to his American mentor, *Henry James: A Critical Study* (1913), in which he poured scorn on 'the botched and amateurish productions of the schools of Scott, Dickens, Thackeray, Reade, Dumas, and George Eliot',[1] comparing them unfavourably with the superior 'continental' tradition of Flaubert and Turgenev, now continued in the novels of Joseph Conrad and of James himself. The British novel has been stultified, he claims, by sentimental moralizing, while the Flaubert–James school has risen above this by taking its artistic goals and methods seriously. Lubbock, who devoted years to editing the Master's letters and novels, was a less polemical Jamesian disciple than Hueffer, and more impartially technical in focus. His book *The Craft of Fiction* (1921) offers a careful codification of James's principles and practice, reviewing the merits and drawbacks of various narrative methods while explaining how the Flaubertian and Jamesian handling of 'point of view' combines the best of these in producing the most vivid effect while reducing their implausibilities to a minimum. Lubbock's larger claim is that with James's refinements of technique the novel has at last evolved beyond its primitive beginnings, to a point at which its stories seem to tell themselves without the intrusion of an old-fashioned narrative commentary. He sees the art of the novel mainly as a process by which the controlling presence of the author is so skilfully disguised that readers feel they are being 'shown' the events and the characters, not merely being told about them. To this end, neither the traditional omniscient third-person narrative nor the constricting perspective of the first-person narrator will serve as well as a cunning blend of perspectives in which the impersonal narrator appears to delegate the witnessing of events to a character within the action while also observing that character externally, this being the method of Flaubert's *Madame Bovary* (1857) and of James's *The Ambassadors* (1903). In such novels, Lubbock claims, the consciousness of the central character is 'dramatized', that is, given an immediacy that would be lost in the retrospective summary of a first-person narrative or in the remoteness of the

---

[1] Ford Madox Hueffer, *Henry James: A Critical Study* (Secker, 1913), 79.

traditional kind of third-person narrative. Lubbock follows James in placing a high value on 'dramatic' or 'scenic' presentation, by which he means a rendering of events through dialogue and through the central character's immediate impressions. If followed to its logical extreme, this method would give rise to novels resembling playscripts in their heavy reliance upon dialogue, as in James's own *The Awkward Age* (1899). This is neither what Lubbock recommends nor what his highest models offer; his advice is rather to balance such 'dramatic' scenes with passages of what he calls the 'pictorial' or 'panoramic' method, in other words description and narrative summaries of events. There is no single superior technique to be preferred at all times, but a variety of techniques that should be deployed in accordance with the fictional materials to be treated, the only golden rule being that the transitions and inconsistencies among them should be so disguised as to maintain an artistically coherent impression.

The positions outlined in *The Craft of Fiction* have been summarized at some length here both because they embody the most carefully developed theory of novelistic technique in this period and because they provide us with concepts according to which we shall come to distinguish between the methods adopted in practice by Lubbock's contemporaries. First, however, we need to register some of the protests made against this Jamesian view of the novelist's art.

As early as 1911, in a lecture later published as 'The Contemporary Novel', H. G. Wells had identified formal perfectionism of the Jamesian kind as a serious obstacle to the liberties of the novelist. He concedes that the sonnet and the short story must aim for a single concentrated impression and must avoid digressive expansion, but argues that the novel cannot be judged by those standards since it is by nature 'a discursive thing, [. . .] a woven tapestry of interests'. Wells commends the novels of Dickens for their amplitude and variety, and detects signs in his own day of a return to those virtues after a period of reaction against them:

I rejoice to see many signs to-day that that phase of narrowing and restriction is over, and that there is every encouragement for a return towards a laxer, more spacious form of novel-writing. The movement is partly of English origin, a revolt against those more exacting and cramping conceptions of artistic perfection to which I will recur in a moment, and a return to the lax freedom of form, the rambling discursiveness, the right to roam, of the earlier English novel, of *Tristram Shandy* and of *Tom Jones*. (*H. G. Wells's Literary Criticism*, p. 195)

Wells is particularly keen to defend, among examples of his 'right to roam', the freedom of the novelist to exhibit his own personality and opinions, to comment openly upon his fiction, to indulge in parody and burlesque, and to discuss contemporary ideas—all of which would be condemned as inartistic distractions by the Jamesian purist. His rhetoric here is unmistakenly Protestant in its implication that English liberties are under threat of curtailment by some pseudo-papal authority, although Henry James himself is not mentioned by name. In *Boon*, though, which is itself a ramblingly discursive collection of fictional diaries, lampoons, and dialogues, James is openly identified as the antagonist, and the difference of aesthetic principle is reduced to the distinction between the single impression afforded by a picture and the mixture of impressions offered over a period of reading time by a novel, the variety of which responds to the diversity of life. James's own fictional characters, Wells alleges, seem to have been artificially cleansed of their human irregularities, their lusts, their whims, their political and religious opinions, and reduced to disembodied minds driven only by curiosity (*H. G. Wells's Literary Criticism*, pp. 207–14).

These Wellsian objections were later endorsed by E. M. Forster in his *Aspects of the Novel*, where Henry James is charged with sacrificing the common stuff of humanity, with gutting and castrating his characters for the sake of rigid aesthetic patterns. Forster also gently rebukes Percy Lubbock for treating the technical problem of 'point of view' as central to the art of the novel. Citing the ability of Dickens and Tolstoy to 'bounce' the reader into accepting their fictional worlds despite inconsistencies in narrative viewpoint, he dismisses 'point of view' as a secondary issue compared with the primary creative task of creating 'a proper mixture of characters' (*Aspects of the Novel*, p. 87). If James and Lubbock tended to confuse novels with paintings, Forster here may be guilty of confusing them with dinner parties. Virginia Woolf's review of Forster's book, 'Is Fiction an Art?' (1927), in turn expressed exasperation at his complacent refusal to recognize novel-writing as an art rather than as a reflection of 'life'. Woolf had her own misgivings about the deficiencies of Henry James's novels, but she objected to Forster's unexamined criterion of 'life' if it failed to include the aesthetic appreciation of pattern and form in fiction (*The Essays*, vol. 4, pp. 457–63).

Woolf had herself repeatedly invoked 'life' as a kind of test that novels might pass or fail in her earlier essay 'Modern Fiction' (1919; rev. 1925), but in a different sense. There she suggests that the novels of the 'materialist' authors Wells, Bennett, and Galsworthy miss something essential that a younger writer like James Joyce does capture: 'the flickerings of that innermost flame which flashes its messages through the brain', or 'the quick of the mind' (*The Essays*, vol. 4, p. 161). In other words, 'life' for Woolf is an indefinite spiritual or psychological quality not to be confused with the sum of describable persons, events, and objects. The 'Edwardian' novelists might be highly industrious in rendering the latter, but a more original artistic energy was required to give us the former. She imagines the 'Edwardian' novelists as slaves of a tyrant who makes them write predictable novels, all solidly lifelike and containing the standard elements of plot, love interest, tragedy, comedy, and denouement: 'The tyrant is obeyed, the novel is done to a turn. But sometimes, more and more often as time goes by, we suspect a momentary doubt, a spasm of rebellion, as the pages fill themselves in the customary way. Is life like this? Must novels be like this?' (p. 160). Woolf's questions are echoed by D. H. Lawrence's in 'The Novel': 'You can put anything you like in a novel. So why do people *always* go on putting the same thing?' (*Selected Critical Writings*, p. 179). Both signal an important sceptical departure from habit and convention, a spasm of rebellion that is felt in the experimental construction not just of their own novels in the 1920s but of many other attempts to escape the imaginary tyrant of novelistic custom.

Most novelists abided by a general agreement that the author should avoid intrusive interruptions of the kind that moralize over the heads of the characters in direct addresses to the reader, this being understood as an antiquated vice associated with Thackeray's *Vanity Fair* (1848). Even Wells and Forster disapproved of that example, although Wells would sometimes begin a chapter—like the sixth and ninth of *The History of Mr Polly* (1910)—with a general moral statement, while Forster had indulged in similar essay-istic digressions in his *Howards End* (1910). Some reversions to this Victorian proprietorial manner are to be found in the novels of D. H. Lawrence, who was an even more aggressive champion than Wells of 'life' against the restrictive protocols of 'art'. Lawrence was fully capable of dramatizing his fictional events through his pro-tagonists' viewpoints in ways that James and Lubbock would have commended, as he does most successfully in *Sons and Lovers* (1913) and *The Rainbow* (1915). Increasingly in the later novels, though, Lawrence grants himself the licence to address the reader directly with sermons disconnected from the fictional events, as in the open-ing paragraph of *Lady Chatterley's Lover* (1928) or at greater length in some chapters of *Kangaroo* (1923).

The prevailing assumption, prompted more by example and instinct than by Jamesian doctrine, was that the author should dis-creetly withdraw from the overt manipulation and interpretation of the story, and play down as far as possible the unavoidable process of telling, so that the events and characters appeared to be objec-tively 'shown' to the reader. If the author's voice were to be muted in the interests of the reader's more direct engagement with the story, there were still alternative strategies by which this could be achieved, some being more drastic than others. A complete elimination of the authorial voice, and in Percy Lubbock's terms a fully 'dramatic' presentation, could be effected, of course, by the perfectly tradition-al means of a fictional first-person narrator or narrators, compos-ing an autobiographical narrative long after the story's events (as in Charlotte Brontë's *Jane Eyre*, 1847) or writing a series of letters and diary entries during or soon after those events (as in Wilkie Collins's *The Woman in White*, 1860). Alternatively, the author's visible role could be reduced to that of a stagehand in novels composed mainly as dialogues between fictional characters, a method for which there were nineteenth-century precedents in T. L. Peacock's *Headlong Hall* (1816) and W. H. Mallock's *The New Republic* (1877).

Novels composed in the fictional first person throughout are un-common in this period, and most of the principal examples belong to the middlebrow kinds of romance, detective story, and thriller: the fictions of John Buchan, Arthur Conan Doyle, Sax Rohmer, and Agatha Christie, along with Michael Arlen's *The Green Hat* (1924),

Mary Webb's *Precious Bane* (1924), P. C. Wren's *Beau Geste* (1924), Robert Graves's *I, Claudius* (1934), Daphne du Maurier's *Rebecca* (1938), and Geoffrey Household's *Rogue Male* (1939). Others were fantastical narratives, like Walter de la Mare's *Memoirs of a Midget* (1921), or Stevie Smith's *Novel on Yellow Paper* (1936). Successful works of these kinds perhaps confirmed an association between pseudo-autobiographical narration and special effects that belonged outside the literary mainstream. Moreover, this kind of narrative demanded a prolonged dramatic impersonation which many authors found uncongenial and restrictive: as Lubbock pointed out, there is a heavy price to be paid for it in a loss of scope and ironic distance. Another critic, Thomas Moult, observed that 'Astute modern novelists have foreseen the pitfalls of the first-person method and usually avoided it altogether.'[2] Indeed, it is notable that most major novelists, from Arnold Bennett to Elizabeth Bowen, use it sparingly or not at all. Moving closer to this mainstream, we find another special group of first-person novels in which the narrator is used for comical or satirical purposes as an observer of the eccentric characters around him: this category includes William Gerhardi's *The Polyglots* (1925), Richard Aldington's *Death of a Hero* (1929), W. Somerset Maugham's *Cakes and Ale* (1930), and Christopher Isherwood's *Mr Norris Changes Trains* (1935). Here the ironic detachment lacking in the 'autobiographical' mode is partly restored by the disposition of the characters.

Another strategy by which the immediacy of first-person narration can be exploited while escaping its limitations is to employ it selectively in 'diaristic' form for certain parts or episodes of a novel, returning to an external vantage point at will. Henry Green's first novel, *Blindness* (1926), for example, opens with the diary of a schoolboy but then shifts into the third person to recount his later fortunes. Conversely, James Joyce's *A Portrait of the Artist as a Young Man* (1916) is told in the third person until the final few pages, where we are given extracts from the protagonist's diary. A more ambitious method is employed in Rosamond Lehmann's *The Weather in the Streets* (1936), where the third-person narrative hands over temporarily to the heroine's first-person account, and

---

[2] Thomas Moult, *Mary Webb: Her Life and Work* (Cape, 1932), 227.

again in Aldous Huxley's *Eyeless in Gaza* (1936), in which chapters written in the third person alternate irregularly with chapters comprising entries in the central character's private journal. It should be stressed that there is nothing especially modernistic in this: Flaubert's *Madame Bovary* also shifts from the first person to the third after its opening pages, while Dickens's *Bleak House* (1854) jumps repeatedly between a lofty omniscient viewpoint and the restricted internal account given by a leading character.

H. G. Wells and Jean Rhys employed the first-person voice recurrently in their fiction, but apart from their cases, one finds in the category of serious 'literary' fiction in this period only a handful of novels that accept the opportunities and restrictions of full-length first-person narration. Among these are D. H. Lawrence's *The White Peacock* (1911), Rebecca West's *The Return of the Soldier* (1918), A. P. Herbert's *The Secret Battle* (1919), George Orwell's *Coming Up for Air* (1939), and Rayner Heppenstall's *The Blaze of Noon* (1939), the last of these being a 'special-effect' fiction, narrated by a blind masseur. Two novels of this kind deserve special notice here because they use the first-person voice in striking new ways: Ford Madox Hueffer's *The Good Soldier* (1915) and Virginia Woolf's *The Waves* (1931).

A fundamental restriction imposed upon first-person narrators is that they cannot read the minds of other characters, as omniscient third-person narrators are freely permitted to do. The feat performed dazzlingly by *The Good Soldier* is to turn this handicap into an advantage by making the inscrutability of other people an explicit theme of the narrative and a leading principle of its construction. Hueffer had learned much about what he came to call 'impressionist' principles of first-person narration from his friend and sometime collaborator Joseph Conrad, and especially from his novel *Lord Jim* (1900), in which the narrator Marlow's parting question is 'Who knows?'—a confession of failure in his quest to unravel the motives of the eponymous Jim's behaviour. Hueffer's and Conrad's belief was that the unfolding of character in fiction would be more credible if it resembled the partial, incomplete process by which we come to know (and inevitably, misunderstand) people in real life, piecing together inadequate and contradictory impressions and second-hand reports from different times of their lives, and revising our views of them too late. This is how Hueffer's narrator, John Dowell, an American widower, goes about reconstructing and reinterpreting the story of his wife Florence, now dead by her own hand, their friend the model English gentleman Captain Edward Ashburnham, his Roman Catholic wife Leonora, and their ward Nancy Rufford. In his opening paragraph the central problems of knowing and telling are thrown into the foreground: 'My wife and I knew Captain and Mrs Ashburnham as well as it was possible to know anybody, and yet, in another sense, we knew nothing at all about them. This is, I believe, a state of things only possible with English people of whom, till to-day, when I sit down to puzzle out what I know of this sad affair, I knew nothing whatever.' It is only now, in writing the story, that he can shape an understanding of it; and this unfolding process itself becomes as much part of the book's human drama as the startling events themselves.

As Dowell's conversational account meanders back and forth in time, it emerges that he had been unaware until after his wife's suicide that she had been Ashburnham's lover, and that Ashburnham's own respectability (so Leonora has since disclosed) concealed a career of tragically compulsive philandering. Worse is to follow in the account of Ashburnham's and Nancy's unconsummated desire for one another, which results in the soldier's suicide and the girl's madness. The events are tragic, but the ironic gulf between what Dowell knew at the time and what he has since learned or guessed colours them with an unusual kind of cruel comedy, of which this baffled narrator is the principal butt. Now alone with his disordered memories and with the deranged Nancy, he still cannot decide what to make of his own tale: 'I leave it to you', he tells his imagined reader (*The Good Soldier*, pt. 4, ch. 6)—an invitation avidly taken up by later interpreters of the novel, who are still in disagreement about the trustworthiness of Dowell's narration. By highlighting the active 'telling' of the story, for whose convolutions Dowell repeatedly apologizes, Hueffer might seem to be disregarding the Jamesian principle of unobtrusive 'showing', but in another sense *The Good Soldier* amply fulfils Lubbock's overriding injunction to dramatize every aspect of a novel, including its own narrative voice.

Woolf's *The Waves* employs a very different version of the first-person voice, one that cannot properly be called narrative at all.

Determined to venture beyond the limits of 'the novel' as usually conceived, she presents us here with a kind of prose poem for six voices. Her six characters 'speak' their parts by turns, although in a shared idiom that does not resemble spontaneous speech; and what they 'say' is, except in the final soliloquy, composed in the present tense as an immediate recording of impressions, thoughts, hopes, and fears rather than as a story. A sequence of events can be inferred from these soliloquies, tracing the growth of seven friends (the seventh remaining silently 'offstage') from childhood to middle age; but these events are not given any more prominence than the characters' momentary sensations, as they would be in conventional novelistic narration. Narrative itself is displaced into a sequence of italicized interludes that describe the rising and eventual setting of the sun over a seascape and a house, composed in the past tense. In one sense *The Waves* is, in Percy Lubbock's terms, more 'dramatic' in method than most novels, because its present-tense soliloquizing debars retrospective narrative from intervening between the characters and the freshness of their experiences. In most other senses, though, drama is deliberately avoided, in that the characters are not speaking to or listening to one another, while their styles of expression are not as differentiated as their private obsessions and habits of perception are. Not quite a poem, not quite a play, and classed as a novel only for want of any other term, *The Waves* stands as one of the most formidably original literary experiments of its time.

A more fully dramatized use of fictional speech is found among those novels that are based upon dialogue rather than soliloquy. Such works resemble playscripts in their reduction of summary and descriptive elements to stage directions, becoming play-novels or novel-plays. Ronald Firbank's novels are composed in this manner, especially the early *Inclinations* (1916) and *Caprice* (1917); while Anthony Powell's first novel, *Afternoon Men* (1931), also privileges the element of dialogue, tending to restrict the narrator's role to that of an impersonal recorder. The more sustained development of the play-novel, however, is to be found in the work of Ivy Compton-Burnett, from *Pastors and Masters* (1925) to *A Family and a Fortune* (1939) and beyond. In these novels, the settings are sketched in very briefly, and the main characters are granted a short paragraph describing their appearance when they first enter the scene; but the rest is conversation of a special mannered kind, in which the arts of polished repartee are on display and dialogue culminates in glittering aphorism. *Pastors and Masters* takes as its subject a group of gossipy dons and teachers in Cambridge, but thereafter Compton-Burnett specialized in late Victorian middle-class family groups, exposing their dynamics of tyranny and rebellion through breakfast-table conversations in which caustic verbal humiliation is answered by barbed sarcasm. The reader is given scarcely any guidance in following these complex patterns of familial conflict and betrayal, and is obliged to develop a new alertness to conversational tone. Often Compton-Burnett's minimal stage directions omit to specify who exactly is speaking or whether a particular utterance is soliloquized or spoken out loud to the assembled family, so the demands on the reader's ability to 'direct' the actors can be heavy. Some justification for this kind of authorial reticence is hinted at in a dialogue between two friends of the Ponsonby family in *Daughters and Sons* (1937):

'What I can't understand about that family,' said Rowland, 'is how they say what they like all the time, and yet seem to be afraid. Can anyone explain it?'

'No one yet,' said Miss Marcon. 'Alfred may be able to presently. But families can seldom be explained, and they make better gossip without any explanation. To know all is to forgive all, and that would spoil everything.' (ch. 3)

Miss Marcon's typically aphoristic twisting of a commonplace saying implies that explanations of motive, as expected in most novels, would simplify what cannot honestly be simplified, detracting from the living drama of human perversity.

The kinds of novel I have discussed so far are those in which special efforts are made to get the author out of the way of the reader's contact with the fictional action and characters. The first-person narrative and the play-novel, however, are exceptions to the general practice, which is broadly that recommended by Lubbock: to avoid drawing attention to the author's narrative voice by presenting the story's events as if observed by one or more characters within it, so that the third-person narrator appears to be hovering at the characters' shoulders rather than looking down upon them from an Olympian height. Of this method and its variations we need remark nothing further here, as we shall encounter several instances in the next two chapters. Some larger implications of this impersonal, oblique, or dramatized approach, however, should be considered at this point. There may be many reasons for subduing the author's personal voice and for suppressing his or her intervenient moral commentary or explanatory omniscience: some of these will have to do with modesty, some with humility in the face of inexplicable human contradictions, others with gaining readers' undistracted involvement with fictional characters, others still with respecting readers' adult powers of inference and autonomous judgement. Whatever the combination of motives, the aspiration towards self-effacement and the accompanying efforts to make the story seem to 'tell itself' carry with them the suggestion that a novel has a life of its own that the novelist may nurture but otherwise not tamper with for his or her own ends. This notion is often implied in the writings of the modern novelists—Hueffer, Woolf, and several others—about their own craft.

No writer was more vehement than D. H. Lawrence in proclaiming the virtues of 'the novel' against attempts by novelists to use it as a vehicle for moralizing or didactic purposes; this despite his own frequent sins in this regard. In the opening chapter of his *Studies in Classic American Literature* (1923) and again repeatedly in his later essays, he accuses Nathaniel Hawthorne, Leo Tolstoy, and others of betraying the true 'passional' life of their fictions by trying to force it into the codes of respectable Christian morality. Fortunately, the novel as Lawrence conceives it is a tremulous but sturdy organism that slithers free of moral abstractions and kicks back at its pious creators. The novelist 'is usually a dribbling liar', as he alleges at the end of 'The Novel' (*Selected Critical Writings*, p. 190), but the novel itself is never fooled by the false absolutes of its author's philosophy, and will assert its own relativistic truths against them. As Lawrence puts it in the same essay, 'There you have the greatness of the novel itself. It won't *let* you tell didactic lies' (p. 180), even if you can get away with them in a drama or a poem. The reasons for this appear more fully in 'Morality and the Novel':

Philosophy, religion, science, they are all of them busy nailing things down, to get a stable equilibrium. Religion, with its nailed-down One God, who says *Thou shalt, Thou shan't*, and hammers home every time; philosophy, with its fixed ideas; science with its 'laws'; they, all of them, all the time, want to nail us on to some tree or other.

But the novel, no. The novel is the highest example of subtle inter-relatedness that man has discovered. Everything is true in its own time, place, circumstance, and untrue outside of its own place, time, circumstance. If you try to nail anything down, in the novel, either it kills the novel, or the novel gets up and walks away with the nail. (*Selected Critical Writings*, p. 174)

Lawrence invokes 'the novel' in such passages not so much as an artistic form with its own rules like the ode or the landscape painting, but as a life form charged with resistant energy, a vital cultural force in a post-Christian world of relativized values.

Writers and critics usually spoke of 'the novel' as if it were a single entity, but the true variety of novelistic practice indicated otherwise. The world of the novel in these decades suffers indeed a serious internal split, or what Raymond Williams in a chapter heading of his *The English Novel from Dickens to Lawrence* (1970) called 'A Parting of the Ways', between fictional traditions devoted principally to 'consciousness' on the one side and to 'society' on the other. In the sphere of novelistic theory that we have been examining here, the split is echoed in the disagreements between H. G. Wells and Henry James, as it is later in the objections raised by Virginia Woolf against the 'materialist' Edwardian novelists. Woolf herself in an essay called 'Poetry, Fiction and the Future' (1927) employs terms of differentiation that were by now familiar to reviewers and novel-readers, referring on the one hand to 'the sociological novel or the novel of environment' in which the houses and incomes of the characters are described in detail, and on the other to 'the psychological novelist' who analyses more closely the characters' feelings (*The Essays*, vol. 4, p. 435). Distinctions of this broad kind had been made in the 1890s between novels of Action (Walter Scott's, for instance) and novels of Analysis (those of George Eliot and Henry James); but the divergent tendencies of early twentieth-century fictional practice reinforced such divisions still further, to the point that one could readily identify two disconnected hemispheres of 'the modern novel', one of them embodying an 'environmental' realism in its stress upon the social circumstances of individual lives, the other practising a 'psychological' realism in concentrating upon the inner worlds of characters in relative isolation from those circumstances.

Since the contents of the next two chapters are arranged according to just that perceived division between novels of social existence and novels of individual consciousness, it is especially important to remind ourselves here that these are not reliable categories in anything but an artificial sense, and all they can indicate are degrees of emphasis in one direction or the other. If we set aside romances and beast-fables (which are to be reviewed in Chapter 10), all novels are concerned with the thoughts and feelings of individual human beings involved in some sorts of social relationship in particular places and historical times. However far any novelist appeared to be pushing in one of these directions, there was no such thing in this period (if there ever could be) as a purely 'sociological' novel that eliminates fictional subjectivities, and equally no such thing as a purely psychological novel that excludes the social existence of its actors. The novel, as Lawrence would have said, does not *let* one tear its essential elements apart into two compartments, so that with very many novels it becomes arbitrary to assign them to one category rather than the other. With that preliminary qualification, we may proceed first to novels of a social emphasis.

8

The Modern Novel as Social Chronicle

New Words, 1910–1940

*averageness   conformism   home-town
interconnectedness   regionalize   socialist realism
sociobiological   underclass   undernourished*

Provincial Chronicles and Sagas

The great Victorian tradition of realistic fiction, devoted to the study of ordinary lives within carefully specified social environments, survived vigorously into this period. Modernist fictional experiment has commanded more critical attention, but the mainstream of the English novel still lay here, inheriting from George Eliot and Thomas Hardy the recognized conventions of realism and its emphases on local community and social change. A strong element of that tradition is its evocation of particular provincial landscapes and ways of life, often thinly disguised under fictional place names: Eliot's 'Loamshire' and Hardy's 'Wessex' are succeeded by Arnold Bennett's Staffordshire 'Five Towns' and after 1910 by a striking assortment of provincial locations offered by the modern 'regional novel': Constance Holme's Westmorland, Hugh Walpole's Cumberland, the Nottinghamshire of early D. H. Lawrence, Sheila Kaye-Smith's Sussex, Mary Webb's Shropshire, Eden Phillpotts's Dartmoor, E. H. Young's Bristol ('Radstowe'), Francis Brett Young's West

Midlands ('Mercia'), and several parts of Yorkshire fictionalized by J. B. Priestley, Winifred Holtby, Phyllis Bentley, Lettice Cooper, and others. The careers of many of these novelists illustrate a process by which steady popularity could be achieved by cornering the market in the fictional celebration of a particular unclaimed territory. Arnold Bennett enthused in these terms about Eden Phillpotts's exploitation of Dartmoor: 'What a district for a novelist—compact, complete, withdrawn, exceptional, traditional, impressive, and racy! Eden Phillpotts found it and annexed it.'[1] By 1940, this process of literary conquest was so far advanced that few English counties, beyond the relatively barren 'Home' counties encircling London, lacked a novelist they could call their own (see Table 2).

Some realistic novels of social observation in this period are set wholly or partly in London and its suburbs, as with Frank Swinnerton's *Nocturne* (1917), Patrick Hamilton's *Twenty Thousand Streets under the Sky: A London Trilogy* (1935), Priestley's *Angel Pavement* (1930), John Galsworthy's *The Forsyte Saga* (1922), and George Orwell's *Keep the Aspidistra Flying* (1936); and each has its own local flavour, whether of Hyde Park in Galsworthy or of Kennington in *Nocturne*. The metropolis, however, was too unmanageable to be shaped into a self-contained 'region' of the literary imagination. The regional novel proper, which means the provincial novel, enjoyed a favoured status, for reasons that combined local and national pride, the urban reader's nostalgia for lost rural 'roots', and the prestige of the nineteenth-century tradition. In that continuing tradition, the regional novelist could compete with the historian in recreating the processes of social and economic evolution as experienced by representative individuals within a particular place and community. This kind of novel could aspire to the standing of a minor epic in commemorating the special customs, dialects, festivities, trades, industries, social hierarchies, and political conflicts of its region, along with its characteristic struggles with Nature (mining, land reclamation, animal husbandry) and with the encroachments of modernity (the coming of the railways, industrial conflict, eviction from the family farm). As in the historical novel, with which it

---

[1] Arnold Bennett, introduction to Eden Phillpotts, *Widecombe Fair* (Widecombe Edition, Macmillan, 1927), p. viii.

Table 2. *Selected English Counties' Regional Novelists,*
1910–1940

County	Novelist
Cornwall	C. A. Dawson-Scott, Daphne du Maurier, Eden Phillpotts
Cumberland	Hugh Walpole
Derbyshire	Thomas Moult, Alison Uttley
Devon	Eden Phillpotts, L. A. G. Strong, John Trevena, M. P. Willcox
Dorset	John Cowper Powys, T. F. Powys
Durham	Harold Heslop
Essex	Samuel L. Bensusan, Jesse Berridge, Victor Bridges
Gloucestershire	E. H. Young
Kent	Sheila Kaye-Smith
Lancashire	J. L. Hodson, Gilbert Cannan, Walter Greenwood, James Hanley, T. Thompson, Howard Spring
Lincolnshire	Bernard Gilbert
Norfolk	R. H. Mottram
Northamptonshire	H. E. Bates
Nottinghamshire	D. H. Lawrence
Shropshire	Mary Webb
Somerset	H. A. Vachell, John Cowper Powys, Walter Raymond
Staffordshire	Arnold Bennett
Suffolk	H. W. Freeman, Doreen Wallace, Adrian Bell
Sussex	Warwick Deeping, Alice Dudeny, Sheila Kaye-Smith, Stuart P. B. Mais, Alfred Ollivant, Ernest Raymond, Victor L. Whitechurch
Warwickshire	Francis Brett Young, George Woden
Westmorland	Constance Holme
Wiltshire	Arthur G. Street, Charlotte Peake
Worcestershire	Francis Brett Young
Yorkshire	Phyllis Bentley, E. C. Booth, Lettice Cooper, J. S. Fletcher, Winifred Holtby, Naomi E. Jacob, M. Storm Jameson, Oliver Onions, William Riley, Halliwell Sutcliffe, Leo Walmsley

Sources: Phyllis Bentley, *The English Regional Novel* (George Allen & Unwin, 1941); Lucien Leclaire, *A General Analytical Bibliography of the Regional Novelists of the British Isles 1800–1950* (Les Belles Lettres, 1954); K. D. M. Snell, *The Bibliography of Regional Fiction in Britain and Ireland, 1800–2000* (Ashgate, 2002).

often overlaps, it places its protagonists within a 'panoramic' vista so that they appear to be overwhelmed by the larger, but still locally specific, forces of Nature and of History: in typical set-piece episodes they are shown to be caught up in floods, storms, strikes, or election campaigns. In schematic terms, environment asserts priority over individuality, this principle being signalled in what had become since Hardy's classic opening of *The Return of the Native* (1878) the conventional scene-setting first chapter.

Glen Cavaliero's critical survey *The Rural Tradition in the English Novel, 1900–1939* (1977) underlines the strength of these conventions in summarizing the usual features of Phillpotts's numerous Dartmoor novels: 'A typical Phillpotts novel will open with a lone figure outlined against a moorland sky or trudging along a moorland road; or else with two lovers deep in converse beside a wooded stream.'[2] Most novelists avoided such obvious borrowings from Hardy, but many still found ways of impressing upon their readers the primacy of environment in their opening pages. Sheila Kaye-Smith's most successful Sussex novel, *Joanna Godden* (1921), for instance, opens with a panoramic prospect of the Kent–Sussex border region, then narrows its focus to describe the 300-acre pastures around a particular farm near Rye, before it homes in upon the farm itself at a defining moment of its history as its ownership passes from the dead farmer to his unmarried daughter. The first sentence of D. H. Lawrence's *The Rainbow* (1915) situates the Brangwen family's Marsh Farm in meadows near the Erewash river at the Nottinghamshire–Derbyshire border; and the second section of this opening chapter gives us an historical account of the transformations of this terrain by industrialization:

About 1840, a canal was constructed across the meadows of the Marsh Farm, connecting the newly opened collieries of the Erewash valley. A high embankment travelled along the fields to carry the canal, which passed close to the homestead, and, reaching the road, went over in a heavy bridge.

So the Marsh was shut off from Ilkeston, and enclosed in the small valley bed, which ended in a busy hill and the village spire of Cossethay.

---

[2] Glen Cavaliero, *The Rural Tradition in the English Novel, 1900–1939* (Macmillan, 1977), 48.

The Brangwens received a fair sum of money from this trespass across their land. Then, a short time afterwards, a colliery was sunk on the other side of the canal, and in a while the Midland Railway came down the valley at the foot of the Ilkeston hill, and the invasion was complete. The town grew rapidly, the Brangwens were kept busy producing supplies, they became richer, they were almost tradesmen.

Although, as we shall see, *The Rainbow* is unusual among regional novels in its departures from realistic conventions, it is credibly located, Ilkeston and the Erewash valley being real places, 'Cossethay' a renaming of Cossall. Its opening chapter also preserves traditional concerns with the enmeshing of individuals and families within networks of economic development, here carefully specified as a contradictory movement by which the Brangwens are simultaneously enriched by the transformed local economy and sequestered from it.

While some kinds of regional fiction offered more or less nostalgic versions of worlds untouched by modern problems—as in Phillpotts's novels or those of Francis Brett Young and Hugh Walpole—there were other uses of this tradition that more seriously represented, as we have seen Lawrence do, the impact of social and economic developments upon recognizable families and communities. Here is the opening paragraph, again conventional in some respects, of Bennett's *Clayhanger* (1910):

Edwin Clayhanger stood on the steep-sloping, red-bricked canal bridge, in the valley between Bursley and its suburb Hillport. In that neighbourhood the Knype and Mersey canal formed the western boundary of the industrialism of the Five Towns. To the east rose pitheads, chimneys, and kilns, tier above tier, dim in their own mists. To the west, Hillport Fields, grimed but possessing authentic hedgerows and winding paths, mounted broadly up to the sharp ridge on which stood Hillport Church, a landmark. Beyond the ridge, and partly protected by it from the driving smoke of the Five Towns, lay the fine and ancient Tory borough of Oldcastle, from whose historic Middle School Edwin Clayhanger was now walking home. The fine and ancient Tory borough provided education for the whole of the Five Towns, but the relentless ignorance of its prejudices had blighted the district. A hundred years earlier the canal had only been obtained after a vicious Parliamentary fight between industry and the fine and ancient borough, which saw in canals a menace to its importance as a centre of traffic. Fifty years earlier the fine and ancient borough had succeeded in forcing the greatest railway line in England to run through unpopulated country five miles off instead of through the Five Towns, because it loathed the mere conception of a railway. And now, people are inquiring why the Five Towns, with a railway system special to itself, is characterized by a perhaps excessive provincialism. These interesting details have everything to do with the history of Edwin Clayhanger, as they have everything to do with the history of each of the two hundred thousand souls in the Five Towns. Oldcastle guessed not the vast influences of its sublime stupidity.

The direct political sarcasm of this passage, prompted by Bennett's anti-Tory mood during the 1910 constitutional crisis, is uncommon. Otherwise this opening exhibits the classical features of provincial realism in weaving together private and public histories and in placing us from the start at the uncertain boundary between rural and industrial landscapes, and between tradition (the church, the borough) and innovation (the canal, the railway). The setting sustains these thematic oppositions upon a basis of historical and geographical accuracy: beneath the barely disguised place names here ('Bursley' is Burslem, 'Hillport' is Porthill, 'Oldcastle' is Newcastle under Lyme, and the river 'Knype' is the Trent) lie acknowledged facts in the history of the Staffordshire Potteries district. Bennett's way of beginning *Clayhanger* and Lawrence's opening chapter of *The Rainbow* have, then, much in common, not just the significant motifs of the canal and the church.

Clayhanger and *The Rainbow* share another significant feature of construction, which is their extended chronological span. The action of Bennett's novel takes place between 1872 and 1892, with some important passages taking us back to the childhood of Edwin's father in the 1830s. Lawrence's novel is a family saga covering a period between the 1840s and 1905, taking us from Tom Brangwen's childhood to the early adulthood of his granddaughter Ursula. The events of this Brangwen saga are unobtrusively linked to historical actuality, from the Polish insurrection of 1863, which brings Tom's future wife to England, to the Boer War of 1899–1902 in which Ursula's fiancé Anton serves. Bennett ties private and public histories more firmly in *Clayhanger*: Edwin falls in love during a potters' strike based on an actual dispute in 1881; his father Darius dies during a by-election campaign, having fallen ill on the day in 1886 on which Gladstone introduced his Irish Home Rule Bill to Parliament; and Edwin is reunited with his mysteriously estranged lover Hilda when her son falls victim to the influenza epidemic of 1892. Both novels fall within the large category of sagas and 'chronicle' fiction in that they attempt to trace the movements of historical change through microcosmic histories of fictional families across two or more generations.

The Rainbow is the more typical of this period's fictional chronicles in bringing its history into the twentieth century, as many novels and novel-sequences of this kind did: Galsworthy's *The Forsyte Saga* runs from 1886 to 1920; May Sinclair's *The Tree of Heaven* (1917) takes its Harrison clan from 1895 to 1916; Phyllis Bentley's *Inheritance* (1932) follows the fortunes of a family of Yorkshire mill-owners, the Oldroyds, from 1812 to 1931; Virginia Woolf's *The Years* (1937) examines the history of the Pargiter family from 1880 to 1936; Rose Macaulay's *Told by an Idiot* (1923) takes the Garden family from 1879 to 1920; and Hugh Walpole's 'Herries Chronicle' sequence of four novels (1930–3) more ambitiously if rather more superficially covers two centuries of family history, from 1732 to 1932. These were all novels that set out to conquer the territory of the social historian by bringing to life the dissolution of the Victorian social order and the painful emergence of modern ways of life, refracted through representative individual and familial fortunes. Such novels have a special significance in this period, indicating both an urgent need to comprehend and revalue the upheavals by which modern readers had themselves been shaped, and the unique capacity of the novel to fulfil it. They account, though, for a small portion of socially oriented realistic fiction, most of which, from *Howards End* in 1910 to the many socialist novels of the 1930s, was set contemporaneously or in the fairly recent past. Here we will note some characteristics of saga and chronicle fiction before passing on to examine novels of contemporary life.

Chronicle and saga fictions are concerned above all with evolutionary processes of change and adaptation, including resistance to change, within property-owning families that represent either the self-assurance of the high bourgeoisie (Galsworthy's Forsytes, Woolf's Pargiters) or the insecurity of the lower middle classes (Lawrence's

Brangwens, Bennett's Clayhangers). Contrasting principles of fixity and flux then tend to be embodied in generational conflict between elders clinging to custom and adolescents welcoming novelty; and along with these come the corresponding psychological features of authoritarian possessiveness in the old, impetuosity and ambition in the young. An emphasis, common to most kinds of realistic fiction, upon money and property takes in modern saga novels a special form in which the solidity of buildings serves to highlight both the transience of passing generations and the new mobilities of modern social history. As the family home, farm, or factory is inherited by the next generation, continuity and change may be represented within the same focus. On the other hand, the family's participation in the flux of modernization may be marked by removal to another habitation: the Brangwens eventually abandon Cossethay for a house in a colliery town; the Clayhangers move to a newly built house equipped, to Edwin's delight, with running hot water and an up-to-date bathroom. Domestic architecture itself carries ironic significance in *The Forsyte Saga*, in which Soames, the 'man of property', has a new suburban house built to keep his attractive wife Irene away from the romantic temptations of London; but its construction only leads her into an affair with the architect.

Architecture as a vocation, as a business, and as the form of art most intimately connected with everday life, looms large in these saga novels, although in different ways. The ambition nursed by the young Edwin Clayhanger is to become an architect, but his father prevents him from pursuing it, and insists that he carry on the family printing business, which he does grudgingly but with some success. In *The Forsyte Saga* architecture is the crucial meeting point of the opposed principles of Art and Property that dominate the personal antagonisms of the Forsyte clan, the property-obsessed Soames being ranged against a succession of other characters who embody artistic talent in various forms: Bosinney the architect, Irene the pianist, Jolyon the watercolourist, and others. In *The Rainbow*, certain architectural features such as porches, pillars, and especially arches are incorporated into the novel's semi-biblical pattern of emblems and symbols. In the seventh chapter, a visit by Will Brangwen and his wife Anna to Lincoln Cathedral exposes the tensions within their marriage as Will's ecstatic absorption in the church's womb-like enclosure is disrupted by Anna's comments upon the gargoyles, which obliquely express her desire for individuality.

Buildings serve as fixed points or milestones all the better to measure human mobility in its dynamics of expansion and aspiration. Edwin Clayhanger starts in an attic room above his father's print shop, later moves to a more spacious house, and finds romantic fulfilment by travelling well beyond Bursley to rescue Hilda from her failed boarding house in Brighton, these movements all corresponding to his emancipation from the confines of paternal tyranny and small-town provincial culture. Similarly in *The Rainbow*, while the patriarch Tom is literally drowned in his farm, the younger Brangwen generations are seen to evolve out of the Marsh into engagement with a wider world: two of the novel's chapters are significantly entitled 'The Widening Circle', and in each of them Ursula is launched outward through the expanding educational system to Nottingham and beyond. The vital centre of these novels is occupied by the figure of the lower middle-class aspirant who seeks a fulfilment that cannot be provided within the narrow limits of his or her birthplace and family. The difference between them lies in the form and scale of the aspirant's goals. Edwin Clayhanger is eventually released by his father's death, assuming responsibility for the business he never wanted to work in; and he attains the emotional reward of marriage to his long-lost fiancée in his mid-thirties. These are the incomplete, compromised victories permitted by realist fiction. Ursula Brangwen, on the other hand, resolutely rejects everything she encounters: home, family, modern industrial society, lovers of both sexes, and the prospect of marriage to Anton. Her liberation, signalled by her vision of a rainbow in the novel's closing paragraphs, is to be a kind of religious transcendence associated with the arrival of another man 'from the Infinite', which is delayed until the sequel, *Women in Love* (1920). *The Rainbow* is throughout more concerned with its characters' individual relation to the Infinite or 'the beyond' than to their observable social existence, and in this important respect it overshoots the terrain of realism that in other ways it seems to occupy. Characterization in its usual forms of human personality is stripped away in order to reveal impersonal forces in whose grip the Brangwens come to resemble predatory birds or angels. The actual people and buildings of Nottinghamshire are finally dismissed as a brittle crust that is to be swept away by some new germination of life, replaced by a heaven-sent 'new architecture'.

The self-improving lower middle-class protagonist had been a major feature of the Victorian novel, in the works of Dickens especially; and this social type regained its significance in the Edwardian and post-Edwardian fiction of H. G. Wells and Arnold Bennett. The eponymous heroes of Wells's fictional romances *Kipps* (1905) and *The History of Mr Polly* are apprentice drapers who are released by implausible coincidences and legacies into sudden wealth and marital bliss. The irrepressible social climber Denry Machin in Bennett's comic novel *The Card* (1911) rises rapidly from the status of rent collector to become mayor and all-round local dignitary through a career of brazen dodges and deceptions. These were sprightly entertainments combining a degree of social satire with a fairy-tale model of social elevation. They identified nonetheless a crucial figure of energetic ambition through which modern mobilities and self-transformations could be dramatized in more serious novels: Edwin Clayhanger is its realistic version, Ursula Brangwen its translation into visionary terms. To look beyond the confines of this chapter for a moment, it may be observed that lower middle-class self-improvement reaches its fullest imaginative treatment in James Joyce's *Ulysses* (1922), by contrast with which the 'Bloomsbury' novelists Forster and Woolf appear especially deficient: even when attempting sympathetic portraits of people from that social stratum (Leonard Bast in *Howards End*, Doris Kilman in *Mrs Dalloway* (1925)), they struggle to see anything more in them than painful vulgarity.

The other tellingly representative figure of social change in modern chronicle fiction is the dissatisfied middle-class woman who seeks release from the self-sacrificing imprisonment of 'Victorian' domestic duty. Lawrence's Ursula Brangwen is the provincial poor relation of this heroine, who appears more often in metropolitan chronicles. In Woolf's *The Years*, for example, we are given a clear contrast between Eleanor Pargiter, who sacrifices individual fulfilment in order to keep house for her father, and her sisters Rose and Delia, who escape the family home to engage in political activism; while in the next generation we find their niece Peggy renouncing domesticity to pursue a medical career. At the centre of Galsworthy's

Forsyte Saga lies the struggle between the lawyer Soames Forsyte, who longs for a son and heir, and his wife Irene, who refuses his marital 'rights' until he rapes her. Estranged from her possessive husband, she lives alone as a music teacher, while Soames likens her rebellion to that of the Boers against British rule in southern Africa (*In Chancery*, pt. 1, ch. 11). Just as the Forsyte clan is offered as a microcosm of the whole English upper middle class in its love of property above all else, so Irene is made to represent the modern quest for individual autonomy, which is increasingly evident in the younger generations of the saga. No fictional chronicle could adequately reflect the times unless it were fairly populated with rebel daughters, runaway wives—like Carmine Oldroyd in Bentley's *Inheritance*—and suffrage activists like Rose Pargiter in *The Years*, Stanley Garden in Macaulay's *Told by an Idiot*, and Dorothea Harrison in Sinclair's *The Tree of Heaven*.

Condition of England, Industrial, and Civic Novels

The closer the action of a saga comes to the present day, the more it assumes the documentary role of the 'Condition of England' novel, a form of fiction that had arisen from the social conflicts of the 1840s and had re-emerged more recently in Wells's *Tono-Bungay* and Galsworthy's *Fraternity* (both 1909). Topical novels addressing contemporary social ills and tensions appeared with special frequency in the 1930s, amid economic slump and mass unemployment, but a few may be found in the previous two decades. Notable and contrasting examples are Robert Tressell's socialist novel *The Ragged Trousered Philanthropists* (1914) and Warwick Deeping's anti-socialist *Sorrell and Son* (1925). Alongside these we may also place Forster's *Howards End*, which examines conflicting values among the middle classes.

Tressell's novel, published posthumously in abridged form, is set in the coastal town of 'Mugsborough' (based on Hastings), and follows a year in the life of a team of men employed by a decorating company to paint and wallpaper the villas of the wealthy. It gives a vividly realistic account of these working conditions, of the fear of poverty that keeps the men in them, and of the cost-cutting practices that produce shoddy results for customers. The hero, Frank Owen, attempts to explain to his fellow workers the iniquities of capitalism in general and of their own exploitation in particular, but to little avail. Owen is a member of the local Trades' Council, but we witness here no unionization nor collective action, as we usually do in the more upbeat socialist fiction of the Thirties. *The Ragged Trousered Philanthropists* is on the contrary a study in working-class isolation, division, and demoralization, in which Owen's only available form of resistance is to preserve artisanal pride in the quality of his own craftsmanship. Despite this bleakness of outlook, it commanded an avid readership in the labour movement, where it had the status of an underground classic that changed people's lives. George Orwell, for example, admired the book, and in *Keep the Aspidistra Flying* he shows Gordon Comstock absorbing Tressell's novel at the impressionable age of 16, and so embarking upon his personal war against the world of money.

Deeping's *Sorrell and Son* was a best-selling novel that dramatized the insecurities of the downwardly mobile middle class in the Twenties through the story of a demobilized gentleman-officer, Captain Sorrell, MC, who cannot find employment befitting his social status and struggles to bring up his son Kit while working as a hotel porter. Abandoned by his materialistic wife, Sorrell finds the post-War world a dangerous one in which to raise his boy, infested as it is with grasping women and the class envy of lazy workmen. He starts by removing Kit from contact with the smelly children at the municipal school and, against all odds, manages before he dies to get Kit privately educated and then established in a medical career, a gentleman at last. This novel is a self-pitying masculine melodrama in which breeding and the stiff upper lip win out against the filthy modern tide of history. Its protagonist has a timely significance in representing the descent of many ex-servicemen into unexpected penury, but Deeping's book offers no convincing view of his society, beyond some incidental ranting against the common crowd.

Howards End is an unusual Condition of England novel because it attempts no representation of working-class life or of conflict between employers and employed. In self-mocking acknowledgement of this restricted scope, its sixth chapter begins: 'We are not concerned with the very poor. They are unthinkable, and only to be approached by the statistician or the poet. This story deals with gentlefolk, or with those who are obliged to pretend that they are gentlefolk.' These remarks introduce the bank clerk Leonard Bast, who occupies the lowest rung of sham gentility, possessing little more than an umbrella and some improving books. Bast and his drunken wife Jacky play important roles in the plot, helping to expose the snobberies and sexual double standards of their superiors, but the pages devoted to them are, as Forster admitted, among the weakest in the book. The novel's central concern, as in Galsworthy's *The Forsyte Saga*, is with the conflict within the propertied classes between practical business and liberal culture, each being represented by a family group. The Wilcoxes are thriving English empire-builders, masculine, businesslike, and unsentimental, while the Schlegels are half-German intellectuals, feminine, impractical, and devoted to the cultivation of art and 'personal relations'. Forster contrives to bring about an unlikely marriage between Margaret, the elder of the two Schlegel sisters, and the businessman Henry Wilcox, a widower. At one level, this alliance suggests a possible reconciliation between the contrasted values they and their families represent; but in practice it provokes further tension, fuelled by extremists in both camps—Margaret's reckless bohemian sister Helen, who has an illegitimate child by Leonard Bast, and Henry's son Charles, a violent champion of respectability who is eventually imprisoned for Bast's manslaughter.

The plot of *Howards End* has many implausible twists and coincidences, serving, as in much Victorian fiction, to stress the interconnectedness of apparently unrelated human destinies, exemplified both in the destruction of Bast by the interference of the Schlegels and in the humiliation of Henry Wilcox when his old affair with Jacky Bast comes to light. The novel's famous epigraph, 'Only connect', upholds with the force of a moral maxim this traditionally revelatory use of linked plots. None of the connections established in this novel is quite as unusual as that between Ruth Wilcox, Henry's first wife, who dies after a few chapters, and Margaret, who later becomes his second wife. They briefly become friends, and Ruth greets with distress the news that the Schlegels are to lose their London house when the lease expires. Shortly before her death, Ruth writes a note to her husband saying that she wishes to bequeath

Howards End, her ancestral vine-covered house in rural Hertfordshire, to Margaret. The Wilcoxes suppress the evidence of this apparently deranged dying request, unaware that Ruth has identified Margaret as her true 'spiritual heir' (ch. 11). The novel's plot, however, ensures that Margaret does become the owner of the house, not just by marriage to Henry but by desert, in that she has a finer appreciation of the continuity it represents.

The prominence of this house, signalled by the title, is one of several features of *Howards End* that echo, despite its much shorter time span, the preoccupations of saga fiction. Complicated family connections emerge, as do themes of mobility and stasis, embodied in the Wilcox motor cars and in their Hertfordshire property. Bricks and mortar, house-lettings and house-removals all occupy the foreground of the action, thereby highlighting the uprootedness of the characters, whether bank clerks, intellectuals, or entrepreneurs. Against this unhealthy modern unrest Forster contrasts the fixity of Howards End with its immemorial wych-elm as a site of rooted values, at which the novel finally comes to settle. The verdict Forster invites us to pronounce upon the condition of late Edwardian England is a pastoralist one that condemns the expansion of London's suburbs into the green fields of the Home Counties, as it regrets the uprooting of rural gentry and yeomanry and their transformation into urban merchants and clerks.

After the General Strike of 1926, and especially with the onset of economic depression and political polarization in the early Thirties, Forster's gently nostalgic liberalism began to look tame, and his fictive 'England' too narrowly southern. Among the new problems concerning many novelists and their readers were severe economic decline, unemployment, and poverty in the industrial regions of the Midlands and the north of England, at a time when most of the south still enjoyed continuing prosperity. One response to this situation, which we shall revisit in Chapter 14, was the appearance of non-fictional books of reportage such as Orwell's *The Road to Wigan Pier* (1937) in which southerners could learn of the deprivations suffered by inhabitants of what was to them almost a foreign land. More widespread was the revival, in markedly regional forms, of the 'industrial' Condition of England novel that had emerged in the 1840s. In this tradition, the contemporary plight of the industrial working class is a central element, and in fully developed versions the novel's action will include strikes or lockouts, and political debates upon the merits of trade unions and socialist activism. It would be mistaken to assume that between the 1840s and the 1930s industrial workers had disappeared from English fiction: on the contrary, the female factory-hand had lived on as a favoured heroine of popular romance. A recurrent minor character in P. G. Wodehouse's Jeeves stories from 1923 onwards is Rosie M. Banks, best-selling author of *Only a Factory Girl*. Even beneath the trenches of the Western Front, Robert Graves had once encountered a coal miner serving with the Royal Engineers, who was reading, in his breaks from digging a tunnel under the German lines, a novelette entitled *From Mill Girl to Duchess* (*Good-bye to All That*, pp. 102–3). The new wave of realistic fiction in the 1930s, by contrast, was dedicated to showing why mill girls could not afford new shoes or even square meals, let alone become duchesses. Fidelity in detail to the facts of contemporary poverty was a leading element in this new fiction, one that gives it a documentary value to offset its sometimes limited imaginative range.

The Hogarth Press had in 1931 an unexpected success with the first novel of a writer from Birmingham, John Hampson: *Saturday Night at the Greyhound* was a family tragedy set in a failing pub frequented by miners on the Derbyshire moors. Hampson himself had experienced casual jobs as a kitchen-hand and waiter; and this close knowledge of low-paid drudgery shows through in his treatment of his 'ordinary' characters, from the lecherous publican to the vengeful cleaning lady. Hampson came to be described as a co-founder of the so-called 'Birmingham Group' along with the novelists Walter Allen and Walter Brierley, although there was little group identity beyond the fact that Hampson and Allen emerged from the same city, jointly discovered the talent of Brierley (who was not from Birmingham but from D. H. Lawrence's part of Nottinghamshire), and wrote realistically about contemporary poverty. The most celebrated production of this group was Brierley's first novel, *Means Test Man* (1935), a fictional exposé of unemployment again based on personal experience, Brierley himself being a former coal miner. The novel describes a typical week in the life of an unemployed miner, Jack Cook, and his family as they await the arrival of the Means Test man, a figure who has the power under recent widely hated legislation to cut the relief payments ('the dole') paid to unemployed workers if they have any savings or wage-earning children. The indignities of this form of inquisition, and the family tensions it stirs up, are evoked in a naturalistic manner devoid of overt political commentary. Another widely noticed novel of this kind was *Love on the Dole* (1933) by the Salford writer Walter Greenwood, which examines a group of characters struggling against poverty in a depressed Northern industrial neighbourhood in the years leading up to the imposition of the Means Test in 1931. Greenwood makes more room for political discussion of working-class problems, but at the same time gives the novel a damagingly sentimental flavour by casting as hero the solitary consumptive Larry, who doubles implausibly as a socialist agitator, and as heroine his fiancée Sally, a mill girl whose rare beauty is suspiciously duchess-like. After Larry loses his job and then dies, having been clubbed by police during a demonstration, Sally nobly offers herself to the local bookmaker in order to secure from him employment for her father and brother. Despite these melodramatic ingredients, *Love on the Dole* succeeded in drawing national attention to the human miseries of the dole queue, both in print and, from 1934, in a stage version.

A curious feature of most English industrial novels in the 1930s, as in the 1840s and 1850s, is that they devote little if any space to the description of work itself. Manual labour is a familiar element of rural and maritime fiction, but novels about factory or colliery life tend to steer clear of the shop floor and coalface in favour of the strike meeting, the pub, or the family kitchen. Given that several prominent novels of working-class life in the Thirties were concerned principally with the the unemployed, the omission of the labour process has an evident justification. Still, if we look for a convincing fictional treatment of life inside a factory, we have to turn back the clock to the late Twenties and read Henry Green's second novel, *Living* (1929). This is a work of striking originality that manages to extract from the world of a Birmingham engineering works a melancholy beauty while remaining true to the unglamorous facts of industrial routine. The book is based upon Green's stint on the shop floor of his father's factory, the management of which he was later to inherit; and from this unusual vantage point Green is able to reveal episodes of the workers' lives contrasted with those of the managers. It offers a realistic study of these working lives and of their everyday rivalries, but in a modernist style whose syntactical oddities jolt us out of habitual perceptions. At times, the narration appears to be a strictly neutral recording of cityscapes and, most memorably, of jocular working-class conversation; at others it veers into elaborately lyrical similes likening human feelings to the flights of pigeons. As in so many works of the Twenties, the skeletal plot involves struggles between older and younger generations: the 26-year-old Richard Dupret inherits the factory from his father, unsettling the managers, who fear the effects of his inexperienced meddling; favouring the younger employees, he condemns the older foundry workers to premature redundancy. One of these old hands, Mr Craigan, heads a household in which young Lily Gates, the daughter of Craigan's unreliable workmate, keeps house while dreaming of self-betterment through marriage and emigration. Her attempted elopement to Canada with a young foundry worker fails, and she returns to Craigan's house apparently defeated but in fact endowed with a new-found if muted self-confidence and power over her elders. The novel offers no romantic escape from industrial Birmingham, implying that the only hope for these workers comes from love of children and respect for the aged, from talk, and from song. Green has no political or sociological point to argue, and there is, by contrast with *Love on the Dole* and several other industrial fictions of the period, no sentimentalizing of workers.

Industrial novels offered detailed representations of working-class characters' daily lives and hardships, as it were in 'close-up'. An altogether more ambitious panoramic view of contemporary society is attempted in certain regional novels of the Thirties, of which the most interesting examples are Winifred Holtby's *South Riding* (1936) and Lettice Cooper's *National Provincial* (1938). These are best described as 'civic' fictions, in that they portray the public life of a town or city, disclosing its contemporary class conflicts by following the fortunes of several representative citizens. Both are Yorkshire novels, the scene of Holtby's being 'Kiplington' in a fictional 'South' Riding (based on Withernsea in the real East Riding), the events of Cooper's taking place in 'Aire' (Leeds). Both are set in the recent past, and both employ as the central observer a Yorkshirewoman returning to her home town after having worked in London: the 39-

year-old Sarah Burton of *South Riding* arrives in Kiplington in 1932 to take up the post of headmistress of the Girls' High School, while the younger journalist Mary Welburn in *National Provincial* comes to Aire for an eighteen-month stint in 1935–6 working for the *Yorkshire Guardian*. Each comes into close contact with the antagonists on either side of local political conflicts, each falls in love with a married man, and each provides the dual perspective of the returning native who is both insider and outsider. For much of the time in these lengthy works, though, we lose sight of the heroines and become immersed in the lives of a large cast of characters representing different social classes, political opinions, and trades or professions. Cooper's novel includes three established middle-class families representing the now-converging Tory and Liberal interests, along with a left-leaning academic couple, an old-fashioned trade-unionist Labour leader, a younger and more radical union activist, a pacifist vicar, a military officer, a Communist student, and a psychoanalyst among its many 'type' characters; and its action includes an unofficial strike that splits the local labour movement, a Fascist march, and a local election campaign. Holtby's *South Riding* is peopled by county councillors of distinct political types, by schoolgirls of contrasting social origins, and by indigent ex-soldiers and lecherous preachers, all connected to one another through complex networks of obligation or indirect influence.

Before Mary Welburn sets off from London to Aire, a journalist colleague encourages her with the reflection that 'We know more about Abyssinia here than we do about the provinces. To us they're either Beauty Spots or Distressed Areas. If something startling happens, we turn the limelight on them for a moment, but we never see their average life.'[3] In seeking to illuminate this 'average life' of their Yorkshire communities, Holtby and Cooper revive the provincial civic realism of George Eliot's *Middlemarch* (1871–2)— a debt acknowledged allusively by Cooper, who has her heroine write a review of a George Eliot biography, and who also mentions the set of Eliot's novels owned by a local Labour leader. Holtby's 'Prefatory Letter' to *South Riding* announces her intention to trace the 'complex tangle of motives prompting public decisions, the

---

[3] Lettice Cooper, *National Provincial* (Gollancz, 1987), 22.

unforeseen consequences of their enactment on private lives', in terms clearly derived from Eliot. More convincingly than Cooper, she emulates the interwoven multi-plot structure of *Middlemarch* and its sympathetic analyses of individuals struggling with historical change and small-scale local reforms; although she also mixes in strong echoes of Charlotte Brontë's *Jane Eyre* (1847) in the romance plot of Sarah Burton's infatuation for the Tory gentleman-farmer Robert Carne, who has a mad wife in a local asylum. Both novels are capacious, allowing plenty of room for opinion and debate both on local conflicts and on world affairs, German concentration camps getting a brief mention in each. Cooper's *National Provincial* is more insistently topical, its air so thick with discussion of contemporary issues that the psychoanalyst Dr Jones finds many of his patients dreaming of strikes and picket lines. Holtby too gives her characters time to worry about impending wars and revolutions, but her technical resources are richer: many of her characters commune with themselves in modernistic interior monologues, and thematic links among the sub-plots are clinched by a structure that follows the agenda items (Finance, Education, Health, and so forth) of a County Council meeting. More Middlebrow than *Middlemarch* as these novels sometimes are, they achieve a certain epic scope that, as Cooper's title suggests, captures living national history in terms of regional self-awareness.

George Orwell, himself a keen student of contemporary social conditions, held a gloomy view of the English novel in his time. He complained that it comprised on the one hand exclusive highbrow fictions about highbrows and on the other lowbrow escapist pulp about gangsters. 'Books about ordinary people behaving in an ordinary manner are extremely rare', he claimed (*Collected Essays*, vol. 1, pp. 259–60), as if the only choice available were between Aldous Huxley and Edgar Wallace. The broad expanse between these poles was in fact crowded with realistic, documentary, and 'sociological' novels, most of them creditably devoted in various ways to the depiction of ordinariness, everyday routine, and unglamorous provincial societies. The one example of an 'ordinary-people' novel that Orwell does mention as a rare exception turns out to be James Joyce's *Ulysses*, which we shall encounter in the next chapter in the company of other fictions predominantly 'psychological' in emphasis.

9

The Modern Psychological Novel

New Words, 1910–1940

*ambivalence   Bildungsroman   introspectionism
montage   multilayer   narcissistic   non-linearity
nuanced   obsessive   Oedipal   psychoanalyse
self-dramatization   self-portrayal   synchronized*

The psychological novel in English has a long history going back to Samuel Richardson's works of the 1740s. The term itself had been introduced by George Eliot in 1855, and was by the 1920s widely used in critical discussion. Novels of the special kind that concentrate on the emotional crises of a protagonist entering upon adulthood were already central to the tradition of English fiction. Although the German word *Bildungsroman* (variously translated as 'novel of formation', 'education novel' or 'coming-of-age novel') was not domesticated as an English term before 1910, the thing itself was prominent in Victorian literature, in Thackeray's *Pendennis* (1850), Dickens's *David Copperfield* (1850) and *Great Expectations* (1861), and George Eliot's *The Mill on the Floss* (1860). Outside this particular genre of subjective fiction, there had been in the late Victorian and Edwardian periods a few distinguished novelists, most notably Henry James and Joseph Conrad, for whom the events of a novel's action seemed less important than the characters' perceptions and interpretations of them in the perplexing mazes of 'consciousness'. By the 1920s, it was accepted by most commentators on fiction that a major tendency of the modern novel in its higher artistic branches was its devotion to analysing subjective states, often at the expense of 'external' action. It was at the same time evident that the popular market for fiction continued to rely on such sensational 'external' ingredients as murder, espionage, revenge, seduction, elopement, mistaken identity, and swashbuckling adventure. The psychological novel of the 1910–40 period was in this context, as it had been for readers of Henry James in the 1890s, a highbrow genre, increasingly differentiated from the lowbrow or middlebrow novel of sensational action.

The special prominence of psychological novels in this period should not be identified exclusively with modernist experiments. Technical innovations developed by Dorothy Richardson, James Joyce, Virginia Woolf, and others for the rendering of consciousness were indeed much discussed by critics and studied by other novelists, as was the new mode of novelistic introspection offered in France by Marcel Proust. These were major developments that extended the imaginative possibilities of prose fiction, in more than a merely technical sense. All the same, such experimental pioneers had no monopoly upon consciousness, subjectivity, or the inner lives of fictional characters. A commonly received view of the modern novel of 'consciousness' and its origins relies heavily on the assertions of Virginia Woolf's essays 'Modern Fiction' (1919/25) and *Mr Bennett and Mrs Brown* (1924), and so regards the modern turn towards the evocation of subjectivity as a post-Edwardian revolt against the 'external' realism of Arnold Bennett and his generation. There are several problems with that simplified history: one is that it ignores the much longer prior evolution of 'consciousness' in the novel, a story in which Henry James plays a major part; another is that it disregards the genuinely psychological element in the fiction of Bennett and his contemporaries. A third, more grievous error, now enshrined in post-structuralist dogma, is the assumption that any adequate depiction of consciousness in the novel is incompatible with nineteenth-century realist traditions and thus requires a radical overthrow of realism. The account offered below of psychological novels will take a contrary approach that regards most such works not as subversions of the realist tradition but as extensions of it into what was often understood at the time to be a 'psychological realism'.

Realism and the Education Novel

The common ground shared by realist fiction and by the novel of subjective life was broad and fertile. Contrary to critical legend, an 'Edwardian' realist such as Arnold Bennett did not just fill up his novels with fussy descriptions of buildings and furniture: like his nineteenth-century predecessors from Austen to Zola, he spent most of his time telling us what was going on in the minds of his characters. His claim to be read seriously as a psychological novelist is most clearly vindicated by *Riceyman Steps* (1923), which probes the private fears and fantasies of an isolated middle-aged couple destroying each other through their obsessions with cleanliness, money, and food. The narrative does include lengthy descriptions of the interior of Henry and Violet Earlforward's living quarters above their bookshop, but these help to focus our attention upon a claustrophobic sphere of domestic tensions and individual delusions. The novel's psychological emphasis is in these terms undeniable, but there is no contradiction in recognizing that Bennett's study of miserliness in *Riceyman Steps* belongs fully in the tradition of Balzac and George Eliot.

Bennett's earlier book, *Clayhanger* (1910), was discussed in the previous chapter in terms of its socio-historical depiction of Staffordshire life, but this work too is a psychological study, in fact a *Bildungsroman* in which the central interest is in Edwin Clayhanger's struggles to overcome his timidity and his resentment against his father. There is no great gulf between that novel and, say, D. H. Lawrence's *Sons and Lovers* (1913), which is about the struggles of a young man in the English Midlands to overcome his timidity and his resentment against his mother. Differences between these two novels certainly remain, but these would not justify any contrast that pitted Lawrence as a novelist of inner reality against Bennett as a novelist of mere external appearances. Lawrence begins *Sons and Lovers*, as Bennett had begun *Clayhanger*, with a description of an industrialized location and of its history. He follows Bennett too in giving his protagonist a familial prehistory: Bennett starts *Clayhanger* on the day that Edwin leaves school, but doubles back to recount his father's childhood experiences in the workhouse in order to account for the kind of paternal tyranny under which Edwin struggles to develop. Lawrence is even more determinedly a realist in the lengths to which he goes in establishing a credible familial context for his hero Paul Morel in *Sons and Lovers*. The first part of the novel, running to over 150 pages, is devoted to the tensions within the marriage of Paul's parents, and within a household that includes his sister and brothers; and none of this is wasted, because the effects upon Paul will show up later. Paul himself is not born until the second chapter, and his independent exploits start to dominate the narrative only in part 2. It is a general rule of the *Bildungsroman* tradition that the weight and solidity of circumstances in which the protagonist grows up must be established and specified if his or her efforts to define a relatively independent selfhood are to yield full significance. In novels of this kind, adolescent desire must come into collision with particular constraints and obligations in its encounters with the disappointments and complexities of adult existence, whether the outcome be defeat, compromise, escape, or rebellion. For these reasons, the coming-of-age novel is closely tied to the values and methods of realism, although there were ways of diverting it into the easier paths of 'romance', as H. G. Wells does in *The History of Mr Polly* (1910).

Sons and Lovers belongs, like *Clayhanger* and its sequel, *Hilda Lessways* (1911), to an extraordinarily fertile decade of fiction in England during which the realistic education novel and its variants arrived at a prominence and an accumulated imaginative power not witnessed before or since. The roster of major *Bildungsromane* in the first ten years of George V's reign includes the three novels just mentioned, along with Compton Mackenzie's *Sinister Street* (1913–14), W. Somerset Maugham's *Of Human Bondage* (1915), Dorothy Richardson's first instalments of *Pilgrimage* (from *Pointed Roofs* in 1915 to *Interim* in 1919), Virginia Woolf's *The Voyage Out* (1915) and *Night and Day* (1919), James Joyce's *A Portrait of the Artist as a Young Man* (1916), and May Sinclair's *Mary Olivier* (1919), to which could be added the latter part of Lawrence's *The Rainbow* (1915). Each of these works contributed something distinctive to the development of 'psychological realism', although, as we shall see below, the realisms of Richardson and Joyce were more experimental in technique. If we seek reasons for such a flourishing of education novels at this time, we are likely to be led back to the same general

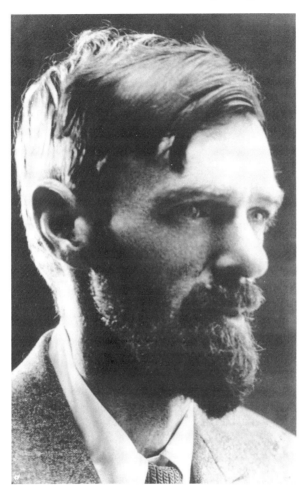

Fig. 5. D. H. Lawrence photographed in 1929
by Ernesto Guardia.

causes that underlie the boom in saga and chronicle fiction: a need to grasp in individualized terms the defining passage from 'Victorian' social conformity to modern autonomous selfhood. Joyce's *Portrait*, for example, clearly identifies the forces constraining its young Irish hero, Stephen Dedalus, as those of Religion and Nationalism, but these large abstractions take on alarmingly vivid life for him in the intimacy of the family dinner table, of the confessional, and of his own agonized conscience. To the extent that an education novel permits an extended time span—twenty years exactly in *Clayhanger* and *Of Human Bondage*, approximately in *Sons and Lovers* and *A Portrait*, as many as forty-five in *Mary Olivier*—it may assume the historically representative qualities of the chronicle novel, while retaining at its core the dilemmas of a unique individual faced with life-changing choices of spouse or vocation.

The inner lives of fictional characters were, then, most often and most convincingly explored within the enduring conventions of realism, and continued to be presented in these accustomed terms in the Twenties and Thirties. Several highly accomplished novelists of that post-War period produced valuable studies of subjective life that are usually now disregarded because they did not involve startling technical innovations: three such cases that are worth briefly reviewing here are those of F. M. Mayor, Rosamond Lehmann, and Elizabeth Bowen. Mayor's novel *The Rector's Daughter* (1924) is an outstanding illustration of surviving Victorian traditions in English fiction. Its subject is the secret emotional turmoil of a lonely spinster in her thirties, Mary Jocelyn, who keeps house for her elderly father in an isolated village. The restricted social setting is similar to those of Jane Austen's novels—two or three households among the rural gentry and clergy—while the quietly sympathetic treatment of the characters is more reminiscent of Elizabeth Gaskell. Were it not for a few passing references to motor cars and Cubist interior decoration, the reader could be forgiven for imagining this novel to be set, and even written, in the previous century. The story offers scarcely anything eventful beyond Mary's own inner wrestlings with the unaccustomed desires and jealousies that follow from her falling in love with a vicar who enters upon an apparently reckless marriage with another woman. Mary learns to live with her disappointment, subsides back into the dull round of Sunday-school meetings and tea parties, and achieves a reconciliation with her emotionally remote father at his deathbed. Mayor presents in this 'spinster novel' a muted individual tragedy of reticence and remorse, in which nobody is finally blamed.

Rosamond Lehmann's first novel, *Dusty Answer* (1927), revived the *Bildungsroman* sub-genre for her own generation, capturing the energies and sexual confusions of post-War youth through the experiences of the dreamy heroine, Judith Earle, as a student at Cambridge. Her later book *Invitation to the Waltz* (1932) returns to the trials of adolescence, but compresses the action into two crucial days in Olivia Curtis's life—her seventeenth birthday, and her first formal dance. In both novels, the focus is upon the heroine's private dreams, doubts, and trepidations, and the treatment is, as with most semi-autobiographical fictions of the period, sensitive and essentially realistic. Elizabeth Bowen's major novels of the Thirties, *To the North* (1932), *The House in Paris* (1935), and *The Death of the Heart* (1938), do not follow the education-novel pattern, but they bring about by other means tense confrontations between innocence and experience, fixity and restlessness. Bowen is a 'psychological' novelist in the tradition of Henry James, and with a similar interest in the analysis of innocence and betrayal, although the mixture she concocts of nervous middle-class social comedy and discomforting scrutiny of characters' moods is altogether her own, inimitable in atmosphere and polished style. Her characters are typically disinherited or dispossessed, orphaned, or bereaved, and thrown into relationships of disorienting opacity, like the young boy Leopold in *The House in Paris*, who is deposited in a strange house to meet his absentee mother for the first time since infancy. They are also, in representatively modern terms, insistently mobile: *To the North* and *The House in Paris* both begin with passengers en route to new lives, and all three of these novels culminate in anxious journeys by car or taxi. It is as if her characters are trying to flee the relentless beam of intelligence with which Bowen lights up their vulnerabilities, often from the oddest of angles.

The more experimental kind of modern subjective novel had emerged, meanwhile, from the flourishing of the realistic *Bildungsroman* during the Great War. James Joyce's *A Portrait of the Artist as a Young Man*, first serialized in the avant-garde London *Egoist* magazine in 1914–15, brought to the education novel a new degree of intimacy with its protagonist, a vividness both realistic and poetically symbolic. Again deploying the modulations of free indirect style as he had in *Dubliners*, Joyce here colours his third-person narrative with the evolving idiom of Stephen Dedalus's own vocabulary, beginning with baby talk about sensations and ending with philosophical jargon about ideas. At the same time he manages to cast over Stephen's humourless self-conceit an ironic perspective that seems somehow to be enhanced by the very force of our identification with his private terrors and ecstasies. In the most rudimentary terms, *A Portrait* is the story of a boy growing up in late Victorian Ireland, undergoing a Jesuit education that leads him to consider entering the priesthood, and eventually rejecting the Church in favour of the similarly priestly vocation of artistic rebel. Unusually for the hero of an education novel, Stephen's rebellion, conducted under the Satanic slogan *non serviam* ('I shall not serve'), is directed not against any tyrannical parent or uncle but against the entire servile condition, as he sees it, of Irish culture. Joyce does not, though, tell a story in the accepted nineteenth-century sense, because the familiar guiding, interpreting, and summarizing roles of the narrator are cunningly underplayed and at times seemingly abandoned, so that the terms in which events are evaluated are Stephen's own, or those of secondary characters within his world. The effect is a powerfully direct involvement in Stephen's perceptions: his infantile sense of the wonder and strangeness of things in the opening pages; his indignation at bullying and at unjust physical punishment as a young schoolboy; his torments of guilt during a hellfire sermon; his rapture upon rediscovering the beauty of the secular world. Certain episodes of this book fulfil perfectly the ambition of nineteenth-century realism as formulated by Henry James—to give the reader the illusion of 'seeing' the fictional world from within rather than just being told about it; others, notably in the final chapter, move in the very un-Jamesian direction of the 'novel of ideas', as Stephen expounds his aesthetic theories in the style of scholastic theology. In many ways a heretically contrary work, *A Portrait* seems to stretch the subjective novel in two directions at once, towards 'fallen' bodily profanity on the one side and towards spiritual exaltation and 'flight' (a theme emphasized by Stephen's mythological surname) on the other; but its climax at the end of the fourth chapter then resolves these apparent opposites into a single revelatory acceptance of mortality, claiming for artistic realism a kind of religious sanction.

An even bolder recasting of the education-novel was to follow quickly in the unfolding autobiographical *Pilgrimage* novel-sequence of Dorothy Richardson, which was conceived, as she later wrote, as 'a feminine equivalent of the current masculine realism' (*Pilgrimage*, vol. 1, p. 9). Richardson's version of realism aims to capture her protagonist's passing impressions of everyday experience, and it disdains the shaping of that experience into the customary patterns of development, climax, or resolution. The accepted structure of a *Bildungsroman* had until now always involved a strong narrative momentum leading to a climax of self-knowledge and of choice, whether in traditional or in more innovatory versions: Maugham's *Of Human Bondage* leads Philip Carey to a settled choice of marriage and professional dedication to medicine, while Joyce's *A Portrait* is marked by its hero's especially decisive adoption of an artistic mission. For Miriam Henderson, the heroine of *Pilgrimage*, though, there are no revelatory climaxes, and any resolution seems constantly to be postponed (eventually, ten years after Richardson's death, a thirteenth and concluding volume appeared, in which Miriam decides to write an autobiographical novel: a Proustian finale that loops back to its beginning). This novel-sequence is set in a recognizably real world of schools, boarding houses, London streets, and dentists' surgeries, and, like so many sagas and education novels of its time, it follows its protagonist across that endlessly fascinating border between the end of the Victorian age and the dawn of the twentieth century: the action is set in London and elsewhere between 1893 and 1907, broadly matching the span (1885–1903) of Maugham's novel. Its most obvious distinction lies in its sheer length—nearly 2,000 pages by 1938, with still no end in sight. More unusual and apparently perverse, however, is its occlusion of the life-changing events that provide both the substance and the significant shape of other education novels. The death of the protagonist's mother is the opening trauma in *Of Human Bondage* and the concluding drama of *Sons and Lovers*; in *Pilgrimage*, on the other hand, the same event happens entirely 'offstage', and we are left to infer that Miriam's mother has killed herself at some time before the close of the *Honeycomb* (1917) instalment. Similarly in the later *Clear Horizon* (1935) volume, Miriam finds herself pregnant, but her subsequent miscarriage goes unrecorded, as a matter of inference rather than of open narrative report, let alone description.

Richardson seems determined, then, to eliminate those peaks and troughs that define the 'fortunes' of a traditionally conceived fictional protagonist, and to offer in their place a level continuum of inconclusive sensations, thoughts, and conversations that captures the quality of Miriam's experience and response without forcing them into patterns of destiny. The point is to give us an impression of how it feels to be alive as Miriam at this moment or at the next, not to arrive at any defining illumination of her position or her progress. This is still an education novel of sorts, but it draws no lessons and attains no graduation. Ideas, of all kinds, are discussed, debated, or privately considered, including those of Miriam's 'Lycurgan' (i.e. Fabian), suffragist, and Zionist friends, and opinion or prejudice—about Germans, English people, and Jews, about men and women—occupies much of Miriam's thinking, but she is not shown to derive from the intellectual ferment of her time any general conclusions. The living process is all, the flow of what quickly became known as Richardson's 'stream-of-consciousness' method, the evolution of which has been remarked upon and illustrated in Chapter 3 above.

Soon after the War, the distinctive experimental challenge of Richardson's evolving sequence was recognized by other writers, although not everywhere applauded even by modernists. Many readers of *Pilgrimage* then and since have found the task of inhabiting Miriam's mind uncongenially restrictive, particularly as it seems impermeable by the reality of other people. Katherine Mansfield complained in her reviews of *The Tunnel* (1919) and *Interim* (1920) that every scene and event in these novels was of equal unimportance, indiscriminately recorded without being subjected to retrospective assessment.[1] Virginia Woolf, also reviewing *The Tunnel*, sought 'in the helter-skelter of flying fragments some unity, significance, or design', but could not find it (*The Essays*, vol. 3, p. 11). For Woolf, the novel was an interesting failure, exemplifying a kind

---

[1] Katherine Mansfield, *Novels and Novelists*, ed. J. M. Murry (Cape, 1930), 3–4, 140.

of realism that could register surface impressions without reaching anything profound.

May Sinclair, who was the first writer to apply the term 'stream of consciousness' to contemporary literary methods in a review of Richardson's work in 1918, is sometimes paired with Richardson, as if their techniques were allied. In fact Sinclair's approach to novelistic construction was more traditional, although increasingly marked by psychoanalytic concerns. Her work shows less interest in the flux of experience, and far more in the larger patterns of individual destiny that Richardson had abandoned. Her novels tend to trace the psychological, spiritual, and sexual development of their protagonists all the way from infancy to death, interpreting and shaping these into explicable designs. Some are family sagas; others are life stories of individuals, notably *Mary Olivier: A Life*, *Life and Death of Harriett Frean* (1922), *Arnold Waterlow: A Life* (1924), and *History of Anthony Waring* (1927). These books push beyond the temporal framework of the coming-of-age novel while still preserving some of its structural features. In one respect, though, they frustrate the expectation of 'development' implied by the *Bildungsroman*, favouring stories of stunted emotional growth, miseducation, and failed aspiration. The most satisfying of these novels, *Mary Olivier*, follows its heroine's inner life from the age of 2 until she is 47, emphasizing both the emergence and the guilty suppression of her philosophical interests under the influence of her grasping mother, who fears Mary's sexual and intellectual independence alike, preventing her from marrying. The novel stands up well as a semi-autobiographical study in the stifling effect of 'Victorian' codes of feminine self-renunciation. It has technically interesting features too, in its switching from third- to first- and even second-person voice, and in the use of stream-of-consciousness style, much more sparingly, though, than in Richardson's work. The last major work in this great decade of education novels, *Mary Olivier* is modern in style and in outlook, but nonetheless recognizably descended from George Eliot's *The Mill on the Floss*.

The flourishing of the coming-of-age novel eventually summoned forth various reactions against its temptations, as familiarity bred contempt. In Aldous Huxley's debut novel, *Crome Yellow* (1921), the young poet Denis Stone confesses that he is writing a novel, 'about the usual things', which prompts the philosopher Scogan to anticipatory précis:

> 'Of course,' Mr Scogan groaned. 'I'll describe the plot for you. Little Percy, the hero, was never good at games, but he was always clever. He passes through the usual public school and the usual university, and comes to London, where he lives among the artists. He is bowed down with melancholy thought; he carries the whole weight of the universe upon his shoulders. He writes a novel of dazzling brilliance; he dabbles delicately in Amour and disappears, at the end of the book, into the luminous Future.'
>
> Denis blushed scarlet. Mr Scogan had described the plan of his novel with an accuracy that was appalling. (ch. 3)

Scogan's mockery here does no real damage to the major education novels of the previous decade, although it manages to summarize Mackenzie's *Sinister Street* neatly enough. It helps to indicate that by the early Twenties the *Bildungsroman* convention had solidified into a readily imitable modern formula with a suspiciously narcissistic appeal. Virginia Woolf had in January 1920 already recorded her private doubts about 'the damned egotistical self' that dominated the autobiographical novels of Joyce and Richardson (*Diary*, vol. 2, p. 14). She was herself experimenting at this time with a new poetic style of prose fiction that could accommodate subjective life without being self-absorbed. Her first fully modernist novel, *Jacob's Room* (1922), is about the early life of a young man who is clearly not a version of the author. In this and in several other respects it occupies the terrain of the education novel while flouting or discarding its conventions.

High Modernism, Memory, and Consciousness

Jacob's Room concerns itself with the short life of one Jacob Flanders, an English boy born in the 1880s and thus of military age when the Great War breaks out. In those minimal terms, the book fulfils the customary expectations of the post-Victorian *Bildungsroman*. Everything else apart from the chronological sequence, though, seems to be distractingly out of place: Jacob has no remarkable adventures; nor does the third-person narrator really tell a connected story that could make overt sense of Jacob's development, so that to speak of its 'narrative voice' is often an exaggeration. Although we have glimpses of Jacob's life as a Cambridge student, his schooldays are omitted entirely, and his profession in early adulthood is never identified. Jacob himself occupies the foreground of the narrative only intermittently, and is significantly absent from the opening and closing scenes of the book. No settled portrait of Jacob is laid before us, and we are obliged to assemble one from fragmentary and unreliable impressions registered by his various admirers, who themselves appear and disappear without explanation. The novel's attention seems to dart with birdlike rapidity from one apparently inconsequential object or incident to another, as in this self-contained episode from the tenth chapter:

Now Jacob walked over to the window and stood with his hands in his pockets. Mr Springett opposite came out, looked at his shop window, and went in again. The children drifted past, eyeing the pink sticks of sweetstuff. Pickford's van swung down the street. A small boy twirled from a rope. Jacob turned away. Two minutes later he opened the front door, and walked off in the direction of Holborn.

Refusing to discriminate between event and non-event, this novel's narrative voice, if we may still call it that, often pays more attention to fleeting impressions of natural movement—of a butterfly, of the wind, of shadow and sunlight—than to human destinies. One contemporary reader, Winifred Holtby, described its disconnected effect as 'a combination of poetic and cinema technique' (*Virginia Woolf*, p. 126), but it also offers more than a modestly neutral record of impressions. In its more traditional aspect, *Jacob's Room* voices general claims and questions about human life, most of them implying a Platonic scepticism about the possibility of knowing another person as a 'character':

How far was Jacob Flanders at the age of twenty-six a stupid fellow? It is no use trying to sum people up. One must follow hints, not exactly what is said, nor yet entirely what is done. Some, it is true, take ineffaceable impressions of character at once. Others dally, loiter, and get blown this way and that. (*Jacob's Room*, ch. 12)

Denied the narrative or dramatic development due to a proper protagonist, Jacob is whisked away from us, leaving a vacant space—

the 'room' of the title—in which such questions of identity echo after him.

As an experiment designed to discover what a novel could be if action and character were evacuated, *Jacob's Room* has its importance, although chiefly as a transition to Woolf's next two novels, which are more coherent and more truly psychological in emphasis. *Mrs Dalloway* (1925) still shows at times some of the abrupt shifts of focus exhibited in the earlier novel, but it has a more secure and recognizably novelistic shape, given to it by the unities of time and place from which the mock-biographical design of *Jacob's Room* could not benefit. Like Joyce's *Ulysses*, which Woolf had absorbed in the meantime, *Mrs Dalloway* is set in a modern city on a single summer's day, and it follows the thoughts and perceptions of two contrasted characters, and of several minor figures, as they live through those few hours. Although it is part of the novel's purpose to revalue fleeting moments of apparent insignificance, this is neither for its protagonist, Clarissa Dalloway, nor for the secondary character of Septimus Warren Smith an 'ordinary day' at all: Septimus, a shell-shocked ex-soldier persecuted by hallucinations and by unsympathetic doctors, commits suicide, while Clarissa, a 52-year-old political hostess, is prompted to review and justify her way of life as old lovers and friends reappear on the day she prepares to throw a big party. The past, whether in the form of war trauma or in the form of recollected adolescent loves, continually haunts and colours the present, flooding it with the changing lights of memory and regret.

The great advance that Woolf makes here upon the method of *Jacob's Room* lies in this exploitation of memory to give characters and events a new depth of significance. Like Joyce, again, Woolf had now moved on from the portrayal of youth to the evocation of middle-aged awareness, in which memory looms larger than aspiration. For both authors, then, as for Ford Madox Ford, Aldous Huxley, and Jean Rhys after them, the psychological novel of maturity required a time-sense quite different from the linear narrative of the education novel; a design in which formative moments of earlier life are not narrated in biographical sequence but are summoned into the character's present thoughts by links of association appropriate to the dramatic occasion. A character's past, in other words, is not to be chronicled as a preamble but integrated into psychological actuality, selectively reimagined as fresh experiences call it to mind while transforming its meanings. In this way Clarissa Dalloway carries on shopping and making domestic preparations for her party while simultaneously reassessing the paths taken and not taken in her life, prompted by the reappearance of her long-absent admirer Peter Walsh, whom she might once have married, by thoughts of her husband Richard Dalloway MP, whom she might not have married, and by conversations with her daughter, a recurrent reminder of her own younger self.

Released from the restrictive 'egotism' of the *Bildungsroman* as it is from the narrow causalities of the traditional plotted novel, Woolf's *Mrs Dalloway* reveals its fictional world from numerous points of view: not just those of Clarissa and Septimus, or of their spouses, friends, or associates, but even of passing strangers whose only connection is that they are in London on that June day in 1923. One character will observe and assess another, only to be observed and assessed by another in turn, as the novel's perspective is passed on and exchanged like a ball in a game. While the novel stresses the isolation of Clarissa and her counterpart Septimus in their private thoughts (both are married yet sexually inactive and essentially solitary), at times it insists upon communal perception, as when people in various parts of London look up to watch the same aeroplane and its indecipherable skywriting. Clarissa and Septimus never meet, but the text links them covertly by symbolic echoes, culminating in the arrival of the suicide's spirit as the harbinger of Death and as the final unwelcome guest at Mrs Dalloway's soirée.

Mrs Dalloway is a novel that delves deeply into the tremulous privacy of its characters' passing thoughts, while also managing to suggest likenesses and permeabilities between one mind and another. The same is true of Woolf's next novel, *To the Lighthouse* (1927). Here the Olympian perspective enjoyed by the narrators of *Jacob's Room* and *Mrs Dalloway*, with its arbitrary power to pluck a stray detail from a cityscape or a domestic scene, is curtailed and confined to a short interlude entitled 'Time Passes'; in the much longer opening and closing sections of the novel, each set in a single day on the same Scottish island, we are immersed more consistently than ever before in the inner reflections of a group of characters. The action is, as before, plotless and almost eventless: in the first section, 'The

Window', the large Ramsay family and its varied guests are holidaying, and the young boy James Ramsay longs to take a boat trip to
the nearby lighthouse, but is put off by his father; in the interlude
the deaths of several characters, including the major figure of Mrs
Ramsay, are recorded; in the final section, 'The Lighthouse', some
of the survivors return ten years later, including James, who at last
reaches the lighthouse with his father and brother, while the artist
Lily Briscoe completes a painting she has been working on. Slender as this story is, it is nonetheless firmly novelistic, an account of
youthful desire deferred and finally fulfilled in the unsought shadow
of death and mutability. The substance of the book, though, lies
in the characters' interior monologues and meditations upon each
other; upon chaos, order, and art; and upon transience and permanence. That two of the characters, Mr Ramsay and his protégé
Charles Tansley, are philosophers assists in the evocation of such
larger themes, although the more likeable and important characters
turn out to be the artists: Lily Briscoe and her painting act as the
central focus of the final section while Mrs Ramsay, who is a kind
of artist of personal and domestic life, dominates the first section,
in which her *chef d'œuvre* is the family gathering at dinner. They
are seen to have recovered order from chaos through their gifts of
sympathy, distance, design, and balance, cultivated in a 'feminine'
mode that is contrasted with the 'masculine' analytic aridity of
Mr Ramsay. Their successes in these terms act also as a reflexive
commentary upon the ambitions of this novel itself, which exhibits
to the full Woolf's powers of sympathetic inwardness with a range
of characters, of distance from her familial memories (Mr and Mrs
Ramsay having been modelled in part on her parents), of formal
design, and of balance between the mentalities of male and female,
youth and age.

Novels that abandon external plotting in order to pitch us into
the eddying 'stream' of individual consciousness are particularly vulnerable to formal disintegration. The shapelessness of which many
readers complained in Richardson's *Pilgrimage* sequence is one
instance of the problem, and the almost random selection of scenes
in *Jacob's Room* is another. One of the qualities that raises *To the
Lighthouse* to a more convincing level of artistic achievement is that
it discovers an organizing principle in the use of a symbol around

which the flux of impressions may congregate into an implicit design: the lighthouse of the title serves variously as such a focus for scattered musings upon remoteness, indifference, illumination, and fulfilment, although it is never allowed in any fixed sense to 'stand for' any one of these ideas. The more boldly the modern novelist discarded the customary frameworks of plot or, in the education novel, of evolution, the more she or he was impelled to shape the novel into coherence around a central symbol or a larger scheme of symbolic oppositions. Such a symbolic method offered not only an alternative route to aesthetic organization but also a means, of vital significance to the psychological novel, for the evocation of non-rational dimensions of the mind. Woolf herself, in her 'Modern Fiction' essay, had predicted that for the emerging generation of novelists the new focus of interest would be 'in the dark places of psychology' (*The Essays*, vol. 4, p. 162). She did so in the knowledge that James Joyce was already exploring those dark places and mapping them with symbolic designs.

Joyce's lengthy novel *Ulysses* is distinguished from all previous novels by the outlandish schematism of its construction. Set on a single day (16 June 1904) in Dublin, the book is divided into eighteen chapters, each of which corresponds in some way with an episode in Homer's *Odyssey*; moreover, each chapter is written in a different style and alludes both to a 'key' symbol and to a different art or science, while most chapters also have their own symbolic colour scheme, hour of the day, and dominant organ of the body. This extravagantly pedantic plan was carefully leaked by Joyce to friendly critics and translators, appearing in Stuart Gilbert's book *James Joyce's 'Ulysses'* (1930) along with the Homeric titles ('Telemachus', 'Hades', 'Circe', and the rest) that are still used by Joycean commentators to designate what are in the text itself unnumbered and untitled chapters.[2] The construction of *Ulysses* betrays an obsessive craftsmanship that finds its formal and aesthetic justification in the abundance of the materials it is called upon to shape. Without some artificial framework of significance to hold them in place, the events, experiences, and thoughts that make up the story would constitute only a surfeit of everyday trivia. The same, of course, applies

[2] Two versions of Joyce's chapter scheme are reprinted as appendices to Jeri Johnson's Oxford edn. of *Ulysses*, at pp. 734–9.

to Woolf's post-Ulyssean novels. Joyce, though, astonishingly sets up not just one or two such frames of symbolic meaning, but several of them, overlaid and mutually illuminating, thereby stretching the limits of 'the novel' towards epic and encyclopedia at once.

I have remarked above that *Ulysses* represented for Joyce the momentous step from youthful education novel to narrative of middle-aged experience. In fact it contains and reworks its antecedents by enfolding Stephen Dedalus, the hero of *A Portrait*, into a new design in which he becomes a mythical 'son' paired with the mythical father-figure Leopold Bloom. At the literal level, Stephen already has a father but is dissatisfied with him, while Bloom mourns the real son who died in infancy some years before, and each is scarcely known to the other. The course of the narrative is plotted, though, as the slow convergence of these two men and of the opposed values they represent into a mock father–son reconciliation. Stephen is a failed medical student trudging idly around Dublin while nursing his literary pretensions, but he is also at the same time a modern counterpart of Odysseus' son Telemachus in search of his wandering father, and an Irish version of Prince Hamlet railing against usurpation, and even an embodiment of God the Son. The same superimposition of quotidian, Homeric, Shakespearian, and theological meanings bestows upon the Jewish advertising canvasser Leopold Bloom the multiple roles of cuckolded husband, long-suffering Odysseus, Old Hamlet/Shakespeare, and God the Father; and he assumes yet further guises in the phantasmagoric fifteenth ('Circe') chapter. Completing this parodic trinity is Bloom's unfaithful wife Molly, a professional singer who plays the travestied parts of Calypso/Penelope, Anne Hathaway/Gertrude, and the profane flesh rather than the Holy Spirit. Whereas Stephen's heroic arrogance had in *A Portrait* occupied the centre of attention, in *Ulysses* it is displaced by the more sympathetic humility of the middle-aged anti-hero. Stephen and his 'medieval abstruosities' (p. 45) dominate the first three chapters, and re-emerge ostentatiously in the ninth, but from the fourth chapter onward, it is the more rounded, experienced, resignedly tolerant, and 'modern' figure of Leopold Bloom that dominates the book. Bloom may appear at first as a comically inadequate version of Odysseus, but the purpose of Joyce's mock epic is not to ridicule him as a figure of modern cheapness by comparison with ancient grandeur. On the contrary, his humane flexibility and his average worldliness are preferred, notably in the twelfth ('Cyclops') chapter, to any available model of heroism.

While the modernist poets T. S. Eliot and Ezra Pound indulged the nostalgically dismissive satire typical of the mock-heroic genre, in which the inadequacies of 'low' subjects are highlighted by a 'grand' style, Joyce adopts in *Ulysses* the opposed—although intimately related—generic principle of burlesque or travesty, in which lofty subjects are stripped of their dignity in mundane surroundings and vernacular language. In this important respect, Joyce continues the levelling mission of nineteenth-century realism, which was to discover in 'ordinary' humanity a dignity equivalent to or higher than that of traditional heroism. Bloom is just the Man in the Street, but the novel persuades us that in his modern context his many-sidedness, his urban wanderings, and his canny evasions of danger are nonetheless Odyssean. As travesty, this book provides numerous belittlings of Homeric material, in which, for example, the Sirens become barmaids, and the boulder hurled at Odysseus by Polyphemus becomes a biscuit tin thrown at Bloom out of a pub. More pervasively still, it travesties the theology and the sacraments of the Church, starting from the very first page, in which a medical student performs a mock Eucharist with his shaving bowl, and climaxing in the thirteenth ('Nausicaa') chapter, in which a church service of supplication to the Virgin Mary is pointedly echoed by Bloom's masturbation at the sight of a teenage girl's underwear. Blasphemy reigns throughout, the sacred is collapsed into the profane, and the spirit is returned grossly to the flesh. Joyce conceived *Ulysses* as, among other things, an epic of the human body, and he pursued this somatic agenda to unprecedented lengths. His characters are more actively embodied than any in previous fiction: they yawn, sweat, belch, snore, sneeze, fart, chew, vomit, defecate, urinate, masturbate, menstruate, and pick their noses; and in set-piece chapters (the fourteenth and the sixth) they pass from gestation to birth and from death to decomposition. This relentless display of physical experience is vital to Joyce's purposes in *Ulysses*, including those of theological travesty (of the Word made Flesh), of unbridled realism, and of psychology.

Ulysses is much more than a 'psychological novel', which also means it is less than one. In several of its chapters, especially in the book's second half, we are not so much entering a state of mind as exploring various conditions of language and style, through parody and reverberant cliché. Although the final ('Penelope') chapter is a continuous interior monologue in 'stream-of-consciousness' style, and the fifteenth ('Circe') is presented in the form of a playscript, most of the story is given as third-person narrative, into which representations of the characters' fragmentary thoughts are woven. Psychological inwardness is to be found in more sustained form in *A Portrait of the Artist* than in this sequel. Despite all these qualifications, *Ulysses* offers the richest exhibition of psychological realism to be found in this period, partly because it is so corporeal and so crowded with indigestibly contingent materials. Mind is not permitted the kind of solo Icarian flight that it attempts in *A Portrait*, but is grounded and bedded in a continuous homecoming to the body, even the intellectual Stephen being obliged to accept in the third chapter the 'Ineluctable modality of the visible' (*Ulysses*, p. 37) and the universal fleshly bond of the navel. In comparison with the minds presented by other 'psychological' novelists, Joyce's are more convincingly earthbound, while those of Woolf, or of Huxley, or of Bowen, or of Sinclair, or especially (despite his theoretical commitment to the body) of Lawrence appear too often to be weightless luminosities innocent of flesh and blood.

Joyce's intermittent use of the stream-of-consciousness technique in *Ulysses* brings to life the novel's theological obsession with incarnation and reincarnation. It is not only more varied and less 'egotistical' than Dorothy Richardson's use of similar devices; it is also more closely adapted to the registration of embodied awareness and of the promptings of the flesh. The scene of Bloom's defecation quoted in Chapter 1 above provides one instance of this, while the whole of the eighth ('Lestrygonians') chapter is an extended exercise in the same vein: as Bloom wanders the streets, his thoughts about people he sees, or advertising gimmicks and slogans that he reads or recalls, constantly switch back involuntarily to food and drink, until he becomes aware that he is hungry and needs his midday meal. Predisposed to a sort of practical utopianism, he ponders the merits and disadvantages of communal kitchens, then of vegetarianism, before rehearsing, in a sequence of broken yet loosely associated phrases, the horrors of butchery:

Wretched brutes there at the cattlemarket waiting for the poleaxe to split their skulls open. Moo. Poor trembling calves. Meh. Staggering bob. Bubble and squeak. Butchers' buckets wobble lights. Give us that brisket off the hook. Plup. Rawhead and bloody bones. Flayed glasseyed sheep hung from their haunches, sheepsnouts bloodypapered snivelling nosejam on sawdust. Top and lashers going out. Don't maul them pieces, young one.

Hot fresh blood they prescribe for decline. Blood always needed. Insidious. Lick it up, smoking hot, thick sugary. Famished ghosts.

Ah, I'm hungry. (*Ulysses*, p. 163)

The passage is thick with the gore of Homeric sacrifice, but it also represents modern urban man in his quest for lunch, his mind hopping among remembered sights and sounds, commonplace sayings, and immediate sensations, before recognizing its shaping bodily needs.

As we have noted in the case of Woolf, *Ulysses* exerted an important influence upon some novelists; but it did not lure many others into Joycean methods, nor redraw the map of psychological fiction in the Twenties. The predominant form of such fiction remained the realistic education novel, usually tracing the emotional development of a young hero or heroine, as in Rosamond Lehmann's early novels, or those of Radclyffe Hall, whose *The Unlit Lamp* (1924) explores mother–daughter conflicts, and whose widely acclaimed *Adam's Breed* (1926) follows the spiritual growth of a boy born into London's Italian community. A secondary development, matching the shift in Joyce's, Woolf's, and Bennett's fiction from youthful to middle-aged subjects, was a kind of education novel examining a phase of life later than the coming-of-age crisis. One of the most ambitious works of this kind is John Cowper Powys's *Wolf Solent* (1928), a very long narrative about a teacher in his mid-thirties entering upon a failed marriage while nursing a hopeless and chaste passion for another woman. This, at least, is the central plot of the book, woven into several sub-plots, but its substance lies in the hero's prolonged bouts of brooding self-analysis, his mystical encounters with the landscape and vegetation of Dorset, his painful abandonment of solipsistic illusions and crude moral simplicities. Although the story is told in an often inflated romantic style and always from the hero's point of view, its underlying realist design is confirmed by its concluding note of disillusionment and resigned acceptance.

Although a redirection of interest from the psychological to the sociological is clearly to be seen among many novelists of the Thirties, this was not and could never have been a complete reversal. Novels devoted to the scrutiny of subjective moods and states were inevitably still appearing, by Bowen and Lehmann, among others; while Aldous Huxley swam against the tide, away from public satire and towards private introspection. His sixth novel, *Eyeless in Gaza* (1936), is, significantly, about a sociologist who is obliged to confront the problems of his own psychological formation. This book absorbs several influences from modern psychological fiction, notably from Proust, Joyce, Lawrence, and the broader *Bildungsroman* tradition. It is a formally splintered education novel, one that reconstructs the early life of its protagonist, Anthony Beavis, in piecemeal flashbacks framed by incidents and diaries of his mid-life crisis in the fictional present. The action starts in 1933 with Beavis on his forty-second birthday looking over a set of family photographs and cursing the name of Marcel Proust—a repudiation of Memory that in fact signals the novel's commitment to Proustian interpenetrations of past and present. The achronological sequence of chapters that follows, interleaving episodes from 1902–3, 1926, and 1912 with diaries from 1934, suggests that Beavis has reshuffled his snapshots, possibly in an evasive shirking of self-knowledge ('only disconnect' might be his motto). We are then given in the twelfth chapter an unforgettable symbolic event that propels Beavis out of his self-protective denials: as he and his young mistress Helen Ledwidge sunbathe naked—we are back to his birthday again, spent on the French Riviera,—a dead dog dropped from a passing aeroplane lands next to them, covering them in its blood. Helen is horror-struck, Beavis coolly unsympathetic, and the startling incident, a symbolic expulsion of the naked Adam and Eve from Eden, ends their affair. As we continue through the sequence of temporally jumbled episodes from six distinct phases of Beavis's life, connections among them become increasingly apparent, and the pattern of his self-inflicted moral blindness (hence the title) up to 1933 and his new-found vision from 1934 emerges. Crucial episodes that have been withheld—notably the young Beavis's betrayal of his friend Brian Foxe, leading to the latter's suicide in 1914—provide delayed illumination towards the close. Most readers have found the diaries dated 1934–5, recording Beavis's conversion to the pacifist mysticism of his guru, Dr Miller, the least satisfactory parts of the book. More impressive is the artfully non-linear unfolding of Beavis's early life, with its powerful shames and repugnances, its debilitating splits between mind and body. Here again we have the material of the *Bildungsroman*, but released from simple evolutionary patterns and intelligently transmuted by mature retrospective analysis.

Eyeless in Gaza is an original novel, but Huxley could not have written such a book without having learned both from the flourishing of the education novel in the 1910–19 period and from the phase of modernist experiment that followed it. His combination of familiar materials with innovatory time schemes is one major example of an important permeability and interchange between 'traditional' and 'experimental' kinds of fiction in the Thirties, but it is far from unique in this. The temporal dislocations of Christopher Isherwood's *The Memorial* (1932), of Elizabeth Bowen's *The House in Paris*, and of Jean Rhys's *Good Morning, Midnight* (1939) could be invoked here, as could the phantasmagoric third chapter of George Orwell's *A Clergyman's Daughter* (1935) and some passages of interior monologue and disconnected reverie in the early novels of Grahame Greene. Although it has often been implied that modernist literary techniques are in some way so revolutionary or subversive that they cannot be accommodated within more conventional kinds of narrative, the evidence of Thirties fiction tends to point the other way. New ways of representing the activities of the mind could quite quickly be adapted to enhance the psychological dimensions of realist novels or even of genre fiction. Interior monologue, for example, can be found plentifully in such a solidly realistic novel as Winifred Holtby's *South Riding* (1936), where every major character is overheard musing in this form. The device even shows up in Dorothy L. Sayers's detective adventure *The Nine Tailors* (1934), when Lord Peter Wimsey's thoughts ramble disconnectedly in stream-of-consciousness fashion (pp. 87–9). It is a sign of healthy cross-fertilization, and equally of widespread interest in matters psychological in the fiction of this period that such initially disconcerting techniques should have been assimilated so readily into the mainstream.

10

Modern Romance, Fable, and Historical Fiction

New Words, 1910–1940

*age-old   anti-self   extra-sensory   fantasist
moonscape   nightscape   paranormal   pie-in-the-sky
primitivism   Shangri-La   surrealism*

In the previous three chapters, developments in the art of the novel have been presented according to a commonly accepted division between fictions of social or 'external' action, mostly realistic in method, and fictions of psychological inwardness, some of them experimental in narrative structure and perspective. As we have noted, there are oversights and distortions involved in such a partition of prose fiction into two distinct continents marked on our map as 'realism' and 'modernism'. One of these problems may be clarified by remarking that the opposite of realism is not modernism; it is, as it has been for centuries, romance, or fantasy, or fable. The preoccupation of literary critics and historians with struggles between realism and modernism, or between social and psychological tendencies in fiction, has its justifications, but it occludes the existence of a third continent of modern fiction that lies beyond both territories: the broad zone of the fabulous, the eccentric, the remote, the fanciful, and the exotic; in short, *romance*. This chapter offers a brief survey of modern romance in its more original forms (popular romances of love and adventure will be considered in Chapter 13). By its nature, this realm of romance and fable is highly variegated, full of freakish surprises. My survey here divides these oddities into four groups, beginning with narratives of holiday escapade or exotic truancy; moving on through a few unusual historical novels; then to more wildly fantastical stories of ghosts, angelic visitations, and humanized animals; and finally to mystical and visionary romances.

Romances of Truancy

There is a modest, semi-realistic kind of romance that releases its characters from routine into colourful adventure without offending its readers' sense of probability. Leading us from the kitchen or office out into the fairground, it offers a holiday from the imprisoning conditions of everyday existence, along with a measure of protest against them. Two such successful prose romances of vagrancy, both clearly indebted to Charles Dickens, are H. G. Wells's *The History of Mr Polly* (1910) and J. B. Priestley's *The Good Companions* (1929). Each provides an image of liberation in triplicate, with Wells presenting his individual hero's escape in three successive phases, each bolder than the last, and Priestley coordinating the awakenings of three different characters. *The History of Mr Polly* concerns the discontents of a small-town shopkeeper who has in his youth sought adventure by taking weekend excursions in the country, and has later graduated to extended romantic holidaying upon inheriting some money from his father. Now unhappily married and failing in business, Alfred Polly plans a final escape through suicide, but is in the event strangely reborn: having set fire to his shop, he rescues a deaf neighbour from the flames, becoming a local hero. Now that his wife can manage on the insurance money, he feels free to set off once more upon rural wanderings, fetching up at a peaceful riverside inn where he settles as odd-job man and companion to the landlady. In a final heroic struggle Alfred disposes both of the landlady's violently threatening nephew and of his own former self, as he is mistakenly declared dead when the nephew is found drowned in Mr Polly's clothes. This is a modern fantasy of escape in which Mr Polly manages not only to walk away from business, marriage, and even his civic identity, but also to bask in that 'Georgian' paradise, an English country pub.

Priestley's *The Good Companions* similarly expands the weekend countryside excursion into a fuller voyage of self-discovery for its three principal characters, a middle-aged working-class Yorkshire-man, a West Country spinster in her thirties, and a young school-master. All three have for different reasons walked away from the restrictions of their previous lives and taken to the road. Eventually their paths converge in the east Midlands, where they surprise them-selves by jointly rescuing a failed theatrical troupe. The shabby world of seaside piers and boarding houses through which they now move is both depressing and at the same time magical, an enchanted route towards self-realization in marriage, professional success, or emigra-tion. Each has been fortified and expanded by the comradeship of the concert-party troupe, and released into life by the 'wonderland' of the footlights. This romance of the stage recaptures some of the atmosphere of Dickens's *Nicholas Nickleby* (1838–9); and so, in a different style, does Ronald Firbank's shorter novel *Caprice* (1917), which similarly enacts an escape into the world of theatre.

Modern romance of this kind takes as its central action a truan-cy from the repetitive dullness of everyday life. A further example of this pattern is provided by W. Somerset Maugham's *The Moon and Sixpence* (1919), which tells the tale, loosely based on Paul Gauguin's life, of an apparently dull English stockbroker who aban-dons his wife and children in order to become an artist in Paris and eventually in Tahiti. Again in H. M. Tomlinson's *Gallions Reach: A Romance* (1927), a shipping clerk who has languished in a City of London office for years suddenly lashes out at his bullying employer, inadvertently knocking him dead, and runs away to sea, ending up in Malaya. Some romances, though, adopt more exotic or fantastical forms of truancy. Sylvia Townsend Warner's *Lolly Willowes* (1926), for example, at first resembles other spinster novels of the period in recounting the uneventful life of its protagonist as a maiden aunt living with her brother's family in London. In its later chapters, how-ever, the book veers off into the realms of the fabulous, as Laura Willowes decides after twenty years of monotony to decamp alone to a small village, where she is initiated into a local witches' coven; she ends the book as a happily liberated convert to rural satanism, holding conversations with the Devil himself. Laura Willowes's romantic wonderland is a village in Buckinghamshire; but the more common and traditional destination for the truants of romance was the enchanted isle. F. Tennyson Jesse's pirate romance *Moonraker* (1927), for instance, has a runaway hero who witnesses the 1802 slave revolt on San Domingo, while Rose Macaulay's *Orphan Island* (1924) takes its Victorian castaways to the South Pacific, where they have to reinvent society without a bible. John Buchan's *The Dancing Floor* (1926), again, is a romance set on the imaginary Greek island of 'Plakos', a land charged with the mystery of ancient rites and pagan superstitions. Norman Douglas's *South Wind* (1917) likewise summons up the paganism of the Mediterranean in the island setting of 'Nepenthe' (based on Capri), where a visiting Anglican bishop becomes so charmed by the 'frolicsome perversity' of the place that he abandons his faith in favour of Nepenthe's 'pantheistic benevolence' (ch. 39). As in *Lolly Willowes*, the change of scene involves a spiritual conversion from Christian respectability to pagan energy.

Sylvia Townsend Warner herself returned in her next novel, *Mr Fortune's Maggot* (1927), to the same subject, this time in the more remote setting of a volcanic Polynesian island. Here an English missionary, the Revd Timothy Fortune, arrives in the hope of bringing the Gospel and decent clothing to a population of happy idolaters who plainly have no need of either. Fortune makes no converts apart from the beautiful adolescent boy Lueli, whom he adopts; but Lueli is in fact carrying on his idol-worship in secret—a discovery that leads the missionary, after an earthquake and volcanic eruption, to lose his own faith and even to carve a new idol for his protégé. The Englishman has been won over by the paradisal innocence of the ever-hospitable islanders, and now regards his failed mission as an unjustifiable intrusion on behalf of a culture whose false claim to superiority is finally exposed by news of the outbreak of the Great War. The central event of this romance, then, is another case of reversed conversion in which the trappings of Christian respectability are cast away as unwanted burdens.

A similar process of unconversion characterizes one of the few positively utopian romances of this period, James Hilton's *Lost Horizon* (1933). This book offers fascinating glimpses into the fears and dreams of a generation forced by the shock of the Great War

Fig. 6. Photo-portrait of Sylvia Townsend Warner in 1930
by Cecil Beaton.

to revise its moral and spiritual bearings. Its narrative acts out an escape from the violence of modern history into the sanctuary of 'Shangri-La', a virtually inaccessible valley in the Tibetan Himalayas governed by an unusual monastery. It levitates its central characters—two young British diplomats, a female missionary, and an American financial swindler—out of a revolutionary uprising in central Asia by means of an airlift that crash-lands the four westerners in Shangri-La, where the hospitable monks evade questions about getting them home. It emerges from conversations between the war-veteran hero, Hugh Conway, and the monastery's High Lama that the new arrivals are guests for life, since Shangri-La has a secret that it cannot risk divulging to a dangerous world outside: miraculous longevity (the High Lama, originally a Catholic missionary from Luxembourg, is at least two hundred years old) achieved by spiritual self-discipline and moderation in all things. By guarding its secret, along with an impressive collection of books and art-works gathered from around the world, Shangri-La hopes to serve as a repository of human culture that will survive the impending self-destruction of the outside world. Anointed as the High Lama's chosen successor, Conway is on the point of assuming the mantle of world-saviour when he makes the disastrous error of agreeing to assist his junior colleague Captain Mallinson—the only newcomer not reconciled to staying in this happy valley for ever—in an escape attempt; after which he is last seen trying to find his way back to Shangri-La. The book's central appeal lies in its dream of an oasis sheltered from world conflagration and cultivating a temperate ecumenical wisdom; but in the opposed figures of Conway and Mallinson it also tries significantly to replace outdated models of heroism with a more modern ideal. From the opening episodes, Mallinson emerges as an unthinkingly impatient English public-school type, constantly irritable in his sense of racial superiority to the orientals. Regarding Conway with boyish hero-worship for his bravery in the initial evacuation, he cannot understand his superior's passive acceptance of their kidnap and imprisonment by lazy foreigners. He has, though, misunderstood the true character of Conway, who is in fact 'not genuinely one of those resolute, strong-jawed, hammer-and-tongs empire-builders' (*Lost Horizon*, ch. 4), but more of a contemplative mystic, sceptical enough about his own culture to reject the restless striving of westerners in favour of what they dismiss too readily as oriental 'indolence': partly as a result of his experiences in the Great War, he agrees with the Shangri-La monks that 'slacking', a vice according to Mallinson's code, should rather be regarded as a virtue (ch. 9). He becomes indeed another convert to non-western values. The setting of *Lost Horizon*, then, may be as exotic as the romance reader could wish, but its central issue lies closer to home, in a struggle over the soul of English masculinity and the meaning of its heroic ideals.

The case of *Lost Horizon*, like those of *Mr Fortune's Maggot*, *The Moon and Sixpence*, and *Gallions Reach*, or even that of *The Good Companions*, may serve to clarify the essential purposes animating the modern romance of exotic escape. A purely formalist critical approach might suggest that the value of literary romance and fantasy lies in its repudiation of the artificial codes of realist fiction, although it would commonly fail to identify the substantial point of such a gesture. The most serious romance writers of this period, however, clearly nursed ambitions among which the mere challenging of an aesthetic convention had only a trivial place. We risk 'romanticizing' romance if we cast it as an underground movement of imaginative liberation for its own sake. It is preferable to see it as a parallel fictional realm in which the social complexities of realism are set aside the better to isolate (often literally, to place upon an island) certain moral or spiritual ideals and to put these to the test. In the aftermath of the nineteenth-century 'death of God', the spiritual values most often scrutinized by modern romance writers were those of established Christianity. A recurrent narrative design of modern romance requires the Christian—or like-minded 'western'—protagonist to undergo a literal or metaphorical divestment, a shedding of ill-fitting garments, and so to step out newly released into an acceptance of pagan sensuality or of 'oriental' spirituality. This pattern of symbolic disrobing can be seen in the fictional careers of Lolly Willowes, of the Revd Timothy Fortune, of the Bishop of Bampopo in *South Wind*, and, in bizarrely literal form, of the eponymous Spanish archbishop in Ronald Firbank's romance *Concerning the Eccentricities of Cardinal Pirelli* (1926), who ends up naked except for his mitre, chasing a pretty choirboy around his cathedral by night. It is found frequently too in D. H. Lawrence's fictions of the 1920s, many of which are clearly romances of exotic escape and religious conversion from the tyrannies of the spirit to the 'dark gods' of the body. A prolonged sequence of fictional truancies begins in the final chapters of *Women in Love* (1920) with Ursula and Birkin throwing up their jobs and dashing to the Alps; it continues in *Aaron's Rod* (1922), in which a colliery worker abandons his job and his marriage, drifting to Italy as an itinerant flautist; and it reaches a 'dark' extreme in the Mexican setting of *The Plumed Serpent* (1926), where an Irish widow becomes involved in the pagan cult of Quetzalcoatl. His shorter fictions of the same period show a similar inclination to romance, notably in the semi-mythological tale 'The Ladybird' (1923) and in 'St Mawr' (1925), in which a married woman rejects her husband and elopes with his horse. The abandonment of false western spirituality in favour of sun-worship and other ancient rites is figured as a literal disrobing in the short stories 'The Woman Who Rode Away' (1925) and 'Sun' (1928), and again in 'The Escaped Cock' (1929), in which the resurrected Jesus of Nazareth repudiates his former denial of the body and fathers a child upon a devotee of Osiris. Where previous romancers had Anglican bishops or missionaries shedding their faith, Lawrence here outdoes them by making Christ himself a convert.

Historical Novels

Lawrence's apparent blasphemy in 'The Escaped Cock' was foreshadowed in an unexpected bestseller by the elderly Irish-born novelist George Moore: *The Brook Kerith* (1916) is a historical fiction in which Jesus has not died on the cross but has been secretly rescued from it and nursed back to health by Joseph of Arimathea, whose narrative of these events makes up most of the story. In the final chapters, Jesus, who has been living obscurely as a shepherd, encounters St Paul, telling him that he now regards his former claim to be the Messiah as blasphemous madness, and rebuking Paul for his fanaticism. Moore's book is unusual in that it poses the spiritual questions familiar to modern romance, but in a form partly resembling the historical novel. A similar hybrid is L. H. Myers's sequence of fictions beginning with *The Near and the Far* (1929): these are novels of ideas in which the nature of spiritual fulfilment is debated in a setting that is ostensibly Mughal India of the sixteenth century, although the intellectual problems can be recognized as those of modern Bloomsbury or Cambridge.

Historical fiction proper, in the traditions of Walter Scott and Alexandre Dumas, has only a minor place in the serious literature of this period. There were indeed several important family-saga novels chronicling recent times, as we saw in Chapter 8; but the fictional study of a particular historical crisis in which typical characters are entangled was not often attempted, except at the relatively trivial level of the 'costume' melodrama or popular historical romance in which history becomes a decorative backdrop to courtship. Hugely favoured in the nineteenth century, the historical novel had before the Great War exhausted itself in the 'Ruritanian' escapism of Anthony Hope's *The Prisoner of Zenda* (1894) and its numerous imitators. In Elizabeth Bowen's *The Last September* (1929), one character recalls 'that she had cried for a whole afternoon before the War because she was not someone in a historical novel' (ch. 9), thus neatly identifying the genre with childishness and with pre-War innocence at the same time. By the 1920s, historical fiction had become associated with the laziest forms of 'escapist' daydreaming: Miss Trant in Priestley's *The Good Companions*, for example, is addicted to historical novels because they give her a colourful respite from the dull routine she treads before embarking on her own adventures.

Among the few novels of this time that lead us credibly into some remote historical moment are Robert Graves's *I, Claudius* and its sequel *Claudius the God* (both 1934). Surprisingly successful in commercial terms, these books brought to life for the modern reader the world of the early Roman Empire through a feat of narrative impersonation in which the Emperor Claudius tells his own story, first recounting the bloody dynastic feuds from which he emerged unexpectedly as emperor, then detailing the successes and failures of his reign. Graves gives his narrator's voice the authentically moralistic and superstitious flavour of the Roman historians—Suetonius, Tacitus, and others—from whom he derives the story. Whereas these early sources portray Claudius as idiotic and cruel, though, Graves reverses their bias by casting him as a well-meaning man who has survived by hiding his true shrewdness behind a mask of stupidity. By contrast with the protagonists of most kinds of historical fiction, this Claudius is markedly unheroic: a bookish stammering weakling with a limp, he appears more as a witness and observer than as a historical actor. His timidity and passivity reflect a 'modern' anti-heroic tendency in Graves's approach to historical fiction, one that also permits the abandonment of the traditionally strong plot. In these two novels, indeed, plot in the narrative sense is replaced by a series of tangled political conspiracies, of such complexity that they require the provision of a fold-out family tree. The narrative resembles, appropriately enough for a supposed 'secret history', a disorded and digressive chronicle rather than a coherent novel; but what it lacks in formal design it makes up for in vivid reconstruction of a remote world in all its strangeness and cruelty.

The world of the Claudius novels is coloured by an element of misogynist dread which casts the Emperor as a victim of the treacherous arch-villainesses Livia, his scheming grandmother, and Messalina, his adulterous wife. An alternative vision of the ancient world seen largely through the eyes of women was available, though, in the work of the socialist-feminist author Naomi Mitchison, an even more industrious and scrupulous student of ancient history than Graves. Mitchison set her historical novels and tales at the questionable boundaries between civilization and barbarism, viewing the empires of the remote past from the viewpoint of the 'barbarian' outsider. Her first novel, *The Conquered* (1923), describes Julius Caesar's invasion of Gaul from the viewpoint of a young Celtic rebel; her second, *Cloud Cuckoo Land* (1925) has its heroine abducted from an Aegean island in the fifth century BCE and taken as a captive wife to Athens, where her husband makes her kill one of their babies because it is a mere girl. Mitchison's major work in this vein is the long romance *The Corn King and the Spring Queen* (1931), a book strongly marked by its author's immersion in J. G. Frazer's anthropological studies of vegetation cults and mystery religions. Continuing here her own fictional investigation of women and power, Mitchison takes her heroine upon a quest for self-healing through three contrasting societies in the Hellenistic world of the third century BCE, starting at the Scythian borderlands by the Black Sea, proceeding to a Sparta riven by political revolution, and thence to the urban decadence of Alexandria. The Spring Queen of the title, Erif Der, is a young witch torn by divided loyalties to her father and to her husband Tarrik, the priestly Corn King who symbolically inseminates her at the annual fertility ritual. Having taken her husband's side, she is punished by her father's murder of her first-born child, and takes her revenge by killing her father in turn, whereupon she loses her magical power to revive the crops. Through the remaining six years of the action, bewilderingly complex as it sometimes becomes (Mitchison supplies a family tree and a summary at the end of each section to explain what has been happening), runs the thread of the exiled Erif's search for purgation and renewal, achieved partially through the worship of the mother-goddess Isis, and eventually after a consolatory vision of her dead mother. Meanwhile the revolutionaries of Sparta have been defeated, betrayed, and sacrificed, but are finally transfigured into the objects of a new proto-Christian cult. This is one of the most ambitious long fictions of the period, based upon sustained research and upon widely varied interests in Hellenic history, art, philosophy, politics, and religion. It has its shortcomings, notably in its somewhat unresolved ending, but its imaginative scope makes most other historical novels look pallid.

It is significant that both Graves and Mitchison achieved outstanding success with works that take the reader back to the 'barbaric' cruelties and religious diversities of the ancient world. While the costume-romancers encouraged their readers to lie back and think of Regency England or of Napoleonic France, Graves and Mitchison enticed theirs into more challenging encounters with unfamiliar customs, languages, and modes of belief, propelling them beyond the merely colourful past of modern European Christendom into realms of violent strangeness. There remains, to be sure, an element of escapism in their appeal, but in serious historical fiction of the Thirties it tends to double back upon the contemporary moment of political menace. Graves and Mitchison both write about living in dangerous times of war, tyranny, and revolution; and so too do Sylvia Townsend Warner in *Summer Will Show* (1936) and Rose Macaulay in *They Were Defeated* (1932), although in more modern English and French settings. *Summer Will Show*, like Warner's earlier books, takes its protagonist on a self-revelatory journey out of a stiflingly conventional existence and into a realm of danger and beauty: this time we follow a young aristocrat, Sophia Willoughby, who sets out from her Dorset estate to seek her errant husband in

Paris in 1848, where she witnesses the February and June revolutions of that year, falls in love with her husband's Jewish ex-mistress Minna, and joins the nascent Communist movement—a trajectory that mirrors Warner's own conversion to Communist activism in the mid-Thirties.

Macaulay's *They Were Defeated* is exclusively English in setting and more conservative in politics, although it makes a clearly feminist case for women's education. Set in Devon and Cambridge on the eve of the English Civil War during the winter of 1640–1, the book has as its heroine the 15-year-old girl Julian Conybeare, whose father, an atheistic physician, has her educated by the clergyman-poet Robert Herrick, one of an implausible number of real literary figures encountered in the developing plot. Julian has two brothers, one of whom has become a Puritan, the other converting to the clandestine Roman Catholic faith; and this familial split mirrors the accelerating division of England and its Church into implacably opposed camps, between which the moderate Royalist Anglicanism of Julian, of her tutor, and of her seducer (the 'Cavalier' poet John Cleveland, who cruelly mocks her intellectual ambitions) will be crushed. The situation, so described, may appear conventional, but Macaulay's handling of it removes this book from the category of light reading to which most historical romances belong. The dialogue is thick with religious, political, and philosophical disputation, all rendered in convincing seventeenth-century English, some of it in almost impenetrable Devonshire dialect: the alleged witch Moll Prowse typically exclaims 'Dowl's come vor Miggle, dowl ull vet mun vore cockleert, hey go. Gar' (*They Were Defeated*, ch. 14). Not just the dialogue but the narrative itself is conducted in period style, so that the reader is obliged to work hard but is rewarded by a fuller absorption into the theological-political mentality of the times.

Historical fiction offered to a number of feminist authors between the wars an opportunity to explore the variety of ways in which women could live their lives, outside the currently legitimate roles of respectable femininity, while also implicitly likening contemporary anti-feminism with the discarded tyrannies of past ages. The serious efforts of Warner, Mitchison, and Macaulay in this field have tended recently to be overshadowed by the celebrity of Virginia Woolf's romance *Orlando* (1928), a more playful work that lies closer to the 'costume' escapade than to the scholarly recreation of a historical moment. The fantastical devices for which *Orlando* is celebrated are the longevity of the protagonist—first seen as a courtier to Queen Elizabeth I, but still youthfully alive in 1928—and the moment nearly halfway through the book when he wakes up transformed into a woman, although still essentially the same person. These devices allow Woolf to conduct a spoof pageant of English history incorporating both masculine and feminine perspectives, along with a parody of biographical and historical narratives that mocks their certainties and solemnities. We may be tempted now to read *Orlando* as a serious or even 'subversive' critique of gendered identity, but this would overlook the whimsical, high-spirited tone of the book, which is a jocular celebration of Woolf's then lover Vita Sackville-West, her country estate at Knole, and the enduring aristocratic spirit of her family. Orlando's longevity here represents, quite unsubversively, the continuity of the English nobility, its unbroken devotion to dogs, gardens, and poetry, its survival through the dark night of Victorian middle-class puritanism, its undiminished glamour.

Fabulous Romances

Orlando takes us from historical romance into the realm of fantastical and fabulous fiction. Here we can do little more than touch upon a few notable curiosities in this category, starting with a rapid review of the kinds of fantasy being published in the earlier years of our period. The strong and varied Victorian and Edwardian traditions of fantastical writing survive into the post-Edwardian years, in such outlandish romances as J. E. Flecker's *The King of Alsander* (1914), in which a bored grocer's son travels in search of adventure and is eventually installed upon the throne of a remote kingdom of the 'Ruritanian' kind with the help of a royal heiress who has fallen in love with him. G. K. Chesterton meanwhile followed up a cycle of popular Edwardian romances about threatened invasions of England with his book *The Flying Inn* (1914), in which a Muslim government has taken control of the land and closed most of its pubs; the Irish rebel hero, armed with an inn-sign and a keg of rum, leads an insurrection of boozers against the killjoy regime. A fabulous form of historical romance based upon time-travelling was adopted ingeniously in Ford Madox Hueffer's *Ladies Whose Bright Eyes: A Romance* (1910). Here a man of the present day is concussed in a train crash, appears to wake up in the fourteenth century amid a bitter struggle among knights and jousting ladies over a precious crucifix, and finally awakens in the present time to recognize his feudal paramour as the nurse who tended him through his coma. A slightly different kind of narrative time-warping was used by Walter de la Mare in *The Return* (1910), dimly echoing the dual-personality theme of R. L. Stevenson's *Dr Jekyll and Mr Hyde* (1886): the unremarkable protagonist dozes off by the gravestone of an eighteenth-century French libertine who had committed suicide, and awakens now possessed by the Frenchman's passionate spirit and by his bodily appearance; he gradually recovers his looks, but his sense of selfhood has been shaken irrecoverably.

After the War, de la Mare adopted more boldly the perspective of the estranged misfit in his *Memoirs of a Midget* (1921), the fictional autobiography of an impossibly tiny woman, Miss M., set in Victorian times. Miss M. is orphaned, then brought up in the household of a former servant, where she falls in love with Fanny, the beautiful but heartless daughter of the house, while also being courted vainly, during her secret forays into the enchanted garden, by a mysterious dwarf called Mr Anon, who later dies while trying to rescue her from the indignity of being exhibited in a circus. The story evokes an old-fashioned 'faerie' delicacy, but still creates its own nightmare world of suicidal despair and masochistic violence, in such disturbing scenes as Miss M.'s vision of death in the shape of a maggot-infested mole, or her burial of a bloodstained nightgown after being scratched by a cat. Angela Carter, introducing the 1982 Oxford edition, committed a forgivable exaggeration in suggesting that *Memoirs of a Midget* could be regarded as 'the one true and only successful English surrealist novel' (p. xiv). It could be better described as a romance of incurable unworldly isolation, at the end of which the narrator is mysteriously 'called away' (p. 5), we know not where.

Memoirs of a Midget is far from unique in this irreversible estrangement of its heroine from human normality. Several other romances of the Twenties and Thirties take us across the boundaries separating the human from the inhuman, and give us a view of *Homo sapiens* seen by some absolute outsider. Edith Olivier's *The Love Child* (1927), for example, offers a fabulous variant upon the spinster novel of the period, bringing to visible life the figure of an Imaginary Friend conjured up from the desperate loneliness of a solitary unmarried woman in a West Country village. Following her mother's death, the 32-year-old Agatha Bodenham revives the memory and the living presence of the fantasized playmate she had in childhood, an elfin, semi-transparent 11-year-old girl she calls Clarissa. As this delightful companion in make-believe games grows up, though, she craves the tangible excitements of motor cars and of boys; when kissed by a real-life admirer, Clarissa vanishes whence she came, tipping Agatha into insanity. An oddly similar female figure, otherworldly, translucent, and asexual, appears in Herbert Read's *The Green Child* (1935), a romance whose central section offers a first-person account of the founding of a utopian state in nineteenth-century South America by an Englishman, Olivero. The opening and closing sections of the story, however, are quite different, telling the story of the disenchanted Olivero's return to his native English village, his following of an upward-flowing stream, and his encounter with the uncanny girl, Siloën, who leads him into a subterranean paradise in which both eventually achieve the transcendence of crystalline petrifaction.

Olivier's Clarissa and Read's Siloën are both sylphs from the Beyond. Other romancers arrived at a different order of strangeness by transforming women into animals, or animals into women. David Garnett's *Lady into Fox* (1922) tells the story of a genteel Victorian couple, Richard and Silvia Tebrick, in rural Oxfordshire a few months after their marriage. Out walking one day, they see fox-hunters and hounds in the distance, whereupon Silvia (née Fox) suddenly and literally turns into a vixen, speechless but capable of communicating by gesture. The rest of the tale recounts Richard's adjustment to his wife's new condition as she becomes increasingly feral, to the point of coupling with a dog-fox and producing a litter of cubs before she is finally killed by a pack of hounds. There is a delicate pathos in Mr Tebrick's uxorious loyalty and indulgence, which leads him even to overcome his religious scruples in extenuating her 'adultery' with the dog-fox. The pathos is balanced and enhanced by the comically straight-faced Victorian respectability of the narrative voice, which assures us that Silvia's cleanliness and strict Protestant rectitude have survived her metamorphosis: she may have difficulty in maintaining her table manners, but she has at least not sunk to popery or card-playing. *Lady into Fox* is a modern kind of beast-fable, one that debars the talking animals of Aesop or of Beatrix Potter and that declines to announce its own meaning in the form of a 'moral' message. The nearest it comes to such a declaration is when Mr Tebrick overcomes his jealousy after Silvia gives birth to her cubs, telling himself that 'she does right to be happy according to the laws of her being' (p. 70), thereby endorsing a liberal 'Bloomsbury' ethic in which the eccentricities of a spouse or friend must be shielded from a hostile public world of fox-hunters.

A similar fabulous device is employed in John Collier's *His Monkey Wife; or, Married to a Chimp* (1930), a more adventurous and sardonic narrative whose heroine, Emily, is a highly intelligent self-educated African chimpanzee. Devoted to an English school-master, Mr Alfred Fatigay, but physically unable to speak her love, she travels with him from the Congo to England, where he is to marry a frivolously heartless girl, Amy; but in an extraordinary sequence of adventures, she outwits and exposes Amy, becomes wealthy as a professional dancer, and returns to Africa as Fatigay's wife. These events are seen almost entirely from Emily's point of view, the reader being made privy (as the unappealing human characters are not) to her secret resources of book-learning, insight, and integrity. The resulting perspective mixes misanthropic satire with sly parody of popular romances in which Love triumphs over Adversity. In certain ways, *His Monkey Wife* reverses the fabulous basis of Garnett's *Lady into Fox*: it ends happily, with the human and the animal united maritally, and it looks into human society through the eyes of the animal outsider. Despite this, the two stories share a common reticence which keeps their meanings close to their furry chests. *His Monkey Wife* could be an allegory of humanity's loss of emotional honesty in its descent from apedom, or a feminist parable about the blind condescension of men to women, but finally it seems to be enjoying itself too much to permit such solemn interpretations.

Before leaving the animal kingdom, we should take note of one writer who took the beast-centred narrative beyond the framework of the fable, let alone the romance or novel. Henry Williamson's animal books of this period—*The Peregrine's Saga* (1923), *Tarka the Otter* (1927), and *Salar the Salmon* (1935)—are fictional renderings of natural history in which the life cycle and habitat of the central creature are described and evoked in the form of an unfolding story. Apart from the giving of names to these animals, anthropomorphic devices such as conversation or narration (as in Anna Sewell's horse-autobiography for children, *Black Beauty* (1877)) are avoided. In the most famous of these works, *Tarka the Otter*, there are no dialogues or even verbal utterances apart from the incidental curses and cries of poachers and huntsmen, human beings having been relegated to the position of malevolent predators. All the rest is description and recorded action, the principal drama in *Tarka* being the prolonged contest between the otter and his enemy, the hunting-dog Deadlock.

Visionary Romances

A fourth and final variety of prose romance remains to be considered here, a sub-genre in which the reader is neither transported to exotic islands nor projected into an imagined past or future, nor confronted by other-worldly sylphs or fabulous beasts, but seems to be placed among human beings in a credible present-day setting. This realistic appearance is then disturbed by the irruption of uncanny influences or mystic vibrations, so that the accepted novelistic boundaries between human and inhuman, or between archaic and modern, are unsettlingly eroded. This kind of romance, whether we call it mystical, visionary, or apocalyptic, typically adopts symbolic, allegorical, intuitive, and 'mythic' methods of evocation and suggestion, irradiating its action with occult significance. It is a rare type, but a few major examples from the Twenties and early Thirties demand attention.

The most celebrated of these, although usually classed as a novel, is D. H. Lawrence's *Women in Love* (1920). A semi-independent sequel to *The Rainbow*, it discards the earlier book's saga design, and develops instead its symbolic use of animal emblems and geometric shapes. Set in England and the Alps just before the Great War,

Women in Love is partly dislodged from that known world into a mythical dimension of symbols, totems, and fetishes in which ancient and modern are as perilously undifferentiated as are the human and animal kingdoms. In this symbolic order, a character can be a colliery owner and an arctic wolf at the same time, or simultaneously a modern motorist and a throned pharaoh. The story is built upon the contrasted relationships of two heterosexual couples: Ursula Brangwen and the school inspector Rupert Birkin are seekers of new life, while her sister Gudrun and the mine-owner Gerald Crich unknowingly crave death. But it soon becomes hard, as contemporary readers complained, to distinguish between these couples. As the primary oppositions of character crumble, we are thrown back upon the grand metaphysical polarities around which Lawrence regroups their dissolving elements: Body against Mind, African South against Arctic North, Female against Male, Growth against Decay, Organism against Mechanism. At times *Women in Love* reads like a novel of ideas, in which these principles circulate as abstract terms of spoken debate, of private meditation, or of sustained disquisition, notably in Birkin's frequent sermons on love or on the death wish of European civilization. At others, it is more clearly a symbolic or apocalyptic romance in which they are integrated into a sequence of powerful symbolic episodes: Gerald's forcing of his mare against the onrush of a freight train (ch. 9), Birkin's shattering of the moon's reflection in a pond (ch. 19), Gerald's entry into Gudrun's bedroom with the mud from his father's grave still clinging to him (ch. 24).

Lawrence attempts in *Women in Love* to depict what he called the 'inhuman' dimension of human subjectivity beneath the superficial conscious personality, and to capture there the movements of unconscious life or of 'blood-consciousness'—a project fraught with difficulties here and in his later fictions. One commonly observed problem is that he struggles to communicate the incommunicable, to make dumb experience speak, to see by the light of darkness; all of which may account for the frenzied iteration that marks his prose style. A similar impasse is involved in the requirement that his characters be both conscious and unconscious at the same time: 'Darkly, without thinking at all, she knew that she was near to death', he writes typically of Ursula (ch. 15). Pressing beyond the limits of mental consciousness as understood by 'psychological' novelists,

Lawrence leads us into a netherworld of solar plexuses and 'suave loins of darkness' (ch. 23) which cannot think or speak for itself, but is sustained by metaphysical assertion combined with a large element of quack physiology. Despite its benignly erotic title, *Women in Love* is a book about doom and dissolution, and among the many self-destructions we witness in it is that of Lawrence the novelist, now sacrificed in order to be reborn as a visionary romancer. Driven to despair by the War, Lawrence was by now embroiled in fantasies of mass extermination and had come to regard humanity as a verminous infestation of the earth. From that position, inevitably, the commitment of the traditional novel to the sympathetic portrayal of human individuals within social relations was no longer Lawrence's, although in the genres of romance and fable he still wrote well on birds and beasts such as those that provide the totemic titles of his variously dehumanized later works—'The Fox', 'The Ladybird', *St Mawr*, *The Plumed Serpent*, *Kangaroo*, and 'The Escaped Cock'. In its furiously unstable fashion, *Women in Love* neverthelesss provides fitful 'prophetic' illumination of the age, comparable in some episodes with the contemporary work of Yeats and Eliot.

In the wake of *Women in Love*, of T. S. Eliot's poem 'The Waste Land' (1922), and of James Joyce's *Ulysses* (1922), the times were favourable in the Twenties to the construction of fictions upon 'mythic' designs. Mary Butts's romance *Armed with Madness* (1928), for example, betrays a Joycean–Eliotic influence, with a Homerically named character called Scylla at the centre of its action, and with repeated allusions to the Holy Grail legend. There are other 'modern' aspects to this book, including multiple viewpoints, interior monologues, and discussions of shell shock and psychoanalysis; but the dominant feature is the foregrounding of a mysteriously symbolic object, a jade cup that might equally be the Sancgrail itself or just a stolen ashtray, a valuable antiquity, or an empty distraction. The cup's meanings shift according to the hopes and fears that the various characters invest in it. They are a group of 'modern' gramophone-playing bohemians sharing an isolated house on the Dorset coast, and beset by post-War malaise, by nervous antipathies and sexual jealousies that culminate, as the title promises, in demented violence. Omen or hoax, the cup catalyses these elements, pitching the participants into a new sense of magic and danger, a 'sacred game'

(p. 43) in which the cup/Grail is less important than the holy wonder reawoken by the quest for it.

Following *Armed with Madness* came another story of West Country Grail-questing in J. C. Powys's *A Glastonbury Romance* (1932), an enormous, sprawling, and overfreighted work, running to nearly twelve hundred pages and prefaced by a list of forty-seven 'principal characters'. This multitude is assembled in present-day Glastonbury, an ancient Somerset town associated in legend with King Arthur and with pre-Christian mysteries. The characters are contrasted in groups (the Crow family of Norfolk sceptics, against the religiously obsessed Glastonburians) and in pairs in order to illustrate the varieties of spiritual, erotic, and socio-economic experience, ranging from lesbian paganism to Christian asceticism, from sado-masochism to anarcho-syndicalism. The action involves the election of a heretical preacher, 'Bloody Johnny' Geard, to the position of mayor; his sponsorship both of an industrial co-operative and of a local religious pageant in which a guilty Welsh sadist re-enacts the passion of Christ; his attempts to found a new mystical cult, during which he becomes a latter-day Merlin and cures a woman of cancer; and his final drowning in a great flood. In linked sub-plots, various characters struggle with sexual temptations and experience magical visions of Arthurian symbols, including the Grail itself: the vicar's son Sam Dekker is granted a revelation of the holy cup while apparently being penetrated anally by a gigantic spear, after which he administers an enema to his elderly neighbour, thus foreshadowing the purgative flood that concludes the book.

As if the action of *A Glastonbury Romance* were not startling enough, the style in which it is treated poses further challenges, of which the book's opening paragraph gives an ominous foretaste:

At the striking of noon on a certain fifth of March, there occurred within a causal radius of Brandon railway-station and yet beyond the deepest pools of emptiness between the uttermost stellar systems one of those infinitesimal ripples in the creative silence of the First Cause which always occur when an exceptional stir of heightened consciousness agitates any living organism in this astronomical universe. Something passed at that moment, a wave, a motion, a vibration, too tenuous to be called magnetic, too subliminal to be called spiritual, between the soul of a particular human being who was emerging from a third-class carriage of the twelve-nineteen train from London and the divine-diabolic soul of the First Cause of all life.

Brewing up an intergalactic storm about a man getting off a train in Norfolk, Powys here introduces his relentless interpenetrations of the trivial and the cosmic, the everyday and the timeless, a method that gives rise more often to bathos and exhaustion than to the spiritual insight it gropes for. His immediate resort to absolutes and superlatives in those opening sentences is matched throughout by insistent exclamation marks and italics; all are symptoms of his reckless disregard for gradations of prose style and narrative tone. Powys does offer in some episodes of this romance genuinely original analyses of motive, and surprising moments of symbolically charged action, but these effects are overwhelmed by an ecstatic flatulence that surpasses even D. H. Lawrence's comparable excesses.

By contrast with John Cowper Powys's verbosity, the work of his younger brother, the Dorset recluse T. F. Powys, appears strikingly self-disciplined and formally consistent. Powys junior specialized in a kind of sinister rustic fable inhabited by allegorical figures derived from Bunyan and from medieval morality plays. The characters of his extended fables are grotesque embodiments of lust, avarice, and cruelty, the settings are sleepy English villages, and the plots are magical and gruesome by turns. In *Mr Tasker's Gods* (1925), the 'gods' are in fact pigs, and they end by devouring the corpse of the title character's father, a murderous vagrant. In the better-known fable *Mr Weston's Good Wine* (1927), God arrives at the village of Folly Down in the shape of a wine merchant driving an old Ford car and dispensing light wine (Love) and dark wine (Death), with varied consequences for the villagers. More extraordinary is the last of Powys's long fictions, *Unclay* (1931), in which God has sent his reaper, John Death, to 'unclay' (that is, to kill) two inhabitants of Dodder village, but Death mislays his written instructions and so passes the time in womanizing and other forms of merriment. An unforgettably grim episode finds Death buying a round of drinks in the pub, whereupon the drinkers appear to each other as worm-infested cadavers. Although Powys clearly derives his allegorical figures from Christian lore, his conversion of them into rustic gargoyles involves a sometimes ferocious travesty of orthodox theology, and throws down repeated heretical challenges to its promises of immortality. While his elder brother conducted his metaphysical explorations in a mode of diffuse rumination, T. F. Powys managed through the economies of allegory to concentrate his heresies into vivid dramatic action.

Romance and fable are in this period the playground of the heretical imagination, and of milder heterodox fancies, as we have seen in a broad range of unusual stories. Leaving behind them the old Victorian dilemmas of Faith and Doubt, such modern romancers as Lawrence, the Powys brothers, Mitchison, Hilton, and Warner move beyond the terms of Christian culture to create fresh dialogues between varieties of mysticism and of scepticism. The rapid collapse of orthodox Christian belief among writers and intellectuals of the post-Darwinian, post-Nietzschean generations had opened up an expanse of fictional possibility that favoured the rediscovery of pagan liberties and magical rites, whether ancient or exotic, as it favoured too the entertainment of fabulous curiosities and eccentric mystical visions. Resisting this larger heretical tide of modern thought, the modernist critics T. E. Hulme and T. S. Eliot upheld at the time what they took to be a 'classical' orthodoxy, Hulme characterizing Romanticism as 'spilt religion' while Eliot called that movement 'a short cut to the strangeness [of life] without the reality'.[1] Both descriptions have their relevance to the realm of modern romance too. We may regard this realm as one of the last redoubts of the nineteenth-century Romantic tradition, sheltering the old cults of strangeness and excess from the now regnant realisms of poetry and the novel. It is also the sanctuary into which the orphaned spiritualities of the period tended to 'spill' themselves and in which they evolved new models of questing pilgrimage and island paradise.

---

[1] T. E. Hulme, *Speculations*, ed. Herbert Read (Routledge & Kegan Paul, 1924), 118; T. S. Eliot, *The Sacred Wood* (Methuen, 1920), 33.

11

Modern Satire

New Words, 1910–1940

*bitchy   bogusness   Colonel Blimp   debag
deglamourize   dimwit   floozie   gigolo   layabout
pip-squeak   poxy   scatological   sick-making
wino   yes-man*

Cyril Connolly observed in 1938 that 'This is a satirical age and among the vast reading public the power of an artist to awaken ridicule has never been so great.'[1] There is a strong sense in which it was the 'age' itself that was satirical, not just its authors. The grim ironies of modern history provided enough mockery of human vanities, even before the literary satirist could get to work on them. Thomas Hardy shared the view that events themselves are the sharpest satirists, an assumption embodied in the title of his verse sequence 'Satires of Circumstance' (1911). Of modern historical ironies, the most cruelly 'satirical' in its perceived implications was the Great War of 1914–18, an event whose moral devastations reverberated long after the Armistice. The War That Will End War (a slogan coined by H. G. Wells), the war that would be over by Christmas, it constituted in the eyes of many writers an unanswerable satire not only upon political blindness, military incompetence, journalistic dishonesty, and the English class system, but upon the higher ideals of European civilization itself. Moreover, from the Marconi scandal of 1909, in which government ministers engaged in 'insider' share-deals, to the

---

[1] Cyril Connolly, *Enemies of Promise* (Penguin, 1961), 112.

achievement of 'peace in our time' by the policy of appeasing Hitler in 1938, public events themselves invited disillusionment and outright derision, while formerly respected institutions covered themselves in ignominy. To write amid all this without some sort of satirical awareness was to belong to the wrong century.

Satire, then, may be said to have been in the air, and the opportunities for satirical writing were clearly auspicious; but where, if this were so, were the satirists to be found? One of their number, Wyndham Lewis, had some difficulty in answering the same question. In his scathing survey of contemporary writing, *Men Without Art* (1934), Lewis declared that 'all art is in fact satire today', but then confessed that he was short of examples to discuss: 'Although there is nothing written or painted today of any power which could not be brought under the head of *Satire* (if you allow a fairly wide interpretation to that term) yet I could not find a fictionist deliberately dealing in satire—either occasionally or all the time—of sufficient significance to use as one of my illustrations—except myself' (p. 15). Part of Lewis's problem here was his usual reluctance to recognize the merits of other writers, but there was a more substantial basis to the enigma: the satirical spirit appeared to have saturated the world of letters to the point at which the traditional distinction between the satirical and the other modes of writing had been almost erased. Satire was invisible because omnipresent.

The writers now usually recognized as the leading satirists of the age were the poet Siegfried Sassoon, and a few novelists of the Twenties and Thirties: Wyndham Lewis, Aldous Huxley, Evelyn Waugh, Christopher Isherwood, and George Orwell. Each of these deserves some recognition for his satirical achievements, as we shall see below, but to isolate them as the representatives of modern satire would be to miss the more important development, which was the pervasion of the satirical impulse across the range of literary genres, movements, and schools. It was a mark of literary modernity to discard as a feature of 'Victorianism' all false respect for the old idols of Home, School, Nation, and Empire, and likewise to subject the old virtues, whether of patriotic heroism or of domestic respectability, to what was now called 'debunking'. As we shall see in Chapter 12, the new fashion of disrespect appeared most strikingly in the genre of biography, where Lytton Strachey's *Eminent Victorians* (1918) substituted a satirical approach to the dead heroes for the formerly reverential mode of panegyric. A more significant development still was the revival of the almost defunct tradition of verse satire, among both modernist and traditionalist poets.

Verse Satire: Hardy, Eliot, and Sassoon

Hardy's 'Satires of Circumstance' are satirical in the sense that they highlight the general and perennial blindness of humanity, rather than any contemporary vices: in one typical poem, bereaved mothers squabble over the positions of their children's graves while the sexton confides that the little corpses have all in fact been moved into a mass grave to make way for a new drain. Other satirists in verse differ from Hardy in concentrating upon the special ills of the modern world, although Hardy himself did at times strike the contemporary note, as in the prophetic 'Channel Firing' of April, 1914, or in his later ditty, 'Christmas: 1924':

> 'Peace upon earth!' was said. We sing it,
> And pay a million priests to bring it.
> After two thousand years of mass
> We've got as far as poison-gas.

Several other leading poets of the period display a more or less prominent satirical vein in their works. In Yeats, it is a minor feature, although significantly heard in such poems as 'September, 1913' and 'The Leaders of the Crowd' (1921). T. S. Eliot's high reputation as the outstanding poet of the Twenties, on the other hand, rested to a great extent upon his achievements as a satirist: 'I think of him as satirist rather than poet', Yeats remarked crushingly in 1936.[2] The polished and allusive wit of Eliot's *Poems* (1919) and *Ara Vos Prec* (1920) presented a modern world in which the grandeur of classical mythology and Renaissance art is displaced by figures of subhuman vulgarity—the feline seductress Grishkin, the ape-like Sweeney. This is an exhausted world of standardized urban despair in which (in 'A Cooking Egg') 'weeping multitudes | Droop in a hundred A.B.C's'—

---

[2] W. B. Yeats (ed.), *The Oxford Book of Modern Verse* (Oxford University Press, 1936), p. xxii.

an A.B.C. being a cheap teashop. These drooping multitudes of the modern metropolis reappear more powerfully in Eliot's 'The Waste Land' (1922), now imagined as the lost souls of a Dantean Hell. 'The Waste Land' is the single most important long poem of modernism in English, and at its heart, in the third section ('The Fire Sermon'), lies a satirical portrayal of modern urban sexuality: an anonymous female typist is visited by a young male clerk, and is too bored either to resist his advances or to notice his speedy departure. Eliot concludes this episode with an echo of Oliver Goldsmith's song of 1766 ('When lovely woman stoops to folly | And finds too late that men betray, | What charm can soothe her melancholy, | What art can wash her guilt away?') that deflates what would formerly have been conceived as the tragedy of seduction and betrayal to a mechanized banality:

> When lovely woman stoops to folly and
> Paces about her room again, alone,
> She smoothes her hair with automatic hand
> And puts a record on the gramophone.

> (ll. 253–6)

The moment also echoes a sequence of similar sexual degradations in the poem, and an overlapping series of suggestions that the human body has become machine-like in its habitual movements: earlier, office workers at the end of the day are likened to the throbbing engines of taxis.

The satirical passages of 'The Waste Land' are unusual in offering an imaginative diagnosis of a general modern malaise. Most verse satire in this period adopts particular targets—individuals or identifiable social types. Of particular importance here is the revival of the hate poem, a minor genre that had withered since the days of Byron and Shelley. It resurfaces often among the poems of D. H. Lawrence ('How Beastly the Bourgeois Is', 'The Oxford Voice', and many of the poems in the splenetic volume *Nettles* (1930)), in the work of the left-wing poet Edgell Rickword ('Hints for Making a Gentleman', 'To the Wife of a Non-Interventionist Statesman'), and even in the light verses of G. K. Chesterton ('Song against Grocers', 'The Aristocrat'). Rickword, an admirer of Eliot's work and editor of the *Calendar of Modern Letters*, called in 1925 for a revival in poetry of those healthy 'negative' emotions such as disgust and scorn, which had enlivened the satirical verse of the eighteenth century before being subjected to conventional taboo in the nineteenth.[3] The hate poem would have come back without the aid of such critical manifestos, but this conscious appeal to a lost Augustan tradition is significant in helping to account for some of the neoclassical trappings in which the modern movement clothed itself between the Wars. Just as one comes across paragraphs of polished mockery in Strachey's *Eminent Victorians* echoing the style of Edward Gibbon, so Eliot's description of the typist and the clerk mimics the quatrains of Gray and Goldsmith, Rickword's 'Hints for Making a Gentleman' employs the octosyllabics favoured by Jonathan Swift, and Roy Cambell's verse satire *The Georgiad* (1931) is evidently a pastiche of Dryden and Pope. The message of the medium here is that the modern satirist is engaged less in venting some private bitterness than in fulfilling the time-honoured duty of the poet in a depraved society.

Among the poets, the most dedicated satirist was Siegfried Sassoon, whose career illustrates more than any other the connections between the Great War and the revival of satire that followed in its wake. His war poems of 1917, collected in *Counter-Attack* (1918), are bitterly satirical, directed against the generals and against various kinds of armchair warriors at home—newspaper editors, clergymen, patriotic parents—whose willingness to sacrifice other people appalled him. 'Base Details', for example, captures the combatants' deep resentment against the 'scarlet Majors' who sent them into the carnage while guzzling in 'the best hotel' (*Collected Poems*, p. 75). In several poems of this kind—'The Father', 'The General', 'Does It Matter?', 'Editorial Impressions', and the sarcastic 'Lamentations'—the clichéd rhetoric of martial glory is mimicked and then answered by the witnessing voice of the truly experienced, which can quickly become the voice of powerfully personal malice. In 'Fight to a Finish', Sassoon dreams of a triumphal home-coming parade in which the soldiers suddenly turn their bayonets on the gathered yellow-press journalists, and then make ready to assault the Houses of Parliament themselves. It is now commonplace to hear all kinds of

---

[3] Edgell Rickword, 'The Re-Creation of Poetry: The Use of "Negative" Emotions', *Calendar of Modern Letters*, 1 (1925), 236–41.

mildly heterodox writings described as 'subversive', but this poem is the real and very rare thing—an openly insurrectionist fantasy.

Sassoon's wartime satires remain well known. Less visible now are the poems of his post-War phase, which include, along with a body of meditative and religious verses, a collection of *Satirical Poems* (1926), and further satires on modern militarism in *The Road to Ruin* (1933). In the early Twenties, Sassoon was a socialist sympathizer marooned among the horse-riding upper classes, struggling to justify to them at dinner parties the real grievances of striking coal miners (in 'The Case for the Miners'), but consoling himself with the thought of their impending extinction as he observed them at their leisure pursuits—fox-hunting (in 'Reynardism Revisited'), watching cricket ('Blues at Lord's'), promenading ('Observations in Hyde Park'), or on holiday, as in 'The Grand Hotel', where the affluent 'can demonstrate by their behaviour | Hotel-de-Luxe aloofness from their Saviour' (*Collected Poems*, p. 135).

Prose Satire: Huxley, Waugh, and Others

Sassoon's significance as a satirist lay in his portraits of an insufferable 'old guard' that had outlived its time and in effect murdered the promise of youth. His red-faced majors, spluttering old colonels, yelping fox-hunters, and jingoistic bishops became in the Twenties the models of caricature by means of which the remnants of a senile 'Victorianism' were laughed away. If we turn to the prose satire of the period, we find that such ossified representatives of the past abound. Wyndham Lewis's lengthy satirical novel *The Apes of God* (1930) opens with the 96-year-old Lady Fredigonde Follett descending into senile delirium. Osbert Sitwell's *Before the Bombardment* (1926) describes the last years of the septuagenarian Miss Collier-Floodgaye in a seaside hotel. Evelyn Waugh's *A Handful of Dust* (1934) includes an elderly vicar, Mr Tendril, who still offers up loyal prayers to his Queen-Empress Victoria, imagining he is still in India, where he has long ago served as a military chaplain. In Aldous Huxley's *Antic Hay* (1923), an unnamed old gentleman, twirling his white military moustache, encounters a young woman muttering to herself in the street, and assumes that she is a drug addict: 'Vicious young women.

Lesbians, drug-fiends, nymphomaniacs, dipsos—thoroughly vicious, nowadays, thoroughly vicious. He arrived at his club in an excellent temper' (ch. 14). Military ogres were a favourite satirical target, and for some reason the colonel was presented by modern writers as the most contemptible of ranks. Katherine Mansfield's story 'The Daughters of the Late Colonel' (1921), for example, describes two middle-aged spinsters who have just buried their father, but who are still so terrified of him that they expect him to leap out of a cupboard to accuse them of mishandling the funeral. In the rogues' gallery of modern satire, the incidence of such fearsome colonels is matched by that of interfering aunts (a speciality both of Saki and of P. G. Wodehouse) and malevolent matriarchs: Ivy Compton-Burnett came to specialize in these figures, for example the 84-year-old Sabine Ponsonby of *Daughters and Sons* (1937), who routinely opens letters addressed to her servants or grandchildren, and drives away a succession of governesses with her sour temper.

To satirize the public or domestic rigidities of 'Victorian' figures such as these may be regarded as working with the grain of the modern temperament, and thus as a task less challenging than the fresh portrayal of the modern age's own distinctively monstrous or ludicrous features, its new human types of folly and delusion. The more adventurous prose satirists of the Twenties and Thirties took up this challenge in the spirit of Eliot, setting out to map the 'waste land' of modern civilization and to caricature the hollow men and women who peopled it. The title of Evelyn Waugh's cruellest satiric novel, *A Handful of Dust*, is, significantly, a quotation from Eliot's 'The Waste Land'; and the Eliotic vision of modern urban life as a limbo of lost souls going through the mechanical motions of their spiritually empty lives is echoed too by Lewis, Huxley, and Isherwood. From this perspective, it was not the old colonels who needed to be held up to scorn—although they might be mocked incidentally—so much as the morally uprooted younger generation that needed to be shown its face in the satirist's mirror.

A typical figure here is Huxley's character Lucy Tantamount in *Point Counter Point* (1928). She is a wealthy young widow, jaded by continuous party-going and by a succession of meaningless sexual escapades, who regards older people as an alien species because they believe in morals. 'Do you genuinely believe that some things are right

Fig. 7. Aldous Huxley photographed in 1934
by Howard Coster.

and some wrong?' she asks another character, in genuine astonishment at the idea (ch. 12). Having amused herself sexually with the novel's anti-hero, Walter Bidlake, Lucy becomes exasperated when he keeps talking of love, which to her is 'absurdly unmodern'; countering his romanticism, she offers a suitably up-to-date metaphor for her alternative code:

'Living modernly's living quickly,' she went on. 'You can't cart a waggonload of ideals and romanticisms about with you these days. When you travel by aeroplane you must leave your heavy baggage behind. The good old-fashioned soul was all right when people lived slowly. But it's too ponderous nowadays. There's no room for it in the aeroplane.' (ch. 15)

Lucy has her counterparts in the charmingly unprincipled gold-digger Sally Bowles of Isherwood's *Goodbye to Berlin* (1939) and in the adultress Brenda Last of Waugh's *A Handful of Dust*, who, in a revelatory moment, expresses spontaneous relief that it is not her temporary lover who has been reported killed in a riding accident, but only her 6-year-old son. As with the typist of Eliot's 'The Waste Land', the figure of the unashamedly promiscuous woman functions in these cases as a central indicator of vertiginous modern mobility in the moral sphere.

It is characteristic of Huxley to make Lucy Tantamount spell out her code of ethical aviation as an explicitly declared and elaborated position. His satirical works of the Twenties, from *Crome Yellow* (1921) to *Point Counter Point*, are all 'novels of ideas' in which highly articulate representatives of various human types (Artist, Scientist, Hedonist, Lecher) are given large scope to debate their views and to speculate upon the way the world is tending. A leading character in *Crome Yellow*, for example, the philosopher Scogan (based on Bertrand Russell), may expatiate freely and wittily upon the nature of aristocracy, the inscrutability of other people, the superiority of books to life, the moral effects of the Great War, and the principles of the coming Rational State. Although the novel includes some inconclusive sexual intrigue among the various guests at Crome (a country house based on Ottoline Morrell's Garsington Manor), and some farcical episodes at the annual fair, the real business is the talk.

By contrast, the early satires of Evelyn Waugh, from *Decline and Fall* (1928) to *Scoop* (1938), manage to embody the restlessness of modern manners in the pace of their action: his characters do not just talk of aeroplanes, they go out and fly in them, even if they then have to reach for the little paper bag, as Nina Blount in *Vile Bodies* (1930) is obliged to do. Waugh's satires are driven by the sort of delirious, panic-inducing speed of disastrous events that belongs to theatrical farce. *Vile Bodies*, the most distinctly 'modern' of these books, makes restlessness, rapid motion, and the resulting nausea its principal modes of action and thus of its satirical theme: it begins with various groups of characters on a rough ferry-crossing from France to England, all attempting to make merry while feeling increasingly sick. Its climax comes at a motor-racing circuit, when Agatha Runcible, the leading spirit among the party-going Bright Young People, drunkenly decides to take the place of an injured driver in the race, careers off the track, and finally crashes in a village fifteen miles away. Recovering in a nursing-home bed, next to a man who has fallen out of an aeroplane, she tells her friends, at an impromptu bedside cocktail party that eventually kills her, about her hallucinations:

'D'you know, all that time when I was dotty, I had the most awful dreams. I thought we were all driving round and round in a motor race and none of us could stop, and there was an enormous audience composed entirely of gossip-writers and gate-crashers and Archie Stewart and people like that, all shouting to us at once to go faster, and car after car kept crashing until I was left all alone driving and driving—and then I used to crash and wake up.' (ch. 12)

The moral application of the dream to the behaviour of Agatha's 'fast' set, and of the journalistic culture that eggs them on, is perhaps too obvious. A more sophisticated feature of Waugh's satire on modern rapidity here is the way in which he echoes the theme in his narrative techniques, intercutting rapidly between events and dialogues to produce a modernist 'montage' effect of constant flickering motion.

Waugh's satires look beyond the follies of youthful revellers to the general and institutional depravities of the age. *Vile Bodies* pokes fun at grasping publishers, at ignorant censors, and at the excessive power of modern journalism. The novel's naïve hero, Adam Fenwick-Symes, unexpectedly lands a job as a gossip columnist for the *Daily Excess*, a position that sometimes seems to give him more power than the government itself. For fear of the libel laws, however, Adam avoids naming real people in his column, and resorts instead to discussing artists and heiresses of his own invention: his fictional Polish sculptor 'Provna', for instance, arouses such interest among the public that a number of fake Provna pieces begin to circulate in the art market. The same joke about life imitating journalistic fiction is expanded in Waugh's later novel *Scoop*, a satire on foreign correspondents. Here, the leader of the journalistic pack is one Jakes, legendary on account of his exploits in the Balkans, where he got himself lost and so filed an invented story about an uprising, thereby provoking an actual revolution. That the truth is the last concern of newspapers is briskly taken for granted. Indeed, the language of newspapermen is so disconnected from ordinary logic that the editors of the *Daily Beast* are unable to say 'no' to their domineering proprietor Lord Copper (a figure based upon the real Lord Beaverbrook): the furthest they will go in qualifying their sycophancy is to mutter 'Up to a point, Lord Copper'. There were many other novels satirizing the world of newspapers in this period—C. E. Montague's *A Hind Let Loose* (1910), and Rose Macaulay's *Potterism* (1920), for example—but Waugh's Lord Copper, who is even today a familiar type, has helped to preserve *Scoop* as the living representative of its genre.

Waugh's usual satirical method is to expose a naïve protagonist to the inner workings of some respected institution, in which he is baffled to discover that the reigning code of conduct is the exact opposite of the professed ideal. As William Boot finds out in *Scoop* that journalists peddle lies and inventions when they are not fiddling their expenses, so in Waugh's first novel, *Decline and Fall*, the naïve Paul Pennyfeather encounters godless churchmen, ignoble aristocrats, and teachers whose only aim is to molest and exploit their pupils. The novel begins with the gathering of an aristocratic dining club, the Bollinger, at the Oxford college where Paul is quietly studying for the priesthood. The Bollinger counts reigning kings among its members, but amuses itself on these occasions by stoning foxes to death with champagne bottles, and by smashing up college property. As the quads echo to the characteristic 'sound of the English county families baying for broken glass' (p. 8), the fellows of the college rub their hands in anticipation of the port they will be able to drink, once they have imposed fines for the ensuing vandalism; one openly prays that the Bollinger rioters will attack the chapel. In fact, they attack Paul, tearing off his clothes, whereupon the fellows decide to expel Paul for indecency of dress rather than throw out his high-ranking assailants. Thus Paul begins a career as scapegoat for the crimes of his social superiors, which, as a loyal respecter of social caste, he refuses to expose. The climax of this career comes as his wealthy fiancée, Margot Beste-Chetwynde, evades well-founded charges of engaging in the white slave trade (i.e. trafficking in prostitutes) by blaming it all on Paul, who is sentenced to seven years in jail, while she vanishes to Corfu and calls off the engagement. Although Waugh provides his satires with cheerfully frivolous surface features such as the characters' improbable names—Lady Circumference, Miles Malpractice, Fanny Throbbing, and the rest—their essential comic quality is one of relentless cruelty.

A defining feature of modern satire is that it exhibits the monstrosities of human behaviour without committing the 'Victorian' impertinence of moralizing upon them. As Wyndham Lewis maintained against received wisdom, 'the greatest satire *cannot* be moralistic at all' (*Men Without Art*, p. 89). The outrages of Waugh's characters are allowed to speak for themselves, and his readers may draw their own conclusions without being instructed openly by the narrative voice. The same is true of the satiric method employed by Huxley, Isherwood, Mansfield, or Compton-Burnett. Satirists of this period may usefully be divided into the 'hot' and the 'cool', according to the degree to which the narrative tone is agitated by overt loathing or rage—or, conversely, the degree to which it maintains a clinical distance from its objects. At the hot end of this spectrum we must place D. H. Lawrence, who habitually condemns his characters as essentially corrupt or reptilian before he has even told us what they do or say. Slightly cooler than this in precept if not in practice is Wyndham Lewis, who maintained that the proper satirical approach must be 'external', like the art of the cartoonist, rather than psychologically 'internal' as Lawrence's tended to be. Lewis's most ambitious satirical novel, *The Apes of God*, exhibits at almost unbearable length a gallery of pseudo-artists and poseurs who appear to us as 'apes' both in their simian repulsiveness and in their desire to imitate genuine artistic bohemianism. A typical descriptive passage may give the flavour:

> With a solemn scowl of scorn the polish lesbian midget squatted aloft upon the model's throne—she was dominating her two sucking doves in attendance who sat like fat odalisks. Her face was with twenty years' hard work as a polish lesbian, with dyspepsia and cosmetics, yellowish—her eyes of an obliquity roughly judeo-tartar. As silent as Dan, she modelled herself upon the asiatic statuette, as seen through the eyes of the Hollywood or West End producer. (pt. 6)

The rendering is indeed 'external', like a formal tableau, but a punitively sneering tone, here and throughout the book, intrudes upon readers' liberty to assess the characters for themselves; and the ornate artificiality of the prose style fails to screen Lewis's personal disgust.

The cooler style of modern satire may be illustrated from Huxley's *Point Counter Point*, in a scene from a party at the home of Lucy Tantamount's father, an eminent biologist:

> In the dining room a rich still-life of bottles, fruits, and sandwiches awaited them. Round the polished flanks of the vacuum flask their reflections walked fantastically in a non-Euclidean universe. Professor Dewar had liquefied hydrogen in order that Lucy's soup might be kept hot for her into the small hours. Over the sideboard hung one of John Bidlake's paintings of the theatre. A curve of the gallery, a slope of faces, a corner of the bright proscenium.
>
> 'How good that is!' said Spandrell, shading his eye to see it more clearly.
>
> Lucy made no comment. She was looking at herself in an old grey-glassed mirror.
>
> 'What shall I do when I'm old?' she suddenly asked.
>
> 'Why not die?' suggested Spandrell with his mouth full of bread and Strasbourg goose liver.
>
> 'I think I'll take to science, like the Old Man. Isn't there such a thing as human zoology? [. . .]' (ch. 12)

There is obviously a lighter touch here, the suggestions of weary narcissism in Lucy and of callous hedonism in Spandrell being carried by the characters' actions and speech. Even the element of defamiliarizing distortion proper to satire appears to come from the vacuum flask rather than from Huxley's own design. Lucy's mention of human zoology is echoed later in *Point Counter Point* by Philip Quarles, himself a novelist who is planning his next book, in which the hero will be yet another novelist, one with a zoological training that provides the basis of his perspective:

His approach will be strictly biological. He will be constantly passing from the termitary to the drawing-room and the factory, and back again. He will illustrate human vices by those of the ants, which neglect their young for the sake of the intoxicating liquor exuded by the parasites that invade their nests. His hero and heroine will spend their honeymoon by a lake, where the grebes and ducks illustrate all the aspects of courtship and matrimony. (ch. 26)

This is a fair description of Huxley's own ambitions as a satirist. The true son of a formidable scientific dynasty (his grandfather Thomas Huxley had been Darwin's greatest champion, and his brother Julian was a prominent popularizer of biological theory), he set out to illuminate human behaviour and make it newly strange from the perspective of an observer versed in modern science. The detachment implied by such a position suits well the traditional satirist's ironic stance, particularly in Huxley's recurrent theme of the absurd discrepancy between spiritual aspiration and bodily needs.

The objective or 'cool' style of modern satire formulated its self-defining ideal in the famous opening page of Isherwood's *Goodbye to Berlin*:

I am a camera with its shutter open, quite passive, recording, not thinking. Recording the man shaving at the window opposite and the woman in the kimono washing her hair. Some day, all this will have to be developed, carefully printed, fixed.

This is a declaration of intentions, and not a reliable description of the book's method. The observer figure, openly named as 'Christopher Isherwood' ('Herr Issyvoo' to his German landlady), is in fact a participant in the fictional events: he becomes emotionally involved with Sally Bowles and the other remarkable people he meets or shares lodgings with in Berlin, where he is working as a teacher of English, and he expresses his own pro-Communist sympathies in the context of the city's increasingly violent political struggles of the years 1930–3. But his willed photographic detachment allows him to show up the blindness both of the nocturnal thrill-seekers and of the Communist youth in their shared conviction that the Nazis can never win power. As a neutral 'camera', Isherwood avoids passing judgement upon his characters. The same is true of his earlier Berlin novel, *Mr Norris Changes Trains* (1935), originally part of the same unfinished book from which the diaristic fragments of *Goodbye to Berlin* emerged. Mr Norris is a shameless old fraudster of 1890s vintage, who is pursued by creditors and whipped by dominatrices, but seems to survive in the very dangerous world of Thirties Berlin by sheer old-fashioned charm, winning the confidence of the impressionable young English narrator. Despite being a disciple of Sade rather than of Lenin, he is warmly cheered when he addresses a Communist rally, but it later emerges that he has been selling information about his Communist contacts, and blackmailing his aristocratic friends, with deadly consequences. Even then, the narrator fails to condemn him openly, and can only marvel at his barefaced fraudulence and grotesque self-pity. Judgement upon Norris is then left to the reader.

The temperature of modern satire tends to rise when it seeks its targets among the author's private enemies. The literary world was a small one, often fetid with intimate rancour and long-nursed grudges, the poison from which was vented in personal lampooning. The major characters of Lewis's *Apes of God* are all caricatures of literary figures whom Lewis resented: Stephen Spender, Lytton Strachey, Osbert Sitwell, and others. D. H. Lawrence's short stories 'Jimmy and the Desperate Woman', 'The Border Line' (both 1924), 'The Last Laugh' (1925), and 'Smile' (1926), all involve personal satires of his disciple John Middleton Murry, whom Lawrence had suspected, falsely, of trying to seduce his wife. Murry also came under more sustained assault in the guise of 'Burlap', a character in Huxley's *Point Counter Point*. Huxley had once worked under Murry when the latter was editor of the *Athenaeum*, and he portrays Burlap as the editor of a literary magazine, one who exploits his male employees financially and his female employees sexually, wrapping his selfishness in a cloud of religiose self-pity and 'spiritual' effusion. Normally 'cool' in his satirical tone, Huxley loads his portrait of Burlap as a man given to 'incessant spiritual masturbation' (ch. 13) with unusual contempt. His gentler earlier satires also draw recognizable figures from the literary and artistic worlds: *Crome Yellow* in particular is a distorted group portrait of Lady Ottoline Morrell's Garsington circle, and the Lady Ottoline figure reappears in different guises in *Those Barren Leaves* and in *Point Counter Point*. This eccentric but harmless literary hostess was probably the most frequently satirized private individual of the period: apart from her appearances in Huxley's works, she is caricatured in Lawrence's *Women in Love* (1920), in Gilbert Cannan's *Pugs and Peacocks* (1921), in Osbert Sitwell's *Triple Fugue* (1924), and in Graham Greene's *It's a Battlefield* (1934). She had done little to deserve this, but her bright orange hair, her flamboyant style of dress, and her gushing manner all made her an easy butt of ridicule. Other literary vendettas of the time had more explicable causes. Roy Campbell, after discovering that his wife Mary was having an affair with Vita Sackville-West, wrote a lengthy verse satire, *The Georgiad*, which rails against Sackville-West, her 'nancy' husband Harold Nicolson, and the Georgian and Bloomsbury writers of their social circle. With some justice, it remarks that

> Cain had more Christian mercy on his brother
> Than literary nancies on each other.
>
> (*Collected Works*, vol. 1, p. 208)

The most widely reprinted, translated, and applauded satirical novel of this period is commonly regarded with undue solemnity as a 'prophecy' of things to come rather than recognized as a satire. Aldous Huxley's *Brave New World* (1932) is set in the late twenty-fifth century by our calendar, or 'the year of Our Ford 632', counting from the birth of Henry Ford, the pioneer of assembly-line methods of car manufacture. It presents an unappealing utopian world-society stratified according to selective laboratory breeding, and governed by a conformist code of compulsory happiness, in which childbirth has been abolished along with monogamy, passion, anxiety, grief, Art, religion, historical memory, scientific truth, and the concept of individual freedom. As far as predictions go, Huxley accurately foresees the coming of helicopters, zip-up garments, and the adoption of television as a mass medium. Rather less probably, the social elite of 'Alphas' five hundred years hence are shown still smoking cigarettes, playing golf, and taking dinner at the Oxford Union, and a suspicious number of them are named after public figures of the

1920s, like 'Benito Hoover' (after the Italian dictator Mussolini and the then serving US President). These are small signs that Huxley's real interest is, as one might expect, in the sociological and moral trends of his own time.

Brave New World is indeed a satire on contemporary notions of progress and modernization, a satire that works by projecting certain aspects of modern culture—mass-production and the arrival of the Hollywood 'talking pictures' in 1927, for example—forward into a future world in which they have eradicated traditional habits and values. The ingenuity with which Huxley has designed this world is unmistakable. The family having been abolished, babies are decanted in large numbers of identical copies, from bottles in state hatcheries, and are then conditioned through 'hypnopaedia' (indoctrination by recorded messages while asleep), and encouraged to take part in 'erotic play' with one another in their crèches. The resulting model citizen is one who engages in promiscuous sex without fear of pregnancy—monogamous pairing is frowned upon—works cheerfully in her assigned industrial role, takes part in approved forms of leisure and entertainment such as the 'feelies' (cinema with tactile sensation), and overcomes boredom by taking the drug 'soma'. Beyond the pale of this civilization, though, there lies the 'Savage Reservation' in New Mexico, in which the novel's rebellious hero Bernard Marx discovers an unusual 'savage' called John, who is in fact the son of civilized parents, and has somehow come across an old copy of Shakespeare's works, learning them by heart. The novel's plot, which is less important than its construction of a consistent world, involves John being brought to civilization as a freakish celebrity, the clashing of his old values—love, monogamy, poetry, individualism—with those of the new civilization, and his declaration of the essential 'right to be unhappy' (ch. 17).

A curious feature of this new world in which all anxiety has been eliminated by conditioning, erotic diversion, or drugs is that its leaders, the 'World Controllers' and their senior lieutenants, seem remarkably anxious about any sign of unorthodoxy, just as they repeatedly rant against evils such as motherhood that have been abolished in the distant past. This aspect of Huxley's design makes his utopia implausible as a prediction, but makes his narrative possible: in a world without worries there could be no story of any interest, no conflict or drama. The repeated sermons in which the rulers of this world defend their system of socially guaranteed contentment against the antique values of individual dignity and responsibility are quite redundant within their context, but they are essential to the satire, if we remember that what are really at issue are the values of 1932, and the uncertainties of Huxley's own age about social engineering, consumerism, sexual mores, or the culture of mass entertainment. Behind the sternly orthodox Director of Hatcheries' homilies on the 'duty to be infantile' (ch. 6), or the more relaxed World Controller's lecture on stability as the highest good, one can hear the voice of an Edwardian public-school chaplain rallying the school spirit, while Bernard Marx's solitary intellectual rebellion against such conformism may be recognized as a version of the bookish schoolboy's hatred of compulsory chapel and cricket. Much of *Brave New World*, indeed, is adolescent in conception and in appeal: its presentation of an entire society—and especially its empty-headed but 'pneumatic' women—as mindlessly conformist except for the solitary bookish rebel relies heavily on the self-flattery of the intellectual and his desire for the glamour of persecution. The stronger side of Huxley's novel is its comedy, and especially the bitter humour of its futuristic language: the constantly iterated hypnopaedic slogans such as 'civilization is sterilization', boastful statistics, lexical taboo (the word 'mother' is regarded as an obscenity), ridiculous secularized forms ('Ford' for 'Lord'), and moronic journalism (the *Delta Mirror* uses words of one syllable only). Set against this are John's vigorous insults and his rapturous quotations from Shakespeare. A major conflict here emerges, then, as in so much of this period's literature, between a journalistic degradation of language and an opposing literary integrity.

The satire of this period was brought to a kind of culmination in George Orwell's *Keep the Aspidistra Flying* (1936), which is, like *Brave New World*, a story about the struggle of a solitary rebel against an overwhelmingly conformist world. The anti-hero of this book, Gordon Comstock, comes from a dull, decaying 'middle-middle-class' family that is subsiding into the lower strata of suburbia. Rather than 'make good', Comstock rebels against his family's respectability, resigns his promising position as a copywriter, and tries to detach himself completely from the 'money-world' which surrounds him, while writing the occasional poem. He occupies, in fact, very much the position of the modern satirist, pouring scorn upon suburbanites from a superior position of artistic self-absorption. One side of the novel involves a partial endorsement of Comstock's view of the modern world as a money conspiracy. Lack of money is shown to affect every aspect of existence, including artistic creativity and sexual capacity: the poorer Comstock gets, the less he can write, while the bus fares and condoms required for sexual trysts become unaffordable. In practice, though, his rebellion means cadging money from friends and from his even more impoverished sister while imagining himself to be superior to the aspidistra-growing suburbanites—an attitude that Orwell despised as a characteristic delusion of the literary intelligentsia. Much of the book, then, exposes the futility of Comstock's solitary rebellion against the taint of money, and the snobbish vanity of his 'satirical' posture. The result of his desire to sink beneath the vulgar respectability of the lower middle class is that he lolls around in a bug-infested bedsit, incapable of writing poetry or of anything else. He is finally brought to his senses by his girlfriend's pregnancy, which impels him back to his well-paid job and to conventional suburban existence complete with aspidistras. In the figure of Comstock, modern literary satire turns upon its own inadequacies, and acts out its own defeat.

12

Modern Essays, Biographies, Memoirs, and Travel Books

New Words, 1910–1940

back-pack   columnist   debunk   desacralization
evaluative   informativeness   non-specialist
psychobiography   self-deprecation
self-exhibition   Stracheyan

Before the Second World War there prevailed among readers, authors, and publishers a shared conception of literature far more capacious than the restricted model of 'imaginative' writing that we now usually entertain. It was taken for granted that Literature included not only poems, plays, and fictional prose, but also biographies, travel books, essays, memoirs, critical studies, historical narratives, philosophical treatises, sermons, political speeches, and even scientific lectures. This breadth can be seen in the scope of the reprinted classics issued by J. M. Dent in their popular Everyman's Library series during this period. These included, along with poetry, drama and fiction, dozens of volumes categorized under Biography, Essays & Belles-Lettres, History, Oratory, Philosophy & Theology, Science, and Travel & Topography; the number of titles published under these categories indeed outnumbered those in the Fiction list. The respect still accorded to non-fictional prose in the period from 1910 to 1940 rests partly upon the prestige of the great nineteenth-century tradition of Carlyle, Emerson, Ruskin, Arnold, Newman, and Mill; partly too upon the continued availability of a wide range of periodicals sustaining a market for travel sketches, reminiscences, reviews, and light essays. It is with the essay, the prose form that underwrites most of the others, that this chapter will begin its sketch map of modern non-fictional writing.

Most magazines of the time, whether particularly literary in emphasis or not, provided room for book reviews, but also for general essays on everything or anything—serious polemics on philosophical, political or artistic matters, sketches of unusual people and places, or trifling meditations about nothing in particular. Numerous writers kept themselves afloat financially by fulfilling the demand for this material. Indeed, publishers were often confident of finding a readership for whole volumes of such pieces, especially collections of the lighter kind of 'familiar' essay. The very titles of these books give away much about the nonchalantly informal, even defiantly trivial, tone of this genre: Hilaire Belloc's *On Anything* (1910) was a sequel to his previous collections *On Nothing* (1908) and *On Everything* (1909), eventually to be followed by *This and That* (1912) and by *On* (1923); G. K. Chesterton's many essay collections include *Tremendous Trifles* (1909), *Generally Speaking* (1928), and *As I Was Saying* (1936); those of A. A. Milne include *Not That It Matters* (1919) and *If I May* (1920); other notable books of essays are A. P. Herbert's *Light Articles Only* (1921), Robert Lynd's *The Pleasures of Ignorance* (1921), E. V. Knox's *It Occurs To Me* (1926), Lord Ponsonby's *Casual Observations* (1929), Augustine Birrell's *Et Cetera* (1930), and Harold Nicolson's *Small Talk* (1937). What is promised by such titles is something like the casual pleasure of intimate fireside chat with a conversationalist capable of conjuring elegant whimsy out of nothing. The perfect type of this verbal exhibition is Chesterton's 'What I Found in My Pocket' (from *Tremendous Trifles*), which unfolds an incident in which the author had been stuck in a train with nothing to read, and had amused himself in contemplation of a few objects plucked from his pocket—a tram ticket, a penknife, a piece of chalk—so underlining his denial 'that anything is, or can be, uninteresting' (*Selected Essays*, p. 125). In the world of the light essay, any trifle can be made tremendous when magnified by a sufficiently assertive display of style and personality.

The demand for reprinted articles of this kind—and of other kinds that we shall soon consider—was strong enough for Everyman's Library to publish an anthology of *Modern English Essays, 1870 to 1920* (ed. E. Rhys, 1922) in no fewer than five volumes, and for the Oxford University Press to respond with two volumes of *Selected Modern English Essays* (1925, 1932), followed by a separate *English Essays of To-Day* (1936). Virginia Woolf, herself an important modern essayist, reviewed the Everyman set in an article later re-worked as 'The Modern Essay' (1925). Here she notes the strong public demand for 1,500-word essays, while regretting the pressures that such a tight word-limit imposes especially upon writers who turn them out every week, leading to strained, affected prose or the dilution of personality into mannerism: she names prolific essayists such as Belloc, Lynd, and J. C. Squire here as victims of their own overproduction. On the other hand she nominates Max Beerbohm, whose essays appeared far less frequently, as 'the prince of his profession' (*The Essays*, vol. 4, p. 220). Other readers, including Arnold Bennett, would have nominated Belloc and Chesterton as the leading essayists of their time: both excelled in the confection of airy trifles, but both also cultivated a more pungent form of argumentative essay in defence of their shared Catholic perspective on the ills of modern civilization: Belloc's 'On Inns' (from *This and That*), for example, typically suggests that the innocent companionship of beer-drinkers is threatened by sinister forces of cosmopolitan progressivism. Beerbohm, Belloc, and Chesterton had all formed their essayistic styles before 1910, and there are good grounds for regarding the light 'familiar' essay of subsequent decades as an Edwardian form of belles-lettres outliving its cultural moment. Certainly by the 1930s it seems to be giving way at last to a new preference for substance over style, for informative reportage over narcissistic rumination. The fully modern prose writer of the Thirties is to be found no longer musing in a book-lined study but investigating some dangerous place as an eyewitness in the open air, as we shall see below when we come to travel-writing and related forms.

The familiar essay, however, is only one prominent species of the genre. Just as well represented in the modern essay anthologies mentioned above, and certainly more enduring in influence, is the literary-critical essay. These were the most fertile decades of literary-critical discussion, both theoretical and applied, in England since the days of Coleridge and Hazlitt; and the favoured form for that discussion, whether in public or in academic spheres, was the essay—including the reprinted review, preface, lecture, or radio talk. Major contributions to the modern reconsideration of literary principles and values include T. S. Eliot's *The Sacred Wood* (1920) and *Homage to John Dryden* (1924), J. M. Murry's *Discoveries* (1924), Woolf's *The Common Reader*, D. H. Lawrence's *Studies in Classic American Literature* (1923) and his posthumous *Phoenix* (1936), G. Wilson Knight's *The Wheel of Fire* (1930), F. R. Leavis's *Revaluation* (1936), and George Orwell's *Inside the Whale* (1940), all of which are gatherings of essays, some of them reworked from book reviews. Other important critical books such as E. M. Forster's *Aspects of the Novel* (1927), Woolf's *A Room of One's Own* (1929), and Eliot's *The Use of Poetry and the Use of Criticism* (1933) are essay-like versions of lecture series. The writings of Murry, Leavis, Knight, and others (such as the Cambridge critics I. A. Richards and William Empson) have their importance in the history of modern literary theory, but the three most original practitioners of the critical essay in this period are Eliot, Woolf, and Lawrence.

By far the most influential critic of his age, T. S. Eliot launched with a handful of reviews and essays for the *Egoist*, the *Athenaeum*, and the *Times Literary Supplement* between 1919 and 1921 a revolution in literary taste. His essay 'Tradition and the Individual Talent' (1919) redirected critical attention away from the personalities of poets and towards the particular qualities of poems, and it announced an 'Impersonal theory of poetry' in which poetry is to be seen not as expression of personality but but as an escape from it (*Selected Prose*, pp. 40, 43). Another essay, on 'Hamlet and His Problems' (1919) proposed that Shakespeare's *Hamlet* is an artistic failure because it fails to establish an 'objective correlative' in action and event for an emotional state that remains inexpressibly obscure, thus giving rise to an over-interpreted enigma (*Selected Prose*, p. 48). In these essays, Eliot attempts to re-formulate the basis of poetry as a transmutation of private emotion into achieved public art, and thus to lead modern criticism away from the nineteenth-century cults of Genius and of Feeling. He then sketched out an alternative history of English poetry that could account for the inadequacies of Victorian verse, proposing in 'The Metaphysical Poets' (1921) that what he called 'a dissociation of sensibility' (*Selected Prose*, p. 64) had in the seventeenth century sundered thinking from feeling, with disastrous results in the next two hundred years. With these few undeveloped hints, Eliot had provided a new generation with a radically altered map of English poetic tradition, raising the reputations of Donne and Dryden while sharply depressing those of Milton, Shelley, and most of the Victorians. The details were to be filled in over the coming years, principally by F. R. Leavis and his associates. As an essayist, Eliot exhibits an Olympian loftiness of tone, especially when dealing with the heresies of romantic individualism, together with a certain feline agility in argument and a highly disciplined concentration of meanings that can illuminate a whole phase of culture with a pair of well-chosen quotations. Some of his most telling points are expounded through paradox or through sudden shift of metaphor, as when he claims, in a 1936 essay on Tennyson, that *In Memoriam* is 'not religious because of the quality of its faith, but because of the quality of its doubt' (*Selected Prose*, p. 245). These surprises can leave an impression more lasting than, for example, the habitual resort to paradox in the essays of Chesterton.

The contribution of Virginia Woolf's essays 'Modern Fiction' (1919; rev. 1925) and 'Mr Bennett and Mrs Brown' (1924) to the critical relegation of 'Edwardian' fiction in favour of modernist experimental novels has already been noticed in Chapter 7. Those two pieces, now among the best-known of Woolf's non-fictional writings, are, however, uncharacteristically decisive and polemical. Woolf wrote more than four hundred essays in this period, most of them book reviews, and they are almost always more hesitantly exploratory than argumentative. Woolf took full advantage of the liberties of the essay form, drawing her readers into playful digressions, allegorical fancies, unanswerable queries, and inconclusive reveries, inviting us through a collaborative 'we' to join in an unchaperoned dance of impressions and ideas. Her 1926 essay 'How Should One Read a Book?' (reprinted in *The Common Reader: Second Series*, 1932), for instance, opens with an insistence that the titular question has no generally applicable answer, and it closes with a dream of the Day of Judgement. An essay of 1931, 'Professions for Women', offers a parable about the Victorian domestic Angel who has to be killed by the modern woman writer if she is to write freely.

A playful element of fiction, then, enlivens Woolf's essays, and lifts them clear of the routines of logical exposition.

The essays of D. H. Lawrence are variously philosophical, topographical, autobiographical, and literary in subject, but distinctive in their nervous, repetitive style. They approximate often both to the raptures of a sermon and to the rhythmic effects of a prose poem, heightening the customary cultivation of pet hates found in the 'familiar' essay to new levels of exasperated violence. His literary essays of the 1920s may be divided into two kinds: those on the nature and possibilities of 'the novel',[1] and those dedicated to individual writers. As a champion of novelistic art against didactic moralism, Lawrence is eloquent and usually persuasive, but when he descends to the examination of particular authors and works, he can be recklessly perverse and unfair, preferring to heckle them rather than assess them according to any critical justice, or to digress into his own theories of blood-consciousness rather than trouble to understand the work before him in its own terms. In this sense Lawrence is not so much a critic as an intuitive interpreter who has granted himself the licence to make a novel or poem mean, as in psychoanalysis, the opposite of what it appears to say. This liberty is announced in the first chapter of *Studies in Classic American Literature*, where Lawrence declares that most artists are damned liars, and that the secret truth of their works has to be 'saved' from their duplicity. The essays that follow distinguish sharply between a manifest sense and a latent or 'passional' meaning in the works of Hawthorne, Poe, Melville, and other American authors, with startlingly idiosyncratic results.

While literary criticism underwent a revolution in this period, the more somnolent genre of biography was swept into its own unprecedented phase of self-consciousness and modern experiment. The leader of what came to be called the 'new biography' was Lytton Strachey, whose sequence of four biographical essays, *Eminent Victorians* (1918), was a landmark publication both for the anti-Victorian iconoclasm that I noted in my Introduction and for its radical redefinition of the theory and practice of biographical writing. The success of this book fed upon a widespread impatience with

---

[1] See Ch. 7, above.

the established conventions of biography, an impatience registered in some fictional works of this period, notably Virginia Woolf's *Jacob's Room* (1922) and *Orlando* (1928),[2] and in the spoof mnemonics ('clerihews') of E. C. Bentley's *More Biography* (1929) and *Baseless Biography* (1939). Strachey himself condemned the depressingly predictable products of the biographical industry in his Preface to *Eminent Victorians*:

Those two fat volumes, with which it is our custom to commemorate the dead—who does not know them, with their ill-digested masses of material, their slipshod style, their tone of tedious panegyric, their lamentable lack of selection, of detachment, of design? They are as familiar as the *cortège* of the undertaker, and wear the same air of slow, funereal barbarism. One is tempted to suppose, of some of them, that they were composed by that functionary, as the final item of his job.

Strachey's principal complaint here is that the standard 'Life' of some Great Man lacked literary artistry; but he and others lamented further shortcomings in the dominant biographical tradition: an uncritical acceptance of the deceased's own self-image and of his widow's reverential reminiscences, a prudish reticence about his private weaknesses, a concentration upon public achievement at the expense of any evoked personality. Strachey's most original successor among the younger English biographers, A. J. A. Symons, continued the assault upon these memorial volumes in 1929:

Constructed on the simple formula of chronological sequence, they begin, for the most part, with their subject's birth, and describe his curly-headed innocence, his sailor suit. Chapters two and three, which show no diminution of the one or discarding of the other, are headed 'Schooldays' and 'Alma Mater', and precede 'Early Manhood' in which a passing reference to 'wild oats' shows that the author also has experienced much; and then chapter five, 'Marriage', sets us on the trail for home. 'Life in London', 'Early Work', and 'Later Work' lead naturally to 'Last Days': a death-bed scene, several moral reflections, a list of the books or acts of the victim, and one more biography is on the shelf, probably to stay there.[3]

Such are the damning verdicts of a collaborative inquest, conducted

---

[2] See Chs. 9 and 10, above.
[3] R. H. Mottram et al., *Tradition and Experiment in Present-Day Literature* (Oxford University Press, 1929), 150.

in a sequence of deliberations upon biographical theory in Woolf's essay 'The New Biography' (1927), in Harold Nicolson's *The Development of English Biography* (1928), and in André Maurois's *Aspects of Biography* (1929), as well as in the writings of Strachey and Symons. Biography and what had gone wrong with it were being discussed as significant problems of modern literature; and the conclusion was that the genre stood in urgent need of renewal.

Strachey was the first to offer radical solutions to these problems. Convinced that biography was an art rather than a science, he insisted that it must bring its sprawling materials under artistic control, clearing away unnecessary public facts about its subjects all the better to grasp the secret springs of their essential personalities. The biographer's first duty, he proclaimed in the Preface to *Eminent Victorians*, was to preserve 'a becoming brevity' that would exclude superfluous materials. The four essays in that volume are nothing if not artistically shapely narratives in which the facts—invented where necessary—are subordinated to the aesthetic demands of selection and formal design. Documents, dates, statistics, factual footnotes, and all such heavy cargo of historical scholarship are pushed aside to allow the new biographer's artistic interpretation to play with intuitive freedom upon the inner life of his subject.

Strachey grants himself a novelist's liberty to make an illuminating episode stand in for a whole phase of life, to embroider events with colourful similes, to transcribe imaginary conversations, to interweave recurrent motifs and allegorical symbols, and above all to imagine his characters' unrecorded inner thoughts. The boldness of his biographical method lay in its aspiring to the condition of the novel. He is prepared to tamper with the facts in the interests of vivid caricature, referring at one point to Dr Arnold's comically short legs (they were in reality longer than average, as Aldous Huxley and others pointed out). A more important novelistic feature lies in Strachey's effort to display the subject's personality 'from within' by a process of impersonation akin to the modern novelist's exploitation of the free indirect style. He raids the subject's letters and diaries to identify his or her characteristic style of self-dramatization, then adapts it freely into a fictional moment of inner debate. A typical passage from the essay on General Gordon mimics the private indecisions of the protagonist at such a moment:

What should he do next? To what remote corner or what enormous stage, to what self-sacrificing drudgeries or what resounding exploits would the hand of God lead him now? He waited, in an odd hesitation. He opened the Bible, but neither the prophecies of Hosea nor the epistles to Timothy gave him any advice. (*Eminent Victorians*, p. 208)

Strachey's next book, the full-length biography *Queen Victoria* (1921), concludes with a celebrated paragraph in which the Empress, on the very point of death, recollects 'in the secret chambers of consciousness' the course of her life in a sequence of fragmentary images. It makes an impressive finale out of a psychic event that is by its very nature unverifiable, finding its justification solely in novelistic convention. In Stracheyan biography, we come to know Florence Nightingale or Queen Victoria by imaginative identification, as we would know Maggie Tulliver or Tess Durbeyfield.

Ruth Hoberman's helpful study of biographical experiment between the Wars, *Modernizing Lives* (1987), summarizes the impact of the Stracheyan revolution in a sentence: 'From Strachey on, biography is aestheticized and psychologized.'[4] Inspired by Strachey's example, several biographers in the Twenties and Thirties—Lord David Cecil, Hugh Kingsmill, Harold Nicolson, and Edith Sitwell among them—attempted to shape their subjects' lives according to what Hoberman calls 'novelistic' principles of narrative form, and thereby to achieve a more direct identification with their inner personalities. Their choices of subject tended also to favour eminent Victorians: Nicolson wrote on Tennyson, Kingsmill on Matthew Arnold, Sitwell on Queen Victoria herself. The trend towards exploring the private foibles of Victorian public figures met its parodist in Virginia Woolf, whose short book *Flush* (1933) offered itself as a biography of Elizabeth Barrett Browning's pet dog, lightly mocking Strachey's methods and along with them the pretensions of the biographical genre as a whole.

The psychologizing ambitions of the new biography are most evident in Lytton Strachey's last major work, *Elizabeth and Essex* (1928), an exhibition both of gorgeously colourful prose style and of Strachey's increasingly Freudian mode of character analysis.

---

[4] Ruth Hoberman, *Modernizing Lives: Experiments in English Biography, 1918–1939* (Southern Illinois University Press, 1987), 13.

Sigmund Freud himself—whose English translators, to whom the book is dedicated, were Strachey's brother James and sister-in-law Alix—was sent a copy, and signalled his approval. This book concentrates upon the enigmatic and deadly intimacy between the ageing Queen and her courtier the Earl of Essex, but it offers an interpretation of Elizabeth's entire life and reign based upon the proposition that her 'sexual organization was seriously warped' (p. 20) by her upbringing, giving rise to a hysterical horror of sexual intercourse, and ultimately to the international conflicts inflamed by her prolonged virginity. The political and diplomatic successes of her reign are thus traced not to the lion-hearted boldness attributed to Good Queen Bess in legend, but to secret vulnerabilities that encouraged her to develop and exploit the high political arts of evasion, procrastination, and equivocation. *Elizabeth and Essex* was not as widely admired as Strachey's earlier books, several of his former admirers finding it distasteful to be invited to 'look below the robes' (p. 13) of a great national heroine.

More scandalous still among the new crop of 'psychobiographies', as they soon became known, was a devastatingly intimate analysis of an English writer only recently deceased. John Middleton Murry's *Son of Woman: The Story of D. H. Lawrence* (1931) avoids Freudian jargon but tells a recognizable tale of sexual malformation and hysterical self-denial that begins with the young Lawrence's domination by his mother's spirituality, proceeds through an agonizing conflict between body and spirit, and ends with sexual incapacity, repressed homosexual longings, misogynist rage, and the cultivation of violent compensatory fantasies of male mastery. In Murry's account, informed by close personal knowledge of Frieda Lawrence and her husband, the author of *Sons and Lovers* was a 'sex-crucified man',[5] a false prophet who blasphemed against his own Christlike gifts of love and tenderness because he was revolted by the female orgasm. Himself riven by thwarted love for his former friend and by guilt at the treachery of his biographical exposé, Murry insists that Lawrence was nonetheless a major symbolic hero of his age, 'the great life-adventurer of modern times' (p. 174). The encounter

---

[5] John Middleton Murry, *Son of Woman: The Story of D. H. Lawrence* (Cape, 1931), 21.

in this book between Murry the penitent Judas and Lawrence the impotent Messiah has the appalling fascination of some ritual blood-letting. 'The victim and the sacrificial knife', as T. S. Eliot put it in his *Criterion* review, 'are perfectly adapted to each other.'[6]

Ruth Hoberman in *Modernizing Lives* distinguishes three principal kinds of modern experimental biography, the Novelistic, the Psychobiographical, and the Mediated. To elucidate that obscure third term, we could add that whereas novelistic biographies have subjects, and psychobiographies have victims, 'mediated' biographies have only traces: the first two kinds of life-writing assume that the personality described is explicable by a sympathetic or analytic omniscient narrator, but this kind discards the conventions of telepathic insight, highlighting instead the silences and riddles that frustrate the biographer's quest for complete knowledge. There is a parallel here with the insistence of some sceptical modern novelists (notably Conrad, Woolf, and Ford) upon the final inscrutability of any human heart. Hoberman has devised the term 'mediated' to cover only one significant instance within our period, A. J. A. Symons's study of the eccentric minor novelist Frederick Rolfe, *The Quest for Corvo: An Experiment in Biography* (1934), but this singular case nonetheless poses a more profound challenge to biographical convention than any of Strachey's novelties, and it has won its followers in later decades. A better term to describe it might be 'investigative' or even 'detective' biography, because it throws into the foreground the biographer's own search for clues and witnesses, and with it the first-person voice of the amateur sleuth. As in a detective story, the chronology follows the order of investigation, not that of the original life events, the difference being that the culprit is not in the end forced to confess his motives, but slips away, taking most of his secrets to the grave. *The Quest for Corvo* does not pretend to offer us the connected and sequential 'story' of Rolfe's life, but rather an account of Symons's own adventures and frustrations as an obsessive bibliophile on the trail of rare books and letters.

Symons's unusual experiment produced a hybrid of biography with autobiography. An earlier experiment by Harold Nicolson had

---

[6] R. P. Draper (ed.), *D. H. Lawrence: The Critical Heritage* (London: Routledge & Kegan Paul, 1970), 359.

gone further by mingling the forms of memoir, biographical sketch, and fiction. His book *Some People* (1927) begins like an autobiography with the narrator's earliest recollection of childhood experience, but it turns out to be a false memory after all. From here on, the uncertain boundaries of truth and fiction are crossed and recrossed in a sequence of character portraits representing the stages of Nicolson's life as the son of a diplomat who eventually follows his father's profession. A kind of self-portrait emerges indirectly from his successive encounters with eccentric types—a governess, a schoolboy hero, a language coach, a literary snob, an incompetent junior diplomat— until we reach the comic climax, at which Lord Curzon's drunken valet absconds with the Foreign Secretary's trousers at an important diplomatic conference. Much of this material is drawn from life, but much too is embroidered, invented, or compounded from features of several real people into a gallery of fictional caricatures and grotesques.

Symons and Nicolson lead us to the borders of the last major category of prose writings to be considered here, that of personal narratives: autobiographies, memoirs, travel books, and works of reportage. These genres do not exhibit such major innovations or revivals as we find in literary criticism or biography, but a few general trends can be noted here. The first of these is the increasing prominence of memoirs, reminiscences, and other autobiographical works written by literary men (literary women were nearly all more reticent). This trend clearly responded to a growing public demand for personal details of literary celebrities and their backgrounds, which is echoed in, for instance, the regular interviews with authors— accompanied by pictures of their homes, families, and pets—published in the *Bookman* magazine. On the authors' part, there were financial temptations here, along with those of self-regard, and sometimes too the prospect of pre-emptive self-vindication in a new age of Stracheyan 'debunking' biographers. Perhaps inevitably, it was the Grand Old Men of Letters, with their eyes on posterity, who led the way in guarded self-exploitation: George Moore's self-justifying narrative of escape from Ireland, *Hail and Farewell* (1911–14) was followed by Henry James's reminiscences in *A Small Boy and Others* (1914) and its sequels, then by W. B. Yeats's *Reveries Over Childhood and Youth* (1916) and his *The Trembling of the Veil*

(1922), by W. H. Hudson's widely admired childhood memoir *Far Away and Long Ago* (1918), and eventually by *The Life of Thomas Hardy* (1928–30), published in the name of the subject's widow but actually dictated by Hardy himself. Further memoirs by literary elders followed in the Thirties, among them Norman Douglas's *Looking Back* (1933), John Cowper Powys's *Autobiography* (1934), H. G. Wells's *Experiment in Autobiography* (1934), G. K. Chesterton's *Autobiography* (1936), and Rudyard Kipling's *Something of Myself* (1937). The more interesting of these reminiscences are those that attempt some analysis of the author's early imaginative development, as Yeats and Hudson do in recounting their occultist and pantheistic tendencies respectively, and as Powys does in a remarkable free-ranging account of his sadomasochistic fantasy life.

A more unexpected feature of this period's autobiographical literature is the sudden rise of the premature memoirist. Autobiographers were getting younger, it seemed, or rather the youth cult of the times was encouraging an early resort to self-portraiture. The minor novelist and librettist Beverley Nichols wrote his autobiography, *Twenty-Five* (1926), while still in his twenties. Less precocious, but still under the age of 40, were Ford Madox Hueffer in *Ancient Lights* (1911), Herbert Read in *The Innocent Eye* (1933), Noël Coward in *Present Indicative* (1937), Christopher Isherwood in *Lions and Shadows* (1938), and Cyril Connolly in *Enemies of Promise* (1938). This trend was further strengthened by the Great War, which had speedily transformed youngsters into seasoned veterans. Herbert Read's *In Retreat* (1925), T. E. Lawrence's *Seven Pillars of Wisdom* (1926), Edmund Blunden's *Undertones of War* (1928), and Robert Graves's *Good-bye to All That* (1929) were all war memoirs or autobiographies culminating in war experiences, and all were written while the authors were still in their thirties. R. H. Mottram (*Ten Years Ago*, 1928), Siegfried Sassoon (*Memoirs of a Fox-Hunting Man*, 1928), and Vera Brittain (*Testament of Youth*, 1933) were in their early forties when they wrote theirs. 'No one, whatever his class or his obscurity,' Virginia Woolf exaggerated in speaking of the 1930s memoir boom, 'seems to have reached the age of thirty without writing his autobiography' (*A Woman's Essays*, p. 174).

By this time it was clear that the War had drastically reduced the qualifications expected of the successful autobiographer: you no longer had to be famous or to have moved among famous people, nor did you need threescore years or more of memories upon which to reflect, the world having changed so much in only two decades. The title of Hudson's *Far Away and Long Ago* is justified by its setting on an Argentine farm in the 1840s, but the much younger Vera Brittain could evoke a vanished age of innocence just by quoting from her diaries written in Derbyshire in 1913. The title of her book indicates the modern autobiographer's chief claim, which is neither fame nor longevity but the ability to witness and interpret the typical shared experiences of one's generation. The memoirs of Graves, Brittain, and Sassoon in particular trace the agonizing passage from late Victorian innocence to post-War disillusionment that also provides the great historical 'matter' of this period's education novels and family sagas: Graves and Brittain both significantly start their accounts with memories of Queen Victoria's 1897 Jubilee, and end with attempts to rebuild their lives after the shocks of war. The subtitles of Isherwood's and Connolly's memoirs—'An Education in the Twenties' and 'A Georgian Boyhood'—also suggest a larger ambition to represent their generation.

A special difficulty faced by the youthful autobiographer is that too many of one's contemporaries are still alive and capable of taking offence. Robert Graves had to omit several names and anecdotes from his life story on this account, while others resorted to semi-fictional ruses. Isherwood's *Lions and Shadows*, for example, provides pseudonyms to disguise the real identities of his friends W. H. Auden and Edward Upward, and advertises itself openly as a half-invented account, while retaining his own name and subjecting his younger self to a merciless analysis of ignorant and neurotic self-importance. Siegfried Sassoon went a step further by devising a fictional identity for himself: the protagonist of his trilogy of memoirs is 'George Sherston', an orphaned only child (which Sassoon was not) and later a simple horse-loving country sportsman who drifts innocently into the hell of the Western Front. Sherston is Sassoon minus the more interesting features (of literary culture, poetic ambition, sexuality, and much else), a two-dimensional figure whose innocence helps to highlight the awful passage into wartime experience, but also hinders fuller self-analysis. Robert Graves's more rounded and candid portrait of his younger self, by contrast, offers a far richer range of self-contradictions, tensions, and ironies.

For the junior writers who had been too young for military service, the 1928–9 boom in war books came as a challenge that could be met only by desperate efforts at emulation. As Isherwood confesses on behalf of his age group, 'we young writers of the middle 'twenties were all suffering, more or less subconsciously, from a feeling of shame that we hadn't been old enough to take part in the European war' (*Lions and Shadows*, ch. 2). Guiltily uncertain of their entitlement to write until they had first suffered, several young authors devised for themselves gruellingly punitive rites of passage into literary adulthood. The salience of travel books, works of reportage, and memoirs of self-exile or self-transformation in the Thirties owes much to this desire for generational penance. George Orwell's first book, *Down and Out in Paris and London* (1933), is clearly a penitential narrative in which this Old Etonian attempts to throw off his class privileges as he first works as an underpaid kitchen-hand in a Parisian hotel, and later shares the life of London's tramps. His first-hand account of the Spanish Civil War, *Homage to Catalonia* (1938) shows Orwell finally earning his red badge of courage when a Fascist bullet pierces his throat. A somewhat lighter work by a near-contemporary is Adrian Bell's *Corduroy* (1930), which recounts the author's renunciation of his former life as a metropolitan journalist and his initiation into the rigours of farm labour in Suffolk.

Others embarked upon more exotic and arduous pilgrimages of self-expiation and self-discovery, both responding to and further inflaming the growing demand for travel narratives in the Thirties. Among the more talented travel writers of that generation, Robert Byron found the need to escape the limits of a discredited European civilization and explore the world for himself an 'impulse so imperious that it amounts to a spiritual necessity' (*First Russia*, p. 10). His best book, *The Road to Oxiana* (1937), recounts a pilgrimage to Afghanistan, a land only recently opened to western visitors, in search of architectural wonders that had never yet been photographed. This quest, recounted in diary form, takes him through an exasperating sequence of tribulations—dysentery, flea bites, obstructive border guards, mud, snow, landslides, and mechanical breakdowns—before he has to abandon his goal of reaching the Oxus river. The narrative's success feeds upon disappointment and frustration, enhancing the book's mixture of ill-tempered comedy, satire, and scholarly enthusiasm. In contrast with Victorian traditions of heroic adventure, the modern travel writer of the Thirties thrived on failure, confusion, boredom, and utterly pointless discomfort. Peter Fleming's account in *Brazilian Adventure* (1933) of his fruitless expedition in search of a lost, and probably long dead, explorer in the uncharted Matto Grosso jungle refers to 'the gathering shadows of anti-climax and fiasco' (p. 52) that hang over the whole reckless enterprise. These same clouds hover above the Thirties travel-book genre more generally; their silver linings are those of comic incongruity and deflation.

Graham Greene set off in 1934 for a trek through Sierra Leone and Liberia for no good reason apart from a publisher's advance, and encountered little but prolonged torment from red ants and malaria. The sheer repetitive tedium of his experiences obliged him to find some angle that would enliven his promised book, and he found it in an allegorical treatment that superimposes an inward journey, into Greene's private memories of childhood terror, upon the outward itinerary. The deficiencies of the real expedition give rise in his *Journey Without Maps* (1936) to a new blend of travel description with autobiographical exploration. Meanwhile another English Catholic convert, Evelyn Waugh, had embarked upon a purgatorial and quite futile attempt to match Fleming's Brazilian exploits, hacking his way through the jungles of British Guiana (now Guyana) to Boa Vista, harried all the way by snakes, insects, vampire-bats, and missionaries. As he recounts the journey in *Ninety-Two Days* (1934), Boa Vista turns out not to be the paradisal gateway to the interior that Waugh had hoped, but a wretched dead end, and in the absence of any boat to the south, he has to turn back. Another failure meant for Waugh another opportunity for comic exploitation. Waugh was a specialist in fiasco, both in his novels and in his travel books, which are accounts of getting nowhere, and reports upon having nothing to report, notably in his African narratives *Remote People* (1931) and *Waugh in Abyssinia* (1936).

The art of wresting literary success from practical failure is exhibited most persistently in Fleming's *Brazilian Adventure*, a book devoted not just to describing a failed expedition but to debunking the glamour and danger of exotic exploration in general through anticlimax and resolute common-sense scepticism. Belittling his own achievements, Fleming insists that 'it requires far less courage to be an explorer than to be a chartered accountant', that 'the dangers which we ran were considerably less that those to be encountered on any arterial road during a heat wave', that tropical jungle exploration 'is a soft option compared with caravanning in the Cotswolds' (pp. 25, 9, 115). In his determination not to succumb to exaggeration or romantic cliché, he informs us that 'São Paolo is like Reading, only much farther away' (p. 57), that witnessing a political revolution is a dull business, that the fearsome reputation of alligators is a fraud, and that the thrill of penetrating untrodden territory is merely a kind of snobbery. Preconceptions about the 'Romance' of travel and exploration are mocked here in a fashion that clearly echoes the cool deflatory realism cultivated by other Thirties writers. As in the case of Auden (himself a travel writer in the late Thirties), though, the anti-heroic stance is not as simple as it looks: the inescapable boastfulness of the travel-writing genre persists, in Fleming, Byron, Orwell, Waugh and their contemporaries, although now in the inverted disguise of understatement and self-deprecation that their public-school education had instilled in them. Defeat borne with ironic equanimity and without ostentation is their great subject, and in this period between two legendary failures—Captain Scott's final Antarctic expedition (1910–13) and the British Expeditionary Force (evacuated from Dunkirk in 1940)—it brings them close to the heart of English national self-consciousness.

The best general account of British travel-writing between the wars, Paul Fussell's book *Abroad* (1980), draws attention in its penultimate chapter to the travel book's generic hybridity, its blending and overlapping of reportage, autobiography, quest-romance, picaresque adventure, pastoral, and satire. Especially interesting is Fussell's suggestion that the travel book in this period was among other things a continuation of the *essay collection* by other means, a device by which readers could be lured with the bait of exotic adventure to join in the free essayistic play of thought and opinion. This important connection is most clearly evident in the early part of our period, in the topographical writings of Norman Douglas and

D. H. Lawrence. These are unhurried works, more loosely digressive than quest-bound, and they range at whim across history, legend, landscape, custom, wildlife, morality, and metaphysics. Lawrence's first and freshest travel book, *Twilight in Italy* (1916) is unmistakably a volume of essays in which people and places by Lake Garda serve as pretexts for musings upon the fate of modern civilization. The eleventh chapter of Douglas's book on the Bay of Naples, *Siren Land* (1912), entitled 'On Leisure', begins in the confidential style of the 'familiar' essay:

Come, let us discourse beneath this knotty carob tree whose boughs have been bent earthward by a thousand gales for the over-shadowing of the Inspired Unemployed, and betwixt whose lustrous leaves the sea, far down below, is shining turquoise-blue in a dream of calm content—let *me* discourse, that is—for if other people are going to talk, as Whistler used to say, there can be no conversation—let me discourse of leisure, the Siren's gift to men. But, first of all, pass nearer those flasks. (p. 155)

Not just in its gaudily archaic style but in its assumption of a rapt reader-companion, this passage betrays the reposeful confidence of the pre-War travel essayist, who takes us on a tour of his own mind as well as of his favourite places, and does so at his own pace.

After the War, the travel writer is still essentially an essayist with a suitcase, most obviously in such miscellaneous volumes as Aldous Huxley's *Along the Road: Notes & Essays of a Tourist* (1925), but also in the more coherent narratives of Waugh, Byron, Greene, Orwell, and Fleming. He is now more likely, though, to be on an arduous journey or mission than on an indolent tour, and his tone is darker and more urgent. In part this arises from political factors, beginning with the strange and sinister new regime of passports and frontier controls imposed during the Great War, and culminating in the menace of renewed world conflict that haunts *Homage to Catalonia*, *Waugh in Abyssinia*, and Auden and Isherwood's *Journey to a War* (1938). A less visible change can be guessed at here on the basis of Fussell's suggestion, which is that the price of the essayist's admission to his pulpit, or to the reader's confidence, has shot up alarmingly. Before the Twenties, a general or topographical essayist like Chesterton or Douglas might charm his readers with a well-stocked mind and a repertoire of anecdote and heterodox opinion; but after them, readers and publishers increasingly expected modern essayists to have earned a hearing by prior ordeal. Before airing their opinions, prejudices, dreams, and pet hates, they had first to expose their scars and their symptoms of tropical disease, and to show us their well-stamped passports.

13

Modern Entertainment: Forms of Light Reading

New Words, 1910–1940

baddy cliff-hanger cloyingly corniness crookery escapism gangland glamourize Holmesian mobster murderee outguess predictably racist repeatability tear-jerker umpteen undemanding weepie whodunit

A major feature of this period's social history was the growth of leisure, particularly in the domestic realm. As middle-class suburbia expanded, countless families were served in the comfort of their well-lit homes by new kinds of leisure industry linking mass-production to private consumption. Away from the 'mass'-entertainment venues of the cinema or football stadium, a transformation of domestic leisure was under way, one that brought standardized products and designs into the private sphere of hobby, pastime, and diversion: whether listening to radio broadcasts from mass-produced wireless sets, or to music from gramophone records, or playing the piano from sheet music, the average middle-class English family was amusing itself with pursuits that were increasingly similar to those of most others, from jigsaw puzzles to board games, from dress-making to crossword-solving. Uniform but non-communal, widely shared but reclusively housebound, this new culture of private recreation had as a central element the consumption of standardized 'light' reading matter.

Most new novels read in this period were undemanding tales of murder, elopement, or heroic adventure, borrowed from one of the various commercial libraries and soon replaced by another book of a predictably similar kind. As we saw in Chapter 1, commercial pressures in the publishing trade were consolidating such formulaic genres as the detective novel, the thriller, and the historical romance, and generating ever more repetitive imitations and sequels to feed the most profitable kinds of demand. The sheer scale of this industry makes it impossible to survey more than a handful of its products in this chapter, but we will be able to dip into a few of the more startling and sometimes legendary cases, divided under the generic heads of detective fiction, thrillers, romances, and comical tales.

Detective Fiction

The most spectacular development in modern light fiction was the rise of the detective story. Formerly a marginal curiosity of the Victorian imagination, crime fiction blossomed in the Twenties and Thirties into a huge national craze. While other middlebrow-to-lowbrow genres languished under shadows of disrepute, the detective story, elevated to new distinction by the success of Arthur Conan Doyle's long cycle of Sherlock Holmes tales (1887–1927), offered a sort of intellectual challenge that made it acceptable to the highly educated, and indeed sometimes addictive. Professors, poets, and priests who would never have read an Edgar Wallace thriller or a Berta Ruck romance joined the larger reading public in devouring the books of Agatha Christie, Anthony Berkeley, Freeman Wills Crofts, Dorothy L. Sayers, Margery Allingham, Gladys Mitchell, and Ngaio Marsh. Respected intellectuals became enthusiastic readers of such stories (the poets T. S. Eliot and W. H. Auden were both confessed addicts), and several even wrote them too: Ronald A. Knox, Roman Catholic Chaplain to the University of Oxford and author of *The Viaduct Murder* (1925); the Fabian economists G. D. H. and Margaret Cole, joint authors of several Superintendent Wilson mysteries; the playwright and children's author A. A. Milne, who also wrote the *Red House Mystery* (1922); the leading leftist poet Cecil Day-Lewis, who, as 'Nicholas Blake', created the well-read detective Nigel Strangeways,

partly based upon Auden, in 1935; and a future contributor to the
Oxford History of English Literature series, J. I. M. Stewart, writing
as 'Michael Innes'. A few isolated voices decried the trend: Arnold
Bennett in his *Evening Standard* column repeatedly complained that
crime novels were just arid puzzles without convincing characters,
while Wyndham Lewis in *Men Without Art* (1934) and Q. D. Leavis
in *Fiction and the Reading Public* (1932) were both more alarmed at
the infection of intellectuals through the detective craze by the values
and tastes of the common mob. Nothing, though, could halt the
general adoption of detective fiction as a national cult.

Historians of crime-writing have often designated the period
1920–39 as the 'Golden Age' of the English detective novel, partly
on the basis of the expanding and appreciative readership it found
in those years, and partly on the strength of the unsurpassed plot-
formulas devised by Christie and others. There are good grounds,
however, for backdating the origin of the Golden Age to 1913. In
that year, the journalist E. C. Bentley brought out a novel intended
as a parodic challenge to the mystique of literary sleuths, but which
inadvertently established a fresh modern tradition of detective fiction. In a deliberate departure from what Bentley regarded as the
'heavy' solemnity and superhuman infallibility of Sherlock Holmes,
Trent's Last Case offers not just an ingenious plot with a daring final
twist, but a new kind of detective hero. Philip Trent is a young English artist who would rather be painting or drinking beer than investigating crime, but he is called in to solve the riddle of an American
millionaire found dead at his English village home. Trent's character
and his conduct of the inquiry are markedly un-Holmesian in several respects. Apart from preferring beer to cocaine, he has interests
more important than sleuthing, and even gives up the investigation
when he thinks, mistakenly, that he has identified a culprit whom he
would prefer to shield. Neither obsessive nor infallible in his quest
for truth, he maintains a cheerful sense of humour even when his
two attempted identifications of the culprit both turn out to be mistaken. He even falls in love, which Holmes would never have done,
with the murdered man's widow, herself a principal suspect or possible accomplice in the crime. Trent is, in short, more recognizably
and sanely human, in his fallibility and emotional breadth, than a
master-sleuth like Holmes. Trent's high-spirited misquotations of

poetry, his jocular banter, and his refusal to take himself seriously distance him from the awe-inspiring gravity of Holmes, aligning him rather with a significant modern preference for coolness and levity.

Other detective writers were seeking alternatives to Holmesian omnipotence; and they too tended to create sleuths whose power was to be worn lightly or camouflaged. G. K. Chesterton's Father Brown, introduced in 1911, is an apparently bumbling, dishevelled, and dumpy little priest who nonetheless performs minor miracles of deduction, laced with theological paradox. Ernest Bramah introduced in 1914 the novelty of a blind sleuth, Max Carrados, whose hypersensitivity to sounds and smells makes up for his disability, as does his typically modern sense of humour. R. Austin Freeman's series character Dr Thorndyke (from 1907) meanwhile pursued the unglamorous but effective path of forensic science, as did Reggie Fortune in the later stories (from 1920) of H. C. Bailey. These detectives were among the more important new arrivals in a short-story tradition notable for the variety of its crimes and enigmas (fraud, theft, abduction, and blackmail were almost as common as homicide), but they came to be superseded by the growing predominance of the full-length murder mystery in the Twenties and Thirties.

As the Golden Age proper arrived with the debut novels of Agatha Christie (*The Mysterious Affair at Styles*, 1920) and Dorothy L. Sayers (*Whose Body?*, 1923), it exploited that curious modern combination foreshadowed by Bentley, of murder with levity. Detective novelists of the inter-war period learned from *Trent's Last Case* the value of the breezy, light-hearted approach to detection. They presented murder as a matter of amusing diversion rather than of tragedy or horror, often by making the victim an unlikeable and conspicuously unmourned character, as in *Trent's Last Case* again, but more generally by converting the murder inquiry into an amateur game or puzzle in which the reader could participate dispassionately. In Sayers's *The Nine Tailors* (1934), for example, the detective attending an inquest into a gruesomely mutilated corpse pronounces it 'A beautiful case. [. . .] Quite charming' (p. 76). Assisting this transmutation of slaughter into light entertainment were an array of modern detectives cast in the decidedly unheroic roles of comedian, clown, or conjuror.

Christie's Hercule Poirot, who dominates her work until the

1940s, is a little man from a little country, pointedly misnamed after the classical Hercules, and ridiculously fussy about his dress and grooming. All of this, and especially his broken English, serves to lower the guard of those murderers who cannot take an eccentric foreigner seriously. His brazenly un-English immodesty and his undignified antics in pursuit of clues make of him a sort of clown who unveils his mastery only in the climactic assembly of suspects. Another form of the deceptively innocuous hero was the type later known as the 'Silly-Ass' sleuth. An extreme amplification of Philip Trent's jocular disposition, this kind of detective appears most famously in the shape of Sayers's Lord Peter Wimsey, whose fancy-dress disguises and idiotic mannerisms of patrician slang mask his formidable powers. Margery Allingham followed the same Wimsical route with her detective Albert Campion (from 1929), another upper-class joker who conceals his brain from all but the deadliest opponents. Both faintly resemble P. G. Wodehouse's Bertie Wooster, but are modelled upon the older Scarlet Pimpernel type of the hero-in-disguise. Considerably less irritating is Blake's Nigel Strangeways, who is given to outbreaks of frolicsome intellectual humour. A mood of witty frivolity or facetiousness also infects the works of Anthony Berkeley, Ronald Knox, and Michael Innes.

Another version of the apparently harmless sleuth is the elderly woman whose true acuity is underestimated by criminals and policemen alike on account of her sex and age. Christie's Miss Jane Marple makes only one appearance in a full-length novel in this period, but she manages in *The Murder at the Vicarage* (1930) to outshine the team of male professionals investigating the murder, despite being disregarded at first as no more than an interfering old gossip. Miss Marple was rested for a further twelve years, during which interval the most impressive female detective was Gladys Mitchell's twice-widowed Mrs Lestrange Bradley, a consultant psychiatrist to the Home Office. Her startling debut in *Speedy Death* (1929) shows her capacity to disconcert all the other characters with her macabre jollity as she not only solves one murder by means of Freudian insight but proceeds to commit another herself, getting away with it at the trial, during which she amuses herself by attempting to psychoanalyse members of the jury. As her frustrated accuser, the aptly named Inspector Boring, bemoans her acquittal, the novel closes with Mrs Bradley's hoots of mirth, which re-echo through many a ghoulishly tongue-in-cheek sequel. Female detectives were not an innovation of the Golden Age, being found fairly often in the decades before Baroness Orczy's *Lady Molly of Scotland Yard* (1910); but Miss Marple and Mrs Bradley do still appear as distinctively modern types of unshockable feminine inquisitiveness.

The knowing flippancy that we have noted as a pervasive feature of Golden Age detection consistently points us away from the heavy Victorian realm of melodrama and towards a sprightly modern game of wits. In the wake of *Trent's Last Case*, self-parody is never far away, and the cerebral detection puzzle teases the reader in full acknowledgement of its artificial conventions, the most important of which is the limited group of suspects, each of whom has both a possible motive and a plausible alibi. In this highly self-conscious genre, it is rare to find a detective novel that does not include some mocking reference to Sherlock Holmes or to more recent fictional detectives, and it is no surprise to meet sleuth characters (Sayers's Harriet Vane, for instance) and even a few murderers who are themselves crime writers. We are more likely still, as in *The Murder at the Vicarage*, to find characters within the fictional world who are just as addicted to detective stories as the intended reader is, not that this helps them through the mazes of bluff and double bluff. As Hercule Poirot warns his conventionally obtuse sidekick Captain Hastings in *Peril at End House* (1932), 'You have a tendency, Hastings, to prefer the least likely. That, no doubt, is from reading too many detective stories. In real life, nine times out of ten, it is the most likely and the most obvious person who commits the crime' (ch. 9). In this novel, as it turns out, it *is* the least likely person who is discovered to be the killer; but the declared principle here does disclose the secret of the puzzle formula that Christie perfected. Some elements of this game are derived from Holmesian tradition, while others had been introduced by contemporaries—for example, the exposure of false alibis based on rail timetables, perfected by Freeman Wills Crofts, a railway engineer by profession, in *The Cask* (1920) and later Inspector French novels. Christie's own superiority is found typically in her ability to lure the reader's suspicions away from the principal suspect by the provision of an ostensibly secure alibi, to throw it upon a less likely candidate, and finally to reveal the principal suspect's alibi as a false one, usually faked by a secret accomplice. The process of deduction is often also confounded by the interference of a second or even third minor crime, leading the reader into tantalizing false trails.

The conventions of the Golden Age detective puzzler, with its two-dimensional characters and its precisely specified times (stopped clocks, rail timetables) and spaces (maps showing the rose garden could be seen from the study window), its plodding policemen who cannot keep up with the superior private or amateur detective, all quickly became matters of common knowledge and common amusement. The rapidly developing sophistication of readers drove the puzzle formula either into daring novelties of plotting or into outright parody. Taking the first route, Sayers devised ever more unlikely means by which her characters could be killed off, while Christie, happy enough with the familiar weapons, devised startlingly unexpected solutions: in one of her better-known works of the 1930s, every one of the suspects turns out to be a murderer, while in another, each suspect becomes a victim. Her most notorious technical feat was to reveal the true culprit in *The Murder of Roger Ackroyd* (1926) to be the narrator himself—a device denounced by Ronald Knox and other rivals as an unsporting trick upon the reader. Knox proposed a set of 'rules of the game' to protect readers against this and other ruses such as identical twins, secret passageways, and supernatural agencies, apparently unaware that underhand deception and foul play constitute most of the fun of this essentially treacherous genre. The second, openly parodic route was followed most tellingly by Leo Bruce's *Case for Three Detectives* (1936), in which the mystery is solved by the patiently industrious working-class policeman Sergeant Beef, despite the ineffectual interference of three socially superior sleuths who are clearly versions of Poirot, Wimsey, and Father Brown.

Christie felt no pressing need to move beyond the puzzle formula in which she excelled. Some other crime writers, though, harboured higher ambitions. Dorothy L. Sayers attempted to exploit the customary 'closed' group of suspects in a more novelistic exploration of special social milieux, and she managed this with some success in *Murder Must Advertise* (1933), which is set in a London advertising agency of the kind in which she had once worked, and again in

Gaudy Night (1935), set in an Oxford women's college. Academic settings, especially fictional Oxford colleges, were much favoured in the Golden Age as ideal enclaves of intrigue and poisonous wit, as in J. C. Masterman's *An Oxford Tragedy* (1933) and Innes's *Death at the President's Lodging* (1936). The semi-satirical observation of particular professional subcultures through detective plots was continued in the late 1930s by Allingham in the haute-couture setting of *The Fashion in Shrouds* (1938) and by the New Zealand stage director Ngaio Marsh, who specialized in artistic and theatrical milieux in *Enter a Murderer* (1935) and subsequent works. In a review of recent crime novels published in 1937, W. H. Auden designated this kind of story the 'Murder on Location', distinguishing its social preoccupations from the more psychological concerns of another new variant, the 'Documentary Murder' (*Prose, 1926–1938*, p. 168). In the latter type of fiction, the puzzle element is abandoned, and the so-called 'inverted' plot divulges the identity and motives of the culprit at an early stage, all the better to concentrate upon the psychology of the criminal. There had been earlier attempts at such an approach, in the stories of R. Austin Freeman's *The Singing Bone* (1912), and in a few novels narrated by murderers, such as Oliver Onions's *In Accordance with the Evidence* (1912), but the recognized master of the form in the Thirties was 'Francis Iles' (a pen name of Anthony Berkeley), in his novels *Malice Aforethought* (1931) and *Before the Fact* (1932)—the titles of which both advertise their emphasis on the prehistory of a crime rather than on its investigative aftermath. Some other crime writers of the 1930s developed this device inventively, in particular 'Nicholas Blake', whose *The Beast Must Die* (1938) consists in its first part of a would-be murderer's diary and in its second part of a third-person account of Nigel Strangeways's inquiry into the case: an ingenious combination, this, of the methods of Iles and of Christie, incorporating also some of the social observation typical of the Murder-on-Location school. It may be observed here that the new directions taken by crime fiction away from the simple puzzle correspond loosely to the divergent paths of the serious literary novel towards social concerns on the one hand and towards psychological analysis on the other; and that more sophisticated practitioners such as Blake found ways to reconcile them.

Many explanations have been offered for the wide appeal of

Golden Age detective writing, some of them religious or 'mythic' (the detective as redeemer or saviour), others psychoanalytic (the detective as Oedipus). A more secular explanation, adopted by Colin Watson in his witty survey *Snobbery with Violence* (1971) and amply supported by numerous examples from the period, is a fantasy of social elevation, by which the lower middle-class reader is granted entry into an exclusive world of aristocratic country-house or Riviera luxury, sustained by chauffeurs, butlers, and countless underservants. Snob appeal, along with condescension (and worse) towards Jews and most foreigners, is a salient feature of much Golden Age writing, especially in the characters of such leading sleuths as Sayers's Lord Peter Wimsey, a Duke's younger brother whose nonchalant mastery of everything from fine wines to cricket is described with besotted adoration. Allingham's Albert Campion is rumoured to be of royal blood, his true identity too dazzling to be revealed in full; and Marsh's Inspector Roderick Alleyn, although a professional policeman, is also the brother of a baronet and a model of aristocratic elegance. Snobbery, while important, cannot account for the distinctive attractions of crime fiction, though, because a similar prostration before high-society glamour is endemic in thrillers and romances as well. It also stumbles against the rather different world of Agatha Christie, which, as Alison Light demonstrates in her book *Forever England* (1991), is notably free from Lord-worship, social condescension towards upstarts, and xenophobia. Poirot is a mere petty bourgeois and of course a foreigner, whose unpretentious cosmopolitanism gives him a great advantage over Hastings, who is blinded by English class prejudices. In *Peril at End House*, for example, Hastings shows instinctive distrust of a Jewish art-dealer while warming to an English naval officer whom he commends as a 'pukka sahib'; and Poirot rightly mocks him for this, as the former turns out to be harmless while the latter is exposed as a crook.

A plainer explanation both for the unsnobbish pre-eminence of Christie and for the genre's distinctive motifs of private investigation would rely more upon the pleasures of intrusive nosiness and domestic snooping. On this hypothesis, the reader dreams less of becoming Lord of the Manor than of being his blackmailing secretary, or, better still, the sleuth who is given carte blanche to pry around the bedrooms and dig up shameful domestic secrets. As Nigel Strangeways's wife remarks to him in Blake's *The Beast Must Die*, 'The nose you have for skeletons in family cupboards is really too indecent. [. . .] I might have married a blackmailer' (pp. 163–4). Modern detective fiction gleefully violates older familial sanctities, opening every privacy to cool inspection. In *Peril at End House*, Poirot rifles through the heroine's underwear drawer in search of her love letters, to the horror of Hastings, who earns the detective's rebuke for his 'Victorian' prudery (ch. 13). In its relish for household secrets and their exposure, the detective genre betrays again its affinities with comedy, even with bedroom farce, as the ludicrous nocturnal substitutions and bed tricks of Mitchell's *Speedy Death*, for instance, help to show. The proximity of these genres was not lost on the Aldwych theatre's farceur-in-chief Ben Travers, one of whose finest comedies, *Plunder* (1928), exploits the conventions of country-house crime and investigation in a farce compounded of burglary, blackmail, bigamy, and homicide.

The Thriller

Leading crime writers in the Thirties had their own exclusive social circle, the Detection Club, which denied membership to authors of mere thrillers and adventure stories. That disqualification reflects the ambition of the detective novelists to preserve their literary values of cool analysis from association with overheated melodramatic action. Detective fiction aspired to be modern, intellectually diverting but light-hearted in tone, while the thriller or action adventure was old-fashioned in its humourless stridency.

Detective writers had good cause to distance themselves from the thriller, because in that more earnest and hysterical genre can be found much of the worst in this period's fiction: slapdash construction, implausible plotting, pasteboard heroes and heroines, and poisonous social attitudes. Worse still, many thriller writers were clearly dabbling in materials derived from detective fiction, notably the villainous master-criminal and his sleuth-like pursuer. In Sax Rohmer's *The Mystery of Dr Fu Manchu* (1913) and its many sequels, for example, the English heroes, Nayland Smith and his narrator-sidekick Dr Petrie, are all too obviously feeble copies of

Holmes and Watson. Here they awaken to find themselves pinned to the wall of the fiendish Fu Manchu's dungeon:

Even at that very moment some venomous centipede might be wriggling towards us over the slime of the stones, some poisonous spider be preparing to drop from the roof! Fu-Manchu might have released a serpent in the cellar, or the air be alive with the microbes of a loathsome disease!

'Smith,' I said, scarcely recognizing my own voice, 'I can't bear this suspense. He intends to kill us, that is certain, but—'

'Don't worry,' came the reply: 'he intends to learn our plans first.'

'You mean—?'

'You heard him speak of his files and of his wire jacket?'

'Oh, my God!' I groaned, 'can this be England?'

Smith laughed dryly, and I heard him fumbling with the steel collar about his neck. (ch. 14)

Disregarding any sense of narrative coherence, Rohmer's Fu Manchu thrillers are frantic sequences of episodes like this, in which Smith and Petrie face certain doom but are released by the Chinaman's alluring slave girl Karamaneh, who happens to have taken a fancy to Petrie. Smith is a secret-service agent rather than a detective, and he spends less time making deductions than in warning of Fu Manchu's evil plan to impose 'Yellow' domination upon the entire white race.

Although Rohmer borrows some elements of classic crime fiction, his works highlight major generic gulfs between the detective novel and the thriller. Even in dangerous situations, the Golden Age detective stands back from the bloody action in dispassionate analysis. The thriller hero, by contrast, is hurled into a relentless series of kidnappings, chases, and hair's-breadth escapes that allow scarcely a moment for reflection. As the Man-Who-Knows-Too-Much, he is a fugitive even in his own land, under constant threat from formidable conspiracies—the Germans, the Bolsheviks, the Yellow Peril, international criminal gangs—whose menace plays upon national anxieties in ways that the detective puzzler tends to avoid. John Buchan's hero Richard Hannay is often matched against German master-spies, while for the much cruder thriller writer 'Sapper' (H. C. McNeile), it is Jewish-Bolshevik diamond thieves who pose the diabolical threat to British civilization. A paranoid and, in the case of Sapper's Bull-Dog Drummond novels, an openly Fascist version of patriotism presents the security of the entire British Empire as vulnerable to foreign subversion; and since politicians are corrupt and police forces ineffectual, only the gentleman-amateur hero prepared to hit first and ask questions later can save it from doom. Operating outside the law, a hero like Hugh 'Bull-Dog' Drummond in *The Black Gang* (1923) may horsewhip foreign pests and even illegally kidnap 'bolshie' agitators, treating these activities as invigorating sport. Drummond is an interesting early example of the Silly-Ass hero, apparently just an idiotic clubland drone but secretly the implacable scourge of socialists and foreign miscreants.

Not all thrillers and action-adventure novels of this period are as alarmingly xenophobic as the works of Rohmer and Sapper. Lighter adventures involving diplomatic intrigue and stolen necklaces in fashionable settings were produced plentifully by E. Phillips Oppenheim and by Dornford Yates, whose gentleman hero Jonah Mansel regularly chases jewel thieves across Austria and southern France in his Rolls Royce. Agatha Christie herself wrote a few playful thrillers in this manner, including *The Secret Adversary* (1922), which includes a Moscow-inspired plot to discredit a Tory statesman and thus bring about the unthinkable horror of a Labour government. An equally preposterous caper is *The Secret of Chimneys* (1925), in which Christie offers a confection mixing Balkan intrigue, stolen diplomatic papers, assassination, royal impersonation, kidnapping, and priceless jewels, all wrapped into a country-house mystery. Some of Margery Allingham's early books belong in this light-thriller category, notably *Mystery Mile* (1930), in which the heroine is chloroformed and kidnapped before Albert Campion brings about a final showdown with the head of an international criminal gang. While Christie, Allingham, and Sapper (who also wrote stories about a Holmesian detective, Ronald Standish) hopped between genres, the most famous and prolific thriller writer of the Twenties, Edgar Wallace, simply jumbled them at random, throwing in whatever melodramatic ingredient came to hand. In *The Black Abbot* (1926), for example, we—and almost certainly the author himself—are never quite sure whether we are in a Gothic novel, a buried-treasure adventure, a detective mystery, or a romantic melodrama, although we are at least spared any foreign plots. It is just as hard to determine whether the characters (bookish squire, gentleman-farmer, plucky heroine, gold-digging secretary, crooked lawyer) are meant to be the same people from one chapter to the next, so rapid are their repentances, double-crossings, and illogical transfers of allegiance. Wallace's stories always rattle along in an energetic, eventful fashion, and the mystery element is sometimes cleverly devised, but they have little else to recommend them.

The thrillers of John Buchan, by contrast, display higher literary accomplishment, in their assured narrative coherence and atmospheric sense of place. Buchan dominated the genre during and after the Great War, having purified it into a paranoid form of masculine quest-romance centred upon the endangered hero. The first of his Richard Hannay adventures, *The Thirty-Nine Steps* (1915), was especially influential in establishing the thriller hero as a hunted man with a quest. Hannay is introduced here as a gentleman at a loose end who is unexpectedly launched, by an assassination in his own London flat, on the trail of an international conspiracy that culminates in the theft of British military plans from the Admiralty. On the run both from the police and from the sinister spy-ring, he survives a punishing sequence of chases across the Scottish Lowlands thanks to his inventiveness in assuming disguises. The story relies heavily upon coincidence, but its tense atmosphere of treachery, in which friends turn out to be foes and sanctuaries become traps, is maintained in compelling fashion. The later Hannay books are marred by moralizing and by allegorical conceits, but the second, *Greenmantle* (1916), retains the essential energy of pursuit and disguise, along with more complex portrayals of the enemy. In this adventure, Hannay is joined by a group of chums who penetrate behind the German lines as far as Turkey in order to foil a plot to stir up a Muslim holy war against the British Empire. Published in wartime, *Greenmantle* distinguishes itself from the xenophobia of Rohmer or Sapper by calling for merciful treatment of ordinary decent Germans. It also pays tribute in passing to the austere beauty of Islamic culture, and even concedes that there are admirable qualities in the arch-villain Colonel Stumm, despite the 'perverted taste for soft delicate things' revealed by his domestic furnishings (ch. 6). Despite some intriguing ambivalence about foreignness in *Greenmantle*, Buchan's thrillers came to be regarded as simple-minded celebrations of British patriotic heroism, especially among liberal intellectuals of the kind Buchan satirizes in *Mr Standfast* (1919).

Writers on the Left in the 1930s had a choice to make about Buchan the literary Tory, who became Lord Tweedsmuir and governor-general of Canada in 1935: either to dismiss him or to steal from him. Much of W. H. Auden's early poetry betrays the imaginative impact of Buchan's espionage adventures; but within the realm of prose fiction the most daring appropriation of the *Thirty-Nine Steps* tradition was found in the political thrillers of Eric Ambler. In *Uncommon Danger* (1937), *Cause for Alarm* (1938), and three further thrillers published in this period, Ambler expertly reproduced the Buchan formula of pursuit and disguise involving a protagonist simultaneously investigating and fleeing from malevolent conspirators; but he endowed it both with an anti-heroic realism and with an anti-Fascist 'Popular Front' message. The Ambler protagonist is not an intrepid man of destiny like Hannay, but an average apolitical English engineer or journalist reluctantly entangled in the murderous intrigues of Fascist Italy or Nazi Germany. Inexperienced in such things, he can escape across frontiers to safety only with the guidance of an admirable Soviet spy, who explains the true economic forces at work behind the scenes. The early Ambler thrillers are designed to impress upon their readers the impossibility of maintaining an innocent neutrality in the face of Fascism. The collective villain of *Uncommon Danger*, for example, is not just the network of Nazi agents but also the Pan-Eurasian Petroleum Company, whose headquarters are in London. Ambler can be credited with the feat of standing the John Buchan thriller on its head, at least in political terms. One element that survives intact from the Buchan canon, though, is the creepily effeminate German spy: General Vagas in *Cause for Alarm* wears cosmetics and perfume, which makes him an obvious descendant of Buchan's Colonel Stumm. Ambler was not alone in updating Buchan during the slide towards a new world war. Two impressive chase-and-pursuit thrillers of 1939 were Nicholas Blake's *The Smiler with the Knife*, in which Georgia Strangeways saves England from a Fascist plot, and Geoffrey Household's *Rogue Male*, written as the diary of an English country gentleman who has made a failed solo attempt to assassinate a European dictator (clearly Hitler, although unnamed), only to be hunted down by spies who trace his underground lair.

Loosely related to the thriller was a popular genre of exotic masculine adventure stories that was now in decline since its hey-day at the time of Rider Haggard's *King Solomon's Mines* (1886) and *She* (1887). The tradition survives in Arthur Conan Doyle's light-hearted romance *The Lost World* (1912), in which Professor Challenger and his team of explorers in the Amazon forests discover a plateau inhabited by dinosaurs and apemen. It reappears too in P. C. Wren's *Beau Geste* (1924), an adventure in which three young English brothers, for the most implausible of reasons, join the French Foreign Legion for service in the Saharan desert. Wren here makes powerful use of a mystery plot akin to the detective puzzle, notably in the famous opening episode recounting the discovery of a desert fort manned entirely by corpses. Wrapped inside this enigma is a second mystery involving the disappearance of a valuable sapphire. Between the initial setting and the eventual solution of these puzzles, the story suffers from tedious and sometimes racist padding, but the scenes of action in and around the desert fort are presented with high melodramatic force.

Thrillers and action adventures, although obliged to be more sol-emn and sinister in tone than detective puzzles, were still not meant to be taken seriously; and nobody looked to them for subtlety or artistic distinction. It was possible, though, for serious literary fiction to reclaim the materials of the thriller for unsensational purposes, as Joseph Conrad had shown in the shabbily unheroic world of his *The Secret Agent* (1907). As we have noted, the glamour of espionage was countered in the Thirties by Eric Ambler's freshly realistic per-spective. An important catalyst of this anti-heroic debunking was provided by the crop of books about the Great War that appeared in the late Twenties, one of which was W. Somerset Maugham's *Ashenden, or The British Agent* (1928), a linked sequence of stories based upon Maugham's wartime intelligence work in Switzerland and Russia. *Ashenden* undermined the cloak-and-dagger mystique of spying by presenting it realistically as a business of drearily incon-clusive routines, inadequate pay, and bungled operations conducted from second-rate hotels:

it must be confessed that for the small fry like himself to be a member of the secret service was not as adventurous an affair as the public thought. Ashenden's official existence was as orderly and monotonous as a city clerk's. He saw his spies at stated intervals and paid them their wages;

when he could get hold of a new one he engaged him, gave him his instructions and sent him off to Germany; he waited for the information that came through and dispatched it; he went into France once a week to confer with his colleague over the frontier and to receive his orders from London; he visited the market-place on market-day to get any message the old butter-woman had brought him from the other side of the lake; he kept his eyes and ears open; and he wrote long reports which he was convinced no one read, till having inadvertently slipped a jest into one of them he received a sharp reproof for his levity. The work he was doing was evidently necessary, but it could not be called anything but monotonous. (ch. 7)

The modern tradition of spy fiction, which recognizes the tedium and confusion of espionage as well as its dangers, begins with this book.

Maugham did not pursue his coolly realistic examination of espionage any further; but the younger writer Graham Greene adopted and reworked the elements of international intrigue in several of his early novels, again stripping them of old-fashioned glamour. In *Stamboul Train* (1932; published in the USA as *Orient Express*), an exiled Serbian socialist leader tries to return home on the Orient Express to reignite a failed insurrection but is arrested at the frontier along with an English chorus girl and an Austrian burglar. In *A Gun for Sale* (1936; USA, *This Gun for Hire*) the professional assassin Raven shoots dead a socialist politician, but then tries to hunt down his employer, who has treacherously paid him in stolen banknotes. Summarized thus, the plots seem to promise sensationalism, but Greene's true focus is on the characters, their complex failings and vulnerabilities, their doubts and duplicities. His fictional mode is psychological realism, although it is coloured by a kind of mythology of espionage—comparable with that found in Auden's frontier-obsessed early poetry—which suggests that we are all double agents, traitors, and fugitives, all damaged as much by our loyalties as by our betrayals.

Romantic Love Stories

The title page of Conan Doyle's *The Lost World* dedicates the book 'To the boy who's half a man | Or the man who's half a boy'. Adventure stories and thrillers were romances, in the broad sense, designed to entertain boys of all ages with tales of heroic action. Girls of all ages were offered increasingly formulaic love stories that came to be known by readers and booksellers simply as 'romances', in a newly specialized usage of a term that has much wider applications. This kind of fiction is the literary dark continent of this period, the soonest forgotten and the least revisited. The novels of Ruby M. Ayres and Berta Ruck, for example, who were in their day hugely successful 'queens' of romance, have vanished without trace, although a few notorious best-sellers such as Ethel M. Dell's *The Way of an Eagle* (1912) and E. M. Hull's *The Sheik* (1919) have been preserved in print. Early works by two romancers who began writing in this period and enjoyed strong sales after it, Georgette Heyer (debut novel, 1921) and Barbara Cartland (1925), can still sometimes be found. Otherwise the love stories once available from Boots', Smith's, and the cheaper libraries are sunk in oblivion, although their conventional contents can easily be guessed at: 'Too much about the same thing. Always love', as Emily, a regular borrower from Boots', complains in Huxley's *Antic Hay* (ch. 12). In this section we will glance over a few formulaic fictions, and then examine three superior tales of jealousy and passion.

Romances of courtship draw upon very old narrative traditions, but in this period the tendency was to pastiche certain classic nineteenth-century novels, principally Jane Austen's *Pride and Prejudice* (1813) and Charlotte Brontë's *Jane Eyre* (1847). In the modern formula, the hero and heroine are destined for one another, but misrecognize their own deeper feelings and bury them under masks of pride that bring about further mistrust, postponing but thereby heightening the climax of their eventual reconciliation. The heroine is dreamily sensitive and preferably well born, while the hero is, as in Brontë, dangerously brooding and violent of temper, his proudly undomesticated roughness standing in need of a taming influence that only one woman can exert. The setting, especially in the more torrid narratives, is, as in most other forms of romance, remote in time or place. Elinor Glyn's *His Hour* (1910) is set in Egypt and Russia, where the widowed heroine meets and becomes fascinated by a Cossack warrior-prince who kidnaps and then pretends to have raped her, thereby eliciting her unwilling acceptance of marriage, but the sheer force of his domineering passion wins her heart. This clearly masochistic pattern of ravishment and surrender was replayed with scandalous success by E. M. Hull in her desert romance *The Sheik*, as we shall see in Chapter 17, and rather more tamely if more successfully in Ethel M. Dell's *The Way of an Eagle*. In this novel, the teenage heroine, Muriel Roscoe, is a brigadier's daughter at a vulnerable British garrison on the Indian north-west frontier. She is rescued from terrible danger by the fort's most trusted subaltern, the ugly and cruelly ruthless Nick Ratcliffe, becomes engaged to him out of gratitude, and then spurns him for reasons of pride. During an interlude in England, Muriel becomes engaged to a kindlier if less forceful officer, but is obliged to recognize that beneath her professed hatred for Ratcliffe there burns the inextinguishable flame of love for him. Hero and heroine are then transported separately back to India, where Ratcliffe goes missing until he emerges from disguise (as a beggar, secretly guarding Muriel from harm) to accept her rapturous surrender. This novel established itself as the model that later romancers emulated. When George Orwell worked as a bookseller's assistant in a 'twopenny' lending library in the mid-Thirties, he found that Dell's novels were still more in demand than any other author's (*Collected Essays*, vol. 1, p. 275).

Even in lighter, semi-comical romances, the theme of submission to the authority of a 'masterful' hero persists, and his final steely embrace comes as a kind of punishment for the heroine's attempts to tame him. Georgette Heyer's *Powder and Patch*, for example, published by Mills & Boon in 1923 and set in the 1750s, offers the entertainment of what we might call today a 'makeover' plot, in which the true-hearted but unpolished young English gentleman Philip Jettan is stung by his beloved Cleone's flirtation with a foppishly fashionable rival who outshines him in the arts of flattery and swordsmanship. Urged by Cleone and by his father to acquire some social graces, he travels to Paris and soon transforms himself into the acme of dress sense and the darling of society hostesses. False rumours of a Parisian *amour* reach Cleone's ears, though, turning her against Philip, as he returns to mock her with the fashionably insolent demeanour she has expected him to acquire. Philip proposes marriage, is refused, and withdraws indignantly, failing to guess her true needs: 'Her hand flew towards him and fell again. Couldn't he understand that she wanted him to beat down her resistance? Did he care no more than that? If only he would deny everything and master her! [. . .] He had not understood that she wanted to be over-ruled, overcome.' These mysteries of the heart are elucidated by the worldly wise Lady Malmerstoke, who urges Philip to assert his mastery of Cleone, because 'women don't want gentle politeness! [. . .] They like a man to be brutal!' (ch. 16). In the final scene, a tearful Cleone begs Philip's forgiveness as he kisses her 'almost fiercely' (ch. 19). The eighteenth-century setting, though, insulates the characters' sentiments from direct application to women of the 1920s, the novel being merely an escape into fancy dress, with much flaunting of wigs and snuff boxes. Along with Jeffery Farnol, the author of *The Broad Highway* (1910) and many other historical romances, Heyer helped to establish the original 'Georgian' age of English history (1714–1830), colourfully pre-Victorian in its amorous liberties, as the romancer's favoured period.

While Heyer and Farnol reimagined the worlds of Henry Fielding and Jane Austen as backdrops for 'costume' romantic comedy, other novelists drew upon the wilder atmosphere of the Brontë sisters' works, reaching well beyond the formulaic love story into more disturbing realms of fantasy and fear. Mary Webb's best-known novel *Precious Bane* (1924) is set in the years just after the Napoleonic wars, but among impoverished farmers and weavers in a rural backwater. It is a love story that revives the fairy-tale motifs of Cinderella and the Ugly Duckling in its tale of the 'hare-beshotten' (hare-lipped) and persecuted heroine Prue Sarn, who is eventually rescued from a witch-hunting mob and swept off on horseback by the handsome weaver Kester Woodseaves, the man she has recognized at first sight as her destined 'maister'. Its evocation of rural penury and superstition, however, is robustly unsentimental, the narrative voice of Prue herself managing to blend homely plainness with poetic pungency in ways reminiscent of Emily Brontë and of Thomas Hardy. Especially Hardyesque is the note of tragedy—Prue's avaricious brother Gideon manages to kill both his parents before following his lover's example by drowning himself—along with a continuous interest in rural customs and folk beliefs suggestive of pre-Christian ritual. Prue's neighbour Mr Beguildy is an atheistic 'wizard' who teaches her to read while preparing to exploit the beauty of his daughter Jancis for financial gain. In the one of the novel's more startling episodes, 'Raising Venus' (bk. 2, ch. 8), Prue substitutes herself for Jancis in impersonating the love goddess, displaying herself naked from the neck down to Kester and others and thus discovering the sexual power she possesses despite her facial blemish. There is an 'earthy' eccentricity to this and other episodes, as in the handling of the narrator's lilting dialect throughout, that marks *Precious Bane* as a more original work than any of the happily concluded love romances of its time.

Echoes of Brontëan romanticism may be heard in love stories set in modern times, too. Margaret Kennedy's best-seller *The Constant Nymph* (1924) acquired an unjust reputation as sentimental 'tosh', but, despite the evasive and operatic aspects of its concluding tragedy, it is a serious and intelligent treatment of conflicts between respectable civility and artistic bohemianism. Its central figure is the young English composer Lewis Dodd, who has fled the bourgeois constraints of his homeland to pursue a musical career in Europe, under the influence of the sexually incontinent genius Albert Sanger. When Sanger dies, the future of his lively but uneducated English children becomes a subject both of Forsterian comedy and of urgent discussion between their friend Lewis Dodd and their deceased mother's cousin Florence Churchill, a handsome young woman of 'good' family. Lewis and Florence unexpectedly fall in love, quickly marry, and take the children to England to be schooled. The romantic nub of the tale, though, lies in the unrecognized fact that it is not Florence but Lewis's ward, the plain and sickly 14-year-old Tessa Sanger, who is the One Who Truly Understands Him. As she and the other children abscond from their schools and Lewis refuses to be domesticated, the marriage is exposed as a misalliance between incompatible temperaments. Reconciliation between artistic anarchy and civilized order proving to be impossible, Lewis returns to the unrespectable Continent, now eloping with the precocious nymph Tessa, who mercifully dies of heart failure just as she is about to consummate her 'ruin'. As in *Wuthering Heights* (1847), the tragedy is precipitated by a rebellious outsider deciding to marry into respectability rather than stay in the wild zone with his true soulmate. The mood of the book, though, is far less Brontëan than *Precious Bane*, as it offers through third-person narration a largely dispassionate, even-handed assessment of the central struggles, sympathizing both with the uncompromising bohemians in their exasperation at English middle-class customs and with Florence's efforts to accommodate these 'impossible' people within social reality. *The Constant Nymph* is not so much a romance as a novel about the destructiveness of romantic nonconformism, and its inevitable expulsion from English civilization.

The most impressive disciple of the Brontës in this period was Daphne du Maurier, who transplanted the romanticism of Haworth to her adopted county of Cornwall. Her first successful novel, *Jamaica Inn* (1936), is a 'Gothic' adventure story set in the early nineteenth century among smugglers and shipwreckers, and in many respects reminiscent of *Wuthering Heights*. Its heroine, Mary Yellan, is faced with a Brontëan choice between contrasting types of 'rough' and 'smooth' masculinity, and predictably she ends up married to the unkempt horse-thief Jem Merlyn rather than to the effete albino vicar Francis Davey, who is revealed to be the master-criminal of Bodmin Moor. Having made a Cornish pastiche out of Emily, du Maurier then moved on to the terrain of Charlotte, reinterpreting both *Jane Eyre* and the Bluebeard myth that underlies it in her most famous novel, *Rebecca* (1938).

The immediate success of *Rebecca*, and its enduring appeal, relies not upon romantic 'escapism', which in fact it smothers in melancholy disillusionment, but upon daring transformations of its source materials that intensify them into highly charged psychological melodrama. The novel offers an autobiographical narrative set in the recent past, like *Jane Eyre*, but it makes its narrator nameless and almost characterless: an English orphan who while still in her teens becomes the second wife of the Cornish landowner Maxim de Winter, she otherwise has no substantial identity. More inventively, du Maurier makes Maxim himself an inert figure, all the better to focus the novel upon his dead wife Rebecca, who uncannily haunts the ancestral mansion, Manderley, both in the recollections of the sinister housekeeper Mrs Danvers and in the apprehensive fantasies of the narrator, for whom Rebecca is an undead rival. In the absence of a commanding Rochester- or Bluebeard-figure, the timid heroine's real struggle is against the invisible predecessor into whose shoes she has stepped, and with whose legendary glamour and self-confidence she imagines her husband (and perhaps more importantly, the servant class) is comparing her unfavourably. For her, paralysing fear lurks in the routines of domestic management, and herein lies the originality of du Maurier's modernized Gothic tale. In this inner battle of jealous fear and envious emulation, deep anxieties about feminine self-definition are stirred up, never finally to be allayed, even after the novel's turning point, at which it is revealed that Maxim detested and even murdered Rebecca in revulsion against her shameless promiscuity. Now confirmed as a good child-wife by contrast with the decadent femme fatale, the narrator enters upon an 'inverted' murder plot in which she and Maxim succeed in covering up his crime with the connivance of friendly coroners and doctors. This is a novel that invites its readers to condone murder, a disturbing conclusion that had to be bowdlerized away in Alfred Hitchcock's film version (1940). The ending, which is also the beginning of the retrospective narration, is far from happy: after the crazed Mrs Danvers has incinerated Manderley, Mr and Mrs de Winter go into foreign exile, read out-of-date newspaper accounts of cricket matches, and long for an England now for ever lost—'Those dripping crumpets, I can see them now' (ch. 2). The Gothic nightmare has been burnt away, but so has the beloved home, leaving the heroine to watch over her diminished modern Bluebeard in a hotel room. As in *The Constant Nymph*, the lawless energies of romance are self-destructively purged, and their contaminated victims are finally ejected from England.

Comical Prose Fiction

The humorous tale is not a clearly defined genre in the sense that the detective novel or the thriller is. Nevertheless, 'humour' constituted a significant category of popular and middlebrow writing, with its own addicts and its own shelves in libraries and bookshops. The comic spirit in this period's literature is a pervasive force, often intimately linked with the anti-heroic scepticism of the times, as we have noticed in previous chapters on drama and satire. Elsewhere it is prominent in certain kinds of short story, notably those of Saki, while we have recorded in this chapter too that it infiltrates the detective story. Here we will review a few specialist practitioners of comical prose, starting with some singular classics of this period's humorous writing before considering more formulaic series of comic tales.

In the sphere of comical fiction, a critical consensus formed through word-of-mouth commendation acts with especially cruel swiftness to sort the mildly or topically amusing works from the enduring gems. Three books in particular emerged from that test covered with acclaim: Max Beerbohm's *Zuleika Dobson* (1911), W. C. Sellar and R. J. Yeatman's *1066 And All That* (1930), and Stella Gibbons's *Cold Comfort Farm* (1932). The first of these, sub-titled 'An Oxford Love Story', is also the most old-fashioned, a late flowering of 1890s Oxonian dandyism written in a highly polished mock-heroic style. The story it tells is a kind of aristocratic apoca-lypse in which the entire male undergraduate population of Oxford, led by the super-dandy the Duke of Dorset, commits mass suicide from unrequited love for Zuleika, granddaughter of the Warden of Judas College and a third-rate conjuror by profession. Zuleika is a parodic version of the late Victorian femme fatale figure, although her cheerful vulgarity, pitted against the strict codes of honour that doom the gilded youth, suggests a more Edwardian sense of class mobility and of exhausted social tradition. Far more modern than this is Sellar and Yeatman's *1066 And All That*, a mock history text-book that dashes through the story of England from Julius Caesar to the Great War while sending up the chauvinist verdicts of school his-tory lessons: 'The Norman Conquest was a Good Thing, as from this time onwards England stopped being conquered and thus was able to become top nation' (ch. 11). Interspersed with multiple howlers and spoof examination questions, the book distilled the post-War generation's irreverent rejection of a providential and moralizing view of history that its Edwardian teachers had forced it to learn by rote.

Among modern comic novels, Stella Gibbons's *Cold Country Farm* has a special importance, as it consciously pits contemporary rationality against regressive primitivism and romanticism, poking fun at the darkly superstitious world of the rural novelists Sheila Kaye-Smith, T. F. Powys, and Mary Webb rather as Jane Austen had mocked Gothic novels in her *Northanger Abbey* (1818). Against the Brontëan romance of elemental passions and violence, Gibbons weaves a modern fairy tale in which Austen's values of reasonableness and good sense prevail. The story is set in the future (*circa* 1950), and its heroine, the city-bred Flora Poste, employs such modern innovations as aeroplanes, the cinema, and contraceptives in order to dispel the archaic gloom of her cousins, the Starkadder family, whom she visits in darkest Sussex. The location is Kaye-Smith country, but the comically sinister family group dominated by an obsessive grandmother is based on the Darkes in Mary Webb's *The House in Dormer Forest* (1920), while the Starkadders' repeated claim to immemorial possession echoes Prue Sarn's boast in Webb's *Precious Bane* that there 'were Sarns about here then, and always have been, ever since there was anybody' (bk. 1, ch. 2). The Starkadders are imprisoned both by their matriarch, Ada Doom, who has at some remote time seen something nasty in the woodshed, and by the implacable call of Nature that tugs them ever earthward. The menfolk are sunk in avarice, suspicion, and lust, while the women are oppressed by fear and fertility. Armed with the virtues of chastity and tidiness, Flora releases them from their family curse one by one, giving brisk instructions in contraceptive techniques to a young woman burdened with illegitimate children, turning the feral urchin Elfine into a marriageable heiress, and packing the stud Seth off to Hollywood to become a matinée idol. The action is interspersed with deliberately overwritten passages in which the surrounding natural elements are hymned in violent metaphors of fecundity and extravagantly personified as 'the all-forgiving and all-comprehending primeval slime' (ch. 5). These purple passages are asterisked in order to assist reviewers in their choice of quotation—a 'literary' joke that is extended into numerous digs at the oversexed treatments of nature and of humanity perpetrated by such contemporary authors as Eugene O'Neill, John Van Druten, and D. H. Lawrence.

A small number of prose humorists managed to build successful careers upon recurrent comic characters. Dornford Yates alternated his light Jonah Mansel thrillers with comical escapades involving

Jonah, his sister Jill, and their cousins Berry, Daphne, and 'Boy' Pley-dell, in a long-running series beginning with *The Brother of Daphne* (1914). Yates's 'Berry' books rely for their humour upon continuous teasing banter exchanged among a group of wealthy chums who appear to be on a permanent holiday, either in Hampshire or near Biarritz, and who are besotted by dogs and fast cars. In their carefree jaunts, nothing is quite so amusing as the sight of a gendarme leaping into a ditch to avoid a speeding Pleydell limousine, or of a crooked 'Hebrew' lawyer being snapped at by a Sealyham terrier. Such no-tions of fun depend upon an Edwardian code of leisured jollity that was already outdated by the Twenties; combined as they are with Yates's leaden pomposity of style, they tend to make these books by now almost unreadable. More sophisticated in outlook, and cer-tainly more elegant in style, are the 'Lucia' books of E. F. Benson, beginning with *Queen Lucia* (1920). These are gentle satires on small-town snobbery, more than a little 'camp' in their relishing of faddish rivalries. Their central character, Mrs Emmeline Lucas, starts off as the autocratic 'Queen' of cultural life in the mock-Elizabethan village of Riseholme, her bogus musical and linguistic accomplish-ments threatened with farcical exposure by the arrival of real musi-cians and Italians and by the treacheries of her narcissistic bachelor sidekick Georgie Pillson. In *Lucia in London* (1927) she overreaches herself by trying to worm her way into metropolitan high society; and by the time of *Mapp and Lucia* (1935), she is attempting to con-quer the town of Tilling—based on Rye, of which Benson was now mayor—against the resistance of her most formidable rival in snob-bery, Miss Mapp. The 'Lucia' series attracted a small cult following in which Noël Coward and W. H. Auden, among others, counted themselves as devotees.

The minor talents of Yates and Benson are overshadowed in this field by the greater achievement of P. G. Wodehouse, who is indis-putably the foremost comic writer of the age. Wodehouse was a seasoned professional who had served a full apprenticeship in com-mercial magazine fiction as the author of school stories and senti-mental tales, before he launched his most successful comical series. A second and more lucrative career as a librettist for musical com-edies on both sides of the Atlantic from 1915 helped to perfect his handling of plot construction and dialogue in the novels and short stories by which he is best remembered. Wodehouse wrote many free-standing comic novels in this period, and tried out several recurrent heroes, but two major cycles stand out as the basis of his international reputation. The first of these, launched with the serialization of *Something Fresh* in the New York *Saturday Evening Post* in 1915, concerns the tribulations of Clarence, ninth Earl of Emsworth, at Blandings Castle in Shropshire. Lord Emsworth is a harmless old soul who only wishes to be left alone with his hobby of preparing pumpkins and pigs for the local agricultural show, but is constantly distracted by his bossy sister and his spendthrift son. At the same time he is ludicrously dependent upon his gardeners, his pig-keepers, and his manservant Beach, all of whom know how to manipulate his obsessions to their advantage. A similar pattern of irresponsible indolence and reliance upon servants characterizes the younger comic hero Bertie Wooster in the even more celebrated cycle of stories beginning with *My Man Jeeves* (1919). Bertie is an idle man-about-town, a 'Drone' whose only exertions are those of evasion and escape from his fearsome Aunt Agatha and from the risk of being married off to some alarmingly 'brainy' young woman. The Wooster code of honour also requires him to come to the aid of fellow drones whose allowances are about to be cut off by rich guardians if they marry chorus girls or, worse still, if they refuse to get a job. In all these adventures, nearly always narrated by Bertie himself, it is the imperturbable manservant Jeeves who gets our hero or his chums out of their farcical scrapes, although his ingenuity and discretion come at a price: to be rescued from the wrath of Aunt Agatha means sacrificing some treasured accessory—a vase, a moustache, a girlfriend, even a pair of spats—if it has failed to meet Jeeves's approval.

The Blandings and Jeeves cycles share certain essential comic features, which tend also to recur in the more varied 'Mr Mulliner' series of tales told in the bar-parlour of the Angler's Rest. The plots are all versions of that centuries-old romantic comedy formula in which Love's Young Dream is obstructed by an elderly tyrant, who is eventually outwitted by a resourceful servant. Fully at home in this tradition, Wodehouse steers it away from the warmth of erotic sentiment and into the cooler atmosphere of farcical action, where the love interest becomes a mere plot device leading to pranks and pratfalls. A second feature deriving from similar traditions has as its central joke an inversion of feudal power-relations such that the master becomes a laughable puppet in the hands of his omnicompetent servants. The collapse of the old aristocracy into a state of helpless buffoonery is presented—to what was in the first place an American readership—as an occasion neither for elegy nor for satire but as a comic premiss that is simply taken for granted, although it may be voiced openly by the more earnest Aunt or Uncle figures: one of these calls Bertie 'a typical specimen of a useless and decaying aristocracy', and another 'an invertebrate waster' (*Carry On, Jeeves*, chs. 5, 7). Social indignation, though, is wasted on a caste so terminally enfeebled that we regard its members less as parasites than as children deserving of an indulgently prolonged exemption from adult responsibilities. Bertie Wooster and Lord Emsworth are never more endearingly ridiculous than when they try vainly to reassert an air of aristocratic command, dignity, hauteur, or condescension.

The essence of Wodehousian humour lies neither in the hackneyed plots, nor in the equally well-worn pantomime characters, nor in the social-satirical possibilities they suggest, but rather in qualities of tone, pace, and style. There are moments of delightful mock-heroic levity in the Blandings stories, along with a more sustained anti-sentimental tone that allows us to follow the course of a romantic-comedy plot from the irritable viewpoint of the obsessive—but happily toothless—ogre-figure Lord Emsworth. In the Jeeves cycle, Wodehouse rises to the more exacting challenge of narrative impersonation, each of these stories being (with one Jeeves-authored exception) a tale told by an idiot, in which irony hovers at length before swooping to deliver its deflatory blow at just the right moment. Dialogue unfolds with a fully theatrical sense of timing, enlivened by stark contrasts between Bertie's jaunty slang and Jeeves's solemn polysyllabic formality of speech (the manservant never aims to please; he endeavours to give satisfaction). Both in dialogue and in narrative, the humour of these stories owes much to Wodehouse's artful handling of cliché, which somehow transmutes exhausted verbiage into sprightly fun. In this gift for making something fresh out of anything stale, Wodehouse merits serious comparison with the James Joyce of *Ulysses*. Both authors exemplify the paradox of creativity formulated by T. S. Eliot: that the true originality of a new literary talent is to be found in its adherence to tradition, not in its departures from it. Wodehouse became the master of modern humorous storytelling not by inventing any new style or form but by repeating himself and thereby recapitulating an entire comic tradition, so that to read him is like a homecoming to a realm of laughter that has always been there awaiting us. In that Wodehousian realm, the embarrassing burdens of popular fiction—its formulaic action, its hackneyed language—become blessings, and 'light' reading can freely levitate.

Part III

Occasions

14

England and the English

New Words, 1910–1940

*Blighty   celebratory   conurbation   cuppa
environmentalist   Georgianism   green belt
mock-Tudor   national grid   nostalgically
pre-industrial   tweedy   walkies*

Names for England

The English had lived for centuries under foreign kings and queens, and since 1714 under the German house of Hanover. Then something remarkable happened in July 1917. Amid rising anti-German war hysteria that now threw suspicion upon the monarchy itself, King George V was persuaded to change his Teutonic name (Saxe-Coburg and Gotha) and renounce his numerous German titles. The new name chosen for the royal dynasty, after alternatives including 'York', 'Lancaster', 'Plantagenet', and even 'England' had been rejected, was 'Windsor', after the quiet Berkshire town and its castle, favoured as a residence by Queen Victoria.[1] Under the pressure of German military might, the British Empire suddenly found itself with a self-consciously 'English' monarchy, its Englishness brandished in the form of a southern rural place name. When the aspirant writer Eric Blair published his first book in 1933, he followed his King's example: disliking his own Nordic-Scottish name, he adopted the

---

[1] See Harold Nicolson, *King George the Fifth: His Life and Reign* (Constable, 1952), 307–10.

reassuringly English pseudonym 'George Orwell' after the Suffolk river; it entitled him to become by the 1940s one of the foremost literary commentators upon England and the English.

Meanwhile England itself had acquired a curious new nickname among soldiers serving overseas in the Great War: 'Blighty' was the new military slang term denoting the longed-for homeland. The word, domesticated by soldiers formerly stationed in India, comes from the Hindi *bilayati*, meaning 'foreign'. Displaced and homesick Englishmen at war renamed their country, then, by a double negation as the place that is foreign to foreigners. Indeed the home country quickly became almost foreign to servicemen themselves when on home leave: 'England looked strange to us returned soldiers', recalled Robert Graves in *Good-bye to All That* (1929, p. 188). Writers in this period repeatedly resort to strategies of estrangement or assumed foreignness in order to bring England into focus at all. 'Look, stranger, on this island now' begins one characteristic W. H. Auden poem of 1936, implying that proper scrutiny of the country is possible only from the eye of an outsider. The many writers who attempted in this period to evoke or define the Englishness of England and the English found too that they could do this best by adopting some such 'alien' perspective, as returned exiles, as anthropologists, or as tourists in their own land. This chapter will examine such attempts under four subdivisions: the encapsulating of England in specially representative places or typical prospects; the exploration of England in tours of inspection; formulations of national 'character'; and the conduct of the Englishman and Englishwoman abroad.

England Epitomized

At the start of our period, E. M. Forster's Condition of England novel *Howards End* (1910) seeks various ways into the heart of Englishness, of which these sentences from the beginning of the nineteenth chapter are among the most striking in their use of an outsider's vantage point:

If one wanted to show a foreigner England, perhaps the wisest course would be to take him to the final section of the Purbeck hills, and stand him on their summit, a few miles to the East of Corfe. Then system after system of our island would roll together under his feet. Beneath him is the valley of the Frome, and all the wild lands that come tossing down from Dorchester, black and gold, to mirror their gorse in the expanses of Poole. [. . .] The valley of the Avon—invisible, but far to the north the trained eye may see Clearbury Ring that guards it, and the imagination may leap beyond that onto Salisbury Plain itself, and beyond the Plain to all the glorious downs of central England. [. . .] Seen from the west, the Wight is beautiful beyond all laws of beauty. It is as if a fragment of England floated forward to greet the foreigner—chalk of our chalk, turf of our turf, epitome of what will follow.

Enlarging from this prospect, Forster concludes that here 'the imagination swells, spreads and deepens, until it becomes geographic and encircles England'. These sublimities are deflated in the next paragraph when the German visitors brought to admire this view remain unimpressed; but the passage is still a remarkable exhibition of poetical prose straining to capture an entire country through a proffered 'epitome' of its qualities. The challenge that Forster sets himself here is the impossible one of representing England as a whole, so his only resort is to epitomize, to depict a fragment and invite the imagination to reconstruct the rest in its image. Known to rhetoricians as synecdoche, this device of making a part stand for the whole is a leading feature of many imagined 'Englands' in the next thirty years.

If a part of England is to stand for the whole of it, the question that arises immediately is which part can best serve as representative. Overwhelmingly, writers of this period answered that question with a favoured enclave of the English countryside, usually presented in pastoral terms as a tranquil idyll. The opening chapters of H. G. Wells's novel *Mr Britling Sees It Through* (1916), for example, take an American visitor to an old Essex village unspoilt by villas or golf courses and persuade him that this is 'the essential England' (bk. 1, ch. 1). The poet Edward Thomas, although himself a Londoner of Welsh descent, selects, in one of his own poems represented in his wartime anthology *This England* (1915), a silent farm with adjacent churchyard as the epitome of Englishness imagined as outside time:

a season of bliss unchangeable
Awakened from farm and church where it had lain

Safe under tile and thatch for ages since
This England, Old already, was called Merry.

('The Manor Farm')

The rural scene is the favoured subject of the 'Georgian' poets, some-times to the exclusion of all else, as in Edmund Blunden's *English Poems* (1922) and Vita Sackville-West's *The Land* (1926); and some of those poets explicitly promote aspects of its landscape or vegeta-tion to represent 'England' at large. W. H. Davies's poem 'England' (1918) and Robert Graves's 'An English Wood' (1922) both suggest that the mild, unthreatening tameness of the countryside can stand, by contrast with the wildness of other lands, for larger national qual-ities. More specific in his choice of idyll (and more self-mocking, too) is Rupert Brooke in 'The Old Vicarage, Grantchester' (1912), which selects the Cambridgeshire village and its stopped church clock as the essence of his homesick version of England.

Howards End itself, as we saw in Chapter 8, holds up a Hert-fordshire village and a particular old house near it, as a haven of true Englishness set against the modern forces of suburban sprawl, motorism, and imperialist commerce. The Potwell inn at the end of Wells's *The History of Mr Polly* (1910) offers another such pastoral oasis in a bewildering world. Country pubs are presented as quintessentially English places by a few of the 'Georgian' poets, and more defiantly as sanctuaries of immemorial English liberty by G. K. Chesterton and Hilaire Belloc in their prolonged campaign against cocoa-drinking puritanism. Chesterton's romance *The Fly-ing Inn* (1914) includes the celebrated drinking song 'The Rolling English Road', in which Englishness appears as a boozy resistance to the linear rationalism of the French Revolution. (A similar opposi-tion is proposed too in Brooke's Grantchester poem between Ger-many, where 'tulips bloom as they are told', and England, where the 'English unofficial rose' blooms 'unkempt' under an 'unregulated sun'.) Belloc had already warned the English in his essay 'On Inns' (1912), 'when you have lost your Inns drown your empty selves, for you will have lost the last of England'.[2] Pastoral oases are com-monly presented not only as refuges but as sites for some imagined last stand of Old England against overwhelming aggression from the

---

[2] *Selected Modern English Essays*, 2nd ser. (Oxford University Press, 1932), 122.

New. Anxieties about new threats to the English countryside led in 1926 to the foundation of the ruralist pressure group the Council for the Preservation of Rural England.

D. H. Lawrence's *Lady's Chatterley's Lover* (1928) is well known as an erotic romance, but it is also fitfully a Condition of England narrative, with some resemblances to *Howards End* in its central misalliance between English industrial wealth and partly un-English aesthetic sensibility: the eponymous Connie Chatterley is the daughter of a Scottish artist, and has been educated, sexually and otherwise, in Germany. But Lawrence's book is far more desperate in its vision of England than Forster's, registering as it does the lasting shock of the Great War and the rapacious triumph of industrialism. Most of the action is set on the family estate of Wragby in Derbyshire, whose ancient woodlands Sir Clifford, a paralysed war veteran in a motorized wheelchair, hopes to preserve as a surviving remnant of Old England:

> 'I consider this is really the heart of England,' said Clifford to Connie, as he sat there in the dim February sunshine.
>
> 'Do you?' she said, seating herself, in her blue knitted dress, on a stump by the path.
>
> 'I do! this is the old England, the heart of it; and I intend to keep it intact.'
>
> 'Oh yes!' said Connie. But, as she said it she heard the eleven-o'clock hooters at Stacks Gate colliery. Clifford was too used to this sound to notice. (ch. 5)

The irony here is that Clifford's determination to preserve the heart of old England is literally undermined by his own colliery, the noise of which disturbs these woods day and night. The fate of a neighbouring landowner's country estate, also linked to its colliery, illustrates what will inevitably happen to the Old England once the gentry sell themselves to industrial development: it is razed to make way for rows of semi-detached houses. There is in this book no secure idyll in the woods, only a temporary hiding place for the lovers, the representative 'heart' of Lawrence's England having been already violated beyond repair. Indeed, as Connie recognizes in her drive through a nearby town that was once part of 'Merrie England', it is now 'on the spontaneous, intuitive side dead, but dead' (ch. 11).

There were other ways of epitomizing England on an even smaller scale, in the person of a representatively English individual. Rupert Brooke's famous war sonnet 'The Soldier' (1915) employs a spectacularly paradoxical synecdoche in imagining the speaker's likely burial as a transplantation of Englishness: 'there's some corner of a foreign field | That is for ever England' (*Poetical Works*, p. 23). Edward Thomas's narrative poem 'Lob' (1915) conjures up an elusive old countryman who appears to be the immortal genius of English folk custom and the minter of curious names for herbs and wild flowers. Dorothy L. Sayers offers her detective hero Peter Wimsey as the essence of English gentility: his newly wed wife Harriet in *Busman's Honeymoon* (1937) dotes on him as the embodiment of an ordered society, to the extent that she persuades herself that she has 'married England' (p. 98). More usual, though, was the evocation of a larger England through significant scenic prospects, as in the Forster passage above, and especially those surveyed at points of departure and homecoming, such as Dover (the subject of a W. H. Auden poem of 1937) or Folkestone, from which the protagonist of D. H. Lawrence's *Kangaroo* (1923) sails into exile, looking back to find that 'England looked like a grey, dreary-grey coffin sinking in the sea behind' (ch. 12). George Orwell adapts this device in the closing paragraph of *Homage to Catalonia* (1938): returning by train through Kent to London after serving in the Spanish Civil War, he is struck by the unchanging tranquillity of southern England, its apparent seclusion from the violent world outside. The inhabitants all seem to be 'sleeping the deep, deep sleep of England', from which only bombs are likely to awaken it.

Writers could view England from shipboard or from a train window, or they could explore it more freely, like Connie Chatterley, by motor car; but they now also had the more modern option of presenting it from the air. The most memorable exploitation of such aerial views comes in Evelyn Waugh's *Vile Bodies* (1930), when the newly-weds Ginger and Nina fly off for a honeymoon in Monte Carlo. Looking down on their homeland, Ginger is inspired to recite snatches of John of Gaunt's speech from *Richard II* about England as 'this precious stone set in the silver sea', and asks Nina whether she too feels patriotic at the sight.

Nina looked down and saw inclined at an odd angle a horizon of straggling red suburb; arterial roads dotted with little cars; factories, some of them working, others empty and decaying; a disused canal; some distant hills sown with bungalows; wireless masts and overhead power cables; men and women were indiscernible except as tiny spots; they were marrying and shopping and making money and having children. The scene lurched and tilted again as the aeroplane struck a current of air.

'I think I'm going to be sick,' said Nina. (ch. 12)

The historical lurch from the beauty and self-confidence of Shakespeare's England to this dismally industrial panorama is nauseating to Waugh, and so it was to many of his contemporaries.

George Bowling, the embittered hero of Orwell's *Coming Up for Air* (1939), is similarly sickened by the transformation of the woods in which he once played as a boy into a suburban estate of mock-Tudor houses: 'doesn't it make you puke sometimes', he asks, 'to see what they're doing to England, with their bird-baths and their plaster gnomes, and their pixies and tin cans, where the beechwoods used to be?' (pt. 4, ch. 5). This desecration of Old England by the vulgarity of the New comes in the late Twenties and the Thirties to the forefront of literary Englishness, replacing the celebratory ruralism of Forster and the 'Georgian' poets. In other words, a defensive pastoralism gives way after the Great War to an aggressive counter-pastoral emphasis on landscapes defaced. Lawrence and Orwell in particular are determined to confront their readers with the dispiriting ugliness of the modern commercial-industrial English scene. 'The real tragedy of England, as I see it,' wrote Lawrence in his essay 'Nottingham and the Mining Countryside' (1930), 'is the tragedy of ugliness. The country is so lovely; the man-made England is so vile' (*Selection from Phoenix*, p. 108). The eleventh chapter of *Lady Chatterley's Lover* surveys the blighting of Old England, the England of Robin Hood and the stately homes, by the encroachments of industrial England: 'One England blots out another. The mines had made the halls wealthy. Now they were blotting them out, as they had already blotted out the cottages. The industrial England blots out the agricultural England. One meaning blots out another. The new England blots out the old England.' Orwell's early novels likewise insist on the shabby, dingy, squalid spectacle that modern England presents to the sensitive beholder, while his book of reportage *The Road to Wigan Pier* (1937), which we will revisit in the next section, remarks that in 'a crowded, dirty little country like ours one takes defilement almost for granted. Slag-heaps and chimneys seem a more normal, probable landscape than grass and trees' (ch. 1). These are responses to a long process of nineteenth-century industrialization, and they belong partly to a long tradition of literary anti-industrialism, descending from Carlyle and Ruskin. The nausea of Nina Blount or George Bowling, though, is induced by a more recent blight, an apparently brighter one of mock-Tudor houses, pylons, and shiny industrial estates.

The epitome of this newest England was no longer Coketown or Wigan but Slough, a modern industrial town that had lately mushroomed around a cluster of wartime supply depots in impertinent proximity both to royal Windsor and to Eton College. The place is mentioned in passing in two of Orwell's novels and again in Aldous Huxley's *Brave New World* (1932), but the incorrigible snob John Betjeman singled it out cruelly in his poem 'Slough' (1937), calling upon 'friendly bombs' to destroy it:

> Come, bombs, and blow to smithereens
> Those air-conditioned, bright canteens,
> Tinned fruit, tinned meat, tinned milk, tinned beans
>   Tinned minds, tinned breath.

In this England of denatured convenience, men 'do not know | The birdsong from the radio', while their wives 'frizz out peroxide hair | And dry it in synthetic air'. Nature has been expelled from this false paradise, and historical tradition is reduced to fakery, in 'various bogus Tudor bars' (*Collected Poems*, pp. 22–3). A long way from Howards End or Grantchester, even from Lawrence's Wragby, here we see epitomized an England so denuded of the poetical that it deserves, in this despairingly inhumane view, to be blasted away.

England Explored

Books about England, and especially about rural England, had emerged as a readily saleable genre of topographical prose in Edwardian times, with Edward Thomas being one of its busiest producers, in such works as *The Heart of England* (1906), *The South Country*

(1909), and *A Literary Pilgrim in England* (1917). Books on England became more plentiful still in the late Twenties and throughout the Thirties. The 'Georgian' poet J. C. Squire edited a whole series of them for the publishers Longmans: the English Heritage Series included volumes on *English Wild Life*, *English Music*, *Shakespeare*, *The English Inn*, *The English Country Town*, *The English Public School*, *The English Parish Church*, *English Humour* (by J. B. Priestley, 1929), *Cricket* (by Neville Cardus, 1931), and *The Face of England* (by Edmund Blunden, 1932). The last of these is a miscellany of notes and sketches of rustic life in Suffolk arranged as a calendar of the year. Similar in structure is T. H. White's *England Have My Bones* (1936), a year's journal of country sports in an unnamed shire, somewhat unbalanced by the author's lengthy accounts of his flying lessons. Along with all these came *The Legacy of England* (1935) with chapters by various hands on 'The Farm', 'The Village', 'The Country House', 'The Country Church', and inevitably 'The Inn'; then W. S. Shears's *This England: A Book of the Shires and Counties* (1936), a fat guidebook with lists of 'places of interest' subdivided into Churches, Castles, and Inns, and recommendations for the sampling of local cuisine. Shears was immediately outdone by Arthur Mee's *Enchanted Land* (1936), which inaugurated the enormous 'King's England' series of county guides. More original in conception was Philip Gibbs's *England Speaks* (1935), a series of interviews with people from all walks of life, published to commemorate King George's Silver Jubilee. A bemused outsider's perspective was provided by A. G. Macdonell's *England, Their England* (1930), a comic novel in which a Scotsman is commissioned to write a book about the English but, after several picaresque adventures among journalists, diplomats, and village cricketers, fails to write it. Sometimes referred to as a satire, this novel is far too mildly indulgent to be called that: it concludes that the English are a kindly and poetical race, and that 'rural England is the real England, unspoilt by factories and financiers and tourists and hustle' (ch. 7)—none of which would have offended Macdonell's employer at the *London Mercury*, J. C. Squire, to whom the book is dedicated.

The more enterprising attempts to capture England between the covers of books were those few in which writers set out to explore the land for themselves like Defoe and Cobbett before them, although now with the help of motor cars, motor coaches, and trains. The three outstanding products of these tours of inspection are H. V. Morton's *In Search of England* (1927), J. B. Priestley's *English Journey* (1934), and George Orwell's *The Road to Wigan Pier*. The first of these recounts a long tour by motor car through most of the beauty spots and tourist shrines of the western and eastern shires, carefully avoiding the industrial regions in between. Morton is an enthusiastic and whimsical guide, determined to add 'romance' to the standard guidebook descriptions by imagining the ghosts of medieval history coming to life, or holding imaginary conversations with abbots and Roman centurions; at Plymouth he closes his eyes and dreams of Sir Francis Drake, at Winchester and Glastonbury of King Arthur. In Berkshire and again in Suffolk he stops to admire the last masters of ancient rural crafts. The England he seeks is almost always an Olde England of ruins, relics, and survivals. For Morton the village and the cathedral are the essential England, while the industrial cities are 'mere black specks against the mighty background of history and the great green expanse of fine country which is the real North of England' (ch. 9). *In Search of England* was a best-seller, running through seventeen editions in five years. A sequel, *The Call of England* (1928), was quickly produced, in part as a peace-offering to slighted northerners: this second tour takes in Hull, Newcastle, Manchester, Liverpool, Sheffield, and Birmingham. Morton, acknowledging in the introduction that the first book had 'deliberately shirked realities', does now pay attention to industry and labour conditions, but at the first opportunity he dashes off again to castles and abbeys.

The great economic depression of the early Thirties quickly changed the ways in which England was surveyed and written up. Several writers became guiltily aware that they knew next to nothing of the northern industrial regions or of mass unemployment. The first to set out on an organized tour of inspection was Aldous Huxley, who visited the Durham coalfield in 1930, returning in early 1931 on a tour that also took in the London docks, Birmingham, Sheffield, and Middlesbrough. The literary fruit of this 'sight-seeing in the alien Englands of manual labour and routine' (*Hidden Huxley*, p. 72) was a sequence of rather anaemic articles on the need for economic planning. Far more thorough was J. B. Priestley's exploration of England in the autumn of 1933, written up in the great domestic tour-book of the period, *English Journey*. Priestley had grown up in industrial Bradford, so the north was by no means alien to him; and he harboured no nostalgia for village greens or cathedral closes. Although his itinerary—westward, then northward, and finally down through the eastern side—broadly resembles Morton's in *In Search of England*, Priestley's destinations and his purposes are strikingly different. Quite uninterested in ancient relics or tourist shrines (even York fails to impress him), he misses out most of the cathedral cities and goes looking instead for the true face of contemporary England in factories, schools, shops, pubs, markets, bingo halls, cinemas, chapels, and fairgrounds, always on the lookout for the state of trade, employment, and civic culture. One chapter is devoted to the Cotswolds and another to East Anglia, but the rest of the book is devoted to ports and industrial centres, from Southampton, Bristol, and Liverpool to Sheffield, the Staffordshire Potteries, and Tyneside. Many of these places he finds depressingly ugly, but it is an important feature of Priestley's moral vision of England that he refuses to follow the intelligentsia's habitual equation of environment with spiritual bankruptcy—as in Betjeman's 'Slough' poem and its easy linking of tinned food to 'tinned minds'. On a tram ride through the dreariest parts of Birmingham, he pauses to reflect that the English here are not getting the England they deserve:

I loathed the whole long array of shops, with their nasty bits of meat, their cough mixtures, their *Racing Specials*, their sticky cheap furniture, their shoddy clothes, their fly-blown pastry, their coupons and sales and lies and dreariness and ugliness. I asked myself if this really represented the level reached by all those people down there on the pavements. I am too near them myself, not being one of the sensitive plants of contemporary authorship, to believe that it does represent their level. They have passed it. (p. 86)

Although as a professional dramatist Priestley worries aloud about the closure of provincial theatres and their conversion into cinemas, he resolutely avoids blaming the debased tastes of the urban masses for the conditions in which they live. The true challenge, rather, is to reconstruct an England that allows those people on the pavement to expand themselves, to work and play more fully.

In the final chapter of *English Journey*, Priestley concludes that he has seen not one but three Englands overlaid: the Old England cherished by conservationists and tourists, the nineteenth-century Industrial England of unchecked despoliation and grime, and a newer post-War England:

This is the England of arterial and by-pass roads, of filling stations and factories that look like exhibition buildings, of giant cinemas and dance-halls and cafés, bungalows with tiny garages, cocktail bars, Woolworths, motor-coaches, wireless, hiking, factory girls looking like actresses, grey-hound racing and dirt tracks, swimming pools, and everything given away for cigarette coupons. (p. 375)

Priestley is glad to report that this newest England is cleaner and safer, and that its popular culture, best represented by Blackpool, is clearly more democratic in its erosion of old deferential hierarchies, but he worries that it is also more monotonously standardized, and lacking in older kinds of individuality, character, or spontaneous enjoyment.

Orwell's *The Road to Wigan Pier* makes no attempt to survey the varied Englands of its time. It offers a more selective inquiry into some surviving enclaves of nineteenth-century industrial squalor. The book falls into two halves, of which the second is a critique of the English Left's puritanical culture of doctrinaire self-righteousness. The first part, though, is a vivid narrative of a middle-class southern-er's investigation of living conditions in what had become known as 'distressed areas' of the industrial north. Orwell picks out Wigan in Lancashire and Barnsley in Yorkshire as representative sites, and re-ports on them both with the eye—and nose—of a novelist and with the factual accuracy of a surveyor or accountant. *The Road to Wigan Pier* begins like a novel, setting its opening scene in a squalid board-ing house where the ever-squeamish Orwell is assailed by bad smells, and absorbs the larger atmosphere of stagnant decay. We move on shortly to a coal mine, where Orwell describes the sheer physical effort of moving and working underground. Having established the physical feel of these places, he proceeds to unfold the practical statistics of poverty: how an unemployed man manages to survive on the dole, how much a miner really takes home after various deduc-tions from his wages, how a working-class family struggles to main-tain hygiene in a back-to-back house, how it scrapes together enough food and fuel. From here he can enlarge upon general questions of social class, the north–south divide, and the condition of the English as a whole: digressing from the poor state of teeth in most Lancashire adults, he recalls standing in the London crowds at the funeral of King George V and being struck by 'the physical degeneracy of modern England' revealed in the puny, sickly specimens around him (ch. 6). The sturdiest of men, he supposes, have been killed off in the Great War, leaving in their place a troglodytic population enfeebled by industrialism and now by a diet of white bread and tinned food.

The physical decline of the English people had been a matter of public anxiety since the time of the Boer War; but in the Thirties bodily infirmity became in the hands of the younger poets a powerful metaphor by which a generally morbid or paralytic condition of English society could be evoked. W. H. Auden's surrealistic medley of verse fantasy and prose parody, *The Orators: An English Study* (1932) attempts a fragmentary diagnosis of 'England, this country of ours where nobody is well' (*English Auden*, p. 62). Likewise C. Day Lewis in section 33 of his *The Magnetic Mountain* (1933) presents a satirical picture of 'our pleasant land' in which decay has 'clogged our bowels, | Impaired our breathing':

> Where is the bourgeois, the backbone of our race?
> Bent double with lackeying, the joints out of place
>
> (*Complete Poems*, pp. 170–1)

English mythology had once treasured its images of masculine corpulence, from Falstaff to John Bull. The tours of inspection conducted by Priestley and Orwell now tended to confirm the poets' intuitive sense of the post-War English as somehow shrunken, inactive, and unwell.

The English Character

To an unprecedented degree, the literature of this period invites its English readers to re-examine their insular certainties by looking at themselves as others see them. The literary world was populated as never before by non-English outsiders and by English writers habituated to foreign customs, many of whom were keen to bring home truths from abroad. Rudyard Kipling, himself originally a colonial outsider, was one: his poem 'We and They' (1926) mocks the childish certainties of Anglocentrism with the relativist conclusion that 'we' are only another 'they' to others. The Irishman Bernard Shaw had long been the chief mocker of English complacency, and in this period he continues his exposure of its blindnesses by adopting not Irish but French vantage points. In *Saint Joan* (1924) he includes among the English conquerors of fifteenth-century France a chaplain, de Stogumber, cast by deliberate anachronism as a jingoist who believes that England's territorial gains have been 'given her by God because of her peculiar fitness to rule over less civilized races for their own good' (p. 100). Yet this stereotype is offered only to be inverted in other respects: against type, the chaplain is emotionally fiery and intemperate, more violent than the French inquisitors both in his impatience to have Joan burned and in self-recrimination after the event. Shaw delighted in overturning all clichés about the English, even the negative ones. His most extravagant exercise in this vein is the long Anglophile eulogy in *Fanny's First Play* (1911), delivered to a conventional English family by a French soldier who believes he has found a paradise of nonconformity:

Your country is a model to the rest of Europe. If you were a Frenchman, stifled in prudery, hypocrisy, and the tyranny of the family and the home, you would understand how an enlightened Frenchman admires and envies your freedom, your broadmindedness, and the fact that home life can hardly be said to exist in England. (p. 171)

This tribute is in one sense an absurd misconception, but Shaw wants us to glimpse a paradoxical truth in it. As other writers noticed too, England was simultaneously the homeland of a Protestant individualism cultivated to the point of eccentricity, and the inventor of stifling conventions of emotional repression and 'good form'. The English were, puzzlingly, both restricted and free, glacial and impassioned, utilitarian and poetical.

   Such contradictions are laid bare by Ford Madox Hueffer's novel *The Good Soldier* (1915), in which the narrator is an American who, as we saw in Chapter 7, confesses from the start his failure to understand the English. The soldier of the title is Edward Ashburnham, the very model of an English gentleman, whose outward poise and nonchalance disguise an inner chaos of sexual passion and despair. The novel avoids presenting the case of this adulterous magistrate as anything so simple as 'hypocrisy': Ashburnham's profoundly conflicted identity is to be seen rather as an inscrutably English condition, one whose roots lie deep in national history. Repeated links between Ashburnham and Henry VIII—he has, for instance, a Catholic wife who will not divorce him—tend to suggest that the modern soldier embodies both the established dignity of the post-Reformation English State and the polygamous incontinence upon which it was originally founded. Destructive passion and rigid self-control cohabit, Hueffer implies, not just in the individual English heart but in the particular Protestant history that nurtures it.

Similar enigmas of the English character were considered in non-fictional writings both by visiting foreigners and by English writers responding to foreign bafflement. The Americanized Spanish philosopher and critic George Santayana was resident in Oxford during the Great War, and he spent his time meditating upon the English scene: its weather, religion, architecture, arts, social manners, and in general its national character, in essays later published as *Soliloquies in England* (1922). While the Englishman, Santayana observes with the confidence of an outsider, 'is the most disliked of men the world over (except where people need some one they can trust) he is also the most imitated'.[3] Some secret of English character produces cultural institutions that are copied elsewhere—football, afternoon tea, and so forth—along with a demeanour that commands universal grudging respect, although plainly this secret cannot be principled intelligence; nor is it likely to be articulate passion; nor even attachment to convention. 'If we tried to say that what governs [the Englishman] is convention, we should have to ask ourselves how it comes about that England is the paradise of individuality, eccentricity, heresy, anomalies, hobbies, and humours' (p. 30). The secret lies somewhere close to this stubborn individualism, as Santayana decides, in a certain inner atmosphere, an imperviousness to the outer world that gives the Englishman steadiness, directness, and self-assurance.

Apart from their exasperation with the hazy muddle of the English

---

[3] George Santayana, *Soliloquies in England; and Later Soliloquies* (University of Michigan Press, 1967), 54.

intellect, Santayana's *Soliloquies* are courteous tributes from a grateful guest. A more intimately troubled brooding upon the strengths and weaknesses of the English appears in E. M. Forster's essay 'Notes on the English Character' (1926; collected in *Abinger Harvest*, 1936), which is in part an attempt to explain to the author's Indian friends in the aftermath of the Amritsar massacre of 1919 why the English are not necessarily to be written off as innately cruel, callous, or perfidious. The essential problem with England, as Forster sees it, is that the middle class has for over a century dominated its culture, and in particular has evolved the unique public-school ethos with its conformist suppression of the feelings. The result is that the Englishman carries about with him an 'undeveloped heart' that inhibits his emotional expression as well as his spiritual and intellectual growth. Taught to bury his feelings deep, he appears to the foreigner as complacent, insensitive, and reserved, although his unimaginative decency also preserves him from conscious malice.

Forster's and Santayana's discussions of 'the Englishman' are clearly not concerned with actual regional and class differences, let alone cultural hybridities, among the English; they are in fact accounts only of a limited but internationally prominent stereotype: that of the upper middle-class public-school alumnus, confident in his practical efficiency and respectability but emotionally inarticulate and unimaginative. The same is true of the provocatively titled *The English: Are They Human?* (1931) by the visiting Dutch academic G. J. Renier, which concentrates on the reticent, pragmatic middle-class male specimen. Given the real social importance of this type, it should not surprise us to find it everywhere in the fiction and drama of this period, most often in minor comic roles but often too in sustained portrayal, from Galsworthy's Soames Forsyte, Forster's Henry Wilcox, D. H. Lawrence's Gerald Crich (in *Women in Love*, 1920), and W. Somerset Maugham's Arnold Champion-Cheney (in his play *The Circle*, 1921), through to Thomas Quayne in Elizabeth Bowen's *The Death of the Heart* (1938). Some treatments of this familiar figure are capable of disclosing its unspoken depths of feeling, as in Katherine Mansfield's story 'The Man without a Temperament' (1920). Some go further in positive endorsement of the English gentleman's virtues, as Ford Madox Ford does with his old-fashioned chivalrous Tory protagonist Christopher Tietjens in

Parade's End (1924–8), whose incorruptible decency exasperates his various enemies even more than his stoically impassive calm. Other writers manage to confirm the stereotype with one hand while retracting it with the other, rather in the manner of Shaw. In Jean Rhys's *Good Morning, Midnight* (1939), the English narrator, Sasha Jensen, is dismissed from her job in a Paris store by its manager, the sternly unsympathetic Mr Blank, a representative Englishman; but she is later questioned by a French gigolo who has never been to England but has been told that half the male population there is homosexual and the other half uninterested in sex. Is it true, he asks, that Englishmen make love with all their clothes on, in deference to respectability? 'Yes, certainly', Sasha responds. 'Fully dressed. They add, of course, a macintosh' (p. 132).

The perfect comic embodiment of 'the Englishman' in this period's fiction is Captain Arthur Hastings, the sidekick of Hercule Poirot in many of Agatha Christie's detective stories and novels. It is appropriate that his surname should recall a historic English defeat at the hands of superior Gallic power, because Hastings spends most of his time being condescended to by Poirot, a French-speaking Belgian whose intellectual and imaginative powers leave the Englishman gasping to catch up. As we noticed in Chapter 13, much of the vitality of these stories derives from Poirot's incidental observations on the oddities of the English—their obsession with sport, their miserable cuisine—and from his effortless humiliation not only of the slow-witted Hastings but of other English characters. The villian unmasked at the end of *The ABC Murders* (1936), for example, is an English xenophobe who repeatedly rails against damned foreigners, including Poirot himself, but the Belgian has the last word, condemning the serial killer's crimes as un-English because they are 'not *sporting*' (ch. 34). Crueller still in the opening chapter of *Peril at End House* (1932), Poirot insists on reminding Hastings of defeats suffered by English tennis players at Wimbledon. The great popularity of Christie's Poirot stories, with their repeated crushing of Hastings's national pride, seems to indicate that English readers commonly looked to fiction not, as is now routinely assumed, for endorsement of any chauvinist arrogance, but on the contrary to take part in a masochistic game of humiliation by flamboyant Continentals.

The English Abroad

In the Great War, English soldiers made it a point of honour to mis-pronounce French and Belgian place names in absurdly Anglicized forms, so that Ypres became 'Wipers' and Etaples 'Eatables'. Noël Coward's famous song 'Mad Dogs and Englishmen' (1931) makes fun of this refusal of the English to acknowledge, let alone adjust to, foreign climates, languages, or customs: while every sane person or animal in the tropics rests in the shade at midday, the English-men, who detest a siesta, go out obliviously into the blazing noon-tide heat. Beneath the surface of the song's light satire there lurks a certain perverse pride in that crazily self-punishing inflexibility upon which the Empire had been built. Coward was at this time lapping up the success of his historical pageant *Cavalcade* (1931), a medley of patriotic song, nobly endured military sacrifice, and flag-waving. Covertly self-congratulatory as it may be, Coward's ditty makes use of a modern convention by which the peculiarities of the English are most fully exposed, once again to an 'alien' viewpoint, under the glare of a foreign sun.

We have noticed already in Chapter 10 that the transplantation of an unimaginative Englishman to some exotic location in which he is absurdly out of place is a favoured device of prose romancers in this period, the clearest case of this being the failed missionary in Sylvia Townsend Warner's *Mr Fortune's Maggot* (1927). Travel writers too delighted in discovering such misfits—missionaries, colonial settlers, big-game hunters, and plain tourists—clinging to their English habits in unlikely climes. In the final essay of *Twilight in Italy* (1916), for example, D. H. Lawrence stages an encounter at the breakfast table of a Swiss inn between himself and a sunburnt clerk from Streatham who has worn himself out walking the mountains on a two-week vacation. This dog-tired young Englishman has put him-self through a needlessly punishing schedule of solitary treks, driven by courageous determination, yet when he is asked a question in Ger-man he hangs his head in shame over his breakfast bowl, reluctantly allowing Lawrence to translate his requests to the innkeeper. Writ-ing a postcard home, he makes sure to turn it so that Lawrence shall not see the address, 'a little, cautious, English movement of privacy' (p. 211). Here as elsewhere in his writings, Lawrence suggests that the all-conquering will-power of the English draws upon and reinforces a fear of spontaneous life which encloses them in a protective shell of reserve. Self-enslaved, they cannot bring themselves to expand under foreign skies and appear rather belittled by them, more to be pitied than envied.

This resolute English refusal to adapt to other cultures is examined mercilessly in W. Somerset Maugham's tales of Borneo and Malaya in *The Casuarina Tree* (1926) and later collections. These stories portray isolated and stultified communities of rubber-planters and colonial administrators trying to preserve outmoded English customs as a defence against the feared moral collapse of 'going native'. In more than one story Maugham dwells on the ritual of the colonist opening packets of six-week-old English newspapers and then reading one each day in the right order. A cultured Englishwoman in 'The Door of Opportunity' (1931) sums up this tropical version of suburbia:

The men had come out to the colony as lads from second-rate schools, and life had taught them nothing. At fifty they had the outlook of hobbledehoys. Most of them drank a great deal too much. They read nothing worth reading. Their ambition was to be like everybody else. Their highest praise was to say that a man was a damned good sort. If you were interested in the things of the spirit you were a prig. They were eaten up with envy of one another and devoured by petty jealousies. And the women, poor things, were obsessed by petty rivalries. They made a circle that was more provincial than any in the smallest town in England. They were prudish and spiteful. (*Collected Short Stories*, vol. 2, p. 456)

In Maugham's other oriental stories, such people are seen succumbing to local temptations and thus losing caste, like Guy in 'The Force of Circumstance' (1924), whose English bride leaves him when she discovers that he already has children by a Malay woman; or they conceal violent passions behind a public mask of respectability, like the murderess Leslie Crosbie in 'The Letter' (1924).

Particularly interesting in this connection is 'The Outstation' (1924), a tale in whose remote jungle setting two contrasting characters come into fatal conflict. The first, Mr Warburton, is an experienced colonial official of the old-fashioned English type: stiffly formal and snobbish in all things, he judges other men according to their public school and regiment, and insists on dressing for dinner in a boiled shirt, high collar, and dinner jacket even when dining alone, and despite the stifling heat. The second, his new assistant Mr Cooper, is a younger man, a middle-class white 'colonial' born in Barbados and resentful of the English public-school sporting code and of the officer class; he arrives for his first dinner with Warburton dressed in old khaki shorts. Cooper is clearly the representative of his generation's modern attitudes, and we might expect him to be the hero of the tale. On the contrary, it is Warburton who comes off better, because he has developed over many years a genuine love and respect for the Malays, while Cooper scorns the natives brusquely as mere 'niggers', and is eventually killed by a mistreated servant, who subsequently enjoys Warburton's indulgent protection. Comically rigid though he may be, the elder man is seen to embody the virtues of a defunct English gentility, while the young iconoclast has no values to fall back upon, only racist egotism.

More often, though, the highly significant figure of the disaffected colonist is presented with fuller complexity than Mr Cooper shows. Usually more cultured and broad-minded than the average English empire-builder, and more open to friendships among the native middle class, this figure is nonetheless tormented by the suspicion that he is fundamentally no better than the gin-soaked bigots of the local whites-only club, as in the cases of Alban Torel in Maugham's 'The Door of Opportunity' and of Flory in George Orwell's first novel, *Burmese Days* (1934), the plot of which is clearly an expansion of Maugham's 'The Force of Circumstance'. A biter of the hand that feeds him, this contradictory modern type is riven by divided loyalties and radical uncertainties of self-definition. His predicament is nowhere more sensitively explored than in the tribulations of Cyril Fielding, the protagonist of E. M. Forster's novel *A Passage to India* (1924). The title and the carefully described setting in and around the fictional city of Chandrapore would suggest that this is a book about India and Indianness, in which case critical accusations of 'orientalist' condescension made against it would have some point; yet the novel itself repeatedly insists that India is both too large to be represented and too various to be personified. What *A Passage to India* does more confidently represent and personify, and what it is truly 'about', is Englishness and specifically the failure of the

English to learn from other cultures. In this it resumes and develops the preoccupations of Forster's earlier novels, *Where Angels Fear to Tread* (1905) and *A Room with a View* (1908), both of which scrutinize the English abroad in Italy. As in those books, so in *A Passage to India* the English characters tend to divide between those who are sympathetically receptive to the local environment and people (the college principal Fielding, along with the elderly Mrs Moore) and those whose undeveloped hearts are hardened against both, their minds blinkered by the prejudices of the Club (Mrs Moore's son, the magistrate Ronnie Heaslop, and several others). This division, indeed, is highlighted as the only significant difference to be found among the leading English participants, who are all drawn from the same narrow caste, while Forster grants far more social and cultural variety to the Indians.

In an important departure from the pattern of his 'Italian' novels, Forster provides in *A Passage to India* a far sharper external perspective upon his English cast, so that Englishness is presented in the form of 'the English problem' as seen and debated by a number of Indians. The story begins in the second chapter with a discussion among a group of Indian Muslims including the physician Dr Aziz about whether it is possible to be friends with Englishmen. One of the party makes the crushingly bathetic claim that with a prominent English official he was 'once quite intimate. He has shown me his stamp collection'. Aziz later adopts Fielding as a friend in a more convincing manner by showing him a treasured photograph of the deceased Mrs Aziz. The opening question about the possibility of such intimacies then hovers over the action until the final page, when Aziz concludes that he can be friends with Fielding again only when the Indians have driven 'every blasted Englishman into the sea'. Between them in the meantime has fallen a cloud of mistrust, embarrassed silence, prejudice, and baseless rumour arising from the melodramatic central episodes in which Aziz is falsely accused of attempted rape by Ronnie Heaslop's fiancée Adela Quested on the basis of a mysterious hallucination, and then acquitted when she sensationally retracts the charge at his trial. Since the reader knows Aziz to be innocent from the start, these events have the effect of placing on trial the English colony, which appears in the twentieth chapter in its worst light as a lynch mob incapable of acting upon the very principles of justice its Empire purports to uphold. Apart from Mrs Moore, who is close to death and too dejected to make a stand, only Fielding, who resigns from the Club protesting his friend's innocence, is exempted from the novel's condemnation at this point, although he discovers that the taint of guilt by association inevitably still clings to him in the eyes of Aziz and his Indian associates, just as lingering English suspicion of Aziz drives the doctor into undeserved and embittered internal exile.

A Passage to India closes with the failure of attempted reconciliation between Fielding and Aziz, and in this withholding of the expected novelistic denouement it serves as a prophecy of Indian independence and of that wider loss of Empire that shaped for decades to come the fate of England (and of Britain: the Scots, it should be recalled, were disproportionately active as imperialists). Among the qualities that place this humane novel among the most important fictional works of its age is its ability to show us in credibly personal terms why the English could not hold on to India, why they did not deserve to, and what it was about the character of their governing classes that guaranteed their historic eviction. Forster manages this by making us see the English through Indian eyes. Once again, the modern perspective adopted is an 'alien' one that succeeds in presenting English people as foreign, *bilayati*, familiar yet freshly strange.

15

The Great War

New Words, 1914–1918

*air-raid ammo anti-aircraft blimp bomber
breakthrough camouflage conchie defeatist gassed
internee nose-dive sand-bagged smoke-screen
storm-troops strafe trench-coat trip-wire U-boat*

The Great War of 1914–18 had a greater impact upon the English imagination and its written forms than any other war in history, or than any other definable event in the twentieth century, and few significant literary works of this period can safely be said to have escaped its shadow. T. S. Eliot's 'The Waste Land' (1922), for example, is an oblique war elegy, Lytton Strachey's *Eminent Victorians* (1918) a satire on militarism, D. H. Lawrence's *Lady Chatterley's Lover* (1928) more directly a fable of the War's consequences, and Virginia Woolf's *To the Lighthouse* (1927) wears the great historical scar of the War years across its divided structure, as if cut in half by a massacre. The novels and plays of the inter-war years are variously peopled by war widows, war veterans, and war refugees: the shell-shocked Septimus Warren Smith in Woolf's *Mrs Dalloway* (1925), the bereaved Sarah Burton in Winifred Holtby's *South Riding* (1936), and the Belgian exile Hercule Poirot in Agatha Christie's numerous detective tales are only three among a multitude.

This pervasive impact of the War upon literature arose not simply from its huge scale and its unprecedented death toll but also from two features that distinguished it from the Crimean and Boer Wars. In the first place, it militarized much of English society, most obviously by converting millions of civilians, including a few hundred writers, into soldiers, medical auxiliaries, munitions workers, or—more often among authors—into war correspondents, spies, and propagandists. Unlike previous wars fought by small standing armies and navies, it drew into its agonies millions of highly literate people as combatants, camp-followers, and anxious relatives. Second, its major theatre of operations, the Western Front of trenches stretching across France from western Belgium, was alarmingly close to home. For civilians in eastern England this meant exposure to the new terrors of aerial bombardment; and throughout the land it meant the permeation of everyday life by the presence of servicemen who had just escaped death or were about to risk it: every English town and village, every theatre, church, and hospital saw uniformed men in training, on leave, or convalescing. By the late Twenties, almost every village had its own war memorial.

This war was all-consuming, inescapable. Its sombre contributions to the vocabulary of modern English give some indication of its far-reaching impact. In addition to the small selection of wartime coinages displayed at the head of this chapter, the period 1910–40 produced, to take *war-* compounds alone, *war-bride, war Cabinet, war casualty, war cemetery, war damage, war diary, war effort, war generation, war graves, war-guilt, war history, war-hysteria, war memorial, war museum, war novel, war orphan, war pension, war period, war-plane, war profiteer, war propaganda, war-rations, war-resister, war-room, war-shattered, war-verse, war-weariness, war-worker, war wound,* and *war zone*; these being just one subset of *war-words*.

Although many writers were ineligible for military service by virtue of being female, over age, or (like Eliot, Lawrence, and Aldous Huxley) physically unfit, the level of participation by literary authors far exceeded that in any previous war. Middle-aged writers worked as propagandists (Wells, Bennett, Galsworthy, Masefield, Kipling, Buchan, Hueffer), as spies (Maugham), or in humbler war work (de la Mare, for instance, toiled in a food-rationing office). Several women who later took up literary careers joined the Voluntary Aid Detachment as nursing assistants, among them Enid Bagnold, Vera Brittain, Agatha Christie, Rose Macaulay, and Naomi Mitchison. Leaving aside a few conscientious objectors (Strachey), absentees

(Wodehouse), and pacifist Red Cross workers (Forster), male writers of military age volunteered in significant numbers. It is surprising, indeed, how few of them were killed in action: only two prose writers of any reputation (the poet-critic T. E. Hulme, and the humorist H. H. Munro, alias 'Saki'), along with five notable poets (Julian Grenfell, Charles Hamilton Sorley, Edward Thomas, Isaac Rosenberg, and Wilfred Owen), most of these being unknown before the War itself. The more famous Rupert Brooke died of disease before reaching Gallipoli. Bereavement was widely felt, though: Kipling lost his only son, whose body was never recovered; the young Christopher Isherwood lost his father; while Katherine Mansfield, T. E. Lawrence, Herbert Read, Ivy Compton-Burnett, and Vera Brittain all mourned the deaths of brothers.

Our inherited legends of the Great War are dominated by accounts of infantry units on the British sector of the Western Front, principally on the Ypres salient and the Somme valley; and with good reason, these being the decisive sites of trench warfare and its appalling costs. Paul Fussell's much-admired book *The Great War and Modern Memory* (1975), for example, concentrates entirely upon the literature of that zone. Yet the War, even as experienced by the English alone, was much wider, and so was its literature. Far-flung battle-lines were to be found on other fronts, and were recorded in literary versions: conflict on the Eastern Front appeared in Hugh Walpole's novel *The Dark Forest* (1916); the disastrous Gallipoli campaign provided the setting for the first part of A. P. Herbert's novel *The Secret Battle* (1919) and for the last part of Ernest Raymond's juvenile romance *Tell England* (1922); the Arab revolt against Turkish rule was the subject of T. E. Lawrence's prose epic *Seven Pillars of Wisdom* (1926); and the forgotten war in East Africa was written up in Francis Brett Young's non-fictional *Marching on Tanga* (1917). The war in the air appears in the *Poems and Rhymes* (1919) of Flight Commander Jeffery Day (killed in action, 1918), and in V. M. Yeates's novel *Winged Victory* (1934). The war at sea, though, did not find adequate literary expression, except in Kipling's tale 'Sea Constables' (1915). Aspects of the intelligence war remained obscure too, the ex-spy Compton Mackenzie's *Greek Memories* (1932) being suppressed for divulging official secrets. More extensive by far, although rather overlooked until recently by literary history, was the literature of the Home Front, of civilian anxiety, bereavement, and war work. This diversity is worth indicating because writers' imaginative grasp of 'the War', within which there were several wars, was open to wide variation according to their positions within it, as we may now see in some special cases.

Survivals of Heroic Literature

There has been little disagreement about one major cultural consequence of the Great War: the collapse, especially in literature, of the heroic ideal as formerly celebrated in the romantic-chivalric tradition that had run from Walter Scott through Tennyson to William Morris. That conception of military glory, already questioned by nineteenth-century writers (Stendhal, Tolstoy, Shaw), had been destroyed by the machine gun, and now lay buried in the Flanders mud. In the 'disillusioned' post-War period, military glory was a discredited slogan of propagandists, a daydream of ignorant schoolboys or cheap romancers, but not a subject of serious literature. And yet there had been aspects even of that war in which special forms of heroism remained available for literary treatment, if only as exceptions confirming the rule. One of these was espionage, romanticized by John Buchan in *Greenmantle* (1916), but later debunked, as we saw in Chapter 13, by W. Somerset Maugham in *Ashenden* (1928). Another was combat in the air, which was glamorously modern and yet amenable to chivalric representation, the individualistic flair of the flying 'ace' making him a knight errant of the skies. The aviator's freedom of movement above the fray, so unlike the trench imprisonment of the troglodytes below, was most memorably affirmed in W. B. Yeats's short heroic poem 'An Irish Airman Foresees His Death' (1919), in commemoration of his friend Robert Gregory, who had been shot down while serving with the Royal Flying Corps in the Italian campaign. The poem insists that this officer's death is a freely chosen destiny, as uncontaminated by political obligation or by self-interest as it is by mud or contact with lower ranks, thereby confirming the helmeted airman—who remained an iconic figure for Auden and the younger Thirties poets—as the aristocrat of modern warfare.

A third exception, and the most 'romantic' in its remoteness from trench-warfare conditions, arose from the alliance between modern British and French forces and a pre-modern warrior caste of Arab tribesmen in their assaults upon the Turkish imperial armies in Arabia, Palestine, and Syria. The literary fruit of this campaign was the most remarkable war memoir of the age, *Seven Pillars of Wisdom*, privately published in 1926 before an abridged version, *Revolt in the Desert*, became a best-seller in 1927, followed by a trade edition of the fuller work in 1935. Its author, T. E. Lawrence, was one of the truly extraordinary men of his time: an academic archaeologist of illegitimate birth, who became a spy, then a theorist and practitioner of guerrilla warfare, the effective leader of the Arab Revolt, a participant in major post-War peace settlements, and a living legend as 'Lawrence of Arabia'. His last major role was as autobiographical historian of his own most famous exploits, and confessional analyst of his own painfully troubled identity. *Seven Pillars* does not pretend to be an objective chronicle of the Arab Revolt, only a subjective account of Lawrence's own role in it; yet it is also much more than a military memoir, as it aspires not just to literary power but to the status of epic. Most literary historians of Great War writing have passed over this book in silence or in parenthetic dismissal, no doubt in part because it will not fit within the Western Front canon, and in part from suspicion of the author's self-mythologizing motives. The temptation has been to hand *Seven Pillars* over to specialist historians, or to psychopathologists. An injustice has been done here to a work of true and sustained literary force, blemished though it is by mannered archaism. *Seven Pillars of Wisdom* is both a fascinating autobiographical work, against which it is idle to press charges of self-obsession, and at the same time the last English epic.

The geographical, cultural, and military circumstances of the Arab Revolt permitted a kind of epic treatment that the Western Front could not offer. It was a guerrilla campaign of daring sabotage against a technologically superior enemy, and of rapid movement by camel across hundreds of miles of open desert between Mecca and Damascus, while its old-fashioned warriors were inspired by high ideals of brotherhood and national aspiration—although low bribery on the part of the British played its part. To this favourably heroic subject Lawrence brought his prolonged study of modern epic writing, from Malory's *Morte d'Arthur* (1470)—a copy of which he carried with him on the campaign—to Melville's *Moby-Dick* (1851) and Tolstoy's *War and Peace* (1865–9). Of these influences Melville's emerges as the strongest, both in Lawrence's alternations between episodes of dramatic action and of introspective meditation, and in his digressions into comparative religion, ethnology, military theory, and topography. Superimposed upon this design is the quest pattern of a 'subjective epic' in the tradition deriving from Dante: complicating the military heroism here are Lawrence's guilt about his duplicitous role in the Arab cause, and his struggles with his own violently ascetic temperament. In accordance with epic precedent, *Seven Pillars* includes its own infernal descents, into a sexualized torture chamber in the eightieth chapter, and into a hospital full of putrescent corpses in the penultimate chapter. The war recorded here is by no means a 'clean' one to be contrasted simply with the filth of Flanders; indeed the final chapters recording the liberation of Damascus show the simultaneous triumph and extinction of the old warrior caste as it encounters the machine guns, artillery, and aircraft of modern warfare.

Even in the literature of the Western Front itself we may find narratives of soldier-heroes, although under these conditions the heroism to be affirmed is one of passive endurance rather than of active energy. The two principal instances here, both long-gestated, both marked by epic ambitions, and both written by Catholic converts, are Ford Madox Ford's *Parade's End* tetralogy of novels (1924–8) and David Jones's long poem in prose and verse, *In Parenthesis* (1937). The protagonist of Ford's sequence, Christopher Tietjens, is a model Christian gentleman of the old Tory school, a chivalrous relic of feudalism, and a good man suffering under multiple tribulations during the War. His only victory, though, is that of surviving with his body and his moral integrity intact in a chaotic world that has no need for his type. Tietjens may represent the remnant of a lost ideal, but Ford's treatment is really too novelistic and ironic to grant him more heroic a status than that. In the final volume he ends up, fittingly, as an antique dealer, no longer even a central character in the tale. Jones's *In Parenthesis* shows a more determined effort to transfigure its soldiers into universal mythic types of self-sacrifice by employing, in the manner of Eliot's 'The Waste Land', a framework of allusions to Arthurian romance (especially Malory), to old Welsh folklore, to Shakespeare's history plays, and to Christian ritual. It produces some striking effects at times, but the larger impression it makes is of a willed medievalizing of the War, in which the heroic values seem to be more borrowed from antique sources than discovered in modern actuality.

Four Phases of War-Writing

For the remainder of this chapter we will be surveying the mainstream of war-writing in its two principal zones, the Western Front and the Home Front. As the best accounts of this literature, notably Samuel Hynes's *A War Imagined* (1990), are careful to point out, the meanings of the War changed significantly over time; so we shall follow here a chronological course through four successive phases—1914–15; 1916–18; 1919–27; and 1928–37.

The writings generated by the first seventeen months after 4 August 1914 scarcely belong to what we now accept as the literature of the Great War. They are for the most part propaganda and patriotic effusion, of historical interest only. While the recruiting offices were mobbed by volunteers in the first weeks of the War, the newspapers, especially *The Times*, found themselves similarly overwhelmed by hundreds of patriotic poems responding to the historic call to arms. Among the few still recalled are Thomas Hardy's 'Men Who March Away', Rudyard Kipling's 'For All We Have and Are', with its terrific slogan 'The Hun is at the gate!', and Laurence Binyon's 'For the Fallen', whose lines 'At the going down of the sun and in the morning | We will remember them' have become lapidary and ceremonial. Countless other versifiers poured out their indignation at Germany's violation of Belgium, and their pride in the impending vindication of English honour, feeding a sudden boom in the production of patriotic verse anthologies.

Meanwhile a formidable propaganda operation had secretly been set up by the government, with literary authors at the forefront of its efforts to proclaim the justice of Britain's participation in the War. By mid-September, the propaganda chief C. F. G. Masterman had rounded up an impressive list of senior literary figures as signatories to an ostensibly spontaneous public declaration of support, published both in *The Times* and significantly in the *New York Times* too, the neutral United States constituting a crucially important audience. The fifty-three signatories included several predictable names of patriotic writers (Hilaire Belloc, Robert Bridges, G. K. Chesterton, Arthur Conan Doyle, Rider Haggard, Rudyard Kipling, Henry Newbolt, Arthur Quiller-Couch, and Mrs Humphry Ward); but along with them appeared some more modern and normally pacific spirits (Arnold Bennett, John Galsworthy, Thomas Hardy, May Sinclair, and most notably H. G. Wells). Wells and Bennett indeed proved to be even more energetic propagandists than their conservative peers: Wells produced a famous pamphlet, *The War That Will End War* (1914), while Bennett wrote some three hundred propaganda articles in the course of the War, eventually becoming director of British propaganda in Europe and deputy minister of information in its closing months. Kipling, Doyle, Galsworthy, Belloc, and John Masefield all contributed works of propaganda to the War effort, and so did the half-German but fully Francophile modernist Ford Madox Hueffer (later surnamed Ford). At this stage the only notable literary dissent came from Bernard Shaw's provocative essay 'Common Sense about the War' (1914), which equated Prussian and British militarisms and recommended that soldiers on both sides turn their guns against their own officers. Having undermined some of the cant about British innocence in the pre-War diplomatic manoeuvres, Shaw soon came round to reluctant support for the British cause.

The sometimes euphoric mood of national vocation and renewal that was felt widely in the opening months of the War was most memorably captured in Rupert Brooke's sequence of five sonnets entitled '1914' but published early in the following year. These soon became the most popular poems of the War, as Brooke became after his death in April 1915 a temporary national poet. The last and most often quoted of them, 'The Soldier', is a rousing patriotic piece, although presumptuously self-glorifying. The third voices the romantic notions of military sacrifice commonly expressed at the time (and bitterly mocked before long), hymning the 'rich Dead' as benefactors who have willingly 'poured out the red | Sweet wine of youth' (*Poetical Works*, p. 21). It is the first sonnet, 'Peace', however, that encapsulates the elation unique to its historical moment:

Fig. 8. Pencil drawing of Rupert Brooke by the sculptor James Havard Thomas, from a photograph taken in 1913 by Sherril Schell. Thomas used this design in the memorial tablet installed in 1919 in the chapel at Rugby School, on which he also carved the text of Brooke's sonnet 'The Soldier'.

> Now God be thanked Who has matched us with His hour,
>   And caught our youth, and wakened us from sleeping,
> With hand made sure, clear eye, and sharpened power,
>   To turn, as swimmers into cleanness leaping,
> Glad from a world grown old and cold and weary,
>   Leave the sick hearts that honour could not move,
> And half-men, and their dirty songs and dreary,
>   And all the little emptiness of love!
>
> (*Poetical Works*, p. 19)

Brooke offers here two sentiments that belong irrecoverably to the 1914–15 phase; the first of these being that his generation is especially fortunate in having this opportunity to fight and to die. A similar sense of privileged destiny is expressed in terms of romantic pantheism in Julian Grenfell's often-anthologized poem 'Into Battle', which appeared posthumously in *The Times* in May 1915.

The second timely feature of Brooke's 'Peace' is the feeling that the War has come as a kind of redemption, rescuing England's youth from decadent frivolity and ennobling it with stern resolve. As Samuel Hynes shows well in *A War Imagined*, this idea of providential purification was widely echoed at the time, especially by conservative commentators who welcomed the War's effect in quelling the distractions of Suffragism, effeminacy, and artistic fads. One of the best-selling books of the War years, *The First Hundred Thousand* (1915) by the Scottish schoolmaster Ian Hay, chronicles the progress of some typical volunteer recruits to 'Kitchener's Army', from training camp to front-line combat, in cheerfully uplifting fashion. Although beginning to grumble by the tenth chapter, Captain Wagstaffe and his comrades decide to look on the bright side:

'My word, it is dark in here! *And* dull! Curse the Kaiser!'

'I don't know,' said Wagstaffe thoughtfully. 'War is hell, and all that, but it has a good deal to recommend it. It wipes out all the small nuisances of peace-time.'

'Such as— ?'

'Well, Suffragettes, and Futurism, and— and—'

'Bernard Shaw,' suggested another voice. 'Hall Caine—'

'Yes, and the Tango, and party politics, and golf-maniacs. Life and Death, and the things that really are big, get viewed in their proper perspective for once in a way.'

'And look at the way the War has bucked up the nation,' said Bobby Little, all on fire at once. 'Look at the way girls have given up fussing over clothes and things, and taken to nursing.'[1]

War could be welcomed as a cleansing return from triviality to fundamental truth. Jane Potter's research into popular women's romances in wartime has unearthed significant examples of this fantasy, in the stories of Berta Ruck's *Khaki and Kisses* (1915) and in Ruby M. Ayres's full-length romance *Richard Chatterton, V.C.* (1915). In these tales, weak, effete, or artistically pretentious men discover in themselves a bedrock of true masculinity in war, awakening in the formerly 'cold' women who once scorned them a responsive return to truly feminine behaviour.[2] Parables of the War as a catalyst of self-renewal were not confined to 'lowbrow' reading, either: the serious and semi-modernist author May Sinclair, who briefly served as secretary to an ambulance unit in Belgium, wrote two wartime novels, *Tasker Jevons* (1916) and *The Tree of Heaven* (1917), in both of which artistic men find themselves heroically revitalized when they enlist for combat.

The most comprehensive literary treatment of the national mood in the War's early months is to be found in H. G. Wells's *Mr Britling Sees it Through* (1916), a best-selling novel that restored Wells's then languishing reputation. Set in an Essex country house resembling Wells's own, and dominated by the central figure of Britling, a famous writer not unlike his creator, this book offers a chronicle of English responses to the unfolding events of 1914–15 as refracted through a single tormented conscience. The shock of the War's unexpected outbreak is enhanced by Britling's prior certainty that such a conflict could never happen in civilized Europe, and it jolts him out of his pacifism into a vengeful anti-Prussian militancy. As the conflict transforms his country, his neighbourhood, and his household (his secretary and his son both volunteer, while his children's German tutor, Herr Heinrich, also a pacifist, repatriates himself unwillingly and is conscripted), Britling struggles to resist the demonizing

---

[1] Ian Hay, *The First Hundred Thousand* (Nelson, 1915), 140–41.

[2] Jane Potter, '"A Great Purifier": The Great War in Women's Romances and Memoirs 1914–1918', in Suzanne Raitt and Trudi Tate (eds.), *Women's Fiction and the Great War* (Oxford University Press, 1997), 85–106.

of Germans and to adjust his world-view amid successive moods of disbelief, alarm, indignation, and despair. At the story's end he is shattered by his son's death in action, and he breaks down into incoherence as he tries to compose a letter of condolence to Heinrich's similarly bereaved parents. As a novel, *Mr Britling* suffers from slap-dash construction and hackneyed plotting, but its narrative of the War's initial impact, and of the passage of English morale from self-confidence to exhausted dejection by the end of 1915, retains a fresh urgency and an unrivalled historical value.

The second phase of war-writing, from 1916 to 1918, is coloured by the collapse of early hopes for swift victory into stalemate and by apparently pointless massacres on a huge scale (notably in the disastrous Somme offensive of 1916 and at Passchendaele in 1917), leading to sharpening resentment among servicemen against Staff and civilians. It produced two important new bodies of work: the verse of a new realistic school of soldier-poets, and a more reflective kind of Home Front fiction, of which *Mr Britling Sees it Through* is a major example.

Early signs of a shift in war poetry away from the rhetoric of national self-vindication and moral mobilization may be found in the 'Georgian' poet W. W. Gibson's collection *Battle* (1915), with its modestly ironic sketches of homesick soldiers shot dead while jesting or boasting of their children; some of these are surprisingly realistic for an author who had never seen active service. Again in the verses of the reluctant young soldier Charles Hamilton Sorley (killed in action, October 1915, aged 20), collected in *Marlborough and Other Poems* (1916), we can see a turn away from declamatory attitudes and towards a sober brooding upon the tragedy of this conflict, notably in the sonnets 'To Germany' and 'When you see millions of the mouthless dead'. The main line of the new soldier-poetry, however, leads by links of personal contact and influence from Robert Graves through Siegfried Sassoon to Wilfred Owen. In *A War Imagined*, Samuel Hynes accurately identifies Graves's short poem 'A Dead Boche' (1916) as a founding work of this new realistic tradition: it is purely and gruesomely descriptive—of a German soldier's stinking corpse that drips black blood—invoking no abstract values, and certainly no red sweet wine. Meanwhile Sassoon, encouraged by Graves to abandon his early romantic style, was discovering a new voice in such early poems as 'The Hero' (1916), which highlights the gulf between the ugly truths known to soldiers and the illusions cherished by civilians. Separate from this group, Isaac Rosenberg published in late 1916 his poem 'Break of Day in the Trenches', a monologue addressed to a trench rat whose indiscriminate crossing of No Man's Land brings the two sides within the perspective of a common mortality. By 1917, with the appearance in that year of Graves's *Fairies and Fusiliers*, Sassoon's *The Old Huntsman and Other Poems*, and Ivor Gurney's *Severn and Somme*, a small but highly significant body of work had emerged that affirmed the priority of the soldier's direct experience. As it developed, it redefined for the modern age what the poetry of war could be.

A shared feature of this new trench poetry is that it seems to recognize no 'just cause' or higher purpose to the War, and, to employ the archaic diction of 1914, no 'foe' either: if there is an enemy at all, it is not the German soldier opposite—now usually respected as a brave fellow-sufferer—but the impersonal machine of the War itself, abetted by the Staff behind the lines and by politicians, journalists, and flag-wavers at home. Suspicious of ideals, slogans, and second-hand opinion, the soldier-poet typically trusts only what he has seen with his own eyes, and endorses no values beyond the immediate promptings of comradeship and compassion. 'Only the love of comrades sweetens all', as Ivor Gurney says in one of his wartime sonnets (*Severn and Somme*, p. 50). In this phase of war poetry, the leading figure was Sassoon, whose *The Old Huntsman* (May 1917) preceded by a few weeks his public protest, published in *The Times* and elsewhere, against the prolongation of the War. Over the next few months, spent at Craiglockhart War Hospital, he composed poems of disturbing realism, collected as *Counter-Attack and Other Poems* (1918), in which he mocks the cosy idealisms of the non-combatants, hurling against them the horrors of combat known to soldiers alone. Sassoon's is a poetry of 'protest', not so much against the War itself (he did after all return to front-line service) as against an increasingly implausible rhetoric of glorious sacrifice.

On the Home Front, novels of civilian life reflected growing dismay and doubt, most prominently in *Mr Britling*, but also in Rose Macaulay's *Non-Combatants and Others* (1916) and in Arnold Bennett's *The Pretty Lady* (1918). Macaulay's novel, set mostly in

London in 1915, portrays the Home Front through the perspective of a young woman, Alix Sandomir, who is studying art while her female cousins engage in nursing work and her brother Paul is at the front. Disappointed in love, she suffers from feelings of uselessness and bewilderment, especially after seeing—in an early and powerful depiction of shell shock—the terrified face of an ex-soldier weeping as he sleepwalks. Alix later learns that her brother has lost his nerve in battle and been killed. Nerves, nervousness, and loss of nerve indeed provide thematic coherence to an otherwise directionless narrative. At the end, Alix has decided to take part in pacifist activity, but with a notable lack of conviction, the pacifists, including Alix's mother, being presented as self-important busybodies. Shell-shocked soldiers feature as important figures in later wartime novels. Rebecca West's *The Return of the Soldier* (1918) uses the device of amnesia affecting an English officer who cannot recognize his own wife but believes he is still attached to an old flame from fifteen years before; but this provides the basis for a sophisticated exploration of love and jealousy rather than for any portrait of a society at war. Much closer to that ambition is Bennett's *The Pretty Lady* (1918), a sombre story of wartime London, in which war profiteers cavorting at charity balls are exposed as frivolous parasites. The title character, a Parisian prostitute living in London as a refugee, comes to the aid of a disturbed soldier on leave, so forfeiting her position as the kept mistress of a wealthy man about town. There are moments of sudden horror in the story (a child's severed arm is found in the street after a bombardment), but more unsettling still is the pervasive atmosphere of corruption and demoralization. The book was banned by the W. H. Smith chain of libraries, and by a number of bookshops.

The third phase of war-writing, from 1919 to 1927, is the most often disregarded and undervalued. Several accounts of Great War literature leap from the fact that there was a boom in war books in the years 1928–30 to the unjustified conclusion that there had been a prolonged silence on the subject in the intervening decade. If true, such an extended forgetting of the War would have sat oddly with the numerous war histories being published and indeed with public acts of commemoration such as the burial of the Unknown Warrior and the unveiling of the Cenotaph (November 1920). In fact 1919 was a year of plenty in the publication of important war-writings, and the Twenties continued the tradition strongly, despite the reported unwillingness of a few publishers to sustain the trend. In 1919, the memorable verse publications included Ivor Gurney's collection *War's Embers*, Siegfried Sassoon's *Picture Show* and collected *War Poems*, Richard Aldington's *Images of War*, Herbert Read's *Eclogues* and *Naked Warriors*, the war epitaphs of Rudyard Kipling's *The Years Between*, and seven poems by Wilfred Owen appearing in the Sitwells' anthology *Wheels*. W. Somerset Maugham's bitter farce *Home and Beauty* showed returning war heroes betrayed by greedy civilians on the stage of the Playhouse for a run of 235 performances, while among the novels of that year we should note Cicely Hamilton's *William, an Englishman* and A. P. Herbert's tragic tale of bravery officially punished as 'cowardice', *The Secret Battle*. The following year saw the appearance of the most admired and influential war book of them all, the *Poems* of Wilfred Owen, edited by Sassoon. It is too often forgotten that during the War itself, Owen had published only four war poems, Rosenberg only two, and Edmund Blunden none at all; in their reception and impact, these three war poets are as much 'poets of the Twenties' as T. S. Eliot or Edith Sitwell. Rosenberg's *Poems* appeared posthumously only in 1922, while Blunden's, many of them written long after the Armistice, were published in successive collections through the Twenties.

Although he wrote few finished poems, Owen is rightly admired as the most talented of the soldier-poets, his imaginative range being broader and his verbal texture being richer than Sassoon's. He can evoke the physical sensations of trench life and death in clotted alliterative lines like these from 'The Sentry':

> Rain, guttering down in waterfalls of slime,
> Kept slush waist-high and rising hour by hour,
> And choked the steps too thick with clay to climb.
> What murk of air remained stank old, and sour
> With fumes from whizz-bangs, and the smell of men
> Who'd lived there years, and left their curse in the den,
> If not their corpses. . . .
>
> (*The Poems*, p. 165)

Owen can also reach beyond the kind of realism shown here and in the famous 'Dulce et Decorum Est' into more fantastical poetic conceits, notably in 'Strange Meeting', 'The Show', and 'Arms and the Boy'. No less impressive, although very different in their complex thought and diction as in their detached tone, are the war poems of Rosenberg. These have been less noticed because they voice no obviously anti-militarist protest, but they exhibit real imaginative force, as in the last stanza of 'August 1914':

> Iron are our lives
> Molten right through our youth.
> A burnt space through ripe fields,
> A fair mouth's broken tooth.
>
> (*Collected Works*, p. 100)

The concentrated metaphorical vision here yields the effect aspired to, but never achieved so well, by the Imagist poets. In another mode again, Edmund Blunden's war poems are traditional in style, often pastoralist in mood, yet still convincing in their descriptive fluency. 'Third Ypres' and 'Rural Economy' (both 1922) are among the poems that best represent his virtues.

The prose-writing of this phase offers weighty evidence against the legend of a post-war decade barren of war literature. *Seven Pillars of Wisdom* alone would refute it, but there is far more: the war stories of Kipling's *Debits and Credits* (1926); Mary Butts's strange tale of shell shock, 'Speed the Plough' (1922); Enid Bagnold's novel *The Happy Foreigner* (1920); Arnold Bennett's novel *Lord Raingo* (1926), based upon his inside knowledge of the wartime Ministry of Information; D. H. Lawrence's novel *Kangaroo* (1923), with its autobiographical chapter of persecution on the Home Front, 'The Nightmare'; Herbert Read's war memoir *In Retreat* (1925); C. E. Montague's sardonic war stories in *Fiery Particles* (1923), and the same author's non-fictional reflections upon the War, published under the significant title *Disenchantment* (1922). R. H. Mottram published three well-received novels about life behind the lines in wartime France, *The Spanish Farm* (1924), *Sixty-Four, Ninety-Four!* (1925), and *The Crime at Vanderlynden's* (1926), later collected with linking narratives as *The Spanish Farm Trilogy* (1927). The major fictional work of this phase, however, is Ford Madox Ford's tetralogy comprising *Some Do Not. . .* (1924), *No More Parades* (1925), *A Man Could Stand Up—* (1926), and *The Last*

Post (1928), better known since 1950 by the collective title *Parade's End* (although there are purists who discount the last volume, recognizing only the first three as the 'Tietjens trilogy').

Ford's ambition in writing the *Parade's End* novels was to compose a history of recent times that could register the destruction visited upon English civilization by the War. He achieves this by building the narrative of the first three volumes upon a central character, the official statistician Christopher Tietjens, who represents, sometimes to a comical degree, the traditional values of the English gentleman, and by setting against him a conspiracy of persecutors (politicians, bureaucrats, senior military staff, bankers) led by his wife Sylvia, who embodies the restless but corrupt energy of the new age. A different kind of foil is provided by the young Suffragette schoolteacher Valentine Wannop: she and Tietjens fall in love and are at last reunited in a romantic climax at the close of the third volume, conjoining Tory chivalry with militant feminism. The chronological span of *Parade's End* makes it less a war novel than a historical fiction that includes the War: its opening episode captures the illusory solidity of the pre-War ruling class, while its final volume is set in a diminished, surrealistically rendered post-War world. The intervening sections of the narrative are set in wartime, combining and alternating the view from the front line, where Tietjens serves as an officer, with various scenes of Home Front life as seen by Valentine and others. This design makes *Parade's End* a more comprehensive fictional treatment of the War and its historical meaning than any other. Ford's handling of the narrative too is innovative, employing complex time-shifts, multiple perspectives, and a fragmentary, impressionistic presentation, as here in the opening page of *No More Parades*:

An immense tea-tray, august, its voice filling the black circle of the horizon, thundered to the ground. Numerous pieces of sheet-iron said 'Pack. Pack. Pack.' In a minute the clay floor of the hut shook, the drums of ears were pressed inwards, solid noise showered about the universe, enormous echoes pushed these men—to the right, to the left, or down towards the tables, and crackling like that of flames among vast underwood became the settled condition of the night. Catching the light from the brazier as the head leaned over, the lips of one of the two men on the floor were incredibly red and full and went on talking and talking. . . .

Such a style is well adapted to evoke the strangeness and confusion not only of trench life but of civilian disruption too, as it does in the whirl of the Armistice Day scenes that conclude *A Man Could Stand Up—*.

The fourth phase of this literature, opening in 1928, is marked by the prominence of satirical prose works presenting the War as essentially a futile waste of life inflicted upon the young by the obtuse or malevolent Old Men: Robert Graves's autobiography, *Good-bye to All That* (1929) is the leading example, sitting alongside Siegfried Sassoon's *Memoirs of an Infantry Officer* (1930) and Richard Aldington's novel *Death of a Hero* (1929); lesser contributions include H. M. Tomlinson's novel *All Our Yesterdays* (1930), Henry Williamson's fable *The Patriot's Progress* (1930), and W. Somerset Maugham's play about a blinded war veteran and his variously war-damaged friends, *For Services Rendered* (1932). On the other hand, it also includes works that are less concerned with protest or recrimination: Edmund Blunden's memoir *Undertones of War* (1928) is unassumingly descriptive in old-fashioned pastoralist manner; Frederic Manning's more powerful novel *The Middle Parts of Fortune* (1929; expurgated version, as *Her Privates We*, 1930) provides realistic portrayal of soldiers' experience rather than any general verdict on the War; R. C. Sherriff's popular play *Journey's End* (1929) is sentimental, not bitter; Vera Brittain's autobiographical *Testament of Youth* (1933) is elegiac; Wyndham Lewis's's memoir *Blasting and Bombardiering* (1937) is flippant, and keen to distance itself from the usual arraignment of military leaders; and, as we have seen, David Jones's heroic poem *In Parenthesis* presents the War in positive, mythically redemptive terms. All the same, it was the noisily 'disillusioned' Graves and Aldington who attracted the most controversy.

Graves clearly intended, in part from financial motives, to be sensationally provocative in *Good-bye to All That*, and he succeeded in offending many ex-servicemen including his friends Blunden and Sassoon, whose outrage at the book's inaccuracies and distortions led to prolonged estrangement. As the title suggests, Graves was preparing to go into exile as he wrote it, and he had larger aims than those of describing his war experiences with the Royal Welch Fusiliers. In fact *Good-bye to All That* is a satirical condemnation of the English social structure, especially its public schools (he and a Charterhouse schoolfellow agree that they should all be demolished) and the senior Army staff; in this it belongs to the modern debunking tradition of Lytton Strachey's *Eminent Victorians*. An autobiography rather than a war memoir, it begins in late Victorian times and proceeds through Graves's schooldays before reaching the War, and later continues the story of the author's post-War penury. The continuities between school and Army are especially significant, as they expose a seamless upper-class culture of bullying, snobbery, and patronizingly rigid regulation, captured perfectly in 'one of those caricature scenes' (*Good-bye to All That*, p. 150) that illuminate the narrative: the colonel summons his officers to a schoolroom in which they squeeze into child-sized desk-benches to hear his outraged lecture on the indiscipline of a lance corporal who allowed a common soldier to address him by his first name. Graves follows this scene up with a brief account of the separate brothels in French towns behind the lines, marked by blue lamps for officers and red lamps for other ranks. *Good-bye to All That* is remarkable for its wealth of grotesquely ironic anecdote: apart from scenes of carnage on the battlefield, we witness an instructor blowing himself up while demonstrating the dangers of mishandling grenades; an Irish soldier's suicide deliberately covered up and reported home as a 'soldier's death'; the looting of dying men's effects by the Royal Army Medicals Corps (RAMC, or 'Rob All My Comrades'); and the mistreatment of corpses and prisoners. Graves was neither a pacifist nor an anarchist: his account of the War exhibits his strong regimental pride and his belief in arms-drill; yet it also gives the impression that almost every official pronouncement during the War was a lie, and that the soldiers were completely irreligious, unpatriotic, and riddled with venereal disease. Edmund Blunden and others objected that he had betrayed his fallen comrades by eliminating the positive virtues of the soldiery—the bravery, endurance, selflessness, and compassion widely attested by other witnesses.

Richard Aldington's *Death of a Hero* directs its satire against the 'Victorian' values of pre-War society more than against the conduct of the War itself. Indeed, although it clearly belongs to this phase of war literature, it feels more like two different books bound as one, the first part being a splenetic sex-novel in the sermonizing manner of

D. H. Lawrence, the second—shorter but superior—portion a more subdued and objective account of life on the Western Front. The tenuous connection between these two halves lies in Aldington's claim that the War was 'the supreme and tragic climax of Victorian Cant' (p. 223). The 'hero' of the title, George Winterbourne, is a young artist who has both a wife and a mistress, and seems to join the army to escape these complications; but the two women soon tire of him, and acquire new boyfriends at home. The first-person narrator, a misogynist comrade of Winterbourne's, observes that many women were sexually aroused by the conflict: 'All the dying and wounds and mud and bloodiness—at a safe distance—gave them a great kick, and excited them to an almost unbearable pitch of amorousness' (p. 18). Similar resentment against women as fickle and bloodthirsty vampires may be found elsewhere in masculine war-writing, notably in Sassoon's poem 'Glory of Women' (1918). It is an extreme symptom of a disconnection generally felt between servicemen and civilians, and between the languages of these dissevered groups.

By comparison with these two iconoclastic books, with their scorn for a whole civilization, the other war-writings of this phase look modestly restricted in scope. Blunden's *Undertones of War*, for example, tells us hardly anything about its author or his opinions, and nothing about his visits home on leave; the focus is entirely upon the landscape of the Western Front and episodes of combat. Manning's *The Middle Parts of Fortune* likewise offers no interpretation of the War, nor any vantage point from which to survey it, but proceeds as a chronicle of the typical experiences of its central character as a common soldier, enriched with convincing psychological insight. Such contrasts of perspective between what we may call the panoramic and the trench-bound modes of war-writing raise certain problems which we should now consider in conclusion.

Passivity, Martyrology, and War Myths

Much of the most celebrated war-writing of the period may better be described as trench literature, in that its strength as well as its weakness is its reliance upon the soldier's immediate view of things, which in trench-warfare conditions often means little more than mud, rats, barbed wire, gas masks, and wounded comrades. The severely restricted vision offered by such trench poems as Rosenberg's 'Break of Day...', Gurney's 'Strafe' (1917), Graves's 'Limbo' (1916), Owen's 'Exposure' (1920), and Sassoon's 'A Working Party' (1917) allows at the same time an intense focus upon the physical sensations and nervous tremors of suffering human bodies, the vulnerability of which replaces and puts to shame any martial abstraction. To be sure, most poems by these soldiers do look beyond the parapet, if only to No Man's Land or to recreations and convalescences behind the lines. Gurney's imagination often reaches back, as his collection's title suggests, from the Somme to the Severn in homesickness for Gloucestershire and a personified maternal England. Sassoon frequently revisits the base camp and the homeland in order to enforce satirical contrasts between their cocooned safety and the raw exposure of the men in the front lines. Nonetheless, in trench poetry, in later memoirs of trench life such as *Undertones of War*, and in soldier-novels such as *The Middle Parts of Fortune* and *The Secret Battle*, the personally witnessed agony or squalor retains its special status as the authenticated truth of war, against which other perceptions of it, especially those of non-combatants, may be invalidated as delusions or lies. In Sassoon's case especially, the rhetoric of a protest poem on trench horrors or the fates of maimed survivors presupposes an improbably deluded reader who, once awoken to the grim truth, no longer needs the poem. Realistic exposé in this sense exhausts itself when most successful, arriving at the redundancy of propagandist writing.

Coming at a related problem from a traditional tragic angle, W. B. Yeats justified his exclusion of Wilfred Owen's poems from the *Oxford Book of Modern Verse* (1936) on the grounds that 'passive suffering is not a theme for poetry'.[3] Yeats indeed kept out of his anthology not only Owen's work but the war poems of Sorley, Gurney, Rosenberg, Brooke, Hardy, and Kipling, along with the protest poems of Sassoon. He did include Grenfell's 'Into Battle', but his preference was clearly for those poems that with calmer hindsight had absorbed the pains of war into tragic or elegiac contemplation:

---

[3] W. B. Yeats (ed.), *The Oxford Book of Modern Verse 1892–1935* (1936), p. xxxiv.

Sassoon's 'On Passing the New Menin Gate' (1928), Blunden's 'Report on Experience' (1929), and Read's 'The End of a War' (1933). His too-rigid application of such principles may be regretted, but the problem of passive suffering to which he referred remains inescapable in any larger consideration of modern war-writing, whether in verse or in prose. With the exceptions of T. E. Lawrence and of Yeats himself that we noticed earlier in this chapter, the reputable literature of the Great War is strongly marked by its displacement of traditional heroic action and by its contrary emphases on passive victimhood, stoical endurance, and even sacrificial martyrdom. To some degree, this development follows inevitably from the military technologies that replaced the cavalry charge with the artillery barrage; but there are additional elements of artistic choice and critical reception at work here too. Andrew Rutherford pointed out in his book *The Literature of War* (1978) that the soldier-poets and memoirists who represented themselves, their comrades, and their German counterparts as sacrificial victims of Old Men's bloodlust were repressing their own active part in the slaughter. These men did not just cower under bombardment while awaiting a chance to play football with 'Fritz'; they went out and killed Germans. Owen and Read are known to have shown bold initiative in assaulting enemy positions, and Sassoon above all, although he is now regarded as a patron saint of pacifism, was in fact a ruthlessly vengeful killer. Some of the later memoirs and novels acknowledge these culpabilities more fully, but wartime soldier-poetry tends to portray active warriors as helpless victims. The common impression of being a cog in an unstoppable machine clearly does have a basis in the new realities of industrialized warfare, but the martyrology of Owen, Sassoon, Aldington, and others also involves a powerfully selective rhetoric that vents resentment against generals and journalists who did not participate in their sufferings. It would be naïve to assume that the realism of the soldier-poets reflects the bare truth while rhetoric is employed only by official propagandists.

The perspectives offered by the war-writings of this period are inevitably partial, incomplete, and selective. The most prominent of these works, especially in the late Twenties and early Thirties, moulded what Samuel Hynes calls 'the myth of the war', myth here meaning not flagrant falsehood but a body of potent simplifications that helped post-War English culture to define its own position.[4] The elements of this war myth include the complete gulf between pre- and post-War periods of history; the sacrifice of the Young to the false ideals of the Old; the sudden loss of innocence and idealism; the discrediting of public slogans and official war aims; the identification of Home Front warmongers as enemies deadlier than German troops; the soldiers on either side as victims of a futile conflict prolonged by incompetent leaders; the War as a juggernaut beyond human control; and the collapse of early patriotic fervour into cynicism and disillusionment. Later accounts of Great War literature have tended to reproduce the myth with variant emphases rather than to question it; and since the Vietnam era of anti-war agitation in the 1960s there has been a tendency to compound the myth, both by favouring overt 'protest' writings over subtler and more ambivalent literary responses and by misreading the latter as if they were the former. So tenacious are the war myths of Martyrdom and Futility that we now need to remind ourselves that most British servicemen (and auxiliaries of both sexes), and most writers among them, took part in the War voluntarily and in what they believed throughout to be a just cause, whatever they may have felt about the manner in which it was conducted. Even Robert Graves, for all his satirical debunkings, continued to insist long afterwards that the War had been a necessary response to German aggression in Belgium.

Military historians are now increasingly sceptical about the lions-led-by-donkeys view of the War as a catalogue of incompetence, although fiasco and appalling waste are of course part of the story. Literary history too needs to reach beyond the easy simplifications of what may be called the futilitarian school, and into the real variety and ambivalence of war-writing, by taking more seriously the literature of zones beyond the Western Front (including works by non-combatant writers), by appreciating the literature of historical reflection as well as that of immediate shock, and by recognizing, in Andrew Rutherford's words,

the fact that much of the finest literature of the war transcends the simplicities of protest to acknowledge a far greater complexity of response

---

[4] Samuel Hynes, *A War Imagined: The First World War and English Culture* (Bodley Head, 1990), 439.

to disturbingly complex experience, and that much of it also reasserts an heroic ideal, stripped of romantic glamour certainly, but redefined convincingly in terms of grim courage and endurance in the face of almost unbearable suffering and horror.[5]

The complexity of response to which Rutherford refers is one in which reluctant acceptance of the War's necessity accompanies revulsion at its devastations, and in which the War could be understood both as a disaster and as a display of positive fortitude on the part of the common soldier. Rutherford rightly points out that even the most disillusioned accounts of the War—Graves's *Good-bye to All That* and Aldington's *Death of a Hero*—pay repeated tribute to the bravery and good humour of the men in the front lines, and cherish the comradeship of the trenches as the chief redeeming feature of the conflict. Other accounts such as Blunden's *Undertones of War* commend individual heroes more fully, while the writings of the officers Owen and Sassoon display an attachment to the men under their command cast in tones of erotic tenderness. Among the many convulsions of the War came unexampled kinds of intimate collaboration between formerly segregated social classes: in the trenches, in hospitals, in munitions factories, on the land. From this experience, upper- and middle-class authors came away with a new respect for, and attention to, the qualities found among the common people. *Death of a Hero* and Manning's novel *The Middle Parts of Fortune* are significant here in that their protagonists both decide to serve as privates, not as officers. The literature of the War and indeed of the decades that followed it is in some important ways anti-heroic and certainly anti-romantic; it is satirical in its view of officialdom and of a jingoist press; but having set aside old illusions and stale catchphrases, it preserves a place for heroism—of a stoical, undemonstrative kind—in its affirmations of the common soldier's endurance.

[5] Andrew Rutherford, *The Literature of War: Five Studies in Heroic Virtue* (Macmillan, 1978), 65.

16

Childhood and Youth

New Words, 1910–1940

anti-authoritarian babysitter child-care inarticulacy infantilization pre-puberty pre-school school-kid school-leaver schoolmistressy teenage weediness youth-leader

As we noted in Chapter 2, modern literary culture echoed and amplified the grievances of the young against the old, especially in the aftermath of the Great War, when many writers presented that calamity as a massacre of youth perpetrated by bloodthirsty elders. By the late 1920s, the blaming of the older generation and the praising of youth for youth's sake had been identified by Wyndham Lewis as central problems of post-War life. Lewis's long satire *The Apes of God* (1930) diagnoses the pseudo-bohemian culture of contemporary art and literature as a bogus 'Revolt of the Children' against imaginary ogrish father-figures, and as a melodramatic '*child-parent-war-game*' (pp. 412, 578). Retarded by self-pitying vanity, the typical modern writer—and reader—is in Lewis's view deeply infantilized, a Peter Pan refusing to assume adult responsibility. One minor character in *Apes of God* is a journalist who makes a lucrative profession from 'sucking-up to the Young' in articles with titles like 'Youth at the Helm!' (p. 290). Whether or not we follow Lewis all the way in his interpretation of the youth cult as the central illusion of his time, we must concede that the period was dazzled by the young, as a few book titles may indicate. This was the period of *Youth* (Isaac

Rosenberg's verse collection, 1915), *The Loom of Youth* (Alec Waugh's novel, 1917), *Testament of Youth* (Vera Brittain's memoir, 1933), *Youth's Encounter* (the first volume of Compton Mackenzie's novel *Sinister Street*, 1913), *A Portrait of the Artist as a Young Man* (James Joyce's novel, 1916), *A Young Man's Year* (Anthony Hope's novel, 1915), *The Young Diana* (Marie Corelli's novel, 1918), *The Young Lovell* (Ford Madox Hueffer's novel, 1913), *The Young Visiters* (Daisy Ashford's juvenile story, 1919), *Young Felix* and *The Young Idea* (both novels by Frank Swinnerton, 1923 and 1910), *The Young Idea* (again, now a Noël Coward play, 1923), *Young Woodley* (John Van Druten's play, 1928), *The Young Physician* (a novel by Francis Brett Young, aptly enough, 1919), and *The Younger Generation* (Stanley Houghton's play, 1910). Wyndham Lewis's own contribution was *Doom of Youth* (1932), a polemic against Alec Waugh and others that was withdrawn by his publishers for fear of libel action.

The origins of the child–parent war game in modern literature lie earlier than 1910, though. The anti-Victorian sentiment of Edwardian writing had been cast in terms of collision between sensitive children and their uncomprehending fathers, notably in Samuel Butler's posthumous novel *The Way of All Flesh* (1903), in Edmund Gosse's memoir *Father and Son* (1907), and in H. G. Wells's novel *Ann Veronica* (1909). Those had been mild by comparison with the 'Maxims for Revolutionists' appended to the published text of Bernard Shaw's *Man and Superman* (1903), which had declared that 'Every man over forty is a scoundrel' and that 'The vilest abortionist is he who attempts to mould a child's character' (pp. 263, 253). Shaw resumed this harsher modern style of parricidal aggression at full length in the essay 'Parents and Children' that prefaces the published version (1914) of his play *Misalliance*. The play itself (1910) features a teenage heroine, Hypatia, whose impatience with her parents vents itself explosively: 'Oh, home! home! parents! family! duty! How I loathe them! How I'd like to see them all blown to bits!' (p. 146). The prefatory essay concerns itself with the inhumanities of Edwardian child-rearing and education, and is at times scarcely more temperate than Hypatia: formal schooling is a 'monstrous system of child imprisonment and torture' notorious for the obscene 'flagellomania' of corporal punishment (pp. 20, 60), while attempts at the moral education of children are worse still:

Were you to cut all of what you call the evil out of a child, it would drop dead. If you try to stretch it to full human stature when it is ten years old, you will simply pull it into two pieces and be hanged. And when you try to do this morally, which is what parents and schoolmasters are doing every day, you ought to be hanged; and some day, when we take a sensible view of the matter, you will be; and serve you right. (p. 102)

Behind the provocative rhetoric here lies a significant revulsion against Victorian notions of compulsorily angelic innocence, not only as artificial but as inhumane. Shaw regarded 'bad' behaviour in children as a healthy and necessary part of their moral growth, and modern literature both for children and for adults increasingly shared his view.

The short stories of 'Saki' (Hector Munro), as we saw in Chapter 6, keenly relish the rebellion of young boys against their aunts and other guardians, notably in 'Sredni Vashtar' (1911), and they scorn the patronizing use of 'improving' moral tales for the edification of the young, as in 'The Story-Teller' (1914). His stories were addressed to adults, but among children's books too a new mood of rebellious energy marks this period, especially in the shape of William Brown, the unkempt hero of Richmal Crompton's long-running series of stories beginning with the *Just—William* collection (1922). To the 11-year-old William, adult codes of behaviour are simply incomprehensible, so whenever he is told not to do something by his sensible middle-class parents and teachers he soon finds a compelling reason to do it, especially if it promises the joys of dirt, noise, and destructive anarchy. The William stories cleverly combine boisterous action that appeals to child-readers with malapropisms and mock-heroic ironies of style that disarm any adults reading over their shoulders. Equally engaging to both is the author's clear preference for her hero, with his band of 'Outlaws', over a succession of sickeningly 'good' children whose parentally approved deportment overlays a spoilt selfishness; the most memorable of these are the lisping heir-ess Violet Elizabeth Bott, who threatens, in *Still—William* (1925), to 'thcream and thcream and thcream till I'm thick' (ch. 8), and the apparently winsome Anthony Martin in *William—The Pirate*

(1932), who is clearly a hostile caricature of A. A. Milne's Christopher Robin. 'There's nothing medieval or romantic about William,' his mother informs a relative who is planning to dress him up as a nuptial pageboy (*Just—William*, ch. 9); and indeed her son is the most distinctively modern hero of this period's juvenile literature.

William's Outlaw chums are all boys, and his experience of the other sex tends to be baffling. The interest that otherwise sensible men show in his irritable elder sister Ethel is a perpetual puzzle, and when William himself succumbs to the charms of the girl next door or of a young teacher, he ends up sorely confused by his failure to impress them. For the most part, girls are dismissed as 'soppy', with the exception of his admirably tomboyish cousin Dorita, who vanishes after the first book. Her absence was eventually made good by the obviously parasitic intervention of 'Evadne Price' (Helen Zenna Smith), who in 1928 launched a rival series with *Just Jane*. Price's heroine Jane Turpin is William's female equivalent, and in some respects an even more determined and violent anarchist in her campaign against soppiness—especially that of her goody-goody enemy Amelia—and her refusal to be dressed up in frilly finery. Jane is an appealing embodiment of feminist rebellion who awaits rediscovery; in her own time, regrettably, she never attained the popularity enjoyed by William.

In serious fiction for adults, the experiences of childhood and youth were often as important as they had been in such classic Victorian novels as *Jane Eyre* (1847), *David Copperfield* (1850), and *The Mill on the Floss* (1860), offering both an imaginative distance from the habitual assumptions of adult civilization and a moral vantage point from which that civilization could be assessed. In these senses, the investment of modern fiction in youthful rebellion retains some strong traditional features, while still seeking to avoid the excesses of Victorian sentimentalism. Especially significant in this context are the education novels of the decade 1910–19, reviewed above in Chapter 9: Arnold Bennett's *Clayhanger* (1910), Compton Mackenzie's *Sinister Street* (1913–14), D. H. Lawrence's *Sons and Lovers* (1913), W. Somerset Maugham's *Of Human Bondage* (1915), James Joyce's *A Portrait of the Artist as a Young Man*, May Sinclair's *Mary Olivier* (1919), and other novels in this tradition all invite the reader to sympathize with a sensitive child growing up within the various constraints imposed by negligent or oppressive parents, guardians, or teachers. In enlisting that sympathy, these books often seek to evoke the strangeness of the world freshly perceived by the infant, as in this passage from the opening pages of Sinclair's *Mary Olivier*:

White patterns on the window, sharp spikes, feathers, sprigs with furled edges, stuck flat on to the glass; white webs, crinkled like the skin of boiled milk, stretched across the corner of the pane; crisp, sticky stuff that bit your fingers.

Out of doors, black twigs thickened with a white fur; white powder sprinkled over the garden walk. The white, ruffled grass stood out stiffly and gave under your feet with a pleasant crunching. The air smelt good; you opened your mouth and drank it in gulps. It went down like cold, tingling water.

Frost.

You saw the sun for the first time, a red ball that hung by itself on the yellowish white sky. Mamma said, 'Yes, of course it would fall if God wasn't there to hold it up in his hands.'

Supposing God dropped the sun— (bk. 1, ch. 1)

Such passages of 'defamiliarization' tend in Romantic fashion to cast the young child as a spontaneously original poet in her response to the world, while the condescending adult utters stale but seductive pieties. In episodes like this, the infant's metaphorical registration of sense-impressions is to be understood as the germ of her authentic selfhood, whose unfolding will be threatened as the prison house of civilized convention closes around it.

Similar moments are to be found in other education novels, notably in the opening chapter of Joyce's *A Portrait*, as they are too in later variations upon the sub-genre like Virginia Woolf's *Jacob's Room* (1922) and Aldous Huxley's *Eyeless in Gaza* (1936). In the short-story form, Katherine Mansfield often employs the estranged perspective of children, most powerfully in the scenes involving Kezia in 'Prelude' (1918), and continuously in the shorter tale 'Sun and Moon' (1920), in which an adults' evening party is witnessed by the children of the house: 'The drawing-room was full of sweet smelling, silky, rustling ladies and men in black with funny tails on their coats—like beetles' (*Selected Stories*, p. 171). Effects of this kind are found too in the stories of Elizabeth Bowen, notably in the opening party scene of 'The Tommy Crans' (1934). In general, the child's-eye view, as we now call it, puts a critical distance between us and the familiar conventions of adult life, encouraging us to see them as artificial and open to justified resistance from the young hero or heroine. In this way it underpins the moral critique of 'Victorian' family values and school regimes, so that the child-protagonist's poetic sensitivity serves to deny legitimacy to the system of values under which she or he is socialized. The child of modern fiction tends thus to occupy the moral high ground marked out for it by Romantic and Victorian literature.

On the other hand, many modern writers were determined to present the child-figure in a more hard-headed manner, stripping it of Wordsworthian clouds of glory and of Dickensian lisping innocence. The angelic child who lectures her tearful elders from her deathbed on her glimpses of heavenly wisdom, as Little Nell does in Dickens's *The Old Curiosity Shop* (1841), was banished in favour of more credibly selfish, callous, and undignified little savages. Evelyn Waugh's contempt for Dickens becomes evident towards the end of *A Handful of Dust* (1934), but his distance from Victorian child-worship is noticeable much earlier, when the 6-year-old John Last is feebly reprimanded by his father:

'Now listen, John. It was very wrong of you to call nanny a silly old tart. First, because it was unkind to her. Think of all the things she does for you every day.'

'She's paid to.' (ch. 2, pt. 1)

Comic cruelty cuts both ways, though: precocious insensitivity of this kind removes child-characters from the sentimental protection of older fictional codes, entitling the modern writer to inflict random violence upon them. As we noticed in Chapter 5, Saki permits his rebellious boy-heroes to harbour murderous thoughts, but his stories claim by the same token a licence to show children killed or maimed with casual flippancy. Waugh indulges in the same kind of fun in *Decline and Fall* (1928) when he has a schoolboy inadvertently shot in the foot by a teacher's starting pistol at the sports day, and in *A Handful of Dust* he kills off little John Last in a riding accident. The deaths of children in modern fiction, as with little Phil's fatal meningitis in Huxley's *Point Counter Point* (1928), can be presented, as never before, as almost meaningless events, quite unlike the moral climaxes that they constitute in Victorian novels.

Some of the best writing about children in this period persuades us that innocence has really very little to do with sweetness. In Elizabeth Bowen's fiction, for example, innocence is treated as a dangerous form of egocentricity or solipsistic blindness to other people's pain, or even to their existence. In her short story 'The Visitor' (1926), a 9-year-old boy remains convinced that the grown-ups he has visited with his mother cease to exist once he has said goodbye to them: they are somehow rolled up and put away for later use. The unconscious cruelty of the innocent is dramatized at full length in *The House in Paris* (1935), in the unnerving scenes between Henrietta, aged 11, and the 9-year-old Leopold, who are left together as strangers and proceed quite casually to rip away each other's fragile sense of identity. 'There is no end', the narrator remarks, 'to the violations committed by children on children, quietly talking alone' (pt. 1, ch. 2). One of the period's foremost writers for children, the author of *Peacock Pie* (rhymes, 1913) and *Broomsticks* (magical tales, 1925), Walter de la Mare shows in his poems and stories for adults a similar sense of children's apparently callous indifference to horror or cruelty. In the short story 'An Ideal Craftsman' (1930), a boy calmly hoists the corpse of his family's manservant from a hook on the kitchen ceiling in order to disguise a murder as suicide. Again in de la Mare's short narrative poem 'Dry August Burned' (1938), a young girl at first weeps at the sight of a dead hare but soon pleads to watch it being skinned. As lay child-psychologists, modern authors tend to ascribe to children two contradictory characteristics: on the one hand a heightened 'poetic' sensitivity to sensations, on the other a reckless insensitivity to—or blessed immunity from—the sufferings of their fellow creatures.

Digressing from his review of an irritatingly 'sweet' novel about a schoolboy, Arnold Bennett remarked in 1929: 'I never yet met a boy, in intimacy, much less a girl, whose make-up had not quite a fair percentage of cruelty and general unscrupulousness. And I am still waiting for a realistic novel whose hero or heroine is a child' (*Evening Standard Years*, p. 294). Although the human child can be the most terrible of creatures, Bennett went on to observe, novelists persisted in covering up this truth and treating the young as enchanting little toys. His demand for a more realistic fictional account of children was promptly answered: within a few weeks he was able to applaud the appearance of Richard Hughes's *A High Wind in Jamaica* (1929; in the USA as *The Innocent Voyage*) as a bracingly unsentimental novel whose author 'knows children for the callous, imperturbable, fatalistic, delightful, imaginative little animals they are' (*Evening Standard Years*, p. 309).

Although Hughes's book deals with the most colourfully romantic materials of historical adventure stories, including piracy, kidnap, and murder, its significance as a minor landmark in modern fiction lies in its soberly realistic treatment of these matters, and in its refusal to sentimentalize his child-characters' responses to them. Set in the Caribbean in the nineteenth century, *A High Wind in Jamaica* is a novel for adults, although its principal characters are children ranging in age from 3 to 13. When a hurricane destroys their Jamaican home, their parents decide to pack them off to England; the ship, though, is soon raided by pirates who make the fatal mistake of abducting the children. These pirates, led by their Danish Captain Jonsen, turn out to be fairly harmless: they are horrified by murder, by blasphemy, and even by attempted insurance fraud, and although the eldest child, a girl of 13, becomes a concubine to some of the crew, the younger children cannot recognize Jonsen and his men as 'wicked', regarding them rather with affection. The children's attitude, especially that of the 10-year-old Emily Bas-Thornton, to their captivity is the central subject of the novel, and Hughes uses it to mock adult delusions. Emily's parents imagine that she adores them and will be heartbroken by being sent away; in fact the family cat occupies a bigger place in her heart, and she hardly notices her parents' absence. Similarly when her brother vanishes (he has died in an accidental fall), she asks no questions and simply forgets him. The standard by which Emily judges the importance of people and of events is indeed alarmingly foreign to adult comprehension: she welcomes a minor earth tremor as the biggest event of her life, but disregards the devastation of her home by the hurricane, too concerned as she is with the problem of whether she herself might be God. As the narrator remarks, children fundamentally 'differ in kind of thinking (are *mad*, in fact)' (*A High Wind in Jamaica*, ch. 7). When the pirates capture a ship carrying a lion and a tiger to a zoo, they drunkenly attempt to stage a fight between them, but the animals are too seasick to oblige. Meanwhile Emily stabs the ship's captain to death in a fit of terror, an action for which Jonsen and his crew are later hanged. The conclusion to be drawn is clear: children are the most dangerous of creatures. Upon the children's eventual release and arrival in England, sympathetic adults assume that they have suffered unspeakable horrors, but Emily and her younger siblings have accepted the whole experience as a kind of game. 'The little angel!' coos one charitable lady to a rescued infant (ch. 9); but the reader by this point knows better.

Hughes's novel embodies the 'debunking' spirit of realism often found in the literature of the Twenties. In books written for children themselves, one would not expect to find such a starkly disenchanted tone, and happily the great Victorian tradition of fabulous literary enchantment survives well through this period in a few children's classics: John Masefield's *The Midnight Folk* (1927) and its sequel *The Box of Delights* (1935) are vividly rendered fantasies involving magic, witchcraft, time travel, piracy, and stolen treasure along with splendidly grotesque grown-up villains; and J. R. R. Tolkein's prolonged fairy tale of dwarves and dragons in *The Hobbit* (1937) created an unusually atmospheric world of its own. Meanwhile younger children could enjoy the whimsical tales of A. A. Milne in *Winnie-the-Pooh* (1926) and its sequel, *The House at Pooh Corner* (1928), in which the characters are cuddly toy animals who act out conflicts between infant joys (Pooh, Tigger) and adult pomposity or gloom (Owl, Eeyore) within the securely self-contained idyll of the Hundred Acre Wood.

Historians of the children's book commonly agree that a 'golden age' of fantasy and enchantment ran from Lewis Carroll's *Alice's Adventures in Wonderland* (1864) to Kenneth Grahame's *The Wind in the Willows* (1908), and that after the Great War such magic, although surviving in the examples just noted, faded away under the pressures of modern realism. And indeed there is a certain momentum towards realism in children's books of the 1910–40 period, of which we have seen one version already in Crompton's 'William' stories. By the 1930s, the realist tendency had assumed several specialized forms. Some of these new realisms were social and political in emphasis: Eve Garnett's *The Family from One-End Street* (1937) broke away from the overwhelmingly middle-class world of juvenile fiction to recount tales involving the children of a dustman in a poor urban neighbourhood; and Geoffrey Trease wrote historical adventures, *Bows against the Barons* and *Comrades for the Charter* (both 1934), with which Leftist parents could prepare their young for the class struggle. In the mainstream of juvenile fiction, meanwhile, realism took the modest form of worldly probability in stories of lifelike children in credible environments. The primary wish-fulfilments of romance still governed these narratives so that the child-protagonist always scores the winning goal, earns the reward, or solves the mystery; but narrative desire is now embedded in circumstantial accuracy to recognizable modern settings uninhabited by goblins or pirates. So a child enthused by outdoor activities could derive from Arthur Ransome's *Swallows and Amazons* (1930) and its sequels a good deal of practical knowledge about sailing and camping, along with some geographical awareness of the Lake District or the Norfolk Broads. The only serious improbability in Ransome's books is the readiness of the grown-ups to devote most of their holidays to assisting the children with elaborate preparations for their adventures. Otherwise the blandness of the action—except in the more exciting *We Didn't Mean to Go to Sea* (1937), few alarming dangers are encountered—is compensated for by a sense that these adventures could really happen.

Part of the appeal of Ransome's holiday adventure stories lay in their fidelity to the technical details of sailing, a kind of accuracy that could win the respect of the early-teenage hobbyist and the approval of parents eager to encourage healthy pastimes. A notable development in children's fiction of the Thirties is the emergence of subgenres addressing quite specific teenage hobbies and obsessions of this kind. The first three juvenile novels of Noel Streatfeild illustrate a new pattern of niche marketing that launched what became known as the 'career novel': the best-selling *Ballet Shoes* (1936), in which one of three orphaned sisters eventually becomes a Hollywood star, was quickly followed by *Tennis Shoes* (1937) and by *The Circus is Coming* (1938), all of them carefully researched, as were the contemporaneous murder-on-location detective novels whose similar adoption of special milieux we noted in Chapter 13. At the same time the cult of ponies among pubescent girls acquired its own literature with Primrose Cumming's *Doney* (1934) and Joanna Cannan's *A Pony for Jean* (1936). The most impressive novel of this kind is Enid Bagnold's *National Velvet* (1935), which tells the story of a 14-year-old girl who wins a piebald horse in a raffle and goes on to ride it to victory in the Grand National. While this plot evidently fulfils a fairy-tale fantasy, Bagnold's handling of the tale is adult in style and richly realistic in presentation, especially in its portrayal of her heroine's family life: Velvet Brown is the daughter of a poor rural butcher, and lives next to the slaughterhouse with her three elder sisters and a pretty 4-year-old brother who has believably disgusting habits. Whether delivering meat for her father, encouraging her sister's canaries to mate, vomiting up her breakfast, picking food out of her dental brace, medicating her mother's injured back, or scrubbing down her horse, she is immersed in the physical 'facts of life' upon which the adolescent reader's apprehensions about mortality and sexuality may feed. Unusually pungent in this respect, *National Velvet* belongs with James Joyce's *Ulysses* among the fleshliest novels of this period.

One special milieu within which realistic children's fiction may be set dominates all others, this being school, especially the kind of private boarding school then favoured by the upper middle class. School stories for girls had been appearing regularly since the 1880s, but they were now assuming a cheerfully modern tone in which demure piety and needlework gave way to the boisterous energy of the hockey field, notably in the works of Angela Brazil, the genre's leading exponent from about 1910 to the 1930s. The Brazil schoolgirl is no dainty young lady but a healthy little Amazon, her cheeks usually glowing both from outdoor sports and from 'hot' bosom friendships. She speaks in slang (*ripping*, *scrumptious*), and although entirely innocent sexually, she is not a model of virtue but an averagely selfish or weak-willed creature struggling to deserve the approval of her teachers and popularity among her chums. To take an example highlighted by Mary Cadogan and Patricia Craig in their affectionate history of girls' stories, *You're a Brick, Angela!* (1976), the heroine of one of Brazil's best early works, *A Fourth Form Friendship* (1911), Aldred Laurence, is a 14-year-old new girl at a small boarding school. There she is thrilled to be chosen by Mildred, the school's most admired pupil, as her intimate room-mate. She soon discovers that Mildred has mistaken her for a similarly named girl who had rescued a boy from a house fire and modestly refused to talk to the press about it. Reluctant to forfeit Mildred's adoration, she cannot bring herself to correct the error, and at the same time she allows herself a succession of minor dishonesties, shirking the blame for various misdemeanours and allowing it to fall on classmates. Eventually she saves Mildred's life in a fire, and can renew their intimacy on a more truthful basis. Clearly this is a moral tale about candour and unmerited reputation, but it avoids heavy didactic sermons, casting the moral dilemmas in terms of the schoolgirls' own code of honour, and allowing the adolescent reader to discern Aldred's weaknesses for herself. The popularity of Brazil's increasingly formulaic novels and stories, like that of Dorita Fairlie Bruce's 'Dimsie' books (from 1920), Elsie Oxenham's Abbey Girls series (from 1920), and Elinor Brent-Dyer's Chalet Girls series (from 1925), rested mainly on their picture of school life as jolly good fun, but partly too on their creation of girl-centred worlds in which parents and teachers play subordinate roles, and the moral values appear to be formulated, negotiated, and enforced by the girls themselves. The books have no literary worth, but they are still recalled with fond condescension as time capsules from an age of uncomplicated wholesomeness.

For boys, the literature of school was becoming altogether more sombre and contentious. The boys' school story was already an established form with its own canon of minor classics (*Tom Brown's Schooldays* by Thomas Hughes, 1857; *Stalky & Co.* by Rudyard Kipling, 1899) and its own romance conventions of initiation and passage (nervous new boy adjusts to arcane customs, passes moral tests, is rewarded with athletic triumph). In the period after 1910 it can be seen to wither under the pressures of social change, educational controversy, and post-War disillusionment, and by the 1930s to be in decline. Before it reached that stage, though, it passed through significant convulsions, most of them arising from novels that questioned the hitherto unmentioned vices lying behind the reputations of the great public schools: their anti-intellectual cult of sport, their toleration of 'cribbing' (academic cheating), bullying, flagellomania, and predatory homosexuality. An early sign of trouble came from G. F. Bradby, himself a master at Rugby, whose novel *The Lanchester Tradition* (1913) recounted a struggle for the soul of a public school between a new reforming headmaster who wants to restore the original ideals of Christian scholarship, and the conservative masters who cling to the supremacy of athletics. Conflict between aesthetically sensitive boys and the bullying elite of sporting 'bloods' was already a staple theme of school fiction, but it was now darkening into satire and exposé, notably in Arnold Lunn's *The Harrovians* (1913), a mocking account of the public-school spirit, its snobberies, petty tyrannies, and its glorification of stupid athletes.

Lunn's boldness in turn inspired the young Alec Waugh (Evelyn Waugh's elder brother), who was suddenly removed—in effect expelled—from Sherborne for homosexual conduct in 1915, and quickly took revenge by writing a novel while still only 17 years old. Rejected by several publishers, it appeared in 1917 as *The Loom of Youth*, provoking bitter controversy in the public schools and in some periodicals, in which Waugh was accused of libelling a sacred English institution. Waugh's story of Gordon Caruthers's schooldays at 'Fernhurst' is an exposé not only of the preference for athleticism over learning but of routine swearing, dishonesty, academic malpractice, and of unspecified 'fast' behaviour. Homosexuality, although never identified openly, is omnipresent, and not only among effete artistic pupils either: it is casually accepted that the sporting 'bloods'—of whom Waugh himself, a promising cricketer, had been one—prey freely on the younger boys. At a time when these demigods of the playing field were dying in large numbers on the Western Front, this was a cruel blow from which the literary romance of public-school life never fully recovered. Positive portrayals of schooldays still kept appearing, but they acquired a defensive note. Beverley Nichols's first novel, *Prelude* (1920), published while he was an Oxford undergraduate, was written as a riposte to Waugh, and sets out to show how even an effeminate aesthete such as himself at Marlborough, or his hero Paul at 'Martinsell', could still be perfectly happy and even popular among the rugby-players. Paul is eventually killed in the Great War, a fitting end for a golden boy. The same fate awaited the hero of Ernest Raymond's best-selling *Tell England* (1922), a sentimental public-school story that carries its joyous mood right through to the bloody disaster of the Gallipoli campaign without any sign of disillusionment, death in battle being greeted as a privilege much like batting for the First XI.

By the mid 1930s, disaffection with the public-school code, and indeed with most other forms of schooling, was widespread among the latest generation of writers. Evelyn Waugh had portrayed the worst of all possible prep schools, Llanabba Castle, in his satirical novel *Decline and Fall* (1928); W. H. Auden—like Waugh, a temporary prep-school teacher—had subjected the school spirit to surrealistic parody in *The Orators* (1932); and Antonia White had exposed the sinister regime of rewards, punishments, and surveillance at her Roehampton convent school in *Frost in May* (1933), ostensibly a novel but really a fictionalized memoir. Graham Greene, who had been suicidally miserable as a schoolboy at Berkhamsted, where his own father was headmaster, rounded up a number of modern writers, most of whom had attended public schools or the nearest girls' equivalents during or shortly after the War, and invited them to reflect upon their schools for a volume of essays, *The Old School* (1934). Greene himself was convinced that the public-school system was justly doomed to imminent extinction and that the book would preserve an image of its dying days. One of his contributors, W. H. Auden, writing about his prep school in otherwise carefully appreciative ways, offered a memorable exaggeration when discussing its 'honour' system whereby boys were encouraged to inform on each others' misdemeanours: 'The best reason I have for opposing Fascism is that at school I lived in a Fascist state' (Auden, *Prose, 1926–1938*, p. 59). In reality, Auden had far better reasons than that, but the remark indicates the readiness with which many Thirties writers saw the world as an enlarged version of the classroom.

Cyril Connolly, an Old Etonian as school-obsessed as any of his contemporaries, developed in *Enemies of Promise* (1938) an analysis of patrician English psychology that he proclaimed as

The Theory of Permanent Adolescence. It is the theory that the experiences undergone by boys at the great public schools, their glories and disappointments, are so intense as to dominate their lives and to arrest their development. From these it results that the greater part of the ruling class remains adolescent, school-minded, self-conscious, cowardly, sentimental, and in the last analysis homosexual. Early laurels weigh like lead, and of many of the boys whom I knew at Eton, I can say that their lives are over.[1]

---

[1] Cyril Connolly, *Enemies of Promise* (Penguin, 1961 edn.), 271.

As for the ruling class, it was presumably busy enough with ruling, rather than wallowing in school memories; but the literary class fitted Connolly's diagnosis only too well, especially in the late Twenties and early Thirties, when a wave of young public-school alumni emerged on the scene with little other than school to write about, at least in their first works: Evelyn Waugh, W. H. Auden, Christopher Isherwood, Stephen Spender, Louis MacNeice, Graham Greene, Henry Green, C. Day-Lewis (whose first detective novel as 'Nicholas Blake', *A Question of Proof* (1935), is set in a prep school), and many lesser writers of their generation were incurably school-minded, and to a greater or lesser degree imaginatively stunted by that obsession.[2]

It was possible to write well about school without indulging the narcissistic glamour of the sensitive pupil. Usually this meant taking seriously the experiences of teachers, a task almost impossible in the school-story tradition, where they are inevitably seen as 'types' through distorting lenses of fear or adoration. James Hilton's sentimental tale of a retired schoolmaster, *Goodbye Mr Chips* (1935) hardly escapes from those distortions. There are, though, some sanely unsentimental and non-satirical novels about teachers in this period, from Hugh Walpole's *Mr Perrin and Mr Traill* (1911) and Dorothy Richardson's *Backwater* (1916) to Winifred Holtby's *South Riding* (1936). There are also impressive portions of novels that take us for a while into the classroom, as in the second ('Nestor') chapter of Joyce's *Ulysses* (1922), the thirteenth chapter of D. H. Lawrence's *The Rainbow* (1915), and the third ('Class-Room') chapter of his *Women in Love* (1920). Not to be forgotten here either are Katherine Mansfield's story 'The Singing Lesson' (1921) and one of W. B. Yeats's greatest poems, 'Among School Children' (1927), set in a classroom observed by Yeats as an official visitor. Proceeding from an assumption of adult responsibility, these writings resisted the youth-cult of the times by placing children at a safe and subordinate distance.

[2] Valentine Cunningham investigates the school obsessions, youth-worship, and Old Boy cliques of that decade with ferocious persistence in his *British Writers of the Thirties* (1988), ch. 5.

17

Sex and Sexualities

New Words, 1910–1940

*birth-control   cross-dressing   curvaceous
eroticize   foreplay   homo-erotic   gigolo   kinkiness
libidinal   masculinist   nookie   nympho   orgasmic
phallocentric   sado-masochism   scopophilia
sexy   strip-tease   testosterone
transvestite   voyeurism*

Sex-Talk in the Freudian Age

Sex was invented in 1929. At least, the first use of the word 'sex' to mean copulation rather than the sphere of differences and attractions between male and female is recorded by *OED2* as appearing in D. H. Lawrence's poem 'Sex and Trust', from his *Pansies* collection of that year. Before then, a couple could have enjoyed a sex-union (from 1898) or sex-relations (from 1911), or the sex act (from 1918), but only now would they be 'having sex'. They might even have regarded themselves as *homosexuals* (since 1912), as *heterosexuals* (since 1920), as *bisexuals* (since 1922), or as *Lesbians* (since 1925), these nouns having arrived later than their adjectives. Whether or not they kept up with the arcane terminologies of *sexologists* (1914), they would soon find it hard to escape the omnipresent *sex-interest* (1911), *sex-awareness* (1925), and *sex-talk* (1931) of their times. This period witnessed an extraordinary dissemination of sexual discourses—medical, legal, popular, and literary—to the point of becoming *sex-obsessed* (1914).

The abandonment of 'Victorian' reticence and euphemism in sexual matters was at the heart of the fully modern experience. One of the legendary episodes in the Bloomsbury Group's self-emancipation from Victorianism involves the discovery of sex-talk as a liberatory release. Virginia Woolf's memoir 'Old Bloomsbury', written in 1922 but not publishable until 1976, recounts a breakthrough in the conversational norms of her social circle, which seems to have occurred in 1909, if at all (Woolf confesses that this may have been an 'invented' memory):

Suddenly the door opened and the long and sinister figure of Mr Lytton Strachey stood on the threshold. He pointed a finger at a stain on Vanessa's white dress.

'Semen?' he said.

Can one really say it? I thought and we burst out laughing. With that one word all barriers of reticence and reserve went down. A flood of the sacred fluid seemed to overwhelm us. Sex permeated our conversation. The word bugger was never far from our lips. We discussed copulation with the same excitement and openness that we had discussed the nature of good. It is strange to think how reticent, how reserved we had been and for how long. (*Moments of Being*, pp. 173–4)

The Bloomsburyites kept such amusements to themselves, though, their published works remaining unstained by explicit sexual vocabulary. It was in the Twenties that a few bolder spirits—James Joyce, D. H. Lawrence, Richard Aldington—tried to bring forbidden words and deeds into literary language, with the result that their books were expurgated or banned. By 1929, Norah James's banned novel *Sleeveless Errand* featured a self-confessed decadent heroine, Paula Cranford, who declares on behalf of her post-War generation, 'We're bored with people who aren't bawdy. We call them prigs and prudes if they don't want to talk about copulation at lunchtime and buggery at dinner.'[1] Although surprisingly chaste in thought and deed, Paula assumes the modern young woman's entitlement to the same verbal liberties as men enjoyed. Women between the ages of 21 and 30 had at last been granted the right to vote in 1928, as their

---

[1] Norah C. James, *Sleeveless Errand* (2nd edn., Paris: Babou & Kahane, 1929), 202.

elders had been in 1918; and they expected equality in other spheres to go with it.

The new assertiveness and self-confidence of the modern woman, pressing beyond the prior rebellions of the 1890s 'New Woman' and the Edwardian suffragists, was widely echoed in literature after 1910. An early indication of things to come can be found in Stanley Houghton's *Hindle Wakes* (1912), a resolutely realistic problem play set in domestic interiors of the mill town Hindle during the August holiday ('Wakes'), and written in Lancashire vernacular. Its initial 'problem' appears to be the stock melodramatic tangle of sex and class: a young weaver, Fanny Hawthorn, has secretly spent the night at a seaside hotel with Alan Jeffcote, the son of a local mill owner. Discovering her shameful secret, Fanny's parents resolve that the seducer must make an honest woman of her, and they appeal successfully to Mr Jeffcote's sense of honour, even though Alan's marriage to Fanny would wreck Jeffcote's planned alliance with another wealthy family through Alan's fiancée Beatrice. Alan and his snobbish mother revolt against the prospect of his marrying a mere mill girl, and Beatrice's father concurs in their proposal to buy Fanny off; but Beatrice herself breaks off the engagement, insisting nobly that Alan's duty is now to Fanny. As the third act begins, all the characters are agreed, reluctantly or not, that Alan shall marry Fanny, but with the exception of the one person who has played no part in these negotiations—Fanny herself, who shocks the assembled families by refusing the financially promising match. Overturning the entire framework of melodramatic assumptions that has governed the play to this point, she rejects Alan as not good enough for her, and shocks him by dismissing the significance of their night together: 'Why on earth should I love you? You were just someone to have a bit of fun with. You were an amusement—a lark.'[2] The chain of assumed connections tying sex to love and marriage is suddenly broken here, and respectability is thrown aside in favour of Fanny's self-respect as a working woman. Threatened with expulsion from the family home by her mother, she reveals that she intends to leave home anyway, as she can support herself on her own wages. In *Hindle Wakes*, a play

---

[2] George Rowell (ed.), *Late Victorian Plays 1890–1914* (2nd. edn., Oxford University Press, 1972), 503.

condemned in some quarters as brazenly immoral, the 'problem' is not, after all, the redemption of a betrayed maiden's tarnished honour, but the readiness of her respectable elders to determine a young woman's future for her without regard to her rights—including here her right to erotic holiday enjoyment. In her rejection of a 'Victorian' feminine passivity in favour of a sexual autonomy underwritten by her economic independence, Fanny represents a new generation of women increasingly active as employees and as citizens.

The exercise of sexual autonomy depended upon the acquisition of sexual knowledge, something usually withheld from young women, and indeed from many young men. In this respect the most important sex-book of the age was not an erotic novel but a sex-education manual, *Married Love*, by Dr Marie Carmichael Stopes, the publication of which in March 1918 unleashed the sex-talk of the Twenties and announced the dawn of modern sexuality. Dr Stopes was neither a qualified physician nor a physiologist but an academic botanist and failed playwright; and even more remarkably she was by her own account a virgin at the time she wrote her book: she had her first marriage annulled in 1916 on the grounds that her husband had never managed an erection. She had, however, studied the works of the English sexologist Havelock Ellis (1859–1939), author of *Studies in the Psychology of Sex* (7 vols., 1897–1928), along with *Love's Coming of Age* (1896) by the socialist sex-mystic Edward Carpenter (1844–1929). Her own megalomanic self-confidence inspired her to overrule the ignorant pronouncements of some medical authorities and to insist upon married women's right to full sexual satisfaction, from which husbands, now instructed in the whereabouts of the clitoris and how to avoid premature ejaculation, would also benefit. *Married Love* quickly became a best-seller, running through eighteen editions in the next ten years and being translated into a dozen languages. More than any other work it exploded the 'Victorian' notion that women had no sexual needs of their own. By now married happily to a wealthy aviator and birth-control campaigner, Stopes proceeded to set up Britain's first birth-control clinic in 1921 and to issue further marital advice in *Wise Parenthood* (1918), *Radiant Motherhood* (1920)—both before she had raised any children herself—*Contraception* (1923), *The Human Body* (1926), and *Enduring Passion* (1928). Despite the lamentable quality of her plays and poems, she acquired a significant following among contemporary authors including Shaw, Wells, Bennett, Coward, and Graves. The most ardent of the disciples was the young Naomi Mitchison, herself the fruit of an alliance between medicine and feminism (her father a physiologist, her mother a suffrage campaigner): after two years of marital disappointment, she gave her husband a copy of *Married Love*, with gratifying results, repaying Stopes by helping to run another London birth-control clinic in the time she could spare from her writing and her six successive pregnancies.

The sex-talk of the times was further encouraged by the intellectual impact of psychoanalysis. A few of Sigmund Freud's works had been translated into English before the Great War, and a handful of writers, including D. H. Lawrence, James Joyce, and Ford Madox Hueffer, had become aware of their propositions through second-hand reports, while Virginia Woolf's husband Leonard wrote in 1914 the first non-medical review of Freud in the English press. Lawrence was annoyed to find his novel *Sons and Lovers* (1913), with its strongly 'Oedipal' story of mother–son attachment, subjected to Freudian interpretation as early as 1915. Meanwhile the more committed Freudian May Sinclair had become involved from 1913 in setting up the first psychoanalytic clinic in London, the influence of Freud upon her novels becoming evident in *The Three Sisters* (1914) and several later works. Rebecca West too introduced a Freudian therapist into her novel of amnesia, *The Return of the Soldier* (1918). It was in the immediate post-War years, however, when shell shock, war trauma, and shattered 'nerves' had become prominent public concerns, that psychoanalytic ideas spread rapidly through English intellectual life. Virginia Woolf, whose brother Adrian later trained as an analyst, complained in 1920, in a review headed 'Freudian Fiction', about the treatment of fictional characters as case studies; and in the same year Lytton Strachey's brother James, with his wife Alix, travelled to Vienna to be analysed by Freud himself, returning as his official English translators. The shell-shocked Robert Graves underwent psychoanalytic treatment in 1922–3, while John Cowper Powys's pamphlet *Psychoanalysis and Morality* (1923) enthused about Freud's world-historic shattering of religious sex-taboos. Few authors actually bothered to read Freud's writings, although the precocious W. H. Auden devoured them while still a schoolboy: even Virginia Woolf, despite being the official publisher of Freud's works in English from 1922, could not bring herself to look through them until 1939. D. H. Lawrence, again, felt moved to publish two anti-Freudian tracts about blood-consciousness and the solar plexus (*Psychoanalysis and the Unconscious*, 1921; *Fantasia of the Unconscious*, 1922) without having read a page of Freud's own works. Woolf, Lawrence, Joyce, and several other authors were dismissive of psychoanalysis, but by the early Twenties there was no ignoring the powerful appeal of its ideas.

As commonly understood by untrained writers and readers, Freudian wisdom amounted to three broad propositions. First, and least controversial among novel-readers at least, was the primacy of the sexual motive in human behaviour. Second was the idea that an oppressive upbringing, or a single shock experienced in childhood, would give you a 'complex' in the form of neurotic behaviour or sexual abnormality: in Stella Gibbons's comic novel *Cold Country Farm* (1932), Ada Doom's repeated claim that she once saw 'something nasty in the woodshed' is a running joke about this simplified notion of early trauma. Third, and most attractive to the promiscuous, was the suggestion, also promulgated independently by Stopes in *Married Love*, that the thwarting of sexual desire would make you ill, both mentally and physically. This last proposition was brought to life in May Sinclair's novella *Life and Death of Harriett Frean* (1922), in which the eponymous Harriett is brought up according to the 'Victorian' ethic of self-renunciation, refuses to marry the man she desires because he is engaged to another girl, thereby poisoning her ex-suitor's marriage along with her own life as an 'old maid', and eventually dies of cancer. The suggested carcinogenic power of sexual abstinence reappears in Arnold Bennett's novel *Riceyman Steps* (1923) with the uterine growth suffered by the frustrated Violet Earlforward; and again in Auden's tasteless ballad 'Miss Gee' (1937), in which a spinster's puritanical disapproval of couples kissing in the park seems to cause her fatal tumour.

A widely read narrative more faithful to Freud's concept of repression was W. Somerset Maugham's 'Rain' (1921), his most successful short story. The tale is set during the rainy season upon a small South Sea island where a party of voyagers are temporarily stranded by quarantine regulations. Among them are the energetic missionary and moral-purity crusader Mr Davidson, and the war veteran Doctor Macphail, both accompanied by their wives. No hotel being available, these respectable couples take temporary lodgings above those of another traveller, a Miss Sadie Thompson, who entertains groups of American sailors late at night. Davidson rightly guesses that Sadie has arrived here from the Honolulu brothels he has recently had closed down. He then takes steps to prevent her receiving visitors, and to have her put on the next boat to San Francisco by the island's American governor. The irreligious Macphail has no sympathy with Davidson's persecution of Sadie, and tries without success to have her expulsion commuted, at which point the prostitute seems to undergo a miraculous conversion, and Davidson spends many exhausting hours in prayer with her. On the morning of Sadie's scheduled departure, which should also be Davidson's triumph, the missionary is found with his throat cut, razor in hand. The real course of events and the true nature of the private prayer-sessions are not spelt out, but Maugham relies on the reader to understand that the struggle between Sadie's sexuality and Davidson's faith has been won decisively by Sadie, reducing the puritan to a suicidal wreck and permitting the prostitute to resume her trade. Clues to the story's spectacular twist are planted for us earlier, in the description of Davidson's sensual lips, and again in a report from his wife that he had been dreaming of the mountains of Nebraska, which Macphail happens to recall are shaped like women's breasts. The dream symbolism here is hardly subtle, but it is an important index of Maugham's confidence in his readers' ability to decode 'Freudian' hints and so to grasp the story's unspoken logic of sexual repression.

The literature of the Twenties and Thirties is peppered with allusions, often nervously jocular, to psychoanalytic ideas, as in *Cold Comfort Farm*, where the erotomaniac intellectual Mr Mybug sees sexual symbols everywhere he looks: 'there were few occasions when he was not reminded of a pair of large breasts by the distant hills' (ch. 11). Sometimes we meet more ambitious incorporations of Freudianism, such as a fictional character undergoing analysis (as in Wyndham Lewis's *The Apes of God* (1930) and Christopher Isherwood's *The Memorial* (1932)), or even a psychoanalyst in the role of detective heroine (in Gladys Mitchell's *Speedy Death* (1929)). The

deliberate construction of narratives upon principles of psychoanalytic revelation, of the kind we have seen in Sinclair and Maugham,
however, remains strictly exceptional. In that sense, the fiction and
drama of this period is only superficially impressed by Viennese sexology, by comparison with biography: as we noticed in Chapter 12,
post-Freudian 'psychobiography' emerged as a significant sub-genre
in this period. Perhaps more deeply affected was the genre of autobiography, in which the impact of Freud seems to have licensed a
new self-analytical 'frankness' about authors' sex-lives. A remarkable case here is John Cowper Powys's *Autobiography* (1934),
which exposes with exhibitionistic relish the author's obsessive
practice of ogling young women's ankles on Brighton beach and his
fantasies about boyishly slender nymphs. Powys devotes hundreds
of pages to the dissection of his abnormality, often in the official
jargon—sadism, exhibitionism, narcissism—of Freudian sexology.
Other autobiographers made their own intimate disclosures: T. E.
Lawrence's *Seven Pillars of Wisdom* (1926) recounts his experience
of homosexual rape; H. G. Wells's *Experiment in Autobiography*
(1934) dwells on his tangled extramarital affairs; and Robert Graves
in *Good-bye to All That* (1929) and Cyril Connolly in *Enemies of
Promise* (1938) both reminisce unblushingly about their adolescent
homosexual crushes. All showed in their revelations of hitherto
unspeakable sexual secrets a distinctively modern candour.

Realism, Deviance, and Censorship

The rapid absorption of psychoanalytic ideas into English literary
culture should not be mistaken for an immediate *cause* of the noticeable sexualization of literature after the Great War, but seen rather as
a fresh and reputedly scientific sanction for it. Sexologists and novelists alike had been pushing at the boundaries of acceptable public
discussion since at least the 1880s, fostering linked subcultures of
sexual unorthodoxy and of literary outspokenness. In the theatre
too, resistance had been launched in the 1890s to the Lord Chamberlain's censorship of dramatic works, which had forbidden public
performance of Henrik Ibsen's *Ghosts* (1881) because it represented
syphilitic madness, and later of Bernard Shaw's *Mrs Warren's*

Profession (published 1898) for its treatment of prostitution. Ibsen's exposure of bourgeois family skeletons had inspired bolder handling of unmentionable sexual topics, as in Harley Granville-Barker's *Waste* (1907), banned by the Lord Chamberlain for including an abortion in its plot. In the realm of the novel, less exposed to official censorship, such works as George Moore's *Esther Waters* (1894) and Thomas Hardy's *Jude the Obscure* (1896) had seemed in their treatment of illegitimacy and alcoholism to echo Émile Zola's French school of naturalist fiction with its scientific interest in the hereditary and environmental bases of deviant behaviour. Naturalist fiction shared with late Victorian sexology a common tendency to present sexual outcasts—unmarried mothers and prostitutes, in the first place—not as moral monsters but as unfortunate victims of Nature or social circumstance. The two trends were indeed linked in the person of Havelock Ellis, who before he undertook his multivolume *Studies in the Psychology of Sex* had been a literary essayist championing Ibsen and Zola, a founding editor of the Mermaid series of unexpurgated Elizabethan plays, and the English translator of Zola's novel *Germinal*. English sexology, established by the lesser literati (Edward Carpenter and Marie Stopes too were very minor poets), exerted in return its own influences upon the modern literary mainstream. Individual affiliations such as the debts owed by D. H. Lawrence, E. M. Forster, and Radclyffe Hall to different aspects of Carpenter's work represent only a portion of the larger sexological legacy, which might be characterized as a post-naturalist agenda for fictional research into abnormal psychology and into hidden worlds of sexual shame and ostracism.

These developments may be encapsulated in travestied form by invoking the common assumption at the end of the Victorian age that French novels and plays were about adultery and prostitution while English novels and plays were about snobbery and ambition. The modernity of post-Victorian English literature consists to an important extent in the combined efforts of authors and publishers to attain Continental standards of free expression in sexual matters, and in so doing to fashion a literature fit for worldly adults. The literary period 1910–40 was a crucial phase in the long-running struggle between literature and the censors that culminated in the liberalizations of the 1960s. Some of its legal battles—the suppression of Lawrence's *The Rainbow* (1915) and *Lady Chatterley's Lover* (1928), the prosecution of Radclyffe Hall's *The Well of Loneliness* (1928)—have become legendary instances of literary martyrdom. These incidents have their importance in helping to define the legal boundaries of obscenity, but so too do the contrary instances of relaxation, such as the 'unbannings' of *The Rainbow* (1926, with some minor expurgation) and of James Joyce's *Ulysses* (in 1936), and the eventual granting by the Lord Chamberlain's office of performance licences to *Ghosts* (in 1914) and *Mrs Warren's Profession* (in 1924). Either way, the arbitrary verdicts of magistrates and censors on particular cases give us only an inadequate impression of the general trend. To the moral-purity crusaders of the day, including the notoriously vigilant Sir William Joynson-Hicks (Home Secretary, 1924–9), there could be no doubt as to the nature of that trend: it was a relentless creeping tendency towards increasingly immodest and indulgent representation of immorality and unnatural vice, all the more insidious for skulking just beyond the reach of successful prosecution. Although rabidly alarmist, these people were still perfectly correct both in their assessment of the direction in which things were heading and in their suspicion that something like a coordinated campaign lay behind it.

A naïve observer might suppose that a few brave writers simply recorded their visions of human love in all good faith and innocence, only to find themselves unexpectedly pounced on by grim philistine persecutors. In fact most of the sexually 'frank' authors of the time knew full well what they were about, how to play the intricate game of second-guessing the prosecutors and censors, and where the boundaries of acceptable expression might be nudged forward at a given time. They understood too the commercial value of notoriety and of the novel or play that was slightly more controversially risqué than last year's equivalent. They engaged in protracted discussions with their publishers and with each other about every last excision, asterisk, and euphemistic synonym, and about the economics of expurgated (London) and unexpurgated (Paris) editions. Some were not above a little dishonesty in their dealings with censors: Noël Coward, for example, managed to persuade the Lord Chamberlain's office that the scandalous immorality of the characters in his *The Vortex* (1924) truly amounted to a stern warning against the dangers of drug-taking, and then laughed all the way to the bank as the play's notoriety launched its international success.

The fact that authors had to be canny and worldly-wise in negotiating this risky territory does not mean that the generalized movement towards freer literary expression was merely a cynical exercise. Under legal and economic pressures, compromises and evasions had to be made by almost all authors (James Joyce, with wealthy patrons backing the publication of *Ulysses*, could afford to be uncompromising); but in their sympathetic treatments of essential human experiences, dispelling the obloquy imposed upon a variety of sexual outcasts, their motives were still genuine. Considered as a collective campaign of enlightened liberalization, the tendency of modern literature—especially in the novel—towards fuller and broader engagement with sexuality and with the social controversies surrounding it is clearly a continuation of the great inclusive project of realism, which in principle welcomes into literary representation every aspect of life, however indecorous or unpleasant. In this light we may here review the range of sexual topics that authors of this period introduced or reintroduced into modern literature.

The principal 'problem' of sexuality widely addressed by modern authors is that of adultery. This being an age-old literary topic, there was no taboo against introducing it, but authors still had to be careful to avoid the appearance of condoning it, especially if it involved married women taking lovers much younger than themselves, as in *The Vortex*, or socially beneath them, as in *Lady Chatterley's Lover*. The Victorian punitive convention whereby adulterers and especially adulteresses must be seen to repent or to come to a bad end still held sway, even over writers who in their own lives were advocates of 'free love'. H. G. Wells, wounded by the controversy over the sexual frankness of his *Ann Veronica* (1909), was careful to bring the fictional adulteries of *The New Machiavelli* (1911) and *The Passionate Friends* (1913) to tragic conclusions, with an errant husband's career ruined in the first and an adulterous wife committing suicide in the second. Ford Madox Hueffer arranges not one but two grisly suicides as the culmination of a doubly adulterous entanglement in *The Good Soldier* (1915). The title character in Daphne du Maurier's *Rebecca* (1938) is murdered with impunity for flaunting her wantonness, while the romantic heroes of Margaret Kennedy's

The Constant Nymph (1924) and of Winifred Holtby's *South Riding* (1936) find that death intervenes to prevent the consummation of their intended adulteries. These were dangerous liaisons indeed, the wages of sin being death or gnawing remorse. The secret lovers in Coward's one-act play *Still Life* (1936; later filmed in bowdlerized form as *Brief Encounter*, 1945) agree nobly to end their affair rather than suffer the guilt of betrayal, while in *The Vortex* the ageing Florence suffers torments of self-loathing over her flings with men young enough to be her sons. Where adulterous characters were not represented as pitifully self-destructive, they were mocked satirically as hypocritical or morally vacuous, as in Maugham's play *Our Betters* (1923), in Richard Aldington's novel *Death of a Hero* (1929), in Vita Sackville-West's novel *The Edwardians* (1930), and repeatedly in the fiction of Aldous Huxley and Evelyn Waugh.

Samuel Hynes has remarked how often in the literature of the Twenties sexual liberation is strangely allied with a mood of depression and ennui.[3] Indeed, it is not only adulteresses who come to rue their sins; even dissolute young widows like Iris Storm in Michael Arlen's *The Green Hat* (1924) and Lucy Tantamount in Huxley's *Point Counter Point* (1928) seem to derive no real enjoyment from their comparatively guiltless promiscuity. It might even have struck readers at the time as a mystery why anyone should come to engage in extramarital sex at all, if it led so inexorably to despair and self-murder. The literature of adultery in this period gives an impression of its authors being more censoriously 'Victorian' than they really were; in most of these cases the apparently punitive plots represent concessions to public morality. Some authors had it both ways: as we saw in Chapter 5, Maugham's play *The Circle* (1921) exhibits the awful fate awaiting a wife who elopes with a lover, in the shape of social ostracism and lifelong recrimination, yet it ends by inviting the audience to cheer just such an elopement after all. To the convention of miserable infidelity there were two major exceptions that proved the rule, these being—not coincidentally—the most scandalous banned books of the period, *Ulysses* (1922) and *Lady Chatterley's Lover*, both of which offer positive portraits of adultresses

---

[3] Samuel Hynes, *A War Imagined: The First World War and English Culture* (Bodley Head, 1990), 365, 378.

who are not only happy but joyously gratified. A further weakening of the wages-of-sin rule is found in Rosamond Lehmann's novel *The Weather in the Streets* (1936), which convincingly portrays an adulterous affair from the perspective of the 'Other Woman': her married lover is involved in a car crash towards the end of the story, but unusually he is allowed to survive it, and even to hint finally at a rekindling of their illicit relations.

Noël Coward's play *This Was a Man* (published 1926) was banned by the Lord Chamberlain not because it featured a serially unfaithful wife but because her husband, upon hearing that she has seduced his best friend, bursts into laughter. To take adultery lightly as a matter of amusement or bored indifference was in the eyes of morality's guardians as reprehensible as the sin itself. Maugham, on the other hand, claimed in 1931 that the solemn melodramatic treatment of marital infidelity was no longer credible to theatre audiences, because 'we do not believe in jealousy any more. We no longer look upon a woman's chastity as her essential virtue. I submit to the dramatists of today that the unfaithfulness of a wife is no longer a subject for drama, but only for comedy.'[4] Maugham suffered some disapproval for saying this, but the shift in public attitudes to which he appeals here had already been confirmed by the success of his own comic plays since 1919, of Coward's since 1925, and of Ben Travers's farces at the Aldwych Theatre. Underlying these changes were important social trends, notably the steeply rising rate of divorce, which ran in the early Thirties at seven times its pre-War level, with a consequent diminution of the disrepute attached to marital breakdown. The increasing visibility and acceptance of the divorced brought along with it widespread awareness of the law's absurdity in this area. Until 1937, divorce could be obtained only on grounds of corroborated adultery, which meant that many separated husbands felt obliged to hire a prostitute to spend the night at a hotel where their presence in the same bed could by pre-arrangement be witnessed by a chambermaid or private detective. This humiliating little ritual was itself a kind of dramatic performance, only awaiting a playwright to turn it literally into farce, which Maugham did in

---

[4] W. Somerset Maugham, *Collected Plays*, vol. 2 (Heinemann, 1952), pp. xix–xx.

Home and Beauty (1919) and Travers did in *A Cuckoo in the Nest* (1925), before Evelyn Waugh used the same comical situation in his novel *A Handful of Dust* (1934). It was the minor novelist A. P. Herbert, serving as an Independent MP, who eventually introduced reforms to the law allowing divorce on grounds of desertion, cruelty, or insanity.

Still within the realm of illicit heterosexual contact, we find more frequent, open, and sympathetic treatments in this period's literature of such problems as bigamy, for example in Arnold Bennett's novel *Hilda Lessways* (1911); brother–sister incest, in Maugham's tragic tale 'The Book-Bag' (1932); and the plight of unmarried mothers, as in E. M. Forster's *Howards End* (1910) and in Rebecca West's novel *The Judge* (1922). Sexual harrassment, molestation, and rape, formerly veiled by euphemism, could now be presented with unsettling directness, notably in Katherine Mansfield's stories 'The Swing of the Pendulum' (1911) and 'The Little Governess' (1915), and again in A. E. Coppard's 'The Tiger' (1923) and in Huxley's *Eyeless in Gaza* (1936). Prostitution too emerges from the scarlet trappings of 'fallen' harlotry to be presented more often now as a commonplace fact of life, although from two different perspectives. In masculine coming-of-age narratives, the protagonist's first nervous encounter with prostitutes becomes a standard rite of passage, as in Compton Mackenzie's *Sinister Street* (1913–14), Maugham's *Of Human Bondage* (1915), Joyce's *A Portrait of the Artist as a Young Man* (1916), and Maugham's tale 'The Facts of Life' (1939). Meanwhile from the other side, the prostitute's own view of her condition is presented in, among other works, Bennett's novel *The Pretty Lady* (1918) and, as we have seen, Maugham's 'Rain'. More fully examined is the life of the *demi-mondaine*, usually an unemployed chorus girl informally trading sex for financial support: a familiar type in French fiction, she is now domesticated in Mansfield's 'Pictures' (1919) and Christopher Isherwood's *Goodbye to Berlin* (1939), and is granted the first-person voice in Jean Rhys's *Voyage in the Dark* (1934).

In the depiction of regular and irregular sexualities alike, modern writers were becoming noticeably more explicit about the physiological facts of life. Venereal disease, for example, had been a dreadful secret, discussed by doctors and social reformers but kept from the ears of respectable young women like Vera Brittain, but when she and others served as wartime nursing assistants, the alarming incidence of these infections among soldiers could no longer be hushed up. Indeed the Great War blew away the official censorship of literary representation in this area: as Nicholas de Jongh reveals in his book on stage censorship, *Politics, Prudery and Perversions* (2001), the censors granted a licence in 1917 to a play about syphilis, Eugene Brieux's *Damaged Goods*, after consultation with the Archbishop of Canterbury and King George himself, on the grounds that it might help to warn servicemen of the dangers. After the War, Michael Arlen's novel *The Green Hat* created a fashionable sensation by employing as the final revelation of its plot a case of syphilitic infection in a respected English family. The more commonplace facts of female physiology also found their way into 'advanced' post-War fiction: characters in Joyce's *Ulysses* and Huxley's *Eyeless in Gaza* are permitted to mention the onset of their menstrual periods, while increasingly realistic accounts of childbirth appear in Mansfield's story 'A Birthday' (1911), in Holtby's *South Riding*, and most extensively—along with the experiences of late pregnancy and of breast-feeding—in Enid Bagnold's novel *The Squire* (1938). Contraception too emerges as an acceptable matter for fictional treatment in, for example, *Cold Comfort Farm* and Orwell's *Keep the Aspidistra Flying* (1936), as does miscarriage, for instance in Rebecca West's novel *The Thinking Reed* (1936). The most 'advanced' writers of the post-War period, beginning with T. S. Eliot in his influential 'The Waste Land' (1922), risked broaching the controversial topic of abortion. Naomi Mitchison's brief description of an aborted pregnancy in *Cloud Cuckoo Land* (1925) is softened by the historical remoteness of its ancient Greek setting, but in the 1930s several writers address abortion as a fact of contemporary life, as Huxley does in *Eyeless in Gaza* and as Elizabeth Bowen does in her story 'Firelight in the Flat' (1934); Jean Rhys in *Voyage in the Dark* and Rosamond Lehmann in *The Weather in the Streets* go further by using their heroines' illegal abortions as the climactic episodes of these novels.

Another range of taboos challenged by writers in this period surrounded the representation of lesbianism, male homosexuality, and bisexuality. Formerly invisible and lacking even the recognition granted by formal illegality, lesbianism suddenly assumed the status of the 'period' vice most often exploited by novelists in the War years and the Twenties. The literary discovery of lesbianism was by no means, though, a liberatory celebration of sapphic love. On the contrary it tended to use lesbian characters as targets against which could be vented public (and some authors' private) anxieties about the general insurgence of women into masculine spheres of economic and professional power. The twelfth chapter—significantly entitled 'Shame'—of D. H. Lawrence's *The Rainbow* describes a passionate and physical attachment between the teenage Ursula Brangwen and her schoolmistress Winifred Inger, which helped bring about the novel's suppression; but the narrative voice treats Winifred scornfully and presents the episode as a sterile sidetrack from Ursula's emotional development. At fuller length, Clemence Dane's novel *Regiment of Women* (1917) devotes itself to exposing the dangers of single-sex girls' schools by portraying a senior schoolmistress, Clare Hartill, as a power-hungry vampiric lesbian preying upon the adoration of pupils and junior colleagues: the heroine is temporarily infatuated with her but is saved by the love of a good man who reclaims her for heterosexual normality. Predatory, monstrous, or grotesque lesbian types appear frequently after this, in Lawrence's 'The Fox' (1923), in the character of Doris Kilman in Woolf's *Mrs Dalloway* (1925), in Dorothy L. Sayers's *Unnatural Death* (1927), in Wyndham Lewis's *The Apes of God*, and in Graham Greene's *Stamboul Train* (1932), while the light satire of Compton Mackenzie's *Extraordinary Women* (1928) presents a group of wealthy lesbians constantly embroiled in petty jealousies.

Where sympathetic treatments of lesbian desire are to be found, they tend to be qualified by reticence or fatalistic dejection. In Rosamond Lehmann's *Dusty Answer* (1927) the shy Judith Earle experiences intense adoration for a more confident fellow student, Jennifer, but this episode in her unfulfilled love life is presented as a chaste infatuation. A fleeting impulse of same-sex desire also agitates a young married woman, Bertha Young, in Katherine Mansfield's enigmatic tale 'Bliss' (1918), although she is abruptly disenchanted by the discovery of her husband making a secret assignation with the very girl she adores. In these cases, lesbian attachment appears as one element within a bisexual range of possibilities that was in the new Freudian age increasingly accepted as the basis of all sexuality. 'We are all, in some degree or another, bi-sexual in our divided impulses', declared the Freudian convert John Cowper Powys in 1923.[5] Just as this fluidity of genders and attractions was becoming absorbed into literature, the exclusively sapphic writer Radclyffe Hall launched her fifth novel, *The Well of Loneliness* (1928), which on the contrary treats lesbianism as an immutable tragic destiny imposed on a few individuals by a freak of Nature. Drawing upon the determinist late Victorian sexology of Ellis and Carpenter, Hall presents the lesbian 'invert' as a biological oddity, a man in a woman's body, fated to love 'real' women who by Nature cannot return her feelings. In this respect as in others, her novel is a throwback to static sexual identities.

The Well of Loneliness became the most famous lesbian book of the twentieth century, banned in Britain following an obscenity trial, and thereafter an underground cult-novel smuggled in from Paris and passed from hand to trembling hand. For years to come, young women coming to terms with their own lesbian inclinations turned to it, often suffering disappointment both from its lack of physical eroticism and from its fatalistic doctrine of inevitable sapphic misery. The very fact of the book's existence must have provided sustaining encouragement to some, but the story itself is a melodramatic tear-jerker of the dullest kind: the young invert Stephen Gordon (so named by a father hoping for a son) grows up encouraged by her wealthy father in the adoption of boyish sports, but rejected by her mother as unnatural; she struggles to become a successful writer, and meanwhile pursues love affairs, first with a married woman who toys with but discards her, then with a younger woman, Mary, who accepts her passionate approaches ('and that night they were not divided' (ch. 38)). However, fearful that Mary will suffer the ostracism meted out to inverts, Stephen selflessly steers her into the arms of a man by pretending to have cooled towards her. The book closes with Stephen in prayer, imploring God's recognition for her kind, and it is coloured throughout by Hall's part-Catholic, part-Spiritualist religiosity, and by her conviction, derived from Carpenter, that 'inverts' constitute a spiritual elite capable of nobler self-sacrifice. Of all the notable novels of the Twenties, this is the most

---

[5] John Cowper Powys, *Psychoanalysis and Morality* (Village Press, 1975), 39.

'Victorian' in outlook. Overshadowed by the notoriety of *The Well of Loneliness*, Sylvia Townsend Warner's portrayal of a love affair between women in *Summer Will Show* (1936) is more confidently modern, although the story is set in the nineteenth century.

Male homosexuality is acknowledged widely but incidentally in English writings of this period, hardly ever emerging as a central theme as it had begun to emerge in France with the works of Marcel Proust and André Gide. Censorship was vigilant on this point, and self-censorship by authors anxious to avoid Oscar Wilde's fate was tighter still. Most homosexual authors, like Lytton Strachey and W. Somerset Maugham, avoided the subject in their public works, although some were eloquent in private. E. M. Forster's novel of same-sex desire, *Maurice*, inspired by a pat on the buttocks from Edward Carpenter himself, circulated clandestinely among his trusted friends from 1914, but was held back for posthumous publication (1971) in more tolerant times. James Hanley's story of the sexual abuse of a cabin boy by older sailors in *Boy* (1931) was at first privately printed for subscribers only, and then legally suppressed when a cheap public edition was attempted in 1934. On the other hand, J. R. Ackerley's homoerotic melodrama *Prisoners of War* (1925) slipped past the censors because it appeared to be about intense comradeship among soldiers. The depiction of love between men was to a degree permissible within military contexts, so that some of Wilfred Owen's and Siegfried Sassoon's poems about beautiful soldier-lads, like those of A. E. Housman before them, could be accepted as innocent. Similarly, an intense platonic friendship between schoolboys, as in E. F. Benson's novel *David Blaize* (1916), could be taken as harmless sentiment. Certain forms of light entertainment too were allowed to present mincing Nancies as stock comic types in non-sexual contexts, as with the group of Wildean aesthetes who sing of green carnations in Noël Coward's operetta *Bitter-Sweet* (1929). Otherwise, homosexual attachments are for the most part invoked by oblique suggestion and sly innuendo of the kind that flickers teasingly through the works of Auden, Coward, Firbank, Forster, and a few other writers. It is not until the end of this period that we find, in Christopher Isherwood's *Goodbye to Berlin*, a literary treatment of homosexual life tentatively acknowledged as a portrait from the inside. The book is set in the years before Hitler's accession to power, in the city that had lately taken over from Paris as the world capital of sinfulness. In its second 'Berlin Diary' fragment, the narrator (who shares the author's name) emerges from a visit to the Salomé, a transvestites' night club, to be confronted by a group of American tourists who are pruriently aghast at the notion of 'queer' men dressing as women.

'You *queer*, too, hey?' demanded the little American, turning suddenly on me.

'Yes,' I said, 'very queer indeed.'

Despite this carefully staged disclosure, the Christopher Isherwood character remains chastely detached from the action as an observer chronicling the sexual behaviour of others. In the 'On Ruegen Island' episode he describes the relationship, which is clearly physical as well as financial, between Peter, a repressed young Englishman of the upper middle class and Otto, a working-class German boy of 16 at a holiday resort as the liaison declines from joyous relaxation to humiliating jealousy. The modern note of this tale lies in its nonchalantly taking for granted the sexual basis of such relationships: homosexuality never presents itself as a 'problem', nor as a scandal, only as an assumed background for the study of individual character.

Isherwood's Berlin writings belong to a small category of works in this period that explore the polymorphous perversity of human sexuality as far as its exotic fringes: his earlier novel *Mr Norris Changes Trains* (1935) peeps on the central character as he writhes under the lash of a dominatrix, while Aldous Huxley's *Eyeless in Gaza* more fleetingly samples the sexual underworld of Berlin with its lesbian bars, its pornography, and its rubber-breasted boy-prostitutes. John Cowper Powys's *A Glastonbury Romance* (1932) offers a gallery of characters variously inflamed by homosexual and sado-masochistic fantasies, and studies of pathological nymphomania appear both in May Sinclair's *The Allinghams* (1927) and in Robert Graves's *Claudius the God* (1934). The most extensive feast of sexual kinks, however, is laid on by James Joyce's *Ulysses* in its portrait of the cuckold Leopold Bloom. For many years debarred by his wife Molly from conjugal fulfilment, Bloom's libido seeks indirect and thus largely fetishistic outlets: he and Molly share a taste for

Fig. 9. W. H. Auden, Christopher Isherwood, and Stephen Spender, photographed together in 1937 by Howard Coster.

pornographic novels of a mildly sadistic flavour, and above their bed hangs a pseudo-classical nude clipped from *Photo Bits* magazine. As he walks around Dublin, he keeps one eye out for exposed female stockings, conducts a furtively titillating correspondence with a woman he has never met, inspects the buttocks of Aphrodite's statue in the museum, and masturbates while a young virgin willingly exposes her legs and knickers. The climactic fifteenth ('Circe') chapter is set in and around a brothel where no directly sexual activity is witnessed, but this is made up for by the extended fantasy sequences in which Bloom's secret desires are acted out in vignettes of voyeurism, shoe fetishism, underwear fetishism, coprophilia, transvestism, and masochism, involving the temporary transformation of Bloom into a woman. None of this detracts from Bloom's representative role as the average man in the street; on the contrary, it confirms this status, as it indirectly corroborates the new Freudian view that abnormality is the norm. Elsewhere the same point is to be heard from Amanda in Coward's play *Private Lives* (1930); 'I think very few people are completely normal, deep down in their private lives' (*Collected Plays: Two*, p. 16).

Erotic Writing

The modern legend of Victorian sexual repression followed by twentieth-century emancipation runs up against two embarrassing literary deficiencies in the period 1910–40. In the first place, the production of pornographic novels of the kind collected by Victorian gentlemen-connoisseurs had declined steeply in the Edwardian decade. After *The Way of a Man with a Maid* (*c*.1910), scarcely any notable new one-handed novels were to follow, *Two Flappers in Paris* (by 'A. Cantab', *c*.1920) representing the last gasp of a once vigorous clandestine literature now wilting under stiff competition from the French dirty-postcard industry. The second, more visible decline is in the writing of erotic verse, at least in the narrower sense. While the Victorian age boasts a number of sex-poems by Robert Browning, A. H. Clough, and A. C. Swinburne, post-Edwardian literature yields little to match them apart from a few of D. H. Lawrence's verses in *Look! We Have Come Through!* (1917). There are indeed poems that philosophize upon sex among such later works of W. B. Yeats as 'Crazy Jane Talks with the Bishop' (1933), poems that argue about it in Lawrence's *Pansies* volume, and others that dwell upon the absurdities of lust, like Robert Graves's 'The Succubus' and his apostrophe to an erection, 'Down, Wanton, Down!' (both 1933). Sardonic disgust, as displayed in T. S. Eliot's account of the typist's seduction in 'The Waste Land', had become the fashionable stance, further discouraging any celebration of sexual pleasures in modern verse. Indeed, Eros is less audible in this phase of English poetry than at any time before.

Culture, however, abhors a vacuum. Erotic narratives of a new kind had emerged in the genre of popular romances written for, and mainly by, women, the pioneer being Elinor Glyn with her sex-scene on a tiger-skin rug in *Three Weeks* (1907). Far less anatomically brutal or repetitive than pornographic fiction proper, these romances linger more patiently over their exotic settings and over their teasingly euphemistic unfolding of masochistic fantasy. E. M. Hull's *The Sheik* (1919) was the most famous of them and the most often imitated—its later rivals including Joan Conquest's *Zarah the Cruel* and Kathlyn Rhodes's *Desert Justice* (both 1923). The story Hull recounts is that of Diana Mayo, a sturdy young Englishwoman raised as an obstinate tomboy interested neither in love (she has never let any man kiss her) nor in the slavery of marriage. Physically strong and an experienced traveller, she sets off unchaperoned to explore the Algerian Sahara, but is almost immediately plucked from her saddle and abducted by the cruelly scowling Sheik Ahmed, who rapes her repeatedly in his luxuriously cushioned tent. The experience quickly transforms her:

For the first time she had met a man who had failed to bow to her wishes [. . .] and she was learning obedience. Obedient now, she forced herself to lift her eyes to his, and the shamed blood surged slowly into her cheeks. His dark, passionate eyes burnt into her like a hot flame. His encircling arms were like bands of fire, scorching her. His touch was torture. Helpless, like a trapped wild thing, she lay against him, panting, trembling, her wide eyes fixed on him, held against their will. Fascinated, she could not turn them away, and the image of the brown, handsome face with its flashing eye, straight, cruel mouth and strong chin seemed searing into her brain. (ch. 3)

When not scorching or scowling, Sheik Ahmed is a famous tamer of unruly horses, and he breaks Diana in likewise after several weeks, until it dawns upon her that she loves him: 'He was a brute, but she loved him, loved him for his very brutality and superb animal strength' (ch. 5). On his non-brutal side too, Ahmed is eligible: wealthy, well read, and unmarried, he boasts an endless supply of cigarettes and an implausibly well-equipped bathroom. He too is surprised by his own feelings for a woman he seized only as a plaything; before long he loves her so much that he plans to restore her to her own people, but she begs to stay, and so the pair end up betrothed.

Although *The Sheik* is clearly a narrative of sexual 'awakening', remotely descended from the fairy tale of the Sleeping Beauty, it relies for its excitement upon sadomasochistic preliminaries while keeping coition itself offstage. Women's romances always observed this rule, and so did almost all other narratives. In real sexual life, a line was recognized between—in the new terms of this period—*petting* (1920) or *foreplay* (1929) and what a character in a D. H. Lawrence story calls going 'the whole hogger' ('The Shadow in the Rose Garden', 1914); so in literature, full sexual intercourse had its assigned place, which was in the gap between two paragraphs, the first of them devoted to passionate kisses, the second commonly beginning 'Afterwards, . . .'. The uniqueness of Lawrence's fiction in this respect lay in its gradual encroachment into that gap. For Lawrence, the challenge was to treat the experiences of petting, coupling, climax, and post-coital reverie with the sacramental reverence he believed they deserved, avoiding the anatomical bluntness and coarse ribaldry of pornographic prose. Before considering his own solutions, we may return briefly to Marie Stopes's *Married Love* and its unusually rhapsodic description of orgasm:

When two who are mated in every respect burn with the fire of the innumerable forces within them, which set their bodies longing towards each other with the desire to interpenetrate and to encompass one another, the fusion of joy and rapture is not purely physical. The half-swooning sense of flux which overtakes the spirit in that eternal moment at the apex of rapture sweeps into its flaming tides the whole essence of the man and woman, and as it were, the heat of the contact vaporises their consciousness so that it fills the whole of cosmic space. For the moment they are identified with the divine thoughts, the waves of eternal force, which to the Mystic often appear in terms of golden light.[6]

Stopes manages here to combine elements of scientific vocabulary (forces, tides, vaporization) with strong metaphysical overtones of eternity and divinity, in a style that owes its 'cosmic' afflatus to the sex-mysticism of Walt Whitman and Edward Carpenter, both of whom were also well known to Lawrence.

In Lawrence's own fiction, sexual consummation commonly occurs between paragraphs, as in the early tale 'Love Among the Haystacks' (posthumously published 1930), and again in the cases of Paul Morel's first couplings with Miriam and with Clara in *Sons and Lovers*, although that novel does permit a mystical recollection of mutual orgasm with Clara in chapter 13. ('It was as if he, and the stars, and the dark herbage, and Clara were licked up in an immense tongue of flame, which tore onwards and upwards.') In the fifteenth chapter of *The Rainbow*, Lawrence describes with greater daring how Ursula and Anton 'take' each other: on one occasion Anton 'came to her, and cleaved to her very close, like steel cleaving and clinching on to her'; on another, Ursula 'vibrated like a jet of electric, firm fluid in response'. Lawrence's coital diction typically wavers between the biblical (cleaving, coming to, loins, womb) and the electromagnetic. By the time of Ursula's climactic encounter with Birkin in the 'Excurse' chapter of *Women in Love*, these two semantic fields have merged in rapturous iteration, almost entirely obscuring the nature of the erotic contact involved:

She had found one of the sons of God from the Beginning, and he had found one of the first most luminous daughters of men.

She traced with her hands the line of his loins and thighs, at the back, and a living fire ran through her, from him, darkly. It was a dark flood of electric passion she released from him, drew into herself. She had established a rich new circuit, a new current of passional electric energy, between the two of them, released from the darkest poles of the body and established in perfect circuit. It was a dark fire of electricity that rushed from him to her, and flooded them both with rich peace, satisfaction. [. . .]

He stood there in his strange, whole body, that had its marvellous

[6] Marie Carmichael Stopes, *Married Love: A New Contribution to the Solution of Sex Difficulties* (18th edn., Putnam, 1926), 102–3.

fountains, like the bodies of the sons of God who were in the beginning. There were strange fountains of his body, more mysterious and potent than any she had imagined or known, more satisfying, ah, finally, mystically-physically satisfying. She had thought there was no source deeper than the phallic source. And now, behold, from the smitten rock of the man's body, from the strange marvellous flanks and thighs, deeper, further in mystery than the phallic source, came the floods of ineffable darkness and ineffable riches.

Anatomically inquisitive readers minded to reconstruct Ursula's dexterities would be wasting their time with such an episode, because Lawrence's characters are not engaged here in sex as we know it, but in a baptismal rite, while the narrative voice is engaged not in description of actions but in intonation of magic formulas. The smitten-rock allusion (to Exodus 17: 6), the fountains, and the floods all evoke Lawrence's constant mythic obsessions with the world-cleansing Flood and with the sacrament of baptism. Some of Lawrence's narratives of sexual awakening, notably 'The Horse Dealer's Daughter' (1922) and 'The Virgin and the Gipsy' (1930), are indeed better understood as parables of baptismal renewal, and the same applies to most of the 'passional' scenes in his longer works.

Although they often take off their clothes, the embracing lovers in Lawrence's fiction never appear naked as real human beings entangled in sweaty copulation. Rather, they are luminous saints wrestling with angels, always wrapped in scripture or in portentous electrical prophecy. The language that wreathes them is remarkable for its rhythmic repetitiveness. Lawrence himself, in a discarded foreword to *Women in Love*, defended this style on the grounds that 'every natural crisis in emotion or passion or understanding comes from this pulsing, frictional to-and-fro, which works up to culmination'.[7] In his scenes of erotic baptism, it is the words and phrases themselves that perform all the heaving convulsions while the characters lie back and think of deluges, as in this passage from the twelfth chapter of *Lady Chatterley's Lover*:

And it seemed she was like the sea, nothing but dark waves rising and heaving, heaving with a great swell, so that slowly her whole darkness was

---

[7] D. H. Lawrence, *Women in Love*, ed. David Farmer, Lindeth Vasey, and John Worthen (Penguin, 1995), 486.

in motion, and she was ocean rolling its dark, dumb mass. Oh, and far down inside her the deeps parted and rolled asunder, in long, far-travelling billows, and ever, at the quick of her, the depths parted and rolled asunder, from the centre of soft plunging, as the plunger went deeper and deeper, touching lower, and she was deeper and deeper and deeper disclosed, the heavier the billows of her rolled away to some shore, uncovering her, and closer and closer plunged the palpable unknown, and further and further rolled the waves of herself away from herself, leaving her, till suddenly, in a soft, shuddering convulsion, the quick of all her plasm was touched, she knew herself touched, the consummation was upon her, and she was gone. She was gone, she was not, and she was born: a woman.

The feats of mimetic repetition here, like the use of Marie Stopes's favoured tidal imagery, are clearly justified by their orgasmic occasion; but another characteristic feature of this style that is more likely to rub the twenty-first-century reader up the wrong way is its priestly solemnity. Lawrence's fictional lovers do laugh sometimes, but not at their sacred rite. The nonchalance of Houghton's Fanny Hawthorn, who, as we saw earlier in this chapter, belittles her night with a boyfriend as a lark and a bit of fun, would in Lawrence's world be counted as high sacrilege.

Even in *Lady Chatterley's Lover*, where Lawrence grants himself the full range of 'four-letter' words and of bodily realism (wilting erections, pubic hair), the narrative rarely goes the whole hogger in identifying specific forms of genital contact. Significantly, one such moment arrives in Mellors's complaints about his estranged wife's demands for clitoral friction. Mellors, and with him Lawrence, recalls with disgust that women 'have beaks between their legs, and they tear at you with it till you're sick' (ch. 14). As John Middleton Murry suggested as long ago as 1931 in *Son of Woman*, and as feminist criticism has pointed out since the 1970s, the legend of Lawrence the benign sexual liberator masks the true complexities of this tormented and often misogynistic author. Some profound revulsion from the clitoris seems to have driven Lawrence's imagination repeatedly into compensatory fantasies of implacable phallic mastery and final feminine submission. The dialogue poem 'She Said as Well to Me' (1917), in which he rebukes his wife for admiring his body instead of fearing its menace, offers an early sign of a pathology that recurs in his fictions of the 1920s about independent women brought to heel by majestic male authority, as in the cruel tale 'The Border Line' (1924) and in the ceremonial sacrifice of white woman-hood acted out in 'The Woman Who Rode Away' (1925). Lawrence's writings are far from being simple outpourings of misogynist dread, though; nor are they straight projections of 'male fantasy', as they almost always invite us, perhaps all the more insidiously, to occupy the feminine position in the drama. As a sexual fantasist and erotic romancer, Lawrence proceeds by cross-dressing impersonation, taking the woman's part in strenuous games of resistance and sur-render. These lead him into unnerving proximity to the masochistic swoonings of *The Sheik* and thus to the popular commercialization of sex against which he raged. But from that, as from Sheik Ahmed's tent, it was too late to escape.

Retrospect: Three Decades of Modern Realism

In the interval between Robert Graves's *Good-bye to All That* (1929) and Christopher Isherwood's *Goodbye to Berlin* (1939) we hear with increasing frequency the valedictory note of reminiscence, mourning over lost innocence, regret, departure for foreign lands, and even contrition. W. B. Yeats in his last years felt the urge to look back over his poetic achievement and his lost friends in 'The Municipal Gallery Revisited' (1937), 'Are You Content' (1938), and 'The Circus Animals' Desertion' (1939), and to draft his own epitaph in 'Under Ben Bulben' (1939). His death in January 1939 was commemorated in W. H. Auden's great elegy 'In Memory of W. B. Yeats' (1939). Auden had written a typically sinister poem of good-byes, 'It's farewell to the drawing-room's civilised cry' (1937; later titled 'Danse Macabre'), and had recently, with Isherwood, taken his leave of England: it was from exile in New York that Auden summed up the end of an era in his sombre 'September 1, 1939'. Among the prose writers, W. Somerset Maugham had conducted a review of his career and literary opinions in *The Summing Up* (1938), and the middlebrow romancers Daphne du Maurier and James Hilton had created memorable myths of irrecoverable paradises, Manderley in *Rebecca* (1938) and Shangri-La in *Lost Horizon* (1932). Hilton, like Auden and Isherwood, emigrated to the United States in 1939, as Aldous Huxley had in 1937.

Emigration and death were breaking up the inter-war literary scene. Some of the elders of late Victorian and Edwardian letters had inevitably passed away: Henry James in 1916; Joseph Conrad in 1926; Thomas Hardy and Edmund Gosse in 1928; Arnold Bennett in 1931; John Galsworthy in 1933; Rudyard Kipling, G. K. Chesterton, and A. E. Housman in 1936. More damagingly for the newer modern schools, several relatively junior writers had died prematurely in addition to the literary victims of the Great War. Katherine Mansfield (1923), Ronald Firbank (1926), and D. H. Lawrence (1930) had succumbed to tuberculosis, all of them dying abroad. Other fevers and ailments had struck down Lytton Strachey (1932), Stella Benson (1933), and Winifred Holtby (1935) while still in their prime, and T. E. Lawrence (1935) had been killed in a motorcycle crash. In 1939, the year of Yeats's death and of Sigmund Freud's, Ford Madox Ford also died. Virginia Woolf and James Joyce would follow only two years later. The modern movement in literature was dying out, and on an international scale, too, the obituarists having seen off Guillaume Apollinaire (1918), Frank Wedekind (1918), Marcel Proust (1922), Franz Kafka (1924), Anatole France (1924), Rainer Maria Rilke (1926), Vladimir Mayakovsky (1930), Arthur Schnitzler (1931), Hart Crane (1932), Luigi Pirandello (1936), Federico García Lorca (1936), Edith Wharton (1937), and Osip Mandelstam (1938).

Mortality aside, the goose-step of world events was clearly accelerating towards another international war, especially after 1938, when Hitler extended his power into Austria and the Czech Sudetenland while Franco defeated the Spanish Republic at the Ebro and prepared to take Madrid. Writers in England became aware then, if not earlier, that a distinct phase of modern history was drawing to a close, and in the years 1938–1940 they looked back at the literary movements of previous decades from a new perspective, now aware that they stood at the end of something. Robert Graves and Alan Hodge, commissioned in 1939 by Faber & Faber to write a social history of the period between the wars, decided to call it *The Long Weekend* (1940), with the suggestion that those twenty-one years amounted to a delusory respite from history's normal business, now resumed. If the years 1910–40, or 1900–40, or 1918–40, make sense to us now as a literary-historical 'period', that is in part because a succession of authors writing between 1938 and 1940 convinced themselves that they were living through an epoch or end-time at which it was fitting to draw up the balance sheet of modern literature. Graves and Hodge in their lively book attempted with the help of newspaper archives to dig up as many of the period's passing fads and crazes as they could, with little thought for the shape of literary history, although they do provide a chapter on Literature, Art, and Religion. The more substantial retrospective works of these years are Cyril Connolly's *Enemies of Promise* (1938), Virginia Woolf's 'The Leaning Tower' (1940), and George Orwell's 'Inside the Whale' (1940).

Connolly's book falls into three distinct parts, the third being a memoir of his boyhood while the second is a warning against the dangers and temptations lying in wait for an ambitious young author. The first part, which concerns us here, is a broad review of major competing tendencies in modern literature since 1900. Its principal argument is that 'the Modern Movement' has within it two contending camps which have alternately dominated its writings, the Mandarins and the anti-Mandarins. The Mandarins are descendants of late Victorian Aestheticism, perfectionists cultivating a subtle, flamboyant, esoteric art for the benefit of an exclusive leisured readership; their antagonists, variously called puritans, realists, or vernacularists, emerge from the new journalistic culture of the same period, and attempt to address a larger readership with a plain-speaking directness. The modern movement indeed began around 1900 with a reaction of puritan realists against the 'decadent' refinement represented by Pater, Wilde, and Henry James. The Mandarin group includes Yeats, Eliot, Huxley, Strachey, Firbank, the Sitwells, Woolf, Bowen, and (in France) Proust; among the vernacularists are numbered Shaw, Kipling, Wells, Bennett, Galsworthy, Maugham, Forster, Wyndham Lewis, Mansfield, D. H. Lawrence, Coward, Evelyn Waugh, Graves, Isherwood, Orwell, and (in America) Hemingway; a few writers, notably Joyce and Auden, have feet in both camps. Connolly distinguishes between these tendencies chiefly on the basis of style, especially prose style, although typical attitudes and postures play their part too: dandyism, introspection, and conservative nostalgia being marks of the Mandarin, social activism and argumentative masculinity marks of the anti-Mandarin. The Mandarin style is often archaic and preciously 'literary' in diction (*nay, lest, sublunary*, and so forth) and elaborate in syntax, while the anti-Mandarin style is usually colloquial, journalistic, plain, and sometimes even hectoring.

A second stage of Connolly's thesis suggests that each camp has benefited in turn from the vagaries of literary fashion, the realists dominating the 1900–18 phase in reaction against the Nineties, giving way to a dominant Mandarinism in the decade between Strachey's *Eminent Victorians* (1918) and Woolf's *Orlando* (1928) but then dethroning it again after 1928. Ten years after the overthrow of the Mandarin reign, Connolly has grown more impatient with the vices of the latest anti-Mandarin dispensation (journalistic flatness of style, philistine insensitivity to beauty, Leftist conformism), but rather than go through further literary revolutions, he hopes for a new synthesis in which the best of both tendencies can be combined and the excesses avoided.

My own account of modern literature in this book has accepted from the start Connolly's basic model of a broad Modern Movement that includes puritan realists as well as 'modernist' Mandarins and at the same time acknowledges conflicts and compromises between these tendencies. His chronological scheme is more open to debate, although it allows fully for contrary exceptions and is not entirely eccentric even in neglecting the 1910–14 watershed, the importance of which Connolly does address at times. The scheme gives us three credible sub-periods: a prolonged 'Edwardian' phase of realism (1900–18); a post-War decade of resurgent Mandarinism led from Bloomsbury; and a slightly premature 'Thirties' revival of vernacular styles. In this design, the significance of some writers now neglected by literary history emerges more clearly: Maugham, for example, whose *The Summing Up* Connolly had just digested, appears as a pioneer of pre-War realism, and later as a leader of the anti-Mandarin reaction after 1928 (although oddly his *Ashenden* (1928), upon which Orwell had modelled his plain style, is overlooked). The clearest distinction, though, remains that between a 'Twenties' literary culture of esoteric and largely apolitical writing, and a 'Thirties' scene marked by political urgency and vernacular realism.

Turning to Woolf's 'The Leaning Tower', a talk given to the Workers' Educational Association and subsequently published, we find the same sort of contrast occupying the foreground. Woolf had long before, as we saw in the Introduction to this book, drawn her thick line between 'Edwardian' (pre-1910) and 'Georgian' (post-1910) literary generations, and here she concentrates on later distinctions between writers of the 1910–25 phase and the newcomers who had arrived since 1925. This succession of phases is interpreted in terms of the talk's major theme, which is educational privilege. Woolf's argument is that virtually all major authors until very recently had been sustained both by expensive education (the metaphorical 'tower' of her title) and by an unquestioned assumption of that privilege; but in modern conditions of war, revolution, and economic slump, the tower of privilege had begun to lean over and so become visible as a problem to be faced by writers. The Auden generation, then, has had the misfortune to be born into interesting times, and has been almost obliged to write in a self-consciously political or class-conscious way, even if that involved the bad faith of rebelling half-heartedly against the basis of its own livelihood. Woolf's verdict upon these unfortunate victims of history is that their poetry and fiction have been blighted by sermonizing and scapegoating, but that their autobiographical writings at least have shown a new kind of honesty.

As a literary historian, Woolf is far less reliable than Connolly, and much more inclined to state 'facts' with little credible evidence. Indeed she doctors her facts not only to fit a thesis but to sustain a public pose, eager as she is to appear before an educated proletarian audience as an ordinary commoner and as an ever-so-humble outsider without the citadel of cultural power. For the purposes of her argument, an expensive education means public school and Oxbridge, but her own form of expensive education conducted at home is passed over in silence. Her claim that all the major nineteenth-century authors (except D. H. Lawrence, who is placed in the wrong century) were launched from elite academies sidesteps the awkward cases of Blake, Keats, the Brownings, the Brontë sisters, the Rossettis, Dickens, Gaskell, Collins, George Eliot, Meredith, and Hardy. When it comes to the leading writers of 1910–25, she offers a conveniently selective list of names and asserts that they were all products of public school and university (in fact one of them, Wilfred Owen, attended neither); omitted from the list are all the period's women writers, along with Shaw, Yeats, Bennett, Ford, Masefield, de la Mare, Davies, Coppard, Wells, Read, and Joyce, none of whom studied at public school, only the three last-named having attended university. Woolf's scope narrows still further in her account of the 1925–40 phase, where the only authors mentioned are Auden, Spender, Isherwood, MacNeice, and Day-Lewis. Again there are no women authors and no working-class writers; but now there are, apart from Isherwood, no novelists either. We have here the first draft of that standard simplified story of 'Thirties writing' in which only one small group matters, its fragile Leftism being the only notable feature of the times.

With Orwell's long essay 'Inside the Whale' we return to seriously informed consideration of recent literary trends, constructed again on the basis of contrasts between the privileged irresponsibility of the Twenties and the narrow earnestness of the Thirties. Orwell begins and ends with a discussion of the American novelist Henry Miller as a portent of some new post-political phase, but he devotes the central part of the essay to the major trends in English literature since about 1910. As in Connolly's *Enemies of Promise*, which Orwell had been reading, there is a tripartite succession, this time from 'Georgian' nature-worship to Twenties disillusionment and then to the political commitments of the Thirties. Rather reductively, Orwell attributes the excesses of each phase to the pampered prosperity of the literati in an age of collapsing religious belief. The bucolic poetry of 1910–25 betrays a comfortable weekend pantheism; the fashionable pessimism of the Twenties and its nostalgia for ancient certainties is the product of leisured boredom; the priggish Stalinophile conformism of the Thirties indicates the literary class's ignorance of real political tyranny and its craving for a substitute religion. Against these various forms of myopia he upholds a wise passiveness before reality, of the kind he admires in Eliot, Joyce, Maugham, Lawrence, and the war poets. The most striking distinction Orwell makes, aligning him partly with Woolf, is between the enduring value of those authors' works in the 1910–30 phase, and the ephemeral worthlessness of almost anything published after 1930. Like Woolf, he takes it as read that Auden and his friends simply *are* the new wave of the early Thirties, as Eliot, Huxley, and Joyce had been 'the movement' of the post-War years. He goes further indeed in asserting explicitly that the best Thirties writers have been poets, the reason being that political orthodoxy is more damaging to prose fiction than to verse. 'No decade in the past hundred and fifty years', he declares with astonishing confidence, 'has been so barren of imaginative prose as the nineteen-thirties' (*Collected Essays*, vol. 1, p. 568). More scrupulous students of English fiction might well nominate the 1820s and 1830s as much leaner years, and might point to the prose fictions of Woolf, Waugh, Bowen, Huxley, Maugham, Lehmann, Wodehouse, Warner, Isherwood, Holtby, Mitchison, Graves, du Maurier, Greene, Rhys, and indeed Orwell himself as symptoms of vitality in the 1930s. Allowance should be made for the fact that it is easier to keep up with four of the latest young poets than with the fifteen leading novelists of one's day. Nonetheless, Orwell's and Woolf's identification of the Thirties literary 'movement' exclusively with Auden and his confederates must strike us as hasty or purblind, especially now that C. Day Lewis's verse collections are all out of print while the principal works of the novelists listed above remain available. It tells us something about the impact that the *New Signatures* circle made at the time, but it betrays too a traditional yet increasingly unreliable assumption that the true voice of any generation will be heard from its poets. The Thirties were the last years in which that assumption was widely shared. Ironically, the contrary view that verse had become a lesser art subordinate to the power of prose genres was expressed at the same time, as we saw in Chapter 4, by W. H. Auden.

Cyril Connolly's strong interest in contemporary prose shielded him from the dazzling prominence of the young poets, and so helped him to outline a more persuasively balanced account of modern literary developments. The other commendable strength of that account is that Connolly allows for the simultaneous currency of different voices, schools, and trends, none of which entirely displaces or supersedes another, even as the Mandarin or anti-Mandarin camp may attain a temporary advantage. I held up *Enemies of Promise* and its conception of a broad Modern Movement as an example for literary history in my Introduction, and I revert to it now because the literature of 1910–40 seems to have been especially vulnerable to distracting and distorting simplifications, of two kinds. The first of these takes the calendar more seriously than it deserves, and wraps literary production into separate decades, each of which is characterized by a single 'spirit of the age' distilled in the voice of one poet. Thus the first Georgian decade is one of pastoral escapism (Brooke); the Twenties are the decade of 'disillusionment' (Eliot); and the Thirties are given over to political engagement (Auden). Squeezing these poets into 'period' attitudes is one harmful consequence, but greater damage still is done by silently pushing the full variety of literary work into a great oubliette of implied irrelevance because it stubbornly fails to express the required spirit of its time. Several recent studies of the Thirties, by Frank Kermode, James Gindin, Jane Dowson, and others, have helpfully indicated ways out of the customary Auden-centred versions of that decade's writing. If we are to achieve a fuller, clearer, and more balanced view of literature in those years, though, we may need to be bolder in dissolving 'the Thirties', both by acknowledging their continuities with earlier and later decades and where appropriate by subdividing them, perhaps to discover that 1928–36 is a phase rather different from 1936–40. As for the earlier part of our period, a curious disparity has long been apparent between the status of the Thirties as a self-contained period in literary history, one to which many books have been devoted, and the two previous decades: the Twenties, although identified by cultural history and in some accounts of American literature as 'the Jazz Age', have in English literary history nothing like the same recognition as a literary decade, while the years 1910–19 lack even an accepted name to which clichés might cling. The reason for this brings us to the second major simplification that distorts our view of the whole period.

In the study of modern English literature, we do not speak much of the Twenties, nor at all of the Teens. This is because we have already, especially in academic discourse since the 1970s, an alternative framework to hand, namely 'modernism'. This term remains a useful one for certain purposes, allowing us to indicate some common features of experimental work in several Western arts (and theories of art) in the first half of the twentieth century; but it also carries its own risks, the gravest of which is that a particular trend or movement comes to stand in for, and in effect to occlude, a whole literary period. In this respect, our concept of modernism is like the older model of Romanticism, only worse. Scholars of early nineteenth-century literature, even when they speak of 'the Romantic period', have usually been careful to avoid implying that all significant literary work of that age must be 'Romantic': the contrary example of Jane Austen alone quells that temptation. The apotheosis of modernism in recent literary studies, though, has been attained in blithe disregard for contemporaneous non-modernist writers and schools, the more important of which have simply been swallowed into an expanded modernist canon. W. B. Yeats and the often scathingly anti-modernist D. H. Lawrence are now routinely discussed as modernist writers, although both could be better understood as late Romantics; and the non-modernist inclinations of such writers as May Sinclair or W. H. Auden are increasingly overlooked, so that the roll-call of eminent modernists can be extended. Meanwhile, books and articles have lately been appearing on Shaw the modernist (he was once with the same assurance classed as a 'naturalist') and even less plausibly on the modernism of E. M. Forster. It cannot be long before we see studies of Brooke the modernist, Christie the modernist, Kipling the modernist, and perhaps even Wodehouse the modernist. Indeed I am tempted to write the last of these myself, if only as a parodic spoiler. Literary modernism in England could without such dubious additions be delimited as a school of poets (Eliot, Pound, Edith Sitwell), novelists (Richardson, Hueffer/Ford, Joyce, Woolf), and polemical outriders (T. E. Hulme, Wyndham Lewis). The recent expansion of its canon beyond credibility seems to arise essentially from an undeclared assumption that other writers are worthy of notice only insofar as they resemble that central avant-garde. This in turn has prompted a defeatist—if you can't beat them, join them—impulse among admirers of non-modernist writers, who fear that nobody will listen to them unless they misapply the 'modernist' label.

The curious result of all this has been that while students of English literature in its pre–1910 periods have been invited to explore all manner of fascinating byways and minor traditions in what is now a much more 'open' canon, the study of literature in the period 1910–40 is ever more firmly locked into the academic framework of modernism alone. One important but generally unnoticed reason for this exception is that modernism as currently understood in literary studies is not just, as with Romanticism, the name of a movement that threatens to subsume a whole period. It is in fact a *cause*, indeed a pseudo-political cause that commands the loyalty of fervent partisans willing to do battle against real or imagined enemies. At one time modernism was, with good reason, although too exclusively, identified with serious literary art, and was to be defended against philistine mockery, which was real enough in the 1920s. (This identification may explain why Henry James, Joseph Conrad, and W. B. Yeats, who were not committed to radical disruptions of form, have nonetheless been treated retrospectively as honorary modernists.) Since the 1960s, under the influence of Parisian literary theorists—notably Roland Barthes and Julia Kristeva—modernism has come to be associated rather with a 'revolution of the word' that radically subverts bourgeois hegemony by breaking the supposed ideological fetters of realism. While the Little Red Book, the cheerleading of the repressive 'Cultural Revolution', and the other shameful follies of Sixties Maoism in the West are mercifully forgotten, its literary dogma (Realism bad; Modernism good—it really is that simple down on Animal Farm) has proved remarkably tenacious in the world of academic literary studies, where admiration for the realist tradition may still be regarded as political backsliding.

In our own time, there is no plausible justification, if there ever was, for the sectarian dismissiveness with which literary modernism has formerly been defended. The reputations of the major modernist writers are secure enough to permit a non-partisan re-examination of the larger Modern Movement within which they worked, of their affiliations to realism and other non-modernist currents, and even of the degree to which they were modernist in the first place, in the sense that Cubist painters were. The age of tense highbrow vigilance against 'Edwardian' tastes and middlebrow entertainment has also passed, so we can afford a relaxed appreciation of significant merit in the work of Shaw, Wells, Bennett, Galsworthy, Kipling, Chesterton, Maugham, Buchan, Coppard, Priestley, Coward, de la Mare, Brooke, Sassoon, Wodehouse, Mayor, Christie, Macaulay, Bagnold, Webb, T. E. Lawrence, Holtby, Greene, and several others without having to fear that we may be betraying the cause of Art. We could also better understand a few writers of 'highbrow' reputation such as Yeats, Ford, Sinclair, Forster, D. H. Lawrence, Strachey, West, Richardson, Mansfield, Huxley, Graves, Read, Lehmann, Rhys, Warner, Waugh, Green, Bowen, Compton-Burnett, Auden, Isherwood, and MacNeice if we approached them on their own terms without straining to justify them as more consistently modernistic than they really were. A formidable range of literary stimulation awaits us in this period's writings, if we only suspend the suspicions and the proscriptions of a century-old culture war.

As an essential step towards seeing this period's literature steadily and seeing it—within reasonable approximation—whole, an amnesty for the alleged crimes of realism, in particular, is long over-due. Realism was never as limitingly 'materialist' as Woolf said its modern exponents were; nor was it a pillar of bourgeois ideology, as the Parisian Maoists pretended; nor was it a Victorian steam-contraption which became obsolete in 1910 or 1922. It was and remains a central impulse in modern literature, one which the modern-ist school never simply rejected. Much of what we call modernism was indeed realism in a new manner, modulated by symbolist or expressionist devices, inflected by new psychological emphases, but still dedicated to puncturing false idealisms and to telling the truth about the world as it is. Modernism did not abolish or supersede realism; it extended its possibilities. Readers who have followed my account through the length of this book will have noticed already that I stress at several points the unexhausted vitality of the realist tradi-tion in the period's literature, not only in prose fiction but in poetry, where, from Brooke to Auden, it stands as the dominant tendency. I have indicated resurgences of realism across a range of genres, from biography and travel-writing to spy thrillers and children's stories, and in the treatment of some major topics, from war to sexuality. I have also, especially in Chapters 4 and 10, made a point of identi-fying the significant departures from realism not among modernist works so much as in the traditions of modern Romanticism (Yeats, D. H. Lawrence) and in the overlooked corpus of the period's prose romances. When I was first invited to write this book, a working title offered to me was 'The Age of Modernism'. The age in ques-tion was certainly adorned and illuminated by a few outstanding works in modernist styles, but they should no longer be permitted to define, let alone monopolize, our understanding of the period. Once we have unlearned some of the distracting dichotomies of twentieth-century criticism, and once we have become accustomed to reading more widely among the overshadowed non-modernist authors, we shall come to recognize this as a great age of literary realism.

New words, 1910–1940

retrospectivity   finalize   fade-out   cheerio

Author Bibliographies

Asterisked editions are those quoted in this book.

ALDINGTON, RICHARD (1892–1962)

Author of poems (*Images* (1915), *Images of War* (1919), *Fool i' the Forest* (1925), *Complete Poems* (1948), *An Imagist at War: The Complete War Poems*, ed. M. Copp (2002)); novels (*Death of a Hero* (1929; *Hogarth repr., 1984); *The Colonel's Daughter* (1931)); short stories (*Roads to Glory*, 1930); biographies (*D. H. Lawrence*, 1950). Biography: Charles Doyle, *Richard Aldington* (1989). Critical study: Charles Doyle (ed.), *Richard Aldington: Reappraisals* (1990).

AUDEN, WYSTAN HUGH (1907–1973)

He was born in York, the son of a doctor, and educated at Gresham's School, Holt, and at Christ Church, Oxford, studying biology, then English. After a year in Berlin, he became a schoolteacher, and then briefly joined the Post Office documentary film unit. His first significant books, *Poems* (1930) and *The Orators* (1932) were followed by the distinctive verse collection *Look, Stranger!* (1936). He briefly visited the Spanish Civil War, wrote three plays for the Group Theatre with his friend Christopher Isherwood, including *The Ascent of F6* (1937), travelled with Louis MacNeice to Iceland, co-writing *Letters from Iceland* (1937), edited the *Oxford Book of Light Verse* (1938), and then visited China with Isherwood, with whom he then emigrated to the USA in 1939, becoming an Anglican. His next major collection was *Another Time* (1940). In New York, he met Chester Kallman, with whom he lived and wrote some libretti. A US citizen from 1946, he published several further volumes of verse, the most important being *Nones* (1951) and *The Shield of Achilles* (1955), and heavily revised many of his earlier poems for the *Collected Shorter Poems 1927–1957* (1966) and *Collected Longer Poems* (1968). In later life, he lived partly in Kirchstetten, Austria, and briefly in Oxford.

The *Collected Poems*, ed. E. Mendelson (Faber, 1976; rev. 1994), incorporates Auden's revised versions of all those poems he wished to preserve. The original versions of his Thirties poems, with some suppressed poems such as 'Spain' and many prose pieces, can be found in *The English Auden*, ed. E. Mendelson (Faber, 1977)—a compendium of his work up to 1939. Edward Mendelson is editing an eight-volume Complete Works (Princeton/Faber): volumes published so far include the *Plays 1928–1938* (1988), the *Libretti & Other Dramatic Writings* (1993), and the *Prose, 1926–1938* (1996). The standard biography is Humphrey Carpenter's *W. H. Auden* (1981). Critical responses to Auden's work are collected in John Haffenden (ed.), *W. H. Auden: The Critical Heritage* (1983), and are surveyed in Paul Hendon (ed.), *The Poetry of W. H. Auden* (2000). Valuable introductions to Auden are provided by Allan Rodway, *A Preface to Auden* (1984), and Stan Smith, *W. H. Auden* (1997). Extended critical studies include Edward Callan, *W. H. Auden: A Carnival of Intellect* (1983); Anthony Hecht, *The Hidden Law* (1993); Edward Mendelson, *Early Auden* (1981); and John Fuller, *W. H. Auden: A Commentary* (1998). Reference: B. C. Bloomfield and Edward Mendelson, *W. H. Auden: A Bibliography, 1924–1969* (2nd edn., 1972).

BENNETT, ARNOLD (1867–1931)

He was born in Hanley, in the Potteries district of Staffordshire, the son of a solicitor. He studied at Newcastle under Lyme Middle School, worked as a legal clerk, and then became a journalist in London on *Woman* magazine, publishing his second novel, *Anna of the Five Towns* in 1902. He moved to Paris in 1903, wrote several minor novels and stories, and married Marguerite Soulié in 1907. His first major novel, *The Old Wives' Tale* (1908) was followed by *Clayhanger* (1910)—to which he later added three sequels—and the more humorous *The Card* (1911). He returned to England in 1912, buying himself a yacht and a large house in Essex, and building upon his commercial successes in the theatre with *The Great Adventure* (1913) and other plays. In the Great War, he was briefly a propagandist in Beaverbrook's Ministry of Information. He separated from Marguerite in 1921, and later lived with the actress Dorothy Cheston, by whom he had one daughter. His last critically valued novel was *Riceyman Steps* (1923). From 1926, he wrote an influential weekly literary column in the *Evening Standard*. Four volumes of his *Journal* appeared between 1929 and 1933, followed by the *Letters*, ed. J. Hepburn, 4 vols. (Oxford University Press, 1966–86).

Annotated editions of *Clayhanger*, ed. A. Lincoln (1989), and

Riceyman Steps, ed. E. Mendelson and R. Squillace (1991), have been published in the Penguin Classics series. Penguin have at various times reprinted *The Card*, *The Grand Babylon Hotel*, two Clayhanger sequels (*Hilda Lessways*, *These Twain*), the short-story collection *The Grim Smile of the Five Towns*, and the **Journals*. A few other minor works have been reprinted by Alan Sutton. Bennett's later reviews are collected as **The Evening Standard Years: 'Books and Persons' 1926–1931*, ed. A. Mylett (Chatto & Windus, 1974). The standard biography is Margaret Drabble's *Arnold Bennett* (1974). Critical responses are collected in James Hepburn (ed.), *Arnold Bennett: The Critical Heritage* (1981). Modern critical studies include John Lucas, *Arnold Bennett: A Study of his Fiction* (1974); Walter F. Wright, *Arnold Bennett: Romantic Realist* (1971); and Robert Squillace, *Modernism, Modernity, and Arnold Bennett* (1997). Reference: Anita Miller, *Arnold Bennett: An Annotated Bibliography* (1977).

BENSON, EDWARD FREDERIC (1867–1940)

Novelist and short-story writer. Principal works: *Dodo* (1893; Hogarth repr., 1986), *The Room in the Tower* (ghost stories, 1912), *Queen Lucia* (1920), *Miss Mapp* (1922), *Mapp and Lucia* (1931), *Lucia's Progress* (1935); the 'Lucia' novels reprinted in Black Swan editions in the 1980s along with *The Tale of an Empty House and Other Ghost Stories*. Biography: Brian Masters, *The Life of E. F. Benson* (1991).

BETJEMAN, JOHN (1906–1984)

Poet. Principal works: *Mount Zion* (1931), *Continual Dew* (1937), *New Bats in Old Belfries* (1945), *A Few Late Chrysanthemums* (1954), *Summoned by Bells* (1960); **Collected Poems* (John Murray, 1958; rev. 1962). Knighted, 1969; Poet Laureate, 1972–84. Biography: Bevis Hillier, *Young Betjeman* (1988), and *John Betjeman: New Fame, New Love* (2002).

BLAKE, NICHOLAS. *See* DAY-LEWIS, CECIL.

BLUNDEN, EDMUND (1896–1974)

Poet, critic, memoirist. Principal works: *The Waggoner* (1920), *The Shepherd* (1922), *Undertones of War* (prose and verse war memoir, 1928; Penguin repr., 1937), *Poems, 1914–1930* (1930), *The Face of England* (prose, 1932), *Poems 1930–1940* (1941). Modern editions: *Selected*

Poems, ed. R. Marsack (Carcanet, 1982); *Overtones of War: The War Poems*, ed. M. Taylor (Duckworth, 1996). Biography: Barry Webb, *Edmund Blunden* (1990). Critical study: Thomas Mallon, *Edmund Blunden* (1983). Reference: B. Kirkpatrick, *A Bibliography of Edmund Blunden* (1979).

BOWEN, ELIZABETH (1899–1973)

She was born in Dublin, into a landed Anglo-Irish family, her father being a barrister. Moving to England at the age of 7, she attended schools in Hertfordshire and Kent, and was then brought up by aunts at the family seat of Bowen's Court, Co. Cork, which she came to inherit in 1930. In 1923 she married Alan Cameron, an educational administrator, living with him in Oxfordshire and London. Her first volume of short stories, *Encounters*, appeared in 1923; several others followed, notably *The Cat Jumps* (1934) and *The Demon Lover* (1945). Her early novels were *The Hotel* (1927), *The Last September* (1929), *Friends and Relations* (1931), *To the North* (1932), and *The House in Paris* (1935). She is better known for the next two, *The Death of the Heart* (1938) and *The Heat of the Day* (1949). Later novels are *A World of Love* (1955), *The Little Girls* (1964), and *Eva Trout* (1965). In 1959, seven years after her husband's death, she sold Bowen's Court, which was then destroyed, and moved to Kent.

Bowen's novels, along with the **Collected Stories* (1980) have appeared in Penguin editions, now reprinted with identical pagination as *Vintage Classics. The standard biography is Victoria Glendinning, *Elizabeth Bowen: Portrait of a Writer* (1977). The principal critical studies are Phyllis Lassner, *Elizabeth Bowen* (1990); Hermione Lee, *Elizabeth Bowen: An Estimation* (1981; rev. 1999); Maud Ellmann, *Elizabeth Bowen: The Shadow across the Page* (2003); and Phyllis Lassner, *Elizabeth Bowen: A Study of the Short Fiction* (1991). Reference: Jonathan Sellery and William O. Harris, *Elizabeth Bowen: A Descriptive Bibliography* (2nd edn., 1981).

BRIDGES, ROBERT (1844–1930)

Poet; founder of Society for Pure English (1913), Poet Laureate (1913–30); editor of G. M. Hopkins's verse. Major work in this period: **The Testament of Beauty* (Oxford University Press, 1929). Modern editions: *Poetical Works* (Oxford University Press, 1953); *A Choice of Bridges' Verse*, ed. D. Cecil (Faber, 1987). Biography: Catherine Phillips, *Robert*

Bridges (1990). Critical study: Donald E. Stanford, *In the Classic Mode: The Achievement of Robert Bridges* (1978).

BRITTAIN, VERA (1893–1970)

Memoirist, novelist, and poet. Principal works: *The Dark Tide* (novel, 1923), *Testament of Youth* (memoir, 1933), *Poems of the War and After* (1934), *Honourable Estate* (novel, 1936), *Testament of Friendship* (memoir of W. Holtby, 1940), *Testament of Experience* (memoir, 1957). The novels and 'Testament' volumes have been reprinted as Virago editions. Biography: Paul Berry and Mark Bostridge, *Vera Brittain* (1995). Critical study: Jean E. Kennard, *Vera Brittain & Winifred Holtby* (1989).

BROOKE, RUPERT (1887–1915)

He was born and educated at Rugby, where his father was a housemaster at the famous school. He read classics at King's College, Cambridge. After a brief stint as a teacher at Rugby, he published *Poems* (1911), and helped Edward Marsh with the first of his *Georgian Poetry* anthologies. He spent 1911–12 in Germany and in Granchester near Cambridge, writing a play, *Lithuania* (1915), and having a nervous breakdown. The *Westminster Gazette* sent him to the USA as a correspondent in 1913, and he travelled on to Tahiti, where he wrote several poems collected in *1914 and Other Poems* (1915)—a volume also containing poems from the early days of his war service with the Royal Naval Division. His sonnet 'The Soldier' was read from the pulpit by the Dean of St Paul's on Easter Sunday, 1915, and published in *The Times*, making Brooke a national hero. But he soon succumbed to septicaemia on his way to Gallipoli, and died on a French hospital ship on 23 April. A Fabian, vegetarian, anti-Semite, and nudist, famed for his beauty, he had numerous female and male admirers. *The Collected Letters*, ed. G. Keynes (Faber, 1968), is incomplete, and has been supplemented by the correspondence collected in *Song of Love*, ed. P. Harris (Bloomsbury, 1990), and *Friends and Apostles,* ed. K. Hale (Yale, 1998).

The standard edition of Brooke's verse is **The Poetical Works*, ed. G. Keynes (Faber, 1946; rev. 1974). Prose writings are collected as *The Prose*, ed. C. Hassall (Sidgwick and Jackson, 1956). Nigel Jones's *Rupert Brooke: Life, Death and Myth* (1999) is now the standard biography. Paul Delaney's *The Neo-Pagans* (1987) is a rewarding biographical study that sets Brooke in the context of his social circle. Reference: Geoffrey Keynes, *A Bibliography of Rupert Brooke* (2nd edn., 1959).

BUCHAN, JOHN (1875–1940)

Author of thriller and adventure fiction. Principal prose romances: *Prester John* (1910), *The Thirty-Nine Steps* (1915), *Greenmantle* (1916), *Mr Standfast* (1919), *John Macnab* (1925), *The Dancing Floor* (1926), *Witch Wood* (1927), *Sick Heart River* (1941), most reprinted as *Oxford World's Classics. Governor-General of Canada (1935–40). Autobiography: *Memory Hold-the-Door* (1940). Posthumous collections include *The Complete Short Stories*, ed. A. Lownie, 3 vols. (Thistle, 1996). Biography: Andrew Lownie, *John Buchan* (1995). Critical study: David Daniell, *The Interpreter's House: A Critical Assessment of John Buchan* (1975). Reference: Robert G. Blanchard, *The First Editions of John Buchan* (1981).

BUTTS, MARY (1890–1937)

Novelist and short-story writer. Principal works: *Speed the Plough* (stories, 1923), *Ashe of Rings* (1925), *Armed with Madness* (1928; *Penguin repr., 2001), *Death of Felicity Taverner* (1932), *Several Occasions* (stories, 1932). Later collections (all published by McPherson): *The Taverner Novels* (1992); *From Altar to Chimney-Piece: Selected Stories* (1992); *Ashe of Rings and Other Writings* (1998); *The Journals*, ed. N. Blondel (Yale, 2003). Biography: Nathalie Blondel, *Mary Butts* (1998). Critical studies: Christopher Wagstaff (ed.), *A Sacred Quest: The Life and the Writings of Mary Butts* (1995); Roslyn Reso Foy, *Ritual, Myth, and Mysticism in the Work of Mary Butts* (2001).

BYRON, ROBERT (1905–1941)

Travel writer. Principal works: *The Station* (1928), *The Byzantine Achievement* (1929), *An Essay on India* (1931), *First Russia, Then Tibet* (1933; *Penguin repr., 1985), *The Road to Oxiana* (1937; Picador repr., 1981). Biography: James Knox, *Robert Byron* (2003).

CAMPBELL, ROY (1901–1957)

South African poet. Principal works: *The Flaming Terrapin* (1924), *The Wayzgoose* (1928), *Adamastor* (1930), *The Georgiad* (1931), *Flowering Reeds* (1933), *Mithraic Emblems* (1936), *Flowering Rifle* (1939), *Talking Bronco* (1946); *Collected Poems*, 3 vols. (1949, 1957, 1960). *Collected

Works, ed. Peter Alexander et al., 4 vols. (Donker, 1985–8). Biography: Peter Alexander, *Roy Campbell* (1982).

CHESTERTON, GILBERT KEITH (1874–1936)

Journalist, essayist, poet, detective fiction writer, critic, biographer. Principal works: *Charles Dickens* (1906), *The Man Who Was Thursday* (1908), *The Innocence of Father Brown* (1911), *The Wisdom of Father Brown* (1914), *The Incredulity of Father Brown* (1926), *Collected Poems* (1927; rev. 1933), *Selected Essays*, ed. D. Collins (Methuen, 1949). Modern editions: *Father Brown* (Penguin, 2001); *The Essential G. K. Chesterton* (Oxford, 1987). Biography: Dudley Barker, *G. K. Chesterton* (1973). Critical study: John Coates, *Chesterton and the Edwardian Cultural Crisis* (1984). Reference: John Sullivan, *G. K. Chesterton: A Bibliography* (1958).

CHRISTIE, AGATHA [née Miller] (1890–1976)

Crime writer. Novels include *The Mysterious Affair at Styles* (1920), *Murder on the Links* (1923), *The Murder of Roger Ackroyd* (1926), *The Murder at the Vicarage* (1930), *Peril at End House* (1932), *The ABC Murders* (1936); all reprinted in *HarperCollins editions, along with *Hercule Poirot: The Complete Short Stories* (1999). Also known for *The Mousetrap* (drama, 1952). Biography: Janet Morgan, *Agatha Christie* (1984). Critical study: Patricia D. Mader and Nicholas B. Spornick, *Murder She Wrote* (1982). Reference: Dennis Sanders and Len Lovallo, *The Agatha Christie Companion* (1985).

COMPTON-BURNETT, IVY (1884–1969)

Novelist. Works include *Pastors and Masters* (1925), *Brothers and Sisters* (1929), *A House and its Head* (1935), *Daughters and Sons* (1937), and *Manservant and Maidservant* (1947), all reprinted in *Penguin editions. Biography: Hilary Spurling, *Ivy When Young* (1974; rev. 1983) and *Secrets of a Woman's Heart* (1984). Critical study: Kathy Justice Gentile, *Ivy Compton-Burnett* (1991).

COPPARD, ALFRED EDGAR (1878–1957)

Short-story writer and poet. Principal collections: *Adam and Eve and Pinch Me* (1921; *Penguin repr., 1946), *Hips and Haws* (poems, 1922),

The Black Dog (1923), *Fishmonger's Fiddle* (1925), *The Field of Mustard* (1926), *Crotty Shinkwin* (1932), *Cherry Ripe* (poems, 1935). Later selection: *Dusky Ruth and Other Stories* (Penguin, 1976). Autobiography: *It's Me, O Lord!* (1957).

COWARD, NOËL (1899–1973)

Born in Teddington, Middlesex, the son of a piano salesman, he was educated privately and became a child actor. He was conscripted to the Army in 1918, but was discharged on medical grounds. As a playwright, he achieved success with his fifth play, *The Vortex* (1924), a melodrama; but it was with his polished comedies that he made his reputation, notably *Hay Fever* (1925), *Private Lives* (1930), *Design for Living* (1939), and *Blithe Spirit* (1941). He himself acted in some of these. He also wrote the musical *Bitter-Sweet* (1929), the patriotic pageant *Cavalcade* (1931), a patriotic family drama, *This Happy Breed* (1943), and the screenplay for the famous film *Brief Encounter* (1945), in addition to numerous songs and short stories. He spent the Second World War cruising with the Royal Navy. Later years were spent as a tax exile in Jamaica, Bermuda, and Switzerland. He was knighted in 1970, and died in Jamaica. *The Noël Coward Diaries*, ed. G. Payn and S. Morley, appeared in 1982.

Methuen publish the *Collected Plays* in 7 volumes, along with *The Complete Lyrics*, ed. B. Day (1998); the *Collected Verse*, ed. G. Payn and M. Tickner (1984); and the *Complete Short Stories* (1985). The standard biography is Philip Hoare, *Noël Coward: A Biography* (1995). The most substantial critical study is John Lahr, *Coward the Playwright* (1982). Jacqui Russell's *File on Coward* (1987) is a handy reference work, as is R. Mander and J. Mitchenson, *Theatrical Companion to Coward* (2nd edn., 2000).

DANE, CLEMENCE [pseudonym of Winifred Ashton] (1888–1965)

Playwright and novelist. Novels: *Regiment of Women* (1917; Virago repr., 1995), *Legend* (1919), *Broome Stages* (1931). Plays: *A Bill of Divorcement* (1921), *Will Shakespeare* (1921), *Granite* (1926), *Wild Decembers* (1933), *Anna Karenina* (screenplay, 1935). Reference: David Waldron Smithers, '*Therefore Imagine . . .*': *The Works of Clemence Dane* (1988).

DAVIES, WILLIAM HENRY (1871–1940)

Poet and autobiographer. At one time a vagrant, he lost one leg while in Canada. *Autobiography of a Super-Tramp* (1908) won him fame. *Nature Poems & Others* (1908) was followed by many volumes of verse. Posthumous volumes: *Complete Poems* (Cape, 1963); *Young Emma* (memoir, 1980). Biography: Lawrence Normand, *W. H. Davies* (2003). Reference: Sylvia Harlow, *W. H. Davies: A Bibliography* (1993).

DAY-LEWIS, CECIL (1904–1972)

Poet and translator (as 'C. Day Lewis'), and (as 'Nicholas Blake') crime writer; Professor of Poetry at Oxford (1951–6); Poet Laureate (1968–72). Modern edition: *The Complete Poems*, ed. J. Balcon (Sinclair-Stevenson, 1992). Detective novels include *The Beast Must Die* (1938; *Penguin repr., 1974) and *Malice in Wonderland* (1940). Biography: Sean Day-Lewis, *C. Day-Lewis* (1980). Critical study: Albert Gelpi, *Living in Time: The Poetry of C. Day Lewis* (1998). Reference: G. Handley-Taylor and T. d'Arch Smith, *C. Day-Lewis, The Poet Laureate: A Bibliography* (1968).

DE LA MARE, WALTER (1873–1956)

Born in Charlton, the son of a banker, he attended St Paul's Choir School in London, and then worked for many years in the offices of the Anglo-American Oil Company. In 1899, he married Constance Igpen; they had four children. He published some children's verse pseudonymously, and the adult *Poems* (1906). Awarded a Civil List pension of £100 per annum in 1908, he retired to Taplow, Bucks., as a full-time writer, further supported by a legacy from Rupert Brooke. His reputation as a poet was established by *The Listeners* (1912) and *Peacock Pie* (for children, 1913), and by the appearance of his poems in the *Georgian Poetry* anthologies. Further verse collections include *The Captive* (1928), *Memory* (1938), and *The Burning Glass* (1945). His most significant prose fiction is *Memoirs of a Midget* (1921). He also wrote several books of short stories for adults, including *Best Stories* (1942), and for children, and edited many anthologies, notably *Behold, This Dreamer!* (1939). He gathered his writings for children in *Collected Stories for Children* (1947) and *Collected Rhymes and Verses* (1944), and his verse for adults in *Collected Poems* (1942).

The 1979 *Collected Poems* (Faber) incorporates later collections; but the *Complete Poems* (Faber, 1969) includes further uncollected material. *Memoirs of a Midget* was reprinted as an *Oxford paperback in 1982.

Faber reprinted the *Best Stories* in 1983. Giles de la Mare has edited and published the *Short Stories 1895–1926* (1986) and *Short Stories 1927–1956* (2001). The standard biography is Theresa Whistler, *Imagination of the Heart: The Life of Walter de la Mare* (1993). The only modern critical study is Doris Ross McCrosson, *Walter de la Mare* (1966), but Henry C. Duffin's *Walter de la Mare: A Study of His Poetry* (1949) still has some value.

DOUGLAS, NORMAN (1868–1952)

Travel writer (*Siren Land*, 1911; *Penguin repr., 1983; *Fountains in the Sand*, 1912; *Old Calabria*, 1915; Picador repr., 1994); novelist (*South Wind*, 1917; *Penguin repr., 1935); autobiographer (*Looking Back*, 1933). Biography: Mark Holloway, *Norman Douglas* (1976). Reference: Cecil Woolf, *A Bibliography of Norman Douglas* (1954).

DU MAURIER, DAPHNE (1907–1989)

Novelist, short-story writer, playwright, biographer. Principal novels: *Jamaica Inn* (1936), *Rebecca* (1938), *Frenchman's Creek* (1941), *Hungry Hill* (1943), *My Cousin Rachel* (1951); all reprinted in *Arrow paperback editions. Biography: Margaret Forster, *Daphne du Maurier* (1993). Critical studies: Avril Horner and Sue Zlosnik, *Daphne du Maurier* (1997); Nina Auerbach, *Daphne du Maurier, Haunted Heiress* (2000).

ELIOT, THOMAS STEARNS (1888–1965)

Born in St Louis, Missouri, he studied literature and philosophy at Harvard, the Sorbonne, and Oxford, settling in London in 1915, when he married Vivien Haigh-Wood. He worked as a schoolteacher, as a bank clerk at Lloyd's, and on the editorial team of the *Egoist* magazine, and began writing for the *Athenaeum* and *Times Literary Supplement*. His early poems appeared in *Prufrock and Other Observations* (1917), *Poems* (1919), and *Ara Vos Prec* (1920). His most important essays were collected as *The Sacred Wood* (1920) and *Homage to John Dryden* (1924). After recovering from bouts of nervous collapse in 1921, he founded the literary journal *The Criterion*, publishing his major poem 'The Waste Land' in its first issue (1922) and continued to edit the journal until 1939. He joined the publishers Faber & Gwyer (later Faber & Faber) in 1925, building up its important poetry list. He joined the Church of England and became a British subject (1927), devoting further prose-writings, such as

After Strange Gods (1934) and *Notes Towards the Definition of Culture* (1948) to the importance of cultural order and tradition. His small body of published poetry was dominated by religious themes in 'The Hollow Men' (1925) and *Ash-Wednesday* (1930), culminating in the major verse sequence *Four Quartets* (1943). He attempted to revive verse drama in several plays, of which *Murder in the Cathedral* (1935) was the most successful. He won the Nobel Prize for Literature in 1948. Ten years after the death of his first wife, who had long been confined as a psychiatric patient, he married his secretary Valerie Fletcher (1957), who as Valerie Eliot edited *The Letters*, vol. 1: *1898–1922* (Faber, 1988).

The standard edition of the verse is *Collected Poems 1909–1962* (1963). The drafts of 'The Waste Land' have been published as *'The Waste Land': a Fascimile and Transcript*, ed. V. Eliot (1971). The most substantial collection of Eliot's prose work is the *Selected Essays* (3rd edn., 1951); some important items not collected there may be found in *Selected Prose*, ed. Frank Kermode (1975). All are published by Faber, as are the *Collected Plays* (1962). There is no authorized biography, but the best attempt so far is Peter Ackroyd's *T. S. Eliot* (1984). Tony Sharpe's *T. S. Eliot: A Literary Life* (1991) concentrates on the writing career. A partly biographical approach to the works is taken by Ronald Bush in *T. S. Eliot: A Study in Character and Style* (1984). Critical responses are collected in Michael Grant (ed.), *T. S. Eliot: The Critical Heritage*, 2 vols. (1982). Helpful introductory works are A. David Moody (ed.), *The Cambridge Companion to T. S. Eliot* (1994); B. C. Southam, *A Student's Guide to the Selected Poems of T. S. Eliot* (1968; 5th edn., 1990); and Ronald Tamplin, *A Preface to T. S. Eliot* (1988). Among the major critical accounts are Gregory Jay, *T. S. Eliot and the Poetics of Literary History* (1983); Hugh Kenner, *The Invisible Poet: T. S. Eliot* (1959); A. D. Moody, *Thomas Stearns Eliot: Poet* (1979; rev. 1994); and Carol H. Smith, *T. S. Eliot's Dramatic Theory and Practice* (1963). Reference: Donald Gallup, *T. S. Eliot: A Bibliography* (1969).

FIRBANK, RONALD (1886–1926)

Novelist. Early works: *Inclinations* (1916), *Caprice* (1917), *Valmouth* (1919). Later novels: *The Flower beneath the Foot* (1923), *Prancing Nigger* (1924), *Concerning the Eccentricities of Cardinal Pirelli* (1926). Modern edition: *The Complete Firbank* (Picador, 1988). Biography: M. J. Benkovitz, *Ronald Firbank* (1969). Critical study: Jocelyn Brooke, *Ronald Firbank* (1951). Reference: Miriam J. Benkovitz, *A Bibliography of Ronald Firbank* (2nd edn., 1982).

FLEMING, PETER (1907–1971)

Travel writer and historian. Principal works: *Brazilian Adventure* (1933; *Penguin repr., 1957), *One's Company* (1934), *News from Tartary* (1936), *Invasion 1940* (1957). Biography: Duff Hart-Davis, *Peter Fleming* (1987).

FORD, FORD MADOX [adopted name from 1919 of Ford Madox Hueffer] (1873–1939)

He was a grandson of the Pre-Raphaelite painter Ford Madox Brown. Born in Merton, Surrey, the son of a German music critic, he attended schools in Folkestone and London. His marriage to Elsie Martindale (1894) was unsettled by his philandering, and broke up after fifteen years. He befriended many writers, notably Joseph Conrad, with whom he collaborated on some works including parts of *Nostromo* (1904). He published several novels, biographies, and volumes of verse before establishing the *English Review* in 1908 and beginning his liaison with the novelist Violet Hunt. He published his best-known novel, *The Good Soldier*, in 1915, and survived the Battle of the Somme the next year. He settled in Paris in 1922 with Stella Bowen, founding the short-lived *Transatlantic Review* there in 1924, conducting an affair with Jean Rhys, and beginning the 'Tietjens' tetralogy of novels (*Some Do Not...* (1924); *No More Parades* (1925); *A Man Could Stand Up—* (1926); *The Last Post* (1928)) later collected as *Parade's End* (1950). His critical works included *Henry James* (1913), *Joseph Conrad* (1924), and *The English Novel* (1930). His later years were spent in France and the USA with the painter Janice Biala. *The Critical Writings*, ed. F. MacShane (University of Nebraska), appeared in 1964, followed by *The Letters*, ed. R. M. Ludwig (Princeton, 1965); and later by *The War Prose*, ed. M. Saunders (Carcanet, 1999), and the *Critical Essays*, ed. M. Saunders and R. Stang (Carcanet, 2002).

Two modern scholarly editions of Ford's *The Good Soldier* have appeared: in the *Oxford World's Classics series is T. C. Moser's edition (1990), while the Norton Critical Edition, ed. M. Stannard, (1995), contains a selection of critical writings on the novel. *Parade's End* has been reprinted by *Penguin, and some of the minor works by Carcanet. The fullest biography is Max Saunders, *Ford Madox Ford: A Dual Life*, 2 vols. (Oxford, 1996), which offers extensive critical discussion of the works; more concise is Alan Judd, *Ford Madox Ford* (1990). Critical articles on Ford are gathered in Frank MacShane (ed.), *Ford Madox Ford: The Critical Heritage* (1972) and in Richard A. Cassell (ed.), *Critical Essays on Ford*

Madox Ford (1987). Full-length critical studies include Richard W. Lid, *Ford Madox Ford: The Essence of His Art* (1964); John A. Meixner, *Ford Madox Ford's Novels* (1962); Ann Barr Snitow, *Ford Madox Ford and the Voice of Uncertainty* (1984); and Sondra J. Stang, *Ford Madox Ford* (1977). Reference: David Dow Harvey, *Ford Madox Ford 1873–1939: A Bibliography of Works and Criticism* (1962).

FORSTER, EDWARD MORGAN (1879–1970)

He was born in London, a few months before the death of his father, an architect, and thus was brought up by his mother near Stevenage. A legacy from his great-aunt gave him a private income. He attended Tonbridge School, and studied classics and history at King's College, Cambridge, forming valuable friendships among the Bloomsbury Group. In 1906 he established a home in Weybridge with his mother. His early novels were *Where Angels Fear to Tread* (1905), *The Longest Journey* (1907), and *A Room with a View* (1908), the first and third of these drawing on his travels to Greece and Italy. He won commercial success with *Howards End* (1910), and followed this with *The Celestial Omnibus and Other Stories* (1911). He travelled to India in 1912–13, and spent part of the Great War working for the Red Cross in Alexandria, Egypt, where he befriended the Greek poet C. F. Cavafy. Returning in 1919, he became literary editor of the *Daily Herald*. After another trip to India, *A Passage to India* was published in 1924, and his Clark lectures at Cambridge as *Aspects of the Novel* in 1927. He became the first president of the National Council for Civil Liberties in 1934. He wrote frequently for the BBC magazine *The Listener*, collecting his essays as *Abinger Harvest* (1936) and *Two Cheers for Democracy* (1951). In 1930 he formed a lasting relationship with Bob Buckingham, a policeman, and from 1946 he lived in King's College. The *Collected Short Stories* appeared in 1947, and his early novel of homosexuality, *Maurice*, was published posthumously in 1971, followed by *The Life to Come and Other Stories* (1972). *Selected Letters*, ed. M. Lago and P. N. Furbank, 2 vols. (Collins, 1983, 1985).

The definitive scholarly edition of Forster's novels and stories is the Abinger Edition, edited by Oliver Stallybrass and published by Edward Arnold in the 1970s. These texts are the basis for the *Penguin editions; Penguin have also reprinted the *Collected Short Stories* and *Aspects of the Novel*. There is also a Norton Critical Edition of *Howards End*, ed. P. B. Armstrong (1998). The standard biography is P. N. Furbank, *E. M. Forster: A Life*, 2 vols. (1977–8). Mary Lago's *E. M. Forster: A Literary Life* (1995) concentrates on the writing career. Critical articles are gathered in Harold Bloom (ed.), *E. M. Forster: Modern Critical Interpretations* (1987); in Joseph Bristow (ed.), *E. M. Forster* (1997); in Philip Gardner (ed.), *E. M. Forster: The Critical Heritage* (1973); in Jeremy Tambling (ed.), *E. M. Forster: Contemporary Critical Essays* (1995); and in Alan Wilde (ed.), *Critical Essays on E. M. Forster* (1985). Useful introductory studies are Christopher Gillie, *A Preface to Forster* (1983) and Nicholas Royle, *E. M. Forster* (1999). Full-length studies include Glen Cavaliero, *A Reading of E. M. Forster* (1979); Norman Page, *E. M. Forster* (1987); and Barbara Rosecrance, *Forster's Narrative Vision* (1982). Reference: B. J. Kirkpatrick, *A Bibliography of E. M. Forster* (2nd edn., 1985); Claude J. Summers, *E. M. Forster: A Guide to Research* (1991).

GALSWORTHY, JOHN (1867–1933)

Born in Kingston upon Thames, the son of a lawyer, he was educated at Harrow and New College, Oxford. He travelled to Australia and the Pacific before completing legal studies and practising as a barrister. He had an affair with Ada Cooper, the wife of his cousin, and eventually married her in 1905. Abandoning the law, he published some short stories pseudonymously in 1897, but his first major work was the novel *The Man of Property* (1906), followed by some successful plays including *The Silver Box* (1906), *Strife* (1909), and *Justice* (1910). He continued the story of the Forsyte family from *The Man of Property* in two more novels to form, with connecting interludes, *The Forsyte Saga* (1922), and in a further trilogy published as *A Modern Comedy* (1929); a third trilogy, *The End of the Chapter* (1934), is devoted to the Charwell family, cousins to the Forsytes. Later plays include *The Skin Game* (1920) and *Loyalties* (1922), collected with others in *The Plays* (1929). He also published many more volumes of short stories. He was awarded the Nobel Prize in 1932. The *Works* appeared in thirty volumes from 1923 to 1935.

There is an annotated edition of *The Forsyte Saga*, ed. G. Harvey (1995), in the *Oxford World's Classics series. *A Modern Comedy* and *The End of the Chapter* have appeared in Penguin editions. *Five Plays was published by Methuen in 1984. The fullest of several biographies is James Gindin, *John Galsworthy's Life and Art* (1987). A modern critical study is Alec Fréchet, *John Galsworthy: A Reassessment* (1982). Reference: Earl E. Stevens and H. Ray Stevens, *John Galsworthy: An Annotated Bibliography of Writings about Him* (1980).

GARNETT, DAVID (1892–1981)

Novelist. Principal works: *Lady into Fox* (1922; *Hogarth repr., 1985, with *A Man in the Zoo* (1924)), *The Sailor's Return* (1925), *Pocahontas* (biography, 1933), *Aspects of Love* (1955).

GERHARDI, WILLIAM (1895–1977)

Russian-born English novelist. Principal works: *Futility* (1922), *The Polyglots* (1925; Prion repr., 2001), *Of Mortal Love* (1936). Later added an 'e' to his surname. Biography: Dido Davies, *William Gerhardie* (1990).

GIBBONS, STELLA (1902–1989)

Novelist, short-story writer, poet. Principal works: *Cold Comfort Farm* (1932; *Penguin repr., 1938), *Bassett* (1934), *Roaring Tower* (stories, 1937), *Nightingale Wood* (1938), *Christmas at Cold Comfort Farm* (stories, 1940), *Westwood* (1946), *Collected Poems* (1950). Biography: Reggie Oliver, *Out of the Woodshed* (1998).

GRAVES, ROBERT (1895–1985)

He was born in Wimbledon of Irish and German parents, his father being a poet and school inspector, and was schooled at Charterhouse. In the Great War he served alongside Siegfried Sassoon in the Royal Welch Fusiliers, was wounded in the Battle of the Somme in 1916, and mistakenly reported as dead, an obituary appearing in *The Times*. His first volume of poems, *Over the Brazier*, appeared in 1916. In 1918 he married the painter Nancy Nicholson, by whom he had four children. They settled near Oxford, where Graves studied for a B.Litt., publishing his thesis as *Poetic Unreason* (1925). He and the American poet Laura Riding published *A Survey of Modernist Poetry* in 1927. In 1929 he set up home with Riding in Majorca, where he spent the next seven years, and published the memoir *Good-bye to All That*. He achieved popularity as a novelist with *I, Claudius* and *Claudius the God* (1934), and published the first of several editions of the *Collected Poems* in 1938. Having spent the war years in England, he returned to Majorca with Beryl Hodge, whom he married in 1950; they had three children. His most important non-fiction works are *The White Goddess* (1948) and *The Greek Myths* (1955). He was Professor of Poetry at Oxford from 1961 to 1966. *In Broken Images: Selected Letters 1914–1946*, ed. P. O'Prey (Hutchinson, 1982).

Good-bye to All That (drastically rev. 1957) is reprinted by *Penguin, along with the *Collected Short Stories*; *Selected Poems*, ed. P. O'Prey (1986); and the *Complete Poems*, ed. B. Graves and D. Ward (2003; based on their three-volume Carcanet edition of 1995–9). Carcanet's projected twenty-one-volume collected edition of the works already includes the *Complete Short Stories*, ed. L. Graves (1995). Carcanet have also reprinted *A Survey of Modernist Poetry* in one volume with *A Pamphlet against Anthologies*, ed. C. Mundye and P. McGuinness (2002). The fullest biography is Richard Perceval Graves's *Robert Graves*, 3 vols. (1986, 1990, 1995). More digestible is Miranda Seymour's *Robert Graves* (1995). Martin Seymour-Smith's *Robert Graves: His Life and Work* (1982) includes critical discussion. Critical works include D. N. G. Carter, *Robert Graves: The Lasting Poetic Achievement* (1989), and Patrick J. Keane, *A Wild Civility* (1980). Reference: Fred H. Higginson, *A Bibliography of the Writings of Robert Graves* (2nd edn., 1987).

GREEN, HENRY [pseudonym of Henry Yorke] (1905–1973)

Novelist. Early works: *Blindness* (1926), *Living* (1929), *Party Going* (1939). Later works: *Caught* (1943), *Loving* (1945), *Back* (1946), *Concluding* (1948), *Nothing* (1950), *Doting* (1952). These have been reprinted in Harvill and in Vintage paperback editions. Posthumous collection: *Surviving: The Uncollected Writings*, ed. M. Yorke (1992). Biography: Jeremy Treglown, *Romancing: The Life and Work of Henry Green* (2000). Critical study: Rod Mengham, *The Idiom of the Time: The Writings of Henry Green* (1982).

GREENE, GRAHAM (1904–1991)

Novelist and travel writer. Principal novels: *Stamboul Train* (1932), *It's a Battlefield* (1934), *England Made Me* (1935), *Brighton Rock* (1938), *The Power and the Glory* (1940), *The Heart of the Matter* (1948), *The End of the Affair* (1951), *The Quiet American* (1955), *Our Man in Havana* (1958), *The Honorary Consul* (1973); all reprinted by Vintage, formerly by Penguin. Travel books include *Journey without Maps* (1936) and *The Lawless Roads* (1939). Biography: Norman Sherry, *The Life of Graham Greene*, 2 vols. (1989, 1994). Critical studies: Cedric Watts, *A Preface to Greene* (1997); Harold Bloom (ed.), *Graham Greene* (1987). Reference: Neil Brennan and A. R. Redway, *A Bibliography of Graham Greene* (2004).

GREENWOOD, WALTER (1903–1974)

Lancashire novelist and playwright, known principally for *Love on the Dole* (1933; Vintage repr., 1993), adapted for the stage with Walter Gow (1934). Autobiography: *There Was a Time* (1967).

GURNEY, IVOR (1890–1937)

Poet and composer. Verse collections: *Severn and Somme* (1917) and *War's Embers* (1919), reprinted as one volume, ed. R. K. R. Thornton (*Carcanet, 1997); *Collected Poems*, ed. P. J. Kavanagh (Oxford University Press, 1982). *Collected Letters*, ed. R. K. R. Thornton (Carcanet, 1991). Biography: Michael Hurd, *The Ordeal of Ivor Gurney* (1978). Critical Study: John Lucas, *Ivor Gurney* (2001).

HALL, RADCLYFFE [pen name of Marguerite Radclyffe-Hall] (1880–1943)

Novelist. Principal novels: *The Unlit Lamp* (1924), *Adam's Breed* (1926), *The Well of Loneliness* (1928; legally suppressed until 1949); all reprinted in *Virago editions. Biography: Sally Cline, *Radclyffe Hall: A Woman Called John* (1997). Critical study: C. S. Franks, *Beyond the Well of Loneliness: The Fiction of Radclyffe Hall* (1982).

HARDY, THOMAS (1840–1928)

Born near Dorchester, this major Victorian novelist, author of *Far From the Madding Crowd* (1874) and other works, renounced novel-writing after the hostile reception given to *Jude the Obscure* (1896), turning to poetry and publishing his first verse collection, *Wessex Poems* (1898), followed by the verse drama *The Dynasts* (3 parts, 1904–8). His first wife, Emma Gifford, died in 1912, and he married Florence Dugdale in 1914. She appeared as the author of the two-volume *Life of Thomas Hardy* (1928–30), which was actually dictated by Hardy himself. His later volumes of verse, all of which include some poems of much earlier composition, are *Satires of Circumstance* (1914), *Selected Poems* (1916), *Moments of Vision* (1917), *Late Lyrics and Earlier* (1922), *Human Shows* (1925), and *Winter Words* (1928).

    The fullest scholarly edition of the poems is *The Complete Poetical Works*, ed. S. Hynes, 3 vols. (Oxford University Press, 1982–5). A good annotated selection is *Selected Poetry*, ed. S. Hynes (1994), in the Oxford

World's Classics series. For this period, the standard biography is Robert Gittings, *The Older Hardy* (1978). Michael Millgate's *Thomas Hardy* (1982) is also helpful. Critical articles are collected in R. G. Cox (ed.), *Thomas Hardy: The Critical Heritage* (1970) and in James Gibson and Trevor Johnson (eds.), *Thomas Hardy: Poems* (1979). Critical studies of the poetry include Donald Davie, *Thomas Hardy and English Poetry* (1973); Trevor Johnson, *A Critical Introduction to the Poems of Thomas Hardy* (1991); and Tom Paulin, *Thomas Hardy: The Poetry of Perception* (1975; rev. 1986). Reference: Richard L. Purdy, *Thomas Hardy: A Bibliographical Study* (2nd edn., 1968); Norman Page (ed.), *Oxford Reader's Companion to Hardy* (2000).

HOLTBY, WINIFRED (1898–1935)

Novelist; director of feminist journal *Time and Tide*. Principal works: *Anderby Wold* (1923), *The Land of Green Ginger* (1927), *Mandoa, Mandoa!* (1933), *South Riding* (1936); all reprinted by *Virago; *Virginia Woolf* (criticism, 1932; *Cassandra repr., 1978). Biography: Marion Shaw, *The Clear Stream* (1999).

HUEFFER, FORD MADOX. *See* FORD, FORD MADOX.

HUGHES, RICHARD (1900–1976)

Novelist, poet, playwright. Principal works: *Danger* (radio drama, 1924), *Plays* (1924), *Confessio Juvenis* (poems, 1926), *A Moment of Time* (stories, 1926), *A High Wind in Jamaica* (novel, 1929; *Penguin repr., 1949), *In Hazard* (novel, 1938), *The Fox in the Attic* (novel, 1961), *The Wooden Shepherdess* (novel, 1973). Biography: Richard Perceval Graves, *Richard Hughes* (1994). Critical study: Paul Morgan, *The Art of Richard Hughes* (1993).

HUXLEY, ALDOUS (1894–1963)

Born in Surrey to a family of intellectuals, he was educated at Eton, where he was afflicted with near blindness, but proceeded to Balliol College, Oxford, studying English. He worked as a farm-hand for Lady Ottoline Morrell, then on the staffs of the *Athenaeum* and other magazines. He married a Belgian refugee, Maria Nys, in 1919; they had one son. His early publications were poems and stories, but he achieved literary fame with his first novels, *Crome Yellow* (1921), *Antic Hay* (1923), and *Those Barren Leaves* (1925), following these with the more ambitious novels *Point Counter Point* (1928) and *Eyeless in Gaza* (1936) and the anti-utopian fantasy *Brave New World* (1932). In this period he published four collections of stories (from *Mortal Coils* (1922) to *Brief Candles* (1930)), three travel books (*Along the Road* (1925), *Jesting Pilate* (1926), and *Beyond the Mexique Bay* (1934)), and numerous essays. He lived mainly in Italy and the south of France, then in 1938 settled in California, where he wrote some screenplays for Hollywood and became involved in mysticism and mescalin, as reflected in *The Doors of Perception* (1954). He married Laura Archera, a psychotherapist, in 1956, and published his *Collected Short Stories* in 1957; the *Collected Essays* followed in 1958. The *Letters*, ed. Grover Smith (Chatto & Windus), appeared in 1969.

The major prose works have been reprinted in paperback as *Flamingo Modern Classics. Robert S. Baker and James Sex are editing a six-volume *Complete Essays* (Ivan R. Dee, 2001–). Meanwhile a selection of articles from the period 1930–6 has appeared as *The Hidden Huxley*, ed. D. Bradshaw (Faber, 1994). The standard biography is Nicholas Murray, *Aldous Huxley* (2002). Critical articles are collected in Donald Watt (ed.), *Aldous Huxley: The Critical Heritage* (1975); in Robert E. Kuehn (ed.), *Aldous Huxley: A Collection of Critical Essays* (1974); and in Jerome Meckier (ed.), *Critical Essays on Aldous Huxley* (1996). A valuable critical account of the early fiction is Robert S. Baker, *The Dark Historic Page: Social Satire and Historicism in the Novels of Aldous Huxley, 1921–1939* (1982). Other critical studies are C. S. Ferns, *Aldous Huxley, Novelist* (1980); Jerome Meckier, *Aldous Huxley: Satire and Structure* (1969); and George Woodcock, *Dawn and the Darkest Hour: A Study of Aldous Huxley* (1972). Reference: Claire John Eschelbach and Joyce Lee Shober, *Aldous Huxley: A Bibliography, 1916–1959* (1961).

ISHERWOOD, CHRISTOPHER (1904–1986)

Born in Cheshire, the son of a soldier, he befriended W. H. Auden at prep school in Surrey, and then studied at Repton School before reading history at Corpus Christi College, Cambridge. He worked as a private tutor, and published his first novel, *All the Conspirators* (1928), before spending four years (1929–33) in the homosexual world of Berlin, where he wrote *The Memorial* (1932). *Mr Norris Changes Trains* (1935) and *Goodbye to Berlin* (1939) are based on his Berlin experiences; the latter includes the story 'Sally Bowles', which was later filmed as *Cabaret* (1972). He collaborated with Auden on three plays for the Group Theatre: *The Dog beneath the Skin* (1935), *The Ascent of F6* (1936), and *On the Frontier* (1938). His autobiography, *Lions and Shadows*, appeared in 1938, when he travelled with Auden to China, writing *Journey to a War* (1939) with him, and then to the USA, where he settled in California, doing some screenplays and becoming the disciple of an Indian guru. The novel *Prater Violet* appeared in 1945. He spent his later life with the painter Don Bachardy. The later novels *The World in the Evening* (1954), *Down There on a Visit* (1962), and *A Single Man* (1964) are openly concerned with homosexuality, as is the memoir *Christopher and His Kind* (1977).

All the Conspirators, *The Memorial*, *Goodbye to Berlin*, *Mr Norris Changes Trains*, and *Lions and Shadows* have been variously reprinted, most recently as *Minerva paperbacks. The plays have been reprinted by Faber, and are collected in W. H. Auden and Christopher Isherwood, *Plays, and Other Dramatic Writings by W. H. Auden 1928–1938*, ed. E. Mendelson (Princeton/Faber, 1988). The standard biography is Brian Finney, *Christopher Isherwood* (1979), and an authorized life by Peter Parker is awaited; another biographical work is Norman Page, *Auden and Isherwood: The Berlin Years* (1998). Modern critical studies include Paul Piazza, *Christopher Isherwood: Myth and Anti-Myth* (1978); Lisa M. Schwerdt, *Isherwood's Fiction: The Self and Technique* (1989); and Stephen Wade, *Christopher Isherwood* (1991). Reference: S. Westby and C. M. Brown, *Christopher Isherwood: A Bibliography 1927–1967* (1968); R. W. Funk, *Christopher Isherwood: A Reference Guide* (1979).

JOYCE, JAMES (1882–1941)

He was born in Dublin, the son of a rates collector, and was schooled first at Clongowes Wood College, Co. Kildare, then at Belvedere College, Dublin, where he abandoned his Roman Catholic faith. He studied modern languages at University College, Dublin, and went to Paris, supposedly as a medical student, in 1902. Returning to Dublin, he met Nora Barnacle in 1904, and took her to live with him in Trieste (1905–15), where they had two children, and Joyce taught English in the Berlitz school. His early poems, *Chamber Music*, appeared in 1907, followed by the stories in *Dubliners* (1914). His first novel, *A Portrait of the Artist as a Young Man*, serialized in 1914–15, appeared as a book in 1916. In Zurich, where he lived during most of the Great War, and later in Paris, where he settled in 1920, he worked on *Ulysses*, which, after some chapters were serialized in 1919–20, was published in a limited edition in Paris in 1922, and could not be published in Britain or the USA for some years. Struggling against failing eyesight, Joyce issued portions of a 'Work in Progress' which was published as *Finnegans Wake* in 1939. Minor works include a play, *Exiles* (1918), and *Pomes Penyeach* (verse, 1927). Joyce and Nora, whom he had eventually married in 1931, returned in 1939 to Zurich, where he died. *The Letters*, ed. S. Gilbert and R. Ellmann, 3 vols. (Viking, 1957–66) omits some letters that are restored in the *Selected Letters*, ed. R. Ellmann (Faber, 1975).

The Oxford World's Classics series provides annotated editions of *Dubliners*, *A Portrait*, and *Ulysses*, all ed. Jeri Johnson; and of *Occasional, Critical, and Political Writing*, ed. K. Barry (2000). Penguin publish a repr. of *Finnegans Wake*, and annotated editions of *Dubliners*, *A Portrait of the Artist*, and *Ulysses*. The definitive biography is Richard Ellmann, *James Joyce* (1959; rev. 1982). Critical responses are collected in Robert H. Deming (ed.), *James Joyce: The Critical Heritage*, 2 vols. (1970). General introductions include Anthony Burgess, *Here Comes Everybody: An Introduction to James Joyce for the Ordinary Reader* (1965; repr. as *Re Joyce*, 1968); Derek Attridge (ed.), *The Cambridge Companion to James Joyce* (1990); Sydney Bolt, *A Preface to Joyce* (1981); and Patrick Parrinder, *James Joyce* (1984). Detailed guides to *Ulysses* are provided by Harry Blamires, *The New Bloomsday Book* (1988); Richard Ellmann, *Ulysses on the Liffey* (1972); and Karen Lawrence, *The Odyssey of Style in 'Ulysses'* (1981). Guides to *Finnegans Wake* include Roland McHugh, *Annotations to 'Finnegans Wake'* (1980), and Danis Rose and John O'Hanlon, *Understanding 'Finnegans Wake'* (1982). Notable modern critical studies of Joyce include Bernard Benstock, *James Joyce* (1985); Richard Brown, *James Joyce and Sexuality* (1985); Cheryl Herr, *Joyce's Anatomy of Culture* (1986); Hugh Kenner, *Dublin's Joyce* (1956); Vicki Mahaffey, *Reauthorizing Joyce* (1988); Charles K. Peake, *James Joyce: The Citizen and the Artist* (1977); Jean-Michel Rabaté, *James Joyce, Authorized Reader* (1981); and John Paul Riquelme, *Teller and Tale in Joyce's Fiction* (1983). Reference: John J. Slocum and Herbert Cahoon, *A Bibliography of James Joyce, 1882–1941* (1953); Thomas Jackson Rice, *James Joyce: A Guide to Research* (1982).

KAYE-SMITH, SHEILA (1887–1956)

Novelist of Sussex. Principal works: *Sussex Gorse* (1916), *Little England* (1918), *Tamarisk Town* (1919), *Green Apple Harvest* (1920), *Joanna Godden* (1921; Virago repr., 1983), *Susan Spray* (1931; Virago repr., 1983). Autobiography: *Three Ways Home* (1937). Biography: Dorothea Walker, *Sheila Kaye-Smith* (1980).

KIPLING, RUDYARD (1865–1936)

Poet, short-story writer, and novelist, born in Bombay. He earned his early reputation with *Barrack-Room Ballads* (1892), *Plain Tales from the Hills* (1888), the school story *Stalky & Co.* (1899), and *The Jungle Book* (for children, 1894), before publishing his best-known novel *Kim* (1901). Principal publications after 1910 are *The Years Between* (verse, 1919); the story collections *A Diversity of Creatures* (1917), *Debits and Credits* (1926), and *Limits and Renewals* (1932); and the reticent autobiography *Something of Myself* (1937). He won the Nobel Prize for Literature in 1907. A thirty-five-volume *Complete Works* appeared in 1937–9; followed more recently by *The Letters*, ed. T. Pinney, 6 vols. (Macmillan, 1990–2004), have appeared so far.

Penguin publish along with *Kim* and the children's books the *Selected Stories* in two volumes, and an annotated *Selected Poems*, ed. P. Keating (2001). The Oxford World's Classics series has several of Kipling's works, including a selected *War Stories and Poems*, ed. A. Rutherford (1990). Daniel Karlin's well-annotated selection of poems and stories, *Rudyard Kipling* (1999) in the Oxford Authors series, is undeservedly out of print. The standard biography is now Andrew Lycett, *Rudyard Kipling* (2000); David Gilmour's *The Long Recessional* (2002) approaches the life in the context of the British Empire. Early critical responses are collected in R. L. Green (ed.), *Kipling: The Critical Heritage* (1971). Critical studies include Sandra Kemp, *Kipling's Hidden Narratives* (1988), and Peter Keating, *Kipling the Poet* (1994). Reference: J. M. Stewart, *Rudyard Kipling: A Bibliographical Catalogue* (1959); Norman Page, *A Kipling Companion* (1984).

LAWRENCE, DAVID HERBERT (1885–1930)

He was born in Eastwood, Nottinghamshire, the son of a coal miner and of a former schoolteacher. After studying at Nottingham High School, he worked as clerk, then as pupil-teacher, training at University College, Nottingham before teaching in Croydon from 1908 to 1911. He published poems and stories in the *English Review*, then his first novel, *The White Peacock* (1911). In 1912 he eloped with Frieda (née von Richthofen), the wife of his former tutor Ernest Weekley, marrying her in 1914. He published *Love Poems* (1913), *Sons and Lovers* (1913), and his first collection of stories, *The Prussian Officer* (1914), after which he wrote the major novels *The Rainbow* (1915) and *Women in Love* (1920). During the Great War, he and Frieda lived for a while in Cornwall, under suspicion of being

German spies; and he published *Twilight in Italy* (1916). In 1919, they abandoned England, living in Italy, Ceylon, Australia, the USA, Mexico, and Italy again. From this period come the novels *Aaron's Rod* (1922), *Kangaroo* (1923), and *The Plumed Serpent* (1926), and several further volumes of poems, essays, stories, and travel-writings. His last novel, *Lady Chatterley's Lover* (1928) could not be published in its full form in Britain until 1960. He died of tuberculosis in Vence, France. An important body of uncollected essays appeared posthumously as *Phoenix*, ed. E. D. McDonald (Heinemann, 1936); *Phoenix II*, ed. W. Roberts and H. T. Moore (Heinemann, 1968); and *A Selection from Phoenix*, ed. A. A. H. Inglis (Penguin, 1971). *The Letters* have been edited and fully annotated in 8 volumes (Cambridge University Press, 1979–2001) by James T. Boulton and various collaborators.

Modern annotated editions of Lawrence's works are now plentiful. The Oxford World's Classics series provides annotated editions of *Sons and Lovers*, ed. D. Trotter; *The Rainbow*, ed. K. Flint (1998); *Women in Love*, ed. D. Bradshaw (1998); and *The Prussian Officer*, along with a *Selected Critical Writings*, ed. M. Herbert (1998). The scholarly Cambridge Edition of his works, which includes unpublished works such as *Mr Noon* (1984) and *Paul Morel* (2003), has been the basis of the more recent Penguin editions, including *Lady Chatterley's Lover*, ed. M. Squires (1994); *Kangaroo*, ed. B. Steele (1997); and *Twilight in Italy and Other Essays*, ed. P. Eggert (1997). Penguin have also published *The Complete Short Novels*, eds. K. Sagar and M. Partridge (1982), and *The Complete Poems*, eds. V. de Sola Pinto and F. W. Roberts (1964). Annotated selections of the short stories have been published by Penguin and Everyman. Of the many biographies of Lawrence, the fullest is the collaborative Cambridge trilogy comprising John Worthen's *D. H. Lawrence: The Early Years, 1885–1912* (1991), Mark Kinkead-Weekes's *D. H. Lawrence: Triumph to Exile, 1912–22* (1996), and David Ellis's *D. H. Lawrence: Dying Game, 1922–1930* (1998). A shorter account is John Worthen, *D. H. Lawrence: A Literary Life* (1989). Selections from the extensive critical literature on Lawrence are available in H. Coombes (ed.), *D. H. Lawrence: A Critical Anthology* (1973) and R. P. Draper (ed.), *D. H. Lawrence: The Critical Heritage* (1979); more recent collaborative surveys are Peter Widdowson (ed.), *D. H. Lawrence* (1992) and Anne Fernihough (ed.), *The Cambridge Companion to D. H. Lawrence* (2001). Valuable introductory works are Gāmini Salgādo, *A Preface to Lawrence* (1983) and Fiona Becket, *The Complete Critical Guide to D. H. Lawrence* (2002). Brief general accounts include Frank Kermode, *Lawrence* (1983); Tony Pinkney, *D. H. Lawrence* (1990); and Linda Ruth

Williams, *D. H. Lawrence* (1997). Important specialist studies include Michael Black, *D. H. Lawrence: The Early Fiction* (1986); Colin Clarke, *River of Dissolution: D. H. Lawrence and English Romanticism* (1969); Paul Delaney, *D. H. Lawrence's Nightmare: The Writer and His Circle in the Years of the Great War* (1979); Anne Fernihough, *D. H. Lawrence: Aesthetics and Ideology* (1993); Sandra M. Gilbert, *Acts of Attention: The Poems of D. H. Lawrence* (1972); and Anne Smith (ed.), *D. H. Lawrence and Women* (1989). Reference: Warren Roberts and Paul Poplawski, *A Bibliography of D. H. Lawrence* (3rd edn., 2001); Paul Poplawski, *D. H. Lawrence: A Reference Companion* (1996).

LAWRENCE, THOMAS EDWARD (1888–1935)

Archaeologist, adventurer, autobiographer; leader of Arab Revolt against Turkish occupation (1916–18), achieving celebrity as 'Lawrence of Arabia'. *Seven Pillars of Wisdom* (privately published, 1926; abridged as *Revolt in the Desert*, 1927; standard edn., 1935). Served anonymously in RAF, the basis of *The Mint* (1936); killed in a motorcycle crash. *Seven Pillars* and *The Mint* have been reprinted in *Penguin editions, *Revolt in the Desert* as a Century paperback. A fuller version of *Seven Pillars* based on a 1922 draft was published by Castle Hill in 1997. Biography: Michael Asher, *Lawrence: The Uncrowned King of Arabia* (1998). Critical study: Jeffrey Meyers, *The Wounded Spirit: A Study of 'Seven Pillars of Wisdom'* (1973; rev. 1989).

LEAVIS, FRANK RAYMOND (1895–1978)

Critic; co-editor of *Scrutiny* (1932-53). Principal works: *New Bearings in English Poetry* (1932), *Revaluation* (1936), *The Great Tradition* (1948), *The Common Pursuit* (essays, 1952), *D. H. Lawrence, Novelist* (1955), *Dickens the Novelist* (with Q. D. Leavis, 1970); all reprinted in *Penguin editions. Biography: Ian MacKillop, *F. R. Leavis: A Life in Criticism* (1995). Critical study: Anne Samson, *F. R. Leavis* (1992).

LEHMANN, ROSAMOND (1901–1990)

Novelist. Principal works: *Dusty Answer* (1927; Penguin repr., 1981), *A Note in Music* (1930; Virago repr., 1982), *Invitation to the Waltz* (1932; Virago repr., 1981), *The Weather in the Streets* (1936; Virago repr., 1981), *The Ballad and the Source* (1944), *The Gipsy's Baby* (stories, 1946), *The Echoing Grove* (1953). Autobiography: *The Swan in the Evening* (1967;

*Virago repr., 1983). Biography: Selina Hastings, *Rosamond Lehmann* (2002). Critical study: Judy Simons, *Rosamond Lehmann* (1992).

LEWIS, C. DAY. *See* DAY-LEWIS, CECIL.

LEWIS, WYNDHAM (1882–1957)

Artist, critic, novelist. Principal fictional works: *Tarr* (1918; rev. 1928; *Penguin repr. 1989), *The Wild Body* (stories, 1927; Penguin repr., 2004), *The Childermass* (1928), *The Apes of God* (1930; *Penguin repr., 1965), *The Revenge for Love* (1937; Penguin repr., 1983). Non-fiction: *Time and Western Man* (1928), *Men without Art* (1934; *Black Sparrow edition, ed. S. Cooney, 1987), *Blasting and Bombardiering* (memoir, 1937). Major works reprinted by Black Sparrow Press, some others by Calder. Modern selection: *The Essential Wyndham Lewis*, ed. J. Symons (1989). Biography: Paul O'Keeffe, *Some Kind of Genius* (2000). Reference: Bradford Morrow and Bernard Lafourcade, *A Bibliography of the Writings of Wyndham Lewis* (1978).

MACAULAY, ROSE (1881–1958)

Novelist, critic, travel writer. Principal novels: *The Lee Shore* (1912), *Non-Combatants and Others* (1916; Methuen repr., 1986), *Potterism* (1920), *Dangerous Ages* (1921), *Told by an Idiot* (1923; Virago repr., 1983), *Crewe Train* (1926; Methuen repr., 1985), *Keeping Up Appearances* (1928), *They Were Defeated* (1932; *Oxford repr., 1981), *The Towers of Trebizond* (1956). Other works: *The Writings of E. M. Forster* (1938), *Fabled Shore* (travel book, 1949). Biography: Sarah LeFanu, *Rose Macaulay* (2003). Critical study: Alice Crawford, *Paradise Pursued: The Novels of Rose Macaulay* (1995).

MACKENZIE, COMPTON (1883–1972)

English—although later would-be-Scottish—novelist. Principal works: *The Passionate Elopement* (1911), *Carnival* (1912), *Sinister Street* (1913–14; Penguin repr., 1960), *Sylvia Scarlett* (1919), *Vestal Fire* (1927; Hogarth repr., 1986), *Extraordinary Women* (1928; Hogarth repr., 1986), *The Four Winds of Love*, 6 vols. (1937–45), *The Monarch of the Glen* (1941), *Whisky Galore* (1947). Autobiography: *My Life and Times*, 10 vols. (1963–71). Biography: Andro Linklater, *Compton Mackenzie* (1987).

Reference: David Thomas and Joyce Thomas, *Compton Mackenzie: A Bibliography* (1986).

MacNeice, Louis (1907–63)

He was born in Belfast, the son of a Protestant clergyman, and educated at Marlborough and then Merton College, Oxford, where he studied classics and published his first volume of poems, *Blind Fireworks* (1929). He was a lecturer in classics at Birmingham and London Universities during the Thirties. In this decade, his verse collections included *Poems* (1937), *The Earth Compels* (1938), and *Autumn Journal* (1939). He also collaborated with Auden in *Letters from Iceland* (1937), and wrote an acclaimed translation, *The Agamemnon of Aeschylus* (1936). After a year's teaching at Cornell University, New York, he returned to London, joining the features department of the BBC in 1941. In this new career as radio writer and producer, he wrote numerous radio plays, notably *The Dark Tower* (1947), and published several more volumes of verse, culminating in the posthumous *The Burning Perch* (1963); a further posthumous work is the autobiography, *The Strings Are False* (1965).

The standard text of the poems is *Collected Poems*, ed. E. R. Dodds (Faber, 1966). Prose works have been edited by Alan Heuser as *Selected Prose* (1990) and *Selected Literary Criticism* (1987), both published by Oxford University Press. The definitive biography is Jon Stallworthy, *Louis MacNeice* (1995). Critical studies include Terence Brown, *Louis MacNeice: Sceptical Vision* (1975); Edna Longley, *Louis MacNeice* (1988); W. T. MacKinnon, *Apollo's Blended Dream* (1971); Peter McDonald, *Louis MacNeice: The Poet in His Context* (1991); Robyn Marsack, *The Cave of Making* (1982); and D. B. Moore, *The Poetry of Louis MacNeice* (1972). Reference: C. M. Armitage and Neil Clark, *A Bibliography of the Works of Louis MacNeice* (2nd edn., 1974).

Mansfield, Katherine [pseudonym of Kathleen Mansfield Beauchamp] (1888–1923)

The daughter of a banker, she was born in Wellington, New Zealand, growing up in rural Karori. After attending Wellington Girls' High School, she was a music student at Queen's College, London (1903–6). She returned to London in 1908, living on a parental allowance. In 1909 she married George Bowden, a singing teacher, but left him the next day; pregnant by another man, she went to a Bavarian spa where she miscarried. Her first collection of stories was *In a German Pension* (1911). In

1911 she met John Middleton Murry, who became her lover and eventually (1918) husband; he published some of her works in magazines he edited. Her brother was killed in the War in 1915, and by 1917 Mansfield was suffering from tuberculosis. She spent most of her remaining life in France and Switzerland. *Bliss and Other Stories* (1920) established her reputation, and was followed by *The Garden Party and Other Stories* (1922). She died, aged 34, while undergoing a doubtful 'cure' at the Gurdjieff Institute in Fontainebleau. Murry edited her *Poems* (1923) and two posthumous collections of short stories, *The Dove's Nest* (1923) and *Something Childish* (1924), followed by editions of her *Letters* (1928), *Journal* (1927), reviews (as *Novels and Novelists* (Cape, 1930)), and *The Collected Stories* (1945; Penguin repr., 1981).

The principal scholarly edition is *The Stories*, ed. A. Alpers (Oxford University Press, 1984). Oxford World's Classics publish an annotated *Selected Stories*, ed. A. Smith (2002). Penguin publish annotated editions of some of the short-story collections including *The Garden Party*, ed. L. Sage (1997), and *In a German Pension*, ed. A. Fernihough (1999), along with a selected *Letters and Journals*, ed. C. K. Stead (1977). Modern editions of the other writings are *The Critical Writings*, ed. C. Hanson (Macmillan, 1987); *Poems*, ed. V. O'Sullivan (Oxford University Press, 1988); *The Katherine Mansfield Notebooks*, ed. M. Scott (Lincoln University Press, 1997); and *The Collected Letters*, ed. V. O'Sullivan and M. Scott, 4 vols. (Oxford University Press, 1984–96). The standard biography is Antony Alpers, *The Life of Katherine Mansfield* (1980). The writing career is covered by Angela Smith, *Katherine Mansfield* (2000). Critical articles are gathered in Jan Pilditch (ed.), *The Critical Response to Katherine Mansfield* (1996). Critical studies include Cherry Hankin, *Katherine Mansfield and Her Confessional Stories* (1983); Pamela Dunbar, *Radical Mansfield* (1997); Sydney Janet Kaplan, *Katherine Mansfield and the Origins of Modernist Fiction* (1991); and Heather Murray, *Double Lives: Women in the Stories of Katherine Mansfield* (1990). Reference: B. J. Kirkpatrick, *A Bibliography of Katherine Mansfield* (1989).

MASEFIELD, JOHN (1878–1967)

Poet, playwright and children's writer. Principal works: *Salt Water Ballads* (1902), *The Tragedy of Nan* (drama, 1908), *The Everlasting Mercy* (1911), *Dauber* (1913), *Reynard the Fox* (1919), *Collected Poems* (Heinemann, 1923), *The Midnight Folk* (children's fiction, 1927). Poet Laureate, 1930–67. Autobiographies: *So Long to Learn* (1952), *Grace before Ploughing* (1966). Modern selections: *Sea Poems* (Heinemann 1978), *Selected*

Poems (Carcanet, 1984). Biography: Constance Babington Smith, *John Masefield: A Life* (1978). Critical study: Paul Binding, *An Endless Quiet Valley* (1998).

MAUGHAM, WILLIAM SOMERSET (1874–1965)

The son of a lawyer, he was born and raised in Paris. Orphaned at the age of 10, he was sent to the King's School, Canterbury. He studied at Heidelberg, then as a medical student at St Thomas's Hospital, London, but became a full-time writer in 1897, having inherited money and published his first novel, *Liza of Lambeth* (1897). In the years 1907–8 he suddenly became a popular dramatist, with several successful West End plays. During the Great War, in which he was an ambulance driver and then a spy, he fathered a child by Mrs Syrie Wellcome, whom he married in 1917, and met his lover Gerald Haxton, travelling with him to Tahiti. His first major novels were *Of Human Bondage* (1915) and *The Moon and Sixpence* (1919). Among his post-war plays, before he abandoned the theatre in 1933, were *Home and Beauty* (1919), *The Circle* (1921), *Our Betters* (1923), and *The Constant Wife* (1927). After extensive travels in the Pacific, and the dissolution of his marriage, he settled with Haxton in a luxurious villa near Monte Carlo in 1928, writing *Cakes and Ale* (1930) and numerous short stories, culminating in *The Complete Short Stories*, 3 vols. (1951). His last major novel, *The Razor's Edge* (1944), appeared in the year of Haxton's death. Having spent the Second World War in South Carolina, he returned to the French Riviera with his new companion, Alan Searle. His memoir, *Looking Back*, appeared in 1962. Uncollected writings appeared as *A Traveller in Romance*, ed. J. Whitehead (Anthony Blond, 1984).

The short fiction was reprinted by Pan in four volumes (1975–6) as *The Collected Short Stories*; these volumes, with the major novels and plays, *Ashenden*, and several non-fiction works, have been reprinted as Mandarin paperbacks; *The Summing Up* has been reprinted by Penguin. Nine of the plays are available in *Plays: One* and *Plays: Two* in the *Methuen World's Classics series; others may be found in *Collected Plays*, 3 vols. (Heinemann, 1952). The standard biography is Ted Morgan, *Somerset Maugham* (1980). Critical articles are collected in Anthony Curtis and John Whitehead (eds.), *W. Somerset Maugham: The Critical Heritage* (1987). Useful critical surveys are John Whitehead, *Maugham: A Reappraisal* (1987); Anthony Curtis, *The Pattern of Maugham* (1974); and Philip Holden, *Orienting Masculinity, Orienting Nation: W. Somerset*

Maugham's Exotic Fiction (1996). Reference: Raymond Toole Stott, *A Bibliography of the Works of W. Somerset Maugham* (1973).

MAYOR, FLORA MACDONALD (1872–1932)

Novelist. Principal works: *The Third Miss Symons* (1913; Virago repr., 1980), *The Rector's Daughter* (1924; Penguin repr., 1973), *The Squire's Daughter* (1929), *The Room Opposite* (stories, 1935). Biography: Sybil Oldfield, *Spinsters of This Parish* (1984).

MEW, CHARLOTTE (1869–1928)

Poet. Collections: *The Farmer's Bride* (1916), *The Rambling Sailor* (1929); *Complete Poems*, ed. J. Newton (Penguin, 2000). Biography: Penelope Fitzgerald, *Charlotte Mew and Her Friends* (1984).

MILNE, ALAN ALEXANDER (1882–1956)

Playwright, novelist, humorist, children's writer. Principal plays: *Mr Pim Passes By* (1919), *The Dover Road* (1921), *To Have the Honour* (1924). Novels include *The Red House Mystery* (1922). Children's books: *When We Were Very Young* (verse, 1924), *Winnie-the-Pooh* (1926), *Now We Are Six* (verse, 1927), *The House at Pooh Corner* (1928). Biography: Ann Thwaite, *A. A. Milne* (1990).

MITCHISON, NAOMI [née Haldane] (1897–1999)

Novelist. Principal works: *The Conquered* (1923), *Cloud Cuckoo Land* (1925), *Greek Stories* (1928), *The Corn King and the Spring Queen* (1931; Virago repr., 1983), *The Blood of the Martyrs* (1939), *The Bull Calves* (1947). Memoirs: *All Change Here* (1975), *You May Well Ask* (1979). Biography: Jill Benton, *Naomi Mitchison* (1990).

MOTTRAM, RALPH HALE (1883–1971)

Novelist, best known for *The Spanish Farm* (1924), *Sixty-Four, Ninety-Four!* (1925), and *The Crime at Vanderlynden's* (1926), collected as *The Spanish Farm Trilogy 1914–1918* (1927; Penguin repr., 1979); also published several volumes of short stories, and some business histories.

Murry, John Middleton (1889–1957)

Critic; editor of the *Athenaeum* (1919–21) and *Adelphi* (1923–30). Principal works: *The Problem of Style* (1922), *Keats and Shakespeare* (1925), *Son of Woman* (1931). Married Katherine Mansfield (1918) and edited her posthumous works. Biography: F. A. Lea, *The Life of John Middleton Murry* (1959). Reference: George P. Lilley, *A Bibliography of John Middleton Murry 1889–1957* (1974).

Orwell, George [pseudonym of Eric Blair] (1903–50)

Born in Bengal, where his father was a civil servant, he went to prep school in Eastbourne, then to Eton. He worked in Burma as a police officer (1922–7), then resigned and spent two years doing menial jobs in Paris before settling in England as a schoolteacher and as a bookseller. His book of reportage, *Down and Out in Paris and London* (1933), was followed by the novels *Burmese Days* (1934), *A Clergyman's Daughter* (1935), and *Keep the Aspidistra Flying* (1936). In 1936 he married Eileen O'Shaughnessy; they lived in Hertfordshire as market gardeners, and adopted a son. *The Road to Wigan Pier* (1937), an account of poverty in northern England, was published while Orwell served in a Marxist militia in the Spanish Civil War, in which he was shot through the throat; *Homage to Catalonia* (1938) is an account of this phase. During the War he published two collections of his essays, served in the Home Guard, worked in the BBC's Eastern Service, and became literary editor of the left-wing *Tribune* newspaper. His anti-Soviet fable *Animal Farm* appeared in 1945, when his wife died. He wrote *Nineteen Eighty-Four* (1949) on the Scottish island of Jura while suffering from tuberculosis. He married Sonia Brownell in a London hospital in 1949.

The definitive scholarly edition is *The Complete Works*, ed. Peter Davison, 20 vols. (Secker and Warburg, 1986–98). The post–1988 *Penguin editions of the novels and non-fiction books incorporate corrections derived from Davison's editions. Penguin also published the often-cited four-volume *Collected Essays, Journalism and Letters*, ed. S. Orwell and I. Angus (1968). The best of several biographies are Bernard Crick, *George Orwell* (1980; rev. 1992) and D. J. Taylor, *Orwell* (2003). Peter Davison's *George Orwell: A Literary Life* (1996) covers the writing career. Early critical responses are collected in Jeffrey Meyers (ed.), *George Orwell: The Critical Heritage* (1975). A useful introduction is David Wykes, *A Preface to Orwell* (1987). Critical studies include Lynette Hunter, *George Orwell: The Search for a Voice* (1984); R. A. Lee, *Orwell's*

Fiction (1969); and Raymond Williams, *Orwell* (1971). Reference: Gillian Fenwick, *George Orwell: A Bibliography* (1998).

OWEN, WILFRED (1893–1918)

The son of a railway clerk, he was born in Oswestry, Shropshire, and studied at Shrewsbury Technical School. Having failed to gain university scholarships, he taught English in Bordeaux from 1913 until 1915, when he volunteered for the army, serving with the Manchester Regiment in 1916. Suffering from shell shock sustained on the Somme front, he recuperated in 1917 at Craiglockhart Hospital near Edinburgh, where he published three poems in the hospital magazine, and met Siegfried Sassoon, who encouraged his work. He returned to the front in August 1918, and was killed on 4 November, only a week before the Armistice. Several of his poems appeared in Edith Sitwell's *Wheels* anthology the next year. Successively expanded collections of his *Poems* were edited by Sassoon (1920), Edmund Blunden (1931), and C. Day-Lewis (1963). *The Collected Letters*, ed. H. Owen and J. Bell (Oxford University Press, 1967).

The best student edition is *The Poems, ed. J. Stallworthy (Chatto & Windus, 1985), which is derived from the same editor's *The Complete Poems and Fragments*, 2 vols. (1983). The standard biography is Dominic Hibberd, *Wilfred Owen* (2002). Critical studies include Dominic Hibberd, *Owen the Poet* (1986); Douglas Kerr, *Wilfred Owen's Voices* (1993); and D. S. R. Welland, *Wilfred Owen: A Critical Study* (1960; rev. 1978).

POUND, EZRA (1885–1972)

American poet resident in London, 1908-20; later in Italy. Early verse collections include *Ripostes* (1912), *Lustra* (1916), and *Hugh Selwyn Mauberley* (1920). Posthumous collections: *The Cantos* (1975); **Selected Poems 1908–1959* (Faber, 1975); **Literary Essays of Ezra Pound*, ed. T. S. Eliot (Faber, 1954); *Selected Prose 1909–1965*, ed. W. Cookson (Faber, 1973). Biography: Humphrey Carpenter, *A Serious Character: The Life of Ezra Pound* (1988). Critical introductions: Peter Brooker, *A Student's Guide to Ezra Pound* (1979); Peter Wilson, *A Preface to Ezra Pound* (1997). Reference: Donald Gallup, *Ezra Pound: A Bibliography* (2nd edn., 1983).

POWYS, JOHN COWPER (1872–1963)

Novelist. Principal works: *Wolf Solent* (1929; Penguin repr., 1961), *A Glastonbury Romance* (1932; *Picador repr., 1975), *Weymouth Sands* (1934; Picador repr., 1980); *Autobiography* (1934; Picador repr., 1982), *Owen Glendower* (1940). Biography: Richard Perceval Graves, *The Brothers Powys* (1983). Critical study: Glen Cavaliero, *John Cowper Powys, Novelist* (1973). Reference: Dante Thomas, *A Bibliography of the Writings of John Cowper Powys, 1872–1963* (1975).

PRIESTLEY, JOHN BOYNTON (1894–1984)

The son of a schoolteacher, he was born in Bradford, where he attended Belle Vue Grammar School and worked as a clerk. After serving in the army in the Great War, he studied English and history at Trinity Hall, Cambridge, and then settled in London as a literary journalist. He published several volumes of essays before achieving success with his third and fourth novels, *The Good Companions* (1929) and *Angel Pavement* (1930). In the 1930s he established himself as a playwright with comedies including *When We Are Married* (1938) and plays about time, like *Dangerous Corner* (1932) and *Time and the Conways* (1937); he wrote more than forty plays, of which *An Inspector Calls* (1946) is the best known. Among his non-fiction works are *English Journey* (1934) and *Literature and Western Man* (1960). He achieved national celebrity during the Second World War with his patriotic radio talks, and was later a co-founder of the Campaign for Nuclear Disarmament.

The Good Companions* and *Angel Pavement* have been reprinted as Mandarin paperbacks. **Time and the Conways and Other Plays* and **English Journey* have appeared in Penguin editions. The authorized biography is Vincent Brome, *J. B. Priestley* (1988). Critical studies include Gareth L. Evans, *J. B. Priestley: The Dramatist* (1964) and Holger Klein, *J. B. Priestley's Plays* (1988). Reference: A. E. Day, *J. B. Priestley: An Annotated Bibliography* (1980).

RANSOME, ARTHUR (1884–1967)

Journalist, travel writer, and children's writer, best known for the children's book *Swallows and Amazons* (1930) and its eleven sequels including *Peter Duck* (1932) and *Pigeon Post* (1936), all now reprinted as Red Fox Classics; also wrote *Six Weeks in Russia* (1919), critical studies of Poe and Wilde, and books about fishing. Biography: Hugh Brogan, *The Life of Arthur Ransome* (1984). Critical study: Peter Hunt, *Arthur Ransome* (1991).

READ, HERBERT (1893–1968)

Poet and critic. Verse: *Songs of Chaos* (1915), *The End of a War* (1933), *Collected Poems* (1966). Prose works include *In Retreat* (war memoir, 1925), *Reason and Romanticism* (1926), *English Prose Style* (1928), *Wordsworth* (1930), *The Meaning of Art* (1931), *Form in Modern Poetry* (1932), *Art Now* (1934), *The Green Child* (fiction, 1935; Penguin repr., 1969), *In Defence of Shelley* (1936), *Selected Writings*, ed. A. Tate (Faber, 1963). Biography: James King, *The Last Modern* (1990). Critical studies: David Goodway (ed.), *Herbert Read Reassessed* (1988).

RHYS, JEAN [pseudonym of Ella Gwendolen Rees Williams] (1890–1979)

Novelist, born in Dominica. Principal works: *Postures* (1928; US title *Quartet*); *After Leaving Mr Mackenzie* (1930); *Voyage in the Dark* (1934); *Good Morning, Midnight* (1939); *Wide Sargasso Sea* (1966); *Smile, Please* (memoir, 1979). Novels all reprinted by *Penguin, along with *Smile, Please*, and the *Letters, 1931–1966*, ed. F. Wyndham and D. Melly (1985). Biography: Carole Angier, *Jean Rhys: Life and Work* (1990). Critical introduction: Helen Carr, *Jean Rhys* (1996). Reference: Elgin W. Mellown, *Jean Rhys: A Descriptive and Annotated Bibliography of Works and Criticism* (1984).

RICHARDSON, DOROTHY (1873–1957)

She was born in Abingdon, near Oxford, to wealthy parents, and was brought up and educated in Worthing and London. From the age of 17, she was employed as a teacher and governess, then, after her mother's suicide in 1895, as a dental secretary in Harley Street. She then turned to journalism as a livelihood. In 1915 she published *Pointed Roofs*, the first instalment of her long-running autobiographical novel *Pilgrimage*. She married Alan Odle, an artist, in 1917, and lived with him in Cornwall and London. Five further volumes of the *Pilgrimage* sequence appeared up to 1921, and another six appeared more slowly over the next seventeen years, incorporated into a collected edition in 1938; an additional volume, *March Moonlight*, appeared posthumously in 1967. Her stories and sketches were collected as *Journey to Paradise* (1989).

Pilgrimage was reprinted in four volumes by *Virago in 1979. The standard biography is Gloria G. Fromm, *Dorothy Richardson* (1977), which includes a bibliography. The principal critical studies are Kristin Bluemel, *Experimenting on the Borders of Modernism: Dorothy Richardson's 'Pilgrimage'* (1997); Gillian Hanscombe, *The Art of Life* (1982); Elisabeth Bronfen, *Dorothy Richardson's Art of Memory* (1999); and Jean Radford, *Dorothy Richardson* (1991). Carol Watts's *Dorothy Richardson* (1995) offers an introductory account.

RICKWORD, EDGELL (1898–1982)

Poet and critic; co-editor of *The Calendar of Modern Letters* (1925–7) and editor of *Left Review* (1935–7). Verse: *Behind the Eyes* (1921); *Invocation to Angels* (1928); *Twittingpan & Some Others* (1931); *Collected Poems*, ed. C. Hobday (1991). Critical essays edited by A. Young as *Essays & Opinions 1921–1931* (Carcanet, 1974) and *Literature in Society* (Carcanet, 1978). Biography: Charles Hobday, *Edgell Rickword* (1989).

ROSENBERG, ISAAC (1890–1918)

Poet and painter. Collections: *Night and Day* (1912), *Youth* (1915), *Moses* (verse drama, 1916); **The Collected Works*, ed. Ian Parsons (Chatto & Windus, 1979). Biography: Joseph Cohen, *Journey to the Trenches* (1975).

SACKVILLE-WEST, VITA [Victoria] (1892–1962)

Poet, novelist, and writer on travel and gardening. Verse: *Orchard and Vineyard* (1921), *The Land* (1926), *King's Daughter* (1929), *Sissinghurst* (1931), *Collected Poems* (1933). Principal novels: *Challenge* (1923), *Seducers in Ecuador* (1924), *The Edwardians* (1930; Virago repr., 1983), *All Passion Spent* (1931; Virago repr., 1983), *Family History* (1932). *Selected Writings*, ed. M. A. Caws (Macmillan, 2002). Biography: Victoria Glendinning, *Vita* (1983). Critical study: Suzanne Raitt, *Vita and Virginia* (1993). Reference: Robert Cross and Ann Ravenscroft-Hulme, *Vita Sackville-West: A Bibliography* (1999).

SAKI [pseudonym of Hector Hugh Munro] (1870–1916)

Short-story writer and novelist. Stories collected in *Reginald* (1904), *Reginald in Russia* (1910), *The Chronicles of Clovis* (1911; Penguin repr.,

1986), *Beasts and Super-Beasts* (1914), *The Toys of Peace* (1919), and *The Square Egg* (1924). Novels: *The Unbearable Bassington* (1912), *When William Came* (1913). Modern editions: **The Penguin Complete Saki* (1982), *Short Stories & The Unbearable Bassington* (Oxford World's Classics, 1994). Biography: A. J. Langguth, *Saki* (1981). Critical study: George James Spears, *The Satire of Saki* (1963).

SASSOON, SIEGFRIED (1886–1967)

Born in Brenchley, Kent, to a landed family of Jewish descent, he was educated at Marlborough and at Clare College, Cambridge. He published eight volumes of poems before the Great War, in which he served as a captain in the Royal Welch Fusiliers, before throwing away his Military Cross and being sent to Craiglockhart Hospital near Edinburgh, where he met Wilfred Owen. He published several anti-war poems, collected in *The Old Huntsman* (1917) and *Counter-Attack* (1918). After the War he published further poems in *Picture-Show*, *Satirical Poems* (1926), *The Heart's Journey* (1928), and other collections. He was for a while literary editor of the *Daily Herald*, and active in Labour politics, but withdrew to Wiltshire as a country squire. After the breakdown of his homosexual affair with Stephen Tennant, he married Hester Gatty in 1934; they had one son, but later separated. His most substantial post-war work is the largely auto-biographical trilogy *Memoirs of a Fox-Hunting Man* (1928), *Memoirs of an Infantry Officer* (1930), and *Sherston's Progress* (1936), collected as *The Complete Memoirs of George Sherston* (1937); further memoirs fol-lowed in *The Old Century* (1938) and other works. The *Collected Poems, 1908–1956* appeared in 1961. *The Diaries*, ed. R. Hart-Davis, 3 vols. (Faber, 1981–5), cover the period 1915–25.

   The Sherston trilogy, the later memoirs, the **Collected Poems, 1908–1956*, and a *Selected Poems* have appeared in Faber paper editions. The standard biography is John Stuart Roberts, *Siegfried Sassoon* (1999). Critical studies include Paul Moeyes, *Siegfried Sassoon: Scorched Glory* (1997); Patrick Quinn, *The Great War and the Missing Muse* (1994); and Michael Thorpe, *Siegfried Sassoon* (1966). Reference: Geoffrey Keynes, *A Bibliography of Siegfried Sassoon* (1962).

SAYERS, DOROTHY LEIGH (1893–1957)

Detective writer, dramatist, translator. Principal works: *Whose Body?* (1923), *Murder Must Advertise* (1933), *The Nine Tailors* (1934), *Gaudy Night* (1935), *Busman's Honeymoon* (1937), all reprinted in *New

English Library editions; *The Man Born to be King* (radio drama, 1943). *The Letters*, ed. B. Reynolds (Hodder, 1995). Biography: James Brabazon, *Dorothy L. Sayers* (1981). Critical study: Terrance Lewis, *Dorothy L. Sayers' Wimsey and Interwar British Society* (1995). Reference: Colleen B. Gilbert, *A Bibliography of the Works of Dorothy L. Sayers* (1978).

SHAW, [GEORGE] BERNARD (1856–1950)

He was born and raised in Dublin, the son of an alcoholic corn merchant. He worked in an estate agent's office, then left Dublin (1876) for London to live with his mother, a music teacher. He wrote five unsuccessful novels, studied Marx and Wagner, and joined the Fabian Society (1884), throwing himself into journalism from 1885 as a music critic and by 1895 as a drama critic. After an affair with the actress Florence Farr, he contracted a celibate marriage with Charlotte Payne Townshend in 1898. His first play, *Widowers' Houses* (1892) was followed by several others including *Arms and the Man* (1894) without great success until the 1904 season at the Court Theatre produced his *John Bull's Other Island*. Meanwhile he published his early plays as *Plays Pleasant and Unpleasant*, 2 vols. (1898) and *Three Plays for Puritans* (1901). Success in the West End followed eventually with *Fanny's First Play* (1911) and *Pygmalion* (1914). He founded the weekly *New Statesman* in 1913. His wartime pamphlet *Common Sense about the War* (1914) met with ostracism. His major post-War plays were *Heartbreak House* (1921) and *Saint Joan* (1924). His non-dramatic works include the novella *The Adventures of the Black Girl in Her Search for God* (1932) and the lengthy prefaces to his various plays, collected as *Prefaces* (1934). He won the Nobel Prize for Literature in 1925. Posthumous collections include the *Collected Letters*, ed. Dan H. Laurence, 4 vols. (Reinhardt, 1965–88).

All the major plays are available in *Penguin 'Definitive Text' editions prepared by Dan H. Laurence, singly or in combinations that include *The Shewing-Up of Blanco Posnet* with **Fanny's First Play* (1987) and *Misalliance with *The Fascinating Foundling* (1984). *The Complete Prefaces*, ed. Dan H. Laurence and Daniel J. Leary, have appeared in three volumes (Allen Lane, 1993–7).

The fullest biography is Michael Holroyd's *Bernard Shaw*, 4 vols. (1988-92); 1 vol. abridgement (1997). More concise is Sally Peters, *Bernard Shaw: The Ascent of the Superman* (1996). Critical responses are collected in T. F. Evans (ed.), *George Bernard Shaw: The Critical Heritage* (1976). A good introductory account of the life and work is Arthur Ganz, *George Bernard Shaw* (1983). Modern critical studies include Maurice Valency, *The Cart and the Trumpet* (1973); Nicholas Grene, *Bernard Shaw: A Critical View* (1984); Margery M. Morgan, *The Shavian Playground* (1972); and Christopher Innes (ed.), *The Cambridge Companion to George Bernard Shaw* (1998). Reference: Dan H. Laurence, *Bernard Shaw: A Bibliography*, 2 vols. (1983); Margery Morgan, *File on Shaw* (1989).

SINCLAIR, MAY (1863–1946)

Novelist. Principal works: *The Divine Fire* (1904), *The Three Sisters* (1914), *Mary Olivier* (1919), *Life and Death of Harriett Frean* (1922); the last three have been reprinted in *Virago editions. Biography: Suzanne Raitt, *May Sinclair* (2000). Critical studies: T. E. M. Boll, *Miss May Sinclair, Novelist* (1973); H. D. Zegger, *May Sinclair* (1976).

SITWELL, EDITH (1887–1964)

She was born in Scarborough to an aristocratic landed family, and grew up in the family mansion in Derbyshire, where she was privately educated. After she left home for London in 1913, her first collection of poems, *The Mother*, appeared in 1915. With her brothers, she launched an annual poetry anthology, *Wheels*, which ran from 1916 to 1921. Following the experimental verses of *Clowns' Houses* (1918), she achieved notoriety with the public performance of her poetic work *Façade* (1923) spoken through a megaphone to the accompaniment of music by William Walton. During her period of residence in Paris (1924–39), further verse collections appeared as *The Sleeping Beauty* (1924) and *Troy Park* (1925), followed by the long poem *Gold Coast Customs* (1929). She published prose studies of *Alexander Pope* (1930), *The English Eccentrics* (1933), and *Victoria of England* (1936); then resumed her poetic career in England in the Forties with *Street Songs* (1942) and other collections. *Collected Poems appeared in 1957. She died as a Roman Catholic and as a Dame of the British Empire in London. *Selected Letters*, ed. R. Greene (Virago, 1998).

The standard biography is Victoria Glendinning's *Edith Sitwell: A Unicorn among Lions* (1981). Reference: Richard Fifoot, *A Bibliography of Edith, Osbert, and Sacheverell Sitwell* (2nd edn., 1971).

SITWELL, OSBERT (1892–1969)

Poet, novelist, autobiographer. Principal works: *Triple Fugue* (stories, 1924), *Before the Bombardment* (novel, 1926; Oxford repr., 1985), *Collected Satires and Poems* (1931), *Selected Poems, Old and New* (1943), *Collected Stories* (1953). *Escape With Me!* (travel book, 1939), *Left Hand, Right Hand!* (autobiography, 1944–8). Biography: Philip Ziegler, *Osbert Sitwell* (1998).

SPENDER, STEPHEN (1909–1995)

Poet, translator, and critic. Verse volumes include *Twenty Poems* (1930), *Poems* (1933), *Trial of a Judge* (drama, 1938), *The Still Centre* (1939), *Selected Poems* (1940), and *Collected Poems 1928–1985* (Faber, 1985). Prose works include *The Destructive Element* (1935), *World within World* (autobiography, 1951), *The Creative Element* (1953), *The Thirties and After* (1978), and *Journals, 1939–83* (1985). Biography: John Sutherland, *Stephen Spender* (2004). Reference: H. B. Kulkarni, *Stephen Spender: Works and Criticism* (1976).

STRACHEY, LYTTON (1880–1932)

The son of General Sir Richard Strachey, an imperial administrator, he was born in London and educated at Leamington College, at Liverpool University, and at Trinity College, Cambridge, where he met Keynes, Forster, Leonard Woolf, and other associates of what later became the 'Bloomsbury Group'. He published two volumes of poems, and worked from 1904 as a literary journalist for the *Spectator* and other magazines. After losing his lover Duncan Grant, he was very briefly engaged to Virginia Woolf in 1909. His first substantial book was *Landmarks in French Literature* (1912). During the Great War he was a conscientious objector. From 1917 he lived with the artist Dora Carrington, and later also with her husband Ralph Partridge. He established his reputation as a biographical essayist with *Eminent Victorians* (1918) and *Queen Victoria* (1921); these works were followed by *Elizabeth and Essex* (1928), *Portraits in Miniature* (1931), and the posthumous *Characters and Commentaries* (1933). He died from cancer, whereupon Dora committed suicide. Diaries and memoirs are collected in *Lytton Strachey by Himself*, ed. M. Holroyd (Heinemann, 1971). Paul Levy's edition of the letters is awaited.

An annotated paperback edition of **Eminent Victorians*, ed. J. Sutherland (2003), is available in the Oxford World's Classics series.

Queen Victoria and *Elizabeth and Essex* have been reprinted in *Penguin editions. Oxford published a selection of essays as *The Shorter Strachey*, ed. M. Holroyd and P. Levy (1980). Michael Holroyd's two-volume biography, *Lytton Strachey* (1967–8), has been revised as *Lytton Strachey: The New Biography* (1994). Critical introductions include John Ferns, *Lytton Strachey* (1988) and Barry Spurr, *Diabolical Art* (1994). Reference: Michael Edmonds: *Lytton Strachey: A Bibliography* (1981).

THOMAS, DYLAN (1914–1953)

He was born in Swansea, where he attended the Grammar School, at which his father taught English, and worked as a reporter on the *South Wales Daily Post* before moving to London in 1934, when his *18 Poems* appeared. Here he worked as a literary journalist in between drinking bouts. After publishing *Twenty-Five Poems* (1936), he married a dancer, Caitlin Macnamara, in 1937; they had three children. His next book, *The Map of Love* (1939), combined poetry and prose sketches, and was followed by a short-story collection, *Portrait of the Artist as a Young Dog* (1940). Unfit for war service, he worked as a screenwriter and broadcaster. His reputation as a poet was enhanced by *Deaths and Entrances* (1946) and the *Collected Poems* (1952). He and Caitlin settled in the village of Laugharne, Carmarthenshire, in 1949. He died of alcoholic poisoning on his fourth tour of the USA. Posthumous works include the celebrated radio play *Under Milk Wood*, the shorter radio pieces in *Quite Early One Morning* (both 1954), and the short-story collection *Adventures in the Skin Trade* (1955). *Collected Letters*, ed. P. Ferris (Dent, 1985; rev. 2001).

Annotated editions of the *Collected Poems*, ed. W. Davies and R. Maud (1993), and the *Collected Stories*, ed. W. Davies (1983), are available in the Everyman Paperback series. The major biographies are Paul Ferris, *Dylan Thomas* (1977; rev. 1999) and Andrew Lycett, *Dylan Thomas* (2003). The best critical work on the verse is collected in C. B. Cox (ed.), *Dylan Thomas: A Collection of Critical Essays* (1966); in Walford Davies (ed.), *Dylan Thomas: New Critical Essays* (1972); in Georg Gaston (ed.), *Critical Essays on Dylan Thomas* (1989); and in John Goodby and Christopher Wiggington (eds.), *Dylan Thomas* (2001). Walford Davies's *Dylan Thomas* (1986) is a useful introductory work. See also Linden Peach, *The Prose Writing of Dylan Thomas* (1988). Reference: Ralph Maud, *Dylan Thomas in Print* (1970); Georg M. A. Gaston, *Dylan Thomas: A Reference Guide* (1987).

THOMAS, EDWARD (1878–1917)

He was born of Welsh parents in Lambeth, his father being a clerk in the Board of Trade, and attended St Paul's School, London. He published his first book of rural essays, *The Woodland Life*, in 1897, and studied history at Lincoln College, Oxford; while there, he married Helen Noble in 1899; they had three children. He worked as a book reviewer for the *Daily Chronicle* and other papers, and as a hack writer of biographies and of topographical books, for which he undertook extensive walking tours across England and Wales. He befriended the American poet Robert Frost in 1913, and began writing his own poems in the next year. In July 1915 he enlisted in the Artists' Rifles, in which he served as a map-reading instructor; the next year he became an officer in the Royal Artillery. He was killed by a shell blast in the Battle of Passchendaele in April 1917, while his *Poems* (1917) were in press. Apart from the prose works *The South Country* (1909) and *In Pursuit of Spring* (1914), his major publications are posthumous: *Last Poems* (1918), *Collected Poems* (1920), and *The Childhood of Edward Thomas* (1938).

The standard edition of the verse is *The Collected Poems of Edward Thomas*, ed. R. George Thomas (Oxford University Press, 1978). Penguin have published an annotated *Selected Poems and Prose*, ed. D. Wright (1981). *The Childhood* was reprinted by Faber in 1983. The authorized biography is R. George Thomas, *Edward Thomas: A Portrait* (1985). The principal critical studies are Michael Kirkham, *The Imagination of Edward Thomas* (1986); Andrew Motion, *The Poetry of Edward Thomas* (1980); and Stan Smith, *Edward Thomas* (1986).

WALLACE, EDGAR (1875–1932)

Thriller writer. Novels include *The Four Just Men* (1905), *Sanders of the River* (1911), *The Crimson Circle* (1922), *The Black Abbot* (1926), *The Double* (1928). Plays include *The Ringer* (1926) and *On the Spot* (1930). Died in Hollywood at work on *King Kong*. Biography: Margaret Lane, *Edgar Wallace* (1938; rev. 1964). Reference: W. O. G. Lofts and Derek Adley, *The British Bibliography of Edgar Wallace* (1969).

WALPOLE, HUGH (1884–1941)

Novelist. Principal works: *Mr Perrin and Mr Traill* (1911), *The Secret City* (1919), *The Cathedral* (1922), *Portrait of a Man with Red Hair* (1925; Boydell repr., 1984); the 'Herries Chronicle': *Rogue Herries* (1930),

Judith Paris (1931), *The Fortress* (1932), *Vanessa* (1933); these four were reprinted by Alan Sutton in 1994–5. Biography: Rupert Hart-Davis. *Hugh Walpole* (1952).

WARNER, SYLVIA TOWNSEND (1893–1978)

She was born in Harrow, the daughter of a schoolmaster, and was educated privately. In the Great War she worked in a munitions factory; for ten years after it, she worked as editor of a ten-volume edition of Tudor church music. Her prizewinning first novel, *Lolly Willowes* (1926) was adopted as the first Book of the Month in the USA, ensuring her reputation there. She became a regular contributor of stories to the *New Yorker*, collecting these and other tales in *More Joy in Heaven* (1935), *A Garland of Straw* (1943), and several other volumes. Following *Mr Fortune's Maggot* (1927), she wrote the historical novels *The True Heart* (1929) and *Summer Will Show* (1936), and the political fable *After the Death of Don Juan* (1938). With her lover Valentine Ackland, she joined the Communist Party in 1935, and travelled to Spain to work for the Red Cross during the Civil War. She later settled in Dorset with Ackland. Later works include the historical novel *The Corner That Held Them* (1948) and *T. H. White: A Biography* (1967). She also wrote poetry, including a verse novel, *Opus 7* (1931).

The major novels, along with the *Selected Stories*, ed. S. Pinney and W. Maxwell (1989), have been reprinted by Virago. Claire Harman edited the *Collected Poems* (Carcanet, 1983) and *The Diaries* (Chatto & Windus, 1994), and has written the standard biography (1989). See also the *Letters*, ed. W. Maxwell (Chatto & Windus, 1982).

WAUGH, EVELYN (1903–1966)

He was born in West Hampstead, the son of the publisher Arthur Waugh, and educated at Lancing College and at Hertford College, Oxford. There he joined a circle of hard-drinking homosexuals, and took a third-class degree in history. His unhappy employment as a prep-school teacher in Wales is echoed in his first novel, *Decline and Fall* (1928). He married Evelyn Gardner in 1928, divorcing two years later. Following his conversion to Roman Catholicism in 1930, he wrote further satirical novels: *Vile Bodies* (1930), *Black Mischief* (1932), *A Handful of Dust* (1934), and *Scoop* (1938). He travelled in Africa as a foreign correspondent, writing *Remote People* (1931) and *Waugh in Abyssinia* (1936). He married Laura Herbert in 1937; they had six children. In the Second World War he served as an officer in the Royal Marines, then in the Royal Horse Guards; this provided the basis for his later *Sword of Honour* trilogy (1952–61). After the war, he took up the life of a country gentleman in Somerset. His most admired post-war novels are *Brideshead Revisited* (1945) and *The Loved One* (1948). His somewhat scandalous *Diaries*, ed. M. Davie (Weidenfeld and Nicolson), appeared in 1976; the *Letters*, ed. M. Amory (Weidenfeld and Nicolson), in 1980; and the *Essays, Articles, and Reviews*, ed. D. Gallagher (Methuen), in 1983. His elder brother Alec Waugh (1898–1981) was also a novelist.

All the novels have been reprinted in *Penguin editions, along with *Remote People*, *Waugh in Abyssinia*, and other travel writings. Annotated Penguin editions include **Decline and Fall*, ed. D. Bradshaw (2001); **A Handful of Dust*, ed. R. M. Davis (1997); and **Vile Bodies*, ed. R. Jacobs (1996). The fullest biography is Martin Stannard's two-volume *Evelyn Waugh* (1986, 1992). Douglas Lane Patey's *The Life of Evelyn Waugh* (1998) offers a more sympathetic riposte to Stannard's view. Humphrey Carpenter's *The Brideshead Generation* (1989) is another important biographical study. Critical articles are collected in Martin Stannard (ed.), *Evelyn Waugh: The Critical Heritage* (1984). Modern critical studies include Ian Littlewood, *The Writings of Evelyn Waugh* (1983); David Lodge, *Evelyn Waugh* (1971); and George McCartney, *Confused Roaring: Evelyn Waugh and the Modernist Tradition* (1987). Reference: Robert Murray Davis et al., *Evelyn Waugh: A Checklist* (1981); M. Morriss and D. J. Dooley, *Evelyn Waugh: A Reference Guide* (1984).

Webb, Mary [née Meredith] (1881–1927)

Novelist of Shropshire. Principal novels: *The Golden Arrow* (1916), *Gone to Earth* (1917), *The House in Dormer Forest* (1920), *Precious Bane* (1924); all reprinted in *Virago editions. Biography: G. M. Coles, *The Flower of Light* (1978).

Wells, Herbert George (1866–1946)

He was born in Bromley, Kent, where his parents were shopkeepers; his mother brought him up at a country mansion where she worked as housekeeper. He was apprenticed to a drapery, but became a student of biology at the Normal School of Science, South Kensington, and then a science teacher. His marriage to his cousin Isabel collapsed when he eloped with his student Amy ('Jane') Robbins, whom he married in 1895; they had two children. In the same year he published *The Time Machine*, the first of a sequence of 'scientific romances'. In the following decade he threw himself into Fabian politics, and published his novels of lower middle-class life, including *Love and Mr Lewisham* (1900), *Kipps* (1905), and *The History of Mr Polly* (1910). Other notable novels include *Tono-Bungay* (1909), *Ann Veronica* (1909), *The New Machiavelli* (1911), and *Mr Britling Sees It Through* (1916). He pursued numerous sexual affairs with, among others, Dorothy Richardson and Rebecca West (by whom he had a son). He was a prolific non-fiction writer, reaching a wide audience with *The Outline of History* (1920), *A Short History of the World* (1922), and *The Shape of Things to Come* (1933). His *Complete Short Stories* appeared in 1927, and his *Experiment in Autobiography* in 1934. Posthumous volumes include **H. G. Wells's Literary Criticism*, ed. P. Parrinder and R. Philmus (Harvester, 1980), and the autobiographical *H. G. Wells in Love* (Faber, 1984).

The major novels and romances are available in annotated **Everyman Paperback editions. Penguin publish the *Selected Short Stories* and *A Short History of the World*, and Faber the *Experiment in Autobiography*. *Mr Britling* and a few other novels are reprinted by House of Stratus.

The standard biography is still Norman and Jeanne MacKenzie, *The Life of H. G. Wells: The Time Traveller* (1973; rev. 1987). *The Correspondence of H. G. Wells* has appeared in four volumes, ed. David C. Smith (1998). Critical articles are collected in Patrick Parrinder (ed.), *H. G. Wells: The Critical Heritage* (1972). An introductory work is John Hammond, *A Preface to H. G. Wells* (2001). Modern critical studies include John Batchelor, *H. G. Wells* (1985), J. R. Hammond's books *H. G. Wells and the Short Story* (1992) and *H. G. Wells and the Modern Novel* (1988), and Patrick Parrinder, *H. G. Wells* (1970). Reference: J. R. Hammond, *Herbert George Wells: An Annotated Bibliography* (1977); W. J. Scheik and J. R. Cox, *H. G. Wells: A Reference Guide* (1988).

WEST, REBECCA [pseudonym of Cicily Fairfield] (1892–1983)

She was born in London, and brought up from the age of 8 in Edinburgh, her journalist father having abandoned the family. She attended George Watson's Ladies' College, then the Academy of Dramatic Art in London. She became a journalist on the feminist *Freewoman* and other magazines, adopting the name of an Ibsen heroine. Her scathing review of H. G. Wells's novel *Marriage* led to her ten-year affair with him; they had a son in 1914. Her critical study *Henry James* (1916) was followed by the novels *The Return of the Soldier* (1918), *The Judge* (1922), and *Harriet Hume* (1929), and by the essay collection *The Strange Necessity* (1928). In

1930 she married a banker, Henry Maxwell Andrews. Another novel, *The Thinking Reed*, appeared in 1936. Her major works after 1940 are *Black Lamb & Grey Falcon* (1942), an account of Serbia, and *The Meaning of Treason* (1949), on the Nuremburg trials. Later novels include *The Fountain Overflows* (1956). She became a Dame of the British Empire in 1959. A valuable collection of her early journalism appeared as *The Young Rebecca*, ed. J. Marcus (Virago, 1982), followed by a *Selected Letters*, ed. B. K. Scott (Yale, 2000).

The early novels have been reprinted as Virago Modern Classics. The authorized biography is Victoria Glendinning's *Rebecca West: A Life* (1987). Critical studies are Harold Orel, *The Literary Achievement of Rebecca West* (1986) and Peter Wolfe, *Rebecca West: Artist and Thinker* (1971). Reference: J. G. Packer, *Rebecca West: An Annotated Bibliography* (1991).

WILLIAMSON, HENRY (1897–1977)

Novelist. Principal works: *The Beautiful Years* (1921), *Dandelion Days* (1922; Faber repr., 1966), *The Dream of Fair Women* (1924; Hamlyn repr., 1983), *Tarka the Otter* (1927; Penguin repr., 1937), *The Patriot's Progress* (1930), *Salar the Salmon* (1935; Faber repr., 1973), *A Chronicle of Ancient Sunlight*, 15 vols. (1951–69). Biography: Anne Williamson, *Henry Williamson: Tarka and the Last Romantic* (1995).

WODEHOUSE, PELHAM GRENVILLE (1881–1975)

Prose humorist. Novels include *Psmith in the City* (1910), *Uneasy Money* (1916), *Summer Lightning* (1929), *Laughing Gas* (1936), *The Code of the Woosters* (1938). Short-story collections include *Carry On, Jeeves* (1925; *Penguin repr., 1957), *Blandings Castle* (1935; *Penguin repr., 1954), *Young Men in Spats* (1936), *Lord Emsworth and Others* (1937). Most works reprinted as Penguin editions, singly and in omnibus volumes. Biography: Frances Donaldson, *P. G. Wodehouse* (1982); new authorized life by Robert McCrum awaited. Critical study: Owen Dudley Edwards, *P. G. Wodehouse* (1977). Reference: David A. Jasen, *A Bibliography and Reader's Guide to the First Editions of P. G. Wodehouse* (2nd edn., 1986); Tony Ring and Geoffrey Jaggard (eds.), *The Millennium Wodehouse Concordance*, 8 vols. (2002).

WOOLF, VIRGINIA [née Stephen] (1882–1941)

She was born in London, the daughter of Sir Leslie Stephen, editor of the *Dictionary of National Biography*, and educated privately. She settled in Bloomsbury, where she and her sister Vanessa Bell were leaders of the 'Bloomsbury Group'. She wrote reviews for the *Times Literary Supplement* from 1905 onwards. She married the political journalist Leonard Woolf in 1912, but later engaged in affairs with Vita Sackville-West and others. After a suicide attempt in 1913, her first novel, *The Voyage Out*, appeared in 1915. With Leonard, she established the Hogarth Press (1917) at their house in Richmond. She published eight further novels: *Night and Day* (1919), *Jacob's Room* (1922), *Mrs Dalloway* (1925), *To the Lighthouse* (1927), *Orlando* (1928), *The Waves* (1931), *The Years* (1937), and *Between the Acts* (posthumous, 1941). Non-fictional works include the selected essays in *The Common Reader* (2 ser., 1925, 1932), her Cambridge lectures on women and literature published as *A Room of One's Own* (1929), and a biography, *Roger Fry* (1940). After the bombing of her London home, she withdrew to her country residence at Rodmell, Sussex, where, fearing the return of mental disturbance that had repeatedly tormented her, she drowned herself. Posthumous collections, all published by Hogarth, include *Collected Essays*, ed. L. Woolf, 4 vols. (1966-7); **The Essays of Virginia Woolf*, ed. A. McNeillie, 6 vols. (1986-); **The Diary*, ed. A. O. Bell and A. McNeillie, 5 vols. (1977–84); *The Letters*, ed. N. Nicolson and J. Trautmann, 6 vols. (1975–80); and **Moments of Being: Unpublished Autobiographical Writings*, ed. J. Schulkind (1978; rev. 1985).

The **Oxford World's Classics series includes annotated editions of all the novels, of *Flush*, of *The Mark on the Wall and Other Short Fiction*, and of *A Room of One's Own* with *Three Guineas*, ed. M. Shiach (1992); Penguin do likewise, along with a 2-vol. selection of essays (ed. R. Bowlby), as **A Woman's Essays* (1992), and *The Crowded Dance of Modern Life* (1993). The definitive biography is Hermione Lee, *Virginia Woolf* (1996); a valuable shorter account of the writing career is John Mepham, *Virginia Woolf: A Literary Life* (1991). Another important biographical work is Suzanne Raitt, *Vita and Virginia* (1993). Critical articles are collected in Robin Majumdar and Allen McLaurin (eds.), *Virginia Woolf: The Critical Heritage* (1975); in Rachel Bowlby (ed.), *Virginia Woolf* (1992); in Margaret Homans (ed.), *Virginia Woolf: A Collection of Critical Essays* (1993); and in Sue Roe and Susan Sellers (eds.), *Virginia Woolf* (2000). Susan Dick's *Virginia Woolf* (1989) and Laura Marcus's *Virginia Woolf* (1997) are helpful introductory accounts. Among the more advanced critical studies are Mitchell A. Leaska, *The Novels of Virginia Woolf* (1977); Rachel Bowlby, *Virginia Woolf: Feminist Destinations* (1988); Maria DiBattista, *Virginia Woolf's Major Novels* (1980); Hermione Lee, *The Novels of Virginia Woolf* (1977); James Naremore, *The World without a Self* (1973); Beth C. Rosenberg and Jeanne Dubino (eds.); *Virginia Woolf and the Essay* (1998); and Alex Zwerdling, *Virginia Woolf and the Real World* (1986). Reference: B. J. Kirkpatrick, *A Bibliography of Virginia Woolf* (4th edn., 1997).

YEATS, WILLIAM BUTLER (1865–1939)

He was born in Dublin, the son of the portrait-painter Jack Yeats, and was schooled in London and Dublin. He studied at the Metropolitan School of Art, Dublin, where he began dabbling in the occult. His first notable works were the folk tales of *The Celtic Twilight* (1893), and *Poems* (1895); several verse collections followed. He associated both with Irish nationalists in Dublin—including Maud Gonne, by whose beauty he became obsessed—and with the London aesthetes of the Rhymers' Club. With Augusta Gregory, he founded the Irish Literary Theatre, staging his verse play *The Countess Cathleen* in 1899. In 1904 he was among the founders of the Abbey Theatre, Dublin. He published his important verse collections *The Green Helmet* (1910), *Responsibilities* (1914) and *The Wild Swans at Coole* (1917), and married Georgie Hyde-Lees (1917), using her dreams and 'automatic writing' as the basis for his schematic symbology, *A Vision* (1925). He spent part of the Irish Civil War (1922-3) in old tower near Lady Gregory's Coole Park estate in Co. Galway, afterwards becoming a senator (1922-8) of the new Irish Free State. In this period he won the Nobel Prize (1923) and published many of his greatest poems in *Michael Robartes and the Dancer* (1921), *The Tower* (1928), and *The Winding Stair* (1929). He underwent a vasectomy (1934) in a failed attempt to restore his sexual vigour, but managed at least to edit the *Oxford Book of Modern Verse* (1936). He died near Monaco, inspiring a memorable elegy by Auden.

The best modern edition of Yeats's verse is *The Poems*, ed. D. Albright (Dent, 1990), which is fully annotated. The dramatic and prose works are available in Macmillan paperback editions. *The Major Works*, ed. E. Larrissy in the Oxford World's Classics series (1997; rev. 2001), offers an annotated selection of poems, plays, and prose writings. An annotated 14-volume *Collected Works* is in progress, ed. Richard J. Finneran and George Mills Harper, published by Scribner and by Palgrave. Also in progress is a multi-volume edition of *The Letters*, ed. J. Kelly (Oxford University

Press). The fullest and richest biography is Roy Foster's much-admired *W. B. Yeats: A Life*, 2 vols. (1997, 2003). Stephen Coote's *W. B. Yeats* (1997) and Terence Brown's *The Life of W. B. Yeats* (1999) cover the life more concisely, while Brenda Maddox's *George's Ghosts* (1999) investigates Yeats's marriage. Critical articles are collected in A. Norman Jeffares (ed.), *W. B. Yeats: The Critical Heritage* (1977); in William H. Pritchard (ed.), *W. B. Yeats: A Critical Anthology* (1972); in Elizabeth Cullingford (ed.), *Yeats: Poems, 1919–1935: A Casebook* (1984); and more fully in David Pierce, *W. B. Yeats*, 4 vols. (2000). Useful introductory accounts are Nicholas Drake, *The Poetry of W. B. Yeats* (1991); Peter Faulkner, *Yeats* (1987); and Edward Malins and John Purkis, *A Preface to Yeats* (1994). Among the more substantial critical works are Harold Bloom, *Yeats* (1970) and Richard Ellmann, *Yeats: The Man and the Masks* (1948; rev. 1978). Reference: Allan Wade, *A Bibliography of the Writings of W. B. Yeats* (3rd edn., 1968).

Suggestions for Further Reading

Among historical accounts of English and British politics and society in this period, the relevant chapters of Peter Clarke, *Hope and Glory: Britain 1900–1990* (1996) offer a good brief overview. A. J. P. Taylor, *English History 1914–45* (1965) is still a vivid if partial account of the political history. John Stevenson, *British Society 1914–45* (1984) is now the standard social history. The classic account of the 1910–14 phase is still George Dangerfield, *The Strange Death of Liberal England* (1935). Arthur Marwick, *The Deluge: British Society and the First World War* (1965) covers the wartime period well. For the inter-war phase, Charles Loch Mowat, *Britain Between the Wars 1918–1940* (1955) is the standard political and economic history. Although thrown together hurriedly, Robert Graves and Alan Hodge, *The Long Weekend: A Social History of Great Britain 1918–1939* (1940) has the freshness of eyewitnesses. Ronald Blythe, *The Age of Illusion: Glimpses of Britain between the Wars* (1963) offers curious vignettes of society and culture. Ross McKibbin's *Classes and Cultures: England 1918–1951* (1998) is a substantial and wide-ranging cultural history. Pertinent specialist works are Deirdre Beddoe, *Back to Home and Duty: Women between the Wars, 1918–1939* (1989) and David Cannadine, *The Decline and Fall of the British Aristocracy* (1990). Handy for quick reference is Andrew Thorpe, *The Longman Companion to Britain in the Era of the Two World Wars, 1914–45* (1994).

The social and cultural contexts of literature are illuminated in specialist chapters by contributors to Michael Bell (ed.), *The Context of English Literature: 1900–1930* (1980); Boris Ford (ed.), *Early Twentieth-Century Britain* (1992); and Clive Bloom (ed.), *Literature and Culture in Modern Britain*, vol. 1. 1900–30 (1993). Malcolm Bradbury offered a survey of these contexts in *The Social Context of Modern English Literature* (1971). A good range of intellectual contexts is reviewed in David Bradshaw (ed.), *A Concise Companion to Modernism* (2003). John Carey in *The Intellectuals and the Masses: Pride and Prejudice among the Literary Intelligentsia, 1880–1939* (1992) offers a controversially caustic analysis of literary arrogance.

The standard history of publishing in the period is Ian Norrie, *Mumby's Publishing and Bookselling in the Twentieth Century* (6th edn., 1982). Victor Bonham-Carter's *Authors by Profession*, vol. 2. *From the Copyright Act 1911 until the End of 1981* (1984) surveys the book trade from the point of view of the Society of Authors; R. J. L. Kingsford's *The Publishers Association 1896–1946* (1970) from the viewpoint of the publishers. Several of the major literary publishers are profiled in J. Rose and P. J. Anderson (eds.), *Dictionary of Literary Biography*, vol. 112 (1991). For the Hogarth Press, see J. H. Willis, Jr., *Leonard and Virginia Woolf as Publishers* (1992). The first major study of reading in the period was Q. D. Leavis, *Fiction and the Reading Public* (1932). More recent and reliable studies of the 'common reader' are Joseph McAleer, *Popular Reading and Publishing in Britain 1914–1950* (1992) and Jonathan Rose, *The Intellectual Life of the British Working Classes* (2001). The publishing history and microeconomic contexts of modernist writing are examined in Ian Willison, Warwick Gould, and Warren Chernaik (eds.), *Modernist Writers and the Marketplace* (1996); in Lawrence Rainey, *Institutions of Modernism: Literary Elites and Public Culture* (1999); and in Joyce Piell Wexler, *Who Paid for Modernism?* (1997). Little magazines and other literary periodicals are described in Alvin Sullivan (ed.), *British Literary Magazines: The Modern Age, 1914–1984* (1986). John Gross's absorbing history, *The Rise and Fall of the Man of Letters* (1969), follows the fortunes of literary journals, editors, and reviewers. Among the more specialized works on literary journals of the period are Mark S. Morrisson, *The Public Face of Modernism: Little Magazines, Audiences, and Reception, 1905–1920* (2001); Wallace Martin, *'The New Age' under Orage: Chapters in English Cultural History* (1967); Jason Harding, *The 'Criterion': Cultural Politics and Periodical Networks in Inter-War Britain* (2002); and Francis Mulhern, *The Moment of 'Scrutiny'* (1979).

On the *OED*, see Simon Winchester, *The Meaning of Everything: The Story of the Oxford English Dictionary* (2003) and Donna Lee Berg, *A Guide to the Oxford English Dictionary* (1993). Theories of language are examined by the contributors to Roy Harris (ed.), *Linguistic Thought in England, 1914–1945* (1988). David Lodge in *The Modes of Modern Writing* (1977) attempts an ambitious analysis of changes in literary language in this period. John Russell's *Style in Modern British Fiction* (1978) and Jacob Korg's *Language and Modern Literature* (1979) both explore individual cases of modern literary style. John Ayto's *Twentieth Century Words* (1999) lists a sample of modern coinages by decade of origin.

General surveys of this period's literature begin with Frank Swinnerton's *The Georgian Literary Scene* (1935; rev. 1938), which is opinionated to the point of flippancy. More soberly reliable if highly selective are A. C. Ward, *Twentieth-Century English Literature 1901–1960* (1964); Christopher Gillie, *Movements in English Literature 1900–1940* (1975); and Harry Blamires, *Twentieth-Century English Literature* (1982). William H. Pritchard's *Seeing Through Everything: English Writers 1918–1940* (1977) surveys aspects of post-Armistice disenchantment, while Julian Symons's *Makers of the New: The Revolution in Literature 1912–1939* (1987) examines aspects of literary innovation.

The secondary literature of the period is increasingly dominated by studies of modernism. David Lodge's published lecture *Modernism, Antimodernism and Postmodernism* (1977) provides the best short account of the basic terms; a revised version appears in his book *Working with Structuralism* (1981). Useful introductory accounts can be found in Peter Childs, *Modernism* (2000) and Peter Faulkner, *Modernism* (1977), while an insider's history is provided in Stephen Spender, *The Struggle of the Modern* (1963). A larger European perspective emerges from Edmund Wilson's pioneering book *Axel's Castle: A Study in the Imaginative Literature of 1870–1930* (1931), and again in the contributions to Malcolm Bradbury and James McFarlane (eds.), *Modernism: A Guide to European Literature 1890–1930* (1976). The best introductory accounts of modernism in its various literary aspects are Michael Levenson (ed.), *The Cambridge Companion to Modernism* (1999) and Peter Nicholls, *Modernisms: A Literary Guide* (1995). More advanced and specialized works of value here include Stan Smith, *The Origins of Modernism* (1987); Michael Levenson, *A Genealogy of Modernism* (1984); Andreas Huyssen, *After the Great Divide: Modernism, Mass Culture, Postmodernism* (1986); and Michael Tratner, *Modernism and Mass Politics: Joyce, Woolf, Eliot, Yeats* (1995).

Several useful studies have appeared of particular phases within this period. Anne Wright's *Literature of Crisis, 1910–22* (1984) examines key post-Edwardian works in context. Harold Orel in *Popular Fiction in England, 1914–1918* (1992) looks at a range of novels and romances, not all of them popular. The underdeveloped field of Twenties studies is best represented by David Ayers, *English Literature of the 1920s* (1999) and John Lucas, *The Radical Twenties: Aspects of Writing, Politics, and Culture* (1997). The two major accounts of Thirties writing are Samuel Hynes, *The Auden Generation: Literature and Politics in England in the 1930s* (1976) and Valentine Cunningham, *British Writers of the Thirties* (1988); other valuable perspectives on that decade are offered by Keith Williams and Steven Matthews (eds.), *Rewriting the Thirties: Modernism and After* (1997); Bernard Bergonzi, *Reading the Thirties: Texts and Contexts* (1978); Janet Montefiore, *Men and Women Writers of the 1930s* (1996); and Frank Kermode, *History and Value* (1988).

Some important studies are devoted to particular groups and circles of writers. The standard works on the Bloomsbury Group are Quentin Bell, *Bloomsbury* (1968) and Leon Edel, *Bloomsbury: A House of Lions* (1979). S. P. Rosenbaum's *Georgian Bloomsbury* (2003) covers the period 1910–

1914, and is a sequel to his earlier studies of the same group. Rosenbaum has also edited a useful anthology, *A Bloomsbury Group Reader* (1993). Peter Stansky's *On or About December 1910* (1996) follows the Bloomsburyites through that momentous year, while the Group's responses to the Great War are examined in Jonathan Atkin, *A War of Individuals: Bloomsbury Attitudes to the Great War* (2002). Miranda Seymour's biography, *Ottoline Morrell: Life on the Grand Scale* (1992) offers another view of that circle. Broader biographical studies of literary-artistic bohemianism of this period include Virginia Nicholson, *Among the Bohemians: Experiments in Living 1900–1930* (2002) and Paul Delany, *The Neo-Pagans: Friendship and Love in the Rupert Brooke Circle* (1987). Important sources for any study of the 'Georgian Poetry' circle are Christopher Hassall's biography, *Edward Marsh, Patron of the Arts* (1959) and Dominic Hibberd's *Harold Monro: Poet of the New Age* (2001). Helen Carr's *The Verse Revolutionaries* (2004) examines the Imagist group, while studies of the wider circle around Ezra Pound include Hugh Kenner, *The Pound Era* (1971); Timothy Materer, *Vortex: Pound, Eliot, and Lewis* (1979); and B. L. Reid, *The Man from New York: John Quinn and His Friends* (1968). A later group is examined in Humphrey Carpenter, *The Brideshead Generation: Evelyn Waugh and his Friends* (1989).

There are several good studies of women's writing in this period. Nicola Beauman's *A Very Great Profession: The Woman's Novel, 1914–39* (Virago, 1983) is an informal but well-documented account, and has been followed by Heather Ingman, *Women's Fiction between the Wars* (1998) and Nicola Humble, *The Feminine Middlebrow Novel, 1920s to 1950s: Class, Domesticity, and Bohemianism* (2001). Alison Light in *Forever England: Femininity, Literature and Conservatism between the Wars* (1991) tackles a few case-studies in depth, as does Sydney Janet Kaplan in *Feminine Consciousness in the Modern British Novel* (1975). For women's poetry, see Jane Dowson, *Women, Modernism and British Poetry, 1910–1939: Resisting Femininity* (2002). The women modernists are examined in Gillian Hanscombe and Virginia L. Smyers, *Writing for Their Lives: The Modernist Women 1910–1940* (1987); in Bonnie Kime Scott, *Refiguring Modernism*, vol. 1. *The Women of 1928* (1995); and in Kathleen Wheeler, *Modernist Women Writers and Narrative Art* (1994).

On the poetry of this period, see David Perkins, *A History of Modern Poetry, from the 1890s to the High Modernist Mode* (1976) and John Press, *A Map of Modern English Verse* (1969) for general surveys. Problems of language and technique are addressed by Jon Silkin, *The Life of Metrical and Free Verse in Twentieth-Century Poetry* (1997) and A. C. Partridge, *The Language of Modern Poetry: Yeats, Eliot, Auden* (1976). C. K. Stead's book *The New Poetic: Yeats to Eliot* (1964) has long been the standard account of the emergence of modernism in verse, later supplemented by his *Pound, Yeats, Eliot and the Modernist Movement* (1986). The best account of Georgian poetry is still Robert H. Ross, *The Georgian Revolt: Rise and Fall of a Poetic Ideal 1910–22* (1967), while Timothy Rogers (ed.), *Georgian Poetry 1911–1922: The Critical Heritage* (1977) is an essential resource. For Thirties poetry, see A. T. Tolley, *The Poetry of the Thirties* (1975) and Adrian Caesar, *Dividing Lines: Poetry, Class and Ideology in the 1930s* (1991). A valuable specialist study is Jahan Ramazani, *Poetry of Mourning: The Modern Elegy from Hardy to Heaney* (1994).

The best introductory surveys of the period's drama are Jean Chothia, *English Drama of the Early Modern Period, 1890 to 1940* (1996) and the relevant chapters of Christopher Innes, *Modern British Drama: 1890–1990* (1992). Earlier surveys that cover some minor dramatists more fully are Allardice Nicoll, *English Drama, 1900–1930* (1973) and Ernest Reynolds, *Modern English Drama: A Survey of the Theatre from 1900* (1949). Special developments in dramatic construction and language are addressed in John Russell Taylor, *The Rise and Fall of the Well-Made Play* (1967) and Alan K. Kennedy, *Six Dramatists in Search of a Language* (1975). The theatrical avant-garde is chronicled in Michael Sidnell, *Dances of Death: The Group Theatre of London in the Thirties* (1984).

Critical works on the short story in this period are not plentiful. The best is Dominic Head, *The Modernist Short Story* (1992). Still useful is H. E. Bates, *The Modern Short Story: A Critical Survey* (1941), as are some parts of Valerie Shaw, *The Short Story: A Critical Introduction* (1983).

For the novel, a good introduction to the leading authors is offered by Douglas Hewitt in *English Fiction of the Early Modern Period, 1890 to 1940* (1988), while a wider range is attempted by Walter Allen in *Tradition and Dream: The English and American Novel from the Twenties to Our Time* (1964). The relations between fiction and gender are examined by Lyn Pykett in *Engendering Fictions: The English Novel in the Early Twentieth Century* (1995). Three stimulating works on the contexts of fiction in the early part of this period are Peter Keating, *The Haunted Study: A Social History of the English Novel 1875–1914* (1989); David Trotter, *The English Novel in History 1895–1920* (1993); and Patricia Stubbs, *Women and Fiction: Feminism and the Novel 1880–1920* (1979). The best introductory account of the modernist novel is Randall Stevenson, *Modernist Fiction: An Introduction* (1992; rev. 1998). Leon Edel's *The Psychological Novel 1900–1950* (1955) remains a sound guide to the same tradition, of which more specialized studies include Michael Levenson, *Modernism and the Fate of Individuality: Character and Novelistic Form from Conrad to Woolf*

(1991) and Erwin R. Steinberg, *The Stream-of-Consciousness Technique in the Modern Novel* (1979). For rural fiction, see Glen Cavaliero, *The Rural Tradition in the English Novel, 1900–1939* (1977). For novels of the Thirties, see Richard Johnstone, *The Will to Believe: Novelists of the Nineteen-Thirties* (1982); James Gindin, *British Fiction in the 1930s: The Dispiriting Decade* (1992); and—for socialist fiction—Andy Croft, *Red Letter Days: British Fiction in the 1930s* (1990).

The pioneering accounts of the period's popular fiction are found in three books by non-academic enthusiasts: Claud Cockburn's *Bestseller: The Books That Everyone Read 1900–1939* (1972) casts a wry glance at a number of forgotten potboilers; Colin Watson's *Snobbery with Violence: English Crime Stories and Their Audience* (1971; rev. 1979) dissects the social assumptions of classic crime fiction; and Richard Usborne's *Clubland Heroes* (1953) does the same for the thrillers of Yates, 'Sapper', and Buchan. The standard history of crime fiction is Julian Symons, *Bloody Murder* (1972; rev. 1992). More specialized academic studies include Stephen Knight, *Form and Ideology in Crime Fiction* (1980); Martin Priestman, *Detective Fiction and Literature* (1990); and Susan Rowland, *From Agatha Christie to Ruth Rendell: British Women Writers in Detective and Crime Fiction* (2001). For the fiction of espionage, see John G. Cawelti and Bruce A. Rosenberg, *The Spy Story* (1987). Another popular genre is explored in Helen Hughes, *The Historical Romance* (1993).

Works addressing the non-fictional literature of the period are relatively scarce, but a good account of biography is given in Ruth Hoberman, *Modernizing Lives: Experiments in English Biography, 1918–1939* (1987), and of autobiography in Brian Finney, *The Inner I: British Literary Autobiography in the Twentieth Century* (1985). The leading account of travel writing is Paul Fussell, *Abroad: British Literary Traveling between the Wars* (1980); this has been followed by the more specialized work of Bernard Schweizer in *Radicals on the Road: The Politics of English Travel Writing in the 1930s* (2001). An introductory survey of the period's literary criticism may be found in the relevant chapters of Chris Baldick, *Criticism and Literary Theory, 1890 to the Present* (1996).

The standard work on Englishness in this period is David Gervais, *Literary Englands: Versions of 'Englishness' in Modern Writing* (1993). Some of the contributions to Robert Colls and Philip Dodd (eds.), *Englishness: Politics and Culture 1880–1920* (1986) are also useful, as is the anthology by Judy Giles and Tim Middleton (eds.), *Writing Englishness 1900–1950: An Introductory Sourcebook on National Identity* (1995).

The three principal surveys of Great War writing are Paul Fussell, *The Great War and Modern Memory* (1975); Samuel Hynes, *A War Imagined:*

The First World War and English Culture (1990); and Bernard Bergonzi, *Heroes' Twilight: A Study of the Literature of the Great War* (1965; rev. 1980). Andrew Rutherford in *The Literature of War* (1978) mounts an important defence of heroic values. A broader background is provided by George Robb, *British Culture and the First World War* (2002). Accounts of war poetry include Jon Silkin, *Out of Battle: The Poetry of the Great War* (1972); Fred D. Crawford, *British Poets of the First World War* (1988); and Dominic Hibberd (ed.), *Poetry of the First World War: A Casebook* (1981). War drama is examined in L. J. Collins, *Theatre at War, 1914–1918* (1998) and in John Onions, *English Fiction and Drama of the Great War, 1918–39* (1990). Specialist works on war fiction are George Parfitt, *Fiction of the First World War* (1988) and Rosa Maria Bracco, *Merchants of Hope: British Middlebrow Writers and the First World War, 1919–1939* (1993). The study of women's writings on the War was opened up by Claire M. Tylee in *The Great War and Women's Consciousness* (1990); since then a number of valuable works on this topic have appeared, including Suzanne Raitt and Trudi Tate (eds.), *Women's Fiction and the Great War* (1997); Sharon Ouditt, *Fighting Forces, Writing Women: Identity and Ideology in the First World War* (1994); and Angela K. Smith, *The Second Battlefield: Women, Modernism and the First World War* (2000). Literary war-propaganda is explored in Peter Buitenhuis, *The Great War of Words: Literature as Propaganda, 1914–18 and After* (1989).

The standard histories of children's literature are John Rowe Townsend, *Written for Children: An Outline of English-language Children's Literature* (1965; rev. 1974); Peter Hunt, *An Introduction to Children's Literature* (1994); and Isabel Quigly, *The Heirs of Tom Brown: The English School Story* (1982). Juliet Dusinberre's *Alice to the Lighthouse* (1987) considers links between modernism and children's books. For the special tradition of girls' fiction, see Mary Cadogan and Patricia Craig, *You're a Brick, Angela! The Girls' Story, 1839–1985* (1986) and Gillian Freeman, *The Schoolgirl Ethic: The Life and Work of Angel Brazil* (1976).

Modern sexuality has been explored well by social historians, the four principal studies in this field being Paul Ferris, *Sex and the British: A Twentieth-Century History* (1994); Cate Haste, *Rules of Desire: Sex in Britain, World War I to the Present* (1992); Steve Humphries, *A Secret World of Sex: Forbidden Fruit: The British Experience 1900–1950* (1988); and Billie Melman, *Women and the Popular Imagination in the Twenties: Flappers and Nymphs* (1988). June Rose's biographical study, *Marie Stopes and the Sexual Revolution* (1992) is also worth consulting. The theatre critic Nicholas de Jongh has written two useful studies of sexuality on stage, *Not in Front of the Audience: Homosexuality on Stage* (1992) and *Politics,*

Prudery & Perversions: The Censoring of the English Stage 1901–1968 (2000). Joseph Bristow covers significant backgrounds to modern male homosexual literature in *Effeminate England: Homoerotic Writing after 1885* (1995). Gay Wachman's *Lesbian Empire: Radical Crosswriting in the Twenties* (2001) focuses on a key period of Sapphic fiction. A good range of essays in this field is offered in Hugh Stevens and Caroline Howlett (eds.), *Modernist Sexualities* (2000).

The standard literary bibliography for this period is I. R. Willison (ed.), *The New Cambridge Bibliography of English Literature*, vol. 4. *1900–1950* (1972), which will eventually be superseded by a new volume in the third edition of the Cambridge Bibliography of English Literature. Useful quick-reference sources for literary biography are Peter Parker (ed.), *The Reader's Companion to Twentieth-Century Writers* (1995) and Jenny Stringer (ed.), *The Oxford Companion to Twentieth-Century Literature in English* (1996). For bibliographical information on poetry, consult Emily Ann Anderson, *English Poetry, 1900–1950: A Guide to Information Sources* (1982) and Catherine W. Reilly, *English Poetry of the First World War: A Bibliography* (1978); interesting critical verdicts are offered by Ian Hamilton (ed.), *The Oxford Companion to Twentieth-Century Poetry in English* (1994). For the novel, Peter Parker (ed.), *The Reader's Companion to the Twentieth-Century Novel* (1994) provides plot summaries and commentaries by year of publication, while bibliographical data is collected in A. F. Cassis, *The Twentieth-Century English Novel: An Annotated Bibliography of General Criticism* (1977) and in Thomas Jackson Rice, *English Fiction, 1900–1950: A Guide to Information Sources*, 2 vols. (1979). Kathleen Wheeler's *A Critical Guide to Twentieth-Century Women Novelists* (1997) is, as the title says, a critical survey, although organized like a reference work. A more specialized compendium of curiosities is Sandra Kemp, Charlotte Mitchell, and David Trotter (eds.), *Edwardian Fiction: An Oxford Companion* (1997), an admirable resource that helpfully extends its period to 1915. For dramatic literature, the standard bibliography is E. H. Mikhail, *English Drama, 1900–1950: A Guide to Information Sources* (1977). Three volumes in J. P. Wearing's long-running series, *The London Stage, 1910–1919* (1982), *The London Stage, 1920–1929* (1984), and *The London Stage, 1930–1939* (1990), provide details of productions and casts. Among the more specialized bibliographies for this period are Lawrence W. Markert, *The Bloomsbury Group: A Reference Guide* (1990); Philip E. Hager and Desmond Taylor, *The Novels of World War I: An Annotated Bibliography* (1981); Sharon Ouditt, *Women Writers of the First World War: An Annotated Bibliography* (2000); and John Cooper and Jonathan Cooper, *Children's Fiction 1900–1950* (1998). Alistair Davies's *An Annotated Critical Bibliography of*

Modernism (1982) is limited in scope and now rather outdated, but still a useful starting point. The multi-volume *Dictionary of Literary Biography* has several volumes on writers of this period, including volumes 15, 34, 36, and 191 on novelists; 20 on poets; 10 on dramatists; 162 on short-storyists; 77 on crime writers; 160 on children's authors; and 98, 100, 155, and 195 on non-fiction writers.

Index

Page numbers given in bold type indicate authors' entries in the Author Bibliographies.